Praise for
Carthage Must Be Destroyed

"A fresh and tantalizing glimpse at a world that was lost when Rome eliminated Carthage." —*The New Republic*

"You know a story is great when it grips you even when you know how it turns out. . . . Miles has written an engaging, richly documented study that merges able storytelling with equally able scholarship. It's quite a tale." —*The Philadelphia Inquirer*

"Historian Richard Miles, of Cambridge, makes telling use of the latest discoveries yielded by Carthaginian ruins in a splendid, comprehensive effort to present the city-state as a dynamic entity and minimize it as a victimized, second-tier society so often portrayed in the histories of Roman and Western interpreters. Bloodcurdling battles receive their pyrrhic due, and Hannibal's trans-Alps adventure and his humbling demise are covered in masterful detail." —*The Star-Ledger* (Newark)

"*Carthage Must Be Destroyed* is a fine, sweeping survey of the rise and fall of an empire and a glimpse into the diversity of the ancient world." —*The Wall Street Journal*

"A monumental history of this lost civilization."
—*Kirkus Reviews*

"Miles breathtakingly narrates Carthage's rise to fame as an ancient cultural and commercial center and its demise before its rebuilding as a Roman city." —*Publishers Weekly*

PENGUIN BOOKS

CARTHAGE MUST BE DESTROYED

Richard Miles teaches ancient history at the University of Sydney and is a Fellow-Commoner of Trinity Hall, University of Cambridge. In 2010, he hosted the BBC television series *Ancient Worlds* and authored the companion book of the same name. He has written widely on Punic, Roman, and Vandal North Africa and has directed archaeological excavations in Carthage and Rome.

RICHARD MILES

Carthage Must Be Destroyed

The Rise and Fall of an
Ancient Civilization

PENGUIN BOOKS

PENGUIN BOOKS

Published by the Penguin Group

Penguin Group (USA) Inc., 375 Hudson Street, New York, New York 10014, U.S.A.
Penguin Group (Canada), 90 Eglinton Avenue East, Suite 700, Toronto,
Ontario, Canada M4P 2Y3 (a division of Pearson Penguin Canada Inc.)
Penguin Books Ltd, 80 Strand, London WC2R 0RL, England
Penguin Ireland, 25 St Stephen's Green, Dublin 2, Ireland (a division of Penguin Books Ltd)
Penguin Group (Australia), 250 Camberwell Road, Camberwell,
Victoria 3124, Australia (a division of Pearson Australia Group Pty Ltd)
Penguin Books India Pvt Ltd, 11 Community Centre,
Panchsheel Park, New Delhi – 110 017, India
Penguin Group (NZ), 67 Apollo Drive, Rosedale, Auckland 0632,
New Zealand (a division of Pearson New Zealand Ltd)
Penguin Books (South Africa) (Pty) Ltd, 24 Sturdee Avenue,
Rosebank, Johannesburg 2196, South Africa

Penguin Books Ltd, Registered Offices:
80 Strand, London WC2R 0RL, England

First published in Great Britain by Allen Lane, an imprint of Penguin Books Ltd. 2010
First published in the United States of America by Viking Penguin,
a member of Penguin Group (USA) Inc. 2011
Published in Penguin Books (UK) 2011
Published in Penguin Books (USA) 2012

10

Illustration credits appear on pages ix–xi.

THE LIBRARY OF CONGRESS HAS CATALOGED THE HARDCOVER EDITION AS FOLLOWS:
Miles, Richard.
Carthage must be destroyed : the rise and fall of an ancient civilization / Richard Miles.
p.   cm.
Includes bibliographical references and index.
ISBN 978-0-670-02266-3 (hc.)
ISBN 978-0-14-312129-9 (pbk.)
1. Carthage (Extinct city)—History.   2. Rome—History—Republic, 265–30 B.C.
3. Hannibal, 247–182 B.C.   I. Title.
DT269.C35M55 2011
939.73—dc22
2011004123

Printed in the United States of America

For my mother, Julie Miles

Contents

CONTENTS

List of Illustrations

1. *Aeneas' Farewell from Dido in Carthage*, 1675–6, oil on canvas, by Claude Lorrain, Hamburger Kunsthalle, Hamburg, Germany. Photograph copyright © Elke Walford, 2005. Photo Scala, Florence/ BPK, Bildagentur fuer Kunst, Kultur und Geschichte, Berlin

2. Panoramic view of Carthage, painting, Musée National de Carthage, Tunisia. Prisma/Ancient Art & Architecture Collection Ltd

3. Finger ring with setting adorned with a woman's head, third century BC, gold, from the Necropolis of sainte-Monique, Carthage. Musée National de Carthage, Tunisia. Photograph: Institut National du Patrimoine, Tunisie (INP)

4. Finger ring with setting adorned with the profile of a man's head, third century BC, gold, from the Necropolis of sainte-Monique, Carthage. Musée National de Carthage, Tunisia. Photograph: Institut National du Patrimoine, Tunisie (INP)

5. Amulets depicting faces, fourth to third century BC, glass, Musée National de Carthage, Tunisia. Photograph copyright © Charles & Josette Lenars/CORBIS

6. Relief depicting the unloading of wood after transportation by sea, eighth century BC, stone, Assyrian, from the Palace of Sargon II, Khorsabad, Iraq. Musée du Louvre, Paris, France/Lauros/Giraudon/ The Bridgeman Art Library

7. Votive Punic stele depicting Priest holding a child, fourth century BC, dark limestone, from the tophet of Carthage. Musée National du Bardo, Tunisia. Photograph copyright © Roger Wood/CORBIS

8. Punic stelae on the cemetery of the tophet, third to second century

Nazionale, Naples, Italy. Photograph: Mary Evans Picture Library

20. Silver double shekel of Carthage showing head of Hercules-Melqart, issued by the Barcid family in Spain, *c.* 230 BC. Photograph © The Trustees of the British Museum

21. *Snow Storm: Hannibal and his Army Crossing the Alps*, exhibited 1812, oil on canvas, Joseph Mallord William Turner. Tate Gallery, London. Photograph copyright © Tate, London 2009

22. *The Battle of Zama, 202 BC,* 1521, oil on canvas, attributed to Giulio Romano. The Pushkin State Museum of Fine Arts, Moscow, Russia. Photograph: akg-images, London

23. Scipio, Publius Cornelius, known as Scipio Africanus the Elder (235–183 BC), marble bust, Roman. Musei Capitolini, Rome, Italy. Photograph: akg-images, London/Erich Lessing

24. Cato the Elder (234–149 BC) in a toga, stone sculpture, Roman. Vatican Museums and Galleries, Vatican City, Italy/Alinari/The Bridgeman Art Libary

25. View of the ruins, Carthage, Tunisia. Photograph: Ken Welsh/The Bridgeman Art Library

26. *Apotheosis of Alexandria with Personification of the Four Parts of the World (Or: Dido Abandoned by Aeneas)*, first century AD, mural painting, Roman, from Casa Meleagro, Pompeii, Italy. Museo Archeologico Nazionale, Naples. Photograph: akg-images, London/Erich Lessing

Every effort has been made to contact copyright holders. The publishers will be glad to correct any errors or omissions in future editions.

List of Maps

Chronology

All dates are BC

969–936 Reign of Hiram I of Tyre.

911 Beginning of resurgence of Assyria.

884–859 Reign of Ashurnasirpal II of Assyria.

830–810 Foundation of Tyrian colony at Kition in Cyprus.

814 Reputed foundation date of Carthage.

800–750 Foundation and early development of Carthage
Foundation of Pithecusa.

800–700 Foundation of Phoenician trading stations and colonies in
Spain, the Balearics, Malta, Sardinia, Sicily and North Africa.

753 Reputed foundation date of Rome.

745–727 Reign of Tiglathpileser III of Assyria.

704–681 Reign of Sennacherib of Assyria.

586–573 Siege of Tyre by Nebuchadnezzar, king of Babylon.

550 (circa) The Magonids come to dominate Carthage politically.

535 Victory of the Carthaginian and Etruscan fleets over the
Phocaeans at Alalia.

509 First treaty between Carthage and Rome.

500 (circa) The Pyrgi Tablets.

500–400 Possible period for Hanno's voyage to West Africa and
Himilco's expedition into the northern Atlantic.

480 Defeat of the forces of the Magonid general Hamilcar by
Gelon, tyrant of Syracuse, at the Battle of Himera.

479–410 Political reforms in Carthage, including creation of the Tribunal of One Hundred and Four, the Popular Assembly and the suffeture.

409 The destruction of Selinus and the recapture of Himera by Carthaginian forces.

405 Carthaginian protectorate in western Sicily acknowledged in a treaty with Dionysius of Syracuse.

397 The destruction of Motya by Dionysius of Syracuse and the subsequent foundation of Lilybaeum (Marsala) by the Carthaginians.

396 Introduction of the cult of Demeter and Core in Carthage.

390s–380s The Magonids lose their political power base in Carthage.

373 Treaty between Carthage and Syracuse.

348 Second treaty between Carthage and Rome.

340 Syracusan forces under Timoleon defeat the Carthaginians at the Battle of the Crimisus.

338 New treaty between Carthage and Syracuse by which the dominion of Carthage in Sicily is confined to the lands west of the river Halycus (Platani).

332 Siege and capture of Tyre by Alexander the Great.

323 Death of Alexander the Great.

310–307 Invasion of Punic North Africa by Agathocles of Syracuse.

308 Failed coup attempt by Carthaginian general Bomilcar.

306 Supposed third treaty between Carthage and Rome.

280–275 The wars between Pyrrhus, king of Epirus, and the Romans and Carthaginians.

279 Treaty between Carthage and Rome against Pyrrhus.

264 The outbreak of the First Punic War between Carthage and Rome.

260 Roman naval victory at Mylae.

256–255 Regulus' expedition to North Africa.

249 Carthaginian naval victory at Drepana.

247 Hamilcar Barca appointed general in Sicily. His son Hannibal Barca is born.

241 Carthaginian naval defeat at the Battle of the Aegates. Carthage sues for peace, and the First Punic War comes to an end with Rome victorious. Carthage loses its Sicilian territories.

241–238 The Mercenaries' Revolt.

237 Annexation of Sardinia and Corsica by Rome.

237–229 Hamilcar Barca establishes the Barcid protectorate in southern Spain.

231 Alleged first Roman embassy to Hamilcar Barca.

229 Death of Hamilcar Barca and the assumption of his generalship by his son-in-law, Hasdrubal.

228–227 Hasdrubal Barca's alleged unsuccessful return to Carthage.

227 Foundation of New Carthage by Hasdrubal.

226 Treaty between Hasdrubal and the Romans.

221 Murder of Hasdrubal. Hannibal Barca is acclaimed as the general of the Carthaginian forces in Spain.

220 Meeting between Hannibal and Roman envoys at New Carthage.

219 Hannibal starts to besiege Saguntum.

218 Roman embassy to Spain and then Carthage.

Rome declares war on Carthage, and the Second Punic War begins.

Hannibal sets off overland for Italy with his army (June).

Battles of the Ticinus and the Trebia (November and December).

217 Battle of Lake Trasimene (June).

Quintus Fabius Maximus becomes Roman dictator.

216 Battle of Cannae (August).

Defection of Capua to Hannibal.

215 Hannibal's treaty with Philip V of Macedon.

Hieronymus becomes king of Syracuse.

214 Hieronymus is murdered. Hippocrates and Epicydes are elected magistrates and ally Syracuse with Carthage.

213 Syracuse besieged by Roman army under the command of Marcellus.

212 Defection of Tarentum, Locri, Thurii and Metapontum to Hannibal.

The Romans besiege Capua.

Marcellus captures Syracuse.

211 Hannibal marches on Rome.

Surrender of Capua to the Romans.

Deaths of the Scipios in Spain.

209 Capture of Tarentum by Fabius.

Capture of New Carthage by Scipio Africanus.

208 Death of Marcellus.

Defeat of Hasdrubal Barca (Hannibal's brother) by Scipio Africanus at Baecula.

Hasdrubal leaves with an army for Italy.

207 Hasdrubal defeated and killed at the Battle of the Metaurus.

206 Hannibal trapped in Bruttium.

Scipio defeats the Carthaginian army at Ilipa.

Gades surrenders to the Romans.

Numidian king Syphax allies himself to Carthage.

205 Philip V of Macedon makes peace with Rome.

204 Scipio Africanus invades North Africa.

The destruction of the Carthaginian and Numidian camps near Utica.

203 Defeat of the Carthaginians and Numidians at the Battle of the Great Plains.

Syphax killed and Masinissa becomes king of all Numidia.

Hannibal recalled from Italy.

202 Battle of Zama (October).

201 End of the Second Punic War.

196 Hannibal elected suffete.

195 Hannibal leaves for exile in the eastern Mediterranean.

184 Rome rejects the Carthaginians' appeal against Numidian incursions into their territory.

183 Hannibal commits suicide in Bithynia.

182 Further Carthaginian appeal over Numidian aggression rejected.

174 The Romans reject another Carthaginian appeal against territorial encroachments by Masinissa.

168 The Macedonians comprehensively defeated by the Romans at the Battle of Pydna.

162 Masinissa seizes the emporia of Syrtis Minor. Carthage's subsequent appeal to Rome is rejected.

153 Roman embassy sent to Carthage.

151 Carthage pays off the final instalment of its indemnity from the Second Punic War.

151–150 Popular party gains power in Carthage.

150 Rome decides on war against Carthage. Third Punic War starts.

149 Oligarchic party led by Hanno returns to power in Carthage.

Start of siege of Carthage.

146 Destruction of Carthage by Scipio Aemilianus.

Destruction of Corinth by a Roman army under Lucius Mummius.

122 Attempted Roman colony on site of Carthage led by Gaius Gracchus fails.

29 Augustus begins the construction of the new Roman city of Carthage.

29–19 Vergil writes the *Aeneid*.

Acknowledgements

This book would not have been written without the support and forbearance of a large number of people.

Particular thanks are due to my editors Simon Winder and Wendy Wolf at Penguin and Viking and Peter Robinson for their patience and advice over the years. I owe an enormous debt of gratitude to Philip Booth, Peter Garnsey, Irad Malkin, Robin Osborne and Peter Van Dommelen, who read and commented on the whole or various sections of this book. I also benefited greatly from discussions with Roald Docter, the late Friedrich Rakob and Dick Whittaker, Henry Hurst, Dexter Hoyos, Tim Whitmarsh, Claudia Kunze, Mike Clover, Jim McKeown, Martin Davidson, and Joseph Maxwell on different aspects of Carthage and the ancient Mediterranean world. Various chapters of this book were greatly improved by the valuable contributions made by participants at seminars at the Universities of London, Illinois–Champaign–Urbana, Wisconsin–Madison, Cambridge and Sydney.

Much of this book was written during sabbatical leave at the Institute of Research into the Humanities at the University of Wisconsin–Madison in 2007 – 8. I am very grateful to the director of the Institute, Susan Friedman, and its fellows and staff for providing such an intellectually congenial working environment. I would also like to acknowledge the support afforded to me over the years by my colleagues in the Faculty of Classics and Trinity Hall at the University of Cambridge.

Lastly, my love and thanks to Camilla, Maisie, Jessamy and Gabriel, who have all lived with Carthage for far too long.

Cambridge
May 2009

Prologue:
The Last Days of Carthage

Carthage had been under siege for nearly three years when one day during the spring of 146 BC the Roman commander, Scipio Aemilianus, ordered the final assault on the stricken city and its increasingly desperate inhabitants.

Even now, with its defences and defenders greatly weakened, Carthage still posed a daunting challenge for the Roman attackers. Situated on the Mediterranean coast of what is now Tunisia, the city was built on a peninsula made up of a series of sandstone hills. On its north-eastern and south-eastern peripheries, two narrow strands of land jutted out like wings, with the latter almost cutting off the sea and creating the large lagoon now known as the Lake of Tunis. The northern area of the peninsula was protected by a series of steep sandstone cliffs, whereas to the south lay a large coastal plain protected by a formidable set of walls, ditches and ramparts.

On the seaward side of the city two magnificent harbours were shielded by a sea wall. A chronic shortage of available living space within the city had meant that security had been somewhat compromised in this area. Whereas previously a gap had been carefully maintained between the wall and the nearest buildings, now houses had been constructed right up to the sea walls, allowing determined attackers the opportunity of setting fire to them with missiles or gaining access by climbing on to their roofs.[1] However, the walls themselves still presented an intimidating obstacle, with some of the huge sandstone blocks weighing over 13 tonnes. The blocks were covered in white plaster, which not only protected the stone from the elements, but also gave the walls a famous shimmering marble effect when looked upon from ships sailing into the city's harbours.[2]

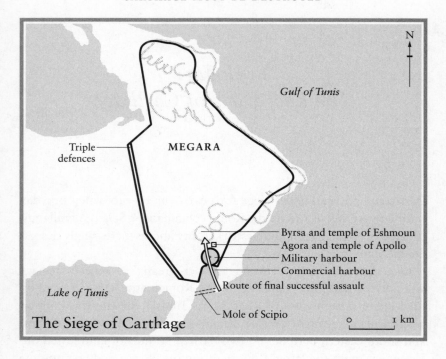

The two harbours – one commercial and one military – stood as a reminder of Carthage's past fame as a maritime superpower. These vast man-made structures, which covered an area of around 13 hectares, had required the manual excavation of some 235,000 cubic metres of soil. The rectangular commercial harbour had extensive quays and warehousing where goods from all over the Mediterranean world and beyond were loaded and unloaded.[3] The circular war harbour was an engineering masterpiece, with storeyed ship-sheds which could hold at least 170 vessels, with ramps to drag them from and to the water's edge.[4] Now the harbours lay idle, because the Romans, after many fruitless attempts, had finally managed to secure their blockade by constructing a mole to block their entrance.

As the Romans had also managed to seal Carthage from its North African hinterland, no further food supplies could be brought into the city – meaning that much of the population was beginning to starve. Physical evidence still exists showing that life for the inhabitants of Carthage had taken a dramatic turn for the worse during the siege. At some point, probably when the siege made them impossible, rubbish collections ceased (a resident's nightmare, but an archaeologist's dream).[5] During the last difficult years of the city, the only waste that seems to have been regularly removed was the corpses of the many who died as starvation and disease took hold. Now, in the last terrible months of the city's existence, in contrast to the care that had traditionally been taken of the dead, the corpses of both rich and poor were unceremoniously dumped in a number of mass graves just a short distance away from where they had lived.[6]

When the attack finally came, the city's defenders were caught off guard, because the Carthaginian commander, Hasdrubal, had gambled on an assault being mounted on the commercial port, whereas in fact the Romans attacked the war harbour first. From the harbour, the legionaries quickly moved to seize control of Carthage's famous agora, or marketplace, where Scipio ordered his men to set up camp for the night. The Roman troops, sensing that final victory was near, began the inevitable plunder by stripping the nearby temple of Apollo of its gold decoration.[7]

Carthage was divided into two distinct but integrated parts. While the lower city was laid out orthogonally in a formal grid, the streets on the slopes of the citadel, the Byrsa, were arranged in a radial pattern.[8] Now that many of the neighbourhoods on the plain had been secured, Scipio called up fresh troops in preparation for the storming of the Byrsa. The soldiers proceeded with caution, as the nature of the hill made it an excellent terrain from which to stage ambushes. Three narrow streets led up the steep slopes. Each was flanked by six-storey houses from whose roofs their inhabitants mounted a desperate last defence by raining missiles down on to the advancing legionaries. However, Scipio, a seasoned siege tactician, quickly regained the momentum by commanding his troops to storm the houses and make their way to the roofs. From there they used planks to create gangways over to the adjacent houses. While this battle raged above, the slaughter on the streets continued.

Once the resistance on the roofs had been neutralized, Scipio ordered that the houses be set alight. So that his troops' progress up the hill should be unimpeded, he also commanded that cleaning parties should keep the streets clear of debris. However, it would not be just stone and burning timber that came crashing down from above, but also the bodies of children and the elderly who had been sheltered in secret hiding places within the buildings. Many, although injured and horribly burnt, were still alive, and their piteous cries would add to the cacophony around them. Some were subsequently crushed to death by the Roman cavalry proceeding up the streets. Others would meet a far more gruesome end as the street cleaners dragged their still breathing bodies out of the way with their iron tools before tossing both the living and the dead into pits.

For six long days and nights the streets of Carthage were consumed by this hellish turmoil, with Scipio conserving the physical strength and sanity of his men by regularly rotating his killing squads. Then, on the seventh day, a delegation of Carthaginian elders bearing olive branches from the sacred temple of Eshmoun as a sign of peace came to beg the Roman general that their lives and those of their fellow citizens be spared. Scipio acceded to their request, and later that day 50,000 men, women and children left the citadel through a narrow gate in the wall into a life of miserable slavery.

Although the vast majority of its surviving citizenry had surrendered, Hasdrubal, his family and 900 Roman deserters, who could expect no mercy from Scipio, still held out. They took refuge in the temple of Eshmoun, which, because of its lofty and inaccessible position, they were able to defend for some time. Eventually lack of sleep, physical fatigue, hunger and terror forced them on to the roof of the building, where they made a final stand.

It was now that Hasdrubal's nerve broke. Deserting his comrades and family, he secretly made his way down and surrendered to Scipio. The sight of their general grovelling in supplication at the feet of his Roman nemesis merely hardened the resolve of the remaining defenders to die a defiant death. Cursing Hasdrubal, they set fire to the building and died in the flames.

It would be Hasdrubal's own wife, with her terrified children cowering at her side, who would deliver the final damning verdict on her disgraced husband: 'Wretch,' she exclaimed, 'traitor, most effeminate of men, this fire will entomb me and my children. Will you, the leader of great Carthage, decorate a Roman triumph? Ah, what punishment will you not receive from him at whose feet you are now sitting.' She then killed her children and flung their bodies into the fire, before throwing herself in after them. After 700 years of existence, Carthage was no more.[9]

Introduction:
Recovering Carthage

HANNIBAL'S SHIELD

In the late first century AD, Silius Italicus, a very rich Roman senator with literary pretensions, wrote the *Punica*, an epic poem that took as its subject the Second Punic War, between Carthage and Rome. At over 12,000 lines long, the work almost made up in sheer ambition for its author's lack of poetic talent. One of its more memorable sections centred on a suit of fine bronze armour and weaponry, strengthened with steel and finished in gold, that skilled Galician smiths presented as a gift to the great Carthaginian general Hannibal while he was on military campaign in Spain. In laborious detail, Silius related how it was not just the excellent craftsmanship of the plumed helmet, triple bossed breastplate, sword and spear that delighted Hannibal, but the intricate scenes from Carthage's past engraved upon a great shield. This medley of historical highlights included the foundation of the city by the Tyrian queen Dido, the doomed love affair between Dido and the Trojan founder of the Roman people, Aeneas, scenes from the first great war between Carthage and Rome, and episodes from the early career of Hannibal himself. These vignettes were adorned with a little local colour in the form of supposedly 'African' bucolic scenes, including animal herding, hunting, and the soothing of wild beasts. Silius went on to describe how, delighted with the gift, Hannibal exclaimed, 'Ah! What torrents of Roman blood will drench these arms.'[1]

Resplendent in his new armour, the Carthaginian general would become a walking, and very deadly, lesson in history. But was it Carthage's lesson or Rome's? Certainly most of this prehistory of the most famous war that Rome had ever fought was complete fiction. So what? one might ask. After all, the *Punica* itself was written not as history, but as a (not particularly good) epic poem. However, by the time that Silius was writing, nearly 250 years after the final destruction of Carthage, the scenes engraved upon Hannibal's shield were part of a very real canon of historical 'fact' that had reduced Carthage to little more than a ghostly handmaid to Roman greatness. Moreover, the 'historical' episodes depicted on Hannibal's shield represented Carthaginians in profoundly negative terms – as impious, bloodthirsty, sly and deceitful. In one scene Hannibal was even represented in the act of breaking the treaty with Rome which led directly to the second Punic War – a reference to the by then established historical orthodoxy that it was Carthage's own perfidy rather than Roman ambition that had brought about its downfall. Such was the emphasis placed by the Romans on Carthaginian treachery that the Latin idiom *fides Punica*, literally 'Carthaginian faith', became a widely used ironic expression denoting gross faithlessness.[2]

The Romans were not the first to develop the powerful negative stereotypes of Carthaginians as mendacious, greedy, untrustworthy, cruel, arrogant and irreligious.[3] As with many aspects of Roman culture, the hostile ethnic profiling of the Carthaginians originated with the Greeks: in particular, with those Greeks who had settled on the island of Sicily and had, before the rise of Rome, been Carthage's main rivals for commercial and political supremacy in the region. However, it had been the Romans who obliterated not only the physical fabric of Carthage but also much of its history, by giving away virtually all the content of Carthage's libraries to their local allies, the Numidian princes,[4] in 146 BC, thereby leaving Rome's own version of events unchallenged.

However, the dispersal and destruction of Carthage's own historical records did not mean that there would be no history of Carthage. The spoils of war included the ownership of not only Carthage's territory, resources and people, but also its past. Carthage was indispensable to Rome because of the central role that it had played in the development of a series of now well-established Roman myths. It was during their wars against Carthage that Romans had first begun to write their own history, and Carthage's subsequent destruction ensured not only the authority of this new (Roman) historical orthodoxy, but also the survival of a defeated Carthage in the popular imagination.

THE LONG SHADOW OF ROME

The most celebrated of Carthage's sons and daughters were little more than mere bit players in the early annals of Roman history. The famous Dido–Aeneas romance, with the latter callously deserting the Carthaginian queen in order to go off to Italy, where his descendants eventually founded Rome, was in fact the invention of the great Roman poet Vergil, long after the destruction of the city. Dido herself, although possibly the product of an earlier Phoenician or Sicilian Greek story, was developed as a character only by later Roman writers.[5] And even Hannibal, the most famous Carthaginian of all, was in part immortalized for his usefulness as a foil for the genius of that great Roman hero Scipio Africanus.

Carthage was just too important to Rome simply to disappear into obliterated obscurity. After all, the great victory over Hannibal in the Second Punic War was considered by many influential Romans to have been their finest hour. Some even believed that the final solution visited on Carthage had been a profound mistake, for the city had provided the whetstone on which Rome's greatness had been sharpened.[6]

Carthage may have been destroyed, but it was never forgotten. Even many years later, the memory of the terrible events that had taken place there still hung heavy over the rubble-strewn site where the city had once stood. Paradoxically, Carthage remained a place that most needed to be remembered by the very people who had so thoroughly destroyed it.[7] For members of the Roman elite, almost any kind of personal reverse or fall from grace could be placed into its correct context by a stroll – usually of the cerebral rather than physical variety – through the pitiful remains of what had been one of the greatest cities of the ancient world. Some, however, had the opportunity of a more direct form of contemplation. Some fifty years after Carthage's final destruction, Gaius Marius, a Roman general who had been forced into exile by his political opponents, was said to have lived a life of poverty in a hut among the city's ruins, prompting one ancient writer, Velleius, to comment, 'There Marius, as he looked upon Carthage, and Carthage as it gazed upon Marius, might well have offered consolation to one another.'[8] However, this regret at Carthage's passing should not be mistaken for respect for a valiant foe. It sprang from a self-indulgent nostalgia for a fantastical golden age when Romans had been proper Romans.

The success of the Roman project to rewrite the history of Carthage is visible everywhere – even in the terminology used by modern scholarship to define the city and its people. For the period from the sixth century BC onward, we use the term 'Punic' to describe not only the dominant culture of Carthage, but also the diaspora of old Phoenician colonies that stretched across North Africa, Sardinia, western Sicily, Malta and the Balearic Islands, as well as southern and south-eastern Spain. It was not, however, a word that Carthaginians or their western Mediterranean peers of Levantine origin used to define themselves, but an ethnic moniker given to them by the Romans. The Latin noun *Poenus*, often used by Romans to describe Carthaginians, and from which the adjective *Punicus* was derived, was hardly a neutral term. As one scholar has pointed out, its use by Roman writers was nearly always 'defamatory and pejorative', and it was 'the term of choice for negative discourse'.[9]

The negative associations surrounding the Carthaginians have proved to be extraordinarily pervasive – particularly the idea that, through its aggression, Carthage had brought its own ghastly end upon itself. When the poet and playwright Bertolt Brecht cast around for a historical metaphor to remind his fellow Germans about the dangers of remilitarization in the 1950s, he instinctively turned to a series of events that had taken place over two thousand years before: 'Great Carthage drove three wars. After the first one it was still powerful. After the second one it was still inhabitable. After the third one it was no longer possible to find her.' [10]

Many of the prejudices first found in Greek and Roman texts were enthusiastically adopted and adapted by the educated elites of eighteenth- and nineteenth-century Europe and America, who had grown increasingly interested in classical antiquity. The attitudes that they found in the Greek and Roman literature that they read quickly became their own. Thus the idea that the British – the inhabitants of 'La perfide Albion' – were in fact the Carthaginians of contemporary Europe firmly took hold in Republican France.[11] The sentiment soon spread across Europe and beyond.[12] Thomas Jefferson, president of the United States in 1801–9, wrote of Britain, 'Her good faith! The faith of a nation of merchants! The *Punica fides* of modern Carthage.'[13] A nation of shopkeepers could not be trusted to keep its word.[14]

For the great powers of nineteenth-century Europe, the emulation of these ancient prejudices was linked to something far more particular than mere admiration for the classical world. During the colonial land-grab of the second half of the nineteenth century, the Roman Empire understandably provided an attractive blueprint for these new imperial powers, and Carthage also had a role to play as an ancient paradigm for the barbarity and inferiority of the indigenous populations that they now ruled over. Similarly, when the French had first started writing of perfidious Albion, it had been as much a way of bolstering their own imperialist claims as it was about undermining British pretensions to be the new Rome.[15]

For the French, in particular, who from the 1830s onward were pursuing long-term strategic goals in the Maghrib, the stories of Carthaginian cruelty, decadence and deceit that abounded in both ancient Greek and Roman literature were eagerly seized upon and projected on to the Arabs who now lived in the region. In North Africa, France would be the new Rome. The most famous product of these colonial assumptions would be Gustave Flaubert's novel *Salammbô*. Published in 1862 and set in ancient Carthage, *Salammbô* was a roller-coaster ride of sexual sadism, extreme cruelty and repugnant luxury.[16] In other words, it played to every western-European stereotype that existed at that time about the decadent Orient. It also served as a sideswipe at the French bourgeoisie, whose religious conservatism, materialism and political bankruptcy Flaubert so despised.[17]

The overarching influence of Roman authors on modern perceptions of Carthage was further reinforced by the trenchant criticism that *Salammbô* received. This had nothing to do with the savagery, sex and licentiousness that appeared on almost every page, but concerned the obscurity of the subject. One critic indignantly wrote, 'How do you want me to be interested in this lost war, buried in the defiles and sands of Africa . . . ? What is this to me, the duel between Tunis and Carthage? Speak to me rather of the duel between Carthage and Rome! I am attentive to it, I am involved in it. Between Rome and Carthage, in their fierce quarrel, all of future civilization is already in play.'[18] The point was that any aspect of Carthaginian history that was not associated with Rome was of no real interest or importance for an educated audience.

Carthage would also prove itself to be as attractive a metaphor for the oppressed as it was for their oppressors. For some, the fate of Carthage, as the victim of brutal cultural vandalism by a ruthless conqueror, appeared so uncannily to resemble their own circumstances that a common heritage could be the only plausible explanation. Eighteenth-century Irish antiquarians, reacting against Anglocentric assertions that the Irish were descendants of the Scythians, an ancient people from the Black Sea famed for their barbarity, counterclaimed that in fact their forebears were the Carthaginians. Serious scholarly attempts were made to attribute megalithic passage tombs in the Boyne valley to the Phoenicians, and to link the Irish language to Punic.[19] These theories predictably attracted the ridicule of many in England, including the following mocking verse from Byron:

> He was what Erin calls, in her sublime
>   Old Erse or Irish, or it may be *Punic*; –
> (The antiquarians who can settle Time,
>   Which settles all things, Greek, Roman or Runic,
> Swear that Pat's language sprung from the same clime
>   With Hannibal, and wears the Tyrian tunic
> Of Dido's alphabet; and this is rational
>   As any other notion, and not national;) –
>
> But Juan was quite 'a broth of a boy,' . . . [20]

In the time of the 'Troubles' in Northern Ireland, although the historical reality of a Carthaginian heritage no longer had any currency, writers such as Seamus Heaney still continued to view Carthage as a powerful metaphor for the situation on the island.[21]

In recent years the ongoing crisis in Iraq has also afforded political commentators many opportunities to equate the situation in that unfortunate land with what had befallen Carthage.[22] The following words by the American sociologist and historian Franz Schurmann are typical of the kind of emotive comparisons that have been drawn:

Two thousand years ago the Roman statesman Cato the Elder kept crying out, 'Delenda est Carthago' – Carthage must be destroyed! To Cato it was clear either Rome or Carthage but not both could dominate the western Mediterranean. Rome won and Carthage was levelled to the ground.

Iraq is now Washington's Carthage.[23]

The inconvenient truth that the Punic world incorporated considerable areas of southern Europe has often been put to one side as a strange historical anomaly as we in the West have become accustomed to seeing ourselves as the heirs of Greece and Rome. Indeed, the casting of Iraq as the new Carthage is emblematic of that close association, which is an admission of the clear distinctions that we draw between ourselves and not only the Iraqis but also the Carthaginians. Schurmann's words, rather than making a convincing case for Iraq being the new Carthage, simply highlight the current (equally bogus) obsession with America being the twenty-first-century Rome. One might legitimately ask, What do modern Iraq and eighteenth-century Ireland have in common with ancient Carthage? The answer is, Very little besides their conquest and suppression by a self-appointed new 'Rome', whether Georgian Britain or present-day America. The continued 'relevance' of Carthage has always been contingent on our abiding obsession with its nemesis, Rome.[24]

WRITING A HISTORY OF CARTHAGE

In the face of such a litany of destruction and misrepresentation, both ancient and modern, one might legitimately ask whether it is really possible to write a history of Carthage that is anything more than just another extended essay on victimhood and vilification.[25] A key difficulty is the lack of surviving literary and material testimony from the Carthaginians themselves.

There are some intriguing but equally frustrating clues to the literature that may have existed. Within the burnt-out structure of a temple (thought by its discoverer, the German archaeologist Friedrich Rakob, to have been the temple of Apollo ransacked by Roman soldiers in 146 BC), were the remains of an archive thought to have contained wills and business contracts, stored there so that its integrity and safe keeping was guaranteed by the sacred authority of the god. The papyrus on which the documents were written was rolled up and string was wrapped around it before a piece of wet clay, then imprinted with a personal seal, was placed on the string to stop the document from unravelling. However, in this particular case the same set of circumstances that ensured that the seal was wonderfully preserved because it was fired by the inferno which engulfed the city also unfortunately meant that the precious documents themselves were burnt to ashes.[26]

When faced with such historical lacunae, there is always a temptation to overcompensate when imagining what has actually been lost. However, we should be wary of assuming that the shelves of Carthage's famous libraries groaned under the weight of a vast corpus of Punic and earlier Near Eastern knowledge now destroyed. Although in the ancient world rumours circulated about mysterious sacred parchments which had been hidden away before Carthage fell, and there are scattered references to Punic histories in much later Roman literature, it is difficult to gauge whether the city was really a great literary centre like Athens or Alexandria.[27]

It was not Punic literature but Carthaginian technical expertise that the Romans were most interested in acquiring. After the capture of the city, the Roman Senate ordered that all twenty-eight volumes of a famous agricultural treatise by the Carthaginian Mago be brought back to Rome and translated into Latin.[28] Unfortunately, although cited in numerous Roman, Greek, Byzantine and Arabic texts, Mago's work has not survived to the present.[29] Its disappearance, however, has not deterred some modern scholars from hailing it as the agronomic bible of the ancient world.[30]

At times, researching a history of the city is rather like reading a transcript of a conversation in which one participant's contribution has been deleted. However, the responses of the existing interlocutors – in this case Greek and Roman writers – allows one to follow the thread of the discussion. Indeed, it is the sheer range and scale of these 'conversations' that allows the historian of Carthage to re-create some of what has been expunged. Ideology and egotism dictate that even historians united in hostility towards their subject still manage vehemently to disagree with one another, and it is within the contradictions and differences of opinion that exist between these writers that the deficiencies of their heavily biased account can be partially overcome.

Of all the ancient commentators on Carthage, none encapsulates the limitations of what remains of the historical record better than the Sicilian Greek Timaeus of Tauromenium. Timaeus, who lived from around 345 to 250 BC, wrote a history of his home island down to 264, the year that the First Punic War broke out between Carthage and Rome.[31] As the Carthaginians were heavily involved politically, militarily and economically in Sicilian affairs throughout much of the fifth and fourth centuries BC, they featured prominently in Timaeus' narrative. Indeed, for much of that important period of Carthaginian history Timaeus provides the only historical narrative we have.

Timaeus' 'testimony' comes with a number of extremely important caveats. First, he is what might be called a 'ghost historian', because none of his oeuvre directly survives. However, his work became immensely influential among later Greek and Roman historians, who used it extensively in their own studies.[32] It has been possible, therefore, for modern scholars painstakingly to retrieve a considerable amount of Timaeus' history of Sicily from the work of his admirers – in particular another Sicilian Greek, Diodorus Siculus, writing in the first century AD – because they often extensively and openly followed his account. Second, as an individual who spent most of his adult life in exile in Athens, Timaeus was often far removed from the events that he described. Lastly, his account of Carthage was coloured by his implacable hostility towards it.

Timaeus' portrayal of Carthage was often predictably negative and clichéd, and there is a marked contrast between the often extremely superficial treatment of Carthaginian motivations and issues and the much more detailed and balanced analysis of the strategies followed by Sicilian Greek leaders.[33] Most significantly, Timaeus very successfully promoted the idea of Carthage as the agent of the barbarous Orient in the West, and of its attitudes towards the Greeks being dictated by ethnic hatred.[34] He typified the Carthaginians as the beneficiaries of almost unlimited resources that allowed them to raise a succession of enormous invasion forces whose sole aim was the destruction of the Greek communities that lived on Sicily.[35]

Timaeus also worked hard to pin negative ethnic stereotypes on to the Carthaginians – such as their alleged softness, proved by their habit of keeping their hands hidden in the folds of their clothing, and their wearing loincloths under their tunics.[36] He lavished particular lurid attention on the supposed Carthaginian enthusiasm for human and particularly child sacrifice, by including in his account the mass killing of infants to appease the gods when Carthage was besieged by the Greek general Agathocles.[37] He was also anxious to portray the Carthaginians as being exceptionally cruel and unmerciful: 'There was no sparing of their captives, but they were without compassion for their victims of Fortune, of whom they would crucify some and upon others inflict unbearable outrages.'[38] Even the mercy shown by the Carthaginians towards women hiding in the temples of the captured Sicilian city of Selinus was explained away by Timaeus as yet another example of their sacrilegious greed, as they feared that those who had taken refuge might set fire to their hiding places, thereby depriving the Carthaginians of the opportunity of plundering them.[39] The impiety of the Carthaginians was a regular theme in Timaeus' Sicilian opus, as they pillaged the temples and even the tombs of the Greeks – for which they were often the subsequent targets of divine retribution such as plague, storms and military disaster.

That Carthage's relationship with Greek culture was typified by greed and theft was a common theme in Timaeus' work. He recounted how the Carthaginian general Himilcar, on capturing Acragas, carefully ransacked the city, sending a vast number of paintings and sculptures back to Carthage, despite some of the citizens' best efforts to stop the looting of the temples by setting them ablaze.[40]

Although what remains of Timaeus in Diodorus' *The Library of History* should be treated with considerable caution, subjecting it to endless postmodernist deconstruction delivers extremely limited returns. One must remain sensitive to the partisan and fragmentary nature of Timaeus' portrayal of Carthage, as well as vigilant with respect to the clichés and exaggerations within it, but there is no reason to dismiss his account as wholesale fabrication. Timaeus' dubious testimony of all-out ethnic conflict in Sicily is very useful precisely because it was so clearly a reaction to a far more complex set of interactions between the Punic and Greek populations on the island.

There had in fact been a number of writers who took an actively pro-Carthaginian position in their histories, such as the Greeks Philinus of Acragas (a historian of the First Punic War) and Sosylus and Silenus (companions of Hannibal in the Second).[41] Although their work has survived only in sparse fragments, we are fortunate that a number of conscientious Roman historians, such as the late-second-century-BC Roman writer Coelius Antipater, made extensive use of it – while Antipater's work has also not withstood the ravages of time, it in turn was heavily used by Livy, whose history of early Rome has mostly survived.[42]

We also owe much to the unfailingly critical eye of Polybius, the best extant historian writing on this period.[43] A Greek aristocrat who had come to Rome as a hostage in the 160s BC, he became a key member of the entourage of the Roman aristocrat commander Scipio Aemilianus. Over the next two decades Polybius travelled around the Mediterranean world with Scipio, and he was actually present at the final siege and fall of Carthage in 146 BC. Although Polybius was fundamentally hostile to Carthage, he was proud of being a thorough and scholarly practitioner of his art. He certainly did not hesitate to point out what he considered to be the errors committed by fellow historians.[44] Nor was it just pro-Carthaginian writers who were the victims of his scorn. His attitude towards Timaeus in some parts of his work has been accurately described as 'consistently abusive'.[45]

But Polybius was happy to acknowledge those who (in his view) upheld the high standards that he demanded of historical scholarship, whatever their standpoint. Thus, although he fundamentally disagreed with Philinus on a number of issues, Polybius clearly respected him as a historian whose didactic approach closely mirrored his own, and he therefore used his work as a basis for his own account of the First Punic War.[46] This means that the modern historian of Carthage gleans some idea of the positions taken up by pro-Carthaginian writers and other historians even if Polybius considered those positions to be erroneous.

As regards other material evidence, the ruins of Carthage have always stirred the imagination of those who have visited them. Rumours that the Carthaginians had managed to bury their riches in the hope of returning to retrieve them in better times had led the troops of one first-century-BC Roman general to launch an impromptu treasure hunt.[47] For the modern archaeologist Carthage can resemble a complicated jigsaw of which many pieces have been intentionally thrown away. Yet history tells us that attempts to destroy all traces of an enemy are rarely as comprehensive as their perpetrators would have us believe.

Although the religious centre on the Byrsa was completely demolished, many of the outlying districts and, as we have already seen, some parts of the hill itself escaped total destruction. In fact the Romans inadvertently did much to preserve parts of Punic Carthage by dumping thousands of cubic metres of rubble and debris on top of it. Even the ominous 60-cm-thick black tidemark found in the stratigraphy of the western slopes of the Byrsa – the sinister archaeological record of the burning down of the city in 146 BC – is packed full of southern-Italian tableware, telling us what pottery styles were in vogue in Carthage at that time.[48]

Then there are the thousands of monuments recording votive offerings made to Baal Hammon and Tanit, the chief deities of Carthage, which, although extremely formulaic in their wording, have furnished invaluable information on Punic religious rites, particularly child sacrifice. There are also a small number of surviving inscriptions relating to other aspects of city life, such as the construction of public monuments and the carrying out of an assortment of religious rituals. This epigraphic evidence has been helpful in aiding understanding not only of Carthage's religious life, but also of the social hierarchies that existed within the city.[49] It is from such writing on slabs of stone that we learn of the faceless potters, metalsmiths, clothweavers, fullers, furniture-makers, carters, butchers, stonemasons, jewellers, doctors, scribes, interpreters, cloak attendants, surveyors, priests, heralds, furnace workers and merchants who made up the population of the city.[50]

LOCATING CARTHAGE

The second problem facing the historian of Carthage is less tangible but equally pressing: where should the historian *place* the city within the wider context of the ancient Mediterranean world, particularly in relation to the acknowledged great 'western' civilizations of Greece and Rome? After all, Carthage may have been physically located in the western Mediterranean, but, even half a millennium after the first Phoenician settlers had established the city, its historic Levantine heritage still played a major role in its cultural, religious and linguistic traditions.

The relationship between the Carthaginians and their Phoenician heritage was particularly strong in the area of religious observance and worship. Right up until the destruction of their city, Carthaginian parents still named their offspring from the same narrow pool as their ancestors had done, based on the names of Phoenician gods (a nightmare for the historian, as we will find out). The most famous Carthaginian name of all, Hannibal, means 'The Grace of Baal', while another popular one, Bodaštart, translates into 'In the Hands of Astarte' (the Punic goddess of fertility). Names may also have been chosen for more precise meanings, such as the woman Abibaal ('My Father is Baal'), whose mother, Arišut-Ba'al ('Object of Desire of Baal'), may have been a temple prostitute or a priestess at the temple of the god.[51]

The importance of Phoenicia in the construction of Carthaginian religious identity is further confirmed by the finely engraved religious monument known as a stele erected by Abibaal as part of a dedication. It shows a priestess (perhaps the supplicant) making an offering of a cow's head to the flames on an altar made up of a capital on top of a pillar base. The woman is dressed in a long robe, and holds an offering box in her left hand, while her right hand is in the traditional pose of supplication. Although this monument has been dated to the last decades of Carthage's existence, it depicts a traditional sacred rite that can be traced right back to rituals that were performed in the Near East a thousand years earlier.[52]

For the Greeks and the Romans, the ambiguity surrounding the identity of Carthage meant that Carthaginians could be represented as the worst of both Western and Eastern worlds: uncultured barbarians *and* effeminate, lazy, dishonest and cruel orientals.[53] This was a judgement that was enthusiastically taken up by many eighteenth- and nineteenth-century western Europeans, in a colonial age when the intermixing of races was frowned upon.[54] However, while highlighting a strong continuity with Levantine traditions and practices, artefacts such as the stele of Abibaal provide only a very partial view of what was actually a far more complex cultural DNA. In particular, what little remains of Punic art and architecture attests to an extraordinary eclecticism and openness to new influences and ideas.

Around the beginning of the second century BC, a wealthy Punic citizen of Sabratha, a city several hundred kilometres to the east of Carthage in what is now Libya that had long been under Carthaginian political and cultural influence, commissioned a mausoleum for himself.[55] This strikingly original three-storey structure, standing at over 23 metres high, was built out of local sandstone blocks and was planned as a truncated triangle with concave facades.[56] At ground level a stepped base led up to a first storey with columns decorated with Ionic capitals on its three corner points and decorative semi-columns in the centre of the facades. The principal facade consisted of a false door decorated with two lions facing each other, and above it a typically Egyptianate architrave with winged solar discs and a stylized frieze. On a second storey were a series of sculpted metopes whose reliefs showed mythological scenes: the dwarf-like Egyptian god Bes (long popular across the Punic world for his ability to ward off evil spirits) overcoming two lions, and the Greek hero Heracles fulfilling the first of his famous ten labours, the subjugation of the monstrous Nemean lion. In a further architectural extravagance, the metopes were flanked by three lions which in turn supported rectangular consoles on which stood 3-metre-tall kouroi (statues of young men). Finally, a pyramidal shaft crowned the structure's apex.

To any Greek contemporary, the Sabratha mausoleum would have managed to look both familiar and alien at the same time. Many of the mausoleum's artistic and architectural elements – including the capitals, columns, kouroi and metopes – hailed from the Greek artistic and architectural canon. Furthermore, the metopes were covered in brightly painted stucco in the same fashion as their Greek equivalents. These colours were used to particularly striking effect on the central panel. The naked flesh of Bes was deep pink. The brilliant white of his loincloth and teeth highlighted the red of his lugubrious lips and the cobalt blue of his beard. Colour also added greatly to the expressiveness of the lions, with their blue manes resting on deep-yellow bodies. The turquoise of their lifeless eyes and the red of their lolling tongues set against the brilliant white of their teeth contrasted with the flaccidity of death.

The heavy use of Egyptian architectural styling and themes also points to the influence of the great new Greek city of Alexandria to the east, where an exciting fusion of native and Greek styles had taken place. And yet other clues suggest that the monument's designer was certainly no Greek architect (the Punic world had in any case been integrating Greek and Egyptian styles into its art and architecture since at least the sixth century BC). The anatomic details on the stocky body of Bes, for example, are articulated on the metope by the use of surface decoration, a typically Punic technique. Another hallmark of Punic art, an obsessive attention to detail and symmetry, is also much in evidence on the Sabratha mausoleum. Thus the two triangles that make up the pointed beard of Bes correspond exactly to their counterparts that mark the lower border of the god's white loincloth on the thighs. Even locks of hair are individually drawn out.

More importantly, one finds that the usual conventions of time and place have been discarded: archaic kouroi jostle with classical and Hellenistic elements.[57] Traditional Greek fable is also given a fresh twist, with Heracles dispatching the Nemean lion with a short sword rather than by strangulation. There is a freedom here that one simply does not find even in the more liberal artistic milieu created by Alexander the Great's conquest of the Persian Empire and the subsequent close contact of the Greeks with the venerable cultures of the East during the third and second centuries BC. Even more heretical to the Greek architectural eye would have been the stunted proportions of the columns on the first floor, which are reduced to being little more than a base for the storey above. One would never find this lack of proportion in a Greek building of that period, however provincial its setting.

However, this willingness to use styles that had long gone out of fashion in the Hellenic world, often in unfamiliar combinations, should be seen not as evidence of boorish gaucheness or a lack of artistic vision, but rather as further evidence of the creative independence that typified the Punic commonwealth. Yet the most surprising aspect of the Sabratha mausoleum was its success as a building. By rights this strange multi-tiered structure crammed with a hotchpotch of cultural references and artistic styles should have been an architectural disaster. However, the bold interplay between shadow and light created by the concave lines and the height of the structure combined with the elegant vertical flow of the colonnades and the kouroi mean that this monument stands as a graceful but unmistakably Punic view of the world.

Too often an overemphasis on the eclecticism of the influences found in Punic art, rather than consideration of the originality of their assemblage, has led to the false assumption that the Carthaginians' engagement with more 'inventive' and 'original' cultures – in particular Greece – amounted to little more than passive consumption or shallow ventriloquism. The considerable evidence that exists for Punic populations speaking Greek, writing works on Greek literature, studying Greek philosophy, wearing Greek clothes, and venerating Greek deities has commonly been taken as confirmation of that view.[58] By the same token, the clear debt that ancient Greek culture owed to the great civilizations of the Near East has often been met with derision and denial.[59]

In fact the Sabratha mausoleum stands as a stunning monument not to the derivative nature of late Punic culture, but to the extent to which the Punic world was part of a wider economically and culturally joined-up community that spanned much of south-western Europe and North Africa long before it was politically united under the imperial aegis of Rome. It was not a world founded on the overwhelming political or military supremacy of one particular power, but a much looser network made up of the diverse peoples – Punic, Greek, Etruscan and others – who lived along its shores. These different ethnic groups were initially linked together by maritime trade – the engine through which goods, people, techniques and ideas flowed across the ancient Mediterranean. Instead of stemming from the domination of one imperial power, the creative and economic dynamism that characterized the West during this period was often forged out of the bitter commercial and political rivalries that existed between near equals: the Punic and Greek populations who had both originally come westward in search of land and trade.

As the dominant commercial maritime power in the region throughout much of the first millennium BC, Carthage was one of the centrepieces of a pre-Roman western Mediterranean defined as much by its cultural, economic and political synergies as by the divisions and enmities which feature so prominently in the surviving textual accounts. A major aim of this book is to recover some of this long-forgotten world. For it is only when Carthage is once more placed within its proper trans-Mediterranean context that the historical significance of this once great North African metropolis can be retrieved from the dead weight of wanton destruction and gross misrepresentation that has for so long subsumed it.

A constant presence throughout this book is the great hero Heracles (or Hercules). It may seen strange, even perverse, that a Greek deity who would also become a major figure in the Roman celestial pantheon should play such a prominent role in a book about Carthage. However, Heracles, better than any other figure, stands as an emblem of the cultural diversity and interconnectivity that typified the ancient Mediterranean. Although, as the great wanderer and strongman of Hellenic myth, Heracles was closely associated with Greek colonial endeavour, he also epitomized the syncretism – the amalgamation of different religions, cultures and schools of thought – that was one of the main results of the contacts that Greek colonists made with other ethnic groups, particularly the Punic diaspora. From the sixth century BC onward, Heracles came to be increasingly associated with the Punic god Melqart in the minds of not only the Punic but also the Greek populations of the central and western Mediterranean. It was no coincidence that, when the great Carthaginian general Hannibal cast around for a celestial figurehead to unite the people of the West against the ever-increasing power of Rome, he should choose the figure of Heracles–Melqart. Indeed, during the Second Punic War, Heracles came to symbolize the spoils of victory for which Carthage and Rome fought so hard and so long: the right not only to dictate the economic and political future of the region, but also to claim ownership of its distinguished past.

Attempts to conjure up contemporary relevance with regard to the ancient world can often appear trite and laboured at best, and fatuous and false at worst. However, the history of Carthage does force us to reassess some of the comfortable historical certainties that underpin many of the modern West's assumptions about its own cultural and intellectual heritage. The 'classical world' still revered as the fount of much of Western civilization was never an exclusively Graeco-Roman achievement, but was the result of a much more complex set of inter-actions between many different cultures and peoples.

Thus Carthage stands not only as an eloquent testament to the cultural diversity that once exemplified the ancient Mediterranean, but also as a stark reminder of just how ruthlessly that past has been selected for us.

I

Feeding the Beast: The Phoenicians and the Discovery of the West

THE LAND OF THE COLOUR PURPLE

Sometime in the second quarter of the ninth century BC, the Great King of Assyria Ashurnasirpal II marched his army to the Phoenician coast, where he ostentatiously washed his weapons in the waters of the Mediterranean and made offerings to the gods. This ominous gesture elicited exactly the response it was supposed to: 'I received the tribute of the kings of the seacoast – namely, the lands of the peoples of Tyre, Sidon, Byblos, Mahallatu, Maizu, Kaizu, Amurru and the city of Arvad, which is in the middle of the sea – silver, gold, tin, bronze, a bronze vessel, multicoloured linen garments, a large female monkey, a small female monkey, ebony, boxwood, and ivory of sea creatures. They submitted to me.'[1]

This was not the first visit that an Assyrian king had made to Phoenicia, but it marked a new chapter in Assyria's interest in the region.[2] Assyria was in the ascendant, and the Phoenician cities would now be expected regularly to provide considerable quantities of tribute in exchange for their continued political autonomy.[3] We are fortunate that the Assyrians understood the power of the image and the authority of the word. In their ruined cities, archaeologists have uncovered considerable numbers of inscriptions and bas-reliefs setting out their blueprint for empire. They present a striking portrait of a formidable military machine manned by legions of warriors sporting trademark carefully curled beards and hair. With their graphic depictions of endless battles, sacked cities, mass deportations and slaughter on a grand scale, the bas-reliefs of Assyria bring home the ruthlessness required to carve out and maintain an empire which at its height took

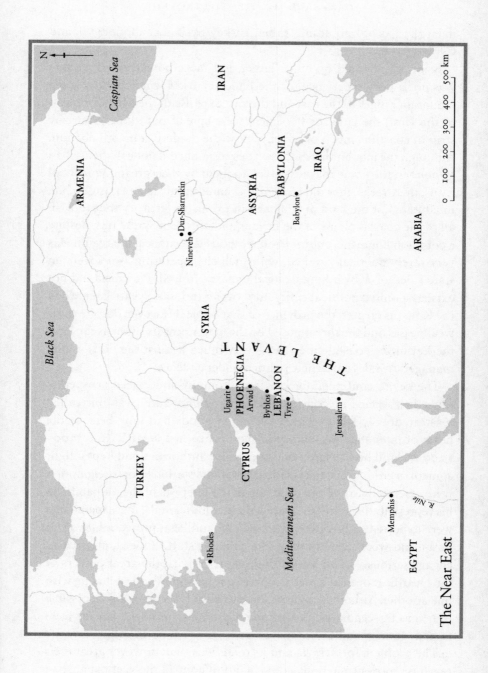

The Near East

in large parts of Iraq, Iran, Arabia, Turkey, Syria, Lebanon, Egypt and Cyprus.[4]

Being intimidated by much larger and more powerful neighbours was not a new experience for the Phoenicians.[5] Hemmed in by steep mountain ranges to the east and the vast expanse of the Mediterranean to the west, the cities of Phoenicia were spread out along a narrow strip of coastline much of which is now the modern state of Lebanon. Although the inhabitants of these cities certainly did not call themselves *Phoínikes*, the name that was given to them by their great commercial rivals, the Greeks, they did recognize a shared ethnic identity as *Can'nai*, inhabitants of the land of Canaan, an extensive territory that took in all of the coastal plains of the Levant and northern Syria.[6] Yet, despite a common linguistic, cultural and religious inheritance, the region was very rarely politically united, with each city operating as a sovereign state ruled over by a king or local dynast.[7] Indeed, Phoenicia did not exist as a united political entity until over a thousand years later, when the Romans created the province of that name. However, despite these weaknesses and the threat posed by the major powers of the Near East, the Levantine coastal cities had – very much against the odds – long managed to safeguard their political independence.

The key to continued Phoenician autonomy and indeed prosperity, often in the face of considerable external pressure, was unrivalled mastery of sea. The exchange of luxury goods had long been at the heart of inter-state diplomacy in the Bronze Age Near East, c.3300–1200 BC, and had ensured that the palace authorities had kept a tight control over long-distance trade. Merchants stationed in foreign ports were essentially royal agents acting in the interests of the monarch. As his representatives and not merely private individuals, these merchants were expected to be offered commercial and legal protection by their hosts, and were treated rather like embassy staff.[8] Indeed, in order to engage seriously in high-level diplomatic activity, the great powers of the Near East needed a ready source of luxury goods to exchange with one another. Although some of these materials were readily accessible – such as the cedarwood for which the mountains of the Levant were famed – others had to be fetched from lands across the sea.

The problem for Assyria and its rivals was that, however great their reach on terra firma, none could claim to control the vast expanse of

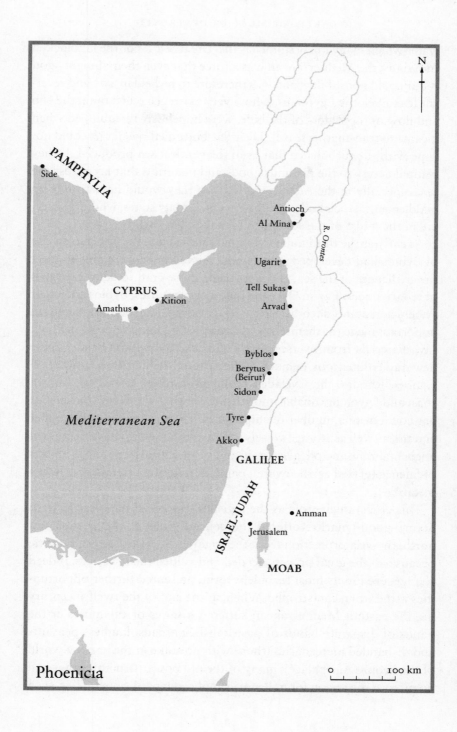

N

PAMPHYLIA

Side

Antioch
Al Mina

R. Orontes

Ugarit

Tell Sukas

Arvad

CYPRUS

Amathus Kition

Byblos

Berytus
(Beirut)

Sidon

Mediterranean Sea

Tyre

Akko

GALILEE

ISRAEL-JUDAH

Amman

Jerusalem

MOAB

Phoenicia

0   100 km

water which many knew simply as the 'Great Sea'.[9] For the landlocked Assyrians, the Mediterranean was a force that even their almighty god Assur could not subdue, and was therefore to be held in awe and reverent fear. Even the Egyptians, whose very existence relied upon the ebb and flow of the waters of the Nile, were hopelessly ill-equipped when it came to transmarine travel. Their flat-bottomed river craft could not cope with the turbulence that even the gentlest sea produced. If they wanted access to the precious goods and materials that lay across the sea, especially in the Aegean world, then they would have to rely on middlemen, a crucial role that the Phoenician city states, whose 'borders are in the midst of the seas', would make their own.[10]

As early as the third millennium BC, sailors from the Phoenician city of Byblos had developed ships whose curved hulls were able to meet the challenges of the sea, and were using those craft to deliver cargoes of cedarwood to Egypt. Over the following centuries, Byblos and other Phoenician states such as Sidon, Tyre, Arvad and Beirut created an important niche for themselves by transporting luxury goods and bulk raw materials from overseas markets back to the Near East.[11] These new trade routes took in much of the eastern Mediterranean, including Cyprus, Rhodes, the Cyclades, mainland Greece, Crete, the Libyan coast and Egypt. Invaluable information on what was being transported has come from a number of shipwrecks. There were ingots of copper and tin, as well as storage vessels which are thought to have contained unguents, wine and oil, glass, gold and silver jewellery, precious objects of faience (glazed earthenware), painted pottery tools, and even scrap metal.[12]

This crucial niche role as the logistics experts of the Near Eastern luxury-goods market offered the coastal cities of the Levant and northern Syria protection from the vagaries of Near Eastern politics, because all the great powers needed and valued their services. Indeed change, even in its most turbulent form, presented further opportunities rather than catastrophe. When, at the end of the twelfth century BC, the eastern Mediterranean suffered a series of calamities at the hands of disparate bands of pastoralists, nomads, landless peasants and disbanded mercenaries (those with no stake in the narrow world of the Bronze Age palace), many of the old power structures that had dominated the region for millennia simply collapsed. Some states, such as the northern Syrian state of Ugarit, and the Hittite Empire in Asia Minor, simply disappeared, whereas others, such as Assyria and Egypt, were seriously weakened.

The top-heavy structure of the priestly scribal and military elites had ultimately provided monarchs with too shallow a power base to overcome any serious challenge. Social problems were exacerbated by a rigidly centralized and controlled economy which simply did not allow enough wealth to trickle down to the poorer classes. Once raiders had made agriculture difficult, and maritime trade in copper and tin impossible, the end for many Bronze Age palace societies was nigh. One might have thought that the dramatic decline of the very structures which they had serviced would have spelled disaster for the Phoenician city states. Instead, it ushered in a golden age of nearly three centuries, during which they were able to operate without serious external interference.

The disappearance of state-controlled commerce liberated traders from the restrictions that had previously inhibited their operations. Long-distance trade was transformed from being a palace monopoly into a commercial venture entered into by businessmen in order to make profits for themselves.[13] In the coastal cities of Phoenicia, groups of traders organized themselves into 'firms', which appear to have revolved around extended families, in order to exploit commercial opportunities. Although commerce was no longer under their strict control, the Phoenician kings were still heavily involved in trading operations. Indeed, the palace often appears to have operated as a bank or moneylender for mercantile ventures. The relationship between business and the state was further reinforced by the presence of the patriarchs of the mercantile firms – referred to in the Bible as the merchant princes or the 'princes of the sea' – on a powerful council of elders who advised the king.[14]

With no threatening neighbour to appease, and many of their commercial rivals in northern Syria destroyed, the Phoenician cities were able to extend their trading networks greatly.[15] The new Phoenician mercantile elite would also increasingly expand its commercial activities to take in the manufacture of luxury goods. Precious materials were unloaded at the docks and transported to workshops to be processed. Ivory from northern Syria, Africa and India was carved into delicate furniture inlays. The most luxurious pieces were further embellished by the skilful insertion of precious stones and coloured glass (Phoenicia was also a centre for the manufacture of glass and faience). Egyptian- and Assyrian-themed designs show the extent to which these luxury products were manufactured for the foreign rather than the home market. Metalwork was another speciality, with Phoenician craftsmen displaying an extraordinary level of skill in producing bronze and silver bowls, often in a bewildering array of different styles. Traditionally, art historians have tended to treat this work as little more than talented mimicry, but what makes it uniquely Phoenician is its extraordinary eclecticism.[16] Gold and silver jewellery, often embellished with semi-precious stones and exhibiting an astonishing degree of detail, was produced in considerable quantities. Favourite motifs included Egyptian magic symbols such as the eye of Horus, the scarab beetle and the solar crescent, and these were thought to protect their wearers from the evil spirits that prowled the world of the living, such as the 'flyers' or 'stranglers' of the night and the serpent demon *Mzh*.[17]

However, not all the goods produced in the Phoenician towns were connected to luxury. Large numbers of ordinary domestic utensils and agricultural tools made of iron were also exported, as well as weapons such as javelins and lance heads. But, the products for which the Phoenician cities would become most renowned were luxuriously embroidered garments and cloth dyed in deepest purple. Their quality would be recognized in ancient literature from the Bible to Homer's *Odyssey*. Indeed, the Greeks would name the people of the Levantine coast after their word for purple or crimson: *phoinix*.[18] The dye was obtained from the hypobranchial glands of two species of mollusc that proliferated in the region. Installations for the production of the dye have been found by archaeologists in a number of Phoenician towns. First the molluscs were caught in nets, before the shells were smashed and the molluscs left for a period of time to dry out. They were then added to salt water in whatever ratio was required to produce a particular purple hue. Although the stench that emanated from the rotting molluscs was so overpowering that the dye factories were located right on the edge of town, production was often on a huge scale, with the mound of discarded murex shells at Sidon measuring over 40 metres high.[19]

It was also during this period of relative freedom that a number of Phoenician cities were able to rise to a position of regional prominence. Indeed, the lack of predators in the political food chain entailed that a reasonably extensive and fertile agricultural hinterland was a distinct advantage, in the Levant as in other regions. Better protected, but therefore more isolated, settlements on an island site, such as Tyre, now tended to be overshadowed by their more richly endowed neighbours who controlled the resources of the mainland, including access to fresh water.

THE RISE OF THE CITY OF MELQART

By the tenth century BC, however, the balance of power among the Phoenician cities had begun to change, for Tyre, under the dynamic leadership of its kings Abibaal and then Hiram, was in the ascendant. Chronic water shortages had been solved by the boring of deep water cisterns into the island rock, and Abibaal had laid the foundations of expansion through astute diplomacy and political awareness.[20] With Egypt still in a period of sustained decrepitude and Assyria and Babylonia also in decline, a new power had emerged in the form of the recently united Jewish kingdom of Israel–Judah. Hiram was quick to realize the potential to outstrip the other Phoenician cities, and sent an embassy to the victorious Israelite king David, with gifts which, of course, included cedarwood.[21] An alliance with Israel was all the more desirable because its territory bordered the narrow hinterlands of Tyre and of other Phoenician cities, effectively cutting them off from the lucrative interior trade routes that led eastward.

When Solomon succeeded David to the Israelite throne in 961 BC, Hiram followed up his father's initial diplomatic work by sending another delegation to congratulate the new king. The overtures appear to have paid off, for Tyre and Israel signed a commercial agreement which contracted the former to supply timber and skilled craftsmen to work on two new magnificent buildings in the city of Jerusalem: a temple to the Israelite god, Yahweh, and a royal palace.[22] Hiram sent large numbers of his subjects to fell cedars and cypresses on Mount Lebanon, while other skilled Tyrian craftsmen dressed stone for the temple in the quarries, before it was transported to Jerusalem.[23] Solomon had also commissioned Cheiromos, a caster of mixed Israelite–Tyrian parentage, to create intricate gold, silver and bronze decorations for the temple.[24]

In exchange, as well as a payment of silver, the Israelites would deliver annual provisions of over 400,000 litres of wheat and 420,000 litres of olive oil – a great boon for Tyre, with its limited territory.[25] The original treaty ran for twenty years, and at its conclusion (marked by the completion of both structures) a new pact was signed. In exchange for a large cash payment of 120 talents of gold, Solomon sold Tyre twenty cities in the Galilee and Akko plain, an area famous for its agricultural production.[26] Tyre now had the hinterland which it needed to consolidate its position in the Levant.

There were other benefits too. Commercially, this deal not only gave Tyre privileged access to the valuable markets of Israel, Judaea and northern Syria, it also provided further opportunities for joint overseas ventures. Indeed, a Tyrian–Israelite expedition travelled to the Sudan and Somalia, and perhaps even as far as the Indian Ocean. Unsurprisingly, when the fleet returned laden with cargoes of gold, silver, ivory and precious stones, this lucrative enterprise was repeated. In the early decades of the ninth century BC, Tyrian–Israelite relations would be further strengthened by the marriage of the daughter of King Ithobaal I of Tyre, the infamous Jezebel, to the new king of Israel, Ahab.[27]

The innovative Hiram also ushered in other radical changes in Tyre. Phoenician religious belief and practice were part of a wider Syrio-Palestinian tradition that encompassed much of western Syria and the states of Israel, Judah and Moab.[28] As adherents to a polytheistic religious system, the Phoenicians worshipped a wide range of deities, although there does appear to have been some kind of hierarchy. At the head of the Phoenician divine pantheon were El and Asherah, while the god Baal, in numerous different manifestations, played the chief executive role in a subordinate but more active day-to-day capacity.[29]

Religious ritual was a central part of the public and private life of the Phoenician cities. The great temples of the gods were the richest and, after the palace, the most powerful institutions in the Near East. They were huge corporations in their own right, employing not just priests but also a host of other professions. Some even had temple barbers for supplicants who wished to offer up their hair as a gift to a particular deity, and temple prostitutes, whose earnings supplemented the income of the temple. This concentration of power and wealth meant that tensions naturally existed between the temples and the other main power structure in the city, the royal palace. Indeed, it seems that a desire to bring the temples to heel lay behind the royal decision to replace the traditional chief deities of Tyre with a new god, Melqart (his name meaning 'King of the City'), who would rule over their pantheon with his consort, the goddess Astarte. According to one ancient source, in order to guarantee the success of his religious putsch, Hiram had the temples of the old Tyrian gods demolished and built magnificent new sanctuaries for Melqart and Astarte. Although the latter part of this account is probably correct, it is unlikely that the religious revolution was quite so drastic as to have required the destruction of the old Phoenician pantheon.

These changes signified not the demise of the old gods, but rather a significant readjustment of the Tyrian religious landscape. Indeed, it appears that El continued as the chief deity of Tyre, and that the three storm gods Baal Shamen, Baal Malagê and Baal Saphon maintained their seniority. However, Melqart was now the undisputed divine patron of the royal house. Thus he was a 'political' god, who acted both as figurehead and as vehicle for the aspirations of the king. The idea may have been imported from the Phoenician city of Byblos, where Baalat Gubal ('the Lady of Byblos') had long been worshipped in a similar manner.[30]

Through the worship of Melqart, the king could portray himself as the bridge between the temporal and celestial worlds, and the needs of the heavenly gods could closely correspond with the political exigencies of the palace.[31] The king even introduced an elaborate new ceremonial to celebrate the annual festival of Melqart.[32] Each spring, in a carefully choreographed festival called the *egersis*, an effigy of the god was placed on a giant raft before being ritually burnt as it drifted out to sea while hymns were sung by the assembled crowds. For the Tyrians, as for many other ancient Near Eastern peoples, the emphasis fell upon the restorative properties of fire, for the god himself was not destroyed but revived by the smoke, and the burning of the effigy thus represented his rebirth. To emphasize the importance of the *egersis* in maintaining the internal cohesion of the Tyrian people, all foreigners had to leave the city for the duration of the ceremony. Afterwards the king and his chief consort would take the roles of Melqart and Astarte in a ritual marriage which guaranteed the well-being and fertility of the king, as well as his legitimate authority. Indeed, the ceremony went far beyond ritual pageantry and role play. It strongly suggested that the king was nothing less than the living embodiment of the great Melqart.[33]

Hiram does not seem to have been alone in his desire to stamp royal authority on the religious identity of his city. At Sidon the king appears to have promoted the role of the deities Eshmoun and Astarte as the guardians and protectors of the royal dynasty, and took up with his immediate family the role of chief priests of their cults.[34] It was also surely no coincidence that Eshmoun, like Melqart, was closely associated with fertility and the cycles of death and regeneration.[35]

Over the centuries, Melqart became increasingly dominant in Tyre, to the extent that he was often given the title of Baal Sôr, divine 'Lord of Tyre', and was even feted as the original founder of the city. When the Greek historian Herodotus visited the great temple of Melqart at Tyre in the fifth century BC, the priests told him that the temple had been built 2,300 years before, at the same time as the city's foundation.[36]

Indeed, in a later Greek story that might have much older Phoenician origins, it was related that the site of Tyre had once consisted of two rocks called the 'Ambrosian stones'. They were uninhabited aside from a solitary flaming olive tree on which perched an eagle and a beautifully crafted bowl. Completing this strange spectacle was a serpent coiled around the trunk and branches. Despite the grave potential for disaster, a peaceful status quo remained in force, with neither the snake nor the eagle attempting to attack the other. Likewise, the blazing olive tree and the creatures which inhabited it were, miraculously, never consumed by the fire. Furthermore, the bowl never slipped and fell from the branches, despite the billowing maritime gales. In contrast to the state of suspended animation that existed on them, the Ambrosian stones themselves drifted rootless around the waters of the Mediterranean. Inspired by the god/hero Melqart, who had come to them in human form, the inhabitants of the mainland built the first ever ship: 'a new kind of vehicle to travel on the brine . . . the chariot of the sea, the first craft that ever sailed which can heave you over the deep' to take them to the itinerant rocks.[37] There they landed, and, as instructed by Melqart, the future citizens of Tyre captured the eagle and sacrificed it to Zeus, splattering its blood on the rocks. Henceforth the Ambrosian stones were anchored to the seabed and wandered no more. The citadel of Tyre was then built on them, with a temple for the worship of Melqart.[38] Herodotus, in his account of the temple, described how it contained twin pillars – one made of pure gold and the other of emerald, perhaps representing the flaming olive tree – which gleamed brightly in the dark of the night.[39]

In this strange tale, the importance of Melqart to the people of Tyre was reflected not only in his role as the founder of their city, but also by his gift of the first boat, which gave them the means to cross the great expanse of the Mediterranean. As the sea was the key to Tyre's prosperity, and at times to its very existence, it was logical that maritime success be attributed to the god who had, in the city's mythology, enabled naval travel.[40] Moreover as Tyrian political influence increasingly extended outside Phoenicia, so did Melqart's visibility. During the ninth century in northern Syria, where Tyre had extensive commercial interests, we find a local potentate erecting a monument to the god and depicting him wearing a horned helmet and brandishing a battleaxe.[41]

The long-term effectiveness of Hiram's policies became clear in the consolidation of Tyrian influence among the Phoenician cities, to the extent that Sidon came under Tyre's control.[42] Indeed, some scholars have argued that a separate Phoenician identity was formed precisely in this period, the product of a powerful Tyrian–Sidonian axis in the southern Levant, and of the subsequent use of the names *Pūt* and *Ponnim* for its cities and peoples. It is at least clear that, as Tyre's commercial influence grew, so it became an important hub for joint ventures involving Phoenicians from other cities along the Levantine coast.[43]

Tyrian commerce was further strengthened by Phoenician advances in navigation and ship construction, which greatly expanded the geographical range and speed of trading operations. The first of these innovations was the use of the Pole Star (which came to be known as the *Phoiniké*) as a navigational tool allowing sailors to travel on the open seas at night. The second involved a series of revolutionary developments in shipbuilding. The keel and the practice of coating the wooden planks of the ships' hulls with bitumen tar so that they remained watertight were both Phoenician inventions. The Phoenician name for merchant ships in Greek (*gauloi*) later also took on the meaning of bathtubs, on account of the ships' huge bulbous hulls. These boats were the perfect marriage between maximum storage space and speed. Despite their size, they were, thanks to their single huge square sail and teams of oarsmen, deceptively nimble, and in good weather conditions they could cover up to 40 kilometres per day.[44]

By the early decades of the ninth century BC Tyre, under the leadership of Ithobaal I, had established itself at the centre of an impressive trading network which took in much of Asia Minor, Cyprus, Armenia, the Ionian Islands, Rhodes, Syria, Judah, Israel, Arabia and the Near East.[45] A new artificial southern harbour was also built to handle the huge volume of goods that passed through the port. It was named the 'Egyptian', for the slumbering giant Egypt had at last woken from its long-term economic stupor and, seeing a new commercial opportunity, the Tyrians had brokered a new alliance, which resulted in a resumption of large-scale trade.[46]

Since at least the tenth century BC, a common modus operandi for Phoenician merchants in the Aegean and the eastern Mediterranean was the establishment of enclaves among the indigenous communities with whom they traded. Over time these commercial contacts developed into more permanent relationships, with evidence of the setting-up of unguent-bottling factories on the islands of Crete, Rhodes and Cos.[47] Some settlements in the region also start to show signs of a more established Phoenician community, such as Kommos in southern Crete, where the remains of a particular type of tri-pillar Levantine religious shrine, probably dating to the early ninth century BC, have been discovered.[48]

It has generally been assumed that the existence of locally made copies of Near Eastern styles of pottery and metalware in the eastern Mediterranean and the Aegean – commonly known as the 'orientalizing' phenomenon – indicates what was originally the work of immigrant Phoenician smiths and potters and their indigenous apprentices.[49] However, it is clear that the Tyrians in particular had, by the end of the ninth century, begun to develop a new set of relationships with the overseas lands with which they traded.

Cyprus had long been linked with the Levantine cities and had been an established part of the eastern Mediterranean trade route since the second millennium BC, mainly on account of the rich copper deposits that were located in the island's interior.[50] The first Tyrian colony was at Kition, on the site of a previously abandoned mercantile settlement. The paucity of Greek pottery and other luxury foreign goods found by archaeologists at Kition shows that it was not set up as a typical trading hub. Other Cypriot ports, such as Amathus, were already fulfilling that function. The primary aim of the settlement was to give the Tyrians access to the rich copper reserves of the Cypriot interior, which could be then smelted and shipped back to Tyre, from a site that would provide its Phoenician settlers with a fertile hinterland for agriculture. Unlike previous overseas commercial enterprises, where Levantine traders and craftsmen had lived within, and under the protection of, the indigenous communities with whom they conducted business, Kition and other Tyrian colonies were treated as Tyrian sovereign territory and were administered by a governor who reported directly to the king.[51] It is clear that the Tyrian king was prepared to protect his interests on Cyprus even with force if necessary. When the inhabitants of Kition rebelled against Tyrian rule, Hiram swiftly sent troops to crush the revolt.[52]

However, there were also more subtle means of control at the Tyrian kings' disposal. Of particular importance was the promotion of the cult of Melqart at Kition, with a substantial temple being dedicated to the god and his celestial consort, Astarte, on the ruins of a late-Bronze Age sanctuary at the end of the ninth century BC.[53] The long-standing importance of Melqart to the citizens of Kition is attested by the fact that the god still appeared on the coinage of the city 400 years later.[54]

While such monuments serve as ample testament to the growing power and assertiveness of Tyre, the visit of Ashurnasirpal II and his army, far from being an isolated event, signalled that the epoch of relative independence for the Phoenician cities was coming to an end, and over the ensuing decades the Levantine coastal cities would find themselves under increasing pressure from Assyria. To ensure their political autonomy, and perhaps even their survival, they would once more return to their traditional role as chief procurers for a potentially threatening neighbour.

FEEDING THE ASSYRIAN BEAST

The Assyrian kingdom, although keen to claim publicly its relationship with other Near Eastern states as a simple matter of total submission brought about by brute military force, with the subsequent provision of tribute, was also engaged in a far more subtle strategic game, which involved the control of inter-regional trade networks.[55] The soldiers, weavers, leatherworkers, farmers, ironsmiths and other workers needed to keep the Assyrian state functioning required raw materials and payment.[56] Courtiers and high-ranking royal officials were granted estates and tax immunities as a reward for their service and loyalty.[57] The Great Kings represented themselves as the great providers. They would boast that the vast spoils that flowed back to Assyria from their conquests were used to bring prosperity to even their most humble subjects.[58]

Precious materials were also required on a vast scale, in order to keep up with a slew of magnificent royal building projects designed to engender both awe and obedience. Of particular note was the 'Palace without Rival', built by the Assyrian monarch Sennacherib at Nineveh in the early seventh century BC. It was massive – over 10,000 square metres in area – and opulently decorated with scented woods ornamented with silver, copper and intricately carved ivory. The exterior walls were decorated with a mass of coloured glazed bricks. Every centimetre of the structure was covered with detailed narrative scenes outlining the king's triumphs. Even the furniture was made of materials of the highest quality, for it was inlaid with ivory and precious metals.[59]

To function successfully, the Assyrian state required a regular supply of high-quality materials and luxury finished goods on a scale that only trade, not conquest, could provide. Increasingly, it was the Phoenician cities that the Assyrian kings expected to meet these heavy demands, as well as to provide a large number of ships and crews for the royal fleet. Of particular importance from the Assyrian perspective was the flow of precious metals – especially silver, which would eventually become the accepted currency throughout the empire – and of the iron required for armaments.[60] The Phoenician cities' usefulness to Assyria meant that some would continue to enjoy a certain degree of political and economic autonomy, instead of incorporation into the empire.[61] Indeed, the establishment of Kition may have been a reaction to the economic pressure that Assyria now exerted on the Phoenician cities, with Tyre no longer able to rely solely on the continued goodwill of its Cypriot trading partners.

However, the real geopolitical watershed was reached when, at the start of the eighth century BC, the Assyrian king Adad-Ninari III conquered northern Syria.[62] This development could be accurately described as a mixed blessing for the Tyrians. On the positive side, the Assyrian seizure of northern Syria had removed at a stroke some of their keenest commercial competitors. On the negative side, however, the loss of an important Tyrian source of precious metals was compounded when the victorious conqueror demanded those very same commodities as Phoenician tribute. If these stupendous demands were to be met, then new sources of mineral wealth had to be prospected and exploited. Moreover, they would also require a vast expansion of the scope and geographical range of previous Phoen-ician commercial operations. It thus appears to have been survival, rather than glory, that provided the motivation for the great Levantine colonial expansion in the far-off lands of the West.[63]

THE 'DISCOVERY' OF THE WEST

There has been much academic controversy about quite when the peoples of the Levant first became involved in trade in the central and western Mediterranean. It seems clear that the first western Phoenician colonies were established during the late ninth/early eighth centuries BC; however, the evidence for 'pre-colonial' mercantile activity is far less certain. Some Near Eastern goods were certainly circulating in the region in the earlier period, but who transported them is unknown.[64]

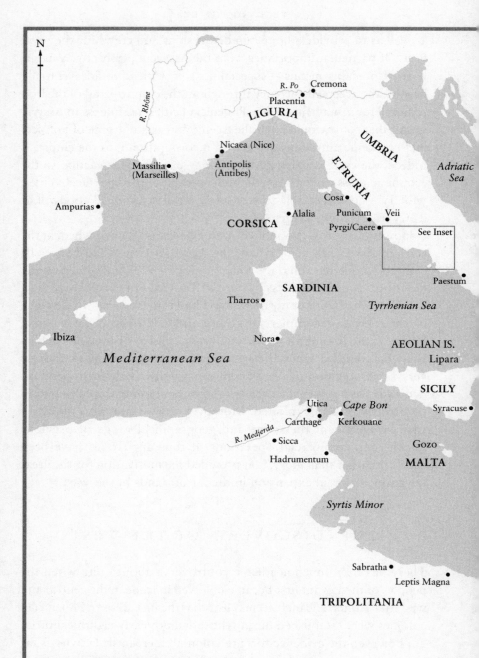

The Central Mediterranean

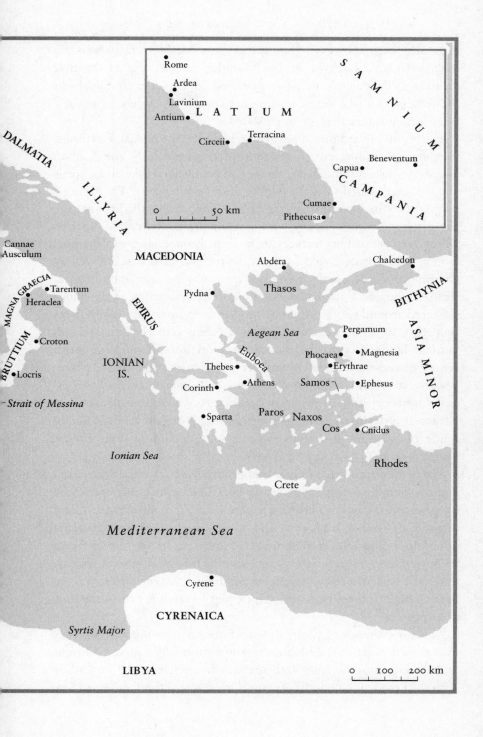

Rome

Ardea

Lavinium

Antium

LATIUM

SAMNIUM

Circeii

Terracina

Capua

Beneventum

CAMPANIA

Cumae

Pithecusa

0   50 km

DALMATIA

ILLYRIA

Cannae

Ausculum

MACEDONIA

Abdera

Chalcedon

MAGNA GRAECIA

Tarentum

Heraclea

BRUTTIUM

Croton

Locris

Pydna

Thasos

EPIRUS

BITHYNIA

Aegean Sea

Pergamum

ASIA MINOR

Phocaea

Magnesia

Euboea

Erythrae

IONIAN
IS.

Thebes

Samos

Ephesus

Strait of Messina

Corinth

Athens

Sparta

Paros

Naxos

Cos

Cnidus

Ionian Sea

Rhodes

Crete

Mediterranean Sea

Cyrene

CYRENAICA

Syrtis Major

LIBYA

0   100   200 km

It is also clear, however, that the central Mediterranean was no unsophisticated backwater, and that the real success of the first identifiable Phoenicians in the area derived not from the establishment of a completely new set of trading networks, but largely from their insertion into ones that already existed.

The island of Sardinia, in particular, had been the nexus of a vibrant transmarine trading circuit that included central Italy, the Aeolian Islands, to the north of Sicily, the Iberian peninsula, Crete and Cyprus and that had existed since the twelfth century or before.[65] The Nuragic people who had dominated the island since the early Bronze Age possessed a complex society with a sophisticated material culture of which the most striking features are intricate bronze figurines depicting, among other things, wild animals, warriors and boats. As well as communal tombs, well-sanctuaries and subterranean monumental shrines, Nuragic settlements usually consisted of circular dwellings clustered around very substantial two- or three-storey dry-wall towers (nuraghi), sometimes enclosed within a defensive perimeter (and still familiar landmarks on the island). More elaborate complexes with central towers surrounded by smaller lateral ones are thought to have been the strongholds of petty chiefdoms, and some of them were eventually transformed into religious shrines.[66] As well as having mastered advanced agricultural techniques such as viticulture, the Nuragic inhabitants of Sardinia also transported goods, including fine pottery, overseas on their own sailing vessels.

The first Phoenician immigrants appear to have arrived on the island in the late ninth or early eighth century BC. Like Cyprus, Sardinia would have been of interest to Phoenician merchants for its substantial inland deposits of copper, lead, iron and silver, which were already being mined by indigenous communities.[67] However, despite the fact that there were also fertile coastal plains suitable for agriculture, it appears that the first Levantine presence on Sardinia was very different from the colonial ventures that were taking place at roughly the same time in Cyprus.

At the metalworking centre of Sant' Imbenia, now modern Alghero, in the north-west of the island, the population was a mixed Nuragic and Phoenician one. Sant' Imbenia was heavily involved in trading with the Etruscan kingdoms of central Italy, across the Tyrrhenian Sea, and it appears likely that its Nuragic and Phoenician inhabitants were cooperating in commercial ventures.[68] Sant' Imbenia and central Italy would also be the scene of Levantine interactions with other newcomers trying to establish their own commercial and colonial networks. At Pithecusa on the island of Ischia in the Bay of Naples, colonists from the Greek island of Euboea had established a settlement which, like Sant' Imbenia, had a diverse demographic that included indigenous people and a sizeable number of persons of Levantine origin. Archaeologists calculate that the latter may have made up as much as 20 per cent of the settlement's population.[69] It is thought that Euboeans were resident at Sant' Imbenia too. It has also been suggested recently that the city of Olbia on the north-east coast of Sardinia may have been a Greek or mixed settlement from the second half of the eighth century.[70] Certainly there was considerable trade, and possibly other interactions, between the two settlements.[71]

The chief object of establishing Pithecusa, like Sant' Imbenia, was to acquire raw materials – particularly iron, which was exchanged with mainland neighbours such as the Etruscans and Campanians for luxury goods from the Near East and the Aegean.[72] The presence of iron-smelting workshops shows that the ore was probably processed on the island. Much of the Phoenician consolidation in the West has been viewed as an emphatic response to aggressive Greek colonization in the region; however, there is in fact good evidence for Phoenician–Greek cooperation in some of these early colonies.[73] Although new dating evidence seems to show that the Phoenicians were trading in central Italy slightly before the Greeks, there is little evidence for tension between the two during this period.[74] At Pithecusa, the Euboeans and the Phoenicians appear to have cooperated with one another because their commercial objectives were complementary rather than competitive. The Phoenicians were interested in acquiring the abundant silver in northern Etruria, a raw material in which the Greeks, despite growing wealth, showed little interest at this time.[75] One can assume that the operations in Sardinia were equally complementary. Indeed, one might argue that it is in these first colonial ventures in the central Mediterranean that one witnesses the growth of the 'Middle Ground' on which Phoenician, Greek and indigenous populations interacted and cooperated.[76]

THE PHOENICIANS AND THE
RECOVERY OF GREECE

The Euboeans and Phoenicians already had a long shared history in the eastern Mediterranean. And it appears that Levantine traders had done much to reconnect the inhabitants of Greece with the Near East after several centuries of insularity and obscurity. After the implosion of the Mycenaean civilization at the beginning of the twelfth century BC, which was part of the wider regional collapse at the end of the Bronze Age, Greece had suffered a huge drop in population, calculated by some at around 75 per cent. Furthermore, its inhabitants had abandoned sophisticated settlements and had forgotten many of the features that we associate with civilized life: monumental architecture, figurative art and even the ability to write had disappeared, and contact with the outside world had all but ceased.[77]

By the tenth century BC, however, the first signs of a quiet revolution can be detected in the archaeological record. At the settlement of Lefkandi on the island of Euboea, a surprising discovery has been made among the pottery and artefacts with which its inhabitants were usually buried. Arranged around the female occupant of Tomb 86 were gilt hair-coils and dress pins, and other bronze objects. Her bleached and brittle finger bones, covered in an assortment of nine gold rings, were placed over a finely crafted gilded bronze bowl. Although it is agreed that these luxury goods had come from the Near East, the question of how they got there is controversial. The Euboeans were the only Greeks during this period with sufficient experience of medium- and long-distance trade, but there is no evidence that they were engaged in contemporary mercantile operations with the Near East.[78] It is far more plausible that the Phoenicians brought these goods to Greece.[79] They had been continuously involved in Aegean trade since at least the fourteenth century BC. Their interest in resource-poor Greece probably lay in the fact that Euboea, through its successful regional trading networks within Greece, was far wealthier than other population centres.[80] There also appears to have been a growing demand for Euboean pottery in the Near East – a market that the Phoenicians would have wanted to control.[81]

At the same time that the flow of goods to Greece from the Near East was increasing – particularly as emerging Greek institutions such as temples and religious sanctuaries grouped together to arrange the import of high-status offerings from the region – so too was the quantity of Greek pottery going in the opposite direction.[82] By the end of the ninth century BC the Euboeans were undoubtedly involved in trans-Mediterranean transportation, for ninth-century archaeological evidence from the north-Syrian coastal trading station of Al Mina, located near the mouth of the river Orontes, points to the existence of Phoenicians and Euboeans residing and trading together in what was most probably an indigenously controlled settlement.[83]

Increasingly scholars have also speculated on the Phoenicians' involvement in joint commercial ventures with Greeks besides the Euboeans. One particularly intriguing case is the city of Corinth, the pottery of which shows a clear 'orientalizing' influence, and begins to be exported in large quantities to both Phoenician and Greek settlements in the central and western Mediterranean during this period.[84]

Luxury goods and artisan techniques were not the only things that the Phoenicians had brought with them to Greece. Although the Phoenicians went to trade and not to deliver an extended tutorial on culture, many aspects of Greek literature, language, religious ritual and art were clearly heavily influenced by the Near East.[85] Perhaps most important was the alphabet.[86] The great strength of the Phoenician alphabetic script was that it could easily be learned by rote, and this was the way that the creator of the first Greek alphabet would have learned it.[87] The first examples of Greek writing, scratched on pottery shards from Lefkandi, on the island of Euboea, date to the second quarter of the eighth century BC, and most scholars agree that the script was an adaptation of the Phoenician alphabet.[88] The loan words which the Greeks borrowed from the Phoenicians – *byblos* (the papyrus reed used as a writing material), *deltos* (a writing tablet), *byssos* (linen), *sakkos* (sack), *gaulos* (ship), *makellon* (market), *titanos* (lime), *gypsum* (plaster), *harpe* (curved sword), *macha* (battle) – give some indication of the scope of these adaptations.[89] Predictably, many of the most important Phoenician innovations adopted by the Greeks related to maritime commerce – such as interest-bearing loans, maritime insurance, joint financing of commercial ventures, deposit banking, and, possibly, weights and measures.[90] The Phoenicians were thus the bridge which brought the economic and cultural advances of the Near East to Greece and which created the foundation not only for future cooperation but also for deep-seated tensions between Phoenicians and Greeks.

The increase in Greek mercantile activities, however, makes it increasingly difficult to separate out the Greeks' achievements from those of the Phoenicians. The best example of this is the invention of the trireme, the dominant warship on the Mediterranean between the seventh and fourth centuries BC, an achievement claimed for both sides by modern academics. The trireme had numerous advantages over its predecessor the penteconter, a narrow craft of around 25 metres in length, powered by a team of around fifty oarsmen and a single sail. The trireme was much more powerful, having space for eighty rowers who were placed at three different levels on either side of the greatly enlarged hull. Equipped also with two sails, one large, one small, in order to catch transverse winds, it was able to cover as much as 340 kilometres without stopping. For combat, the sails and other heavy equipment would be left ashore to give the ship more manoeuvrability. On the end of its prow it had a ram made of bronze, used for smashing holes in the sides of enemy ships. The trireme's military capabilities were further enhanced by the presence of a foredeck close to the prow, on which archers and slingers would be stationed during sea battles, raining missiles on to the enemy crews.[91]

A number of ancient Greek writers claimed that the trireme had been invented by the Corinthians in the eighth century BC. In fact, with some notable exceptions, most Greek authors assert that all ancient warships were invented by their fellow Hellenes.[92] However, there is no artistic representation or any other evidence for Greek triremes before the late sixth century BC.[93] The first unambiguous reference to the construction of triremes concerns the Egyptian pharaoh Necho II building them for use on both the Mediterranean and Red seas around the start of the sixth century BC. As the Egyptians had no previous record of constructing any kind of sea craft like the trireme, it has long been assumed that Necho must have needed outside expertise. While there is little evidence of a strong Greek connection with Egypt during that period, the Phoenicians are known to have long supplied timber for boatbuilding there.[94] Furthermore, the earlier development of the Phoenician bireme, with a deck clearly constructed over the rowers below, appears to show the genesis of the design which would lead to the trireme's upper level of oarsmen.[95]

More generally, the futile scholarly quest for the trireme's origins merely serves to mask the fact that the diverse ancient claims to originality were a product of the simultaneous use by several seafaring peoples of broadly similar vessels, showing that cultural interactions were taking place throughout the Mediterranean.[96]

Throughout history, the Mediterranean Sea has acted as an agent of both diversity and unity. Although often perceived as a collection of interconnected seas – Ionian, Aegean, Adriatic, Tyrrhenian etc. – which all possess their own identities and histories, the Mediterranean has also provided the means for those peoples who live on its edges to interact with one another.[97] The building of craft that could travel on its waters, meant that goods, people and ideas could be, and were, exchanged between areas many thousands of kilometres distant.[98] Like the Mediterranean itself, those who managed to master the complex crafts and skills associated with shipbuilding and maritime navigation acted not only as agents of cultural interaction and acculturation but also as symbols of cultural distinctiveness. It was these seemingly contradictory dynamics that provided the basis for Phoenician–Greek relations. Thus, the archaeological evidence of commercial cooperation is counterbalanced by the growing ambivalence towards Phoenicians in early Greek literature.

In Homer's *Iliad* and *Odyssey* – each a product of a time when both Greek and Phoenician colonial expansion in the Mediterranean was reaching its zenith during the eighth and seventh centuries BC – a clear distinction is drawn between the Phoenicians as a people and the exquisite artefacts that they produced. In the *Iliad* a large silver cup, a 'masterpiece of Sidonian craftsmanship', is offered as a prize by the Greek hero Achilles as 'the loveliest thing in the world'. In another episode, Hecuba, queen of Troy, is described as possessing richly embroidered robes woven by Sidonian women and so precious that they are kept in the treasure chamber of the palace and considered worthy to be offered up to Athena.[99] This admiration for Phoenician workmanship is in stark opposition to the characterization of the Phoenicians as dishonest, greedy and sly.[100] In one famous episode from the *Odyssey*, Eumaeus, the faithful swineherd of Odysseus, explains how he ended up as a slave looking after his master's pigs. He had in fact been born a prince in his native land, before being kidnapped by his Sidonian nurse, who had given him to Phoenician traders. Odysseus himself would almost suffer the same fate at Phoenician hands. He recounts how he had been persuaded by 'a dishonest Phoenician, a thieving wretch who had already performed a great deal of mischief in the world', to travel with him to Phoenicia, where he had a house. However, the invitation turned out to be nothing more than a ploy to kidnap and sell him into slavery.[101] Rather than expressing genuine hostility towards Phoenicians, these depictions might be viewed as representing a general deep-seated disapproval of traders among the Greek aristocratic elite, who wanted to create a clear distance between mercantile activities and themselves. However, the weight of evidence does seem to show that this antipathy was based on *pre-existent* negative attitudes towards the Phoenicians, rather than their acting simply as the random fall guy in a literary discourse on Greekness or its absence. It is also generally thought that the *Odyssey* was written down later than the *Iliad*, perhaps indicating that Greek attitudes towards the Phoenicians had hardened as their commercial rivalry developed. Yet, equally, the degree of cultural assimilation and appropriation that had already been taking place between Greeks and Phoenicians strongly suggests that such entrenched views were by no means universally held.[102]

During the second half of the eighth century BC there was a marked change in the nature of Phoenician activities overseas, particularly in the central Mediterranean. In Sardinia a number of settlements were founded in the south and west of the island, at Sulcis, Tharros and Nora. These colonies were very different from Sant' Imbenia, because they were very much Phoenician settlements with little evidence of Nuragic residents. They conformed to the topographical particularities of Phoenician foundations located on islands, promontories and peninsulas, with two natural harbours so that wind direction would not inhibit use. Each provided good anchorage and easy access to the hinterland, where metal ores and agricultural produce could be acquired through trade with the Nuragic population.[103] These new commercial relationships appear to have brought about a marked increase in competition for land and resources among the Nuragi, as different groups sought to control the lucrative business of supplying the Phoenicians with raw materials. This led to the clustering of populations into more nucleated settlements, a more complex social stratification, and the creation of a series of complex socio-political divisions.[104]

Pottery found at Sulcis clearly shows that trade with Pithecusa and Etruria, probably in conjunction with the Euboeans, was an important aspect of the economic life of these early Phoenician colonies.[105] Sardinia also served as a platform for more ambitious trading strategies, especially by the Tyrians. As the most distant of all the Mediterranean islands from the European and African mainland, and with its long stretches of coastline, Sardinia was a natural 'stepping stone' to the far western reaches of the great sea, where far greater mineral riches could be found.[106] Indeed, the Phoenician emporium at Huelva in south-west Spain was receiving goods from Sardinia in the eighth century.[107]

THE SPANISH SILVER MOUNTAIN

The oldest piece of Phoenician writing discovered in the western Mediterranean is on a fragmentary monument known as the Nora Stone, dated to the late ninth/early eighth century BC and from south-west Sardinia. Some scholars have interpreted the text as a vote of thanks to the god Pummay by a Phoenician high official, Milkaton, after he and the crew of his ship had survived a storm while on their way to the land of 'Tarshish'. There has been much speculation on the actual location of 'Tarshish'; however, easily the most convincing claim is that it refers to Tartessus, the ancient name for that region of southern Spain which now roughly covers Andalusia.[108]

Phoenician interest in Tartessus primarily centred on the vast mineral wealth found in its interior. Although the Greek author who claimed that during forest fires streams of molten silver ran down the hillsides may have been guilty of more than a little exaggeration, the mines of southern Spain appear to have offered a seemingly limitless supply of silver, iron and many other metals.[109] Once again, the Tyrians had been quickest to recognize the huge possibilities presented by the mines

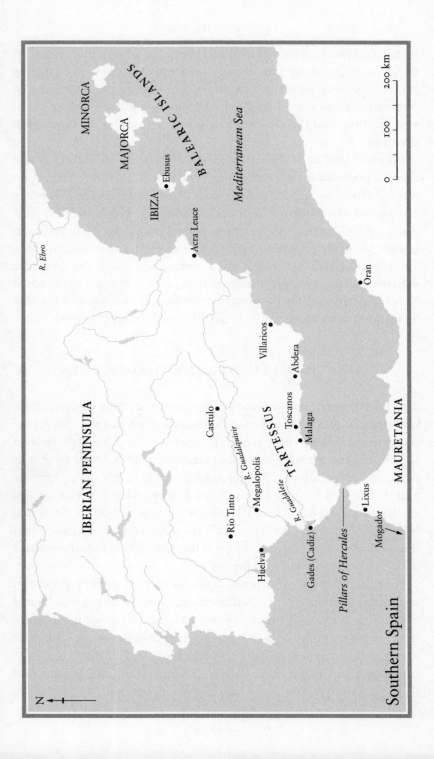

Southern Spain

of Tartessus, although other Phoenicians, from Sidon, Arvad and Byblos, are also recorded as taking part in Tyrian mercantile ventures.[110] The Tyrians were the first to push to the furthermost limits of the Mediterranean Sea, establishing the colony of Lixus on the west coast of what is now Morocco after passing through the Pillars of Hercules (the Strait of Gibraltar) into the Atlantic Ocean, after which they established another trading station on the island of Mogador.[111]

The Phoenicians had first reached Tartessus by the first half of the ninth century BC.[112] The Tyrians had quickly struck up an extremely successful economic relationship with the local Tartessian elites, with their new partners controlling the actual mining and processing of the metal ores, while the Tyrians concentrated on the transportation of the ingots back to the Levant. At Huelva, a native Tartessian port, archaeologists have discovered huge smelting furnaces used for the production of metal ingots on an almost industrial scale.[113] The metal trade was only one part of this lucrative enterprise. On the voyage from Phoenicia to southern Spain the ships would carry luxury goods such as jewels, ivories, bronze statuettes, cut glass, ornate jugs, unguents and perfumes packaged in alabaster vessels made in Tyrian workshops, which would be traded with the Tartessian elite.

In the late eighth century BC the Tyrians set up a colony at Gades (modern Cadiz), just beyond the Pillars of Hercules on the south-western coast of Spain, as the main transport hub for the trade. It would later be claimed that they had set out to found a settlement in the region under the orders of an oracle. However, it would take three separate expeditions before the right site was confirmed by a propitious sacrifice to the gods.[114] Some would even say that the Phoenicians had reached Gades only after being blown off course in a storm.[115] The site, like that of Tyre, was chosen because of its fantastic natural harbour. Situated at the end of a long, narrow promontory, it was surrounded on three sides by water, making it defendable from the land and accessible from the sea. Most importantly of all, it was situated opposite the mouth of the river Guadalete, down which the ore from the mines in the interior could be transported. In fact Gades was not just a one-industry town: it would also become famous for its garum, a strong-tasting sauce made out of decomposing mackerel mixed with vinegar, considered to be a great delicacy in the ancient world. It was, however, the metals – primarily silver – that were mined from the Spanish earth that kept the increasingly demanding Assyrian state satisfied and Tyre, therefore, relatively free to operate without excessive external interference.

The favoured route from Tyre to Gades took ships over the northern Mediterranean first to Cyprus, then to the southern coast of Asia Minor. The fleet would then travel to the islands of Rhodes, Malta, Sicily and Sardinia. The final leg of the journey went from Ibiza around the coast of Spain and then through the Pillars of Hercules to Gades. The least complicated return route was to follow the coast of North Africa, then Egypt and the Levantine coast.[116] It was no coincidence that many of the Phoenician colonies that sprang up in North Africa, Sardinia, Sicily, Malta and the Balearic Islands in the late ninth and eighth centuries were located on these vital trading arteries, like links in a giant chain. These colonies also acted as a defensive line that cut across the southern Mediterranean, effectively locking commercial competitors, particularly the Greeks, out of the most lucrative metal-ore market in the ancient world. Although a Greek sea captain from Samos, Colaeus, had made it to southern Spain in the seventh century BC and picked up a cargo of sixty talents of silver (the equivalent of between 1 and 2 tonnes of metal ore), this was an isolated incident.[117]

Along the Mediterranean coast of Andalusia a series of small Phoenician trading settlements, spaced out at a distance of every 10 kilometres or so, sprang up. Like their larger counterparts, they tended to be situated on promontories and small islands at river mouths, which provided good locations for harbours. It has been plausibly argued that each of these settlements was associated with a particular Phoenician trading firm. Although at first the economic activity that took place in these colonies was centred almost exclusively on their role as marketplaces where local goods would be traded, later some developed their own specialist industries often associated with the production, storage and transport of goods, such as pottery and metalworking. Moreover, many appear to have supported themselves not only through manufacturing and trade, but also through agriculture, fishing and animal husbandry.[118] However, the prosperity and indeed very existence of these modest Phoenician settlements and many others in the central and western Mediterranean relied heavily on the metal-ore mining and processing operations that were taking place further to the west.

Gades was set apart from the other Phoenician colonies on the southern Spanish coastline not just by the scale of the city and its population, but also because it was the only urban centre with public buildings. The city appears to have acted as the centre of Tyrian interests on the Iberian peninsula, and it even established a number of secondary colonies such as fishing, transit and trading stations in North Africa and what is now Portugal.[119] Unlike Kition, these new colonies in the western Mediterranean would not be administered by a governor sent from Tyre. Their distance made such close control impossible. Instead, it appears that the Tyrian king appointed commercial agents from the Tyrian mercantile elite to oversee the trading operations and governance of the colonies.[120] As individual initiative took over from palace monopolies in regard to foreign trade and the Tyrian commercial empire was extended to the far-off lands of the West, the influence of these merchant princes increasingly grew at the expense of the king's own authority.[121] As the king could not safeguard his interests through direct control, it therefore became increasingly important that he find another way of maintaining his power over a city which was many thousands of kilometres away. In these difficult circumstances, Melqart, for whom a magnificent temple would be built in the city, would become the embodiment of Tyrian royal power at Gades. The elision between god and king that had been such a key element of the veneration of Melqart since his emergence under Hiram meant that the worship of the god at Gades was also a recognition of Tyrian royal authority.

Melqart would stand at the epicentre of this dynamic new settlement. His sanctuary would take up the whole of the eastern half of the island site on which it was built, and it appeared to awed later visitors that the bedrock on which it sat resembled a huge polished platform.[122] Within the sacred precinct was a famous sweet-water spring.[123] The magnificent adornments for which the temple at Gades would become as famous as its Tyrian counterpart emphasized the sacred bonds that linked colony to mother city. Indeed, the presence of the temple of Melqart at Gades may have been a symbol of the city's position as the centre of the Tyrian colonial community in the western Mediterranean.[124] The temple contained an olive tree made of solid gold, whose branches held fruit made from glittering emeralds – surely a reference to the famous foundation myth of Tyre. The sanctuary also contained twin pillars, standing over a cubit (45 centimetres) high and square in shape, which were made of gold and silver fused into one colour and were covered in writing the meaning of which would eventually be lost.[125] It was said that, after being instructed to in a dream, the people of Gades had brought relics of the god from Tyre to their new sanctuary.[126]

The sacred rites that were practised at Gades followed the Phoenician tradition. Women and swine were forbidden from entering the inner sanctum of the temple precinct. The barefoot priests, who wore linen robes with a band made of Egyptian flax over their shaven heads, were expected to remain celibate. When offering incense at the altar they wore their robes unbuckled, and while sacrificing they wore a garment embroidered with a broad stripe. In the temples there were no statues or other imagery of the gods. Most importantly, the fires on the sacred altars were kept continually alight.[127] The sacred rite of the *egersis* was also enacted at Gades.[128] Later writers would tell strange stories of foreigners being required to leave the city while the great ceremony was being held, and on their return 'they found cast ashore a man of the sea, who was about five roods in size, and burning away, because heaven had blasted him with a thunderbolt' – a clearly confused reference to the effigy of the great god which was put on a raft and set ablaze out at sea.[129]

The temple of Melqart at Gades also served as the vital umbilical cord through which wealth flowed from Spain back to Phoenicia, acting as an important financial guarantor, with business deals being concluded with oaths sworn to the god. As the Phoenicians had no coinage in this early period, Melqart was also called upon to guarantee the weight and purity of the metal ingots and bars through special temple hallmarks. The Gaditans also paid a substantial annual tribute of a tenth of the public treasury to the temple of Melqart at Tyre.[130]

A CRUEL LESSON IN SUPPLY AND DEMAND

By the last decades of the eighth century BC it might therefore have looked as though the Tyrians were the clear winners in the great Phoenician expansion into the western Mediterranean. They had certainly succeeded in securing the means to keep the Assyrian beast's ravenous hunger for precious metals sated and thereby maintain a fragile political independence that other, less productive, neighbours had already lost. Moreover, their relentless quest for raw materials had directly led to the establishment of a substantial network of trading emporia and colonies stretching from Cyprus to Spain. However, in this instance appearances were deceiving. During the 730s the Assyrian king Tiglath-pileser III, breaking with the policy of his royal predecessors, who had left the Phoenicians to their own devices as long as hefty tributes continued to be paid, attacked and captured a number of cities, including Tyre. On this occasion the Tyrians, who had initially joined an anti-Assyrian alliance with some Syrian and other Phoenician cities, suffered a lighter penalty than most others because of their swift capitulation and the huge tribute of 150 talents of gold that was then paid. This unusual leniency on the part of the Assyrians was also surely connected to the crucial role that the Tyrians continued to play in maintaining the supply of precious metals and other goods into the Near East. However, Tyrian commercial activities did now start to come under much closer Assyrian scrutiny and supervision. The freedoms that the Tyrians had jealously guarded for centuries would be gradually eroded as Assyrian customs officials became increasingly involved in the administration of the famous twin harbours, enforcing the payment of heavy customs duties on products such as wood and ensuring that Phoenician merchants did not break the ruinous trade embargo that had been placed on the Great King's enemy, Egypt.[131]

It was perhaps these clear signs of weakness that led to a series of revolts by Tyrian satellites in both Phoenicia and Cyprus, and to the eventual annexation of the latter by the Assyrians, making Tyre ever more reliant on its commercial operations in the West. A Tyrian revolt against Assyrian rule led to the Tyrian monarch Luli having to flee the city and go into exile in Cyprus – an act beautifully caught on a royal Assyrian bas-relief from Dur-Sharrukin (Khorsabad) that depicts the king with his family and retainers being bundled on to ships as the Assyrian army under the vengeful king Sennacherib is about to break into the city after a five-year siege. In a further sign of Tyre's decline, it appears that a number of Phoenician cities that had previously been under its rule supplied the Assyrians with sixty ships so that the island city could be blockaded. Certainly Sidon was no longer under Tyrian control, and nor was most of Tyre's former territory on the Levantine mainland. Although Tyre was still nominally an autonomous kingdom, the powers of its monarch were now severely curtailed. A new 'agreement' signed sometime in the second half of the 670s placed restrictions on whom the Tyrians could trade with and its famous ports were now directly administered by Assyrian officials. Moreover, a governor was stationed in Tyre to oversee Assyrian interests. The Tyrian king was now not even allowed to open official communiqués without Assyrian officials being present.[132]

Yet, even after several more unsuccessful rebellions during the seventh century, Assyria still resisted incorporating Tyre, along with the cities of Arvad and Byblos, into one of the three provinces into which the rest of Phoenicia had been divided. Pragmatism dictated that Assyria could not risk disrupting the Tyrian trading network in the western Mediterranean, which now supplied the bulk of the silver and other metals that the Great King relied on to maintain his rule over his diffuse domains.[133] The incorporation of Tyre would in no way have guaranteed the acquiescence of colonies thousands of kilometres over the sea. Furthermore, the modes of control that the Tyrians had developed in relation to their western colonies very much centred on the figure of the king himself and his relationship with Melqart. It was much more efficient for Assyria to maintain a strictly controlled but nominally independent Tyrian monarchy.

Yet, conversely, the pressures that Tyre increasingly faced during the seventh century BC undoubtedly played some part in creating favourable conditions for the growth of a number of its western colonies. With a founder often distracted by the ongoing battle for its own political survival and an environment in which there were as yet no big predators at the top of the political food chain, these fledgling communities could develop in a way that was simply unimaginable in the old world of the Near East. Moreover, the commercial exploitation and colonization of the central and western Mediterranean by both Phoenicians and Greeks, and their subsequent interactions with indigenous populations, based as they were on both cooperation and competition, would set an important precedent for how this new world would subsequently develop. Indeed, the greatest legacy of Tyre would not be Gades, the silver routes, or the diplomatic high-wire act with Assyria, but a colony situated on the North African coast in what is now Tunisia, whose renown would soon come to far outshine the faded lustre of its Phoenician parent.

2

New City: The Rise of Carthage

ELISSA'S REFUGE

Great cities often attract great foundation myths, and Carthage was no exception. It was said that Mattan, king of Tyre, had dictated that on his death, in 831 BC, the kingdom was to be split between his son Pygmalion and his daughter Elissa (Elisshat). However, the people of Tyre, perhaps concerned about the instability that such an equitable settlement might ferment, had protested, and Pygmalion had been crowned sole monarch. In a ruthless show of strength, the new king quickly moved to snuff out any potential opposition by ordering the assassination of his uncle Acherbas (Zakarbaal), high priest of the god Melqart and husband of Elissa. To secure her own safety Elissa pretended to bear her brother no ill will for his actions, but secretly planned to flee the city with some similarly disaffected Tyrian nobles.[1]

Elissa then successfully allayed the suspicions of Pygmalion by requesting that she be allowed to move into his palace, as her late husband's residence brought back too many painful memories. Her brother was delighted, as he thought that she would bring Acherbas' gold with her. In a wonderful psychological ruse, Elissa then took the attendants that Pygmalion had sent with her to collect her belongings on a ship out to sea, where she threw a number of sacks overboard which she claimed were full of her dead husband's gold. She then persuaded these royal retainers to join her in flight, claiming that a painful death now awaited them at the hands of her brother, who would be enraged at the loss of this treasure. After being joined by her noble companions and offering prayers to Melqart, the party fled the city and travelled to Cyprus. There the exiles were joined by the high priest of the goddess Astarte, who, as a reward for his loyalty, demanded that the office would stay within his family for all time. Eighty girls who had been chosen to serve as sacred prostitutes at the temple of Astarte were also added to the group, so that the men should have wives and their new settlement a future population.

The expedition then set off for Africa, where they were welcomed and presented with gifts by the citizens of Utica, a Tyrian colony. Elissa and her fellow refugees were also initially well treated by the local Libyan people, for their king, Hiarbus, freely let them enter his territory. But, perhaps wary of ceding too much land to these newcomers, he offered to sell them only as much as could be covered by an ox hide. The resourceful newcomers cut the hide into very thin strips, and were therefore able to mark out a much larger area than Hiarbus had surely imagined.

According to one Graeco-Roman ancient tradition, the new settlement – Carthage – was an immediate success, and people from the surrounding area came both to trade and to settle there. Yet, as the city became ever more populous and wealthy, so the resentment felt by Hiarbus grew, until eventually the Libyan king threatened war unless Elissa agreed to marry him. The elders of Carthage, hesitant to report such unwelcome news, were coerced into telling the truth by the queen, who demanded that they should not shirk a hard life if it was beneficial to their new homeland. The elders, after making the queen aware of Hiarbus' ultimatum, skilfully turned the tables on her by pointing out that if she shirked the hard life of marriage then the city would be destroyed. Trapped by her own rhetoric, Elissa had little choice but to comply with the wishes of her people. But first she ordered a massive pyre to be erected so that she could make sacrifices to appease the spirit of her first husband. Once the great fire was ablaze, however, the queen climbed atop of it and, turning to her people, announced that she would now go to her husband as they had desired. She then stabbed herself to death with a sword.

It is, of course, doubtful whether any of this baroque tale of love, loss and cunning correlates with the actual reality of Carthage's foundation. The earliest roots of the story cannot be traced any further back than a Greek source of the third century BC, and the fullest rendition comes from Trogus Pompeius, a Romano-Gallic historian who wrote in the last decades of the first century BC.[2] Moreover, the Elissa myth not only conforms to the stylistic diktats of Hellenistic literature, but also serves as a wonderfully dramatic vehicle for virtually every Greek and Roman prejudice about Carthage and its inhabitants. The ruses that Elissa uses to circumvent the obstacles that impede her progress intentionally jar with the virtues and characteristics that the Romans attributed to themselves for much of their history – particularly *fides*, or faithfulness.[3] The Carthaginians in the legend are portrayed as treacherous and deceitful practitioners of doublespeak. Like their Phoenician cousins, they are overly controlled by women and liable to suffer from such dangerous feminine traits as hysteria and envy. They are also cruel and unhealthily obsessed with death, as well as sexually lascivious and with an overdeveloped love of wealth.

A number of scholars have considered the tempting possibility that buried within an essentially Greek story are genuine Carthaginian memories of that much earlier age. It has been argued that in fact the Carthaginians themselves may have consciously played a part in the creation or promulgation of the Elissa myth, constructing and embellishing it rather like Thanksgiving in modern America.[4] However, it seems extremely unlikely that they would have bought into a story that projected so many negative character topoi on to them. In fact it was the first half of the third century BC – and many have seen the hand of Timaeus of Tauromenium in it – when the elements that made up the Elissa myth appear to have crystallized into an accepted narrative.[5]

Some have pointed to a second-century-AD history of the Phoenicians whose Levantine author, Philo of Byblos, claimed to have studied the ancient annals of Tyre. Those annals apparently referred to the Tyrian king Mattan I leaving his throne to his 11-year-old son Pygmalion in 820, which in turn had led to the subsequent flight of, and foundation of Carthage by, his sister Elissa in 814 BC. Moreover, a gold pendant had been found in a tomb in Carthage inscribed with the names Pygmalion and Astarte, which led to the theory that the tomb's incumbent, Yada'milk, must have been a military officer from the original Tyrian expedition, and that the presence of Pygmalion's name on the pendant proved that it had probably been the king himself who had encouraged the dissidents to found Carthage.[6]

However, any such hopes for the partial historical veracity of the Elissa story were dashed by the discovery that the tomb of Yada'milk was not from the late ninth century BC, but from up to three centuries later.[7] Indeed, the earliest occupation layers found by archaeologists in Carthage stretch back only as far as 760 BC, although new advances in our extremely limited knowledge of the first phases of the city may yet push that date further back.[8] Moreover, significant doubts exist about Philo's historical testimony, and most suspect that, rather than having gleaned his information from ancient Phoenician texts, he simply took the story from the same Hellenistic Greek authors as those Roman writers who mention Elissa.[9]

We may suspect, however, that, even if much was fabricated by later Greek writers, some elements of the myth were based on information or even misunderstandings gleaned from contacts with the city. Thus another version of the foundation of Carthage, told by the fourth-century-BC Sicilian Greek historian Philistus, named the leaders of the first settlement as the Tyrians Azoros and Carchedon, clear derivations of the Punic/Phoenician words *sor* ('rock') and *Qart-Hadasht* ('Carthage').[10]

A similar confusion might also explain the story about Elissa and the ox hide. The Byrsa, the hill which remained the centre point of Carthage throughout its history, was most likely named from an Akkadian word, *birtu*, which meant 'fortress'. However, the Greek word for ox hide was *bursa* – hence, perhaps, the bovine association with the city's foundation made by Greek writers.[11]

The central importance of Tyre in the construction of Carthaginian elite identity was more than a figment of the Greek imagination. Throughout the city's history there are epigraphic references to *bn Sr* ('sons of Tyre') or *h Sry* ('Tyrians') which may have alluded to the Tyrian origins of these individuals, or be a sign that descent from the mother city denoted some kind of status.[12] Tyrian heritage was perhaps an important signifier of status in a rapidly growing city where the population was not only drawn from all over the Phoenician world, but also had a significant Libyan element.[13] Moreover, the traditional ties with Tyre continued to be articulated through the worship of Melqart, Astarte, Eshmoun and other deities, who were all well established there.[14] Indeed, the debt that Carthage owed to its founder was explicitly acknowledged each year when a flotilla carrying members of the Carthaginian elite made the long journey eastward to Tyre, where they presented a tithe of a tenth of Carthage's earnings to Melqart.[15]

THE EARLY CITY

The Elissa story shows that the Carthaginians and Greeks considered the city to have been founded in exceptional circumstances, which made it immediately stand out from the other Phoenician colonies in the West.[16] There is, of course, a large element of hindsight in such a judgement, but archaeology confirms that the early settlement did develop extraordinarily quickly. Its Phoenician name, *Qart-Hadasht* or 'New City', certainly suggests that Carthage was set up as a colonial settlement and not just as a trading post.[17] Strategically, the site could not have been better chosen, for it stood on the nexus of the two most important trading routes in the region: the east–west route from the Levant to Spain and its north–south Tyrrhenian counterpart. As with Gades, it appears that some Tyrian colonies were established with the aim of providing a market and, possibly, a civic focus for other, smaller, Phoenician trading stations. This may well explain why Carthage grew so quickly.

The north–south route would be of particular importance for Carthage, as it linked the city not only with Sicily, Sardinia and Italy, but also with mainland Greece and the Aegean region. Indeed, a considerable amount of Greek pottery, both Euboean and Corinthian, has been found in the earliest habitation layers of Carthage.[18] It is clear that Carthage had, during the eighth century BC, become a key coordinate on a Tyrrhenian trading circuit that included Sant' Imbenia, Pithecusa and Etruria. The links with Pithecusa appear to have been particularly strong, and a number of ceramics from there have been found in early Carthaginian archaeological contexts. (The Carthaginians were also exporting goods and ceramics to Pithecusa.)[19]

During the eighth and seventh centuries, there is also good archaeological data for the importation of goods from central Italy into Carthage.[20] Similar Greek-style pottery was actually made in Carthage itself, suggesting either that a community of Euboean potters was active

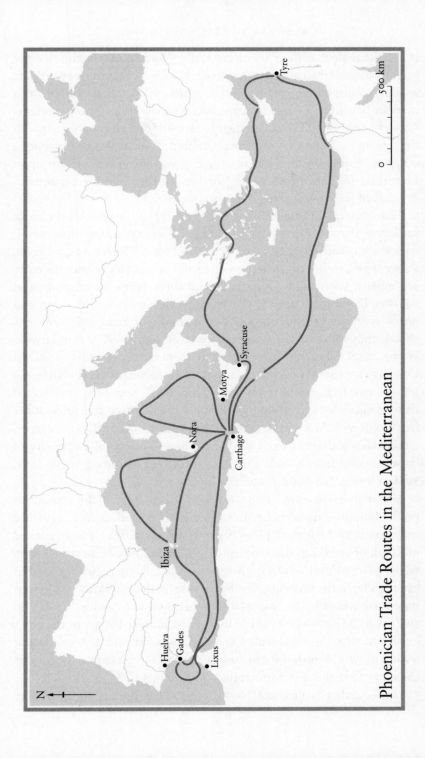

Phoenician Trade Routes in the Mediterranean

in Carthage or that the Phoenician settlers had swiftly begun to copy such forms.[21] It thus appears that from its earliest beginnings Carthage was a cosmopolitan trading centre which attracted settlers from a number of different ethnic constituencies (while still carefully preserving its institutional 'Tyrian' heritage). Furthermore, although trade with the Levant and Spain would remain an important aspect of Carthage's economy throughout its history, the city was in no way reliant upon Levantine–Iberian metal routes, for much of its commercial activity was keyed into the thriving Tyrrhenian circuit.[22]

Palaeobotanical research has ascertained that the diet of the early settlers was made up of barley, wheat of several different varieties, oats, grains, lentils, pulses, olives, fruits and wine.[23] There was, however, a complete absence of domesticated birds such as chickens in the early settlement, with wild goose and wild duck being important food sources. Domestic livestock was mainly made up of cattle, sheep and goats, with the bovids being used as a source of meat. Bone analysis shows that most of these animals were slaughtered at a relatively young age.[24] Where this produce came from during the early phase of Carthage's existence has been a particular focus for recent archaeological research, because, as the Elissa myth suggests, the size of its hinterland was clearly very limited in the first two centuries of the city's existence. Analysis of amphorae in which foodstuffs were carried clearly shows that the early settlement had to import the majority of its sustenance from a wide variety of locations, including Spain, Italy, Sicily, Greece, the Aegean and the Levant.[25]

Although archaeologists have yet to locate any of the important public buildings or harbours from that early period, current evidence indicates that the littoral plain began to fill up with a densely packed network of dwellings made of sun-dried bricks laid out on streets with wells, gardens and squares, all situated on a fairly regular plan that ran parallel to the shoreline. By the early seventh century the settlement was surrounded by an impressive 3-metre-wide casement wall.[26] So swift was the development that in the first hundred years of the city's existence there is evidence of some demolition and redevelopment within its neighbourhoods, including the careful relocation of an early cemetery to make way for metalworking shops.[27]

Three further large cemeteries ringing the early city indicate that, within a century or so of its foundation, Carthage was home to around 30,000 people.[28] The deceased had been generally buried with great care and attention to detail in underground tombs or cist graves – slab-lined graves, usually covered by a single larger slab – depending on their material circumstances.[29] From the objects left with the dead – razor blades, perfumes and perfume flasks, make-up, little bowls, lamps, statuettes and altars – it is possible to reconstruct something of the rituals that were performed to ease entry into the afterlife. The dead body was first washed and anointed with oil before make-up was applied to the face. The corpse was then laid out, after which offerings of food and drinks were placed upon a special altar, followed by a banquet and a funeral procession involving the mourners.[30] Finally the dead person was interred with objects that it was thought would be needed in the afterlife: tools, weapons and seals, food, perfumes, herbs and imported pottery. Amulets and other apotropaic objects to protect the deceased from evil spirits were also included.

The everyday nature of these offerings strongly suggests that the Carthaginians expected the afterlife to be similar to the life that they had lived on earth. Grave inscriptions support this theory, speaking of a soul that eats and drinks, and warning the living against opening the grave and disturbing the deceased.[31] The Carthaginians appear to have believed that the soul split into two when a person died. The *néphesh*, the physical part of the soul, stayed in the tomb and had the same needs as a living person, whereas the spiritual embodiment of the dead person's soul, the *rouah*, left to reside in the world of the dead.[32]

Wealthier individuals were often buried with a number of luxury items that tell us much about Carthage as a consumer and increasingly a producer of such goods. Although at first luxury goods were imported from the Levant, Egypt and other areas of the Near East, by the mid seventh century Carthage had become a major manufacturer itself through the establishment of an industrial area just outside the city walls, with potters' kilns and workshops for purple-dye production and metalworking.[33] The city now became a major manufacturer of terracotta figurines, masks, jewellery and delicately carved ivories, which were then exported throughout the western Phoenician colonies.[34]

However, the growing regional importance of Carthage cannot be measured by its industrial output alone. The city was now a major consumer of food and raw materials that the limited nature of its hinterland meant it could not produce for itself. This in turn would have had a major impact on the organization of other Phoenician colonies in the central Mediterranean. In Sardinia during the seventh century BC, for instance, Phoenician colonists built a series of new settlements, some of them clearly fortified, at Othoca (near Tharros), Bithia, Cuccurredus, Monte Sirai and Pani Loriga (built by Sulcis). These new foundations were very different from the older colonies, in that they lacked religious and public buildings, as well as significant populations. Their intended purpose appears to have been to secure access to the fertile plains and metal-ore-rich mountains of the interior.[35] The growth of these settlements coincided with the disappearance of Nuragic-manufactured amphorae, used for the transport of metal ore and foodstuffs, from Carthage's archaeological record.[36] This suggests that these new settlements were part of a deliberate Phoenician strategy to take control of the means of production on the island, in order to service the growing Carthaginian market.[37]

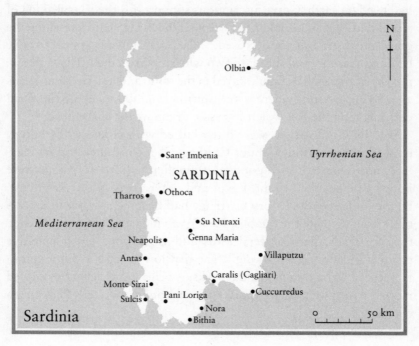

Sardinia

The intricate construction of some of the early tombs in Carthage and the richness of the burial goods – including gold medallions, pendant necklaces and earrings, delicately carved ivory mirror handles and combs, as well as large numbers of enamel-coated or faience amulets and scarabs, often depicting Egyptian deities and pharaohs used to ward off evil spirits – confirm that the opportunities the city presented had attracted members of the Phoenician mercantile class, and that this group of leading citizens quickly accrued even more wealth.[38] Carthage therefore appears to have been established as a proper colonial foundation with a core group of the Phoenician mercantile elite, and it was this group that would control Carthage for most of its existence.

Later Greek claims that Carthage was a monarchy ruled by 'kings' until the sixth century BC appear to have been built on a misunderstanding of its oligarchic government.[39] From its earliest beginnings the city was ruled by an aristocratic cabal referred to as the *b'lm*, the lords or princes, who controlled all the important judicial, governmental, religious and military organs of state.[40] At the apex of this hierarchy was a family whose wealth and power set them above fellow members of the elite at that particular time. Greek writers would call them 'kings', and they seem to have held some kind of executive power over their fellow citizens, particularly in regard to the command of the Carthaginian military. From the last decades of the sixth century to the first decade of the fourth the supreme family was the Magonids. The Carthaginian 'kings', however, were apparently not confined to one particular family, which strongly suggests that, although they may have held monarchical powers, the 'kings' were not hereditary, and that their powers were allotted by a consultative council of elders.[41] The Elissa story would have acted as a powerful tool for legitimizing the privileged status of a Carthaginian elite who were unlikely to have such exalted origins as hers. At the same time, the idea of a first female queen who died childless not only stood as a neat justification for the oligarchic system, but also denied any hereditary right to autocratic power.

The obvious pride that the Carthaginian elite took in their Tyrian heritage should not be mistaken for a slavish adherence to the mother city's economic and political agenda. Carthage very quickly showed that it would plot its own course through the choppy waters of

Mediterranean power politics by maintaining a strong trading relationship with Egypt at a time when the Phoenician cities had been forbidden from such activities by their Assyrian 'ally'.

CHILD SACRIFICE AND THE TOPHET

The same autonomous character is also seen in the religious life of the city. Religious ritual lay at the heart of Carthage's developing identity, not least because it provided a vital tool for elite political control. As in the Near East, the temples were Carthage's greatest and wealthiest institutions, and it was members of the elite who constituted the chief-priesthoods that governed them. The larger temples employed considerable numbers of specialist staff. The scribes, choristers, musicians, light attendants, barbers and butchers were needed to ensure the correct performance of the sacred rites due to the deity whose dwelling it was. Such was the level of organization that tariff lists were issued setting out the cost of particular sacrifices, with offerings banded into different price categories. Such documents not only guaranteed the livelihoods of the legion of Carthaginian priests and temple workers, but also provided some consumer protection to supplicants, as they gave notice of the fines that could be levied against those priests who abused the pricing structure.[42] Not only did members of the elite oversee these sprawling organizations and their vast resources, but the temples also served as the venues for the dining clubs with ritualistic functions to which they belonged.

Melqart, despite his pre-eminence in the Tyrian pantheon, and in other major western Phoenician colonies such as Gades and Lixus, never held the same dominant position in Carthage, although he remained a senior member of the gods, with his own temple in the city, and priests who practised the sacred rite of *egersis*.[43] Instead, the two most significant deities in Carthage were Baal Hammon and his consort, Tanit. The latter, although often referred to as the 'Face of Baal' on Carthaginian inscriptions, does not appear to have played a junior role to her husband. The distinctive sign of Tanit – an outstretched stylized figure – is found on many of the steles in Carthage, and she was often represented as the patroness and protector of the city, a significant promotion for a goddess who had previously been a minor deity in Phoenicia.[44] In contrast, Baal Hammon, who was often represented by a crescent moon, was a major god in the Levant. The term 'Baal' was a title or prefix meaning 'Lord' or 'Master', and was given to a number of different gods. The meaning of 'Hammon' is less clear. It may come from the Phoenician linguistic root *hmm*, meaning 'hot' or 'burning being', indicating that he was 'Lord of the Furnaces'.[45]

The separate development of Carthage is demonstrated not only in the promotion of a new celestial order distinct from that of Tyre, but also in the ways in which that order was honoured. From the third millennium BC onward Near Eastern texts allude to the practice of *molk* (*mlk*), which simply meant 'gift' or 'offering'. The word was often used for the sacrifice of firstborn children to appease the gods when communities were facing a particularly calamitous situation. The Old Testament provides a number of examples of *molk*. In the Book of Exodus the Israelites are given the command that 'the firstborn of thy sons shalt thou give unto me'. The sacrifice of sons by two Judaean kings is also referred to, as is a Jewish backlash against the (supposedly) foreign practice.[46]

Some rather dubious later Greek sources claimed that the Phoenicians, in times of grave peril, had also resorted to the sacrifice of the sons of princes by beheading them in honour of their god El, in pious emulation of the deity himself, who had offered up his only son, Ieud, to save his land from disaster.[47] In terms of archaeological evidence, however, only one confirmed tophet – the name given by modern scholars to the sacred enclosures where these sacrifices are supposed to have taken place – has so far been discovered in the Levant, and only one stele that alludes to a *molk* sacrifice.[48] In the Book of Genesis, Abraham, after being tested by God, was allowed to sacrifice a ram as substitute for his son Isaac, and scholars have thus argued that in most instances young animals were sacrificed in place of human children. Indeed, it appears that the practice of *molk* sacrifice had completely died out in Phoenicia by the seventh century BC.

Nevertheless, a number of ancient Greek references to the Carthaginian practice of child sacrifice have survived.[49] The fullest and most dramatic description comes from the pen of the Sicilian historian Diodorus: 'There was in their city a bronze image of Cronus [the Greek equivalent of Baal Hammon], extending its hands, palms up and sloping towards the ground, so that each of the children when placed thereupon rolled down and fell into a sort of gaping pit filled with fire.'[50] The third-century-BC philosopher and biographer Cleitarchus also evoked the ghastly image of the limbs of the children contracting and their open mouths looking as if they were laughing as they were consumed by the fire.[51] According to the first-century-AD Greek writer Plutarch's *On Superstition*, parents avoided sacrificing their own infants by replacing them with purchased street children, whose mothers would lose the fee they had been paid if they cried or mourned for their lost offspring. Loud music was also played at the sacrificial area to drown out the victims' screams.[52]

These accusations might have been put down to nothing more than Greek slurs if it had not been for the determined sleuthing of two minor French colonial officials, François Icard and Paul Gielly, in the 1920s. Icard and Gielly had become increasingly suspicious of a Tunisian stone-dealer who kept on appearing with very fine Punic steles. One example had particularly grabbed their imaginations. It was engraved with the image of a man wearing the cloak and headdress of a priest, his right hand raised in supplication and his left cradling a swaddled infant. The inscription bore the letters *MLK*. Had the stone-dealer stumbled across the sacred precinct where the Carthaginians had continued the macabre traditions of their Phoenician ancestors? One night, acting on a tip-off, the two Frenchmen surprised their quarry digging up steles in a field not far from the site of the great rectangular harbour. After coercing the owner of the land into selling them the plot, the two men set to work. What they found further fuelled their suspicions: a series of votive offerings, each consisting of a stele listing dedications to Baal Hammon and Tanit, and usually accompanied by a terracotta urn containing calcified bones and sometimes jewels and amulets. When the contents of the urns were analysed, it was ascertained that virtually every one contained the burnt remains of young children. The tophet had been found. Later French excavations confirmed this as one of the oldest areas of Phoenician Carthage.[53]

Further analysis showed that the tophet at Carthage had been in use since at least the mid eighth century BC. It was also clear that the western Phoenicians had continued with *molk* sacrifice long after their

Levantine cousins. There had been three distinct phases of activity at the site. The first dated from around 730 to 600 BC and was marked by increasingly elaborate votive monuments, which eventually included crude obelisks and L-shaped throne monuments called *cippi*. Analysis of the contents of the urns and others found later showed that they contained the burnt remains of both young humans and animals.[54]

The tophet at Carthage has been so badly disturbed by the generations of archaeologists who have worked there that it is almost impossible to re-create the physical environment in which the rites took place. Other tophets elsewhere in the western Mediterranean are much better preserved. For example, the tophet at Sulcis off the coast of Sardinia consisted of a large rectangular enclosure delineated by massive blocks of the local trachyte on a rocky outcrop. With its thick walls and water cistern, it appears that this tophet also doubled up as a defensive refuge for the inhabitants of Sulcis in times of trouble.

Analysis of the human bones and burnt remains at Carthage has shown that the vast majority come from either stillborn or newborn infants, which is strongly suggestive of death by natural causes. These findings have been backed up at the tophet of Tharros on the island of Sardinia, where only 2 per cent of the children were more than a few months old.[55] One suggested explanation is that the *molk* sacrifice involved not human sacrifice per se but rather the substitution of the dead for living victims, and that when none of the former was available a bird or animal was sacrificed instead.

Those who are sceptical of claims that the Carthaginians and other western Phoenicians practised child sacrifice also point to the supposed lack of children's graves found in cemeteries during this period (of more than 2,000 graves so far discovered, only about 100 have contained the bones of infants) – odd when one considers that infant mortality rates in this period have been calculated at as high as 30 to 40 per cent. These objections lead to the theory that the tophet was in fact a place of burial for those who had not reached the age of a fully fledged member of the community. The customary placing of tophets at the fringes of the city suggests that the victims were considered to be on the fringes of society. The *molk* ceremony would therefore have acted as an introduction of the dead child to the god or goddess, rather than as a sacrifice.

Although such conclusions correlate with the material from the early phases of activity at the Carthaginian tophet, they work far less well with later evidence. When the contents of the urns from the fourth and third centuries BC were analysed, they were shown to contain a much higher ratio of human young. Furthermore, whereas the human remains from the seventh and sixth centuries BC tended to be of premature or newborn babies, the single interments from the later period were of older children (aged between one and three years). Some urns from this phase even contained the bones of two or three children – usually one elder child of two to four years, and one or two newborn or premature infants. The age difference between them (up to two years) suggests that they may have been siblings. One possible explanation is that neither stillborn children nor animal substitutes were now considered enough to appease Baal or Tanit, and that an elder child had to be sacrificed as a substitute when a particular infant promised to the deity was stillborn. In inscriptions incised on to the steles, Carthaginian fathers would routinely use the reflexive possessive pronoun *BNT* or *BT* to underline the fact that their sacrificial offering was not some mere substitute, but a child of their own flesh. One of many such examples from the Carthaginian tophet makes the nature of the sacrifice explicit: 'It was to the Lady Tanit Face of Baal and to Baal Hammon that Bomilcar son of Hanno, grandson of Milkiathon, vowed this son of his own flesh. Bless him you!'[56]

The argument that the tophet was some kind of cemetery for children is undermined by the fact that the ratio of children's burials found in cemeteries in Punic Carthage correlates well with comparative evidence from elsewhere in the ancient world. In fact, the lack of recorded remains may well be the result of archaeologists simply not recording small and often badly preserved children's bones. Contemporary Greek writers thought that the Carthaginians were performing child sacrifice, and the archaeological evidence means that their claims cannot merely be brushed aside as anti-Punic slander.

The conclusion to be drawn is that during periods of great crisis the Carthaginians and other western Phoenicians *did* sacrifice their own children for the benefit of their families and community. The archaeological evidence also clearly shows that the tophet was no dark secret but a symbol of western Phoenician prestige. The possession of a tophet was a mark of great distinction, limited to the largest and wealthiest settlements, and the children who were offered up for sacrifice were mostly the offspring of the elite.[57] The rites that took place in the tophet were, however, considered central to the continued well-being of the *whole* community, and were officially sanctioned by the public authorities.[58]

Place of Child Sacrifice

The continuing significance of the tophet in Carthage and in other western Phoenician settlements shows the continuing importance of Levantine heritage to their citizens, but at the same time the growing political and cultural cleavage between the new and old communities. The fact that the tophet thrived as a religious institution in the West, centuries after it had become defunct in the Levant, was more than a mere reflection of the innate conservatism of immigrant communities. Indeed, it was a symbol of the vibrancy and coherency of a western Phoenician world that was beginning to emerge from the shadow of its beleaguered Levantine cousins.

THE RISE OF A MERCANTILE SUPERPOWER

In 573 BC, after a thirteen-year siege, Tyre was forced to sign a humiliating peace with the Babylonian king Nebuchadnezzar. Traditionally, scholars believed that it was the demise of Tyre as an independent mercantile power that sent the Phoenician colonies of the far West into the economic crisis that enveloped them around the same period.[59] In fact both events were symptoms of the same malaise: the collapse of the value of silver. Such had been the oversupply of silver to the Near East that by the beginning of the sixth century BC, the trans-Mediterranean traffic between Spain and the Levant had dramatically declined.

Tyre thus no longer received its former protection from its reputation as the dominant player in the precious-metals market, and many of the smaller Phoenician trading stations along the southern coast of Spain now faced doom. The only reason for the existence of many of these settlements had been the small-scale trade facilitated by the cargo ships which passed by on the Gades route, and once these ships were gone these communities were quickly abandoned. In contrast, the

Phoenician colonies of the central Mediterranean seem to have emerged from this economic crisis relatively unscathed, probably because their primary focus was the north–south Tyrrhenian axis and its links with the Aegean.[60]

For Carthage, the disappearance of Tyrian shipping in the region appears to have presented a major opportunity to expand further its own trading networks, particularly in regard to the supply of goods and raw materials from the eastern Mediterranean, Egypt and the Levant.[61] The collapse of the Levantine–Spanish trade routes, which had played such an important part in the early development of Carthage, would now be the catalyst for what one German scholar has termed 'Der Aufstieg zur Grossmacht' – 'the rise of a superpower'.[62]

The nature of this new superpower has been much debated. Many historians, influenced by the great empires of both the ancient and the modern worlds, have been content to view Carthage as an imperialist power which quickly sought to dominate the lands of the western Mediterranean through military and economic pressure.[63] Hostile ancient Greek historiography and more modern prejudices have combined to create an image of the Carthaginians as aggressive and pernicious oriental interlopers whose one clear aim was to overrun an ancient world already imbued with Western civilization. This is particularly true in the case of Spain, where the Carthaginians have often been blamed for the demise of the old Tartessian kingdoms. Keen to promote the idea that Tartessus had been a great Western civilization – indeed an occidental Troy – some scholars have argued that ancient Andalusia was subjected to a brutal invasion by the Carthaginians in the late sixth century BC.[64] These claims appear to be validated by much later Roman sources, who report that the Carthaginians had treacherously seized Gades after its hard-pressed citizens had begged them to provide help against hostile Spanish forces.[65]

These were not the only accusations of imperialism levelled at Carthage's actions during this period. According to the third-century-AD Roman historian Justin (himself drawing on the lost *Philippic Histories* of Pompeius Trogus), Malchus, a Carthaginian general or 'king', after overrunning much of the island of Sicily was heavily defeated in Sardinia in the mid sixth century BC. Unwilling to accept such a humiliation, the Carthaginian Council of Elders punished the general and his remaining troops by sending them into exile. However, Malchus and his soldiers, indignant at the severity of the sentence – especially as they had enjoyed considerable success in the past – rebelled. After putting Carthage under siege, Malchus captured the city, although eventually he was himself put to death after being accused of plotting to be king.[66]

Justin would also report that later in the sixth century BC another Carthaginian general, named Mago, supposedly sent an armed force to Sardinia under the command of his sons Hasdrubal and Hamilcar. This expedition almost ended in disaster when Hasdrubal died of battle wounds, but the Carthaginians eventually managed to establish themselves in the southern half of the island, and forced several of the indigenous tribes to withdraw into the mountainous interior.[67] There is indeed good archaeological evidence for unrest on the island in the mid sixth century BC. The Phoenician stronghold settlements at Monte Sirai and Cuccurredus were both abandoned, the latter after being burnt down, and the major Nuragic settlement at Su Nuraxi was violently destroyed.[68]

These dramatic stories of a tyrannical and acquisitive Carthage in the sixth century BC must be treated with a good deal of scepticism, particularly as they were written both in a much later period and at a time (after the Punic wars) when such negative stereotyping was firmly fixed in the Greek and Roman cultural imagination. On Sardinia, there is no sign of a long-term Carthaginian occupation during this period. The violence and unrest evident in the archaeological record might well indicate disturbances between the Phoenician and indigenous populations, or even internecine conflict between Nuragic groups.[69]

If the stories concerning Malchus and Mago have any basis in truth, then they may be literary embellishments of long-distant memories connected with a short-term Carthaginian intervention to protect Phoenician interests on the island. In the first half of the sixth century BC, Carthage was still reliant on overseas imports for around 50 per cent of its food, and Sardinia remained an important source of supply.[70] Indeed, Carthaginian strategy on the island during the sixth century BC, rather than being one of aggressive conquest, appears to have centred on improving the collection and transportation of agricultural produce and other raw materials from the interior though the foundation of two new towns, Caralis (Cagliari) and Neapolis.[71]

In southern Spain there is also no convincing evidence for a Carthaginian invasion. The collapse of the Tartessian kingdoms has nothing to do with a Carthaginian invasion and everything to do with internal feuding and the collapse of the Levantine metal trade, the main source of wealth for the elite.[72] Even if the Carthaginian military interventions mentioned in later sources did take place, they must have been of a temporary nature, for there is no archaeological evidence of a prolonged occupation of southern Spain. Carthage did partially step into the economic vacuum created by the collapse of the Levantine–Iberian metal trade, but only in a strictly limited way. There was some Carthaginian colonization in Andalusia (such as at Villaricos), but most efforts appear to have been directed towards the reorganization and expansion of existing Phoenician settlements such as Malaga and (on Ibiza) Ebusus.[73] It was not until the late fifth/early fourth century that Carthage began to acquire direct control of overseas territory, and even then this did not fit comfortably into any model that we might view as 'imperialistic'. There is little evidence of territorial conquest, administrative control, collection of taxes, commercial monopolies or the appropriation of foreign policy.[74]

EXPANSION INTO AFRICA

Carthage's commercial expansion during this period has traditionally been ascribed to its chronic lack of agricultural hinterland.[75] However, new archaeological evidence from Carthage itself conclusively shows that, while maintaining and indeed strengthening their overseas trading networks during this period, the Carthaginians were gradually moving away from their previously heavy reliance on overseas imports of food-stuffs. Palaeobotanical analysis has revealed the extraordinarily varied diet that the citizens of Carthage enjoyed: wheat, barley and other cereals, numerous kinds of vegetables, pulses, lentils and fruits such as pomegranates, figs, grapes, olives, peaches, plums and melons, as well as almonds and pistachios. Fish and other seafood, sheep, goats, pigs, chicken, and even on occasion dogs were also eaten.[76] From the second

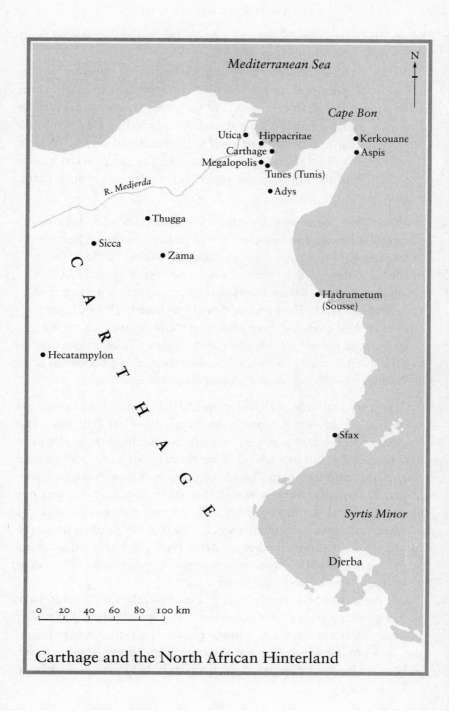

Carthage and the North African Hinterland

half of the sixth century onward most of this sustenance hailed from Carthage's own North African territory.[77]

We do not know how this new land was acquired – whether by alliances struck with local Libyan leaders or by aggressive military action – but during the sixth century Carthage clearly began to expand its authority over the fertile Medjerda valley and the Cap Bon peninsula through the construction of a number of forts and settlements.[78] A later Greek account of Cap Bon (now north-eastern Tunisia) provides a clear explanation of the allure of the region for a city with a burgeoning population:

> All the lands . . . were set with gardens and orchards watered by numerous springs and canals. There were well-constructed country houses, built with lime along the route, announcing widespread wealth. The houses were filled with things that contribute to the enjoyment of life and had been stored up by the inhabitants thanks to a long peace. The land was cultivated with vines, olive trees and a whole host of fruit trees. On both sides there were herds of oxen and sheep grazing on the plain, and near the main pastures and the marshes there were studs of horses. To be brief, in these lands was the varied prosperity of the most distinguished landowners of Carthage who enjoyed using wealth for the pleasures of life.[79]

Over forty years ago, archaeologists had the good fortune to stumble upon one of the new Carthaginian foundations on Cap Bon. The wonder of Kerkouane is not its magnificent buildings or its exquisite material culture, but its survival. Whereas many of its counterparts lie inaccessible under Roman, Byzantine, Arab and now Tunisian settlements, Kerkouane, when it was destroyed by the Romans, was not even considered worth rebuilding. We do not even know what the Carthaginians called this small town, for 'Kerkouane' (a name bestowed by archaeologists) does not appear in the surviving historical accounts from the ancient world. Kerkouane nevertheless provides a rare window into small-town life in Punic North Africa.[80]

Life for most of the inhabitants of Punic North Africa would have been a gruelling struggle for subsistence, and it is this world that Kerkouane represents. Its water, though plentiful, is rather brackish, and the land around it too thin for extensive agriculture. What is more, although it lies on the water's edge, Kerkouane has no natural harbour.

Kerkouane is the town that history forgot, lying under the dunes for over two millennia, waiting to be rediscovered.

Although much of what remains of the town dates to the early third century BC (just before it was finally destroyed), Kerkouane still gives us a full picture of a small Punic town in North Africa.[81] It is unlikely that its population was ever more than 1,200 people, who made their living as fishermen and craftsmen. The main industries of the settlement seem to have been salt-making, the manufacture of purple dye (many murex shells have been found on the site), and the production of garum.

Despite its modest size, the town was planned on a loose grid system, with buildings lining a series of wide streets interspersed with public squares. The most prominent public building in the city was the temple, and it must have been a fine sight. The handsome entrance was flanked with pilasters and contained a vestibule which led into a large court-yard, divided into two distinct spaces by an altar and a podium. The sacrificial altar was located in the front part, and behind was an area for ritual banquets. Although archaeologists do not know for sure which deities were worshipped at the temple, artefacts found at the site (including a votive arrowhead) hint at an emphasis on Melqart, his son Sid and Tanit – perhaps an indication of Kerkouane's original status as a 'colonial' foundation on foreign land. Two male terracotta heads of an older bearded deity and a younger clean-shaven one, both wearing rounded-off conical hats, bear a striking resemblance to the iconography of Sid and Melqart at the temple of Antas in Sardinia.[82]

Undoubtedly the most impressive features of Kerkouane were some of the private residences that lined its generous avenues. The walls were built in the traditional Punic way, with rubble fill strengthened at regular intervals by large and upright rectangular stones. Most of these houses consisted of a series of rooms, including living and storage spaces, built around a central courtyard. The finest of them had inbuilt cupboards and chests, and some contained built-in bread ovens (similar to the *tabourna* ovens still found in Tunisia today). Many had an upper storey with rooms and a terrace.

However, what really surprised the archaeologists who excavated Kerkouane was the sheer number of bathrooms, and their technical ingenuity. Unlike in Carthage, where the hip baths were free-standing, many of those in Kerkouane were built into the room, with the most elaborate having a stepped seat, arm rests and a basin, all of which were covered in water-resistant render. Some bathrooms were split between changing and washing facilities. Whereas in many Greek houses the bathroom was connected to the kitchen area, in Kerkouane many were situated off the entrance vestibule or passageway leading from the street into the house. Although there were pragmatic reasons for such a location, such as the availability of drainage and water, the choice also suggests that in the Punic world the washing of the body was seen as an important ritual act of purification that marked the transition from the public sphere outside the house to the private space of the family.[83]

The town also provides invaluable clues about the interaction between the Carthaginian and the indigenous Libyan peoples.[84] Although the religious practices and architecture of the town show a strong Carthaginian blueprint, and the written language used was Punic, strong native Libyan elements are still evident. This is particularly marked in certain funerary practices. In the tomb of Zybac, a metal-smelter, the burial arrangements correlate with the Libyan name of its occupant, for Zybac was buried in the foetal position (as was Libyan custom). His tomb also showed traces of the red ochre used in native Libyan burial practices.

The inhabitants of this little town were also connected into the wider Mediterranean world. An Attic black-figure wine jug depicting the Homeric hero Odysseus escaping from the cave of the Cyclops Polyphemus has been found with an Ionian cup in a tomb dating to the sixth century BC. Greek architectural features such as Ionic capitals were also widely used, and a number of the more impressive private dwellings show significant Greek influence, such as peristyle courtyards and the use of ornate stucco plaster. Even outside the territory beyond its direct control, Carthaginian influence over wider areas of North Africa increased in the sixth century as new emporia were established along the coast through compacts with local indigenous leaders, while its commercial relations with the older Phoenician colonies such as Lixus continued.[85]

The fifth century saw further Carthaginian expansion into Africa, with the fertile regions of the Sahel (the area around the modern

Tunisian towns of Sousse and Sfax) and Syrtis Major (modern north-west Libya) being added to the Carthaginian dominion.[86] It was during this period that Carthage became as celebrated an agricultural producer as it was a mercantile power. Recent studies of the amphorae used to convey foodstuffs into the city clearly show that, even by the last decades of the sixth century BC, the vast majority of those foodstuffs originated from Carthage's own hinterland.[87] A land survey has also shown that in the fifth and fourth centuries new farms and agricultural centres began to appear on Carthage's near hinterland, including on the peninsula itself.[88] These included one particularly fine villa estate at Gammarth, in the north of the Carthage peninsula, which possessed a substantial olive-pressing operation.[89]

A name strongly associated with the Carthaginian agricultural revolution is Mago, an expert whose advice on trees, fruits and viticulture, as well as animal husbandry, was often cited by both Greek and Roman authors.[90] Mago was particularly deferred to in regard to trees, fruits and viticulture, as well as being one of the first advocates of fertilizers and the need for regular pruning. Archaeologists working in the area of the commercial ports in Carthage found physical evidence of this expertise through the existence in a water channel (silted up sometime in the mid fourth century BC) of numerous seeds of fruits such as grapes, olives, peaches, plums and melons, as well as almonds, filberts and pistachios, a number of which require the use of complex horticultural techniques such as grafting.[91] Wine was also produced in considerable quantities.[92] Of particular fame was a sweet wine made from sun-dried grapes (rather like the *passito* which is still drunk in Italy today). Large numbers of Carthaginian transport amphorae have been found all over the western Mediterranean, and probably contained either wine or olive oil, also produced in large quantities in North Africa. The region was also famous for both figs and the pomegranate, the latter known by the Romans as the *malum Punicum* or 'Punic apple'. The Carthaginians were also celebrated for certain technological advances in agriculture, such as the *tribulum plostellum Punicum* or Punic cart, a primitive but highly effective threshing machine.[93]

ATLANTIC ADVENTURES

Intriguing stories exist that suggest Carthaginian activities in far more distant parts of Africa too. Greek and Roman authors reported that, over a century before the first recorded Greek voyage into the Atlantic Ocean by Pytheas of Massilia in the second half of the fourth century BC,[94] two contemporaneous state-sanctioned Carthaginian expeditions set out to explore its African and European coastlines.[95] So little was known about the Atlantic in antiquity that it was generally believed it was part of a giant river that encircled the whole earth.[96]

The first of these Carthaginian Atlantic ventures, involving a single ship captained by a senior Carthaginian commander named Himilco, is found in a poetical work of geographical instruction written in the fourth century AD by a Roman nobleman, Festus Rufus Avienus, for a young relative. Although it is unlikely that Avienus had read an original Punic text, he probably picked up the information from an earlier Greek account of Himilco's adventures.[97]

Avienus recounts that, after passing through the Pillars of Hercules, Himilco's ship turned north along the western coastlines of the Iberian peninsula and Gaul (modern France). The voyage took four long months, owing apparently to the shallow becalmed seas, vast areas of seaweed, and huge marine monsters which they encountered along the way.[98] Eventually the party arrived in what is now Brittany, where lived the Oestrymnians, a trading people who ventured out on to the ocean in their hidebound boats. The Oestrymnians were renowned for their special relationship with the inhabitants of the mysterious tin- and lead-producing Cassiterides islands (variously identified as islands off Spain or in the Gulf of Morbihan, the Scilly Isles or Cornwall).[99] Afterwards the party travelled further north, with Himilco visiting both Ireland and Britain before making the return journey to Carthage.

Like the account of Himilco's northern mission, the second of these reported Carthaginian Atlantic expeditions is found not in a Punic text, but in this case in an anonymous Greek work called the *Periplus* (voyage) of Hanno, most recently dated to the fifth century BC, but purporting to be a faithful copy of an inscription put up in the temple of Baal Hammon in Carthage itself.[100] This expedition was a more

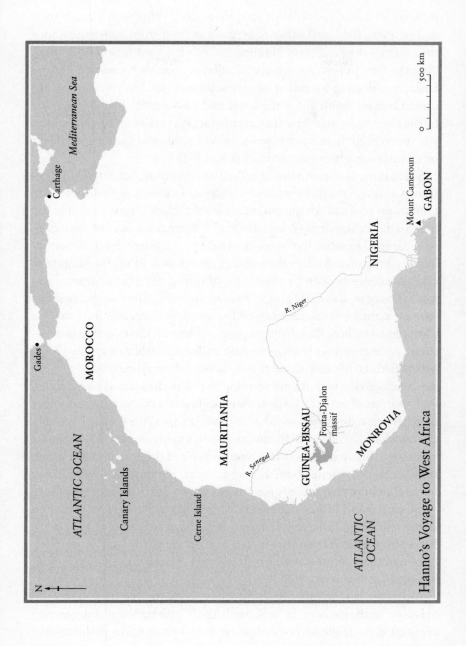

Hanno's Voyage to West Africa

substantial affair. A flotilla of sixty-five oared ships with 30,000 men and women, food and other equipment set sail from Carthage under the command of a certain Hanno, and headed west into the Atlantic. First the fleet followed the coast of what is now Morocco and Mauritania, establishing a number of new settlements along the way, before sailing further south along the coast and past a great river, thought to be the river Senegal, where they sometimes met resistance from natives who prevented them from disembarking by throwing stones (while on other occasions they merely ran off and hid).[101]

Eventually, the author of the *Periplus* recounts, after twelve days from Carthage the Carthaginians anchored close to a series of large mountains covered with aromatic, colourful trees – most probably the Fouta-Djalon massif in Guinea-Bissau.[102] When, a number of days later, they camped in what has been identified as the Niger delta, the crews became very afraid when the evening gloom was lit up by camp fires and the silence broken by the sound of music, the beat of drums and loud shouts in the dark jungle around them.[103] After witnessing the strange sight of large torrents of fire emptying directly into the sea (thought to be lava flow from an active volcano), the expedition eventually came to a very high mountain called the 'Chariot of the Gods' (identified as Mount Cameroun), where they witnessed yet more volcanic activity, with flames seeming to rise to the stars at night. Later, in the forests of perhaps Gabon, they would come across a large number of what were described as 'hair-covered savages' (in reality probably chimpanzees).[104] The Carthaginians were unable to capture any male specimens, because of their climbing ability and the ferocity with which they defended themselves; however, they managed to seize three females, whom they were forced to kill owing to their fierce resistance – a later Roman source claimed that their flayed hides were exhibited in the temple of Tanit at Carthage, until the destruction of the city.[105] It was now that Hanno was forced to turn back, for lack of supplies, although there is no account of the return journey: the *Periplus* ends abruptly at this point.[106]

Although it is impossible completely to guarantee their historical veracity, such voyages fit well with the Carthaginians' burgeoning reputation for trade and colonization during this period. Although the reported numbers on board must be exaggerated, the account makes it clear that the establishment of emporia and workshops in the coastal regions of what is now western Morocco – an area particularly abundant in sea life and therefore a good place for the establishment of factories producing purple dye, salted fish and garum – was an important component of the voyage.[107] As regards metal ores, there were sources of copper in Mauritania and of gold in Gambia and Guinea-Bissau, as well as large quantities of easily accessible tin in the Bauchi region of northern Nigeria.[108]

There has long been a vigorous academic debate over these accounts of Carthaginian exploration and trade out into the Atlantic. The French scholars Jean-Gabriel Demerliac and Jean Meirat have gone as far as to argue that the voyages were part of a coordinated attempt under the Magonids to control Atlantic trade.[109] To prove this theory they have 'reconstructed' a carefully planned rotation system whereby smaller, more manoeuvrable, craft were used to carry tin, lead, amber, flax, hides and copper from the northern Atlantic coast, and gold, tin, ivory, hides, jasper, resin, rubber, purple garments and fish products from the southern, before the goods were transferred at Gades into large merchant ships for the journey on to Carthage.[110] Moreover, they view Himilco's expedition as an attempt to arrange the sea transport of tin from Gaul and Britain through an alliance with the Oestrymnians, thereby trumping attempts by the Greek colony of Massilia (Marseilles) to strengthen its own commercial networks in Gaul.[111]

These theories have, however, been hotly contested by other specialists, most recently Victor Bello Jiménez, who point to the lack of accurate geographical knowledge relating to these particular regions in ancient Greek geographical works (on which we are entirely reliant for these accounts, despite the reference in the Hanno text to a Punic inscription in the temple of Baal Hammon at Carthage) and the complete lacunae in archaeological evidence for Carthaginian trade on either the northern or the African Atlantic coasts.[112] Others have voiced serious doubts about the veracity of these accounts, arguing that they are full of tropes and clichés commonly associated with Greek fantastical literature.[113] Yet, although Jehan Desanges has rightly argued that the *Periplus* 'cannot be divested of its Greek mantle without blurring its outlines into utter pointlessness', the Greek paradigm within which the account is expressed does not necessarily challenge its basis in actual events.[114] Seemingly informed descriptions of African topography, fauna and flora cannot be explained away simply as the product of the fertile Greek imagination.

In regard to the lack of material evidence for a Carthaginian presence in West Africa and the northern Atlantic, it would be more surprising if vestiges of such a transitory presence *had* survived in coastal areas, which are likely to have endured significant topographical changes in the past two and a half millennia. However, a more serious objection lies in the powerful winds and currents that any ship would have to travel against on the way back to the Pillars of Hercules. But, although an extended period of rowing would have been required to get the ship to the Canary Islands, this would not have been an impossible feat.[115] And, although by no means conclusive, there is some indication of sporadic use of the Canary Islands for shelter and resupply by sailors.[116]

It is also clear that West Africa was not completely terra incognita by this period. As early as the seventh century BC, the circumnavigation of the continent had been successfully accomplished by a group of Phoenician sailors, under the aegis of Necho II, pharaoh of Egypt.[117] Herodotus also describes an unusual system of barter developed by the Carthaginians so that they could trade with African tribes:

> The Carthaginians also relate the following: – There is a country in Libya, and a nation, beyond the Pillars of Hercules, which they are wont to visit, where they no sooner arrive but forthwith they unlade their wares, and, having disposed them after an orderly fashion along the beach, leave them, and, returning aboard their ships, raise a great smoke. The natives, when they see the smoke, come down to the shore, and, laying out to view so much gold as they think the worth of the wares, withdraw to a distance. The Carthaginians upon this come ashore and look. If they think the gold enough, they take it and go their way; but if it does not seem to them sufficient, they go aboard ship once more, and wait patiently. Then the others approach and add to their gold, till the Carthaginians are content. Neither party deals unfairly by the other: for the Carthaginians themselves never touch the gold till it comes up to the worth of their goods, nor do the natives ever carry off the goods till the gold is taken away.[118]

Another later Greek travel writer, the anonymous Pseudo-Scylax, described how merchants would arrive at Cerne Island, one of the sites mentioned in Hanno's expedition, from where they would take their merchandise to the mainland by canoe, to show it to the native 'Ethiopians'.[119] These were described as being extremely tall and beautiful, with beards, long hair and tattoos. They lived in a great city, where they were ruled over by the tallest among them. Their diet consisted of meat and milk, and they drank wine. In war, their forces were made up of horsemen and of javelin-throwers and archers who used fire-hardened tips. Their drinking bowls, bracelets and decoration for their horses were made of ivory. The Phoenicians/Carthaginians traded perfumed oil, Egyptian stone, and Attic tiles and pitchers, and in exchange received domestic animals and the skins of deer, lions and leopards, as well as hides and ivory from elephants.[120]

There is no good reason to discount the voyages of Hanno and Himilco as nothing more than products of the baroque fantasies of Greek writers. It nevertheless seems very unlikely that Carthaginian merchants made the long and extremely hazardous journey to West Africa on a regular basis. A more plausible scenario is that the first leg of Hanno's expedition (which involved the setting-up of new settlements and trading stations along the Atlantic coast of what is now Morocco) was the major aim of the enterprise, whereas the latter stages of the journey, once the flotilla passed Cerne, were solely concerned with exploration and discovery.[121] Indeed, these new Carthaginian settlements on the Atlantic coast of Morocco may have been the source of the large quantities of pickled and salted fish, packed in Punic amphorae from that particular region, which began to be shipped to Corinth around 460 BC, from where they were presumably distributed to other destinations in Greece.[122]

The establishment of these new settlements along the Atlantic coast of Morocco fits the broader pattern of Carthaginian colonization with a particular emphasis on agricultural exploitation during this period. Indeed, Aristotle emphasized the dispersal of surplus, poor inhabitants to colonies as an established method used by the Carthaginian elite to avoid potential political unrest.[123]

THE EMERGENCE OF A PUNIC MEDITERRANEAN

Although Carthage was not exercising any direct political control over the lands of the old Phoenician disapora in the central and western Mediterranean, this does not mean that its influence was not felt. The advent of what we call the 'Punic' era is notoriously difficult to define, but during the second half of the sixth century BC one witnesses the growing influence of recognizably Carthaginian cultural traits in other western Phoenician colonies.[124]

The most significant of these traits was the adoption of Punic, the Levantine dialect spoken in Carthage, and the replacement of cremation by burial as the favoured funerary practice.[125] Furthermore, it is noticeable that the tophet became an increasingly prominent part of the religious life of those western Phoenician colonies where that tradition had previously been less strong.[126] In regard to material culture, and specifically luxury goods, there was a clear change in taste away from imported eastern-Greek fineware pottery to ceramic ware from Athens (long favoured in Carthage).[127] Politically, there was a growing sense of community, with elites enjoying some citizenship rights in other western Phoenician cities.[128] In Carthage it appears that a minority of foreigners and freed slaves were also able to attain a status called 'Sidonian rights'($\check{s}$ $\dot{s}dn$), which appears to have been a partial bestowal of some rights and privileges associated with Carthaginian citizenship.[129]

However, the 'Punicization' of the old Phoenician western diaspora was never simply the imposition of 'top-down' cultural conformity. Indeed, in some areas it led to greater diversification as the influence of Phoenicia waned. Thus it is noticeable that the dinner service of bowls, plates, perfume jars, pots, and trefoil- and mushroom-shaped jugs which had been the standard grave goods for generations began to disappear, to be replaced with a far more diverse set of ceramic goods.[130] Moreover, the same variegation is found in other art forms, such as the designs and motifs found on the steles produced in considerable numbers across the new Punic world.[131]

The emergence of what we might term a 'Punic world' was not a linear progression from the old Phoenician one, but a complex and multifarious series of hybridizations with other indigenous and colonial cultures throughout the western Mediterranean.[132] This is particularly evident on the island of Sardinia, where the large number of oil lamps left as offerings at Punic sanctuaries (following an indigenous Sardinian custom) shows a complex interaction between Punic and local traditions.[133] The fact that many of these shrines were built into previous Nuragic structures may also indicate the absorption of indigenous customs into Punic religious practice, or the introduction of Punic elements into traditional native rites.[134]

Initially in diverse locations such as Spain, Sardinia and Sicily, these distinct micro-cultures were 'common mutually comprehensible' worlds inhabited by both Phoenician/Punic settlers and native populations. Initiated through commercial exchange, these communalities were often built on misperceptions of each other's cultures. However, out of mutual incomprehension a shared understanding was born that was very particular to its participant groups but which often excluded those, even of the same ethnicity, who lived outside the particular region.[135] What we refer to as 'Punic' culture is an umbrella term for a whole series of diffuse cultural experiences that took place all over the western and central Mediterranean. It is only really later, in the fifth and fourth centuries BC, as Carthage imposed greater political and economic control over certain areas, such as Sardinia, that one begins to witness greater, but by no means total, cultural uniformity.

At Antas, for example, an isolated inland site in the south-west of Sardinia, a temple to the Punic god Sid was established. Sid was originally a Levantine god who had made the long journey west with Phoenician traders. Although only a minor member of the Carthaginian pantheon, by the fourth century BC he appears to have been widely recognized by the Punic population of Sardinia as the divine protector of the island.[136] The temple was a typical Punic design, consisting of a large walled enclosure which contained a north-facing rectangular structure with an open air altar where incinerated offerings were made to the god.[137] Although it was situated in a remote valley surrounded by steep wooded hills, the temple still attracted large numbers of people, including many of high social status, from as far away as Caralis.[138] Its importance lay in the rocky outcrop on which it had been situated, which had been a sacred site to the Nuragic god Babi long before the Phoenicians had arrived on the island.[139] Archaeologists excavating the site found a bronze statuette of a naked warrior figure, identified as Babi, holding up his right hand in benediction and brandishing a large spear in his left, dating to sometime around the ninth and eighth centuries BC. There are striking resemblances between this warrior figure and the iconography of Sid, who was also often presented with his right hand raised and a lance in his left.[140] Moreover, a connection with Babi might also explain the presence of a large number of iron arrowheads and javelins among the votive offerings left for Sid, as these were artefacts that were strongly associated with the former.[141] Antas, therefore, stands as a striking example of the cultural hybridization that took place on the island during the Punic period.

NEW FRIENDS AND OLD ENEMIES

Relations between Punic and Greek populations on Sicily developed along similar lines. By the early eighth century BC the Phoenicians had established colonies on the island, of which the most important were Panormus, Solus and Motya. At the island site of Motya, located in a sheltered bay just off the coast and attached to the mainland by a narrow promontory, the first buildings were warehouses and workshops, which were gradually joined by a number of dwellings and religious structures, of which the most substantial was a sanctuary now known as the Cappidazzu.[142] However, the Phoenicians on Sicily soon came under increasing pressure from a deluge of Greek colonists who arrived during the last decades of the century, attracted by the island's position on key Mediterranean trade routes and its abundance of fertile coastal land.[143]

According to Thucydides, of the populations who already lived on the island, the Sicans had originally arrived in Sicily from Iberia in the distant past. The Elymians, another people living in western Sicily, were supposedly refugees from Troy. The Sicels had arrived from Italy, and after defeating the Sicans had taken over much of Sicily, restricting the latter to southern and western parts of the island.[144] In contrast to the good relations that the Phoenicians had built up with the native

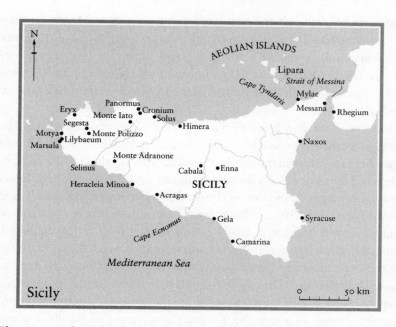

Sicily

Elymians and Sicels, the Greek colonial modus operandi often involved the violent expulsion of indigenous communities.[145] This led to threatened Phoenician and Elymian cities forming alliances against Greek aggression and territorial incursions, and the colonial landscape of Sicily was thus framed from its outset by competition for precious resources, often leading to conflict. Despite such animosities, these different ethnic communities also developed strong commercial and cultural ties. A pattern of economic interdependence punctuated by periods of both inter- and intra-communal violence was quickly established on the island.[146] None of the colonial or indigenous ethnic groups in Sicily ever attained a permanent upper hand over one another, which meant that the cultural syncretism and politico-economic synergy typified by this colonial 'Middle Ground' were sustained for far longer than in other colonial settings such as Italy.

Many of these interactions and collaborations were carried out against the backdrop of increasing competition between different communities for commercial markets and raw materials. Carthage's main concern was to protect its lucrative Tyrrhenian commercial interests.[147] The Greeks already controlled much of eastern Sicily and southern Italy (the latter being known in antiquity as Magna Graecia – 'Great Greece'). Now, in the sixth century, a new wave of Greek colonists would establish settlements right across the northern shores of the Mediterranean, at Massilia, Antipolis (Antibes) and Nicaea (Nice), as well as on the eastern coast of Corsica and on the Aeolian Islands.

On Sicily, the sixth century was a period of general prosperity. The collapse of the Levantine–Spain metal trade had little impact on the old Phoenician colonies in the south-west of the island, which had traditionally relied far more heavily on mercantile ties with their Greek neighbours and their strategic position on the sea lanes between Greece, Italy and North Africa. Signs of new-found wealth can still be seen in the archaeological record. At Motya, a new causeway was built to the mainland, and a dry dock (the *cothon*) was constructed for overhauling shipping. At the same time the Cappidazzu temple was monumentalized and the tophet was enlarged. The city during this period possessed two industrial zones equipped with kilns and wells for the large-scale manufacture of pottery, as well as a complex for the manufacture of purple dye and leather goods.[148]

Motya's Greek and indigenous neighbours had also prospered. At Greek Selinus, the civic centre had been redeveloped by the construction of a series of magnificent temples built on a huge new dual level pyramidal terrace, while at Elymian Segesta a temple was commissioned so large that it has been estimated that it took over thirty years to complete.[149]

Yet wealth brought with it heightened tensions. The southern and eastern coastlines that had been the traditional preserve of Greek settlers began to reach saturation point in terms of settlements, with the inevitable consequence that eyes began to turn towards the less crowded north-western and western areas of the island (already under the sway of the Phoenicians and the Elymians). In 580, Greek colonists originally from Cnidus and Rhodes had attempted to establish a settlement on the mainland opposite Motya, and were driven away by a joint Phoenician and Elymian force.[150] In such circumstances, it is no surprise that Motya and Selinus were now fortified with sturdy perimeter walls and watchtowers.[151] Conflict between the two neighbours can be seen in objects such as the tombstone found at Selinus of

Aristogeitos, son of Arcadion, who was killed near or under the walls of Motya at some point during the sixth century BC.[152]

Sicily was not the only place where Greek expansion created tensions. Concern over this new wave of Greek colonization in the central and western Mediterranean was probably a key factor in the formation of a Carthaginian alliance with the Etruscan kingdoms of central Italy, also key players in the lucrative Tyrrhenian trade routes. Carthage had already developed strong diplomatic ties in Etruria, for Phoenician merchants had long operated out of Etruscan ports; now these same privileges were extended to Carthaginian merchants.[153] Indeed, the second port of the Etruscan kingdom of Caere, modern Santa Marinella, came to be known as Punicum, probably because of the number of Punic merchants there.[154] In addition to the delicate *bucchero nero* drinking cups and other Etruscan fineware found in the tombs of wealthy Carthaginians, further evidence of commercial relations has been provided by a small ivory plaque discovered in a Carthaginian cemetery, on which was written, in Etruscan, 'I am Punic from Carthage.'[155]

In a complex of twin temples at Pyrgi, a port also in Caere, archaeologists made a spectacular discovery of three inscribed, beaten gold sheets, two written in Etruscan and the third in Punic. These documents, commonly known as the Pyrgi Tablets, allude to the grant by the ruler of Caere of a specific space for the worship of the goddess Astarte in a temple dedicated to the Etruscan goddess Uni. This was probably about providing a place of worship for a resident group of Punic and/ or Cypriot Phoenician merchants.[156]

Although the alliance between Carthage and the Etruscans appears to have dealt predominantly with matters of trade, joint military action was also envisaged if their interests were threatened.[157] As a city which relied so heavily on maritime trade, Carthage was famed in antiquity for its uncompromising attitude towards those who attacked its shipping.[158] Thus, when in 535 BC a group of Phocaeans – Greek refugees from Persian aggression in Asia Minor who had founded a colony at Alalia on Corsica – started attacking Carthaginian vessels, the response was as forceful as it was rapid. A joint Carthaginian and Etruscan armada made up of 200 ships attacked the Greek fleet off the southern coast of Corsica, in what would become known as the Battle of the

Sardinian Sea. Although both sides sustained heavy losses, the Greeks were eventually driven off and forced to abandon their Corsican colony. Those who were captured were triumphantly transported to Etruria, where they were stoned to death.[159] The Phocaeans had been brutally warned to keep out of the Tyrrhenian Sea.

In their efforts to secure commercial advantage in the central Mediterranean, the Carthaginians also signed a treaty with another emerging power in the region, the Latin city of Rome. For the Carthaginians this was probably just one of many such bilateral agreements with local rulers and states designed to guarantee the security of the Punic emporia that dotted the central and western Mediterranean region.[160] However, for the Romans this was clearly an important acknowledgement of their growing influence in central Italy.[161] Indeed, the accord with Carthage was considered to be significant enough to be inscribed on a bronze tablet.[162]

The terms of the agreement, signed in 509 BC, were remarkably detailed and wide-ranging. The Romans and their allies were forbidden from sailing past the 'Beautiful Promontory', the area to the north of Carthage now called Cap Bon. This effectively barred access to the fertile heartlands of Syrtis Major (the modern Tunisian Sahel) further east. If any crew were driven past that point by bad weather or enemy actions, their movements were strictly restricted:

> It is forbidden to anyone carried beyond it by force to buy or carry away anything beyond what is required for the repair of his ship or for sacrifice, and he must depart within five days. Men coming to trade may conclude no business except in the presence of a herald or town clerk, and the price of whatever is sold in the presence of such shall be secured to the vendor by the state, if the sale takes place in Libya or Sardinia. If any Roman come to the Carthaginian province in Sicily, he shall enjoy equal rights with the others.

In exchange, the Carthaginians undertook not to harm Latium's coastal cities of Lavinium, Ardea, Circeii and Terracina, or any other Latin city which was subject to Rome. (If they did capture any such city, they were to hand it over to the Romans.) They were also forbidden from building any forts in Latin territory, and if they entered such territory in arms they were not to pass the night there.[163]

Although Rome was still only a minor Italian power, the city was nevertheless considered to be strategically important enough for the Carthaginians to conclude this treaty with it. Situated 20 kilometres inland, on the banks of the river Tiber, the main transport artery into central Italy, Rome was already one of the major mercantile centres in northern Latium. The city had grown quickly, and had been one of the first in Latium to adopt urban planning, as well as substantial public buildings and well-built private residences. Although its early history was hidden in the mists of obscurity, later Roman historians generally agreed that the city had been initially ruled by a lineage of seven kings. They also claimed, through the use of Greek genealogical projections, that Romulus, the first of these kings, had come to the throne in 753 BC. Rome's dalliance with kingship would eventually be poisoned by the high-handed, rapacious and brutal behaviour of its regal incumbents.

However, one of the results of the Romans' growing dissatisfaction with their kings was the gradual creation of a political constitution that centred on a new, aristocratic, council called the Senate, which acted as both an advisory body and, increasingly, a counterbalance to the king's autocratic power. By the last decade of the sixth century BC, the citizens of Rome had finally had enough of their monarchy, and in 509 Tarquinius Superbus, 'the Proud', was driven out of Rome. In his place a new Republic was established, with two executive officers called 'consuls' at its head, annually elected from Rome's original aristocratic, patrician clans.[164]

Yet these accounts of grand strategic alliances can paint a very misleading picture of the central and western Mediterranean in the sixth century BC. This was no archaic version of the Cold War. Across the region, Greek, Punic, Phoenician, Etruscan and other indigenous peoples traded and interacted with one another with a freedom that stands in stark contrast to the power politics of the period. Indeed, it was often the deep and long-standing relationships that existed between supposedly bitter rivals that were the driving force in the creation of a surprisingly cohesive and interconnected world. In the lands of the West, nowhere was this better represented than in the curious relationship that developed between a belligerent Greek superhero and a Punic god.

3

The Realm of Heracles–Melqart: Greeks and Carthaginians in the Central Mediterranean

HEROIC WANDERERS: THE LEGACY OF HERACLES

When the first Greek traders arrived on the shores of the central and western Mediterranean, they had not come alone. They had brought with them not only their gods, but also many of the great heroes of the Greek mythological canon. Homeric figures such as Odysseus, Menelaus and Diomedes were portrayed as trailblazers who had roamed throughout the lands of the West in the long-distant past.[1] Over the decades that followed, these heroes would play an increasingly important role not only in lending legitimacy and antiquity to subsequent Greek claims to newly settled land, but also in forging links with local indigenous elites, some of whom came strongly to identify themselves with particular Greek heroes. Thus the Etruscans in central Italy adopted the Greek hero Odysseus initially as their founder and then as the leader who had brought them to Italy.[2]

The most high-profile role in helping these new Greek communities as they sought to assert themselves over new and unfamiliar landscapes was played by the legendary strongman Heracles. As a famed terrestrial wanderer who roamed the lands of the West civilizing the indigenous inhabitants by abolishing savage customs and clearing away brigands and monsters, Heracles set something of a precedent for the Greek colonists' sometimes aggressive dealings with the indigenous peoples.[3] The developing relations between the colonists and the native populations were also reflected in the numerous offspring that the legendary womanizer was said to have sired through his congress with well-born local females.[4] He was viewed not so much as a founder of colonies but rather as their initiator, who chose and secured locations before restlessly moving on, leaving it for those who followed him to settle there.[5]

Yet Heracles was far more than just a violent enforcer. The protection that he provided for the Greek colonists also encompassed the well-being of their harvests and livestock.[6] Indeed, the succour that he afforded ranged from the highest-sounding heroic deeds to the absurdly mundane. In the Greek colonies of southern Italy, the hero was revered not only for slaying giants, but also for warding away the flies that plagued the summer flocks, and for keeping locusts away from the crops. Such was the enduring influence of the great hero that by the end of the sixth century BC, when the memories of the first settler leaders had begun to dim, and the desire to be considered as the equals of the Greek cities of their forefathers grew, a number of communities in southern Italy and Sicily began to claim Heracles as their actual founder.[7]

Souvenirs and relics long associated with his heroic labours in mainland Greece started to appear in these western Greek settlements. Thus the hide of the monstrous Erymanthian boar, the victim of one of Heracles' famous labours ordered as a penance for his killing of his wife and children in a fit of madness, made the long journey from the Peloponnese to the temple of Apollo in the southern Italian town of Cumae. Colonists from the Greek city of Chalcedon relocated not only themselves but also Heracles' famous battle against the giants to their new home in Italy.[8] Heracles was thus gradually transformed from a talismanic figure strongly associated with terrestrial wandering and mercurial violence to an exuberant symbol of the success of the Greek colonial project in the West. The message that these legendary associations proclaimed was as clear as it was powerful: these colonists were no alien arrivistes. This was Greek land, bequeathed to them by none other than the son of Zeus.

By the sixth century BC western Greek writers – most notably the Sicilian poet Stesichorus, in his epic poem the *Geryoneis* – had associated Heracles' presence in the West with the tenth and eleventh of his famous labours: the theft of both the red cattle of the monstrous ogre Geryon and the golden apples from the garden of the Hesperides.[9] In the fragments of the *Geryoneis* that still exist, Heracles travelled to

Tartessus, where he borrowed a golden cup from the sun and floated across the ocean to Erythia, the mysterious island in the westernmost reaches of the world where lived Geryon. After killing his herdsmen and guard dog, Heracles eventually dispatched Geryon, took his cattle, and then returned to Tartessus to give the cup back to the sun, before driving the cattle overland to Italy and making his way back to Greece.[10]

Heracles' epic journey took him and his cattle up through Spain, the Pyrenees and Gaul, and then over the Alps. Faced with such a challenge, Heracles dispensed with his usual gung-ho approach and prepared himself properly. After carefully spending three days loading supplies on to the backs of his cattle, he successfully crossed the mountains before passing through Italy and on to Greece. Thus, by the sixth century BC the legend of the Heraclean Way, the route of the extraordinary journey that the hero made with Geryon's cattle, had begun to develop. For centuries it stood as a monument not only to Heracles the great traveller, but also to the hero who had tamed the West. And

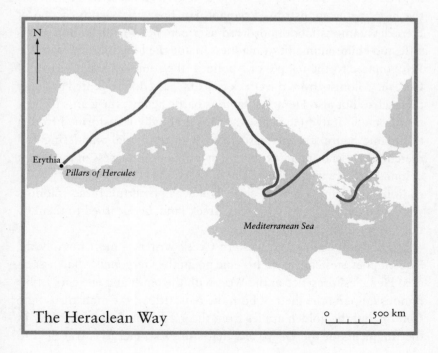

The Heraclean Way

because the story of Heracles in the West had become so tied to the ongoing process of Greek colonization in the region, the Heraclean Way itself was always a 'work in progress', forever taking new eccentric detours and doubling back on itself as new settlements and authors staked a claim to this seductive inheritance.[11]

It is probably because of Stesichorus that his home island of Sicily became part of Heracles' itinerary, despite it making no geographical sense at all in the context of travelling from Italy to Greece. The story told how an errant bull from the herd had supposedly broken free in southern Italy and swum across the Strait of Messina to Sicily, with the hero in hot pursuit.[12] Eryx, a local Sicilian king – founder of a settlement on a mountain which both took his name – and a son of Aphrodite, the goddess of love, had found the bull and placed it into his own herds. Heracles eventually tracked it down, but the king would return it only if the hero could beat him in a wrestling bout. After defeating Eryx three times, Heracles brought the competition to an emphatic end by killing the monarch. Reclaiming his errant bull, Heracles agreed to hand over Eryx's territory to the local indigenous people, as long as they gave it back to his descendants if they ever presented themselves in Sicily.[13] Before leaving the island, Heracles engaged in an eclectic variety of activities, including the foundation of cults and shrines, the creation of a lake, and a great victory over the indigenous Sicans, an indication of his centrality to the Greek settlers' claims to the ownership of the colonial landscape that they inhabited.[14]

The next episode within the Heracles and Eryx story highlights the extent to which the stories of Heracles' wanderings in the West were open-ended reflections of current geopolitical realities. The Greek historian Herodotus, among others, related how Dorieus, a prince of the royal house of Sparta, in 514 BC received permission to go to found a new settlement on the Libyan coast. Dorieus chose the location of his colony well, for Cinyps fell between the influence of the powerful Greek city of Cyrene to the east and of Carthage to the west. Dorieus' endeavours were, however, soon cut short by a combined Carthaginian and local Libyan force, which drove him and his followers out during the third year of their occupation.[15] Carthage's aggressive response appears to have stemmed less from the geographical position of Dorieus' settlement than from his ambitions to extend the territory of his colonial foundation westward into the fertile region of Syrtis Minor (a major object of Carthage's own territorial ambitions). Indeed, soon after this Carthage founded the city of Leptis Magna 50 kilometres away from the ruins of the abandoned Greek settlement, partly in order to head off any future Greek attempts to colonize the area.[16]

The late sixth century BC was, however, a period when the possibilities provided by the western Mediterranean still seemed limitless to many adventurers from the East. Defeated but unbowed, Dorieus and his companions returned to Sparta, where plans were soon hatched for another expedition, this time to the island of Sicily. According to Herodotus, the story of Heracles' agreement with the people of Eryx regarding the claims of his descendants to the territory was well known in Greece. The Spartan royal family claimed direct descent from Heracles, and, after receiving advice to 'found Heraclea, the one in Sicily', and receiving what he perceived as confirmation of success from the oracle at Delphi, Dorieus set off with a new expeditionary force. After he had taken Eryx and established a new colony, however, the settlement was attacked and destroyed by a combined Punic and Elymian force, and Dorieus and most of his fellow colonists were killed.[17]

The legacy of Heracles could be extremely threatening to both Punic and indigenous populations on the island. It is surely no coincidence that Pentathalus, the leader of the earlier Cnidian/Rhodian attempt to found a colony near Motya, also claimed descent from Heracles.[18] What these stories show is that, as western colonization had become inextricably bound with the Heraclean story in the Greek cultural imagination, myth came to legitimize colonization and colonization created new myths.

The long reach of Heracles was certainly not restricted to Sicily. Across the sea in North Africa, the Carthaginians also gained first-hand experience of his legacy, which provided the ideological rationale for a Greek colonial endeavour which saw cities sprouting up on the Libyan coast, to the east of Carthage.[19] North Africa now became the supposed location for Heracles' epic wrestling bout against the brutal giant Antaeus, who was said to have drawn his huge strength from his mother, the Earth. All those who were unfortunate enough to cross the path of this giant bully were forced into a wrestling match with him.

After he had defeated and killed them, their skulls were then added to his extensive trophy collection. Heracles vanquished Antaeus by depriving him of his power source, holding the giant off the ground while he throttled him. Ominously for the Carthaginians, the precise spot where this brutal encounter was meant to have taken place crept ever westward as Greek colonies sprang up ever closer to their territory.[20] The capture of Geryon's cattle was thus not the only Heraclean labour that provided a mythological canvas for Greek colonization in North Africa. The closest Greek settlement to Carthaginian territory was the city of Euhesperides, founded around the middle of the sixth century BC and named after its supposed proximity to the garden of the Hesperides, from which Heracles as his eleventh labour was tasked to steal its golden apples.[21]

MELQART AND HERACLES IN SICILY

Heracles was, however, always more than just a vehicle for aggressive Greek colonial expansion. In the frontier lands of the West, he developed as a multifaceted and indeed wildly contradictory figure, who accurately represented not only the aspirations of the Greek community, but also their often complex relations and interactions with the other populations of the region. On Sicily, Greek, Punic and indigenous communities intermarried and worshipped each other's gods and goddesses as well as trading and making war and political alliances with one another. Heracles, that seemingly most belligerent of Greek heroes, came to reflect those geopolitical realities too.

Sometime in the late sixth century BC, a large temple with a double frontal colonnade of six columns and with a further seventeen side columns was built on the acropolis of the Greek city of Selinus, near-neighbour and often fierce rival to Carthaginian Motya. It is thought that the temple was dedicated to Heracles, since one of the metopes on its capacious frontage shows the Greek hero fighting against the giant Cercopes. This was Sicilian Greek art at its very best, for it was not a slavish copy of current fashions in the wider Hellenic world. As David Asheri has commentated, 'the ferocious expression and the heavy, almost rigid, figures in these metopes . . . show a conscious local attempt to break away from the mere elaboration of imported idealistic models.'[22] It was thus in the very frontier lands of the island that Sicilian art came of age. The Heracles of the Selinuntine metope might resemble 'a [Greek] colonial symbol of civilizing power grappling with wild beings', but the artist that created this marvellous relief was heavily influenced by the brutal expressionism of Punic art, particularly as found on terracotta masks. This piece represented the central paradox of Greek Sicily, namely that the culture which was its greatest threat and enemy was also an integral part of its very being.[23]

The complex, multilateral processes of acculturation discussed earlier are also much in evidence in the adoption by the Sicilian Punic population of new, Greek, artistic forms. Terracotta figurines of goddesses in classical Greek style, wearing the *peplos*, a richly embroidered garment that hung in intricate folds, and carrying the *calathus*, a type of basket, were produced in large numbers across the island.[24] Rather than leading to mere mimicry, this familiarity with Greek art allowed the Punic population of the island to express themselves in new and powerfully original ways. Traditional Phoenician art forms such as anthropoid sarcophagi – stone coffins whose human heads, arms and feet protruded out from a piece of smooth stone like human pupae – acquired Greek dress and hair decoration.[25]

The most striking example of Punic art in this period comes from Motya. In 1979, archaeologists working on the island city discovered an oversized marble statue of a young man, standing at 1.8 metres tall without his missing feet. Although the arms had gone, it was relatively simple to reconstruct the pose of the left arm, as the hand had been carved resting on the hip. The head was framed by a fringe of curly hair, and had once worn a crown or wreath kept in place by rivets. All in all, the statue appeared to conform to the severe Greek sculptural style of the early fifth century BC, and indeed a very similar statue of an ephebe, a young man of military-training age, has been discovered at the Sicilian Greek city of Acragas.

It was argued that only a Greek sculptor could have created such a high-quality piece, and that the Motya ephebe was a looted Greek work.[26] However, there was a problem with this. Unlike the ephebes represented in other statues from this period, who are depicted nude, the Motya young man is clothed in a fine long tunic, with flowing pleats bound by a high girdle. Many ingenious solutions have been proposed to explain this anomaly. The strange girdle and the hand position have led to the suggestion that the young man was either a Greek charioteer or a sponsor of a chariot race. However, the Motya figure is very different from other surviving statues of Greek charioteers. In fact the closest parallels are found within the Punic world. First, despite the clearly Greek sculptural form, the statue clearly follows the Punic convention of not displaying the nude body; second, the clothes and headgear worn by the young man bear a marked resemblance to the ritual garments worn by priests of the cult of the Punic god Melqart, with whom Heracles would enjoy an increasingly close association in Sicily.[27] Neither Greek nor Punic but Sicilian, the Motya ephebe stood as a glittering testament to cultural syncretism.

From at least the seventh century BC, in the eastern Mediterranean Heracles had come to be increasingly associated with the Tyrian god Melqart. When Herodotus travelled to the great temple of Melqart at Tyre, he found compelling evidence that the temple of Heracles on the Greek island of Thasos had in fact started out as a sanctuary to the Tyrian god. In order to verify this information for himself, Herodotus then travelled on to Thasos, where the story was confirmed.[28] Intriguingly, Herodotus commented that the Thasians perceived their Heracles as having two very distinct identities, who needed to be worshipped in different ways. The worshippers offered to one whom 'they called the Olympian the sacrifices due to an immortal, whereas with the other they delivered funerary honours as with a hero'.[29] On another Greek island, Erythrae, locals told how Heracles had come to them after a raft that was carrying him from Tyre ran aground in a shallow channel – surely a dimly recollected communal memory of the rites of egersis.[30] The Phoenician world was clearly also struck by the synergies that existed between Heracles and Melqart, particularly on the island of Cyprus, which, like Sicily, also had a large Greek population. By the sixth century BC, workshops in the Phoenician Cypriot town of Kition were producing statuettes of a lionskin-clad male figure with a club, in a clear replication of the established Greek iconography of Heracles but posing in the manner of a Near Eastern or Egyptian deity, with his weapon raised in his right hand while holding in his left a lion ready for the kill.[31]

What were the similarities that Greek and eastern Phoenician and Punic populations saw in Heracles and Melqart? All were, of course, polytheistic religious cultures that actively sought to forge syncretistic connections between their own gods and foreign deities.[32] More particularly, a bilingual inscription from Malta is dedicated by two Phoenician brothers in the third/second century BC to 'Melqart, Lord of Tyre' in Phoenician and to 'Heracles *archegete*' in Greek.[33] The Greek word *archegete* was usually used in the context of a founder or progenitor, a role with which both Heracles and Melqart were strongly identified.[34] Melqart was as synonymous with colonization for the Tyrians as Heracles was for the Greeks. As protector of both the mother city and the new colonial foundations, Melqart helped to foster lasting links between the two. The temples in the newly founded colonies also provided a neutral and sacred space for the first contacts between Phoenician settlers and local indigenous peoples. Although Melqart was not the chief deity in Carthage, the god continued to fulfil his traditional role as the city's influence over the new Punic community in the western Mediterranean developed.

Punic colonization and economic consolidation on Sardinia had a notable impact on the religious landscape of the island. Indeed, there is some evidence for an organized initiative to represent Carthage's new relationship with the island through the establishment of new religious centres. This is well illustrated at the temple of Sid at Antas, where archaeologists have also discovered a dedication to Melqart.[35] The close relationship between Melqart and Sid on Sardinia is confirmed in the work of the second-century-AD Greek travel writer Pausanias, who claimed that 'The first sailors to cross to the island are said to have been Libyans. Their leader was Sardus, son of Maceris, the Maceris surnamed Heracles by the Egyptians and the Libyans.'[36] 'Sardus Pater' was the name that Sid Babi came to be known by in the Roman epoch, and 'Maceris' almost certainly refers to Melqart, the Libyan Heracles.[37] Indeed, epigraphic evidence points to the two gods having been closely linked with one another in Carthage.[38] Unlike Sid, who was particularly associated with Sardinia, Melqart represented the overarching sweep of Punic colonization, and hence why the relationship between the two was represented as being unequal – with Sid as the son of Melqart – in Sardinia and in Punic iconography.[39]

The worship of Melqart on Sardinia was self-consciously linked with Tyre during the Punic period, for the epithet '*L HSR* (literally, 'that is on the Rock') was often applied to the god – surely a reference to the great sanctuary.[40] This emphasis on Melqart in a period when the Carthaginians were exporting their own population to Sardinia, and strengthening their economic ties on the island, was a way of articulating the increasingly paternalistic relationship with the older Phoenician population while at the same time emphasizing a common Tyrian heritage.[41] Indeed, an inscription dating to the third century BC refers to a series of monumental improvements to the sanctuary of Melqart at Tharros, lists the senior officials of *Qrthdšt* (Carthage), and thereby explicitly links the god with the North African metropolis.[42]

Heracles and Melqart shared a number of striking characteristics. Most importantly, both transcended the boundaries between humanity and divinity: Heracles, the son of Zeus and a human mother, had to earn the right to become a god himself through his heroic feats; Melqart, although a god, was also the first mythical king of Tyre and ancestor of its royal lineage.[43] Other striking connections included the crucial regenerative role that fire played, for Melqart at the *egersis* and for Heracles during his apotheosis, when his body was burnt on a pyre before his spirit ascended to heaven and he took his place among the gods. Each year, after the ritual burning of his effigy, Melqart was symbolically reborn, thereby making the same journey between humanity and divinity.[44] Indeed, the syncretism between the two can be detected at the temple of Heracles in the Sicilian Greek city of Acragas, built around 500 BC, which contained twin staircases that led up to the attic of the structure. A recent study has suggested that this unusual architectural feature, although unlikely to have still have been used for such purposes in the fifth century BC, was originally associated with the ritual celestial ascent of deities found in Phoenician–Punic religion, such as the *egersis*. The temple at Acragas was just one of a number of archaic-era temples found with these staircases in Sicily and southern Italy.[45]

Ironically, the likelihood is that the tradition of Heracles and Eryx was derived not from the Greek but from *Phoenician* occupation of a site. Dorieus' mission may have been represented as the championing of Greek Heracles against the 'non-Greek' Heracles who at that time occupied Eryx.[46] The mountain, which rises to 750 metres above sea level, had been a sacred site for the indigenous Elymians before it had become the location for a temple to the goddess Astarte sometime in the second half of the sixth century BC.[47] Melqart was widely recognized as the consort of Astarte.[48]

Indeed, even the Heraclean Way, that seemingly most strident of monuments to Greek colonial endeavour in the West, was not quite what it first seems. Its tortuous and often nonsensical itinerary reflected the rivalries and shared interests of both incomers and indigenous populations who sought to stamp their mark on what was clearly, in the sixth century BC, a region of unrivalled opportunity. Thus the terminus of the Heraclean Way may have been the city of Argos in Greece, but by the sixth century BC Greek authors were generally in agreement that Erythia, the legendary home of Geryon and the starting point of Heracles' great western odyssey, was Gades, the oldest Phoenician settlement in the far West and site of the great temple of Melqart.[49] Even the accounts of Heracles' visit to Sicily, which could be construed as little more than the most aggressive kind of Greek colonial chauvinism, often contain small pieces of evidence that point to a far more complex set of relationships between the Punic and indigenous populations of the island. For instance, the genesis of Heracles defeating and killing the indigenous king Eryx very probably lay in the introduction of the Punic cult of Astarte into Eryx in the second half of the sixth century BC, which replaced a native Elymian shrine that had previously stood there. In this context, the story of Heracles appears to have been originally related to Melqart, who, as the consort of Astarte, was often worshipped in her temples.[50] The Heraclean Way, rather than merely being the superhighway of Greek colonial ambition, instead represented the ubiquity of cultural exchange and religious syncretism in the archaic central and western Mediterranean. Nowhere was this clearer than on the Italian leg of Heracles' great odyssey, which, with the Sicilian stage of the great hero's journey, was already being written about by the fifth century BC.[51]

HERACLES AND EARLY ROME

According to the first-century-BC Greek writer Dionysius of Halicarnassus, who was using earlier lost sources, after he had crossed the
Alps Heracles was supposed to have made his way down through the
Italian peninsula until he eventually pitched camp on the left bank of
the river Tiber, at the settlement of Pallanthium, the future site of the
city of Rome. While he slept, an ogre named Cacus, who had for many
years terrorized the other inhabitants of the locality, stole several of
his cattle. In order to cover his tracks, Cacus dragged the beasts to his
cave on the Palatine hill backwards, by their tails. Heracles, on waking
and discovering the theft, searched for his bovine charges in vain.
However, eventually he found them by driving the rest of the herd past
the entrance of Cacus' cave, from where the stolen cows bellowed when
they heard and smelled the others. Cacus then suffered the same grisly
fate as all those who tried to separate the cattle of Geryon from Heracles: he was beaten to death with the giant club, before his cave was
smashed down on top of his lifeless corpse.

Heracles then purified himself by washing in the Tiber and erected
an altar to Zeus, where he sacrificed a calf in thanks for finding the
cattle. When the indigenous peoples and Arcadians who lived in the
neighbourhood discovered what had happened, they rejoiced at
the fate of Cacus, whom they had long hated because of his thefts,
and made garlands for themselves and Heracles. The hero was then
invited to dine with their joint kings, Evander and Faunus.[52] On
discovering Heracles' true identity, Evander in obeisance to a long-
standing prophecy about the hero's coming, erected an altar to the
hero and sacrificed a calf upon it. Thus it was on the future site of
Rome that the first altar to Heracles was set up. After performing the
initial rites and sacrificing some of his own cattle, Heracles decreed
that, 'since they were the first who had regarded him as a god, they
should perpetuate the honours they had paid him by offering up every
year a calf that had not known the yoke and performing the sacrifice
with Greek rites'. The remainder of the story told how Heracles had
then taught two distinguished families, the Potitii and the Pinarii, the
sacrificial rites that were to be performed in his honour at his altar,

the Ara Maxima ('Great Altar') in the Forum Boarium, the ancient cattle market of Rome.[53]

Central Italy was the location of a large number of sanctuaries dedicated to Hercules and Hercle, the Italian and Etruscan interpretations of Heracles. Many of these temples were located on important links in key communication and transport arteries that traversed the Italian peninsula and acted as centres for trade, salt production and the seasonal movement of lifestock (an intriguing parallel with the myth of the hero and the cattle of Geryon).[54] The popularity and growth of the cult have tended to be seen as a reflection of the strong influence of Hellenic culture on the inhabitants of central Italy, through their frequent interactions with Greek merchants and the cities of Magna Graecia.[55]

However, part of the story of Heracles in Rome appears to be an adaptation of a much earlier Latin tale. Originally the hero figure had been Recaranus, a local shepherd of Greek origin, with whom our wandering hero has been amalgamated.[56] Cacus also appears to have started not out as the ogre of the Heracles myth, but as an indigenous divine seer. In fact the first identifiable artistic representations of Cacus were found not in Rome but in Etruria.[57] In the earliest version of the story he was not a brigand but a dishonest slave of King Evander, whom the monarch himself unmasked as the thief.

At first sight, the Ara Maxima dedicated to Hercules in Rome appears to conform completely to this analysis.[58] Its prestige and antiquity are proved by its position within the Pomerium, the traditional sacred boundary of the city. Furthermore, the old cattle-market district where it stood was on the nexus of two major transport links: the river Tiber and the land route which joined central Italy and the Sabine hills to Etruria (and thus fitting well with the familiar Herculean themes of cattle droving and trade). That it was Greek merchants who first brought the cult to Rome is strongly suggested by the widespread evidence that exists for their presence in the city during the archaic period, as well as the emphasis on the implementation of Greek rites for the cult in the Hercules and Cacus story.

This view appears to be confirmed by the discovery of a shrine dating to the mid sixth century BC in the Forum Boarium, under the church of Sant' Omobono.[59] The shrine was replaced by a more substantial temple with a podium in the late sixth century, reflecting both the growing prosperity of the city and the importance of the cult that was housed there. The presence of an almost life-size statue of Hercules with another of an armed female goddess strongly suggests that this is the archaic temple dedicated to the hero. As well as a large quantity of imported Greek pottery, the temple received a wide variety of offerings that included grains, hazelnuts, piglets, goats, sheep and cattle, as well as turtles, fish, geese and doves. The dedications left at the temple included loom weights, spindle whorls, perfume bottles, bronze pins, figurines, and carved amber and ivory plaques, and were also of a wide variety and exceptional quality for the period.[60]

The Sant' Omobono temple, however, does not vindicate but rather questions the scholarly orthodoxy that the cult of Hercules was simply a Latin/Roman adaptation of a purely Greek rite. The statue of Hercules discovered there, while following some of the standard Greek iconography associated with the hero, also shows clear artistic parallels with a series of statuettes of Heracles–Melqart produced in Kition. This raises the strong possibility that the Sant' Omobono male figure is Heracles–Melqart, and the armed goddess his divine consort, Aphrodite–Astarte.[61] The discovery of a deposit of Euboean, Pithecusan, Cycladic and Corinthian pottery dating to the eighth century BC close to the temple also strongly suggests that early Rome may have been connected into the Tyrrhenian trading circuit. Was early Rome, like Pithecusa and Sant' Imbenia, a mixed community where Greek, Phoenician and indigenous populations lived and economically cooperated with one another, and is the Sant' Omobono temple evidence of the same kind of cultural and religious syncretism that we witness in archaic Sicily?[62]

There are certainly other interesting parallels between the cult of Hercules at the Ara Maxima and what we know of the religious practices associated with the worship of Melqart at Tyre, Thasos and Gades, of which the most striking are the banning of flies and dogs from the precinct, the exclusion of female celebrants and pork from the sacrifices themselves, the giving of tithes of 10 per cent of profits by merchants and other wealthy individuals, and the choice of the autumn equinox – the time of the annual rebirth of Melqart – as the season to practise many of the rites associated with the cult.[63] Other famous landmarks around the Forum Boarium hint at the presence in archaic Rome of deities and religious rituals associated with the Phoenician/Punic world, and Melqart was certainly not the only Punico-Phoenician deity to have a considerable impact on the central-Italian religious landscape of the archaic period. His consort, Astarte, came to be closely associated with a startling array of Greek, Etruscan and Italian goddesses, including the Latin warrior goddess Juno, later queen of the Roman divine pantheon.[64]

Another important Roman connection was between Astarte and the goddess Fortuna. Scholars have long recognized the intriguing parallels between the twin temples supposedly built in Rome by the seventh-century-BC king Servius Tullius for Fortuna and Mater Matuta, a fertility goddess, and the religious complex at Pyrgi, where famous tablets promising part of one of the twin temples to the worship of Astarte were found. Indeed, the strange story that Servius Tullius actually engaged in sexual relations with Fortuna in her new temple may be an allusion to sacred prostitution taking place there.

Then there was the tomb of Acca Laurentia, which stood in the same area. A beautiful young woman of reputedly loose morals, Acca Laurentia had been won by Hercules in a game of dice and had been subsequently locked up in his temple with his other prize, a sumptuous feast. Later she would take Hercules' advice and marry a rich man whose considerable wealth she bequeathed to the Roman people on her death. In gratitude, the Roman king Ancius Marcus supposedly set up a tomb for her in the Forum Boarium, as well as an annual festival that was held in her honour on 23 December. Another version of this story merely records that she was a prostitute who used her vast wealth for a public feast for the Roman people. Were these strange stories a distant memory of a time when Phoenician/Punic sacred prostitution was practised in Rome?[65]

Once again the sanctuary at Pyrgi provides some interesting parallels. It has been argued that the Pyrgi Tablets themselves allude to the sacred marriage of Melqart and Astarte through which the welfare of the people and the fecundity of the new season were guaranteed.[66] The presence of a series of small rooms within the temple complex may confirm a brief Roman textual reference that sacred prostitution, a custom strongly associated with the worship of Astarte, was practised at Pyrgi.[67]

Later, Rome's ancient history would be comprehensively rewritten in order to provide the city with a pedigree that befitted its new position as a great Mediterranean power. However, these fragmentary and often obscure reminders of a very different, long-forgotten past would remain embedded within this new triumphant narrative, hinting at an archaic Rome where the Carthaginian ambassadors sent to conclude the 509 treaty would have found much that was familiar to them. Whether in the end it was Phoenician, Punic or eastern-Greek merchants who first brought Heracles to Rome is in fact relatively unimportant.[68] What is striking is the extent to which both Phoenicians and Greeks had brought to this new world not just the age-old rivalries that existed between them, but also the syncretism that had developed over the long centuries of interaction in the eastern Mediterranean.[69]

Very soon, however, these synergies would be challenged, and eventually eclipsed, by a far more dramatic, if erroneous, narrative of inter-ethnic hatred, and the brooding threat that Carthage supposedly posed to the very survival of the western Greeks.

4

The Economy of War:
Carthage and Syracuse

CARTHAGE THE COLONIAL POWER

Although during the fifth century BC there was still no sign of what we might conventionally view as a Carthaginian imperial structure, with the old western Phoenician settlements apparently keeping their political autonomy, there is plenty of evidence that Carthage was becoming increasingly assertive and interventionist, particularly in pursuing its economic goals in the central Mediterranean.

On Sardinia and Ibiza, territorial occupation and agricultural exploitation by a new influx of Punic settlers from North Africa rapidly took place during the later decades of the fifth century.[1] As well as the farmsteads built by these settlers to exploit the fertile plains, larger fortified settlements were also established to act as market centres and to control the countryside.[2] Such colonial ventures would have served a number of key purposes. First, they allowed the relocation of surplus populations who were potential malcontents with few prospects in Carthage or its North African territory. Second, they helped to expand the agricultural base of Sardinia – a key exporter of food to Carthage – by increasing the amount of land under intensive cultivation. Finally, they helped secure Carthaginian influence in a territory that was strategically vital in terms of both trade and food production.

Although most of Carthage's foodstuffs continued to come from North Africa, from the 430s onwards Sardinia became an increasingly vital source of food, its agricultural economy seeming to have become ever more keyed into the needs of Carthage. Large numbers of Sardinian 'sack'- and 'torpedo'-shaped amphorae used for the transportation of foodstuffs such as wine, olive oil, corn, salted meat and fish, and salt are found in Carthage during the fifth and fourth centuries BC.[3] According to a treatise by Pseudo-Aristotle, the Carthaginians were even supposed to have ordered the destruction of fruit trees in Sardinia and forbade the planting of new ones, presumably because they did not fit into the wider economic plan for the island as Carthage's main producer of cereals.[4]

The strengthening of the economic ties between Carthage and Sardinia brought great prosperity to the Punic cities on the island, as shown by the large number of opulent public and private buildings that were now built, and the fine imported objects and other luxury goods with which the wealthy elite were now buried.[5] At the city of Tharros, the fifth century BC in particular brought about a dramatic change in the cityscape, with the construction of a new quarter consisting of private residences and temples, as well as the building of imposing new fortifications on its landward side.[6] The source of this new wealth was not only agricultural produce and other raw materials, but also, increasingly, the manufacture of luxury goods such as decorated precious stones, amulets, jewellery, ceramic statuettes, perfume burners and masks, which were then exported throughout the Punic world.[7] Indeed, the increase in manufacturing output at Tharros may have been connected to the construction of a new industrial quarter in the fifth century.[8]

There were also very close ties between local Punic elites and Carthage, including the apparent bestowal of a type of honorary citizenship of the city.[9] Despite the increasing influence that Carthage wielded over the island, however, there is no evidence of a Carthaginian provincial administration ruling over Sardinia, and each city and its hinterland was governed by its own autonomous municipal authority.

Punic colonization had a far less beneficial impact on the island's indigenous population. Throughout the fifth and fourth centuries BC, the Nuragi were pushed further and further into the mountainous central and northern areas of Sardinia, as new settlers took over their land and founded new fortified settlements not only as market areas, but also to control the countryside.[10] Other sites pushed even further into Nuragic territory, and probably acted as commercial emporia for the exchange of goods.[11] However, this trade was increasingly one-way, with Phoenician goods beginning to predominate over indigenous artefacts in many Nuragic sites. Other important aspects of this ancient culture were also steadily eroded. Large numbers of the 'complex' multi-towered nuraghi that had studded the plains and hills of the island were abandoned by their inhabitants, suggesting that the chieftains that had controlled the territory and population were no more.[12]

Punic colonization and economic consolidation on Sardinia also had a notable impact on the religious landscape of the island, and there is some evidence for an organized initiative to represent Carthage's new relationship with the island through the establishment of new religious centres. The temple of Sid Babi at Antas, although on one level a symbol of the cultural and religious syncretism that had developed between colonial and indigenous communities on the island, was also a sophisticated attempt to inculcate a Punic god with the properties and authority of a Nuragic deity, which also played into the wider project of legitimating the Punic colonization of the island.

HIMERA AND THE CREATION OF THE 'CARTHAGINIAN MENACE'

At the same time that the Carthaginians were becoming increasingly involved in Sardinia, they also intervened militarily in Sicily. The catalyst was a plea for assistance made in 483 BC by Terillus, the Greek autocrat of Himera, a city in the north of the island, to his guest-friend Hamilcar, the leader of the Magonids, the pre-eminent political clan in Carthage. Terillus had been driven out of Himera when it had been attacked and captured by the forces of Gelon, ruler of Syracuse, the most powerful Greek city in Sicily, who with his allies had been engaged in a campaign of aggressive expansionism directed mainly against other Greek cities on the island.

The Magonids had close ties with Sicily, and Hamilcar's own mother was Syracusan. The solemn ties of guest-friendship (which involved the bestowal of hospitality and gift-giving), perhaps combined with concerns for the island's western ports (vital for Carthaginian trading operations), prompted the Magonids into action. Yet it appears that the expedition remained a private enterprise, underwritten by the Magonids rather than by the Carthaginian state. The huge army that

Hamilcar raised contained not only Carthaginians but also large numbers of mercenaries from across the central and western Mediterranean, including Libya, Spain, Sicily, Sardinia and Corsica.[13] These forces were further supplemented by those of Anaxilas, the Greek tyrant (autocratic ruler) of Rhegium in southern Italy, who was married to Terillus' daughter.

In 480, after disembarking his army at the port city of Panormus, Hamilcar, wishing either to maintain an element of surprise or to advertise the very limited scope of this operation, marched directly to Himera. However, any hoped-for advantage created by catching Gelon unawares was lost when secret letters, setting out the Carthaginian tactical plans, were intercepted. Furthermore, by setting off in such haste, Hamilcar had not spent sufficient time preparing his troops. The two forces met at Himera, and the result was a total disaster for the Magonids, their army being obliterated and Hamilcar killed. One version of events, by Polyaenus, a later Greek writer, told how Gelon had ordered his commander of the archers, who closely resembled him, to impersonate him. Leading out his company of archers dressed as priests, with their bows hidden behind myrtle branches, the commander went out to make a sacrifice. When Hamilcar similarly came forward, the archers pulled out their bows and killed the Carthaginian general as he was making a libation to the gods.[14] In another version of this story, recounted by Herodotus, during the battle Hamilcar remained in his camp, where he sought to enlist divine assistance by burning the bodies of whole animals on a great sacrificial pyre.[15] Yet even as he received favourable signs, his defeated men were fleeing from the battlefield, making it clear that these divine omens were false. Seeing that all was lost, Hamilcar made a new offering to the Punic gods by throwing himself into the searing flames. The defeat was so total that only a few bedraggled survivors made it back to Africa to bring news of the disaster.

Diodorus goes on to emphasize the scale of the defeat that the Magonids suffered at Himera. On learning of the terrible disaster, the Carthaginians kept close guard over their city, terrified that Gelon would now mount an attack there.[16] Labouring under this false expectation, they also immediately dispatched their ablest citizens as ambassadors to Sicily. These envoys sought the assistance of Gelon's queen, Damaretê, and when a satisfactory peace had been concluded they showed their gratitude by giving her a crown created from 100 gold talents. The audience that the Carthaginian embassy had with Gelon himself was later portrayed as a triumph for the Syracusan tyrant, with his Punic visitors tearfully begging that their city be spared.[17]

The victory brought great material wealth to Gelon and his allies. Not only was there a huge quantity of war booty to be distributed among the victors, but an enormous number of prisoners of war were available to labour on a number of ambitious building projects.[18] At the city of Acragas, a series of giant columns depicting what are thought to be the sculpted figures of Punic slaves were built as supports for the architrave of a temple to the Olympian gods.[19]

In Carthage itself, after the initial panic had subsided, the political fallout was surprisingly mild. In the decades that followed, there were political changes, including the creation of many of the political institutions that would operate throughout the remainder of the city's existence: the Tribunal of One Hundred and Four, the suffeture and the Popular Assembly.[20] Although the creation of the Popular Assembly, in which all citizens, whatever their socio-economic status, could participate, might seem to hint at some form of democratization of Carthage's political apparatus, this was very far from being the case. Rather, the main aim of these constitutional reforms was the establishment of a new, more clearly defined, senior executive council and officers. The Popular Assemby's ability to act was extremely limited, and, as the Athenian political scientist Aristotle noted approvingly, wealth remained as the defining factor in judging an individual's fitness to hold political office.[21] The Sardinian cities also adopted many of the political reforms that had originated in Carthage.[22]

Further proof that these changes were part of a reorganization by the existing elite comes from the Magonids remaining the dominant political clan in Carthage, suggesting that they may have had a major hand in the formulation and implementation of these reforms. Although the suffeture was non-hereditary, and incumbents were selected from any elite family, Aristotle nonetheless observed that particular individuals monopolized a number of state offices simultaneously, which suggests that it was still possible for the particular clans to dominate many important posts.[23] As a measure of undiminished Magonid influence, the posthumous reputation of Hamilcar was spared the opprobrium that was the usual lot of those commanders who had presided over military defeat on this scale. In fact his reputation appears to have been enhanced rather than diminished: monuments were built in his memory and sacrifices were offered up in his name all over the Punic world.[24] Perhaps the tale of his martyrdom on the altar of guest-friendship played well with the Carthaginian public. And Magonid prestige was probably protected by the surprisingly modest terms that Gelon had demanded. Carthage was to pay 2,000 talents of silver as reimbursement for war costs, and was compelled to build two temples where copies of the peace treaty were to be kept. Himera was now recognized as part of the Syracusan bloc.[25]

No Carthaginian force would enter Sicily for over half a century. In fact the Carthaginians rejected a number of opportunities – including an overture from the Athenians for an alliance against their great nemesis, Syracuse – to become involved once more in Sicilian affairs.[26] There are, however, few signs of Carthage suffering any kind of economic decline due to the defeat. Indeed, it was during the fifth century that the physical fabric of the city was transformed, with the creation of a coordinated street grid that took in both the old and the new districts of the city. The undulating topography of Carthage was integrated within this plan by the creation of a fan-shaped series of streets climbing the southern and eastern slopes of the Byrsa hill. New residential districts were built close to the shoreline, where a sea wall and a monumental gate were constructed.[27] Although greatly hampered by the belt of cemeteries around the city, the spatial integrity of which continued to be respected, other new residential and industrial zones were also established.[28]

Himera would, however, have repercussions that affected Carthage in other, less direct, ways. Momentous events a long way away in Greece gave Carthage's enemies in Sicily the opportunity to recast Himera in a grand narrative of how a barbarous invader had attacked and attempted to destroy the western Greeks, rather than the reality of a failed attempt by one of the Carthaginian political clans to come to the aid of a Greek ally. During the first two decades of the fifth century, the notoriously quarrelsome city states of Greece had twice united to repel the invading armies of Persia, the greatest superpower of the age. The result of Greece's 'finest hour' was the crystallization of a set of ideas about what it meant to be Greek. In particular, the exclusivity and superiority of Greek ethnicity was defined against the 'barbarian' world (made up of all non-Greeks) around it.[29]

Gelon had in fact been conspicuous for his lack of support for the mainland Greeks when they had appealed for help in their efforts to defend themselves against the Persian invasion in 480. When Greece had first been menaced by the Persian expeditionary force, the mainland Greek cities had sent out messengers in order to enlist support from the wider Hellenic community. Syracuse was one of the first cities to be visited, but Gelon met the call for Greeks to stand shoulder to shoulder against the barbarian threat with an offer which skilfully exposed the snobbery of the Greeks towards their western cousins. He would come to their assistance as long as he could be the commander-in-chief of the Greek forces. This proposal was designed to be unacceptable to those it had been offered to. Gelon went on to express his anger and disappointment at his fellow Greeks' past refusals to assist him in his struggles against the Carthaginians and the indigenous Sicilians, and in his proposal to liberate Greek trading stations from barbarian hands. Quite simply the Sicilian Greeks had not been treated as proper members of the Hellenic club, and the Greek envoys returned home empty-handed. After rebuffing their pleas, Gelon compounded this lack of pan-Hellenic solidarity by sending an envoy, Cadmus, to Greece with three ships and a large sum of money with instructions to wait for a victor to emerge. If the Persian Great King was victorious, then Cadmus was to give him the money and assurances of Gelon's loyalty. If the Greeks were victorious, then he was swiftly to bring the money back to Syracuse.[30]

The fact that the allied Greeks under Athens and Sparta went on to win a series of resounding victories over the Persian invader made it even more important that Himera should be claimed as the equivalent of these great victories. The promotion of Himera and the idea of a 'western front' against a Persian-led alliance not only showed that the great tyrant of Syracuse deserved a place on the top table of Greek states, but also provided a convenient explanation for Syracuse's telling absence from the war effort.[31] Carthage could be linked to the Persians through the Phoenicians, who, as vassals of the Persian king, were obliged to provide a large number of levies and ships for the naval armada. Furthermore, the Greek Cypriot city states had recently rebelled and been put under the control of the Cypriot–Phoenician kings of Kition by their Persian overlords.[32] Over the next few decades, the Deinomenids, the ruling family of Syracuse, would use the huge wealth that they had accumulated to press their claims for Himera across the Greek world. Magnificent monuments were put up in prominent Greek religious sites such as Delphi and Olympia, and famous poets were commissioned to write paeans celebrating the victory – such as the following lines by Pindar, in praise of Gelon's brother and successor Theron:

> I pray, son of Cronus, that the battle cry of the Phoenicians and Etruscans remain quietened at home, since they have seen arrogance bring grief to their ships before Cumae [a Syracusan naval victory over the Etruscan fleet in 474 BC]. They suffered such things after being subdued by the ruler of the Syracusans, he who hurled their youth into the water from their swiftly moving ships, and drew Hellas out of overbearing slavery.[33]

Among the wider Greek community, there were some signs that this extraordinary publicity campaign was successful, for the historian Herodotus believed that Salamis – the famous naval victory that the joint Greek fleet won against a far larger Persian force in September 480 – and Himera had taken place on the same day, and the later Athenian scholar Ephorus embraced the idea that the battles had in fact been the result of a wider conspiracy between the Carthaginians and the Persians.[34] Yet within the wider Greek intellectual community there was still little enthusiasm for viewing Carthage as a western surrogate for Persia, despite the best efforts of the Syracusans.[35] Aristotle dismissed the theory of any collusion between the Carthaginians and the Persians, arguing that, apart from their timing, the two events were unconnected.[36] Indeed, in contrast to the opprobrium that Persia's autocratic monarchy usually attracted, the Carthaginian political constitution was widely admired in Athens.[37] Aristotle would include Carthage with Sparta and Crete on the very short list of contemporary city states that he considered had an excellent system of government.[38]

His comment that it was because of the high quality of their political system that the Carthaginians had never suffered from rebellions and had never been under the rule of a tyrant may have been a sideswipe at the Syracusans, who were likely to have still been peddling the idea of Carthage as the Persia of the West.[39]

Earlier, Aristotle's own teacher, the Athenian philosopher Plato, would present the image of an extremely well-ordered state when he referred to the strict laws in Carthage forbidding the drinking of wine for magistrates, jury members, councillors, soldiers and ships' pilots while on duty, and for slaves at any time. Moreover, all Carthaginians were supposedly banned from imbibing wine during the day, unless in connection with exercise or medicine, while couples who were attempting to procreate were also covered by these restrictions at night.[40]

In fact, a few decades after Himera, the Athenians would try to broker an alliance with the Carthaginians against Syracuse. Carthaginian trading relations with Greece and the wider Aegean region appear to have strengthened in the interim, with large quantities of Attic fine pottery being transported to Carthage and other Punic towns.[41] The fifth-century Athenian poet Hermippus mentioned Carthaginian multicoloured carpets and cushions that were presumably exported to Greece.[42] Punic traders were also involved in the shipping of Greek goods to Spain, and of Spanish tuna fish to Greece. Indeed, a recent study of fourth-century BC transport amphora from an excavation in Carthage produced the surprising statistic that over 20 per cent of them hailed from the Ionian Islands – four times more than those from the Levant.[43] Further evidence of healthy trading relations comes from the presence of a resident community of Punic merchants operating in mainland Greek and Aegean cities.[44]

On Sicily itself, Himera had little immediate impact on the cultural and religious synergies that had long existed between different ethic groups on the island. Politically, there was also little change, as Greek city states continued to seek political alliances with Carthage in disputes with their neighbours. However, for influential early-fourth-century Syracusan historians such as Antiochus and Philistus, Himera marked the genesis of a new set of ideas that ignored the complex mix of political allegiances and cultural interactions between Syracusan, Punic and indigenous populations that had for long been a major part of the colonial landscape of the central Mediterranean.[45] In its place came a grand narrative that erroneously emphasized inter-ethnic rivalry and the brooding threat that Carthage posed to the very survival of the western Greeks.

THE REVENGE OF THE MAGONIDS

It was not until 410 BC that Carthage's seventy-year sabbatical from Sicilian affairs came to an end, when it was decided to lend help to the city of Segesta in a dispute that had flared up with its Greek neighbour Selinus.[46] The reason for this foreign-policy volte-face probably had more to do with increasing concerns over the growing influence of Selinus' ally Syracuse than it did with solidarity with Segesta. After the death of Gelon in 478, Syracusan power had quickly waned and Sicily had once more become a patchwork of feuding city states and minor warlords.[47] Economic and demographic decline had quickly followed, with many mainly Elymian settlements in western and central Sicily contracting greatly in size or even being completely abandoned. However, by 410, after spectacularly repelling an Athenian invasion, Syracuse began to re-emerge as a major power on the island – one that might potentially take advantage of the continuing turmoil in western Sicily.[48]

Segesta and Selinus were located in the west of the island, close to the Punic cities of Motya, Solus and Panormus, which, although politically independent of Carthage and neither significant markets for Carthaginian goods nor major exporters to the city, were still of great strategic importance to Carthage, being key coordinates on the trade routes that linked the North African metropolis with Italy and Greece.[49] The sense of a renewed Syracusan threat may have been the stimulus for the construction of a new system of fortifications at Panormus.[50] The Greek cities of Sicily were also important trading partners. Diodorus, taking his information from earlier Sicilian Greek historians, explained that the enormous wealth of the city of Acragas in the late fifth century came in part from supplying olives to the Carthaginians.[51] The Carthaginian economic hegemony in the central Mediterranean appears to have been built around the control of foreign trade. Profit was gained not only through Carthage's own participation in this trade, but also from taxing foreign merchants who wished to operate in markets for which Carthage increasingly provided 'protection', such as the Punic cities on Sardinia and Sicily. Moreover, allies could be rewarded by the grant of trading rights in ports over which Carthaginian influence extended.[52] Initially, at least, Carthaginian intervention in Sicily was driven by the desire to protect this system.

For the Magonids, there were other, more personal, considerations. Carthage might have become the richest and most powerful state in the western Mediterranean under their stewardship, but the disaster at Himera remained a blemish on that proud record. Magonid prestige at home would undoubtedly be boosted by a triumphant return to Sicily. Now that major domestic constitutional reforms had been bedded in, the Magonids may have considered this a good time to act abroad. Unsurprisingly, it was Hannibal, the present leader of the Magonids and the grandson of Hamilcar, the defeated commander at Himera, who was the main advocate within the Council of Elders for Carthage lending assistance to Segesta. When that assistance was agreed, in 410, he was put in command of the expeditionary force.[53]

In an attempt to ensure that the Syracusans did not become militarily involved in the dispute, the Carthaginians sent envoys to Syracuse requesting their arbitration. This strategy delivered the desired result when the Selinuntines refused Syracusan intervention. The Syracusans then decided to renew their alliance with Selinus while maintaining their peace treaty with Carthage, thereby staying neutral.[54] The Carthaginians then sent 5,000 Libyan and 800 Campanian mercenaries, supplying them with horses and high salaries, to assist the Segestans.

After the Segestans with their hired military help had routed a Selinuntine army, both sides turned to their respective allies, Carthage and Syracuse, for help, which was granted, thereby putting the two great powers on a collision course. Preparing himself for war, Hannibal mustered a formidable army made up of Libyan levies and Iberian mercenaries, and started to prepare the necessary sea transportation to carry his army across to Sicily.[55] After these troops, siege engines, missiles and all the other equipment and supplies that were needed had been loaded into 60 ships and 1,500 transports, in 409 the armada set off.[56]

Once it had safely landed, the army was joined by Carthage's Greek and Segestan allies, before marching directly to Selinus, where Hannibal, aware that the Selinuntines were holding out for the arrival of Syracusan allies, did everything in his power to capture the city as quickly as possible. Giant siege towers were dragged up to the walls, and battering rams were taken to the gates. Archers and slingers were also employed to keep up a constant stream of missiles. (Unfortunately we are almost completely reliant on the extremely hostile (and much later) testimony of the Sicilian Greek historian Timaeus for information on this, and later, Carthaginian military campaigns in Sicily. Though he provides a considerable amount of information on Carthaginian troop movements, much of his analysis needs to be treated with extreme caution.)

The Selinuntines had recently spent so much effort and expense on the construction of a series of magnificent temples that they had neglected the repair of their city walls. The Carthaginian siege engines soon punched holes in these fragile defences, and battalion after battalion of fresh troops were thrown at the breaches. However, knowing how catastrophic the consequences of defeat would be for them, the citizens of Selinus mounted a desperate defence that held the Carthaginians at bay for another nine days. Indeed, it was only when, in a moment of confusion, the defenders withdrew from the walls that the Carthaginians gained access to the city. Despite this piece of good fortune, progress was still painfully slow, as each street had to be taken by fierce hand-to-hand fighting while women, children and old men rained stones and missiles down upon the heads of the Carthaginian troops. The end arrived when the Selinuntines, who had at last run out of options, made a futile last stand in the marketplace. After a fierce fight, they were all cut down. Diodorus (once more following Timaeus' hostile testimony) then provides a vivid, but one suspects highly partisan, account of the supposed outrages inflicted on the city and its surviving inhabitants by the Carthaginian troops, which he contends left the streets of the city choked with 16,000 corpses and many buildings burnt to the ground.[57]

Hannibal's next target was surely no surprise to its inhabitants. Using the same tactics that had been so successful at Selinus, the Carthaginian army hit Himera with a sustained, high-tempo assault. However, the Himerans, deciding that attack was the best form of defence, marched out of the city and, as their families cheered them from the walls, attacked the Carthaginian army. Although initially startled by this unexpected tactic, the numerically superior Carthaginian forces eventually managed to drive the Himerans back into their city. There the decision was now taken to evacuate as many of the citizenry as possible on Syracusan ships. Those left behind were instructed to hold out as best they could and wait for the Syracusan fleet to return for them. It never did, and on the third day the city fell. Once more Diodorus provides a lurid account of the outrages committed, on the orders of Hannibal himself, by the Carthaginian troops. Unlike Selinus, which had only its walls destroyed, Himera was to be razed to the ground and its famous temples pillaged. Hannibal then supposedly rounded up the 3,000 men who had been taken prisoner and, in a bloody memorial to his grandsire, slaughtered them at the very spot where it was said that Hamilcar had fallen. After that, rather than pressing on and taking full advantage of the Sicilian Greeks' disarray, the Magonid general paid off his army and returned to Africa.[58]

Despite the strictly limited nature of Hannibal's Sicilian operation, there is little doubt that it had set an important precedent for future Carthaginian intervention. Carthage's extensive use of mercenary troops resulted in the production of the city's first coinage to pay them. Previously Carthage had resisted the introduction of coinage, which had first appeared in the Greek world at the beginning of the sixth century. However, the Punic cities of Sicily, clearly influenced by their Greek counterparts on the island, had started minting their own coinage much earlier, in the last three decades of the sixth century.[59]

As their chief purpose was to pay mercenaries, who wished to have high-value Greek-looking coinage, the new Carthaginian coins borrowed heavily from western Greek designs and weight standards.[60] They were decorated with two motifs that became increasingly associated with Carthage: the horse and the palm tree. They carried one of two superscriptions: *Qrthdst* ('Carthage') or *Qrthdst/mhnt* ('Carthage/ the camp'). The latter term, which basically meant 'Carthaginian military administration', is surely confirmation that the coins were only for a specific purpose.[61] Carthage's lack of a permanent presence in Sicily at this time is highlighted by the fact that the troops were recruited and drilled in Africa, and it appears that the supplies and coinage were also shipped from Carthage.[62]

There were now clear signs that Hannibal's actions had further destabilized the island. Within two years, in 407, Carthaginian troops were back on Sicily after Hermocrates, a renegade Syracusan general, had attacked the Punic cities of the south-west.[63] Despite Diodorus' assertion that their aim was the conquest of the whole island, the Carthaginians were wary of taking further unilateral action.[64] The discovery of a partial inscription in Athens shows that the Carthaginians sent envoys there to seek an alliance. The Carthaginian heralds received a warm welcome, and were invited to participate in civic entertainment. The inscription appears to have been a positive recommendation from the Athenian council that steps should be taken to cement such an alliance if the wider citizen assembly ratified it. The council also recommended the dispatch of a diplomatic mission to Sicily to meet with the Carthaginian generals and assess the situation. However, even if this alliance was sanctioned, the Athenians, stretched by long years of conflict with Sparta, provided no practical assistance to Carthage.[65]

After collecting together another sizeable army, made up of Carthaginian citizens, North African allies and levies, Hannibal and a younger colleague, Himilcar, set out for Sicily.[66] However, the campaign got off to an inauspicious start. First the fleet was attacked by the Syracusans, with the resulting loss of a number of ships and the remainder of the flotilla having to flee into the open sea.[67] Then, after the army had managed to land on Sicily and had started to besiege the exceptionally wealthy Greek city of Acragas, it was struck by an outbreak of plague that killed many men, including Hannibal. Diodorus, taking his cue from Timaeus, records the questionable detail that Hannibal's fellow general, Himilcar, in order to appease the god's anger, sacrificed a young boy to Baal Hammon.[68] Subsequently, after suffering a defeat at the hands of the Syracusan army, the Carthaginians managed to retrieve the situation sufficiently that they forced the citizens of Acragas hurriedly to evacuate their city.[69] Diodorus/Timaeus describes how Himilcar and the Carthaginian army then went on a looting session, seizing all manner of works of art and other precious objects from the abandoned temples and mansions.[70] However, this is one of the few occasions when we possess a document – a Punic inscription from the tophet at Carthage – which, although incomplete, provides a Carthaginian view of these events:

> And this *mtnt* at the new moon [of the month] [P] 'It. year of Ešmunamos son of Adnibaal the i [Great?] and Hanno son of Bodaštart son of Hanno the *rb*. And the *rbm* [general] Adnibaal son of Gescon the *rb* and Himilco son of Hanno the *rb* went to [H]alaisa. And they seized Agragant [Acragas]. And they established peace with the citizens of Naxos.[71]

Despite the limited nature of the information that it imparts, the inscription stands as an important reminder of how one-sided and partial our usual historical view of these events actually is.

Eventually, in 405, the Carthaginian generals, having lost over half their army to plague but having gained a strategic advantage, offered Syracuse a treaty of peace, which was accepted by their hard-pressed foes. Understandably, the terms were very favourable to the Carthaginians. Their authority over the indigenous and Punic areas of west and central Sicily was recognized, and the payment of an annual tribute to Carthage by a number of cities on the island was ratified.[72]

DIONYSIUS AND THE END OF SINGLE-FAMILY DOMINATION

However, this peace treaty, agreed to at a time of mutual weakness, was not destined to hold long. In the political turmoil that followed the military reverses against Carthage, Dionysius, a young man of modest birth but endowed with charisma and brilliant political instincts, managed to establish himself as tyrant of Syracuse.[73] Bolstered by the news that Carthage itself was ravaged by plague, and anxious because a number of cities previously under Syracusan control had defected to the Carthaginians, Dionysius had almost immediately begun stockpiling weapons, building warships and hiring soldiers and crews.[74] By 397 he was ready to strike. Brazenly taking up the mantle of Greek liberator, he summoned the Syracusan assembly and arranged that it issue a declaration threatening war if Carthage did not immediately set free the Sicilian cities that it had supposedly subjugated. At the same time, the Punic populations of Syracuse had their property seized and were expelled from the city. Across Greek Sicily, towns and cities were now purged of their Punic inhabitants in an ugly orgy of ethnic cleansing that included atrocities and massacres.[75] Joined by forces from a number of the Greek cities who saw this as an opportunity to cease paying tribute to Carthage, Dionysius assembled a substantial army and marched on the Punic city of Motya, which he put under siege.[76]

The Carthaginians were caught completely by surprise, and had not had sufficient time to raise a force to come to the aid of their Motyan allies. On seeing the Syracusan advance, the Motyans had broken down the causeway which joined their island city to the mainland. Dionysius, however, countered this by having a giant mole built, so that battering rams and huge siege engines could brought right up to the city walls. Despite the efforts of the Carthaginians, who created a diversion by raiding the harbour of Syracuse, the situation became increasingly hopeless for the island city, with the walls being eventually breached. Still, the defenders, knowing that no mercy would be shown to them, made the Syracusan forces fight for every street by building great barricades across the narrower streets, and hurling missiles down from their tall buildings on the advancing Greeks. But Dionysius now constructed giant six-storey siege towers, specially designed to be the same height as the tallest Motyan buildings, so that his soldiers were able to bring the fight to the defenders even in the most inaccessible of places.

The Sicilian Greek historian Diodorus, although hostile to the Carthaginians and writing many years after the event, gives a powerfully evocative if rather generic insight into the state of mind of the desperate Motyan defenders:

> The Motyans, as they took account of the magnitude of the peril, and with their wives and children before their eyes, fought the more fiercely out of fear for their fate. There were some whose parents stood by entreating them not to let them be surrendered to the lawless will of victors who had been brought to such a state of mind that they now set no value on life; others, as they heard the lament of their wives and helpless children, sought to die like men rather than see their children dragged off into slavery. Flight, of course, from the city was impossible, since it was entirely surrounded by the sea, which was controlled by the enemy. Most appalling for the Phoenicians and the greatest cause of their despair was the

thought of how cruelly they had used their Greek captives and the prospect of their suffering the same treatment. Indeed, there was nothing left for them but fighting bravely, either to conquer or to die.[77]

The city was given over to dreadful scenes of barbarity and slaughter. Diodorus reports that when Dionysius saw that not even the women or children were being spared, he decided to act – not out of any pity, but because he desperately needed the funds that could be raised by selling them into slavery. When his orders to stand down had no effect on his rampaging troops, he instructed heralds to announce throughout the city that the stricken Motyans were to make their way to the temples of deities which were revered by the Greeks, and take refuge there. Those who successfully made it to those sanctuaries were subsequently sold into servitude. The Greeks who had fought on the Motyan side were crucified.[78] Such was the devastation visited upon it that Motya was never rebuilt.[79]

The next year, Diodorus/Timaeus relates, Dionysius moved to ravage other areas of Carthaginian-held Sicily.[80] However, the Carthaginians, who had initially been caught out by the ferocity of the assault, raised sufficient troops to counter Dionysius' advance. After a series of victories which included the capture and complete destruction of the city of Messana, the Carthaginian general, Himilco, forced Dionysius' troops out of western Sicily, and even managed to advance as far as Syracuse itself.[81] Dionysius was saved by the onset of what was very probably typhus in the Carthaginian camp – an occurrence that the hostile Greek historical tradition explained as divine punishment, due to the sacrilegious acts that the Carthaginians had committed, particularly the sacking of the temples of the goddesses Demeter and Core.[82] Diodorus has left us with a graphic account of its symptoms:

> The plague began with catarrh; then came a swelling in the throat; gradually burning sensations ensued; pains in the sinews of the back, and a heavy feeling in the limbs; then dysentery supervened and pustules upon the whole surface of the body. In most cases this was the course of the disease; but some became mad and totally lost their memory; they circulated through the camp, out of their mind, and struck at anyone that they met. In general, as it turned out, even help by physicians was of no avail, because of both the severity of the disease and the swiftness

of death; for death came on the fifth day or on the sixth at the latest, amid such terrible tortures that all looked upon those who had fallen in war as blessed.[83]

At the onset of the epidemic the Carthaginians buried their dead, but as increasing numbers succumbed to the sickness their bodies were left unburied to rot where they fell.[84] Dionysius quickly took advantage of the calamity that had befallen the Carthaginians by sending both his naval squadrons and his land forces to attack the Carthaginian ships and army. Himilco, now in desperate straits, was forced to negotiate a truce. In a secret deal, which was struck without the knowledge of the citizenry of Syracuse or of much of the Carthaginian army, Dionysius agreed to let Himilco and the Carthaginian troops under his command escape in exchange for money.[85] In fact only a few ships made it back to Carthage, for they were attacked as they fled the harbour by Syracusan forces unaware of their leader's underhand negotiations. Of the Carthaginian allies who were left behind, the native Sicels managed to escape back to their homes in the interior, and one group of Spanish troops massed together in sufficient numbers to be able to negotiate their recruitment into Dionysius' army. The vast majority, however, were captured and enslaved.[86]

Diodorus/Timaeus portrayed the political fallout in Carthage as considerable. Supposedly, on hearing the news of the disaster, the city went into mourning, with private houses closed to visitors, business dealings suspended, and temples shut. The whole population converged on the harbour in order to get news of their relatives as the boats carrying the survivors limped into the port. On learning of the full scale of the catastrophe, the wails and shrieks of the bereaved could be heard all along the shoreline. For the Magonids, the threat to their political dominance in Carthage was very real. Once more their name would be linked with failure overseas.

Himilco, disgraced and defeated, spent the rest of his days dressed in cheap robes going around the temples of Carthage accusing himself of impiety and offering himself for divine retribution. He then starved himself to death.[87] This public act of repentance was still not enough to preserve Magonid power in the long term, and within a few decades another elite clan, led by Hanno 'the Great', had taken over as the dominant political force in Carthage.[88]

However, the old political status quo was not maintained for long after this takeover, as the elite classes within Carthage were clearly hungry for more change. During the early years of the fifth century a new constitutional body had been established: the Tribunal of One Hundred and Four. Made up of members of the aristocratic elite, it oversaw the conduct of officials and military commanders as well as acting as a kind of higher constitutional court. At the same time the Council of Elders remained in existence, and may even have had its powers enhanced, with treasury and foreign affairs coming under its control.[89] At the head of the Carthaginian state were now two annually elected senior executive officers, the suffetes, and a range of more junior officials and special commissioners oversaw different aspects of governmental business such as public works, tax-collecting and the administration of the state treasury.[90] Panels of special commissioners, called pentarchies, were appointed from the Tribunal of One Hundred and Four; they appear to have dealt with a variety of affairs of state.[91]

The war with the Syracusans continued without either side really gaining the advantage.[92] The Carthaginians attempted a number of new tactics, including opening up a second front against Dionysius in southern Italy.[93] Both sides won crushing victories, the Syracusans at Cabala and the Carthaginians at Cronium, but neither managed to sustain a consistent military advantage.[94] Eventually, in 373, exhausted by their losses, a new treaty was signed that recognized the previous status quo of Carthaginian and Syracusan territorial influence.[95] But by merely reacting to threats as they appeared, and doing only enough to defend their interests, Hanno's faction proved, like the Magonids before them, that they could never provide any lasting security in the region. After each setback Dionysius was given sufficient time and opportunity to rebuild his support and military forces, before launching another attack.

The seemingly never-ending war grew ever more unpopular with the citizens of Carthage. Their discontent was further fuelled by another outbreak of plague in the city, as well as unrest in Sardinia and among the Libyans. Increasingly the political leadership of Hanno was called into question.[96] Even the death of Carthage's long-term nemesis, Dionysius, in 365 (after a marathon drinking session), and success in having Suniatus, Hanno's chief political rival in Carthage, condemned for treason, did not silence the criticism.[97] Unused to his supremacy being questioned, Hanno resorted to the desperate measure of trying to overthrow the constitution. At a banquet to celebrate his daughter's marriage, he unsuccessfully attempted to murder his fellow councillors by poison.

Perhaps reading the Council's failure to act decisively in this matter – its only response had been to pass a decree that limited expenditure on weddings – as a sign of weakness, Hanno now plotted an uprising of 20,000 slaves and conspired with the local Libyan and Numidian tribes to try to overthrow the Carthaginian state. Such treachery could not be overlooked, and Hanno, when captured after his rebellion failed, was subjected to merciless punishment. After suffering scourging and terrible torture, he was finally nailed to a cross.[98] All the male members of his clan, whether innocent or guilty, were rounded up and executed.[99] Although some aspects of this story, reported by hostile Greek sources, appear far-fetched, it is clear that for the time being Carthage had at last grown tired of being dominated by a single clan.

CARTHAGINIAN SICILY

The end of the Magonids' political domination in Carthage did not conclude the Sicilian strategy of which they had been the main architects, for Carthage was now simply too embroiled in Sicilian affairs to withdraw. During the first half of the fourth century, Carthage's relationship with western Sicily had profoundly changed – a transformation noted by the Greek historians who had begun to talk of Carthage's zone of influence in western Sicily in terms of an eparchate, basically an imperial province.[100] Although there is no evidence of the older Punic cities on the island being directly governed from Carthage, newer establishments show extremely close links with the North African metropolis.[101] The Carthaginians were without doubt the driving force behind new settlements in Sicily such as Halaisa and Thermae Himerae.[102]

Carthage's most significant foundation on Sicily was the port of Lilybaeum.[103] Situated on the western Sicilian mainland, not far from the island where Motya had once stood, Lilybaeum had been

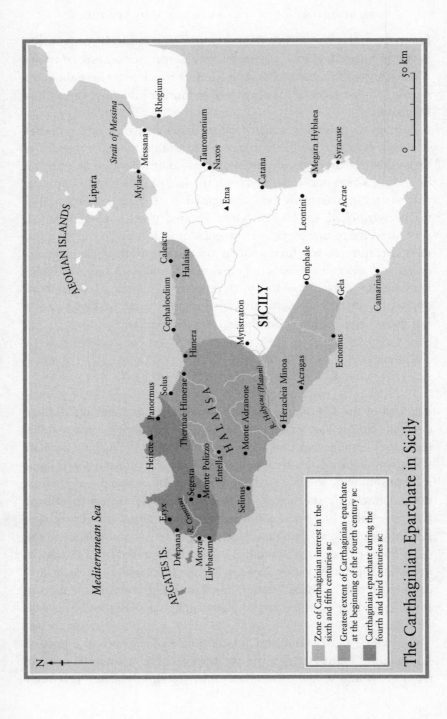

The Carthaginian Eparchate in Sicily

Mediterranean Sea

AEOLIAN ISLANDS

Lipara

Strait of Messina

Rhegium

Messana
Mylae
Tauromenium
Naxos
Megara Hyblaea
Syracuse
Catana
Acrae
▲Etna
Leontini
Omphale

Caleacte
Halaisa
Cephaloedium
Gela
Camarina

SICILY

Myttistraton
Heraclea Minoa
Acragas
Enomus

Himera
Solus
Panormus
Heircte ▲
Thermae Himerae
H A L A I S A
Monte Polizzo
Monte Adranone
R. Halycus (Platani)
Segesta
R. Crimisus
Entella
Eryx
Drepana
Motya
Lilybaeum
Selinus

AEGATES IS.

N

50 km
0

Zone of Carthaginian interest in the sixth and fifth centuries BC

Greatest extent of Carthaginian eparchate at the beginning of the fourth century BC

Carthaginian eparchate during the fourth and third centuries BC constructed as a new home for Motya's surviving citizens. However, analysis of the city's material culture suggests that immigrants from Carthage significantly supplemented its population.[104] Unlike the older Punic cities in Sicily, Lilybaeum had strong commercial links with Carthage. Strategically placed on Cape Boeo, the westernmost point of Sicily, the city soon became the major hub for commercial traffic between North Africa, Sicily, Italy and Greece.[105]

Perhaps the most striking aspect of Lilybaeum, apart from its strategic significance, was its defences, for it was built as a maximum-security port. Its solid walls were 5.8 metres high, and made from tufa reinforced by stone and mud brick. In front of these walls was a cavernous ditch over 28 metres wide. In addition, rectangular towers, fortified gates and posterns punctuated the walls, so that the defenders could rain missiles down on any attacker who made it over the ditch. There were also underground passages, galleries and communication trenches that went beneath the defences so that surprise sorties could be launched to attack enemy lines from the rear.[106] In one particular tunnel, the walls were filled with the doodling of bored military personnel: a warrior, ships, weapons, a mountain with Punic symbols and letters and, of course, erotic scenes.[107]

The coinage which is thought to have been minted in Lilybaeum reflected the port's position as a Carthaginian military base rather than a Sicilian Punic city. The tetradrachms bear the superscriptions of the Carthaginian military authorities: *qrthds*, *mmhnt* and *s'mmhnt* ('the people of the camp'). Indeed, Lilybaeum appears to have been administered by a military governor rather than by suffetes or a city council.[108] It was built to act as a heavily fortified commercial enclave, even if all the territory around it was in enemy hands.

One also finds the establishment of new Punic settlements in the Sicilian hinterland during this period, particularly on the sites of former Greek cities. At Selinus in the fourth century BC the old Greek acropolis was given a new urban system by Punic settlers who often used the old Greek city for building materials. The main street was widened, and the new structures were built on a different orientation from the former Greek ones. Diodorus mentions that Hannibal, the general who had taken the city, had let the survivors of the original city return there; however, it is noticeable that many of these new houses display the typical Carthaginian construction techniques and architectural plans which were also a feature of the houses at Lilybaeum.[109]

A marked transformation can also be detected in the religious life of the city. Many of the sacred shrines of the old Greek city, such as the sanctuary of the goddess Demeter Malaphorus, were once again in use, but it is clear that very different religious rites were being practised there. The most striking example of this was the sacred enclosure of Zeus Meilichios, an amalgam of the Greek king of the gods and a pre-Greek subterranean spirit of death and regeneration, an important fixture in the religious life of the old city.[110] All around the site, archaeologists have found strange double-headed steles portraying the Punic deities Baal Hammon and Tanit, whom the new settlers considered to be the parents of Zeus Meilichios.[111] In the Greek temples and sanctuaries, typical aspects of Punic worship such as betyls (sacred stones) and open-air altars were introduced. In another temple, originally dedicated to the Greek underworld goddess Hecate, a new altar was built on which large numbers of small animals were sacrificed and incinerated according to Punic religious rite.[112] Furthermore, Punic religious emblems such as the sign of Tanit and the sacred caduceus plant now adorned the streets of the city.[113]

At Monte Adranone, a fortified town founded by the Selinuntines in the sixth century BC, there are also clear signs of Punic resettlement. It had been destroyed at the same time as Selinus, in 409 BC, but during the fourth century BC its walls were reconstructed and two new temples were built, as well as an industrial complex. The more impressive of these temples was located on the original acropolis. It was built to a classic Punic tripartite plan, with a central sacrificial area open to the sky. Typically for the period, it showed an eclectic mixture of Punic and Greek architectural styles, including elegant Doric columns that held up the entrance portico, and a triangular frontage replete with Egyptian cornicing.[114] In this period, much smaller settlements in the region also show Punic influence for the first time. At Monte Polizzo, which had previously been deserted, there are clear signs of a Punic reoccupation of the site, with a stele, altar and offerings all discovered in a reused temple.[115]

However, despite this evidence of Punic urban development in Sicily, many of these new settlements were mere shadows of the towns and cities that they replaced. Notwithstanding the exaggerations of Greek historians, who describe fourth-century-BC Sicily as replete with cities inhabited only by wild animals and vegetation, there can be little doubt that decades of violent upheaval had left their mark not only on the physical fabric of the cities, but also on their inhabitants.[116] The archaeological data that have been gathered in Sicily suggest that some of the literary descriptions of deserted cities with dilapidated walls and desecrated temples may be more than mere dramatic fiction.[117]

The primary function of many of these sites appears to have been military defence rather than urban regeneration. The new settlement of Monte Adranone appears to have been little more than a large Carthaginian military garrison, with an extremely small civilian population.[118] At Monte Polizzo the archaeological evidence also strongly suggests that the later Punic occupation took the form simply of a watchtower or a military observation post.[119] More fortresses appear to have been established in the area between the Belice and Platani rivers.[120] Even Punic Selinus, with its shops and houses, still covered only a fraction of the old Greek city, although clearly more than just a military fort. Indeed, most of the city remained in ruins during this period. In fact the striking feature of many of these high-ground sites in central and western Sicily is the paucity of Punic artefacts aside from bronze coinage and imported torpedo-style amphorae – both signs that suggest a military rather than a civilian occupation.[121]

We know that, as in Sardinia, much of what we might view as Carthaginian 'imperialist' action in Sicily was connected with the acquiring of the resources that a great city like Carthage relied upon.[122] However, quite what these resources were, and where they came from, is perhaps not as clear as one might assume. The direct benefit that Carthage appears to have derived from the agricultural hinterland of western Sicily was not extensive. A series of recent studies on amphorae imported to Carthage from the fifth and fourth centuries BC has shown that the quantity of imports from Punic Sicily was minute when compared with those from Sardinia.[123] Similarly, Carthaginian exports to western Sicily were equally modest during the period.[124] Of course, for the Carthaginians the economic value of western Sicily was its ports, through which a huge amount of Tyrrhenian and Aegean commercial traffic passed.[125] The large quantity of fine pottery from Athens dating from the end of the fifth and the first half of the fourth centuries BC found in Carthage probably means that cargoes were being shipped directly between the two cities during this period.[126] Later in the fourth century these luxury imports were gradually replaced by fineware from Greek Sicily and southern Italy, which relied on the continued occupation of the Sicilian ports.[127] It is clear that by the fourth century BC these regions were the largest overseas exporters of wine (and perhaps other foodstuffs) into Carthage.[128] Indeed, without Panormus and Lilybaeum, Carthage would have faced the risk of economic disaster. These ports were therefore worth protecting at almost any cost. Carthaginian interest in much of the hinterland of western Sicily was based not on the local agriculture, as it was on Sardinia, but on fortified settlements which created a defensive buffer for the main object of Carthaginian economic interest on the island: the ports of the west.

The other major factor in Carthage's economic and political organization of western Sicily was its very large standing army that remained on the island for considerable periods of time. Owing to the lack of economic input from the territory that it was meant to be protecting, the Carthaginian army on Sicily had to be largely supplied with foodstuffs from Sardinia.[129] One must assume that the profits made from the Tyrrhenian and Ionian trade could be offset against these expenses, and that the Punic cities in western Sicily may have been paying some form of taxation in coinage.[130]

THE CORINTHIAN THREAT

It was Carthage's determination to hold on to the western Sicilian ports that made it resist any potential external threats with such dogged determination and disregard for the heavy cost in manpower and other resources that it entailed. In the 340s the threat was from the Greek city of Corinth, which was becoming increasingly involved in the internal affairs of its daughter city Syracuse.[131] The Carthaginians attempted to warn off Timoleon, the Corinthian representative sent to Sicily, but without success.[132] Subsequent efforts militarily to intimidate him also failed, with Timoleon successfully establishing a new democratic government in Syracuse as well as creating a broad anti-Carthaginian alliance among a number of the Sicilian Greek city states.[133]

Further disaster struck when in 340 a large Carthaginian army – unusually, made up of a large contingent of citizen troops – was successfully ambushed by Timoleon.[134] Marching deep into enemy territory, the Syracusans waited for the Carthaginians at the river Crimisus. According to Diodorus, on that summer morning the river valley was covered in a thick mist. The only sign that the Carthaginian army was on the move was a deep rumble which rose up to the Syracusans through the swirling mist. Later in the morning, as the gloom lifted, the Crimisus below came into view – and with it the awe-inspiring sight of the Carthaginian regiments crossing the river.

First came four-horse chariots fitted out for battle, and then the elite citizen regiment, the Sacred Band, distinguishable by their white shields, heavy bronze and iron armour, and the ordered discipline of their march. Anxious to catch these crack battalions before they had a chance to clear the river, Timoleon sent his cavalry in among them. During the battle a terrible hailstorm came to the aid of the Greeks, who had their backs to it. The Carthaginian line was broken, and many were trampled underfoot and drowned in the river. The Sacred Band, perhaps mindful of their citizen status, or knowing that their heavy armour ruled out any chance of flight, valiantly stood their ground until they were cut down to a man. Crimisus, in terms of citizen lives lost, stood as the worst military disaster that the Carthaginians suffered in Sicily. Over 10,000 Carthaginian soldiers were reported to have been killed, with a further 15,000 captured. The loss of the Sacred Band, the flower of Carthage's citizen elite, ensured that citizen regiments would now be mobilized only in the gravest crises.[135]

The Carthaginians, however, did manage to recover from this terrible setback by continuing the war against the Syracusans by proxy. Fresh mercenaries were sent to Sicily to help various autocrats, the natural enemies of democratic Syracuse. This tied up the Syracusan forces so that the Carthaginians could quietly reconsolidate their hold on the western half of the island, and the tactics were vindicated when in 338 BC a new treaty was signed with Syracuse. Much of western Sicily was recognized as a zone of Carthaginian influence, and in return the Carthaginians jettisoned their new allies.[136]

THE ECONOMY OF THE
SICILIAN WARS

By the 330s BC it may have looked as though the strategic 'long game' first initiated by the Magonids in Sicily had paid off. After all, there were few who did not now recognize the western half of the island as a zone of Carthaginian influence. Yet, despite all its impressive developments, questions must still remain concerning the true extent of Carthage's hold on western Sicily. Particularly troublesome were the bands of mercenaries and buccaneers who had flocked to Sicily to fight for either side. After they had been paid and discharged from service, these mercenaries often became a real problem. Many had few prospects in their home states, and preferred to stay on the island and make new lives for themselves, often at the expense of its lawful inhabitants.[137]

There can also be little doubt that the military investment needed to protect the Carthaginian zone of influence was very considerable. The Carthaginian military authorities in Sicily found themselves having to mint vast amounts of high-value coinage in gold, silver and electrum (gold–silver alloy) to pay the wages of their mercenary armies.[138] Also, issues of overvalued bronze coinage produced by both Syracuse and Carthage in the fourth century BC strongly indicate that continual warfare was an enormous drain on their financial resources.[139]

The importance to Carthage's long-term economic interests of controlling the western ports; the shorter-term needs of the Carthaginian army; and the acquisitiveness and insecurity that provided the Sicilian Greek autocrats with the necessary motives and conditions to maintain their rule: all these ensured that the relentless cycle of Sicilian violence continued unabated. Through the enslaving of the defeated, the capturing of cities, and war reparations, conflict provided the funds to preserve the bloody status quo between Carthage and Syracuse on the island. The real victims were the Punic, indigenous and Sicilian Greek cities in whose name this bloody process was perpetuated. Such was the brutal economy of war.

5

In the Shadow of Alexander the Great: Carthage and Agathocles

ALEXANDER, TIMAEUS AND CARTHAGE

During a twelve-year period in the 330s and 320s BC, a young Mace-donian king, Alexander ('the Great'), had by the tender age of 31 succeeded in becoming master of an empire that stretched from Greece to Pakistan. Many of Alexander's contemporaries and those who came after him understandably struggled to make sense of his extraordinary success. After all, what Alexander had achieved had never been done before and, it was thought, could never be matched again. Stories swirled around the towns and cities of the ancient Mediterranean and Near East that Alexander was not just descended from celestial lineage, but was actually a god himself.

His meteoric career would be marked out not just by an astounding sequence of military victories, but also by an ability to write his own headlines. Alexander's 'heroic' image was carefully worked on by the coterie of advisers, diarists and historians who accompanied him on campaign. Portrayed as the new Heracles, he had stormed across Asia capturing all in his path. After he stopped his great march eastward in what is now Pakistan, the question for all the peoples of the West was whether they would be the next targets in his seemingly endless thirst for glory and conquest. The terrifying speed with which Alexander had built up his huge Asian empire meant that the idea of his turning his attention westward was a distinct and unsettling possibility. Alexander made the world seem like a small place.

Envoys from all over the lands of the western Mediterranean there-fore made the long and arduous journey to the royal court at Babylon to strike up friendly relations with Alexander and to find out what his future intentions were. From Italy there came Bruttians, Lucanians and Etruscans. From the northern climes there were Celts and Scythians. Iberians came from the far West, and Nubians from the depths of Africa. Among this gaggle of supplicants was a Carthaginian, Hamilcar 'Rodanus', who had probably learned his Greek while living on the island of Rhodes. Unlike the others, however, Rodanus had not been sent to find out if Alexander wished Carthage well: events at the finale of the siege of Carthage's mother city of Tyre had emphatically answered that question.

Alexander and his armies had approached Tyre in 332 BC. After being refused entry to the sacred sanctuary of Melqart, Alexander had besieged and then sacked the city, massacring its defenders and enslaving its remaining population.[1] Melqart, the god whose annual cycle of death and rebirth took place in the heat of the sacred fire, would be smothered in the smoking ashes of the city which had for centuries nurtured him. Generations of Tyrian tradition and religious observance would be buried under the martial pomp of self-consciously Greek/Macedonian ceremonial: military parades, gymnastic competitions, and a torchlight procession of Alexander's army. The solemn burning of the effigy of Melqart would be set aside for yet another set of anodyne athletic competitions in honour of the Hellenic Heracles. Alexander also seized the sacred boat in which the Carthaginians had first brought their offerings to Melqart many centuries ago, and inscribed it with a Greek dedication.[2]

Diodorus, clearly following Timaeus, digressed from the history of his Sicily to tell how a group of thirty Carthaginian emissaries, who had brought the annual tithe from their city to be offered to Melqart, had found themselves stranded in the besieged Tyre. When the city fell, Alexander had spared the Carthaginians' lives, sending them home with the ominous warning that Carthage's turn would come once the conquest of Asia was complete.[3] So Rodanus' mission at the court in Babylon was to discover quite *when* rather than *if* Alexander would launch an attack on Carthage.

According to the Roman historian Justin, Rodanus, considering it unwise to present his credentials in the normal fashion, managed to secure an audience with Alexander by convincing his close associate Parmenion that he was in fact an exile and that he wished to join the

Macedonian army. On finding out the Great King's intentions, Rodanus sent secret missives back to Carthage. However, such was the paranoia that had gripped the panic-stricken city that no one was above suspicion. Rodanus would be rewarded on his return from this potentially perilous mission with execution, because his fellow citizens were convinced that he must have tried to betray Carthage to the Macedonian king.[4]

Alexander's early demise, in Babylon in June 323, has made it impossible to know if he really did plan to attack Carthage. However, western-Greek and, later, Roman historians certainly wanted their readerships to think so. It suited their anti-Carthaginian agenda to conflate Alexander's war against the Persian Empire with the Syracusan struggle against Carthage. During his long years of exile in Athens, Timaeus had become deeply influenced by the increasingly hawkish attitudes towards Persia that many Athenian writers had developed against the backdrop of Alexander's great campaigns in the East.[5] It is highly pertinent that Diodorus, once more following Timaeus, described how, after capturing Tyre, Alexander liberated a statue of the god Apollo which had been sent as an offering to Tyre by the Carthaginians after they had plundered it from the Greek Sicilian city of Gela. Diodorus also took from Timaeus one of the temporal synchronicities of which the latter was so fond, namely that the capture of Tyre had occurred on exactly the same day of the month and hour of the day as when the Carthaginians had stolen the statue from Gela.[6]

Diodorus/Timaeus, like other eastern-Greek commentators, was aware of the association between Melqart and Heracles. He states that it had been Alexander's initial intention to 'sacrifice to the Tyrian Heracles'.[7] However, he was certainly not inclined to dwell upon the syncretism that had developed between the Greek hero and the Phoenician god in the minds of many in the Mediterranean world. Instead, as the Carthaginian military became a permanent presence on Sicily, he and other Sicilian historians promoted the association between Carthage and that other supposed great enemy of the Greek world, Persia.

To that end, we know from Diodorus that Timaeus restated the old fabrication that Himera had been the western front of a coordinated attack on the Greeks organized between Carthage and their Persian allies.[8] Then, by pushing back the date of the battle so that it now fell on the same day as Thermopylae, when 300 Spartans had heroically resisted but eventually been overwhelmed by a huge Persian force, Timaeus could portray Himera as the vital turning point in this Mediterranean-wide war between the barbarians and the forces of Hellas.[9] Moreover this also obscured the Syracusan tyrant's failure to send any help to the mainland Greeks by creating enough delay for a further fabrication: that Gelon had actually sailed to Greece to help the war effort against the Persians, only to be conveniently met by news of the great victory at Salamis.[10]

In Timaeus' account of the later wars between Carthage and Syracuse, the complex strategic reasons why it was important for Carthage to intervene militarily in Sicily, like those of the Persians in Greece, were reduced to little more than a wish to enslave Hellas, beautifully articulated in one episode by the apparent discovery of 20,000 pairs of manacles in the Carthaginian camp after a Greek victory, or simply a hatred of all Greeks.[11] In another wonderfully evocative but surely manufactured vignette, Timaeus described how Greek mercenaries fighting for Syracusans while fraternizing with their fellow countrymen who were in the employ of the Carthaginians asked them how they could serve a state whose sole aim was to barbarize a Greek city.[12]

Yet what remains of Sicily's material culture tells a very different story from the tales of ghastly inter-ethnic conflict and total war propagated by hostile Sicilian Greek historians.[13] Decades of bloody conflict had in fact done little to impede the processes of acculturation and accommodation between the Greek and Punic communities on the island. Indeed, the wars between Carthage and Syracuse had directly led to the export far beyond its shores of the religious and cultural syncretism that was long one of the defining characteristics of colonial Sicily. In particular, such ideas had found fertile ground in Carthage, where they had probably been introduced both by members of the Carthaginian elite who had served as officers in the army in Sicily and by the sizeable Sicilian Greek community who were now resident in the city.[14]

One particularly prominent example was the growing prominence in Carthage of the cult of the Greek deities Demeter, a fertility goddess, and her daughter Core, the consort of Hades, king of the underworld.

In his history, Diodorus, thought to be following Timaeus, strongly emphasized the Sicilian Greek origins of the cult by insisting that the abduction and rape of Core by Hades actually took place on the island, even though Greek cities in southern Italy had claimed that the heinous event had taken place there.[15] When in 396 BC the cult was officially adopted in Carthage, Diodorus later portrayed this merely as a panic-stricken attempt to appease the goddesses after they had punished the Carthaginians with a visitation of the plague, after the sacking of their temple at Syracuse by the hapless general Hamilcar. At the same time, Diodorus emphasized the indelibly Hellenic nature of the cult by reporting that the Carthaginian authorities had sought out Greeks living in Carthage and assigned them to the service of the goddesses, while those aristocratic Carthaginians who were appointed to be priests of the cult were instructed to follow 'the ritual used by the Greeks'.[16]

CARTHAGE: A CENTRAL-MEDITERRANEAN MELTING POT

Diodorus' account of the relationship between the Carthaginians and the cult of Demeter and Core was in fact very partial. The goddesses had long been worshipped by the Punic population of Sicily as fertility and underworld deities, and it was most likely from this source that the cult had first come to Carthage.[17] Core, in particular, became a ubiquitous presence on Carthaginian coinage.[18] The two goddesses were two of the most popular motifs of the Punic world – especially on terracotta incense-burners, where they were depicted wearing concave headdresses in which perfumed pellets were placed.[19] Indeed, within a very short period of time during the fourth century BC the cult would also proliferate across other Punic areas of the western Mediterranean, such as the rural shrine of Genna Maria in Sardinia, where the worship of Demeter was clearly amalgamated with that of indigenous deities.[20] What is also clear is that, despite Diodorus/ Timaeus' insistence to the contrary, this was no mere replication of the Greek cult, but one that had already been mediated through the extensive cultural and religious borrowings that had been taking place between the diverse communities that inhabited the island of Sicily, before being tailored to the diverse religious needs of its adherents across the Punic world.

Then there was the syncretistic figure of Heracles–Melqart, who became increasingly popular in Carthage during the third century BC. Of particular significance are a series of engraved bronze hatchet razors (a traditional part of the Punic funerary assemblage) dating to this period and found in the cemeteries that ringed the city. Although the images that were engraved on many of the blades of these hatchets show traditional Levantine representations of Melqart dressed in a long tunic and headdress, with a double-sided axe resting on his shoulder, new representations of the god had also begun to appear.[21] Indeed, one particular example shows Heracles complete with a lionskin, a club and a hunting dog at his feet, in the classic iconography of the hero that had developed in the Greek cities of southern Italy.[22] Yet, as the French scholar Serge Lancel has rightly observed, this was really only an 'Italianate veneer' on Punic Melqart. For on the reverse side of the blade was an image of Ioloas, Heracles' nephew and companion, holding a branch from the kolokasion plant in one hand and a quail in the other.[23] This was a Greek interpretation of the Phoenician/Punic rite of *egersis*. The story, preserved by the Greek writer Athenaeus, summarizing a story told by an earlier fourth-century Greek author, Eudoxius of Cnidus, told how 'Tyrian' Heracles lay dying and was soothed by his faithful companion with the leaves from the kolokasion plant, before being brought back to life by the smell of roasting quail meat.[24] Another hatchet razor dating to the third century BC found in Carthage displays a possible Sardinian connection, with an engraving of Heracles naked under his lionskin leaning on his club on one side of the blade, while on the other side Sid, wearing a plumed headdress, spears a kneeling figure wearing a breastplate and a short tunic.[25]

Thus, rather than proving the existence of an unbridgeable divide between Greek and Punic populations in the West, Timaeus and the other Sicilian Greek historians used by Diodorus represented a shrill xenophobic reaction to the growing political, cultural and religious syntheses that governed not only their home island, but also the whole central Mediterranean. For Timaeus in particular, the attraction of this model of ethnic conflict between Greeks and barbarians was clearly the result of his long absence from Sicily and the continually shifting compromises and allegiances that made up the political landscape there.

AGATHOCLES: THE ALEXANDER OF SICILY

Despite the fact that these sweeping generalizations bore little resemblance to the geopolitical realities on the ground, they did increasingly have an impact on the local Sicilian potentates who were Carthage's rivals on the island: much better to portray oneself as the saviour of western Hellas from oriental barbarism than as yet another feuding warlord. After Alexander's untimely death, his generals had quickly divided up his vast dominions in Asia, Europe and Egypt, and many bullishly adopted the heroic public persona of the Great King. As Peter Green has remarked, 'They stood long after his death, in his [Alexander's] tremendous shadow still. He made them what they were: and however consciously they might try to jettison his alleged ideals ... their fierce ambitions forced them to follow where he had led.'[26]

Beneath the top tier of the *diadochi* – the senior Macedonian military commanders who had carved up the great empire between them – was a jostling group of minor princes, junior officers and other adventurers, many with the most tenuous connections to Alexander. Self-conscious about their peripheral position on the fringes of this gilded world, some ardently desired to be included in the dazzling club of A-list Hellenistic monarchs. Such a figure was Agathocles, a dashing cavalry commander with a shady past that included spells in exile and as a mercenary captain, who had risen to autocratic power in Syracuse in the 320s through popular demagogy and military thuggery.[27] Like Gelon and Dionysius, Agathocles would use the almost continuous round of warfare that he provoked with the Carthaginians as a way to consolidate his regime.

The conscious connection that had been made by Alexander between his great victories in the East and the earlier Persian invasion of Greece (at first he mooted his campaigns in Asia as a revenge mission) also breathed new life into the perennial conflict between Carthage and Syracuse. Once more the totally erroneous but seductive idea that the

Sicilian wars were a western extension of the age-old struggle between the civilization of Greece and the dark forces of the barbarian East would have renewed capital. Throughout a long and eventful career, Agathocles consistently chose to present himself as the western heir to Alexander.[28] His coinage, like that of other post-Alexander Greek leaders, self-consciously reproduced the motifs favoured by the Great King of Macedon and self-styled Lord of Asia.[29] A century later, the Roman playwright Plautus would mockingly refer to Agathocles' desperation to ape the imagery and antics of Alexander.[30]

However, Agathocles' talent stretched to more than an ability to present himself as the heir to Alexander in the West. Carthage's long sojourn on Sicily meant that many Sicilian Greeks had a very good knowledge of Carthaginian military institutions. Indeed, one of Agathocles' most potent weapons was his understanding of Carthage and his awareness of the tensions that existed between the city and its army in Sicily. Carthage's use of mercenaries to fight its wars engendered a feeling of suspicion towards its generals, and the ruling elite in particular felt threatened by the perceived unconstitutional ambitions of the men who were sent to command the Carthaginian armies. During the fourth century BC it appears that Carthage's generals, particularly in Sicily, had acquired a wide range of powers that allowed them to operate with a certain amount of autonomy while on campaign, including the authority to negotiate for peace and to form alliances (although it is likely that these agreements then needed to be formally ratified by the Council of Elders, who also approved the resupply of armies).[31] Indeed, such was their mandate for independent action that the fourth-century-BC Athenian politician Isocrates was moved to comment that the Carthaginians were 'ruled by an oligarchy at home, by a king in the field'.[32]

Although these generals were drawn from Carthaginian ranks, they had been chosen not by the Tribunal of One Hundred and Four, but by the whole citizenry of Carthage in the Popular Assembly.[33] This fact alone placed them under suspicion by the elite. The development of the Carthaginian army in Sicily into a quasi-independent institution with its own coinage and administrative structure made the situation even more tense. The ports of Sicily were hundreds of kilometres away from Carthage, and news of events on the island was sporadic and often inaccurate. In such circumstances it was easy for a military commander to forget that he was answerable to his peers.

Though Carthaginian army commanders made decisions with considerable autonomy while on campaign, these decisions were retrospectively subject to a rigorous audit carried out by the Tribunal of One Hundred and Four. Many years of campaigning in Sicily meant that these generals could scarcely have failed to notice how some of their Syracusan equivalents – men who like themselves had first gained their commands through their popularity with the general citizenry – had managed to shed the awkward scrutiny to which they were subjected by their peers by seizing autocratic power. The harsh punishment of military commanders who had failed to show sufficient skill or courage on the battlefield was a long-standing feature of Carthaginian political life. The Carthaginians were certainly not the first in the ancient world to use crucifixion; however, whereas others reserved this horrific punishment for the lowest of the low – runaway slaves, common criminals, and foreigners – Carthage would periodically nail its generals to the cross. This was not just a grim warning against failure, but also acted as a gruesome form of political decapitation.

The feelings of distrust were reciprocated by the military commanders themselves, who complained of the hostile treatment that they received from their fellow citizens on their return from campaign. As Diodorus/Timaeus acutely observed when providing an explanation for a later attempted army coup:

> The basic cause in this matter was the Carthaginians' severity in inflicting punishments. In their wars they advance their leading men to commands, taking it for granted that these should be the first to brave the danger for the whole state; but when they gain peace, they plague these same men with suits, bring false charges against them through envy, and load them down with penalties. Therefore some of those who are placed in positions of command, fearing the trials in the courts, desert their posts, but others attempt to become tyrants.[34]

Agathocles was portrayed by Diodorus (as usual taking his information from earlier Sicilian Greek sources) as ruthlessly exploiting the tensions between the Carthaginian generals and the politicians at home. In this he was following historians such as Timaeus (who particularly disliked Agathocles because he had been responsible for the exile of the historian's father), who showed Agathocles in a poor light as a political opportunist who willingly entered into compacts with the hated Carthaginian intruders.[35] However, it also points to Agathocles' understanding of the fears and ambitions of the Carthaginian military commanders on Sicily as a key element in his own rise to power.

On one occasion early in his career, in the 320s BC, when his hopes of political power in Syracuse had been seemingly dashed, Agathocles raised an army of discontented Sicels with the intention of seizing the city with violent force. Finding that a large Carthaginian army was blocking his path, Agathocles used his considerable talent for diplomacy with the Carthaginian commander, Hamilcar. Learning that Hamilcar had ambitions of seizing autocratic power in Carthage, Agathocles agreed a secret arrangement with him whereby the Carthaginian army would stand aside so that he could take Syracuse, in exchange for which he would help the general in any future attempt to seize power in his home city. Indeed, Hamilcar went even further in his cooperation with Agathocles, by supplying him with 5,000 troops to assist in the massacre of his political opponents in Syracuse.[36] A peace treaty was then agreed that appeared to be immensely favourable towards Agathocles, even though he was hardly in a strong position. Under its terms, the eastern Sicilian cities were compelled to acknowledge Syracusan suzerainty, while the Carthaginians gained nothing aside from confirmation of the territory that they had already held before the conflict.[37] The situation was made even worse by Hamilcar's appearing to turn a blind eye to Agathocles' continued harassment of Carthage's Sicilian allies.[38]

The Greek and Roman sources which record this pact suggest that the crafty Agathocles duped Hamilcar. A more realistic explanation may be that continued violence and instability in Sicily was in the interests of both the Carthaginian army and Agathocles. The instability was an indication both of the lack of control that Carthage had over its army and of the level of collusion between its forces in Sicily and its Syracusan foes. The reaction of the Carthaginian Council is revealing. Rather than recalling Hamilcar and openly confronting him with his treachery, the Council voted on the matter but suppressed their judgement until such time as they felt confident to act against him.[39]

The Carthaginian army in Sicily was beginning to act as a semi-autonomous force, and its supposed masters in Carthage had little power to control it.

In fact Hamilcar died before justice could be dispensed, and the confrontation that the Carthaginian Council had obviously feared was avoided. In an attempt to seize back the agenda, the Council sent a delegation directly from Carthage to warn Agathocles that he should respect the existing treaties between the two states. But, in an effort to reassert the Council's authority over their forces in Sicily, a fresh army was recruited under a new commander, Hamilcar, son of Gisco.

Hamilcar's campaign did not get off to an auspicious start. As the army crossed over to Sicily, a number of ships carrying Carthaginian noblemen were sunk in a storm.[40] However, on his arrival on the island, in 311, Hamilcar quickly proved to be an excellent general. After winning a comprehensive victory, the Carthaginians managed to blockade Agathocles and the remainder of his forces in Syracuse.[41] Hamilcar then followed up these military successes with a diplomatic initiative among the Greek Sicilian states which left Agathocles increasingly isolated. In a marked departure from his predecessors, Hamilcar attempted to end the war through the final defeat of Agathocles and the capture of Syracuse.

THE INVASION OF AFRICA

Faced with this desperate situation, Agathocles would decide upon a course of action so bold and indeed reckless that he caught the Carthaginians completely by surprise. He would take the war to the Carthaginians where they least expected it: in the Punic heartlands of Africa.[42] Once more Agathocles showed a sound understanding of Carthage and its people. He knew that most Carthaginians had no experience of war. Their armies were made up largely of mercenaries, and as yet they had never been forced to fight any major conflicts in their North African homeland. By launching a surprise attack there, he would be able quickly to acquire supplies and booty, and thus pay his troops from land that had, unlike Sicily, been spared the ravages of war. He was also hopeful that the Libyans, for so long discontented by the treatment that they had received from the Carthaginians, would rise up and join with him. Faced with such a crisis at home, he reasoned, Hamilcar and his forces would quickly be compelled to evacuate Sicily.[43]

Agathocles quickly recruited Syracusan levies, mercenaries and even slaves to serve in his army. Money for the expedition was acquired by murdering his surviving aristocratic opponents and confiscating their property, pillaging orphans' inheritances, appropriation of temple offerings and women's jewellery, and compulsory loans.[44] After assembling a fleet of 60 ships and a very modest force of 13,500 men, Agathocles managed to slip through the Carthaginian blockade. Carefully disguising their route to ensure that the Carthaginians remained oblivious to the real objectives of the mission, in 310 the Syracusan flotilla landed on the Cap Bon peninsula a mere 110 kilometres from Carthage, after six days at sea. Knowing that he was finished if this venture failed, Agathocles set fire to the ships so that any thought of escape was discounted.[45] He dedicated them to the goddesses Demeter and Core – surely as a way of propagandizing this campaign as Sicilian Greek revenge for previous outrages committed by the Carthaginians on their island.[46] After a final exhortation to his troops, they moved against and captured with ease the towns of Megalopolis and Tunes (Tunis).[47]

Buoyed by the ease of these successes, Agathocles' army then pitched camp not far from Carthage, whose citizens started to panic because they wrongly assumed that Agathocles' presence in Africa meant that the Carthaginian forces in Sicily must have been totally destroyed.[48] Male citizens were now drafted into the army under the joint command of two political rivals, Bomilcar and Hanno.[49] The campaign opened disastrously for the Carthaginians, with a heavy defeat in which their most able commander, Hanno, was killed. Bomilcar, seeing this as an opportunity to seize autocratic power for himself, retreated to Carthage with his troops.[50]

Diodorus recounted how, with their city under siege and their best general far across the sea in Sicily, the Carthaginians sent a large sum of money and expensive offerings to the temple of Melqart at Tyre, in the belief that their present misfortunes were due to the god being disgusted with the miserly nature of their recent tithes. Now the terrified

Carthaginians were also supposed to have tried to appease their vengeful gods by offering up 200 high-born children for sacrifice. Later another 300 citizens, who were thought to have particularly offended the gods, were reported to have voluntarily sacrificed themselves in the fire.[51] In perhaps a further sign of the Carthaginians' fears of having provoked divine anger, an inscription dated to around this period refers to the construction of new temples to the goddesses Tanit and Astarte, replete with decorations, gold statuary and furniture. Tellingly, the inscription also refers to the construction of fortification walls around the sanctuary, and probably also around the hill where it was sited.[52]

Soon disastrous news arrived in Carthage from Sicily. Its general Hamilcar had been captured and killed while attacking Syracuse, with the result that the Carthaginian army in Sicily had fragmented into several warring factions.[53] Agathocles was said to have carefully displayed Hamilcar's head, which had been sent over from Sicily, within sight of the already demoralized Carthaginians.[54]

On the brink of a great victory, it is perhaps hardly surprising that Agathocles' Alexander complex became ever stronger. Certainly his coins from the period clearly aped those of the Macedonian king, especially in their use of the thunderbolt as a motif.[55] His troops, however, mutinied, upset by their general's pretensions and increasingly high-handed behaviour and, more importantly, by his failure to pay them.[56] The Carthaginians now quickly seized on Agathocles' difficulties and offered the leaders of the mutiny enhanced pay and a bonus if they brought the Sicilian Greek army over to them. Agathocles, whose troops still held him in great esteem, only just managed to save the situation by theatrically threatening to commit suicide.[57]

After once more bolstering his position by defeating a Carthaginian force, Agathocles, distrusting the local Libyans and Numidians, cast around for an additional ally with whom to deliver what he believed would be the final victory. He successfully enticed Ophellas, the ruler of the Greek city of Cyrene and a man with a real Alexandrian pedigree (he had served in the army of the Macedonian king), to join the campaign with the promise of all the Carthaginian territory in North Africa if they were successful. However, true to form, Agathocles quickly murdered his new ally and incorporated his large and well-equipped army into his own forces.[58] Yet the greatest danger to Carthage would come from those whom it had entrusted with its own defence.

The Carthaginian general Bomilcar, who had long held autocratic ambitions, at last judged the time had come to act. First he sent out a force made up of many of Carthage's most distinguished citizens to fight against the Numidian tribes, thereby removing from the city many of those who might oppose his coup. He then mustered his troops, made up of citizens and mercenaries, in an area of Carthage called the New City. Diodorus left a vivid account of what occurred next:

> Dividing his troops into five groups, he sounded the attack, massacring those who opposed him in the streets. Since an extraordinary disturbance broke out everywhere in the city, the Carthaginians at first thought that the enemy had broken in, and that the city had been betrayed. When however the true situation became known, the young men gathered together, formed groups, and moved against the tyrant. However, Bomilcar, slaughtering those in the streets, moved quickly into the marketplace. Discovering many unarmed citizens there, he killed them. The Carthaginians, however, took over the tall buildings around the marketplace, and hurled down missiles which struck the rebels. Hard-pressed, the plotters closed ranks and forced their way through the narrow streets of the New City, all the time being struck by objects thrown from the houses that they passed by. Once they had occupied higher ground, the Carthaginians, who had now mustered all the citizens, rallied their forces against the rebels. At last, sending older citizens as envoys, and offering an amnesty, terms for surrender were agreed. Against the rebels they demanded no restitution, on account of the dangers presently facing the city, but Bomilcar himself was cruelly tortured and then put to death, with no attention being paid to oaths that had been given. Thus, in this way, the Carthaginians, having faced the gravest danger, saved the constitution of their forefathers.[59]

Diodorus, whose sources were ever hostile to Carthage, could not resist the temptation of highlighting the treachery of the Carthaginians at the end of this account, although on this occasion the victim was a traitor. There is, however, no reason to dispute his account of the attempted coup.

Although he now found himself in control of a huge swathe of Carthaginian territory in North Africa, Agathocles now received alarming news of renewed conflict in Sicily, where several vassal cities had decided to take advantage of the lengthy absence of the Syracusan army to declare their independence. Agathocles was forced to return to try to retrieve the situation, leaving his son Archagathus, who had inherited little of his father's political or military talents, in command of his army.[60]

The Carthaginians, clearly re-energized by the defeat of the coup and the absence of their talismanic opponent, intelligently refocused their military strategy away from set-piece battles, in which they had fared so badly. They now split their forces into three combat groups with explicit areas of operation: the coast, the interior and the deep interior. Faced with this fresh challenge, Archagathus made the catastrophic decision to match this move by dividing his own forces in the same way. Soon the two battalions that had been sent into the interior to hunt down their Carthaginian foes were ambushed and cut down.

Deserted by his fickle Libyan allies, Archagathus rallied the remainder of his forces at Tunes, and sent messages to his father requesting urgent help.[61] Although Agathocles did return, he found the situation irretrievable. A further defeat at the hands of the Carthaginians was followed by a terrible conflagration, which Diodorus – surely fancifully – states was started by the Carthaginians incinerating the fairest of their Greek captives as sacrificial victims to their gods. Many Sicilian Greek troops were killed, which led the Syracusan general to decide to leave Africa. Knowing that a large-scale evacuation would quickly come to the attention of the Carthaginians and lead to an attack, after one failed attempt to flee, Agathocles eventually managed to slip away, leaving his army and at least two of his own sons behind.[62] This last detail, probably taken from Timaeus, whose loathing of Agathocles made him want to portray him in as poor a light as possible, may well have been false. A Roman account, clearly using other sources, related that Agathocles tried to take Archagathus with him, but they became separated during the night and the latter was captured and brought back to the Syracusan camp.[63]

After killing their erstwhile general's progeny, Agathocles' deserted army swiftly negotiated surrender with the Carthaginians. The latter offered them generous terms: all the army received cash donatives, and those who wished to be were co-opted into the Carthaginian army; the remainder were transported to Sicily and allowed to settle at the

Punic city of Solus. Those who, out of misguided loyalty to their old leader, refused to cooperate were set to work to restore the lands which as soldiers they had laid waste. The most recalcitrant were crucified.

After settling with his troops, the Carthaginians then concluded a peace with Agathocles himself, which superficially offered surprisingly generous terms. Carthage agreed to pay Agathocles a large amount of gold and grain, in exchange for which he would recognize Carthage's rights over all the territory that it had previously controlled in Sicily.[64]

A DUBIOUS 'FINAL' VICTORY

The question remains as to why the Carthaginians did not press home their clear advantage in the treaty. The answer probably lies in the fact that the wars against Agathocles had brought Carthage to the brink of financial ruin. To pay for this protracted conflict, there had been an enormous increase in the production of electrum coinage in Carthage, yet the gold content of the new coins had fallen dramatically.[65] In a further sign of economic difficulties, the Carthaginian and Sicilian mints had started producing larger amounts of very heavy large bronze coinage, probably meant as substitute for gold and silver currency.[66]

The strategy of trying to capture Syracuse and completely dismantle the Agathoclean regime had backfired spectacularly. Agathocles, left with nothing to lose, had simply transported the conflict to North Africa, where Carthage's discontented Numidian, Libyan and Greek neighbours had been more than happy to join the attack. Of even greater concern had been the conduct of those elements of the Carthaginian army who had participated in Bomilcar's coup attempt. Having large Carthaginian armies operating in North Africa for long periods of time clearly posed a threat to the current political regime. All these factors must have persuaded the Carthaginians that the old territorial status quo in Sicily was preferable to the tumult that they had just experienced. By resettling and incorporating Sicilian Greek soldiers who were extremely hostile to Agathocles (after he had deserted them in North Africa), Carthage may have been already preparing for the next round of conflict with Syracuse.

A change in the named minting authority that issued military coinage in Sicily may be a sign of a wider change in Carthage's relationship with its army on the island. There is little reason to think that the army's actions during the Agathocles crisis had done much to promote confidence in either its loyalty or its military capabilities. Indeed, the armed forces on Sicily had been in complete disarray, and had contributed nothing to the defence of North Africa. Moreover, senior military commanders such as Bomilcar had been involved in the planning and execution of coup attempts.

These concerns may explain the gradual transferral of minting authority for the military from *mhmhnt* ('the people of the camp') to *mhsbm* ('the controllers').[67] Were the *mhsbm* Carthaginian officials sent to take over the financial administration of the army in Sicily, so that the authorities in Carthage could reassert their authority?[68] After all, mercenary soldiers tended to be loyal to those who paid them. Tellingly, all Carthaginian military coinage production had ceased by the end of the first decade of the third century BC, with troops presumably being paid with electrum shekels which were now being minted in Carthage.[69] More importantly, it is clear that the disruption caused by Agathocles' African onslaught had left Carthage on the brink of financial exhaustion.

In fact there was no new war with Agathocles. Clearly unchastened by his recent humiliation in North Africa, in 306 Agathocles declared himself a king, before turning his attention northward to the Italian peninsula in an attempt to build up a new empire which might be able to challenge the dominance of the Carthaginians.[70] However, his dreams of an Adriatic/southern-Italian empire were dashed, as were his hopes of contracting a grand alliance with Ptolemy, king of Egypt, and several other Hellenistic potentates. Eventually a terrible illness, most likely to have been cancer of the jaw, finally robbed Agathocles not only of his Carthaginian ambitions, but also of his life.[71] As a final irony, the man whose silken tongue had propelled him to such notoriety was reputedly burnt alive on his funeral pyre, because the disease had robbed him of the capacity to move or speak.[72]

In eventually prevailing over this most persistent of enemies, the Carthaginians had shown resilience and resourcefulness. Over two decades, they had survived coup attempts, disastrous military defeats,

Libyan and Numidian rebellions, an invasion, and a siege of their home city. Yet, despite his grand pretensions, Agathocles was no Alexander, and the grave difficulty that the supposedly dominant power of the western Mediterranean had in finally overcoming the threat that he posed suggested that it might struggle even more against a better-resourced and more consistent opponent. Other Hellenistic warlords would now view Africa as a viable target in a way they had not done before Agathocles.

Thus the Greek biographer Plutarch's account of the African ambitions of the Molossian general Pyrrhus, who spent 278–277 attacking Punic interests in Sicily, may have been apocryphal, but it probably accurately reflected contemporary opinion: 'For who could keep his hands off Libya, or Carthage, when that city got within his reach, a city which Agathocles, slipping stealthily out of Syracuse and crossing the sea with a few ships, narrowly missed taking?'[73]

6

Carthage and Rome

THE RELENTLESS MARCH OF ROME

By the late fourth century BC, the treaty that Carthage in 509 BC had concluded with what had then been a small city in upper Latium must have begun to look like an inspired piece of forward-thinking diplomacy. Although Rome had faced a number of serious setbacks, including internal political stasis, catastrophic military defeat, and the humiliating capture of much of the city by a Gallic war band in 387, its successes had been extraordinary.[1] Latium had been brought under Roman control through a seemingly endless round of military and diplomatic initiatives. This had been followed by three terrible wars of attrition against the powerful Samnite confederation who lived in the mountainous Apennine region of central and southern Italy, which had eventually led to the latter's subjugation. At the same time, the regions of Etruria and Umbria were brought under Roman control, and an alliance with the city of Capua brought much of the agriculturally rich region of Campania into the Roman sphere of influence.[2]

Such had been the scale of Rome's conquests that one general, Manius Curius Dentatus, issued the famous boast that it was unclear which was the greater: the amount of land which had been taken or the number of people captured. It has been calculated that by the early third century BC Rome controlled 14,000 square kilometres of territory – more than two and a half times more than it had just under half a century before. The Roman domain spread right across the expanse of central Italy, and decades of war and conquest had brought considerable wealth to the city. It was recorded that during the great triumphs of 293 BC, to celebrate the final victory over the Samnites, one consul brought back 830 kilograms of silver and 1,150,000 kilograms of bronze.

It was not just the scale of Roman expansion that was extraordinary, but also the manner in which it was achieved. Perhaps the most striking feature that emerged from these years of conquest was not the incredible run of military triumphs, but the fact that these victories had been interspersed with some devastating defeats. Rome in this period is conventionally defined above all by its extreme aggression and acquisitiveness, but it is clear that these were precisely the characteristics required not only to thrive, but even to survive, in Italy during this period.[3] As the historian Arthur Eckstein has commented, 'The Roman experience of competition for influence, power and security, first in Latium, then in central Italy, and then in the wide western Mediterranean, was a harsh experience, against formidable and warlike rivals.'[4]

Rome quickly developed a marked capacity to absorb the loss and shock of defeat. The Roman state responded to defeat not with offers of peace treaties and truces, but with the sending out of new armies to recover what had been lost. It was often the relentless pressure that Rome was able to exert which led to final victory. One of the key problems which Rome presented for its enemies was that no one individual or clan had such a monopoly on political power that a lasting or meaningful peace treaty could be negotiated. All regular senatorial offices were held for only a year, and consecutive terms were forbidden. It was also exceptional that any Roman held the consulship more than once. The competition to hold the top job in Roman politics was so ferocious, and the tenure of office so short, that no Roman general would risk the disapproval and opprobrium of his peers by daring to negotiate when facing defeat.

However, military success was only one part of the equation. There was also the extraordinary efficiency with which the Romans asserted their control over the newly subjugated territory. This was achieved in a number of different ways. First there was an emphasis on the implementation of new physical infrastructure to connect the new lands to Rome. Within a short period of time a network of roads was cut through the countryside connecting the city to all the major settlements in the region, both old and new. Large-scale movement of the population was instigated, with colonists from Rome being sent out to establish new settlements and Latin peoples being moved from their traditional homes to new territories.[5] But Rome's greatest strength in this regard was an extraordinary ability to integrate quickly and efficiently the native populations of the newly subjugated lands and thereby create a large and very stable territory for itself. By using newly created legal statuses rather than ethnicity or geography as the basis for membership of the state, Rome quickly drew on a huge reservoir of human resources to fight its battles, rather than relying on mercenaries like most of the Mediterranean world.[6]

A new body of knowledge was created that represented these newly won lands in explicitly Roman terms, and divine portents and signs which occurred in these lands were carefully recorded and expiated by Roman ritual practice. The cities of Latium enjoyed the same legal rights that they had previously enjoyed in respect to Rome, but they were now bound by a series of treaties to provide Rome with troops whenever they were required. The ancient Latin identity survived, but only as a set of duties, rights and privileges enshrined in Roman law. Thus Rome sought to display its mastery and indeed *ownership* of this territory. Italy would never be just a piece of conquered territory that could be evacuated if circumstances dictated.[7] It was Roman land that was to be defended as if it were within the city itself.

The Roman genius for appropriation and redefinition extended also to the religious sphere. Latin religious cults and practices were sustained by the Romans, but only under strict supervision and with an agendum that placed Rome at the heart of Latin identity. The religious ritual of *evocatio*, for example, designed to entice an enemy deity from its native land to Rome (where it could expect due and, indeed, greater reverence), was now used to great effect. The first instance of the *evocatio* being used by a Roman general occurred in 396 BC at the siege of the Etruscan city of Veii, where Iuni/Juno was the chief deity. After the fall of the city, the cult of the goddess was transferred to Rome, where she was worshipped as the queen of the Roman divine pantheon. Superficially this process appears comparable to the religious syncretism that took place in central Italy in the archaic period, but in fact it was an abrupt departure. Foreign gods were incorporated on strictly Roman terms.

CARTHAGE IN ROME

Now that Rome was emerging as an important regional power, the Carthaginians were clearly anxious to maintain and indeed strengthen diplomatic relations between the two city states. Thus in 351 BC a Carthaginian embassy was sent to Rome in order to present a massive gold crown weighing 11 kilograms as congratulations for victory against the Samnites. So proud were the Romans of this recognition of their growing stature by the most powerful state in the western Mediterranean that it was decided to place the crown in their most important temple, that of Jupiter Optimus Maximus on the Capitoline Hill.[8]

This was followed in 348 by a fresh treaty between the two cities, the terms of which were a more detailed and expanded version of the first (with Spain now added to the zones of Carthaginian influence). Carthage had plenty of reasons for maintaining friendly relations with Rome. The terms of the treaty afforded both Roman and Carthaginian merchants the same rights and privileges as citizens in each other's city, and there is reason to believe that there was a significant Punic mercantile presence in Rome and in the wider area of Latium.[9] Certainly the placing of copies of this and the previous treaty in the Treasury of the Aediles – senatorial officials whose roles included the supervision of Rome's commercial markets – adds to the picture of a thriving trading relationship between the two states that would have probably involved fish products, salt, Sardinian fleeces and African garlic, as well as almonds and pomegranates.[10]

There are also several other intriguing clues that point to a Carthaginian presence in Rome. Varro, a Roman writer of the first century AD, mentions an area of Rome called Vicus Africus on the Esquiline Hill, which he said had got its name from resident hostages of the Punic wars.[11] However, recent research has shown that this 'African quarter' must have dated to well before that period.[12]

Further clues to a Carthaginian presence in Rome exist in the description of a strange monument called the Columna Lactaria, the Milkers' Column, at Rome's vegetable market, the Forum Holitorum: this may have actually been a sacred betyl originally worshipped by the Punic inhabitants of the district.[13] Varro described the Forum Holitorum as 'the old Macellum where vegetables were the provender', assuming that *macellum* was a Greek word.[14] However, it is in fact a Semitic word for a market that was much used in the Punic world. Indeed, the word *macellum* can be linked to several towns in Latium, suggesting that they also possessed Punic commercial enclaves.[15] Moreover, there is strong evidence for a Punic presence elsewhere in the region at the town of Ardea, where a votive deposit containing Punic pottery and two Punic inscriptions has been found in the locality of the temple of Hercules.[16]

Carthage also had major mercantile links with Bruttium (modern Calabria) in the toe of Italy. Recent archaeological research into the provenance of transport amphorae found in Carthage has shown that in the fourth century BC Bruttium was a greater source of goods and materials even than Sardinia.[17] Carthage had certainly developed strong links with the region, and had even sent troops to help the people of the town of Hipponium refound their city after they had been displaced by Dionysius, tyrant of Syracuse.[18] To the north, the region of Campania also had close links with Carthage, with a considerable number of mercenaries from the region fighting in the Carthaginian armies in Sicily.[19] The new treaty was recognition of Rome's growing influence in the Tyrrhenian region and also of Carthage's interests on the peninsula.

The terms of the new treaty made allowance for Carthage to intervene again in Italy if it needed to. If the Carthaginians captured any Latin cities, they were to hand them over to the Romans while keeping any property or captives (although if any of the latter were brought to Rome they would be set free). North Africa (excepting the city of Carthage itself) and Sardinia would remain strictly out of bounds to Roman merchants, but the treaty terms seem to suggest that trade on Sicily was allowed. Militarily, the Carthaginians probably saw Rome as an important regional ally to counter the influence of Syracuse, and Rome may have seen Syracuse as a potential threat. Both Dionysius and Agathocles had displayed ambitions to extend their authority into Italy, and indeed the Romans had recently beaten off an unwelcome visit by a Sicilian Greek fleet.[20]

PYRRHUS

By the early decades of the third century BC the Romans had turned their attention to the wealthy cities of Magna Graecia, the area of southern Italy that had been colonized by Greek settlers. After clashing with Roman troops in several border incidents, Tarentum, the most powerful city in the region, started to cast around for allies both inside and outside Italy. Eventually a potential saviour was found in the form of Pyrrhus, king of Epirus, a small Hellenistic kingdom roughly where Albania is now.[21] Now thirty-eight, Pyrrhus had already led a very eventful life, which had included several depositions and restorations to the throne, a spell as a hostage at the Egyptian court, and a short-lived interlude as king of Macedonia.[22] Once more confined to his small kingdom, he found the Tarentines' invitation to save them from the clutches of Rome too good to refuse.

On the face of it Pyrrhus was an exceptional ally. He was widely considered by his peers (and by later admirers) as one of the finest generals of the ancient world. Moreover, many other Hellenistic monarchs – anxious to see the back of such an indefatigable creator of trouble as he strived to establish a powerful kingdom for himself – furnished him with troops, elephants, ships and money. The campaign started rather inauspiciously, with his armada being scattered by a severe storm in the Adriatic. However, after his forces had regrouped, and he had himself been appointed by the Tarentines as supreme commander with unlimited powers, Pyrrhus vigorously prepared his new charges for war with Rome.

The Romans had now faced the best military opposition that Italy had to offer, in the form of the tough Samnites, but Pyrrhus and his core of battle-hardened Molossian troops from Epirus were a different proposition altogether. Now, for the first time, Rome met Hellenistic troops on the battlefield, and it came off worst in two battles at Heraclea in 279. (Aside from his tactical nous, Pyrrhus was greatly aided by the panic and disarray of the Roman cavalry at the sight of the combat elephants that he had brought with him.) In the wake of his victory, Pyrrhus was even able to advance to within a relatively short distance of Rome itself.[23]

Carthage, which had watched the initial stages of the war from the sidelines, now decided to intervene. Any obligations that the Carthaginians may have felt towards their Roman allies were almost certainly increased by the fear of Pyrrhus' ambitions towards Sicily. In 280 a Carthaginian commander named Mago had arrived at Ostia, the port of Rome, with a fleet of 120 warships and offered to lend assistance to the Romans. The Romans, clearly wary of leaving themselves open to future Carthaginian interference, politely rejected the offer.[24] After almost agreeing to the peace terms that Pyrrhus had dictated, the Roman Senate, chastened by the defiance shown by one of its oldest and most distinguished members, Appius Claudius Caecus, at the last minute showed the resilience for which it would become famous, by rejecting them and voting to continue the war. Although Pyrrhus won another victory against the Roman legions, at Ausculum in 279, it came at such a cost to the king that he was said to have pithily exclaimed that if he won one more victory like that then he would be utterly ruined.[25] With his army seriously weakened, he had little choice but to retreat back to Tarentum.

This devastating 'Pyrrhic victory', while positive for Rome, had serious ramifications for its Carthaginian allies, for Pyrrhus, his enthusiasm for the Roman campaign now at an ebb, was invited by the Syracusans to take a command against the Carthaginians. What made this proposition particularly appealing was that his wife, who was the daughter of no less a figure than Agathocles, had borne him a son, thus giving him a legitimate claim over Syracuse and its territory at a time when it was weak and politically divided.[26]

It was probably at this juncture that a third treaty between Carthage and Rome was signed. As well as renewing the terms of the 348 treaty, it also added several new clauses. Any peace negotiations with Pyrrhus would be entered into jointly, thus pre-empting an attempt on the part of the Epirote king to make an alliance with one against the other. Provisos were also included for limited military cooperation if either Carthage or Rome came under direct attack, and it was agreed that each side would supply and pay for its own troops (although Carthage would provide the naval support).[27]

Although Pyrrhus had initially landed in Sicily in the summer of 278 with a very modest force, he was quickly provided with troops, money and supplies by the anti-Carthaginian group of Sicilian cities. After a triumphal entry into Syracuse, where his mere approach had led to a substantial Carthaginian fleet abandoning their blockade of the harbour, Pyrrhus was able to acquire an army of 30,000 infantry and 2,500 cavalry for the campaign ahead. Indeed, he quickly discovered that the Carthaginian army on Sicily did not present the same kind of stiff challenge as the Roman legions.

Pyrrhus showed himself to be an extremely effective propagandist, for he quickly appropriated the mantle of a Hellenic liberator who would rid Sicily of the barbarous Carthaginians once and for all. Indeed, in familiar fashion, he made a vow to institute games and a sacrifice in honour of Heracles if he captured the Punic stronghold of Eryx – a promise that he carried out 'in magnificent fashion' after the attack was successful.[28] Of course Eryx was a central Punic religious site, sacred to the goddess Astarte and therefore also linked to her celestial consort, Melqart. It seems very unlikely that Pyrrhus' evocation of Heracles was a mere coincidence: more probably it was a specifically targeted reference that associated his assault of Eryx with Alexander's celebrated siege of Tyre, the city of Melqart, after the fall of which Alexander had instituted games and a festival in honour of Heracles.

The cities and strongholds in the Carthaginians' zone of the island quickly fell, until only Lilybaeum remained under Carthaginian control. Increasingly desperate to see Pyrrhus return to Italy, the Carthaginians suggested a peace deal in which they offered a large sum of money and a supply of ships (presumably to ensure his withdrawal). The move, which must have surely outraged the Romans, was rejected. Ominously for Carthage, Pyrrhus had now begun to make preparations to cross to Libya, reminded of the success of Agathocles when he had invaded North Africa directly. The continued resistance of Lilybaeum, however, gave reason for Carthaginian hope, and Pyrrhus moreover had alienated his Sicilian allies through increasingly high demands and arrogant behaviour. Invited once again by the desperate Greeks in Italy to protect them against Rome, he finally left Sicily in 276.[29]

In Italy, Pyrrhus met with little of his previous success. Although the Roman legions earned most of the credit for driving him out, the Carthaginians appear to have provided logistical support. On one occasion the Carthaginian fleet transported a force of 500 Romans to Rhegium, where they destroyed a stockpile of wood earmarked for building boats for Pyrrhus.[30] Carthaginian warships also managed to defend the Romans from further attack by intercepting Pyrrhus' fleet while it sailed back to Italy from Sicily.[31] After a comprehensive defeat at the hands of the Roman army at Beneventum in 275, Pyrrhus left the shores of Italy never to return.[32] He eventually met a humiliating end at a siege in Greece three years later, for an old woman knocked him unconscious with a tile thrown from a rooftop. Captured by the enemy, he was then beheaded.[33]

AN INEVITABLE WAR?

With Pyrrhus gone, the Romans wasted little time in subduing Magna Graecia. In 275 a group of Campanian mercenaries, originally sent by the Romans to protect the city, had seized Rhegium, killing or expelling its male citizens and taking over their property and families. It was five years before they were dislodged by the Romans, who restored the city to its surviving citizens and took the captured mercenaries to Rome, where they were flogged and beheaded in the Forum, probably as a warning to others.[34] Finally, in 270 Tarentum was besieged and captured. Soon afterward the process of territorial absorption honed by the long hard years of struggle in Latium swung into action. The road network was rapidly expanded, with the Via Appia being extended from Capua through the newly conquered lands of Samnium and Magna Graecia. The conquests of such wealthy cities meant a huge influx of war booty into Rome, much of it spent on providing the ever-growing citizen body with a better infrastructure as well as a series of magnificent new temples and victory monuments.

However, once the common threat of Pyrrhus had been seen off, it did not take long for the Roman–Carthaginian alliance to start to unravel. Indeed, the Roman refusal of Carthaginian naval assistance at a time of desperate crisis (when Pyrrhus had only been a few kilometres from Rome) suggests a level of distrust between the two allies before the defeat of the Epirote king. The impressive way that the Romans had eventually defeated Pyrrhus, a general whose talents were widely recognized across the Mediterranean world, had certainly caught the attention of the larger Hellenistic kingdoms in the East, and in 273 Ptolemy II Philadelphus, ruler of Egypt, the most powerful of the Hellenistic states, sent envoys to Rome to establish diplomatic relations, an initiative reciprocated by the Romans. This would suggest that Rome was casting around for new Mediterranean allies, perhaps already with the idea of jettisoning its relationship with Carthage. Roman suspicions of Carthaginian intentions were underlined in 270 when a Carthaginian fleet appeared at Tarentum while the Romans were besieging the city, leading to accusations it had been endeavouring to help the beleaguered Tarentines, although it is far more likely that the flotilla was merely on a reconnaissance mission.[35]

Some scholars, in particular William Harris, have argued for the inevitability of conflict between Carthage and Rome once Pyrrhus was defeated. Rome now had control over Magna Graecia, and the affairs of the Greek cities in southern Italy had long been intertwined with those of their counterparts on the island of Sicily. Such scholars point to the Roman capture of Rhegium (just across the Strait of Messina from Sicily), in 270, the foundation of two new Roman colonies at Paestum and Cosa on the Tyrrhenian coast, in 273, and the confiscation of the Bruttian forests (a source of timber ideal for shipmaking) as signs of Roman designs on Sicily.[36]

All these developments have been seen as evidence of the growing influence of a cabal of several Roman senatorial families of Campanian origin who wanted to provoke a war with Carthage so that they could control the flow of Campanian goods, especially wine and fine black-glaze pottery, into Punic Sicily and North Africa.[37] However, there is little evidence for the export of substantial quantities of Campanian goods into either Punic Sicily or Carthage during this period.[38] In fact these initiatives probably had far more to do with Rome's growing concerns over its lack of a maritime defence, especially as the capture of Magna Graecia had greatly increased the amount of Tyrrhenian coastline under its control.[39]

It is extremely unlikely that any significant grouping in either Rome or Carthage actively sought war with the other; however, new political realities meant that tensions between the two states were bound to arise. The Sicilian cities had a long tradition of playing off the larger regional powers against one another, and now that Rome had joined the number of the latter it would be only a matter of time before it became embroiled in the affairs of the island. Furthermore, any Roman reticence about challenging Carthage on land must have been diminished by the Carthaginian army's unimpressive showing against Pyrrhus in Sicily. Despite the lack of overt warmongering, therefore, by the early 260s the central position of a divided Sicily within the influence and interests of both cities, and the apparent swing of contemporary military might away from Carthage and towards Rome, made for a highly combustible situation.

Behind the political pragmatism and strategic diplomacy lurked a growing sense among the Roman senatorial elite that the Carthaginians inhabited a different side of an important ethno-cultural divide. By the fourth century, the Roman elite had become increasingly interested in a number of theories propagated by Greek authors on the origins of their city. The earliest known example of such ethnographical speculation, by the fifth-century-BC writer Hellanicus of Lesbos, claimed that the great wandering hero Odysseus, king of Ithaca, and the Trojan prince Aeneas, who had come to Italy after Troy had been destroyed by the Greeks, were the joint founders of Rome.[40] Superficially this may have looked like a strange combination, as it was the enmity between the Greeks and the Trojans which had been the subject of the most famous Greek epic ever written, and, theoretically at least, Trojans were in Greek eyes barbarians.

In fact in much Hellenic literature the Trojans were often characterized as possessing many of the same qualities and virtues as the Greeks.[41] Indeed, by the late fourth century the Roman aristocracy appears to have embraced the idea of a Trojan heritage precisely because, while it allowed them to maintain their own ethnic distinctiveness, it also permitted them to share in the prestige of the Hellenic cultural tradition.[42] Over the next century, as the western-Greek intelligentsia, especially in Sicily, had become increasingly aware and interested in Rome, so the number of stories that linked the city's foundation to either Greek or Trojan settlers would be multiplied into a bewildering number of versions.[43]

Although the Romans had their own indigenous foundation myth, which centred on the twin foundlings Romulus and Remus, by the end of the fourth century BC those stories that associated the origins of the city with Trojan and Greek settlers had become very influential among sections of the Roman aristocratic elite who were beginning to show a deep interest in Greek language, art and politics.[44] Indeed, over time this diffuse set of stories concerning Rome's origins was skilfully incorporated into a prehistory that emphasized different waves of Greek and Trojan incomers, eventually leading to the foundation of the city by Romulus and Remus, now considered to be the direct descendants of Aeneas. These stories were not just quaint pieces of cultural narcissism. They came to have important political ramifications, for instance in the appeal to common kinship made by Demetrius Poliorcetes, king of Macedonia in the early third century, in an attempt to gain Roman assistance in dealing with Etruscan pirates.[45]

THE RISE OF HERCULES, THE INVINCIBLE

Among these Greek foundation myths, the cult of Hercules began to have an increasingly high profile by the time of Rome's great Italian expansion in the fourth century BC. Although, as we have seen, the cult at the Forum Boarium stretched back into the archaic period, it had by this period divested itself of its earlier syncretistic properties, and especially any connections with Melqart. In 399 BC the cult of Hercules was accepted into the Roman religious calendar, and then in 312 it received the ultimate accolade of becoming an official state cult. The first official temple to Hercules Invictus, 'the Invincible' – a clear nod to the triumphalism of the Hellenistic world – was also built around this time. And it is clear that the Herculean legacy had seeped into the private familial histories of Rome's aristocratic elite, with one of the major senatorial families, the Fabii, claiming the hero as their progenitor.[46]

Although the story of Hercules' association with Rome was a very old one, the myth of his visit to Pallanthium and the subsequent killing of Cacus may have been refined as late as the last decades of the fourth or the early third century BC, which suggests that the association of Hercules with Rome was very closely linked to Roman political aspirations in Italy.[47] The claim that Pallanthium (the future site of Rome) was the location for the slaying of Cacus by Hercules certainly lent the city some prestige among its Latin neighbours. Indeed, in some versions of the story Hercules fathered Latinus, the eponymous founder of the Latin people, at the site of Rome.[48] Armed with their own Herculean legacy, the Romans could not only claim a distinguished Greek pedigree, but also legitimize their political ambitions over the rest of Italy as establishing a Herculean commonwealth. Then there were the obvious connections with the venerable cities of Magna Graecia, many of whom claimed the great hero as their founder. With a Herculean legacy of their own, not only could the Romans claim to hail from as distinguished an ancestry as their Greek counterparts, but the association also promoted Rome's political ambitions in the region.

Thus, through their investment in a supposed Trojan heritage and the promotion of the cult of Hercules Invictus, the Roman senatorial elite had by the late fourth/early third century BC come to culturally ally itself increasingly with the Greek world, a development which had important ramifications for Roman attitudes towards the Carthaginians. Romans certainly never thought of themselves as Greeks, but they had begun to view themselves as inhabiting the same side of the Greek-authored ethno-cultural divide that separated the civilized Hellenic world from the barbarian world, a category into which Carthage was emphatically placed. These foundation theories represented something far more potent than mere obtuse scholarly speculation. They were a body of ideas in which there had been considerable material and political investment, for they increasingly came to provide the intellectual justification for war being waged, territory being conquered, and treaties being signed. Rome's membership of the club of civilized nations by dint of its Trojan antecedents was inherently a political decision open to periodic revision by opportunistic Hellenistic leaders (if circumstances dictated it). Indeed, the Romans themselves had been the target of a brilliant propaganda campaign waged by Pyrrhus, for silver tetradrachms that were minted under his authority were clearly designed to create a firm link in the minds of contemporaries with Alexander the Great. Among the portraits on them were the Greek heroes Heracles and Achilles.[49]

These images were aimed at the idea that Pyrrhus, like his heroic forebears, would lead the Italian Greeks in crushing the barbarian menace that now threatened them. Pyrrhus tried to use Rome's supposed Trojan provenance as a propagandistic weapon to marshal the Italian Greeks under his banner, by declaring that he would copy the example of his famous ancestor, the great Greek hero Achilles, by conquering the Romans, the descendants of the Trojans.[50] The political importance of ethnic categories was also highlighted later when in 263, during the diplomatic manoeuvring that signalled the escalation of the First Punic War, the Elymian city of Segesta killed its erstwhile Carthaginian allies and defected to the Roman side, citing their common descent from the Trojan prince Aeneas.[51]

The Romans' growing interest in their Trojan and Herculean 'inheritance' was not in itself a major reason for the breakdown of the relationship with Carthage, although the Roman elite may have become more susceptible to Sicilian Greek stereotyping of Carthage as an aggressive and acquisitive power. It did, however, provide a powerful intellectual model for explaining the growing tensions and final breakdown of that relationship in the early decades of the third century BC. From the remaining fragments of his work, it appears that this was the particular historiographical approach that Timaeus favoured. Despite decades of exile in far-off Athens, he had grasped that, after the failures of Agathocles and Pyrrhus, the future of the central Mediterranean would now be decided between the Carthaginians and the Romans, with the Greeks very much on the sidelines.[52] With that painful (for western Greeks at least) reality very much in mind, he had constructed the elaborate fiction that Carthage and Rome had in fact been founded in exactly the same year, 813 BC.[53] Through diligent research that had supposedly involved the actual interviewing of informants, Timaeus had satisfied himself of the Trojan origins of both the Romans and the Latin people.[54]

In the Timaean world view, Rome, as a Trojan–Greek city, was both the new counterweight to the menacing threat of Carthage and the potential champion of the western-Greek world – a view that the Romans may have been happy to encourage. Although very little survives of Timaeus' account of Pyrrhus, we may speculate that a major theme was the terrible mistake that the western Greeks had made in allying themselves against Rome, a Trojan–Greek city, and a true heir of the Heraclean tradition (in contrast to Pyrrhus, who had falsely tried to claim that tradition for himself), rather than focusing their energies against their common enemy, Carthage.[55] It was surely no coincidence that Timaeus was careful to emphasize the Heraclean antecedents of Italy in his work, with particular attention paid to the Greek hero's progress down through the peninsula and Sicily with the cattle of Geryon.[56]

The focus on the southern-Italian and Sicilian travels of Heracles in Timaeus' work may have been deployed in order to emphasize the western Greeks' and Romans' shared investment in the great hero's legacy. Indeed, we know that this connection was not just the product of Timaeus' imagination, but an idea in which the Romans themselves also had a growing investment. In 270 Rome minted an issue of silver coinage in commemoration of the final victory over Tarentum, and the obverse showed the famous image of Romulus and Remus suckling from the she-wolf. The reverse, however, featured Hercules in the Greek iconographical tradition wearing a lionskin. The city states of southern Italy had a long and proud tradition of putting Heracles on their coins, and the hero had long epitomized the success of Greek colonial endeavour in the region. Now Roman coinage proclaimed Rome's membership of the Heraclean tradition.[57]

THE COUNTDOWN TO CONFLICT

The catalyst for hostilities between Carthage and Rome was a group of troublesome mercenaries who had decided to make Sicily their home once their services were no longer required by Agathocles. The Mamertines, or 'followers of Mamers' (the Italian god of war), had originally hailed from Campania, but on demobilization they had made a new home for themselves by massacring the citizens of the Sicilian city of Messana and taking over their wives and property. However, by the mid 260s they were themselves under sustained pressure from Syracuse, which was enjoying a resurgence under the dynamic leadership of a new populist leader, Hiero. In 265, with their future in serious jeopardy, the Mamertines hedged their bets by appealing for assistance not only to Carthage but also to Rome.

This diplomatic initiative achieved the desired result. The Carthaginian military command on the island eagerly took up the invitation and sent a small force to garrison Messana.[58] Later Greek and Roman sources, hostile to Carthage, made the erroneous claim that this was just the first stage of a new attempt by the Carthaginians to seize control of Sicily, after which they had designs on Italy.[59] However, the real attraction for the Carthaginian army was most likely to have been that Messana gave them a base in an area that was traditionally considered to be a Syracusan zone of influence. Indeed, this episode was probably nothing more than another of the frequent Sicilian defections between Carthage and Syracuse that occurred on the island. Nevertheless, in Rome a fierce debate took place in the Senate as to how they should respond to the Mamertine plea. If help was provided then it would almost certainly lead to some kind of diplomatic confrontation with Syracuse – which, as we shall see later, may have been the very hope of some senators.[60]

In an account clearly coloured by historical hindsight, the Greek historian Polybius described the opposing points of view put forward during the debate. The Roman consuls, anxious for the chance to earn military glory, were said to be in favour of sending a force to provide help. However, other senators reminded their colleagues of the unsavoury nature of the Mamertines' seizure of Messana and the charge of hypocrisy that would be justifiably levelled at Rome after the harsh treatment that they had meted out to the Campanians who had attempted to seize Rhegium. With the Senate deadlocked, the consuls now turned to the Popular Assembly, who were easily convinced by the promise of war booty. It was decreed that a force should be sent to aid the Mamertines, with the consul Appius Claudius Caudex at its head.[61]

Clearly aware that the Romans were raising an army and arranging transport among their new allies in Magna Graecia, the Carthaginians stationed a naval squadron to block any crossing of the Strait of Messina from Rhegium. However, rather than risk a naval battle against the much stronger Carthaginian navy, Appius Claudius covertly sent one of his tribunes, Gaius Claudius, across in a small boat to persuade the Mamertines to eject the Carthaginian garrison from their city.

After a second visit, during which he received enthusiastic assurances from the Mamertines, Gaius Claudius attempted a crossing with several ships. However, weather conditions and a Carthaginian attack forced the Romans back to Rhegium. In a conciliatory gesture, Hanno, the commander of the Carthaginian garrison at Messana, sent the ships that he had captured back to the Romans, and even offered to release the men that had been seized once hostilities had ceased. When these overtures were rejected, Hanno then boasted that he would not allow the Romans even to wash their hands in the sea. He was soon to be made to regret such a bold statement. Gaius Claudius attempted the crossing again, and this time was successful. After calling an assembly of the Mamertines in the city, he managed to persuade them to request a meeting with Hanno, who had by then taken refuge in the citadel. After reluctantly agreeing to this assignation, Hanno was promptly seized, but was then allowed to leave the city unharmed with his men. He was later crucified by the Carthaginians 'for both his lack of sense and his lack of courage'.[62]

The Roman occupation of Messana, although a limited operation, sent shock waves through the island. With their bloody diarchy now under threat from a third force, Carthage and Syracuse quickly forged an alliance of convenience against Rome.[63] The Carthaginian forces under the command of another Hanno, son of Hannibal, blockaded Messana in conjunction with the Syracusans. In a deliberate stalling tactic, Appius Claudius, who was waiting in Rhegium with the main body of the Roman army for an opportunity to cross into Sicily, sent envoys to both Hiero and the Carthaginians offering a ceasefire. These overtures were quickly rebuffed, with Diodorus – possibly once more armed with historical hindsight – presenting Hiero as mocking the Romans' justification of their actions as merely maintaining the bond of *fides* that they owed to their new allies, the Mamertines.[64] However, soon Carthaginian confidence in their naval supremacy was undermined when Appius Claudius and his army managed to cross the Strait of Messina in a ragbag flotilla of ships largely borrowed from Rome's allies in southern Italy. A later historical tradition stated that Appius Claudius had managed to hoodwink the Carthaginian naval command by feeding false information to their agents (who hung around the harbour at Rhegium on the pretext of trade).[65] The situation was made worse by the fact that one of the Carthaginian warships detailed to halt the crossing ran aground and fell into Roman hands, with serious future consequences.[66]

In fact the first stages of the land war in Sicily appear to have been inconclusive, with both sides loudly claiming victory.[67] The next year, 263, Rome sent the new consuls with a fresh army of 40,000 men to the island, and once again the Carthaginian fleet failed to prevent the Roman army from crossing. As a consequence, a larger number of Greek Sicilian cities defected to the Romans, and Hiero, now increasingly isolated and unsure of victory, sued for peace. The Romans, who had problems of their own in maintaining supplies for their troops on the island, were willing to offer extremely generous terms. Hiero was allowed to keep his throne and a large chunk of territory in eastern Sicily in exchange for becoming a friend and ally of Rome. Syracuse was also to hand over all Roman prisoners of war and a sum of 100 talents in war reparations. Most importantly for Rome, it now had a secure base in eastern Sicily from which to launch any future offensive.[68]

For Carthage the loss of Syracuse was a blow, but not a devastating one. After all, its alliance with the city had always been based on convenience, and it had long been a major competitor on the island. In fact it was the second-century-AD historian, and former Roman consul, Cassius Dio who appears to have best understood the underlying reasons for the outbreak of hostilities between the two powers:

> As a matter of fact, the Carthaginians, who had long been powerful, and the Romans, who were now growing more rapidly stronger, kept viewing each other with jealousy; and they were led into war partly by the desire of continually acquiring more – in accordance with the instinct of the majority of mankind, most active when they are most successful – and partly also by fear. Both sides alike thought that the one sure hope for their holdings lay in obtaining also those of others. If there had been no other reason, it was most difficult, if not impossible, for two free peoples, powerful and proud, and separated from each other by a very short distance considering the swiftness of the voyage, to rule alien tribes and yet be willing to keep their hands off each other. But it was a chance incident of the following nature that broke their truce and plunged them into war.[69]

Most probably there was little political will on either side for war. But equally there was seemingly little will to stop the progression towards full-scale conflict. While Carthage was most probably now not a Roman target, it is difficult to read Rome's intervention on the side of the Mamertines as anything less than a desire to be more closely involved in Sicilian affairs.[70] Roman ambitions most likely now looked not to North Africa but to Syracuse, control over which might be justified as an extension of Roman military policy in southern Italy.[71] Indeed, by this period the Roman people's appreciation of the material benefits of conquest had become highly developed, as had the connection between the winning of military glory and elite status. Combined, these two motivations made for an ominous mix, and fears of a Carthaginian backlash may have been dampened by Carthaginian military complacency and the failure of Carthage's navy to repel the Romans from the Strait of Messina.

The aggressive and acquisitive nature of Rome had been undeniably proven by its conquest of Italy.[72] Yet, as Rome expanded its territory through its own aggression, it increasingly came to fear the greater proximity of its larger neighbours. The possibility that Carthage might intervene in southern Italy was probably a very real concern, fed by insecurities over Rome's recent experience with Pyrrhus.[73]

For their part, however, the Carthaginians were probably concerned less about attacking southern Italy than with defending their territory in Sicily. Their original involvement there had been prompted by the pragmatic desire to control the lucrative Tyrrhenian and Ionian trade routes. However, after 150 years of a Carthaginian presence on the island, there was now a strong sense that Punic Sicily was *their* land, that Lilybaeum, Panormus and Solus were as Carthaginian as the farms of the Cap Bon peninsula or the olive groves of the Sahel. When war did break out, the pro-Carthaginian historian Philinus would accuse the Romans of breaking a treaty signed sometime after the 348 accord which explicitly debarred them from interference in Sicily, although Polybius, who claimed to have researched all such treaties, would hotly deny that such a treaty existed.[74] Whether that treaty existed or not, the claim of Philinus nonetheless demonstrates that Roman interference in Sicily was, for the Carthaginians, a legitimate cause for war.[75]

Initially, therefore, neither Rome nor Carthage planned to attack the other, but the respective strategies of Italian expansion and Sicilian defence boded ill for the maintenance of peace.[76] In fact the main antagonists of the First Punic War drifted into the conflict less for reasons of grand strategy, and more for the lack of political will to prevent it.[77] Those who predicted that this dispute would be settled swiftly with honours shared would prove hopelessly wrong. It was no accident that Timaeus chose to end his history in 264 BC with the start of the First Punic War. Looking back on events, he knew that the central-Mediterranean world was about to change for ever.[78]

7

The First Punic War

CARTHAGE RULES THE WAVES

As Carthage's stock as the pre-eminent power in the central Mediterranean had fallen ever lower, one arm of its military still remained with its exalted reputation intact. The Hellenistic kings may have built ever larger and more pointless ships, but everyone in the Mediterranean world in the early third century BC knew that Carthage ruled the waves. Yet it had been a very long time since that much-vaunted maritime supremacy had really been tested. Apart from a few minor skirmishes, the Sicilian wars had produced little in the way of naval warfare. But nothing about Rome – a land power with virtually no fleet of its own – suggested any challenge to Carthage's navy.

In all its dealings with Carthage after the defeat of Pyrrhus, Rome clearly considered itself to be an equal. Only in one area did this Roman perception of parity with Carthage not exist: the sea. Polybius described the Carthaginian position at the beginning of the First Punic War as one of 'undisputed command of the sea'.[1] The Carthaginians had been the pacesetters in naval technological innovation throughout the fourth century BC. They had been the first to develop the quadrireme, which was both bigger and more powerful than the trireme, the ship that had dominated naval warfare for the previous 200 years. Indeed, a veritable arms race developed, with different Mediterranean powers vying with each other to develop larger and larger warships, to the extent that some of these craft were so huge that they were of no use at all for naval warfare.[2]

However, the quadrireme was fairly quickly replaced by the larger quinquereme, which was first developed under the aegis of Carthage's old enemy Dionysius of Syracuse. The quinquereme (from the Latin for 'five', *quinque*) took its Roman name from the number of men required to power each section of it: two pairs of men operated the upper two tiers of oars, while a single man operated the lower. Although they were not the original inventors of the quinquereme, the Carthaginians quickly adopted it and did much to improve its original design. It is thought that one of these innovations was to house all three levels of oars and their rowers in a single oar box that projected from the hull. This meant that the hull was exceptionally wide and could also be strengthened.[3]

These innovations were particularly important for contemporary naval warfare, in which the two main aggressive tactics were boarding and ramming. The latter involved driving the ram, a long blunt-headed metal implement that was fixed to the ship's keel, into the side of the enemy ship, so that it would start taking in water and be abandoned or taken or sink. The reinforced hulls of the Carthaginian quinqueremes gave them extra protection from ramming, but made what was already a difficult manoeuvre even trickier to complete successfully themselves. In fact the size of the quinquereme made it too unwieldy for this tactic to be really effective.[4] Increasingly, war fleets tended to rely on securing themselves to enemy ships with grappling hooks before boarding parties attempted to overpower the enemy crew. Once again the quinquereme offered an advantage for this form of combat, because its wide deck could accommodate a larger number of marines for hand-to-hand fighting.

Marine archaeologists have found the remains of several Carthaginian ships dating to this period, of which one in particular, found lying on the seabed just off Marsala on the west coast of Sicily, has excited much interest. It was a small military craft in use sometime around the mid third century BC. On close inspection, archaeologists were amazed to discover that each piece of the boat was carefully marked with a letter which ensured that the complex design could be easily and swiftly assembled. The Marsala wreck had, in effect, been a flat-pack warship.[5] The excavators were also able to provide invaluable insights into the crew's diet, which appears to have consisted of preservable foods such as meat (horse, beef, venison, poultry, pork and goat) and nuts (almonds and walnuts). Wine appears to have been drunk in response to the lack of fresh water.[6]

Rome, on the other hand, although not quite the maritime virgin that Polybius (who was generally sympathetic towards the Roman cause) tried to portray it as, had very little experience of naval warfare.[7] After all, the Roman army had never fought outside the confines of the Italian peninsula. By the last decade of the fourth century the Romans had officials whose responsibility was the building and main-tenance of a small number of warships, but when this fleet had seen action against the Tarentines in 282 BC it had been soundly defeated. After that embarrassment the Romans had preferred to rely on their allies to provide shipping for troop transportation.

THE WAR ON SICILY

It was in part this tremendous inequality between respective naval strengths that lay behind Carthage's bullish attitude, despite recent reverses. If a land war on Sicily went the way of all the other Sicilian campaigns, then it would prove bloodily inconclusive, but Carthage would continue with its control of the seas. Carthage could survive, indeed prosper, indefinitely while its merchant ships had the free run of the Mediterranean. As long as there was gold and silver to pay them, there would never be a shortage of military adventurers willing to enter service in the Carthaginian army. Hence Carthage's confidence as a new army was hired and transported to Sicily after the defection of Syracuse in 263 BC.

Acragas was chosen as the new Carthaginian headquarters, owing to its strategic location as a transport hub, and the easy access that it offered to enemy-held eastern Sicily. Alert to the danger that a Carthaginian-held Acragas posed, the Roman commanders on the island quickly besieged the city. After five months, and with the defenders growing increasingly desperate, a substantial Carthaginian relief force, reported to have consisted of 50,000 infantry, 6,000 cavalry and 60 elephants, landed in Sicily. Its commander, Hanno, son of Hannibal, swiftly marched the army to Acragas.

However, any hope that the defenders of Acragas may have had of decisive action was quickly dashed. After a skirmish against the Roman forces, Hanno – who appears to have had little confidence in his as yet untried troops – simply camped on high ground nearby and waited. The ensuing stand-off dragged on for two months, until eventually even Hanno could procrastinate no longer, and prepared for open battle. In another clear sign of his lack of faith in his soldiers, he placed his elephants behind his infantry in the battle line. This meant that, when the Roman forces managed to drive the Carthaginians back, the elephants panicked and stampeded on to their own men. In the resulting rout, the Carthaginians lost not only a considerable number of men and elephants, but also the whole of their baggage train.

The commander of the Carthaginian garrison in Acragas was now left with little option but to attempt a breakout. The night after the battle, he and his mercenaries crept out of the city and escaped, according to Polybius and Diodorus, by coming up with the ingenious ruse of filling up the Roman trenches with either straw or earth so that they could safely cross. Most of the Carthaginians got away; however, the hapless citizens of Acragas were left to their collective fate. The Romans quickly took the undefended city and promptly sacked it, before selling its 25,000 citizens into slavery.[8] Diodorus would report that Hanno was eventually recalled to Carthage in disgrace for failing to relieve the city. In addition to losing his command, he was punished with the loss of his civil rights and a fine of 6,000 gold pieces.[9]

ROME BUILDS A FLEET

For Polybius this was the real turning point in the conflict, for he later claimed that it was the capture of Acragas that first alerted the Roman Senate to the possibility of forcing the Carthaginians completely out of Sicily.[10] According to Polybius, it had been decided that this could be achieved only if the Carthaginian dominance of the sea was successfully challenged. In fact the Romans had already identified their lack of a navy as a significant weakness. By 260, four years into the war, it had been decided to build a fleet of 100 quinqueremes and 20 triremes. The catalyst had been the preceding year, when the

Carthaginian fleet had started raiding the Italian coast, possibly from bases in Sardinia. There was also some suggestion that Carthage's maritime dominance had discouraged many of Sicily's coastal cities from siding with the Romans.

It appears that the Romans took as their model the Carthaginian quinquereme that ran aground and had been captured at the start of the war. New crews, made up of both poorer Roman citizens and Italian allies, were trained on land using unorthodox methods, described here by Polybius: 'Making the men sit on rowers' benches on dry land, in the same order as on the benches of the ships themselves, they accustomed them to fall back all at once bringing their hands up to them, and again to come forward pushing out their hands, and to begin and finish these movements at the word of command of the chief crewman.'[11] The boats themselves were constructed at breakneck speed, taking just sixty days to complete, perhaps by copying the Carthaginian method of construction by numbers.[12]

The new fleet was tested at sea as soon as it was completed, so that its crews could gain some experience on water before they were called on to fight. However, the new admiral, the consul Gnaeus Cornelius Scipio, anxious like all Roman aristocrats for military glory, was in no mood to wait around. In 260 BC, while at Messana with an advance guard of seventeen ships, he got news that the citizens of Lipara, the main town on the Aeolian Islands, were ready to surrender their city to the Romans. However, the Carthaginians soon received intelligence of the plot and sent a force to the city, where they trapped Scipio and his ships in the harbour. The panic-stricken Roman crews quickly showed their inexperience by deserting their ships and fleeing to the shore, where they were promptly captured, along with their commander.[13]

Unlike his Carthaginian counterparts, who would have been severely reprimanded or worse for presiding over such a debacle, Scipio's career seems to have been unaffected. After he was ransomed, a story was put about that he had actually been a victim of treachery rather than his recklessness, and he went on to hold the consulship for a second time in 254. While public honours continued, however, the more cynical members of the Roman population privately bestowed on him a mischievous new nickname – Asina, or She-Donkey.[14]

For the Carthaginian admiral, yet another Hannibal, this was clearly a good start. However, as he sailed with a reconnaissance squadron of fifty ships to locate the remainder of the Roman fleet, he suffered the misfortune of encountering it head on as it sailed towards Messana. Heavily outnumbered, many of the Carthaginian ships were lost, although Hannibal himself managed to escape.[15] The victory over the impetuous Scipio now looked like less of a triumph. Not only had he been replaced by his more competent consular colleague, Gaius Duilius, but the wait for Duilius' arrival at Messana had given the novice Roman fleet more time to train.

While they prepared for active service, the fleet became increasingly conscious of the poor construction and unwieldy nature of their hastily built ships. Polybius describes how, in order to counter these short-comings, an ingenious new device called the *corvus* ('the crow') was developed. The crow was a type of boarding bridge 1.2 metres wide and 11 metres long with a low parapet on either side. The first 3.6 metres of the bridge was made up of two prongs separated by a channel into which slotted a tall vertical pole on the deck such that the bridge could be raised up at an angle against the pole by a pulley system. When in battle, the bridge could then be released so that it fell on the enemy ship's deck. A heavy pointed spike on the underside of the bridge would pierce the timber of the deck, so that the ships were now effectively fixed together, and the Roman marines could then use the bridge to board the enemy. The beauty of this system was that it negated the Roman fleet's manifold disadvantages, particularly its lack of manoeuvrability, its slowness and the inexperience of its crews.

In a clear sign of Roman recognition that Carthage would be completely defeated only if the war at sea were won, Duilius handed over control of the Roman land forces in Sicily to his lieutenants and took personal command of the fleet. Knowing that the Romans possessed the element of surprise through their new invention, he now risked a full-scale confrontation. The Roman fleet caught up with the Carthaginians off Mylae, on the northern Sicilian coast. Polybius vividly recounts what happened next:

> The Carthaginians on sighting him put to sea with 130 ships, quite overjoyed and eager, as they despised the inexperience of the Romans. They all sailed straight towards the enemy, not even considering it even

worthwhile to maintain order in the attack, but just as if they were falling on a prey that was obviously theirs ... On approaching and seeing the crows nodding aloft on the prow of each ship, the Carthaginians were at first nonplussed, being surprised at the construction of the engines. However, as they entirely gave the enemy up for lost, the front ships attacked daringly. But when the ships that came into collision were all held fast by the machines, and the Roman crews boarded by means of the crows and attacked them hand-to-hand on deck, some of the Carthaginians were cut down and others surrendered from dismay at what was happening, the battle having become just like a fight on land. So the first thirty ships that engaged were taken with all their crews, including the commander's galley, Hannibal himself managing to escape by a miracle in a rowing boat. The remainder of the Carthaginian fleet was mustering as if to charge the enemy, but seeing, as they approached, the fate of the advanced ships they turned aside and avoided the blows of the engines. Trusting in their swiftness, they veered round the enemy in the hope of being able to strike him in safety either on the broadside or on the stern, but when the crows swung round and plunged down in all directions and in all manner of ways so that those who approached them were of necessity grappled, they finally gave way and took to flight, terror-stricken by this novel experience and with the loss of fifty ships.[16]

Duilius was rewarded for Rome's first major naval victory with a triumph and the construction of a monument, the Columna Rostrata, on which his achievements were listed.[17] According to Diodorus, the defeated Carthaginian admiral, Hannibal, escaped punishment for defeat by sending a post-battle message back to Carthage, pretending to ask if he should engage the Roman fleet. When the affirmative answer came back, he was able to claim that he was merely following orders.[18]

The victory at Mylae, although by no means decisive, emboldened the Romans to extend their field of operation to Sardinia and Corsica, where they launched a number of raids. It was one of these operations that led to Hannibal, the defeated Carthaginian admiral, being executed by his own subordinates. Zonaras, citing the historian Cassius Dio, claims that Hannibal was tricked into open water by the Roman admiral, who had planted false reports of an invasion of Africa. Hannibal had rashly chased after the Roman fleet, only to be ambushed in the fog, and with the majority of his ships sunk he took refuge with the remainder of his forces in the Sardinian city of Sulcis. According to the same source, however, his disaffected men then turned on their commander and crucified him.[19]

CARTHAGINIAN 'HIT-AND-RUN' IN SICILY

Although the sea war had been a disaster for the Carthaginians, their land forces on Sicily were doing surprisingly well. The defeat at Acragas had convinced the Carthaginian high command that they should stick to the strategy of attrition that had been such a feature of their wars against the Syracusans. Sicily's hilly terrain favoured such tactics, and the endemic violence and instability on the island meant that most of its population lived in heavily fortified towns. Indeed, the Sicilian wars between Carthage and Syracuse had mainly consisted of sieges interspersed by lightning raids.

This type of warfare did not suit the Romans. Their political system meant that their consuls/generals held their commands for only one year, so that there was considerable reason to force the pace of conflicts by decisive action. The Carthaginian generals, who were often kept in post for years, could afford to play a waiting game. Thus, in the land war at least, Carthage was able to dictate the pace and style of the conflict, and the Romans could do little about it.

A protracted campaign of attrition began with the Romans having to fight for each fortified town, sustaining heavy losses along the way. Indeed, a number of long sieges ended in defeat – that of Mytistraton, for example, which had to be abandoned after seven months. As had always been the case in Sicily, both sides found themselves favoured by different political factions within each city, which led to frequent changes of allegiance (the town of Enna, for example, changed hands three times in five years). Furthermore, frustration led to the harsh treatment of captured populations, which no doubt helped the Carthaginian cause. Although smaller towns such as Camarina and Enna did fall, the larger and more strategically important urban centres, such as Panormus and Lilybaeum, stayed in Carthaginian hands. The Carthaginian forces were also able to conduct a number of hit-and-run raids.

The most successful of these, at Thermae Himerae in 260, led to the slaughter of 4,000 unsuspecting Syracusan troops, who were caught completely by surprise.[20]

In the war at sea, however, the much-vaunted Carthaginian navy chronically underachieved. After its unexpected victory at Mylae, the Roman fleet continued to perform well. Successful raids were launched against targets on Malta and the Aeolian Islands, and it scored another notable victory over the Carthaginians off Cape Tyndaris, on the northern coast of Sicily. Once more a Carthaginian admiral was at fault, underestimating the number of ships that the Romans had in reserve.[21]

REGULUS AND THE ASSAULT ON AFRICA

The lack of progress in Sicily, coupled with their surprising naval success, in 256 BC led the Romans to decide to bypass the island and attack North Africa itself. It was an extremely risky enterprise, especially as the initial crossing to Sicily marked their only previous overseas campaign. Carthage was over 600 kilometres from Rhegium (where the troops would embark), meaning that supply lines would be stretched to the limit. Throughout the voyage the fleet, especially the animal transporters, was extremely vulnerable to attack.

However, none of these concerns deterred the Roman effort, and a huge armada of 330 ships was mustered, under the joint command of the two consuls, Lucius Manlius Vulso and Marcus Atilius Regulus. The flotilla first sailed south to Sicily, where crack Roman infantry were picked up to serve as marines. Polybius informs us that 120 were assigned to each quinquereme (a total of 140,000 men). The Carthaginians had themselves assembled an even greater fleet (of 350 ships, with 150,000 men), which it is generally thought may have been intended to attack the Roman fleet and seize control of Sicilian waters, in order to land a new army.[22]

The two sides clashed at Cape Ecnomus off the southern coast of Sicily, in what was the largest naval battle of the ancient world. The Roman fleet was split into four different groups, shaped into a triangular formation with one squadron providing a rearguard. The Carthaginian fleet took on a far more conventional formation: a straight line, with the left wing angled towards the Sicilian shoreline. The Carthaginian plan seems to have been to attack the Roman formation and break it up, thereby provoking confusion. However, once again the Roman *corvi* served as the great equalizers, negating centuries of Carthaginian skill and experience.

The Carthaginian centre was the first to flee, leaving the remaining Roman ships free to assist their colleagues who were having difficulties against the Carthaginian left. Now over fifty Carthaginian ships found themselves surrounded. Some in their desperation to escape pretended to run aground in the shallows, but nothing could disguise the fact that Ecnomus was a total disaster for the Carthaginians.[23] In all, 94 of their ships had been either sunk or captured, against Roman losses of just 24.[24]

The defeated Carthaginian fleet regrouped, probably at Lilybaeum, and played for time by sending Hanno, one of its commanders, with peace terms to the Romans. According to a story told by the Roman writer Valerius Maximus and others, the Romans were said to have considered arresting the Carthaginian, but Hanno argued that if the Romans did seize him then they would be no better than the Carthaginians, and then made good his escape.[25]

Realizing that if they confronted the Roman fleet on its way to North Africa they would be at a grave disadvantage numerically, the Carthaginian commanders decided to split the surviving fleet, with Hamilcar remaining in Sicily while Hanno returned to Carthage with the larger number of ships. Meanwhile the Roman flotilla carried on to North Africa, and landed near the town of Aspis, probably the modern town of Kebilia on the Cape Bon peninsula. Quickly capturing the city, they waited for further instructions from Rome.

The order that came back from Rome was that one consul, Manlius Vulso, was to return to Italy, leaving the other, Regulus, with a force of 40 ships, 15,000 infantry and 500 cavalry. The Roman Senate was clearly not yet ready to chance everything on such a risky enterprise. For the Carthaginians, the delay and subsequent evacuation of a considerable part of the Roman force was an unforeseen boon. Hamilcar was recalled from Sicily with 5,000 infantry and 500 cavalry, and a three-man commission, made up also of Hasdrubal and Bostar, was given command of the Carthaginian forces.

By now Regulus and his army had advanced to the town of Adys (possibly the modern town of Oudna), which he put under siege. The Carthaginian army approached and built a fortified camp on a nearby hill, but this proved to be a tactical blunder, as the high ground negated the advantage that their elephants and cavalry might have given them. At the same time, it allowed them no opportunity to indulge in the hit-and-run guerrilla tactics that had worked so well in Sicily.[26]

The Romans were so confident of success that they quickly launched a dawn assault on the Carthaginian camp. The Roman vanguard was driven back by the defenders, but this advantage was soon lost when the Carthaginian troops chased the retreating Romans down the hill, whereupon they were promptly surrounded. The Carthaginian army now fled in disarray, leaving the victorious Romans to plunder their camp.

Tunes, just a few kilometres from Carthage itself, was the next city to fall to Regulus. Carthage was now crammed with refugees from the surrounding area fleeing not only the Romans but also Numidian attacks. Soon famine set in.

At this point there seems to have been peace negotiations between the two sides, although it is not clear who made the first overture. Polybius reports that it was Regulus, who was anxious to secure a triumphal victory before his term of office came to an end. Other sources, among them Diodorus and Livy, are equally adamant that it was a Carthaginian initiative, in a bid to avoid complete destruction. In fact the terms put forward by Regulus were so harsh that they were completely unacceptable to the Carthaginians. The Roman general demanded total Carthaginian withdrawal from Sicily and Sardinia, the release of all Roman prisoners, the paying of ransoms for all Carthaginian captives, the payment of all Rome's war expenses, and an annual tribute. Furthermore Carthage would be allowed to make war or peace only with Roman consent, it would be permitted to retain only one warship for itself, and it would be expected to supply Rome with fifty triremes whenever Rome requested them. The terms themselves are a clear indication of how confident Regulus was of inflicting a decisive victory. Unforeseen circumstances, however, would give the lie to Roman confidence.[27]

The Carthaginians at last accepted the manifold shortcomings of their own commanders. New mercenary soldiers had been recruited in mainland Greece, and among their number was an experienced Spartan commander, Xanthippus, who quickly identified the tactical mistakes that the Carthaginian generals had made. He soon won over the high command, who appointed him to a senior advisory position overseeing the training of the troops. The army was now properly drilled under his tutelage outside the walls of Carthage, and, with morale restored, it was decided immediately to engage the enemy.

The Carthaginian force, which numbered 12,000 infantry, 4,000 cavalry and nearly 100 elephants, was deployed by Xanthippus to play upon its natural strengths. The main phalanx of the Carthaginian citizen levy was positioned in the centre, with the cavalry on the right and mercenaries on each wing. The elephants were drawn up on a single line in front of the infantry. These were intelligent tactics, because Regulus' failure to strike an alliance with the Numidians, who might have been able to supply specialist horsemen, had left the Romans short of cavalry.

Although the massed Roman infantry withstood the elephant charge, their wings were quickly overwhelmed by the Carthaginian cavalry. The battle soon descended into a slaughter, with only 2,000 Roman troops managing to fight their way to safety. The only other survivors were Regulus and a further 500 soldiers, who were captured alive. The Roman general (despite a later canard that had him sent to Rome on a peace mission before returning to Carthage to an extremely painful death when the terms were rejected) probably died in captivity.[28] Xanthippus did not remain long in Carthage to enjoy this triumph, for, aware of the jealousy that his great victory would provoke among the Carthaginian nobility, he returned home to Greece.

North Africa had been saved, but the victory was hardly decisive. Regulus' army was not large, and Rome still had plenty more troops, and ambitious senators eager to lead them. More importantly, Rome was still dominant at sea, a fact compounded by another terrible defeat when a Carthaginian fleet had attempted to stop its Roman counterpart from evacuating its remaining troops from North African soil. Out of a total of 200 Carthaginian ships, 114 were lost or captured.

After this, Carthage again benefited from outside assistance, although this time it came not from a foreign mercenary captain, but from the weather. Against the advice of their most experienced captains, in 255 BC Roman admirals had decided to show their dominance by sailing down the Punic-held south-western coast of Sicily, but the fleet was caught up in a violent storm that resulted in many ships being driven on to the rocky shore. The Roman fleet was decimated, with only 80 out of 364 ships surviving. It has been calculated that around 100,000 Romans and Italians died in this catastrophe. Although the fleet was quickly rebuilt, it was to suffer another disastrous loss in a storm on the way back from raiding North Africa in 253, in which 150 ships were lost.[29]

DÉJÀ-VU DEADLOCK

The Carthaginians nonetheless failed to capitalize on these Roman setbacks. Although in North Africa the Numidians had been brought back into line, the situation in Sicily had begun to unravel.[30] The key port of Panormus had fallen to the Romans in 254, followed by both Thermae Himerae and Lipara in 252. Compounding this growing crisis was the decision by a number of other small cities, calculating that the tide was turning against the Carthaginians, to defect to the Romans. Although Acragas had been retaken, the Carthaginian commander recognized that he did not have the forces to hold it, and simply burnt it to the ground, razing its walls and scorching its hinterland, while its citizens cowered in the temple of Zeus. A large force was sent to try to retake Panormus, but the attempt ended in debacle when Caecilius Metellus, the Roman commander, cleverly enticed the Carthaginian attackers to venture too close to the city walls.[31]

> Once the Carthaginians had got their elephants and other forces across [the river], he kept sending out skirmishers to molest them, until he had forced them to deploy their whole force. When he saw that what he had planned was taking place, he stationed some of his light troops before the wall and the trench, ordering them, if the elephants approached, not to spare their missiles, and when driven from their position they were to take refuge in the trench and, sallying from it again, shoot at those elephants which charged at them. Ordering the lower classes of the

populace to bring the missiles and arrange them outside at the foot of the wall, he himself with his maniples [divisions of legions made up of about 120 men] took up his position at the gate which faced the enemy's left wing and kept sending constant reinforcements to those engaged in shooting. When this latter force engaged with the enemy, the drivers of the elephants, anxious to exhibit their prowess to Hasdrubal and wishing the victory to be due to themselves, charged those of the enemy who were in the vanguard and, putting them easily to flight, pursued them to the trench. When the elephants charged the trench and began to be wounded by those who were shooting from the wall, while at the same time a rapid shower of javelins and spears fell on them from the fresh troops drawn up before the trench, they very soon, finding themselves hit and hurt in many places, were thrown into confusion and turned on their own troops, trampling down and killing the men and disturbing and breaking the ranks. Caecilius, on seeing this, made a vigorous sally and falling on the flank of the enemy, who were now in disorder, with his own fresh and well-ordered troops he caused a severe rout among them, killing many and forcing the remainder to quit the field in headlong flight. He took ten elephants with their mahouts, and after the battle, having penned up the others who had thrown their mahouts, he captured them all. By this exploit he was acknowledged by all to have caused the Roman army to take courage again and gain control of the open country.[32]

Twenty to thirty thousand Carthaginian troops were lost, and Metelus made sure that the elephants, which were captured alive, were the centrepiece of his triumphal parade in Rome.[33]

While the defeated Carthaginians offered up various excuses for the disaster – including the accusation that the army's Celtic mercenaries were drunk – it had nevertheless been a terrible mistake to engage the Romans in open warfare when the latter were so clearly superior. The Carthaginian authorities agreed – Hasdrubal, the commander of the army, was put to death.[34]

Since the capture of Panormus, Lilybaeum had become the chief Roman target, and in 250 a combined consular army with a fleet of 200 ships laid siege to the city. The ships were to blockade the harbour so that no reinforcements or supplies could be sent in, but in a series of daring Carthaginian missions the blockade was breached. On the first occasion 50 Carthaginian warships, loaded with supplies and

10,000 fresh mercenaries, raced into the harbour to replenish and reinforce the city. Contact with the Carthaginian commander in Lilybaeum, Himilco, was maintained through a series of smaller scale operations. Not only did these help to bring supplies into Lilybaeum, they also served as a morale-booster for its besieged population.

The star performer was a ship's captain, Hannibal 'the Rhodian', who ran the Roman gauntlet on two occasions by using the element of surprise to speed into the harbour on a strong favourable wind before rowing out under the cover of nightfall. Hannibal further bolstered his heroic reputation by stopping and challenging the pursuing Roman ships to combat, an offer which they declined. Encouraged by this bravado, other sea captains also launched similar missions, meaning that Lilybaeum received sufficient supplies and remained in contact with Carthage. Eventually, however, the Carthaginians' luck would run out, as one of their quadriremes ran aground at night on obstacles which had been laid for exactly that purpose by the Romans. Recognizing the superior speed and agility of this ship, the Romans remanned it, and used to it to hunt down other Carthaginian vessels attempting to break the blockade. The captured quadrireme would eventually snare the ultimate prize when it out-ran and captured Hannibal the Rhodian as he issued another of his proud challenges. His ship was recrewed and commissioned by the Romans to patrol the harbour. Lilybaeum was now effectively sealed off.[35]

While Roman naval power was thus in the ascendancy once more, the Carthaginian fleet enjoyed at least one success against its counterpart. In 249 BC the Roman consul Publius Claudius Pulcher – a man variously described as being mentally unstable, an arrogant snob and a drunk – decided to launch an attack on the Carthaginian-held port of Drepana. The mission got off to a rocky start when the sacred chickens used to gauge divine favour went off their feed, prompting the impetuous Claudius to throw them overboard with the pithy remark that perhaps they were thirsty. Setting out at night, the Roman fleet hugged the coast. Adherbal, the Carthaginian admiral in charge of the defence of Drepana, made the bold decision to confront the enemy in open combat, rather than endure a blockade. Claudius was apparently a poor commander, and the Roman ships do not appear to have been equipped with the *corvus*, allowing the Carthaginians to use their superior maritime skill to ram the Roman fleet. Only thirty Roman ships (including the flagship with Claudius on board) managed to escape. Claudius was later prosecuted for his part in this disaster, and heavily fined. His negligence indeed became proverbial – so much so that, according to several later writers, his sister was later punished for expressing the wish, when hemmed in by the populace on her way through Rome, that her brother would lose another battle (and thus clear the streets of Roman citizen soldiers).[36]

A further disaster quickly followed for the Romans when a fleet of 120 ships escorting 800 transport craft, bringing supplies to the Roman troops at Lilybaeum, was almost completely lost in a ferocious storm. The respective responses of the two powers were markedly different. On the model of previous wars between Carthage and Sicily, these mutual disasters would have provided a juncture at which to make peace and consolidate, but the Romans did not adhere to such diplomatic norms. While the Carthaginians did little to capitalize on Roman maritime disasters, the loss of almost their entire fleet prompted the Romans not to retreat but to redouble their efforts on land, and they soon captured the famous Carthaginian fortress at Eryx. The Roman troops at Lilybaeum continued to be supplied by overland routes, and pressure was thus relentlessly applied to a Carthage unused to such trial by endurance.

This unprecedented warfare without respite economically exhausted Carthage. The fighting in western Sicily, the capture of Panormus and, most importantly of all, Roman naval dominance must have severely disrupted its economy. Taxation from the hard-pressed cities of Punic Sicily would have been hard to collect, and the important centres of Drepana and Lilybaeum remained effectively blockaded despite desperate Carthaginian efforts to divert Roman forces by attacking Italy. In contrast, most of the Roman war effort had been paid for by Syracuse, where Hiero had been minting huge quantities of silver and bronze coinage.[37] Much of the war had been fought in western Sicily, meaning that the Syracusan economic base had remained relatively undamaged.

Most of the Carthaginian coinage during the war was minted in either North Africa or Sardinia, probably because their security could be better guaranteed.[38] The Sicilian mints produced only two series of heavy gold coins, in addition to high-value electrum and silver money, which were shipped over to Carthage during the Roman invasion of 256–255.[39] The Punic superscription on the coins, *b'rst* ('in the territory'), is probably a confirmation that the coins could be used throughout all Carthaginian territory in North Africa and overseas.[40] After this huge effort to produce the money to pay for the war effort in North Africa, Carthage appears to have succumbed to economic exhaustion. The electrum coinage that was produced thereafter contained silver of very poor quality and was often underweight.[41] Indeed, Carthaginian mercenaries in Sicily would eventually mutiny because they had not been paid. In 247 Carthage would be reduced to asking for a loan of 2,000 talents from Ptolemy of Egypt – a request that was quickly rejected.[42]

HAMILCAR BARCA AND THE END OF CARTHAGINIAN SICILY

In the same year, in an effort to break the deadlock, a new commander was sent from Carthage to take over the troops in Sicily. Hamilcar would live up to his nickname, 'Barca', which appears to have meant 'Lightning' or 'Flash'. The situation that faced him was grim. Carthage was confined to just two strongholds, while the remainder of the island was controlled by Rome and its allies. What was more, Hamilcar had few troops and no money to hire any fresh mercenaries. As one historian has recently put it, 'Realistically then, his [Hamilcar's] task was not so much to win the war as to avoid losing it.'[43]

After first bringing his mutinous troops into line by executing the ringleaders, Hamilcar was ready to make his presence felt. After a first attack on an island close to Drepana was easily rebuffed, he wisely switched to softer targets with which to boast his own prestige and his troops' morale. He launched a naval raid on the southern toe of the Italian peninsula, where there were no Roman forces. But Hamilcar Barca's real genius lay not on the battlefield, where he appears to have been a proficient but not exceptional tactician, but in knowing how to generate an appropriate public image for himself. Faced with the overwhelming military superiority of the enemy, a hit-and-run strategy was to some extent forced upon him, but that strategy nevertheless suited a man who appears to have appreciated profoundly the symbolic capital which could accrue through a series of eye-catching, if strategically pointless, raids.[44]

On the way back from the successful but ineffectual Italian expedition, he seized the height of Heircte, which most scholars now think was the mountain range centred around Monte Castellacio to the west of the Roman-held city of Panormus.[45] From this easily defended point, which had access to fresh water, pasturage and the sea, Hamilcar planned a series of lightning strikes against enemy-held territory. His initial raid on the Italian mainland delivered morale-boosting booty and prisoners; thereafter things settled down to a 'cat-and-mouse' war of attrition with the local Roman forces. By launching swift raids from his mountain refuge, Hamilcar was able to disrupt Roman supply lines and tie down a large number of Roman soldiers who could have been well used elsewhere. However, this strategy also tied down much-needed Carthaginian troops too. Thus, under Hamilcar, the Carthaginians came no closer to re-establishing their control of their old possessions on the island, let alone capturing new territory. Recognizing this, Hamilcar withdrew from Heircte in 244 BC and planned an even bolder venture: the recapture of Eryx.

Sailing in under the cover of night, Hamilcar led his army up to the town and massacred the Roman garrison there. The civilian population was deported to nearby Drepana, one of Carthage's last outposts, but curiously Hamilcar seems to have made no initial attempt to capture a further Roman garrison stationed on the summit of Mount Eryx. The town, which lay just inland from Drepana, certainly had strategic advantages, for, at over 600 metres, it provided an incomparable view over the coastal plain and the sea. Yet taking it was a odd choice, since it left Hamilcar and his force perched halfway up a mountainside between Roman forces at the top and at Panormus. The one route to his anchorage, following a narrow twisting path, only added to his problems.

In terms of military strategy, Eryx would prove as fruitless as the heights of Heircte had done. Although Hamilcar continually harried the Roman forces who were besieging Drepana, his own side suffered as many losses as his opponents. Once again Hamilcar's military strategy yielded a high profile for the dashing leader, but mixed results. At one point he was even forced to ask his Roman opposite number for a truce so that he could bury his dead. This was followed by a thousand-strong group of Gallic mercenaries in his army, fed up with the unrewarding war of attrition in which they were involved, attempting to betray Eryx and the Carthaginian army to the Romans.[46] What Eryx lacked in strategic advantage, however, it more than made up for with its strong association with those halcyon days when the Carthaginians had been the dominant force on the island, rather than a defeated contender desperately clinging on to its last few enclaves. What could be better for the burgeoning reputation of a young ambitious general than seizing back a town which the Carthaginians had held for so long and in which they had such emotional investment? Eryx was the holy site where the goddess Astarte had for centuries held sway under the protection of her divine companion Melqart.

In fact matters were soon taken out of Hamilcar's hands. In Rome, it had been decided that the only way of breaking the deadlock was to rebuild the fleet. As treasury funds were low, much of the money for this ship-construction programme had to be borrowed from private individuals. The result was a fleet of 200 quinqueremes modelled on the superior design of Hannibal the Rhodian's ship. In a conscious attempt to create a confrontation, the blockade of Lilybaeum and Drepana was tightened, thereby forcing the Carthaginians to act. It took the Carthaginians nine months to assemble a fleet of 250 ships. Although they outnumbered the Romans, the ships were poorly prepared and the crews lacked training. Furthermore, the admiral, Hanno, hardly had a distinguished record against the Romans, having presided over previous defeats at Acragas and Ecnomus.[47] The plan was to drop off supplies for the army in Sicily before taking on troops to serve as marines.

In 241 the fleet crossed over to the Aegates Islands, just to the west of Sicily, and waited for a favourable wind to carry them to Sicily itself. But the Roman fleet, already aware of their location, caught up with the Carthaginians as they were preparing to cross. For the first time, the Roman fleet had no need of the *corvi*, as it was superior in all areas of seamanship and naval warfare. The Carthaginian crews – poorly trained, with too few marines, and burdened down with supplies –

stood no chance. The Romans sank 50 Carthaginian ships and captured 70 before the remainder managed to escape.[48]

The disaster broke the Carthaginians' resolve, and they sued for peace. The terms agreed in 241 were harsh, but not unexpected. The Carthaginians were to evacuate the whole of Sicily, to free all Roman prisoners of war, and to pay a ransom for their own. Lilybaeum, which had held out to the bitter end, was surrendered to the Romans. A huge indemnity of 2,200 talents was to be paid to Rome over a period of twenty years. Lastly, neither Carthage nor Rome was to interfere in the affairs of the other's allies nor recruit soldiers nor raise money for public buildings on the other's territory. When the treaty was put before the Roman Popular Assembly to be ratified, the terms were made even stiffer. The indemnity was raised to 3,200 talents, with 1,000 due immediately and the remainder within ten years. Carthage was also to evacuate all the islands between Sicily and North Africa, but was allowed to hold on to Sardinia. Faced with ruin if the war continued, the Carthaginians had little option but to accept.[49]

There is, however, compelling evidence that the Carthaginians had begun to prepare for a future without Sicily. One of the reasons for the lack of resources to pursue the conflict against Rome in the latter stages of the war was that, astonishingly, the Carthaginians were concurrently fighting another war – against the Numidians in North Africa, and a great deal more successfully than the Sicilian campaign. Sometime in the 240s the Carthaginian general Hanno 'the Great' conquered the important Numidian town of Hecatompylon (modern Tebessa), which lay some 260 kilometres south-west of Carthage.[50] Dexter Hoyos has suggested that the capture of Hecatompylus was part of a broader campaign of territorial acquisition marshalled by Hanno, which also included the subjugation of another significant Numidian town, Sicca, approximately 160 kilometres to the south-west.[51] Was this part of a deliberate change of policy on the part of the Carthaginian ruling elite, and was it a reflection of the victory of those who wished to concentrate on Africa over those who wished to maintain the hold in Sicily?

Certainly there were interesting changes in the Carthaginian rural economy. In the third century BC the hinterland of Carthage experienced a dramatic increase both in population and in levels of agricultural production. As a result of an archaeological survey, Joseph Greene has argued that this was the result of dispossessed Punic farmers leaving Sicily and Sardinia and settling in North Africa, but there is reason to think that this reorganization of Carthage's rural territory was part of the same process as the military action against the Numidians, for it seems that some members of the Carthaginian elite had finally decided that there were easier ways to prosper than the retention of the western Sicilian ports.[52]

Trade between many of the Sicilian cities appears to have all but ceased. Local wine and agricultural products, which had previously dominated the market, were replaced by imports from Campania as Rome took control; but, even so, large numbers of amphorae from Carthage simultaneously start appearing in the archaeological record.[53] It seems that the Carthaginians were now exporting large amounts of their own agricultural surplus to Sicily, so it was paradoxically its loss that finally created the circumstances under which Carthage could profit less problematically from the island.

Apart from a brief interlude of three years during the Second Punic War, Carthage would never regain a foothold on Sicily. The Carthaginians had been defeated by an enemy who had simply refused to play by the rules of engagement which had for so long held sway on the island. The destructive march of the Sicilian wars had continued for the best part of 130 years, but it had always been punctuated by intermittent periods of peace which allowed both Carthaginians and Syracusans to regroup. However, Rome, with its extraordinary ability quickly to integrate the human and material resources of those whom it had subjugated, had proved to be a very different proposition. Such had been its ability to sustain a war effort for decades, and at a high tempo without any respite, that it had been able to exhaust the stamina of Carthage, one of the best-resourced states of the ancient Mediterranean.

Moreover, after the first year of the war any chance that the Romans might have accepted some kind of territorial division of Sicily had completely disappeared. The Syracusans, who had been relatively content to maintain a strategic stand-off, had now been replaced by an uncompromising, expansionist enemy who demanded nothing less than the total retreat of the Carthaginians from the island. The latter, despite their initial advantage particularly in terms of sea power, had simply been unable to adapt to this new challenge.

PLUS ÇA CHANGE, PLUS C'EST LA MÊME CHOSE

In other ways, the First Punic War was less of a departure from the past than later Greek and Roman historians, aware as they were that it was merely the first of a sequence of clashes between Carthage and Rome, presented it. Telling local testimony has been recently provided by a series of bronze tablets which came to scholarly attention in rather murky circumstances in the early 1980s.[54] All the inscriptions are connected to the inland Sicilian town of Entella, situated around 19 kilometres from modern Corleone. Although the script is Greek, the names of the citizens recorded on the tablets as a result of brutal turmoil during the Sicilian wars were clearly of Italian origin. In 404 the original male inhabitants of the city had been slaughtered by a group of Campanian mercenaries in the employ of the Carthaginians, who had then taken the city for themselves. The citizens of Entella mentioned on the tablets were their descendants. The tablets themselves record a series of decrees in which those who had helped the Entellans in their darkest hour were recognized and granted honorary citizenship of the city for themselves and their children. The decrees themselves were probably issued over a period of just thirty-six days sometime in the later stages of the First Punic War, to mark the refoundation of Entella after a disastrous interlude. Earlier in the conflict, the Entellans had allied themselves against the Carthaginians, who had subsequently attacked and captured the city. Many of its citizens, both male and female, had again been made captive or deported.

Among those honoured for helping the Entellans were a number of neighbouring cities which had provided military support, grain, refuge and, in some cases, ransoms for captives. There were also individuals such as a Mamertine and even a Roman official, Tiberius Claudius of Antium. It is noticeable that, even though Rome was soon to become the dominant power on the island, the tablets artfully construct a picture of this small Sicilian town as an independent city state making its own decisions and honouring its friends (among whom the Roman official is given no particular precedence). Indeed, the text suggests that we are in fact merely witnessing the fallout from the latest episode of the conflicts that had flared up on the island over the previous two centuries, with Entella having to deal with the usual brutal consequences of having to take sides in the war between two great powers. Little did the Entellans know that this episode marked the start of centuries of exclusively Roman domination.

8

The Camp Comes to Carthage: The Mercenaries' Revolt

THE HEAVY PRICE OF PEACE

Despite having been charged with negotiating Carthage's surrender, Hamilcar Barca emerged from the end of the disastrous conflict with his reputation not merely intact but enhanced.[1] In an early sign of his political astuteness, he had sent the governor of Lilybaeum, Gisco, to discuss terms with the Roman consul Lutatius, thereby distancing himself from Carthage's capitulation.[2] Hamilcar was reportedly furious that the Carthaginian Council had surrendered in such meek fashion.[3]

In fact the Council had, by its actions, probably saved him from further defeat and the steady diminution of his already overblown reputation as a military commander. Hamilcar's own actions, although undoubtedly publicly impressive, had done little to help the Carthaginian war effort, and there is little indication that he would have been a saviour if he had been given more time. But, while he skilfully avoided association with a surrender which seemed to many Carthaginians overly swift, he would not be able so adeptly to avoid the chaos that followed in its wake.

The greatest problem facing the Carthaginian government at this time was what to do with its army in Sicily. A catastrophic defeat in Sicily might have excused Carthage of its financial obligations to these men, but the fairly orderly end to the First Punic War had paradoxically put Carthage in a very dangerous situation. Its Sicilian army was more or less intact, and one of the terms of the peace was that Carthage should evacuate all its forces from Sicily. Carthage was faced with the threat of a large mercenary army returning to North Africa, and demanding to be paid.

The economic situation could not have been bleaker. At a time when revenues had been cut by the loss of Sicily and disruption in Sardinia, Carthage was expected not only to pay off the mercenaries, but also to meet the huge war reparations owed to Rome. The amount owed to the mercenaries has been the subject of much scholarly speculation, but the ancient sources are clear that the arrears were substantial, and may have amounted to as much as 4,368 talents or 26 million drachmas – an astronomical sum, which the Carthaginians could not pay easily.[4]

The best option open to the Carthaginians was to evacuate the mercenaries in a piecemeal fashion and thereby perhaps avoid negotiating a collective pay deal. Their erstwhile commander, Hamilcar Barca, washed his hands of the problem by resigning his command and quickly leaving the island. In fact the policy of shipping the mercenaries in smaller groups seemed at first to be successful. It was nevertheless soon undone by allowing the troops then to recongregate in Carthage, where they quickly began to misbehave.

Unwilling to pay the whole sum owed, the Carthaginian authorities stalled for time by paying a small proportion of what was due in order to persuade the mercenary captains to take their troops, camp followers and baggage train to the town of Sicca, a good distance from Carthage, where they should wait to receive the balance. This was a disastrous mistake. At Sicca, the troops, with time on their hands, calculated the exorbitant sums that they thought were owed them.

In Sicily, their generals, in order to maintain morale, had promised rewards that now, in defeat, could simply not be delivered. The Carthaginian envoys who arrived to negotiate the necessary pay cut, led by Hanno, were understandably given a very hostile reception when their intentions became clear, and the argument that the Carthaginians themselves were suffering under the heavy financial exactions placed on them by Rome was not received with much sympathy.[5] Furthermore, the folly of not sticking to the original plan of dealing with the mercenaries in smaller groups soon became apparent when negotiations were hampered by serious communication problems.

Polybius, who is the main source for this conflict, explains that the Carthaginian practice of hiring troops of many different nationalities was 'well calculated to prevent them from combining rapidly in acts of insubordination or disrespect to their [Carthaginian] officers'.[6] However, this inability to communicate with one another was a serious setback in this situation. As Polybius recounts:

> It was therefore impossible to assemble them and address them as a body or to do so by any other means; for how could any general be expected to know all their languages? And again to address them through several interpreters, repeating the same thing four or five times, was, if anything, more impracticable. The only means was to make demands or entreaties through their officers, as Hanno continued to attempt on the present occasion, and even these did not understand all that was told them, or at times, after seeming to agree with the general, addressed their troops in just the opposite sense either from ignorance or from malice. The consequence was that everything was in a state of uncertainty, mistrust and confusion.[7]

It was at this juncture that the rebels, sensing the weakness of their employer's position, marched en masse to the town of Tunes near Carthage itself, and there tried to increase the back pay that they were owed by adding on the cost of their equipment, horses and backdated corn rations, as well as recompense for those of their number who had been killed in service.

Now that 20,000 disgruntled mercenaries were camped just a few kilometres away from their capital city, the Carthaginians understood that they had made two major blunders. First, they should never have mustered such a large group of mercenaries in one place, when they had no citizen force to oppose them. Second, they should have held on to the wives and children of the mercenaries, to serve as hostages for their menfolk's good behaviour and as potential bargaining chips in the pay negotiations. Despite the growing mistrust between the mercenaries and the Carthaginians, both sides now sought some kind of compromise solution, and indeed the former's exaggerated claims may have been an opening ploy to obtain the best deal possible.[8]

In an attempt to retrieve the situation, the Carthaginian authorities sent food and other supplies to the mercenary camp, and envoys from the Council of Elders promised to meet all the mercenaries' demands if it was in their power to do so. It was agreed between the parties that Gisco, late of Lilybaeum, the Carthaginian commander who had successfully evacuated the mercenaries to North Africa, should negotiate with them, on the grounds that they had some trust in him.

Gisco brought money with him, and started to pay the mercenaries off. Perhaps in an effort to create divisions within the ranks of the rebels, he paid off each ethnic group separately.[9] Among the mercenaries, however, there were runaway slaves and army deserters who proved to be very difficult to deal with, because they feared retribution from the Romans. The punishment for runaway slaves under Roman law was harsh in the extreme: torture and then usually crucifixion. Many may have hoped to start a new life in Punic Sicily as soldier settlers, but the Carthaginian ejection from the island had put an end to such aspirations.[10]

UPRISING

Among these men was a Campanian runaway slave called Spendius, who did all in his power to persuade the rebels to reject the settlement. Others equally feared a deal being done with the Carthaginians, but for different reasons. Mathos, a Libyan, had taken a leading part in the disturbance and feared that, once the mercenaries had disbanded and returned to their homelands, Carthage would seek revenge on those whose home was Africa. It did not take him long to convince the majority of the Libyans in the camp that peace would not serve their future interests. Spendius and Mathos, in order to further their aim of wrecking any pay deal, called a number of meetings and, using the excuse that not all due payments had yet been made, stirred up the assembled mercenaries. Polybius relates how anyone who stood up to oppose Spendius and Mathos found himself under attack from a hail of stones thrown by their supporters.

Unsurprisingly, the argument went their way. Spendius and Mathos were appointed generals of the mercenary force, and immediately ordered the seizure of Gisco and his staff. The commanders were further able to consolidate their authority by using the funds that Gisco had brought, to meet the arrears themselves.[11] To prepare themselves for the confrontation with Carthage that lay ahead, the rebels began to cast around for allies. They did not have to look very far.

In order to fund their war effort, the Carthaginians had placed harsh exactions on their subject Libyan populations. Hard-pressed farmers were forced to hand over half their crop yields to Carthage. In the towns, taxation had been doubled without exemptions, even for the poor. Carthaginian governors were expected to strip the Libyan people of whatever they could get their hands on to meet burgeoning war costs. In order to tap into the resulting discontent, the rebels sent envoys to the Libyan towns to stir up unrest. The Libyans needed little encouragement to join the revolt. Polybius reported that such was their enthusiasm that Libyan women were willing to donate all their jewellery to the mercenaries' war fund. He estimated that around 70,000 Libyans came to join the mercenaries, increasing the number of troops available to Spendius and Mathos by threefold.[12]

Although the Libyan rebellion gave the uprising ethnic overtones, this was far more than the clash of one ethnic group against another. It is striking, for instance, that at no time did the rebels try to induce the many slaves who lived and worked in Punic North Africa to revolt.[13] The newly strengthened rebel army was made up of many different peoples. As well as Libyans, there were Ligurians, Iberians, Balearic islanders, Gauls and what Polybius terms as 'mixhellenes', a name more usually associated with Hellenized Thracian and Scythian peoples from the Black Sea region.[14] In this context the term probably refers to Campanians and inhabitants of Magna Graecia, some of whom were runaway slaves or deserters from the Roman army.

When one surveys the coinage that the rebels produced, it becomes clear that this was anything but an undisciplined rabble, for what the Carthaginians were really confronted with was a decapitated version of their own Sicilian army. The money that Gisco had brought with him was not simply distributed among the rebels, but was restruck into new coinage. By overstriking Carthaginian coinage with their own motifs, the rebel leadership sent out a bold statement of intent. What had started as a dispute over wages had become a full-blown rebellion which sought to throw off the Carthaginian yoke. The rebel forces were paid under their own authority with their own money, silver coinage that carried the Greek legend *LIBUWN* ('[coin] of the Libyans').[15] The eclecticism of the motifs used on the coinage shows that the Greek superscription 'of the Libyans' was not meant to refer to one particular ethnic group, but acted rather as an expedient umbrella for the diverse constituencies that made up the rebel force.

At the same time, the apparent inclusivity of the term 'Libyans' may have signalled that ethnically non-Libyan mercenaries now had ambitions of conquering and settling Carthaginian settlements in North Africa, rather like Campanian privateers had done in Sicily.[16] In fact the motifs used on both the silver and bronze coinage formed two quite distinctive groups. Those which portrayed agricultural themes such as corn ears and a plough were most probably aimed at the Libyans, while those that followed traditional Syracusan, southern-Italian and Carthaginian Sicilian military designs were directed at the non-Libyan mercenaries.[17]

Among the latter group of coins Heracles figured prominently, with the majority showing the standard Alexandrian portrait of the hero wearing a lionskin headdress, with a prowling lion on the reverse.[18] Despite some minor stylistic differences, it was surely no coincidence that these coins reproduced the iconography of the last series of coinage issued by the Carthaginian military authorities in Sicily in the first decade of the fourth century. Although the army had been paid with coinage from Carthage decorated with the now conventional symbols of the city – the head of Core and the horse – Heracles–Melqart had remained an important emblem for the Carthaginian army in Sicily. When the rebels began to produce their own coinage, they naturally turned to a figure who had come to represent their martial vigour. The 'camp' had truly come to Carthage.[19]

A WAR WITHOUT PITY

Ancient war was a brutal business, and the First Punic War certainly had its moments of savagery. Nevertheless, it had been the hapless Sicilian cities which had borne the brunt of such atrocities, and not the Romans or the Carthaginians themselves. Both sides had aimed largely at securing Sicily, and the total destruction of the other had not been a strategic goal. Yet, within a year of signing a humiliating peace, Carthage would be fighting for its very survival in a conflict that was brutal even by ancient standards. This conflict became a fight to the death with no mercy shown by either side. For Polybius it was *polemos aspondos* – quite simply, war without a chance of a truce.[20]

Through poor decision-making, the Carthaginians had allowed a pay dispute to escalate into full-blown rebellion, the avowed aim of which was nothing less than the overthrow of Carthaginian hegemony in North Africa. This revolt highlighted in the most harsh way just how over-reliant Carthage had become on the efforts and resources of others. The funds that Gisco had brought with him to pay off the mercenaries had probably represented the last vestiges of good-quality silver coinage left at Carthage's disposal.[21] Now the Libyan revolt had cut off another important source of revenue. Polybius, with his customary adroitness, articulated the precariousness of the Carthaginians' situation:

> Neither had they a sufficient supply of arms, nor a proper navy, nor the material left to construct one, so many had been the battles in which they had been engaged at sea. They had not even the means of providing supplies and not a single hope of external assistance from friends or allies. So it was now that they thoroughly realized how great is the difference between a war against a foreign state carried on overseas and civil discord and disturbance.[22]

Desperate times warranted desperate measures. The Carthaginians had no option but to mobilize and train a citizen army. Some money was scraped together to pay for new mercenaries, and the few ships that remained were also made ready for service. Command of this modest force was handed over to Hanno, who, like Hamilcar, had also escaped the blame for the series of debacles that had brought defeat on Carthage in the First Punic War, by winning several important military victories on the home front. This appointment soon proved a costly mistake. Polybius would judge that Hanno may have had enough talent to defeat Libyans and Numidians (who would turn and run once defeated), but an enemy of well-trained professional soldiers was a different proposition.[23]

Hanno's military expertise was no match for a well-drilled army which had spent years honing its skills on the battlegrounds of Sicily. On the rebel side one might have expected a lack of leadership skills, for the Carthaginians had always supplied their own senior officers for the Sicilian army. In fact the Libyan Mathos showed himself to be an excellent military strategist. Hanno gained the advantage of surprise by attacking the rebels while they were occupied in besieging the city of Utica, which was allied to Carthage. However, instead of capitalizing on the rebels' disarray, Hanno had then complacently gone into the city to celebrate his victory. The rebels quickly rallied, and launched an attack which caught the Carthaginians completely unawares. Killing many Carthaginian soldiers, they captured all the baggage and siege artillery that Hanno had brought from Carthage to use against them.

This sort of carelessness characterized virtually the whole campaign, with Hanno snatching defeat from the jaws of victory on several further occasions. In contrast, Mathos quickly proved a dangerous opponent. First, he divided his large army into several smaller, more mobile, forces. His aim seems to have been to try to cut the Carthaginians off from their supplies and allies. As well as besieging Utica and Hippacritae, two of the largest cities in the region, a rebel force also seized control of the head of the isthmus that Carthage was situated on, thereby effectively blocking off the city from its African hinterland, and putting it under siege. Although the Carthaginians were not yet ready to get rid of the ineffectual Hanno, Hamilcar Barca was given a small army of 10,000 men and some 70 elephants with which to try to repel the rebels.[24]

The campaign started well for Hamilcar. First he managed to beat the rebel blockade by sneaking out of the city at night with his force and fording the river Medjerda. He then captured the one bridge over the river, even though his forces were heavily outnumbered. To achieve this victory he used a tactic that his famous son, Hannibal, would later use to great effect. Feigning retreat, Hamilcar provoked the enemy into ill-disciplined pursuit. Once the enemy had completely lost their formation, the Carthaginians turned on them in battle order and a rout ensued.[25]

Over 8,000 of the enemy were either killed or captured. However, this initial morale-boosting success was followed by a near-disaster brought on by Hamilcar's impetuosity. The rebels, knowing that they stood little chance against the superior Carthaginian cavalry and elephants in open battle, used their old general's own guerrilla tactics against him. Thus Hamilcar found himself being continually harried from the foothills, making progress very difficult. Eventually, he and his army found themselves surrounded by enemy forces on a mountainous plain where they had set up camp. Total destruction loomed. Yet it was now that all those dashing but futile raids in Sicily would pay off in spectacular and unexpected style. Among the massed enemy ranks closing in for the kill was a Numidian chief, Navaras, who had long admired the Carthaginian general.[26] This high regard and other family loyalties ensured that Hamilcar and his army lived to fight another day when Navaras and his 2,000 horsemen switched sides.[27]

It was now that the war between the Carthaginians and their rebel troops was dramatically transformed into a conflict infamous for its brutality. Ironically, this butchery was provoked by an act of calculated clemency. After his surprise victory, Hamilcar had cannily offered positions in his own army to the 4,000 mercenaries whom he had captured; those who declined this overture would be set free and allowed to return home. This had the potential to break up the potentially fragile coalition between the mercenaries and the Libyans, for if the rebels knew that they could swap sides with no recriminations then this might have led to mass desertions.

Spendius, Mathos and the other rebel leaders, knowing that they would not be included in the amnesty, took a course of action that was guaranteed to ensure that their troops stayed loyal to their cause. Through persuasion and coercion, a motion was passed at a rebel assembly that Gisco and the other Carthaginian prisoners should be executed. In order that no further avenue for rapprochement with Carthage remained, the rebel leaders had the men tortured to death in the most hideous way. Their hands were cut off, they were castrated, and their legs were then broken. While they were still breathing, they were flung on top of one another in a big pit and buried alive. The rebel leaders then declared that all Carthaginian prisoners could expect the same repulsive fate. The time for compromise was now truly over.[28]

This atrocity had the desired effect, for Hamilcar responded by killing all his prisoners. Now no rebels could expect any mercy if they fell into the clutches of the Carthaginians. They had to stand and fight. There is, however, little reason to think that many of the mercenaries would have defected, for the war was going well for them, and Carthage had been hit by successive misfortunes. A number of its ships carrying essential supplies had been lost in a terrible storm, and news had then come that Sardinia, which it had held for over three centuries, was in revolt. Finally and most seriously, Carthage's Punic allies began to turn against it: the cities of Hippacritae and Utica had massacred their Carthaginian garrisons and defected to the rebels.

The situation was not helped by Hamilcar and Hanno, who were long-standing political rivals, not agreeing on military strategy. Yet succour now came from the most unlikely source, for Syracuse agreed to provide much-needed supplies.[29] Polybius explained this development purely in terms of political pragmatism: for Hiero, the removal of Carthage from the central-Mediterranean power equation might have led to his status as a key strategic ally of Rome (and hence his independence) being called into question.

The response of Rome is at first more difficult to understand. During the years of the revolt, it had refused to capitalize on a number of opportunities that would have very probably led to the complete demise of Carthage as a regional power. An offer from the citizens of Utica to turn their city over to Rome was rejected. In addition, Italian merchants were banned from trading with the rebels but permitted to export vital supplies to Carthage, while the Carthaginians were even allowed to recruit fresh mercenaries from Italy.[30] This was despite there having recently been some tension between the two cities. Rome had sent an embassy to North Africa to protest after the Carthaginian authorities had arrested some 500 Italian merchants delivering supplies to the rebels. The matter had been resolved amicably, however, and as a token of goodwill the Romans had freed all remaining Carthaginian prisoners of war from the Sicilian campaigns. This release of 2,743 fighting men without ransom was an unexpected boon for Carthage, and allowed it to maintain the war effort.[31]

The reasons for Rome's supportive stance towards Carthage are complex. It has been argued that, after such a long and debilitating conflict, Rome was in no shape to embark on yet another war. Although much of the expense of the First Punic War had been met by Rome's Syracusan and Italian allies, Polybius clearly states that both Carthage and Rome were financially exhausted by the conflict.[32] In fact it is very unlikely that there was much appetite in Rome for further pressure to be brought to bear on Carthage. Much of Sicily may now have been nominally under Roman control, but two decades of war had severely damaged the local economy of the island. It would naturally take time for Rome to assert itself politically there, and it was unlikely that Rome wanted to create even more of a reputation for itself as a state that habitually supported mercenary uprisings.[33]

Outside assistance for Carthage marked a crucial turning point. The rebels now found themselves short of supplies, and were forced to raise their siege of the city. They had been previously relying on both the funds that had been collected from the Libyans and the coinage that they had seized from the Carthaginians. It was probably now, with their stocks of silver and bronze exhausted, that the rebels started using arsenic to make their debased, copper-alloy coins look like valuable silver money.[34] Hamilcar had by this time been given sole command of the Carthaginian army, after consultation with the troops. This seems to have greatly improved military performance, as decisions could now be swiftly made and executed. The policy of total war was continued, with all those rebels who were captured being trampled to death by Hamilcar's troop of elephants.

THE RECKONING

Eventually Hamilcar managed to trap the majority of the rebel army in a pass called the Saw, and, with no way in or way out, the starving mercenaries turned to cannibalism in order to survive. After eating their way through their prisoners of war and their slaves, the rebels realized that there was little chance of their comrades sending a relief force. Knowing that to stand and fight would be futile, their leadership decided to try to negotiate with Hamilcar. The Carthaginian general received ten envoys, who included Spendius and other rebel leaders. Hamilcar once again showed what a shrewd political operator he was. The terms that he offered seemed extremely mild. All he demanded was that he should be able to choose ten men from among the rebels to detain, and then the rest would be free to leave with one tunic each. The rebel leaders agreed, but Hamilcar then promptly chose them as the hostages. Thus, without breaking the sacred rules of parley, which did not permit the seizure of enemy envoys, Hamilcar managed to detain most of the rebel high command. The remainder of the rebel army, which numbered nearly 40,000 men, was quickly cut to pieces.[35]

Understandably, after this disaster the revolt began to collapse. The native Libyans saw that the tide had now turned against the rebels and deserted in droves to the Carthaginian side. Hamilcar was now free to turn his attention to Tunes, the last rebel stronghold. To dampen the morale of the besieged rebels, Spendius and the other captured leaders were brought in front of the walls and crucified in full view of their comrades. Mathos had, however, noticed that Hamilcar's co-general Hannibal, now confident of victory, was no longer guarding his own camp properly. The rebels launched a surprise attack, and not only managed to kill many of the Carthaginian troops, but also captured Hannibal himself. The unfortunate general was terribly tortured before being nailed up on to the cross which had previously held Spendius. As a macabre farewell offering to his fallen comrade, Mathos is said to have had thirty high-born Carthaginians slaughtered around Spendius' body.[36]

Chastened by this gruesome reverse, the Carthaginian leadership pulled together once more. A committee of thirty councillors was formed which managed to persuade Hamilcar and his great political rival, Hanno, to put their differences aside so that the enemy could finally be crushed. A new force was raised, comprising all the remaining citizens of military age. The rebels, depleted of men and supplies, had realized that their only chance of victory lay in throwing everything into one final battle, but their strength was spent and they were easily defeated. The Libyans were then quickly pacified. Utica and Hippacritae, fearing Carthaginian vengeance, held out for a while, but were both soon captured and forced to accept terms. All those rebels who were unlucky enough to be captured alive were crucified – all bar Mathos, who in 237 was led through the streets of Carthage in a mocking charade of the triumphal procession of which he had perhaps dreamed. As he was dragged through the city, its young men inflicted all kinds of terrible tortures on his body. Thus a war which, in the words of Polybius, 'far excelled all wars we know of in cruelty and defiance of principle' was perhaps fittingly concluded with a hideous death.[37]

THE INCREASINGLY UNACCEPTABLE PRICE OF PEACE

The hard-won victory over the mercenaries earned the Carthaginians only a brief respite from their troubles. In Sardinia, their last significant overseas possession, a mercenary rebellion every bit as brutal as the African insurrection had broken out in 240 BC. After the rebels killed Bostar, the military governor on the island, and other Carthaginians, a force was dispatched from Carthage. After arriving, however, its mercenary troops mutinied and crucified their Carthaginian general, then massacred all the Carthaginians in Sardinia.[38]

What made the situation even more precarious was that there seems to have been some coordination between the two revolts. Polybius recounts how a letter from the Sardinian mutineers was sent to the African rebels which appeared to impart information about persons in their camp who were secretly negotiating with the Carthaginians.[39] Although Polybius believes that the letter could have been a fabrication, it is possible that the mercenary troops sent out from Carthage to Sardinia may have had some knowledge of this. Alarmingly for Carthage, in 240 the mercenaries offered to hand over the island to Rome. For the time being the Romans declined this invitation, and without powerful allies the mercenaries were soon driven off the island by indigenous Sardinians. Taking refuge in Italy, they once more approached the Romans to aid their enterprise, and this time their offer was accepted.

In 238 BC Rome let it be known that it was planning an expedition to occupy Sardinia. When the Carthaginians quite justifiably objected – on the grounds that the 241 treaty recognized their sovereignty over the island – and then stated their intention to retake it, the Romans declared that they would consider this a declaration of war. Severely weakened after years of conflict, Carthage had to back down. In 237 both Sardinia and the neighbouring island of Corsica were seized, and matters were made even worse by the Roman demand of a further indemnity of 1,200 talents from Carthage.[40]

Even Polybius strongly condemned the Roman annexation of Sardinia, which was in his words 'contrary to all justice' and an action for which 'it is impossible to discover any reasonable pretext or cause.'[41] These were sharp criticisms from one of Rome's strongest supporters. Why did Rome, after initially turning down the inducements of the rebels, eventually break its own treaty and take Sardinia for itself? Later writers, perhaps buying into Roman propaganda of the time, argued that this was retaliation for Carthage's imprisonment, and in some cases execution, of the Italian traders who were caught profiteering from the Mercenaries' Revolt.[42] This seems highly implausible given the earlier amicable agreement between the two powers. The answer very probably lies in the aggressive and acquisitive behaviour that had been the hallmark of Roman foreign policy for some time, and there were a number of reasons why the Romans had now taken up an invitation that they had first refused in 240.[43]

Carthage had in 238 defeated the rebels in North Africa and could now turn its full attention to reclaiming Sardinia (indeed, a further force was being prepared under the command of Hamilcar Barca for that purpose).[44] Rome, therefore, annexed the island to prevent Carthage from reasserting itself in the central Mediterranean.[45] It should also be noted that it was the Roman Popular Assembly – a body which had already proved itself willing to take a far more hawkish attitude towards Carthage – that voted for the annexation of Sardinia.[46] The fact that the mercenaries had massacred the Carthaginians on the island before being driven out also made it easier for the Romans to present this as a simple occupation of neutral territory.[47]

The annexation of Sardinia had a seismic impact on future events. Economically, Sardinia had been a very important part of the Carthaginian zone of influence. As the Carthaginian hold on western Sicily had become increasingly insecure, Sardinian mints had increasingly taken on the production of Carthage's bronze coinage.[48] The loss of Sardinia was a blow not merely to Carthage's economic prospects, however, but also to its sense of pride. Rome's annexation of the territory and demand for indemnities were a brutal reminder that Carthage's former status as a major player in the central Mediterranean, disingenuously acknowledged in the 241 treaty just a few years before, was no more.

THE RISE OF HAMILCAR BARCA

In order to conserve its hold on power, the Carthaginian elite looked around for a scapegoat to blame for the mercenaries debacle. Hamilcar Barca, who had rashly made his soldiers promises that he could not keep, and whose military command in Sicily had been unsuccessful in meeting any of Carthage's immediate strategic aims, was the obvious candidate.[49] Yet Hamilcar's glamorous but ineffectual raids against the Romans, and his eventual defeat of the rebels, had earned him great popularity among the citizen body. Although he had been the commander of the Carthaginian armies in Sicily, and had indeed been in charge of the peace negotiations, he had not been tainted by the abrupt surrender like other members of the Carthaginian elite. As the Roman historian Livy records, he felt that 'Sicily had been surrendered too soon, before the situation had become really desperate.'[50] Hamilcar was also by far the most popular general among the Carthaginian troops – as emphatically proved when they voted for him, rather than Hanno, as their leader during the Mercenaries' Revolt.[51]

Hamilcar was also well connected to wealthy individuals who had great influence with the general citizenry, such as his new son-in-law, Hasdrubal.[52] By using his connections, he was able not only to escape attempts at prosecution, but also to obtain a military command over all Libya that was granted him by popular vote.[53] Carthaginian generals on overseas campaign had long enjoyed wide powers, and now it appears that Hamilcar would enjoy them in North Africa itself. Indeed, Hamilcar Barca appears to have been the main beneficiary of sweeping political changes in the crisis-hit state. According to Polybius, it was in this period that 'in Carthage the voice of the people had become pre-dominant in deliberations and that for the Carthaginians it was the opinion of the greatest number that prevailed'.[54]

Although many of the details remain opaque, there is no doubt that the sequential catastrophes of the defeat in the war against Rome, the loss of Sicily, near-extinction at the hands of their own mercenaries and the further loss of Sardinia had ushered in a period of profound political transformation in Carthage. The delicate balance of aristocratic, oligarchic and democratic governance, so admired by Aristotle, had relied to a large extent on the forward momentum of the overseas success that Carthage had enjoyed in the fourth century.[55] The loss of the empire was a devastating blow to that effective political status quo. The Mercenaries' Revolt had already strengthened the Carthaginian officers, who during the conflict had been heavily involved in the selection of their commander-in-chief. This now became a jealously guarded privilege, rather than a one-off piece of crisis management.

Moreover, within the mass of the ordinary citizenry or the s'rnm ('little ones') were ambitious groups who were clearly no longer willing to accept a political system that gave them so little influence.[56] Previously, some limited opportunities for social and civic advancement had existed for a select few of Carthage's non-citizen male inhabitants. (As was the norm right across the ancient Mediterranean world, no such opportunities for enfranchisement were open to the female population of the city, whatever their social status.)[57] For instance, it had been possible for some very highly valued slaves legally to gain their freedom, although they were still bound to their ex-masters by a formal set of obligations.[58] However, there is no evidence of the s'rnm being accepted into the exalted ranks of Carthage's elite.

That did not mean that they had no influence. In particular, the tradesmen and artisans, who were the most dynamic sections of the s'rnm, were extremely well organized and belonged to powerful guilds and corporations which had sufficient resources to contribute to major construction projects in the city.[59] The main political vehicle for the ordinary citizens of Carthage since at least the end of the fourth century had been the Popular Assembly, although its original powers were strictly limited. The Assembly could debate issues only when they had been expressly invited to do so by the suffetes and the Council of Elders, or when the two chief officials were in disagreement with one another. Now it appears to have acquired more influence over the decisions of the Council of Elders and the Tribunal of One Hundred and Four, including an extension of its influence over the annual election of the two suffetes. It was because of these developments that Polybius, who was vehemently unsympathetic to democracy, considered post-war Carthage as exhibiting all the worst aspects of a slow drift into demagogy.[60] Diodorus went even further in his description of Hamilcar Barca's growing political influence in Carthage: 'Later, after the end of the Libyan War, he created a political faction of the basest sort of men, and from this source, as well as from war booty, amassed a large amount of wealth; sensing that his successes were gaining him great power, he gave himself over to demagogy and to earning favour with the people.'[61]

Indeed, the tactics supposedly used by Hamilcar Barca to amass political power would have been very familiar to any of the Sicilian Greek historians (such as those used as sources by Diodorus), as they were similar to those that had been deployed by many autocratic leaders in Sicily. In Syracuse, Dionysius, Agathocles and now Hiero had all seized and maintained political power through the support of three key constituencies of the Syracusan state: the Popular Assembly, the mercenary army, and a number of the rich and influential elite. Although both Agathocles and Hiero would later proclaim themselves kings, both had initially used their appointments as *strategos autokrator* (sole commander of the armed forces) as a power base from which to gain control of the political process.[62]

The growing political influence of the Barcids – Hamilcar's clan – was further displayed when, immediately after the African command, he received permission from the Council to take an expeditionary force to southern Spain.[63] The southern and south-eastern coasts of the Iberian peninsula were certainly not unknown to the Carthaginians. Since the fourth century BC, Punic products as well as considerable amounts of Campanian and Athenian pottery had been arriving in Spain courtesy of Carthaginian merchants often operating through the Ibizan town of Ebusus. Indeed, in the second treaty with Rome, in 348, southern Spain had been listed as an area of Carthaginian influence, although there is no evidence of any direct intervention.[64] Carthage's main interest in the region, like that of Tyre before it, appears, un-surprisingly considering its huge war expenses, to have been silver.[65]

A further connection between the Iberian region and Carthage existed through the recruitment of mercenaries. On the island of Majorca there exist fortified enclosures built by the Carthaginians which archaeologists have suggested were mustering points for the famous Balearic slingers, whom the Carthaginians used to such deadly effect in their armies.[66] Hamilcar's reasons for targeting Spain were simple: it was blessed with enormous natural resources of metal ores, people and food. Indeed, the Greek geographer Strabo reported the unlikely tale that the Barcids had first become aware of the great mineral wealth in the region when they witnessed the Turdentani, the tribe on whose territory the richest mines were located, using silver feeding troughs and wine jars.[67]

Polybius and Livy, the two major historical sources for this period, agree that the dominant motivation for the Barcid expedition to Spain was to build up the necessary resources to gain revenge on Rome for recent humiliations that Carthage had suffered. But the actions of Hamilcar were probably driven as much by the need to restore Carthage's ruined economy as by any hatred of Rome. The deeply debased coinage that was minted in Carthage during this period tells a story of economic hardship and personal privation. Heavy bronze coinage was being used as a poor substitute for silver, and generally there seems to have been a dramatic drop in the amount of coinage being minted in Carthage during this period.[68]

Carthage also had a huge indemnity to pay off. One incentive for the Spanish expedition was to rescue the city from this economic quagmire, but the meeting of Carthage's punitive debts to Rome was only ever one of a number of motivations for Hamilcar's Spanish expedition. Perhaps the most crucial lesson that had been learned from the First Punic War was that any successful resistance to Rome required a huge reservoir of human and material resources. With its extraordinarily rich mines and large pool of warriors, southern Spain had the potential to supply such resources at a level that far exceeded the combined output of Sardinia and Punic Sicily.[69] This does not mean that a new war with Rome was already at the forefront of Hamilcar's thinking; nevertheless, among the Barcid faction there was already a steely determination that Carthage would never again be humiliated by Rome as it had recently been.

9

Barcid Spain

GLORY IN SOUTHERN SPAIN

For Hamilcar, the last commander of the Carthaginian army in Sicily, the expedition to Spain offered the opportunity not only to be cast as the saviour of his homeland, but also to increase the opportunities for autonomous action.[1] Despite his own supporters dominating the Council of Elders and the Popular Assembly, Hamilcar could still expect opposition from the political clique led by his arch-rival, Hanno.[2] For Hanno and his faction it was not foreign adventures but the harnessing of the huge agricultural resources of North Africa which would provide the answer to Carthage's economic woes.[3] The Greek historian Appian reports that Hamilcar defied the wishes of the Council of Elders when in 237 he set off for Spain.[4]

The Carthaginian elite had traditionally relied on two methods for managing their armies in Sicily. First, they controlled the flow of reinforcements, supplies and, latterly, money sent from Carthage. Second, the decisions and actions of their commanders were reviewed at the end of their service, and harsh punishments for mistakes could be meted out. Hamilcar would make sure that there were no such opportunities for scrutinizing his actions in Spain, for he recruited and paid his own troops. Also, Hamilcar never returned to Carthage to answer for his actions, instead relying on partisans in the Council and the Popular Assembly to speak for him. The wealth of Spain was used not only to pay off Carthage's war debts, but also to ensure the support of his army, the Popular Assembly and his own faction in the Council of Elders. Despite his absence from Carthage, Spanish gold and silver guaranteed Hamilcar's political influence by proxy.[5]

In a depressing sign of Carthage's diminished maritime status, the expeditionary force did not have the means to sail directly to Spain, as it would have done in previous times, but marched along the coast of North Africa before making the short crossing at the Pillars of Hercules.[6] Nor, once it got to Spain, could Hamilcar expect that the task that lay ahead would be an easy one. Carthage had maintained trading relations with the old Phoenician settlements of the Iberian peninsula as well as the Greeks at Ampurias, but it was not certain that Hamilcar and his army would receive a warm welcome, and the Iberian and Celtiberian tribes of the interior proved almost uniformly hostile.[7]

For Hamilcar, the lack of united political leadership in Spain may have made military campaigning easier, but it made diplomacy far harder, as an ad-hoc patchwork of individual treaties had to be agreed with the different tribal confederations and communities. Understandably, his priority was to secure control of the all-important gold and silver mines of the Sierra Morena.[8]

To start with, even those Spanish tribes who had previously cooperated with the Phoenician settlers resisted the Carthaginian advance. In his dealings with the hostile Celtiberian tribes Hamilcar exported much of the brutality of the Mercenaries' Revolt. While releasing many of the defeated enemy so that they could return home, he publicly tortured and then crucified one of the chieftains. By carefully juxtaposing clemency with this display of severe punishment, Hamilcar sent out a powerful message to the Spanish tribal leadership of the rewards of cooperation and the consequences of further resistance. This strategy soon bore fruit, as the Turdentani capitulated.[9] Hamilcar quickly set about a thorough reorganization of the mining operation. In contrast to the old Tyrian system, which had left production under indigenous control, a number of mines were taken over by the Barcids.[10]

Furthermore, in order to increase efficiency and production, new techniques were brought in from the eastern Mediterranean. Large numbers of slaves, controlled by overseers, did the manual labour. Underground rivers were redirected through tunnels and shafts, and new technology was used to pump water out of shafts. The process by which the metal ore was extracted was laborious. First the rock containing the silver ore, usually mixed with lead, was crushed in running water. It was then sieved, before going through the same process twice more. The ore was then put in a kiln so that the silver could be separated out from the stone and lead before being transported, often by river, to the main cities on the coast.[11] For the Carthaginians these mining operations were hugely profitable. Although no actual figures exist for the Barcid era, in the Roman period from the second century BC to the fifth century AD it was calculated that at any one time some 40,000 slaves toiled in the Spanish mines, producing 25,000 drachmas of profit a day.[12] Indeed, the colossal scale of both the Punic and the Roman mining operations can be ascertained by the 6,700,000 tonnes of mainly silver slag found at Rio Tinto that can be dated to those periods.[13]

For the next four years, and despite fierce local opposition, Hamilcar consolidated his hold over the coastline of lower Andalusia, and the essential Guadalquivir and Guadalete river routes, as well as pushing eastward to the coastline opposite the island of Ibiza. In order to strengthen further his control over the region, he founded a new city, Acra Leuce ('White City' in Greek), near to the modern town of Alicante.[14] As the occupation of southern Spain progressed, there is some evidence that the relationship between the Barcids and Carthage began to change. The annual military campaigns in Spain required a huge standing army of mercenaries, and one Greek historian even puts the figure at 50,000 infantry, 6,000 cavalry and 200 elephants.[15] Now that the metal mines had been brought under control and production greatly increased, the Barcids could pay their own mercenaries with their new coinage, which was of exceptional purity.[16]

A NEW KINGDOM OF HERACLES–MELQART

The first silver Barcid coins, probably minted in Gades around 237 BC, used the weight standard of the Phoenician shekel (unlike in Sicily, where the Attic drachma had been used).[17] However, in terms of their iconography these early issues displayed clear connections with the wider Hellenistic community. On the obverse they showed the head of a clean-shaven man wearing a hairband, who has been identified as the syncretistic figure of Heracles–Melqart. The portrait itself was a clear copy of one that was being used on the coinage being issued by Hiero, now king of Syracuse.[18] The Hellenistic theme continued on the reverse of this coinage issue, which featured the prow of a war galley equipped with a triple ram and a wreathed forepost ending in a bird's head, a motif used on the coinage of the Macedonian king Demetrius Poliorcetes in the first two decades of the third century BC. There may also have been a self-conscious connection with the Levantine world, however, as coinage minted in the Phoenician city of Arvad in the mid fourth century BC also displayed the head of Melqart on its obverse and a warship on the reverse.[19]

This design may have been selected simply because it would be attractive to the mercenaries in the Barcid army, or because the coin-makers were Syracusan and could therefore have reproduced it quickly from existing templates.[20] However, the subsequent emphasis that the Barcids placed on the projection and control of their image warns against such a theory.[21] As we have already seen, by this period the syncretism between Melqart and Heracles, long a hallmark of the island of Sicily, had become increasingly influential in Carthage itself, and had even come to play an important role in articulating the North African metropolis' relationship with other cities in the Punic community.

There were also more particular local concerns that may have come into consideration in Hamilcar's choice of coinage. Melqart was the patron god of Gades, but as chief deity of Tyre he also emphasized the Phoenician heritage which that city shared with Carthage. The desire to stress that association most probably explains why the god appears without his customary lionskin headdress on contemporary Barcid coinage, in accordance with local iconographic conventions.[22] At a time when the Barcids needed the support of the Phoenician cities in Spain, the promotion of an association with Melqart was thus a clever choice. At the same time, Melqart was strongly associated, through Heracles, both with the martial legacy of Alexander the Great and with the Carthaginian army on Sicily, of which Hamilcar had been the last commander. The Carthaginian military mints in Sicily had started producing silver tetradrachms with a portrait of Heracles in lionskin headdress during the last decade of the fourth century, but it is unlikely that such a design was meant merely as a copy of similar coins produced by Greek mints, or simply to satisfy the tastes of mercenaries within the Sicilian army.[23] For within a Phoenician context the Heraclean image had strong associations with Melqart, and the new coin succeeded an issue with Melqart's more traditional iconography on its obverse. Redeployed in Spain, the multivalent image of Melqart–Heracles proved an excellent and enduring emblem of Barcid power.[24]

Hamilcar's growing autonomy must have been further highlighted by Carthage's reliance not only on his mining operation, but also on his military assistance. When a serious mutiny broke out in North Africa, Hamilcar sent his son-in-law Hasdrubal from Spain with a contingent of Numidian cavalry to suppress it. The strength of the Barcid position on the Iberian peninsula was further underlined by the events that followed the death of Hamilcar in the early years of the 220s. The circumstances of his death are confused, and different stories have him variously killed on the battlefield, drowned while attempting to divert enemy pursuers away from his two sons, or killed in the panic caused by the Spaniards driving burning carts into the Carthaginian ranks.[25]

THE ESTABLISHMENT OF THE BARCID PROCTECTORATE

Traditionally, the Council of Elders should have selected his successor; however, that precedent had been ignored since the tumultuous events of the Mercenaries' Revolt. Before any decision could be made in Carthage, the army in Spain took matters into their own hands and acclaimed Hasdrubal, Hamilcar's son-in-law, as their new leader. The Popular Assembly then enthusiastically endorsed this decision.[26] Appian relates that tensions were generated when, after he had been appointed commander of the Spanish armies, Hasdrubal returned to Carthage, with the express aim of overthrowing the constitution and introducing his own monarchical rule. After the Council of Elders managed to rebuff this putsch, Hasdrubal returned to Spain in high dudgeon and henceforth ruled the Iberian dominions without taking instruction from the Council. Polybius hotly denied the veracity of this story, but

Hasdrubal's previous history of buying public support, and his subsequent actions, suggest it is true.[27]

Increasingly the modus operandi pursued by Hasdrubal in Spain came closely to resemble that of the Hellenistic kingdoms that succeeded the empire of Alexander the Great in the East. Like there, in Barcid Spain a small population of an alien elite backed up by a large mercenary army ruled over a much larger indigenous population. As in the successor kingdoms, considerable emphasis was placed on the founding of new urban centres and the replenishment of old cities in order to consolidate power over conquered territory and generate much-needed markets and transport hubs. The fiscal structure of the state also reflected a form of apartheid within it, with the coinage being divided between high-value issues for the troops and copper for the local market.[28] There were also similarities in the way that the Barcids ruled through a patchwork of alliances made with the tribal leaderships of both the peninsula and the old Phoenician cities. Like Alexander, Hasdrubal attempted to make himself more acceptable to the indigenous population by marrying

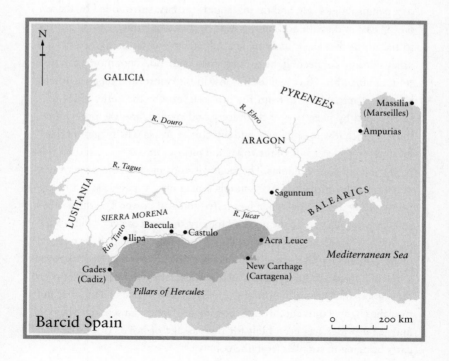

Barcid Spain

the daughter of a local king. Diodorus states that Hasdrubal was acclaimed by all the Iberians as *strategos autokrator*, a title which (as we have already seen) had strong associations with Syracusan tyranny and kingship. Most strikingly of all, Hasdrubal built a new city on the south-eastern coast of Spain. Founded in 227 BC, it carried the same name as the mother city, *Qart-Hadasht* (Carthage).[29]

This new foundation, modern Cartagena, was built to be no ordinary city. Polybius has supplied a vivid description of what it was like in his day:

New Carthage lies halfway down the coast of Spain, in a gulf which faces south-west and is about twenty stades [3.7 kilometres] long and ten stades broad at the entrance. This gulf serves as a harbour for the following reason. At its mouth lies an island which leaves only a narrow passage on either side, and as this breaks the waves of the sea the whole gulf is perfectly calm, except that the south-west wind sometimes blows in through both the channels and raises some sea. No other wind, however, disturbs it as it is quite landlocked. In the innermost nook of the gulf a hill in the form of a peninsula juts out, and on this stands the city, surrounded by the sea on the east and south and on the west by a lagoon which extends so far to the north that the remaining space, reaching as far as the sea on the other side and connecting the sea with the mainland, is not more than two stades in breadth. The town itself is low in the centre, and on its southern side the approach to it from the sea is level. On the other sides it is surrounded by hills, two of them lofty and rugged, and the other three, though much lower, yet craggy and difficult of access. The biggest of these hills lies on the east side of the town and juts out into the sea, and on it is built a temple of Aesculapius. The second is opposite it on the western side in a similar position, and on it stands a magnificent palace said to have been built by Hasdrubal when he aspired to royal power. The three other smaller eminences are to the north of the city, the most easterly being called the hill of Vulcan, the next one the hill of Aletes, who is said to have received divine honours for his discovery of the silver mines, while the third is known as the hill of Saturn. An artificial communication has been opened between the lagoon and the neighbouring sea for the convenience of shipping, and over the channel thus cut through the tongue of land that separates lagoon and sea a bridge has been built for the passage of beasts of burden and carts bringing in supplies from the country.[30]

Strategically, this Spanish Carthage was perfectly placed not only for fishing and trade, but also as a transit point for the precious silver brought from the interior. Although it is unlikely that Hasdrubal had any pretensions to become a Hellenistic-style monarch by adopting the trappings of kingship, the Barcids nonetheless added to their prestige and their aura of personal power, essential in their dealings with the leadership of the Spanish tribes and their own mercenaries, many of whom were drawn from lands where charismatic autocracy was the rule. It is also clear that the Barcids increasingly saw the Spanish territories as their own personal fiefdom, and any outside intervention, even from Carthage itself, was unwelcome.[31] This situation was only exacerbated by the economic discrepancy between Barcid Spain and Carthage. The former enjoyed an economic boom, with many settlements being enlarged in this period, and a triple-shekel coin was added to the currency, indicating that after 228 BC, when the final indemnity payment was made to Rome, there was plentiful silver in circulation. In contrast, the silver content in the bullion coinage being minted in Carthage appears to have continued to diminish, and overvalued bronze coinage was still the main currency.[32]

Indeed, when the Roman Senate, probably after receiving reports from their concerned allies in Massilia, decided to find out more about what the Barcids were doing in Spain (first in 231 and again in 226), they did not travel to Carthage, but went directly to Hamilcar and then later to Hasdrubal in Spain.[33] On the first occasion Hamilcar had stated that his sole intention was to pay off Carthage's war indemnity.[34] On the second visit, according to Polybius, the hard-pressed Romans played for time through flattery and conciliation, and an agreement was reached with Hasdrubal that the Carthaginians would not 'cross the river Hiberus [now generally thought to be the river Júcar] bearing arms'.[35]

In 221 BC the question of succession arose again, when a vengeful servant whose previous master had been murdered on the general's orders assassinated Hasdrubal in his palace in New Carthage.[36] The succession was, however, never in doubt. The Spanish army quickly acclaimed Hannibal, the 26-year-old son of Hamilcar, as their new leader, and the Carthaginian Popular Assembly then ratified the appointment.

HANNIBAL

In many ways Hannibal represented the growing chasm between Barcid Spain and Carthage. He was a product of 'the camp'. He had left North Africa at the age of 9, and his formative years had been spent among the troops on campaign in Spain. The later Roman historian Livy described the young general's martial qualities as follows:

> Power to command and readiness to obey are rare associates; but in Hannibal they were perfectly united . . . Reckless in courting danger, he showed superb tactical ability once it was upon him. Indefatigable both physically and mentally, he could endure with equal ease excessive heat or cold; he ate and drank not to flatter his appetites but only so much as would sustain his bodily strength; waking and sleeping he made no distinction between night and day; what time his duties left him he gave to sleep, nor did he seek it on a soft bed or in silence, for he was often to be seen, wrapped in an army cloak, asleep on the ground amid common soldiers on sentry or picket duties. His clothing in no way distinguished him from other young men of his age; but his accoutrements and horses were eye-catching. Mounted or unmounted he was unequalled as a fighting man, always the first to attack, always the last to leave the field.[37]

With the appointment of Hannibal, the perception that the Spanish command was a Barcid family possession was confirmed. In his account Livy emphasized the sense of resentment towards the Barcids that had built up among some of the Carthaginian political elite, in a diatribe supposedly delivered by Hamilcar's old enemy Hanno in the Carthaginian Council of Elders. Although the words are undoubtedly Livy's, the sentiments that they impart are probably genuine:

> Are we afraid that it will be too long before Hamilcar's son surveys the extravagant power and the pageant of royalty which his father assumed, and that there will be undue delay in our becoming slaves of the despot to whose son-in-law our armies have been bequeathed as though they were his patrimony?[38]

It is clear from the Barcid coinage of this period that Hannibal was keen to promote his familial links with Hamilcar. A series of silver coinage issues appeared showing a portrait of Heracles–Melqart depicted with a number of elements associated with the Greek Heracles, including a club resting on his shoulder and a laurel wreath.[39] The figure is a clean-shaven young man, and on the reverse is an African elephant. At roughly the same time a double-shekel silver coin was released which showed a similar figure with laurel wreath and club. Although this Melqart displays very similar characteristics, he sports a beard and is clearly older. On the reverse there is again an African elephant, but here with a driver on its back. These coins are a progression from earlier coins depicting Melqart, in that they attempt to associate the Barcids and the god.[40] The war elephant was a symbol that came to be increasingly linked with the Barcids during this period.

Hellenistic kings and leaders had long blurred the division between personal and divine portraiture. There often appears to be an almost deliberate ambiguity between the human and the divine in the portraits on the coins of Alexander and his successors, which bolstered the issuers' claims to divine protection and favour. In the Barcid context there also appears to be the added focus on articulating the legitimacy of Hannibal taking command as Hamilcar Barca's son. That legitimacy over the Spanish realm was further bolstered when, as his predecessor Hasdrubal had done, Hannibal married an Iberian woman, from Castulo, 'a powerful and famous city', which was in close alliance with the Barcids.[41]

Hannibal spent the first two years of his generalship mopping up opposition and expanding Barcid territory towards the north-west of Spain. He would soon prove his genius as a military commander. Not only did he storm a number of important Celtiberian strongholds, but he also showed great cunning in his destruction of a dangerous enemy force. In the spring of 220 BC, finding themselves threatened by a formidable foe, Hannibal and his army feigned retreat by crossing the river Tagus and set up camp on its left bank. The trap was now baited by leaving enough space between his trenches and the banks of the river to encourage the enemy to attack. When the enemy started to cross the river, they found themselves under attack from the Barcid cavalry. Those who managed to struggle across found forty of Hannibal's war elephants waiting to trample them underfoot. Hannibal then crossed the river with the rest of his army to deliver the *coup de grâce*. This victory was so emphatic that others now knew not to test the military worth of the young general.[42]

SAGUNTUM

Hannibal now held much of the territory north of the river Hiberus, with the important exception of the city of Saguntum, which a few years previously had reacted to the creeping northward advance of the Barcids by entering into an alliance with Rome. The Saguntines proved a useful source of information about Barcid activity in Spain, and the relationship was evidently close enough for Roman envoys to be invited to adjudicate when pro-Roman and pro-Barcid factions clashed within the city. Unsurprisingly, the Romans found in favour of the pro-Roman party, and a number of Barcid supporters were executed. The message was clear – any attack on Saguntum would be viewed in Rome as a serious provocation.[43]

Undeterred, over the next few months in 220 Hannibal slowly tightened his control over the territory around the city. Alarmed, the Saguntines sent increasingly persistent requests for assistance from their ally Rome. Eventually, after much prevarication, the Roman Senate dispatched envoys to parley with the Barcid general. Once again the Carthaginian Council of Elders was sidelined as the Roman embassy made its way directly to Spain.

The meeting that was held in the great palace at New Carthage was very different from the one six years previously, when the hard-pressed Romans had played for time by, in the words of Polybius, 'flattering and conciliating'. The young general was solemnly warned not to attempt anything that would harm Rome's ally Saguntum, as its citizens lay within Roman trust (*fides*). It was perhaps the hypocrisy of the ambassador's pious reference to Roman *fides* which riled Hannibal into retaliation. The young general retorted that Rome itself had not delayed in interfering in the affairs of Saguntum, including the driving out and execution of pro-Carthaginian members of its elite. He then bitterly turned the whole question of faithfulness back on to the Romans: 'The Carthaginians, he said, would not overlook this violation of good faith, for it was from old the principle of Carthage never to neglect the cause of the victims of injustice.'[44] Hannibal did not even deign to mention the second Roman demand, that he respect Hasdrubal's agreement not to cross the Hiberus, and he dismissed the envoys – who then sailed to Carthage to make their protests there.[45]

Hannibal's rather high-handed treatment of the Roman ambassadors surely gives an indication of his growing confidence in the Barcid position in Spain. After all, the resources at his disposal were greater than any Carthaginian general had previously enjoyed. Hannibal now controlled almost half of the Iberian peninsula, an area of roughly 230,000 square kilometres. He had inherited an excellent fighting force of 60,000 infantry, 8,000 cavalry and 200 elephants, honed by over sixteen years of campaigning against a determined and ferocious enemy. A series of alliances had been signed with the leaders of powerful Celtiberian tribes that added to his military strength. Huge mining production meant that there was enough money to meet war costs. A later Roman writer estimated that one mine at Baebelo, whose shafts ran for more than a Roman mile and half (2.2 kilometres) into the mountain, produced an enormous 135 kilograms of silver a day for Hannibal. Indeed the weight and purity of the silver coinage that was being produced for the troops was a reflection of robust economic health.[46]

It was perhaps with these great resources in mind that Hannibal now decided to defy Rome and attack Saguntum. The Saguntines resisted doggedly, and progress was very slow. They made particularly good use of the *falarica*, a type of oversized javelin, whose metre-long iron spike was bound with material covered in flammable pitch and sulphur and then set ablaze and hurled down on to the Punic attackers. Hannibal himself was wounded in the thigh by a javelin when he strayed too close to the city walls. Not long after, a new Roman embassy landed a short distance away from the Carthaginian camp, but Hannibal refused even to grant them an audience, explaining that he could not guarantee their safety and that he was in any case too busy commanding the siege.[47]

THE ROAD TO WAR

Knowing that the Roman embassy would now again journey on to Carthage, Hannibal sent messengers with a letter addressed to the heads of the Barcid party there, warning them and requesting that they prevent his opponents in the Council of Elders from making any concessions to Rome.[48] Hannibal's action here suggests that, despite the strength of the pro-Barcid faction in Carthage, he feared that some members of the Council of Elders might have been swayed by what the Roman envoys had to say.[49] When one looks at the debased coinage still being minted in the North African metropolis in this period (against the magnificent silver issues being produced in Spain), it could be argued that the beneficial effects of the Barcid economic miracle had not yet reached Carthage.[50]

There were also signs that the alternative policy of developing Carthage's African territory – the strategy that had been pushed by Hanno and his supporters – was beginning to pay dividends. Indeed, archaeological survey of Carthage's African hinterland has revealed an increase in its occupation and agricultural production levels, with considerable amounts of produce being exported from the city to western Sicily.[51] Tyrrhenian trade was also booming, with large quantities of Campanian black-glaze pottery, which was mostly used as common tableware, being found in Carthage during this period.[52] Certainly some of the more perceptive members of the Roman Senate appear to have been aware of the tensions between the Barcids and some in the Carthaginian Council of Elders, and to have actively sought to exploit those differences.[53] Hannibal was thus perhaps mindful of the importance of bringing Barcid Spain completely back into the Carthaginian fold, to remove any danger of being disowned as a renegade. Most importantly of all, however, he would have wished for the diplomatic agreements that his father and brother-in-law had entered into to be accepted and given the official authority of the Carthaginian state.[54]

In Carthage, the Roman ambassadors at last found somebody who took their complaints and threats seriously. The great Barcid opponent Hanno stood up in front of the Council of Elders and launched a blistering attack on Hannibal. In the speech that is attributed to him by Livy, the focus of his assault is not Hannibal's hatred of Rome, but rather his all-consuming ambition:

> 'I urged you', he [Hanno] said, 'and warned you not to send Hamilcar's son to the army. That man's spirit, that man's offspring cannot rest. As long as any single representative of the blood and name of Barca survives, our treaty with Rome will never remain unimperilled. You have sent to the army, as though supplying fuel to fire, a young man who is consumed with a passion for sovereign power, and who recognizes that the only way to it lies in passing his life surrounded by armed legions and perpetually stirring up fresh wars. It is you, therefore, who have fed this fire which is now scorching you . . . It is against Carthage that Hannibal is now bringing up his penthouses and towers, it is Carthage whose walls he is shaking with his battering rams. The ruins of Saguntum – would that I might prove a false prophet – will fall on our heads, and the war which has begun with Saguntum will have to be carried on with Rome.'[55]

Hanno finished with an exhortation that the siege of Saguntum should be lifted immediately, and Hannibal be handed over to the Romans. But on this occasion his words had little impact, and even his own supporters sat in silence.[56] However, we should be wary of taking this as a ringing endorsement of Barcid unilateralism. Even those councillors who were no friends of the Barcids were still political realists, and if the Carthaginian Council of Elders attempted to relieve Hannibal of his command, that decision would have to be ratified by the Popular Assembly, still very much a Barcid political stronghold.

It also remained to be seen how a man who commanded such a huge standing army and controlled the resources of an area greater than Carthage's African territories could be dismissed and detained. Such a move might momentarily appease Rome, but the Spanish territories in which so much of Carthage's hopes were invested would surely be lost for ever. The native tribes swore their allegiance to the Barcids, not to Carthage. They would certainly not meekly accept a replacement overlord from the ranks of the Carthaginian Council. Confronted by their own impotence, the anti-Barcid faction pragmatically elected to keep their counsel.[57] Hannibal's relationship with some members of the Carthaginian elite clearly remained a marriage of convenience. As the Roman historian Cassius Dio would so astutely point out, 'He was not sent forth in the beginning by the magistrates at home, nor later did he obtain any great assistance from them. For although they were to enjoy no slight glory and benefit from his efforts, they wished rather not to appear to be leaving him in the lurch than to cooperate effectively in any enterprise.'[58]

In regards to Saguntum, however, it appeared that Hannibal's calculation had paid off. Despite the later efforts of Rome's historians to conceal the procrastination, the Roman Senate debated what should be done about Saguntum until it was too late.[59] As the siege entered its eighth month, there was still no sign of a Roman relief force. The starving people of Saguntum eventually gave up hope and committed mass suicide by incinerating their town. Hannibal split the spoils of war three ways. The captives were handed over to the soldiers to be sold as slaves or ransomed, and the proceeds from the sale of all the looted property were sent back to Carthage. As for the gold and silver, Hannibal set that aside for what lay ahead.[60]

In Rome, the Senate was split between those who wanted to declare immediate war on Carthage and those who wished to send another embassy. Although Rome would be able to muster a formidable army – and, more importantly, control the seas – the senators knew that by taking on Hannibal they were now subjecting the city to considerable risk against a large and well-trained force led by an energetic and talented leader. After a debate, it was decided to send a mixed delegation of hawkish and dovish senators to Carthage. Their mission was simple: the Carthaginian councillors were to be asked whether Hannibal had acted on his own initiative or whether the attack on Saguntum had been officially sanctioned. If their answer was the former, then a request would be made that Hannibal be handed over for retribution. The latter would be treated as a declaration of war. When the Roman ambassadors were led into the Carthaginian Council, they met a united body.

The Carthaginian councillors had nominated their most talented orator (whose name is not recorded) to act as their spokesman. He contrived to give a subtle answer to the rather blunt question posed by the Roman delegation. Livy presents the speaker cleverly turning the Council's powerlessness into a virtue. He argued that the treaty that Rome had struck with Hasdrubal, in which the Carthaginian general had agreed not to cross the Hiberus, was invalid, because the Council had not been consulted.[61] On the question of Carthaginian perfidy, the tables were then neatly turned on the Romans, who had of course broken the terms of the treaty that had ended the First Punic War by annexing Sardinia. The Carthaginian spokesman followed this up with the argument that Hannibal had not broken the terms of this treaty, because Saguntum had not been a Roman ally when the treaty had been signed. To prove the point, the relevant sections of the treaty were read out aloud. This rhetorical tour de force was finished off with a searching question for the Roman envoys when he demanded that they tell the assembled Carthaginian councillors quite what Rome's intentions were.

But the Roman envoys were not interested in entering into dialogue. Fabius, their chief negotiator, stood up and pinched the cloth of his toga between two fingers so that he created a fold as a symbol of the stark choice that the Carthaginians faced, saying, 'We offer you here war or peace: choose which you please.' The Carthaginians would not be drawn, and they replied that it was for Rome to choose the course. Fabius then smoothed out the fold of his toga, and retorted that it would be war, thereby beginning perhaps the most famous conflict of the ancient world.[62]

Few scholars now accept the Polybian line that Hannibal's combative stance was the realization of his father Hamilcar's plan to marshal the resources of Spain and then renew the war with Rome.[63] It is nevertheless true that the Barcids were the main driving force in the growing tensions between Rome and Carthage. It is doubtful whether the Carthaginian Council had the political authority or military capability to force Hannibal from his confrontation with Rome, and in any case the Barcid intervention in Spain had been an economic necessity driven by the need to pay off Carthage's war indemnities and to compensate in the long term for the loss of Sicily and Sardinia. Economic stability was nevertheless as much about security as prosperity, and opposition to Rome must have been a further motivation for resistance.

At the same time, the Spanish command presented an opportunity to the Barcids not only for defence against Rome but also to attack it, and thus to restore Carthaginian military prestige, with which the Barcid self-image had been so intertwined since Hamilcar and the First Punic War. That a potential confrontation with Rome was central to Barcid thinking may be gleaned from the actual organization of the Spanish command, which revolved around little more than war and conquest, and thus military training and the acquisition of booty. Indeed, the restoration of Carthage's old central-Mediterranean empire appears to have been an important strategic aim once war was declared.[64]

The Romans, for their part, had shattered any hope of a sustained status quo with the annexation of Sardinia, and their aggressive, expansionist policy must have been well recognized in Carthage. Whether the Romans actually cared about Saguntum is debatable, judging from the protracted period that it took them to come to its defence. Renewed Roman interest in southern Spain in 220 BC probably had less to do with the protection of small allies than with concern at the growing Barcid influence in the region.[65] The capture of Saguntum gave the hawks within the Roman Senate the opportunity to press for a war which they were highly confident of winning. Even those senators who opposed the move appear to have been less concerned with the prevention of war than with Rome's potential image as an unprovoked aggressor.[66] Indeed, the last Roman embassy sent to Carthage had so presented its terms that the Carthaginian Council could not possibly have complied with them.[67] War between the two powers was now unavoidable.[68]

10

Don't Look Back

THE CARTHAGINIAN ARMY
UNDER HANNIBAL

The aftermath of the dramatic declaration of hostilities between Carthage and Rome was anticlimactic. Rome could not launch an attack, because its armies were not yet mobilized, but Hannibal was already making plans. The military strategy that was taking shape in his mind was so bold that the Romans never once considered it as a possible plan of action. Aware of the long ordeal that lay ahead, Hannibal wintered his army at New Carthage, and sent his Iberian contingents on leave. He also deployed a large contingent of his Spanish troops – 13,850 infantry, 1,200 cavalry and 870 Balearic slingers – to North Africa, to 'protect' Carthage and other cities in Punic Africa, and perhaps to ensure the continued goodwill of the Carthaginian Council. In return, a similar number of African troops were sent to replenish Hannibal's army in Spain. The defence of Spain was entrusted to his brother Hasdrubal, who was put in command of a force of foot soldiers, slingers and twenty-one war elephants. This was a case not just of protecting the peninsula from Roman attack, but also of guaranteeing the fickle loyalties of the Spanish tribes, who might take advantage of Hannibal's absence.[1]

The overland route to Italy offered Hannibal the element of surprise. It was not that the Roman commanders were not expecting an attack, but rather that they never imagined that he would try to take his army to Italy via the Alps. The consuls for 218 BC were Publius Cornelius Scipio and the equally blue-blooded Tiberius Sempronius Longus. The Roman plan was simple: Scipio, with 22,000 infantry and 2,200 cavalry, was to proceed to Spain to take the war to Hannibal. Longus,

with a combined force of over 27,000 men and a fleet of 160 quinqueremes and 20 lighter boats, was to launch an invasion of Africa.
There can be little doubt that the Roman Senate reckoned on their
Carthaginian counterparts, true to past form, hurrying to negotiate at
the first sign of real trouble. However, on this occasion, Carthaginian
nerve held, and Hannibal himself had no intention of meeting the
Roman challenge in Spain.

Historians have long pondered over Hannibal's motivations in
deciding on the arduous land route to Italy. Potential disaster lurked
at almost every step. It meant crossing the two highest mountain chains
in western Europe – the Pyrenees and the Alps – and passing, often
uninvited, through the territory of hostile tribes who did not welcome
such intrusions. This might have seemed daunting enough, even for
an army of highly trained professional soldiers, but once 12,000
extremely reluctant Spanish levies and a troop of African elephants
were factored into the equation this mission stretched the realms of
possibility.

Even though taking the overland route gave Hannibal the invaluable
advantage of surprise, it was nevertheless an incredibly risky enterprise,
born as much from a lack of viable alternatives as from buccaneering
endeavour. Carthage may have ruled the waves for over 300 years, but
since the disastrous defeat in the First Punic War the western Mediterranean had become a Roman sea. Hannibal himself was a living
embodiment of just how much the situation had changed, for it was
solely as a land general that he had earned his reputation. Indeed, the
Punic fleet in Spain at the start of the Second Punic War consisted of
only thirty-seven seaworthy quinqueremes and triremes. Between them
Scipio and Longus had over three times that number of ships. Moreover, the Romans controlled many of the bases and much of the
coastline by which any fleet would have had to pass in making its way
from Spain to Italy.[2] The brutal truth was that for Hannibal to transport his army to Italy by sea would have been even more hazardous
than the land route. There was no other option than to take his army
overland through Spain and Gaul, over the Pyrenees and the Alps and
into Italy.

What of the army itself? When describing Hannibal's troops, Polybius
made the dismissive observation that '[The Carthaginians] depend for

the maintenance of their freedom on the courage of a mercenary force but the Romans on their own valour and on the aid of their allies . . . Italians in general naturally excel Phoenicians and Africans in bodily strength and personal courage.'[3] In fact, the force that Hannibal mustered for the march to Italy was far from an inferior rabble, and Polybius himself describes a formidable command of the army overall. Its most senior tiers were made up of members of the Carthaginian elite, supplemented by a number of Numidian and Libyan commanders. At its apex was an inner circle of key advisers mainly drawn from the Barcid clan, including Hannibal's two brothers Mago and Hasdrubal and his nephew Hanno.[4] Polybius also mentions other close confidants who were not close family members, such as Hannibal Monomachus and Mago the Samnite. Despite his fame as a military leader, one of the keys to the future military success that Hannibal would enjoy was the excellence of these lieutenants, themselves excellent generals.[5]

In its diverse make-up of levies and mercenaries, Hannibal's army bore a strong resemblance to the armies of the Hellenistic world. The core of his expeditionary force consisted of experienced troops who had fought under him in Spain for a considerable amount of time. Of these, the majority of the heavily armed line infantry which Hannibal brought to Italy were Libyans from areas of North Africa which were subject to Carthage. Famous for their endurance and agility, they were equipped similarly to Roman legionaries, with large oval or oblong shields, short cutting and stabbing swords, and throwing spears. A large number of infantry also came from Spain. The Iberian peninsula supplied at least 8,000 infantry and 2,000 cavalry for Hannibal's war effort. Iberian levies from areas of southern Spain which had been pacified by the Barcids over the previous twenty years made up a large part of this contingent. Although many of the Iberian tribes had sworn an oath of allegiance to Hannibal and his predecessor Hasdrubal, their loyalty was not a given. In 218 BC Hannibal's recruiting sergeants, who had been sent to raise troops for the war against Rome, were roughed up by Oretani and Carpetani tribesmen angered at what they perceived as the Barcid general's excessive demands.[6]

The Iberian infantry wore no body armour over their national dress of a white linen tunic with purple borders, although the leather caps that they wore may have afforded some protection. They were armed with a large oval shield, throwing javelins, and swords of which the most common was the dreaded *falcata*, curved and sharpened on both sides near the point, so that its handler could inflict maximum damage by cutting and thrusting at the same time. The Iberians were joined in Hannibal's army by a small number of their wilder cousins, the black-cloaked Celtiberians and sure-footed Lusitanians, who, as they had not been conquered by the Barcids, had to be paid for their services. Hannibal's force also contained over 1,000 highly specialized mercenaries from the Balearics, who fought as slingers. These troops carried a range of different size slings and shot, depending on the range which was required. The majority of Hannibal's cavalry came from Numidia, whose two main kingdoms were Carthage's neighbours, and bound to it by alliance. The Numidians were renowned as superb horsemen, who controlled their pint-sized ponies without saddle, bit or bridle. As Hannibal's best cavalry, they would prove to be crucial on a number of occasions.[7]

These Spaniards and Africans, who had often fought for years under the Barcid standard and were tied to Hannibal by a personal bond of loyalty, provided the core of his expeditionary force. They were his most effective and exceptional troops, and Hannibal used them sparingly – only when their discipline and experience were needed.

All ancient armies required a large number of troops who were dispensable. For the Carthaginians it was the Celts, through whose lands Hannibal would have to pass on the way to Italy, who provided the necessary cannon fodder. The Celts who fought with Hannibal came mainly from the two largest tribal confederations from the Po valley in Cisalpine Gaul (now northern Italy), and they fought in large numbers at a number of key battles. At Cannae, for example, there were 16,000 Celts in the Carthaginian ranks, with a further 8,000 in reserve. Most appear to have been mercenaries recruited through diplomatic treaties agreed with their chiefs, who along with their noblemen fought as cavalrymen. The majority of the Celts of more humble status fought in the massed infantry ranks, often in the front line and armed with long swords sharpened on both sides and designed for slashing. Rather than fighting in formal regiments, war bands of retainers gathered around charismatic leaders selected for both their courage and their fighting prowess. When one looks at the equipment carried by Celtic fighters, it immediately becomes clear why they suffered such high casualties in battle. In the infantry line they appear to have worn trousers, but generally fought bare-chested. They received some protection from their long oak shields, although some sources suggest that these were very narrow and so left the warriors terribly exposed to the spears, javelins and swords of their opponents.[8]

Although Hannibal would become famous for his use of elephants in battle, it was Alexander the Great who had first introduced them into Mediterranean warfare, having encountered them while campaigning in India. His successors seem to have been equally impressed by the intimidating presence of these giant beasts, to the extent that elephants were used in ever-increasing numbers in set-piece battles. Seleucus I of Syria mobilized 480 elephants – a gift from his new ally the Indian king Chandragupta – at the Battle of Ipsus in 301 BC. It was the 'shock and awe' factor of 3 tonnes of trumpeting elephant flesh, its huge ears spread out like dark canopies, that made them such a 'must have' for most Hellenistic armies. One terracotta statuette from Asia Minor, which was perhaps a commemoration of the Seleucid king Antiochus' famous victory over the Galatian Celts in 275 BC, shows a war elephant complete with driver and howdah on its back throttling an unfortunate barbarian warrior with its trunk and impaling him with its giant tusks while trampling him underfoot. Yet other evidence throws doubt on their effectiveness as killing machines, and the Romans, for example, never considered it worthwhile to use them on the battlefield. African elephants were considered to be particularly unreliable in battle, often turning on their own side with devastating results when panicked or wounded. In an attempt to prevent this, their drivers carried a metal spike which they were expected to plunge into the soft nape of the elephant's neck with a mallet at the point when they lost control of their charges.[9]

The Carthaginians had first come across battle elephants when fighting against Pyrrhus in Sicily. They had then added elephant troops to their own military arsenal, and used them with some success both in the First Punic War and in subsequent campaigns in North Africa and Spain. For the Barcids the elephant seems to have become an emblem of their power on the Iberian peninsula: its image appears on many high-value coins minted under the authority of Hasdrubal and Hannibal.

The choice of the war elephant for battle was a fitting bridge between the martial aspirations of the Barcid clan and the great Hellenistic tradition of which these great beasts had long been a symbol. But the Barcid use of elephants differed from that of the Hellenistic kings in one important respect, for the former's elephants were not of the larger Asian or bush African variety, but the smaller, now-extinct, forest species which dwelt in the foothills of the Moroccan Atlas mountains and the Rif valley. Their relatively small size (forest elephants measured around 2.5 metres high at the shoulder, against the Asian and bush African species, which often reach over 3 metres) meant that they had to be used in different ways. There has been much academic debate over quite how Hannibal used his elephants on military campaign, other than as a way of intimidating the enemy. Recent research has suggested that, contrary to the previously held orthodoxy, Hannibal's smaller African forest elephants may have been able to carry a howdah with archers, as their larger Indian cousins did.[10]

Hannibal's greatest strength as a military commander was his ability to transform what initially appeared to be his major weakness, the lack of homogeneity in his army, to his advantage. He did not attempt to standardize how his troops fought, but used their variety as a way of offering up a diverse range of military options.[11] Indeed, flexibility was the byword of Hannibal's armies. Tactical orthodoxies were thrown to the wayside as the Carthaginian general frequently bewildered his opponents with new and often rapidly changing formations. Although since the First Punic War the Carthaginian army appears to have adopted the phalanx – the rectangular massed infantry formation that had long been a favourite in the Hellenistic world – Hannibal introduced some important modifications. The long spears and pikes, which could be used effectively only after many years of specialized training, were discarded in favour of heavy-bladed thrusting swords which could be quickly mastered by his assorted body of troops. Moreover, the heavy-infantry phalanx, though undoubtedly an effective bludgeon on the battlefield, could also be unwieldy and slow, and so was customized into a number of different tactical models, including the introduction of a hollow core with the strongest troops deployed on the wings – excellent for effecting an encirclement of the enemy.[12] Conscious of his army's shortcomings, Hannibal managed to transform them into strengths through intelligent generalship. In essence, the Second Punic War was one of the first in which the tactical awareness and abilities of its generals would override other, more conventional, military strengths such as numbers and weapons.[13]

THE PROPAGANDA MACHINE

In his comparison of the Carthaginian and Roman forces at this time, Polybius had been eager to point out what he saw as the key differences between the armies: 'Carthaginians entirely neglect their infantry, although they do pay some slight attention to their cavalry. The reason for this is that the troops they employ are foreign and mercenary, whereas those of the Romans are native of the soil and citizens.'[14] We have already seen how Polybius distinguished the Roman and Carthaginian forces – the former as composed largely of solid citizen soldiers, the latter of naturally weaker mercenaries – and how inappropriate his characterization was in respect of the Carthaginian army. For the Roman forces too his neat assessment does not stand up to scrutiny. While Polybius' description of the composition of Roman forces may well have been accurate for his own period, it did not reliably represent the situation in 218.[15] The inner core of the army indeed consisted of Roman citizens, but around half the strength of each legion was provided by various allied troops, and in a number of military engagements allied troops outnumbered their citizen counterparts.[16] These allies were divided into two broad groups: the Latins and the Italians. The former had long-standing and close associations with Rome, for many of them were descendants of Roman settlers who had forsaken their citizenship for the opportunity of a more prosperous future. Indeed, the Latin states shared much with Rome, including language, religion and political institutions, and their people enjoyed certain rights under Roman law.[17] The Italians, however, were a different matter. Many had relatively recently been compelled into becoming 'allies' of Rome, and their loyalty could not be guaranteed.

The support of the Celtic tribes in Cisalpine Gaul was therefore extremely important, particularly as the Carthaginian army would be passing through their territory.[18] These peoples were not directly ruled by Rome, and Polybius reports that, when Roman envoys attempted to gain their support after war had been declared against Carthage, the response was hardly favourable, with frequent interruptions and derisive laughter. One of the reasons that the Gauls gave for their unwillingness to come to Rome's aid was that 'they heard that men of their race were being expelled from Italy, and made to pay tribute to Rome, and subjected to every other indignity.'[19]

Another potential ally was Rome's eastern neighbour, Macedon. The king, Philip V, was a young man who had ascended to the throne in 221 BC. He had quickly proved that he possessed all the qualities required of anyone who was to make a success of ruling that restless and violent land. A ruthless political operator and shrewd military tactician, Philip had quickly become embroiled in a vicious war against the Aetolians, a powerful political confederation in central Greece. A succession of military victories soon followed, which brought him great plaudits within Greece, including the flattering title of 'darling of Hellas'. However, Philip's plans also involved securing a permanent outlet on to the Adriatic Sea. It was this particular ambition that brought him into direct contact with Rome, and to the attention of Hannibal. At the same time that Hannibal was besieging Saguntum, Rome had made its first intervention into territory which traditionally fell within the Macedonian sphere of influence. The Romans had previously attempted to maintain influence in the key area of Illyria (modern day Slovenia and Croatia) by supporting a local warlord, Demetrius of Phalerum. By 219, however, the Romans had terminally fallen out with their erstwhile ally, who had set himself up as the pirate prince of the Dalmatian coast and begun to menace Italian shipping. Rome sent a fleet to Illyria and Demetrius fled, seeking refuge with his other protector, Philip of Macedon.[20]

At the point when Hannibal was starting out upon his great expedition, therefore, several of Rome's key strategic alliances appeared insecure. Hannibal, however, needed equally to guarantee the support of the Punic world, whose enthusiasm for his venture was far from assured. Punic communities on Sicily and Sardinia would need the confidence to rebel against their new Roman masters, especially considering the inevitable high price of defeat. In Carthage, too, the continued support of the Council of Elders was a vital precondition of military success, for Hannibal required not only troops and money from North Africa, but also authority. His ability to attract the support of others required that he be seen as the representative of the Carthaginian state, not just another rootless military adventurer. Indeed, the growing influence of the Carthaginian Council of Elders on the campaign was reflected by the presence of their representatives in Hannibal's camp. Their officials – referred to in Greek as *synedroi* – accompanied the Carthaginian army in Spain and Italy, and were co-signatories to the treaty that Hannibal eventually struck with Philip in 215 BC.[21]

Faced with the necessity of continued appeal both at home and abroad, therefore, Hannibal could not rely solely upon new battlefield tactics to sustain the Carthaginian war effort. The term 'propaganda', with its apparent emphasis on the production and dissemination of a strictly controlled message, often appears out of place in the context of the ancient world, where distance and the lack of effective transport and communication systems worked against such techniques' effective deployment.[22] Nevertheless, despite such limitations, later, retrospective, accounts demonstrate a remarkable consistency in their presentation of the general, and all were based in part upon stories already in circulation at the time of the Second Punic War.[23] During that period, a body of stories developed around Hannibal which had been produced by individuals who were broadly sympathetic to his cause, or who at least saw him as a viable or necessary bulwark against the growing power of Rome. Although there was no central 'Ministry of Information' directly overseeing this artistic output, the uniformity which one finds in the way that Hannibal and his campaign against Rome were represented by his supporters suggests a studied Carthaginian interest in image and opinion.

It was Alexander the Great who had first developed this aspect of ancient warfare, as he travelled across the lands of the East not only with his well-trained armies but also with a coterie of special advisers, writers and intellectuals. Although a number of their accounts of his campaigns were written up after his death, many of the stories with which Alexander was associated, particularly in regard to the divine favour shown to him by his heroic ancestors Heracles and Achilles, were circulated while hostilities were still ongoing, as a way of encouraging friends and potential allies and demoralizing enemies.[24]

For Hannibal, the support of the Greek cities in Magna Graecia was particularly essential if his expedition was to be successful. The long and arduous march to Italy, as well as the fierce resistance that the Romans would undoubtedly put up, meant that reinforcements, supplies and bases would be sorely needed on the peninsula. He thus gathered around himself a small group of trusted confidants, including Sosylus of Sparta, his old teacher, and the Sicilian Greek Silenus of Caleacte, who both 'lived with him as long as fortune allowed'.[25] Polybius, who was generally disparaging towards Hannibal's historians, nevertheless respected Silenus, whose work he may have used as a source for Hannibal's campaigns in Spain.[26] A number of Roman writers certainly rated Silenus, and used his work extensively. Indeed, the famous Roman writer and politician Marcus Tullius Cicero was moved to comment that Silenus was a 'thoroughly reliable authority on Hannibal's life and achievements'.[27]

That Greeks should be such close associates of Hannibal is unsurprising when one considers the long-standing and close contacts between Carthage and the Greek world, particularly in Sicily. From the end of the fourth century BC considerable numbers of Greek mercenaries had fought in the armies of Carthage,[28] and there were close cultural connections. Members of the Carthaginian elite had long been educated in Greek literature, and Hamilcar had ensured that Greek tutors carefully educated Hannibal, to the extent that he had been able to write several books in the language.[29] Hannibal's knowledge of Greek was recognized by later historians as one of his great strengths. According to Cassius Dio, 'He [Hannibal] was able to manage matters . . . because in addition to his natural capacity he was versed in much Punic learning common to his country, and likewise in much Greek learning.'[30]

Little of Sosylus' work has survived beyond an account of an unidentified naval defeat which the Massilians and their Roman allies had inflicted on the Carthaginian fleet.[31] Yet even this brief fragment appears to show an anti-Roman inclination, for Sosylus gives all the credit for the victory to the Massilians. Moreover, by justifying the defeat in terms of Massilian tactical genius, Sosylus may also have hoped to deflect any criticism of Carthaginian tactics.[32] There is therefore a dismissive reaction to Sosylus by Polybius, who describes his work as nothing more than 'the common gossip of a barber's shop'. Sosylus and a fellow historian, Chaereas, appear to have stirred Polybius' indignation by reporting that, after the fall of Saguntum, the Roman Senate had long debated and procrastinated over potential courses of action, even allowing their young sons to attend the session if they swore not to divulge what had taken place there.[33] The reported episode once again reveals Sosylus' pro-Hannibalic stance, for it is clearly designed to demonstrate that some Roman senators were deeply unsure of the rectitude of their position with regard to Saguntum.

We know far more about Silenus, who was very much part of a long Sicilian Greek literary tradition that stretched back past Timaeus to the Syracusan historians of the fourth century BC. In addition to his work on Hannibal, Silenus also wrote a four-volume study of his home island, in which nuggets of topographical and encyclopedic information seem to have been interspersed throughout the text.[34] In his account of Hannibal's great journey to Italy and his subsequent campaigns there, Silenus appears to have used a similar style, with descriptive vignettes of places interspersed with accounts of the events that took place. As in Timaeus' history, the heroic figure of Heracles also featured prominently in Silenus' work, a reflection most probably of the importance of the god/hero to the Hannibalic image. In this Hannibal imitated the Molossian king Pyrrhus, whose policies while campaigning in Italy and Sicily proved somewhat prototypical for Hannibal's own. Pyrrhus, like Hannibal, also wrote several works, and members of his entourage recorded his campaigns as they travelled.[35] Like Alexander the Great before him, and Hannibal after, Pyrrhus, through a judicious mix of legend, speeches, pageantry and iconography, had successfully promoted himself as the saviour of western Hellas against Rome.[36] Within that ideological programme, the image of Achilles had proved central, for it recast the conflict as a further episode in the Trojan War. On Sicily, however, Pyrrhus had identified himself with Heracles, as one of several heroic figures through whom he had attempted to mobilize the Sicilian Greeks against the Carthaginians.[37] Hannibal's appropriation of the Heraclean image thus had a long history, but within a Carthaginian context that image was rather different, perhaps more potent, for Hannibal could appeal both to the salvific qualities of Heracles, as contained within the Greek tradition, and to his syncretistic qualities and associations with Melqart within the alternative, central-Mediterranean tradition.

A NEW HERACLES FOR AN OLD WORLD

Silenus therefore presented Heracles–Melqart as companion and guide to Hannibal and his army on the long journey that the god/hero had himself undertaken with the cattle of Geryon.[38] The similarities between Silenus' account and the work of Timaeus was not lost on Polybius, who criticized the former for suggesting that some unnamed god or hero had actually aided Hannibal, and the latter for bringing accounts of dreams and other superstitious nonsense into his work.[39] Silenus' work was, however, in many respects an explicit rejection of the Timaean position. The Heracles that appeared in Silenus' narrative, as on Hannibal's coinage, was not the Greek colonial adventurer, but the product of an equally old Sicilian tradition, the syncretistic figure of Heracles–Melqart. This strong emphasis on Hannibal's close association with the god was clearly designed to present the Carthaginian leader as the saviour of the old West, with its long history of cultural interaction between its Greek, Punic and indigenous populations. That history was now under terminal threat from a dangerous interloper, Rome. Silenus thus turned on its head the old Timaean thesis, which had used the wanderings of Heracles through the West as a vehicle for promoting a Greek–Roman cultural and ethnic axis against Carthage. Hannibal was presented as the champion of a central-Mediterranean world that had existed *before* Rome had taken the stage, and whose passing was now increasingly regretted in diverse quarters.

Among the western-Greek intelligentsia, the Timaean view had never completely held sway. One important dissenting voice had been another Sicilian Greek, from Acragas, Philinus, who had written a history of the First Punic War that was sympathetic to Carthage. Indeed, Philinus was well respected by his peers, and his work was used by a number of later scholars, including Polybius.[40] One of Philinus' main themes, which appeared in a number of later Greek writers, was that it was the Romans' acquisitiveness and greed that had led to their assistance to the Mamertines and the subsequent outbreak of hostilities with Carthage, rather than any noble desire to protect the underdog. Indeed, this may have been a commonly held view among Sicilian Greeks, who must have looked with some cynicism towards the intentions of both the Carthaginians and the Romans. Diodorus reports that Hiero, king of Syracuse, said that by coming to the help of the Mamertines 'it would be clear to all of mankind that they [the Romans] were using pity for the endangered as a cloak for their own advantage.'[41]

One identifiable theme in Philinus' history is the focus on those Greeks who had fought on the Carthaginian side in the First Punic War, which might be seen as an implicit rejection of the ethnic divisions propagated by Timaeus.[42] Many western Greeks may now have looked back with a certain nostalgia to the days when it was they who had vied for supremacy of the central Mediterranean with Carthage. Now the cities of Magna Graecia had been firmly under Roman control for over half a century. Moreover, the decades after the end of the first conflict between Carthage and Rome had definitely shown that there was to be no renaissance of Greek Sicily. Hiero's Syracuse was both prosperous and powerful, but, although it was nominally an independent sovereign realm, it was in reality little more than a Roman client state. And, after years of relatively light Roman government, in which Sicilian cities were effectively left to their own devices in the western section of the island, 227 BC saw the strengthening of Roman control with the appointment of two new praetorships, senior senatorial posts, with special authority over the islands of Sicily and Sardinia.[43]

Polybius' trenchant criticism of Rome's annexation of Sardinia from the Carthaginians (an act which, as we have seen, he described as being 'contrary to all justice' and for which the Romans had no 'reasonable pretext or cause') demonstrates that it was not well received by some in the Greek community, who must have seen it as a sign of Roman intentions to take the whole of the central Mediterranean under direct control.[44] Even in Syracuse (supposedly a staunch Roman ally), the subsequent realignment of Hiero's successor Hieronymous with the Carthaginians demonstrates a good deal of disillusionment with Rome among Sicilian Greeks.[45] Silenus' portrayal of Heracles–Melqart as Hannibal's divine companion was thus designed to send out a message to the western Greeks that it was the Carthaginian commander who represented their last opportunity to restore their diminished freedoms.[46]

The influence of Sicily on the Hannibalic propaganda campaign can also be seen in that campaign's strongly euhemeristic tenor. During the late fourth century BC the philosophical tradition of euhemerism – which maintained that gods were deified human beings, and that mythology was based on traditional accounts of real people and events – had developed on the island. The figure of Heracles had played an important role in that development, not only through his ability to transcend the boundary between humanity and divinity, but also as a powerful syncretistic figure who, through his long-standing association with Melqart and Sicilian deities, brought the diverse constituencies on the island together.[47] Indeed the euhemeristic emphasis on the permeability between the temporal and the celestial worlds would surely have been attractive to Punic as well as Greek populations, particularly in relation to the religious rites connected with Melqart. Euhemerism had thrived in the Hellenistic world, where Alexander and his successors had worked hard to blur the boundaries between the temporal and the celestial in their efforts to prove a heavenly sanction for their rule.

Now Hannibal's journey from Spain to Italy was connected with what appears to have been a euhemeristic account of Heracles' journey with the cattle of Geryon. Such euhemeristic treatments of the hero's tenth labour and return to Greece exist in two later Greek texts, of which one and perhaps both can be connected with an earlier Sicilian Greek tradition.[48] In the fuller of these two accounts, which appears in the work of the Greek teacher of rhetoric Dionysius of Halicarnassus, who worked in Rome during the last decades of the first century BC, Heracles was transformed from Greek superhero into 'the greatest commander of his age'.[49] At one point Dionysius suggests that Heracles' main aim was the subjugation of the peninsula; however, as the story unfolds it is clear that the aim is in fact the liberation of its inhabitants from tyranny:[50]

> [Heracles] marched at the head of a large force through all the country that lies on this side of the Ocean, destroying any despotisms that were grievous and oppressive to their subjects, or commonwealths that outraged and injured the neighbouring states, or organized bands of

men who lived in the manner of savages and lawlessly put strangers to death, and in their room establishing lawful monarchies, well-ordered governments and humane and sociable modes of life. Furthermore, he mingled barbarians with Greeks, and inhabitants of the inland with dwellers on the sea coast, groups which hitherto had been distrustful and unsocial in their dealings with each other; he also built cities in desert places, turned the course of rivers that overflowed the fields, cut roads through inaccessible mountains, and contrived other means by which every land and sea might lie open to the use of all mankind. And he came into Italy not alone nor yet bringing a herd of cattle (for neither does this country lie on the road of those returning from Spain to Argos nor would he have been deemed worthy of so great an honour merely for passing through it), but at the head of a great army, after he had already conquered Spain.

Dionysius then proceeds to describe how Heracles pacified the barbarous Ligurians, who had tried to block the Alpine passes so that he could not proceed into Italy.[51]

In Italy, Heracles clashed with Cacus, who in Dionysius' story was 'an exceedingly barbarous chieftain reigning over a savage people, who had set himself to oppose Heracles . . . and on that account was a pest to his neighbours. He, when he heard that Hercules lay encamped in the plain hard by, equipped his followers like brigands and, making a sudden raid while the army lay sleeping, he surrounded and drove off as much of their booty as he found unguarded.' Afterwards Cacus was besieged by Heracles' army and his forts were stormed and demolished before he himself was killed and his land given to a group of Greeks and indigenous inhabitants of the area under their respective kings Evander and Faunus.[52] Dionysius identifies one of the main reasons for Heracles' success in Italy as

his practice of carrying along with him for a time on his expeditions the prisoners taken from the captured cities, and then, after they had cheerfully assisted him in his wars, settling them in the conquered regions and bestowing on them the riches he had gained from others. It was because of these deeds that Hercules gained the greatest name and renown in Italy, and not because of his passage through it, which was attended by nothing worthy of veneration.[53]

Some obvious correspondences with Hannibal's Italian expedition immediately present themselves. First, there is the heavy emphasis on Heracles' role in defending and indeed saving states that were being attacked and taken over by tyrannical neighbours, a situation analogous to the subjugation of Magna Graecia and the rest of Italy by Rome. Second, there is the reference to uniting Greeks and barbarians under the banner of the hero, which once more reflects a central tenet of Hannibal's campaign in regard to Greeks and Carthaginians. Third, there is the focus on Heracles crossing vast rivers and cutting a route through seemingly impenetrable mountains, which are both themes that appear in the narrative of Hannibal's journey to Italy. Finally, the confrontation with Cacus, the robber chief, becomes a far more conventional ground war in the euhemeristic account, with battles and sieges, and is followed by Heracles' release of prisoners of war and their re-settlement on recently conquered land. Heracles' generous treatment of his captives mirrors similar methods later used by Hannibal to attempt to detach the Italian allies from Rome (cast here as the evil Cacus).

The numerous correspondences between Dionysius' euhemeristic story and the Hannibalic campaign are thus too obvious to be ignored, and would surely have resonated with contemporaries. While the precise origin of Dionysius' story is unfortunately unknown, an account told by Diodorus points tantalizingly towards a Sicilian origin, most probably from the period of the Second Punic War, when (as we have seen) contemporary Sicilian writers and Carthaginian coin-makers made similar associations. Hannibal's message was, however, not aimed exclusively at Greeks, for other important communities on the Italian peninsula had strong links with the hero. The cult of Hercules, the Italian interpretation of Heracles, was particularly strong in the central Apennines and Samnium, and the Samnites had a notoriously difficult relationship with Rome and might become useful allies.[54] If Hannibal took the fight against Rome to Italy, then these groups would be critical for providing bases, supplies and other logistical support, as well as much needed reinforcements.

Away from the grand narratives of trans-Mediterranean diplomacy, Hannibal's association with Heracles–Melqart served a more pressing day-to-day purpose in creating cohesion among the disparate ranks of his soldiery. The figure of Heracles–Melqart was already power-fully emblematic for the Barcid army, and Hannibal endeavoured to maintain that association between the god and his troops through the issue of large quantities of coinage bearing the god's head.[55] The fiercely contested conflict ahead, however, would naturally involve large-scale casualties and the necessary recruitment of large numbers of reinforcements – men who would need swiftly to be integrated into Hannibal's force. The multivalent symbol of Heracles–Melqart provided a potent shared symbol not only for the culturally diverse troops who already comprised the Carthaginian army, but also for potential new recruits.

The Heraclean image attributed to Hannibal by his propagandists may well have created cohesion among the Carthaginian army not only by its diverse appeal, but also by the sense of divine favour that it conveyed. An ancient-Greek military strategist, Onasander, writing 300 years after Hannibal, made the following observation: 'Soldiers are far more courageous when they believe that they are facing dangers with the good will of the gods; for they themselves are watchful, each man, and they look out keenly for omens of sight or sound and an auspicious sacrifice for the whole army encourages even those who have private doubts.'[56] As Gregory Daly has recently pointed out, 'Hellenistic armies apparently developed their *espirit de corps* based on the mystique of their leaders who could be seen as having almost "super-natural powers" as they were granted triumphs by the gods.'[57] The claim to divine endorsement was a key element of Hannibal's campaign against the Romans, and certainly played to the expectations of Hanni-bal's Celtic allies, whose chieftains were often accompanied by bards who eulogized their deeds in song.[58] In the writings of the later Roman historian Cassius Dio, the equation between successful leadership and divine sanction is made explicit. Dio attributes Hannibal's ability to predict future events to the fact that 'he understood divination by the inspection of entrails.'[59] At those critical moments when confidence in their mission had begun to ebb away from his troops, Hannibal seems to have ensured that some evidence of divine favour was presented by which the stocks of Carthaginian self-belief were replenished and the troops were reminded that they were literally following in the footsteps of Heracles and his army. Indeed, when a late-Roman military writer,

Vegetius, mistakenly claimed that Sosylus served as a military tactician under Hannibal, he was only partly wrong. The role that Sosylus and other writers within the general's circle played in propagating Carthaginian propaganda was central to the early success of the campaign.[60]

On the eve of the army's departure, Hannibal journeyed to Gades, that first great Phoenician bridgehead in the West and the supposed site of Geryon's home island of Erythia. There he made solemn vows at the altar of Melqart.[61] It appears that this episode was Silenus' work, and it is surely no coincidence that what has survived from his account is a description of the Heracleium, a sacred spring located in the sanctuary of Melqart. Thus, once more, the extent to which Heracles–Melqart, along with Hannibal, was the central character in Silenus' narrative is highlighted.[62] For Hannibal himself this visit was far more than a public display of pious devotion, for the rites that he performed in the sacred precinct marked the first steps of a carefully choreographed journey.

The Heraclean association forced home by Silenus can also be seen in another famous anecdote concerning a supposed dream of the Carthaginian general. Below is the version supplied by Cicero, which is thought to be the most accurate rendition of Silenus' original:

> The following too is found in the Greek history of Silenus, whom Coelius follows and who gave a most thorough account of Hannibal's career. Hannibal (he says), after taking Saguntum, dreamt that he was being called away by Jupiter into a council of gods; when he arrived, Jupiter ordered him to invade Italy, and gave him one of the assembly as his guide. He had begun the march together with his army, under the guide's leadership; then that guide told him not to look behind him. He could not carry that through, and borne away by desire, he had turned to look back, and saw a vast monstrous wild beast, intertwined with snakes, destroying all of the trees and shrubs and buildings wherever it went. Staggered, he had asked the god, what such a monstrous thing could be. 'The devastation of Italy,' answered the god; 'go forward and do not worry about what is happening behind your back.'[63]

Although other versions of this episode were adapted by their Roman authors to place Hannibal in a sinister and ultimately flawed light, the original story appears to have hailed from the sympathetic pen of Silenus.[64] The pro-Hannibalic tint of the initial version is indeed confirmed by the hostile reaction of the Roman writer Valerius Maximus, who described it as a 'definite prediction, hateful to any person of Roman blood'.[65] Indeed, the fact that it was so widely reported and discussed would suggest that it had a considerable impact. The main emphasis of the dream is that Hannibal has divine sanction to pursue a war with Rome, a sanction confirmed by the approval of Jupiter/Zeus and his provision of a divine guide (who must surely be Hercules/Heracles).[66] The beast that Hannibal sees wreaking the 'devastation of Italy' has been variously interpreted, but most plausibly as the Hydra, the many-headed serpent which Heracles was commanded to kill as his second labour. The problem in fulfilling that task, so it proved, was that the beast's heads would spontaneously reappear once severed – a problem eventually overcome by cauterizing the wounds to prevent regrowth.

In Silenus' tale, therefore, as Hannibal is represented by Heracles, so Rome is represented by the Hydra, the self-perpetuating monster which the western hero is called to overcome. Indeed, one of Pyrrhus' advisers had once likened Rome to the Hydra precisely for the city's extraordinary capacity for self-renewal. The original story therefore signified not only the divine sanction and Heraclean quality of Hannibal, but also Rome's monstrous nature and destruction of its allies' territory.[67] The message of Silenus' vignettes may therefore have been that the great god/hero of the old Mediterranean world had risen once more and called the faithful to muster, for now the time had come to civilize the barbarous and drive the Roman monster into the sea. Other scholars have argued that Coelius had deliberately doctored Silenus' tale, omitting an important detail about a terrible storm that appears in the versions given by Livy and Cassius Dio. They contend that Coelius' intention was to change the location of the dream from its original place – as Hannibal's army crossed the Alps – to earlier, just after the final fissure with Rome. This would mean that, in its proper context, the point of the dream was to encourage the Carthaginian army in their efforts to keep moving forward and to master the difficult conditions and terrain that faced them.[68]

Both Polybius and Livy acknowledge a Hannibalic propaganda campaign which attempted to surround the Carthaginian general with divine associations. In fact their complaints serve as confirmation of just how successful Hannibal's literary entourage had been in pushing the idea of the expedition as divinely sanctioned. As the stories of how Hannibal had tamed this wild land and its even wilder peoples multiplied, so his claim to be heir to Heracles became ever more sure. Thus Polybius condemned certain anonymous writers because

> While . . . introducing Hannibal as a commander of unequalled courage and foresight, they incontestably represent him to us as entirely lacking in prudence, and again being unable to bring their series of fabrications to any conclusion or issue they introduce gods and the sons of gods into the sober history of the facts. By representing the Alps as being so steep and rugged that not only horses and troops accompanied by elephants, but even active men on foot would have difficulty in passing, and at the same time picturing to us the desolation of the country as being such, that unless some god or hero had met Hannibal and showed him the way, his whole army would have gone astray and perished utterly, they unquestionably fall into both the above vices.[69]

Livy, in turn, has a Roman commander exhort his troops before battle against the Carthaginian general to find out 'whether this Hannibal is, as he gives out, the rival of Hercules in his journeys, or whether he has been abandoned by his father to pay tax and tribute and to be the slave of the Roman people'.[70] Indeed, the heavy emphasis that Livy places on the impiety of Hannibal throughout his account of the war is probably connected with the disquiet that the Carthaginian's association with Heracles–Melqart engendered in Rome.[71] What made Hannibal such a potent threat was not merely his military might, but the challenge that he presented to the previously successful Roman model of territorial conquest and incorporation. The relentless divine associations attributed to the Carthaginian general by his literary entourage represented something far more potent than mere self-indulgence.

Hannibal was intent on setting out a clear alternative not only to Roman political hegemony, but also to the Roman mythology by which that hegemony was justified. The Romans' own promotion of the cult of Hercules had provided a much-needed mythical and historical affirmation for the huge territorial gains in Italy and in the old Carthaginian colonial possessions in the central Mediterranean. Hannibal's appropriation of Heracles placed a large question mark over such claims. Hannibal appears to have been determined to wrest from Rome not only the military but also the propagandistic initiative. The Romans found themselves recast by Hannibal's literary entourage in a new and unfamiliar role: as the agents of a tyranny from which the great hero was destined to liberate Italy. Rome, it appeared, was the new Cacus. In attempting to unite the Punic, Greek and Italian communities under the banner of Heracles–Melqart, Hannibal was attempting to drive Rome out of the god/hero's ancient realm. Timaeus had underlined the 'historic' ties that supposedly bound the Romans and the western Greeks against the Carthaginians, but now his heirs embarked on a bold project to dismantle that proposition. From the outset, Hannibal's assault on Rome aimed not only to reduce the city's present formidable power base in the central Mediterranean, but also to undermine increasingly confident Roman claims to a distinguished past that foretold Rome's emergence as a regional superpower.

I I

In the Footsteps of Heracles

A HERACLEAN LABOUR

The enormity of the task ahead must have struck Hannibal the moment the Hiberus had been crossed. He may have received welcome messages of support from Celtic chiefs in the Alpine regions and the Po valley, to whom he had sent emissaries laden with presents, but the Spanish tribes who lived in north-eastern Spain were certainly not so well disposed towards his presence.[1] His armies met particularly fierce resistance in the foothills of the Pyrenees, resulting in heavy losses. So hostile was the reaction of the local peoples that Hannibal was forced to leave a force of 10,000 foot soldiers and 1,000 cavalry there in order to hold the mountain passes and protect his rearguard. His army was further diminished when 3,000 infantry from the Carpetani, a tribe that had been recently subdued, deserted. Realizing that they would be even more of a liability if they remained in his force, Hannibal sent away another 7,000 men whose loyalty was unsure.[2]

On crossing the Pyrenees, the situation did not improve, for the Gallic tribes who lived in south-western France, fearful of subjugation, mustered their fighting men in order to repel the Carthaginian army.[3] It is hardly surprising that some of the peoples who inhabited the region saw the Carthaginians as being far more of an immediate threat than the Romans. Full-scale conflict was averted only by the distribution of gifts.[4]

Following the line of the Mediterranean coast, Hannibal and his army passed through Gaul,[5] and by the close of August 218 they had arrived at the next great natural barrier between them and Italy: the Rhône.[6] This would be Hannibal's greatest challenge yet. The Rhône was a vast expanse of water, and on the other side waited an army of hostile Volcae tribesmen. To counter this, Hannibal sent his nephew Hanno with a detachment of his Spanish troops to cross the river 40 kilometres upstream, with the intention of attacking the Gauls from the rear. When they were in position, they would let Hannibal and the main army know by smoke signal.

The next day, as the main army started to cross the river on a flotilla of small craft and rafts, some of the horses swam across (led by long reins), while others travelled on the boats, saddled and ready to spring into action once they reached the other side. On being attacked by Hanno and his troops, however, the Volcae panicked and fled. The elephants within Hannibal's entourage nevertheless presented another problem. Most ancient writers were of the opinion that elephants were frightened of water and could not swim, and Polybius even repeated a story that some of Hannibal's elephants, panicked by the water, plunged into the river, and crossed to the other side by walking underwater on the riverbed and using their trunks as snorkels. To get their elephants across to the other bank, the Carthaginians came up with an ingenious solution. Huge rafts were constructed covered with a thick layer of earth so that the elephants would be tricked into thinking that they were still on terra firma. To encourage the bulls, two females were led on to the rafts first. Thus the whole squadron crossed safely.[7]

The crossing of the Rhône would very much set the tone for the other events which provided the narrative links in the chain of the long march to Italy. Each story had as a common theme both the conquest of seemingly insurmountable natural obstacles and the taming of wild beasts and barbarous peoples. Thus Hannibal's journey to Italy came increasingly to resemble a series of Heraclean labours. Indeed, the strong association between the expedition and the Heraclean odyssey may have injected some awkwardness into overtures towards indigenous peoples, for, while the Carthaginian general eagerly sought out their friendship in order to gain access to manpower and supplies, Hannibalic ideology placed a heavy emphasis on the pacification of the land not only as a physical barrier but also in regard to the people who lived there. Hannibal's elephants played a starring role in these adventures, and on the battlefield they would stand for the seemingly unstoppable might of the Carthaginian forces. However, the stories connected with the crossing of the Rhône and, later, of the Alps also played on the essential vulnerability of these giant beasts in unfamiliar territory. Through being able to control these formidable and mercurial creatures in even the most difficult of circumstances, Hannibal would prove himself equal even to the great Heracles, who had led Geryon's cattle over the same route.

Before embarking on his account of Hannibal's epic journey over the Alps, Polybius provided his readership with an impromptu geography lesson. In typically censorious style, the Greek historian voiced his disapproval of those fellow writers who bamboozled their audience with a daunting list of strange names. Whether they liked it or not, those who read the histories of Polybius would know exactly where Hannibal and his armies had been.[8] In addition, Polybius particularly emphasized the precedents for Hannibal's supposedly unique feat: 'Similarly in what they [other historians] say about the loneliness, and the extreme diffi-culty and steepness of the road, the falsehood is manifest. For they never took the trouble to learn that the Celts who lived near the Rhône not on one or on two occasions only before Hannibal's arrival but often, and not at any remote date but quite recently, had crossed the Alps with large armies.'[9] According to Polybius, crossing the mighty Alps was an almost mundane exercise, easily within the capabilities of a large Celtic rabble. The feat for which Hannibal was most celebrated thus became a mere cipher for barbarity. Hannibal, rather than being a new Heracles taming the wild Alps, was just one in a long line of barbarian invaders hoping to break into Roman territory.

Polybius had felt able to pass such a damning judgement on Hanni-bal's achievement because he had, according to his own account, actually visited the Alps and painstakingly gathered evidence by talk-ing to the locals, even walking some of the route that Hannibal had taken. The truth, however, was that Polybius' account of his Alpine research trip was really an indication of the gaping distance between himself and his subject. The area known as Cisalpine Gaul and Liguria had been radically transformed by the time that Polybius visited it. The 'locals' whom Polybius grilled were not the Celts who had peopled that region during the time of Hannibal's crossing, but Roman settlers sent there long after the Second Punic War, when the region had at last been militarily subdued by Rome and many of its previous Celtic inhabitants deported. For the Greek historian wandering around the new farmsteads and settlements of the Roman colonists, the idea that this place had just a few short years ago been a dangerous and hostile environment could be dismissed as alarmist nostalgia. In 218 BC, however, the situation had been very different.

The Celtic people who lived in the Alpine regions had long been a thorn in the side of Rome. Commonly known as 'Gauls' in both Latin and Greek texts, they had in 387 BC swept down into central Italy and inflicted the terrible humiliation of occupying Rome. The Po valley, where these tribes lived, was worth fighting for. By the mid third century BC it was the largest parcel of fertile land on the Italian peninsula outside Roman control. If it were captured, new homes and cheap food could be provided for Rome's dispossessed and discontented poor.[10] There were also other, more defensive, strategic considerations that informed Rome's northern-Italian policy. Ancient commentators appear to have been united in their analysis that while Rome did not control this area 'not only would they [the Romans] never be the masters of Italy but they would not even be safe in Rome itself'.[11] In 225 BC a large force of 50,000 infantry and 20,000 cavalry mainly made up of two Gallic tribes, the Boii and the Insubres, had again marched down the Po valley and had advanced on Etruria. It was only after an emphatic Roman victory over this force in battle that the Roman Senate decided on a systematic plan for conquering the region. Two new Roman colonies were established on Gallic territory, at Cremona and Placentia, and by 220/219 the Via Flaminia, which connected the region to Rome, was also completed.[12] Now the approach of Hannibal put these hard-fought gains in jeopardy, with the Boii and the Insubres once more in open revolt (no doubt encouraged by the ambassadors whom Hannibal had instructed to foment unrest). The Roman armies sent to subdue the revolt suffered humiliating defeats and were driven from the region, and an attempt to recover the strategically crucial Po valley was also a catastrophic failure, with the Roman forces annihilated.[13]

Although the Celts were generally denigrated by Roman and Greek authors for their lack of endurance, tendency to panic and lack of military discipline (as well as their drunkenness), it was also recognized that they could be a very effective fighting force.[14] The intimidating mixture of their wild appearance, blood-curdling war cries and ferocious charges made them a tough proposition, even for a disciplined

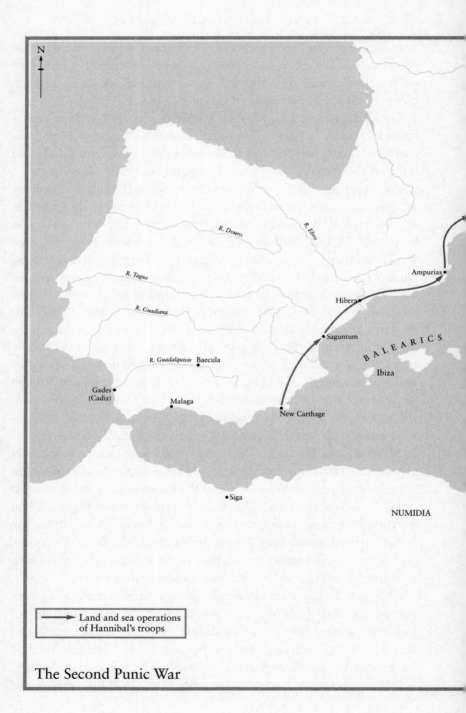

N

R. Douro

R. Ebro

R. Tagus

R. Guadiana

Ampurias

Hibera

R. Guadalquivir   Baecula

Saguntum

BALEARICS

Gades
(Cadiz)

Malaga

Ibiza

New Carthage

Siga

NUMIDIA

Land and sea operations
of Hannibal's troops

The Second Punic War

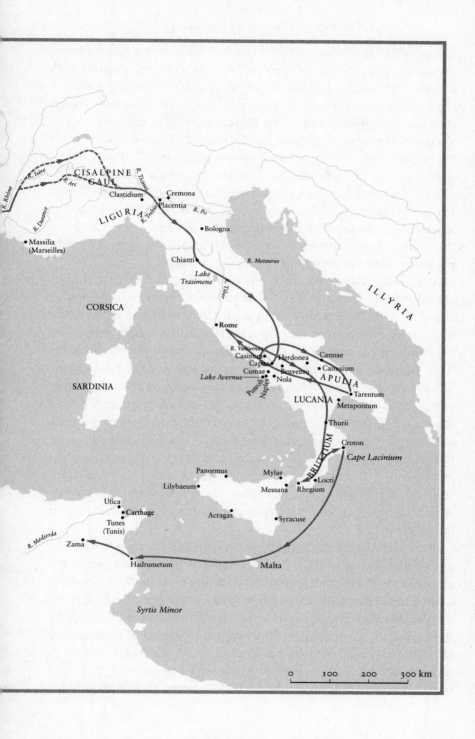

and experienced Roman army.[15] Their menace to Rome had, however, previously been diluted by their inability to maintain alliances with one another,[16] and in later Greek and Roman historians the perfidy of the Celts became proverbial. According to one damning assessment, they were 'naturally more or less fickle, cowardly or faithless ... And the fact that they were no more faithful to the Carthaginians will teach the rest of mankind a lesson never to dare invade Italy.'[17] The potential danger for the Romans was that Hannibal might manage successfully to unite the Celtic tribes under his charismatic command. While Hannibal himself never really trusted the Celts (it was said that he possessed several wigs and other disguises to guard against treachery), many of the alliances he made with them gave him invaluable access to much-needed reinforcements and front-line shock troops.[18]

At the same time as Hannibal was approaching the Alps, the Roman consul Publius Cornelius Scipio had landed his army near the port of Massilia, with the intention of attacking Barcid Spain. Scipio might have arrived there much more quickly if he had not been delayed by the rebellion of the Boii and the Insubres, in response to which the Romans were forced to use one of the legions given to him for his new Spanish campaign. Scipio had therefore been obliged to recruit another new legion, and had arrived in southern Gaul three months behind schedule.[19] On landing, he quickly sent out 300 horsemen to ascertain the whereabouts of Hannibal and his forces. These Roman scouts soon ran into a group of Numidian cavalry who were fulfilling the equivalent role for Hannibal, and, after a skirmish in which the Numidians suffered fairly heavy losses, the Roman cavalry returned to their camp to pass on the location of the Carthaginian army. Scipio quickly set off in hot pursuit.[20]

Hannibal initially vacillated between engaging with Scipio's legions and continuing on to Italy, but his mind was finally made up by the arrival in the Carthaginian camp of emissaries from the Boii, who both offered to act as guides across the rugged terrain ahead and promised an alliance. When Scipio arrived at the site of Hannibal's camp, he found that the Carthaginians had long gone. Instead of rushing after Hannibal in pursuit of glory, however, he returned to northern Italy in order to defend the Po valley. At the same time, he decided to raise fresh troops for this mission and left the greater part of his original force under the command of his brother Gnaeus, with orders to proceed with the original mission of invading the Iberian peninsula. This decision proved crucial, for it effectively ended any chance of Hannibal receiving reinforcements from Spain.[21]

Hannibal approached the Alpine region at some speed, hoping to put as much distance as possible between Scipio and himself. For both topographical and propagandistic reasons, he must surely have desired to continue on the Heraclean way via the river Durance and Mont Genèvre, but Scipio's retreated army now blocked that route. Hannibal's subsequent route is unclear, but it is most likely that he travelled north following the river Rhône. There in the territory of the Allobroges he made valuable allies by adjudicating in a dispute between two royal brothers over who should rule. Aided by guides given by the grateful new ruler, and provided further with supplies, warm clothes and food, he and his troops then set off across the Alps.

By now it was October and winter was fast closing in, and as the Carthaginian army prepared its ascent through the valley of the Arc, probably after marching through the Isère valley, it lost its friendly guides, who returned home.[22] Despite Polybius' claims to the contrary, the Alps presented possibly the most formidable barrier on the European continent. One later Roman historian described how in the spring season men, animals and wagons slipped and slithered on the melted ice towards precipitous ravines and treacherous chasms. In the winter, conditions were even worse. Even on the level ground, lines of posts were driven through the snow so that travellers knew where it was safe to tread to escape being swallowed up by the treacherous voids which lurked just under the surface of the snowfall.[23] Ominously, other Allobrogian chiefs, sensing easy pickings to help them through the harsh winter ahead, had started to muster their tribesmen on the high ground, ready for an attack on the vulnerable Carthaginian column below.

Now Hannibal showed that he was as skilled in mind games as in armed combat. Finding out from his scouts where the Alpine tribesmen were planning an ambush, he and a group of select men occupied a nearby site while the complacent Allobroges slept in their village. When the tribesmen started to attack his army, Hannibal and his troops rushed down and drove them off, killing many of them. He then stormed the Gallic settlement, and not only freed a number of his men and animals who had been captured the previous day, but also seized the contents of the tribesmen's corn store. A few days later, Gallic chieftains came forward and offered friendship, hostages and guides. Hannibal, suspicious of their motives, accepted their overtures while at the same time preparing for treachery. Two days later, as the Carthaginians travelled through a narrow pass they were ambushed by a strong force of Gauls. Fortunately Hannibal had prepared for this eventuality by moving his vulnerable baggage train and cavalry to the front of the column, and positioning heavy infantry at the rear where the tribesmen attacked. The tribesmen were eventually repulsed, but nevertheless they continued in small groups to make isolated attacks on the column, rolling boulders down the steep slopes on to the men and animals below.[24]

Finally, nine days into their march, the Carthaginians reached the top of the pass. After waiting two days for stragglers to catch up, Hannibal rallied his exhausted and dispirited troops by showing them the panorama of Italy below and, according to Livy, delivering a spirited exhortation.[25] Such encouragement was sorely needed. It was now late October, and the winter snows had begun to fall. What was more, the descent into Italy was even steeper than the past ascent. The track was precipitous, narrow and slippery, and it was almost impossible for men or beasts to keep on their feet.

Eventually the army reached what at first looked like the premature end of their odyssey. In front of them was a steep precipice, which a recent landslide had turned into a vertical drop of some 300 metres. Livy dramatically describes the attempt to bypass it:

> The result was a horrible struggle, the ice affording no foothold in any case, and least of all on a steep slope. When a man tried by hands or knees to get on his feet again, even those useless supports slipped from under him and let him down; there were no stumps or roots anywhere to afford a purchase to either hand or foot; in short there was nothing for it but to roll and slither on the smooth ice and melting snow. Sometimes the mules' weight would drive their hooves through into the lower layer of old snow; they would fall and, once down, lashing savagely out in their struggles to rise, they would break right through it, so that as often as not they were held as in a vice by a thick layer of hard ice.[26]

The situation was now critical, and Hannibal ordered that snow be cleared high up on the ridge so that camp could be pitched. It had been decided that the only way of proceeding down the sheer slope would be by cutting a stepped route through the rock. The means by which this was achieved became one of the most famous tales in the Hannibalic canon:

> It was necessary to cut through the rock, a problem that they solved by the ingenious application of heat and moisture; large trees were cut down and logged, and a huge pile of timber was built up; this, with the opportune aid of a strong wind, was set on fire, and when the rock was sufficiently heated the men's rations of sour wine were flung upon it in order to render it friable. They then proceeded to work with picks on the heated rock and opened a sort of zigzag track, to minimize the steep gradient of the descent; they were, therefore, able to get the pack animals and even the elephants down it.[27]

Many aspects of this story of course appear fanciful, and it may reasonably be doubted whether the Carthaginians were able to acquire such quantities of wood, let alone to heat rock to a sufficient temperature. Nevertheless, the dissemination of such tales from the Carthaginian camp served a vital agenda. Quite simply, the heroic creation of a new Hannibalic way through impermeable Alpine rock was a brilliant piece of propaganda. Through the production of such heroic tales, Hannibal ensured that his name would be indelibly linked with the great mountain chain that he had successfully crossed. Despite Polybius' denigration of this stupendous achievement, it would not be until the reign of the emperor Augustus (31 BC–AD 14) that a Roman would traverse the Alps.[28] Indeed, Hannibal's Alpine adventures would remain a source of wonder for both Greek and Roman writers, producing a vast number of different theories on the actual route that the Carthaginian troops took through the mountains.[29] Even 600 years later the section of the mountains through which Hannibal passed was still called 'the Punic Alps'.[30]

THE DIE IS CAST

The great Alpine trial was now at an end, and the plains of northern Italy stretched out before the Carthaginian army. Yet heroic grandeur and the element of surprise had come at a high price. The journey that had taken the Carthaginian army from Spain to northern Italy had been epic in every sense, including the scale of human loss. Hannibal had left the Iberian peninsula with 50,000 foot and 9,000 horse, but by the time he had reached the river Rhône those numbers had dwindled to 38,000 and 8,000 respectively. The crossing of the Alps had cut those figures down to just 20,000 infantry and 6,000 cavalry.[31] Whether or not the original size of the Carthaginian army was exaggerated, the collateral damage of Hannibal's Alpine crossing was as breathtaking as his feats of valour. Like many armies on epic journeys, however, the majority of soldiers were lost not to enemy steel, the cold, hunger or, in this case, even the steep precipices of the Alpine peaks. Many, confronted by extreme hardship, exertion and danger, had simply deserted. But, for all the losses, there could be no doubt that this daring enterprise had been a glittering success. After all, new troops could now be recruited and supplies gathered. More importantly, if the Hellenistic world and the Italian city states had not taken the young Carthaginian general seriously before, they certainly would now.

Before the battle for Italy began, however, Hannibal engaged in a little housekeeping. The loyalty, or at least the compliance, of the Celts could not be guaranteed by blandishments and expensive gifts alone. An example had to be made so that the price of hostility to the Carthaginian cause could be gauged and understood. Once the Roman armies were successfully engaged, there would be little time to keep the northern Celts in check. The Taurini, a tribe who had attempted to resist the Carthaginian advance, were picked out as the poor unfortunates who would provide the painful lesson. Their capital was besieged and soon taken, and its inhabitants – men, women and children – were massacred. Thus a brutal, bloody message which spelled out the consequences of resistance was sent out to the Gallic tribes. However, the massacre also served another purpose, for, as the final act of the great Alpine crossing, the slaughter of the Taurini stood as a further reminder of Hannibal's claim to the lionskinned mantle of that great hero who had first tamed the wild peoples of this barbarous land.[32]

In Rome, the news that Hannibal had successfully crossed the Alps was met with grave alarm. The consul Tiberius Sempronius Longus was recalled from Sicily to assist his colleague Publius Cornelius Scipio, who was now marching towards the river Po in order to confront the Carthaginian army.[33] Before the first confrontation between the two armies, at the river Ticinus, a tributary of the Po, Hannibal, in order to prepare his army psychologically for the hardships that undoubtedly lay ahead, took the unusual step of offering his Gallic prisoners the opportunity of freedom if they emerged victorious from a series of bouts of single combat. Previously he had ensured that these young men had been ill-treated and starved, in order to create the maximum impact when they were led out in front of his assembled troops. To exaggerate further the contrast between the present miserable plight of the captives and the possibilities which both triumph and defeat would offer, Hannibal also brought forth some suits of armour, rich military cloaks and horses as rewards for the victors. All the prisoners clamoured to take up Hannibal's offer, for both victory and, through death, defeat offered release from their present servitude. After the bouts, the Carthaginian troops found themselves pitying those who had not been chosen for combat but remained captive even over those who had been killed. Polybius gives an account of what happened next:

When Hannibal had by this means produced the disposition he desired in the minds of his troops, he rose and told them that he had brought the prisoners before them with the purpose that, clearly seeing in the person of the others what they might themselves have to suffer, they would better understand the present crisis. 'Fortune', he said, 'has brought you to a pass, she has locked you into a similar battlefield, and the prizes and prospects she offers you are the same. For either you must conquer, or die, or fall captive into the hands of your foes. For you the prize of victory is not to possess horses and cloaks, but to be the most envied of mankind, masters of all the wealth of Rome. The prize of death on the battlefield is to depart from life in the heat of the fight, struggling until your last breath for the noblest of objects and without having learned to know suffering. But what awaits those of you who are vanquished and for the love of life wish to flee, or who preserve their lives by any other means, is to have every evil and every misfortune as their fate. There is not one of you so dim and unreflecting as to hope to reach his home by flight, when he remembers the length of the road he traversed from his native land, the numbers of the enemies that lie between, and the size of the rivers he crossed. I beseech you, therefore, cut off as you are entirely from any such hope, to take the same view of your own situation that you have just expressed regarding that of others. For as you all considered both the victor and the dead fortunate and pitied the survivors, so now should you think about yourselves and go all of you to battle resolved to conquer if you can, and, if this be impossible, to die. And I implore you not to let the hope of living after defeat enter your minds at all. If you reason and decide as I urge upon you, it is clear that victory and safety will follow; for none ever who either by necessity or choice decided on such a course have been deceived in their hope of putting their enemies to flight. And when the enemy has the opposite hope, as is now the case with the Romans, most of them being sure of finding safety in flight as their homes are near at hand, it is evident that the courage of those who despair of safety will carry all before them.'[34]

Later, just before the battle, Hannibal called his men together for some final words of encouragement. He promised land, money, Carthaginian citizenship and freedom to the massed ranks of his troops if victorious. Then, as a sign of the inviolability of his oath, Hannibal picked up a lamb in one hand and a stone in the other and sent up a prayer to Baal Hammon and the other gods that they should kill him if he broke his word. He then dashed the animal's brains out.[35]

The battle itself ended in a complete rout of the Roman forces. Hannibal, realizing the great advantage that he possessed in both numbers and quality of cavalry, had recalled the Numidian prince Maharbal and his squadron of 500 horsemen from a raiding mission. Perhaps overconfident in the ability of his javelin-throwers to keep the Carthaginian cavalry at bay, Scipio had placed them in front with his own horse in reserve, but the Roman cavalry were called quickly into action when the javelin-throwers retreated behind them. Eventually a party of Hannibal's Numidian horse managed to outflank the Roman cavalry, and rode down the foot soldiers behind, who panicked and fled. The Roman horse soon followed. Matters were made worse for the Romans by the fact that Scipio was badly wounded, and Livy reports that the general's 17-year-old son Publius, fighting in his first battle, saved the life of his father, although the historian also alludes to an alternative version of the events, in which Scipio suffered the indignity of being rescued by a Ligurian slave.[36]

In pain, and lacking confidence in his inexperienced troops, Scipio

1. *Aeneas' Farewell from Dido in Carthage*, 1675–6, oil painting by Claude Lorrain.

2. Panoramic view of Carthage, reconstruction painting from the Musée National, Carthage.

3. and 4. Gold finger rings with settings adorned with a woman's head and a man's head, third century BC, from the necropolis of sainte-Monique, Carthage.

5. Amulets depicting faces, fourth or third century BC.

6. Relief depicting the unloading of wood after transportation by sea, eighth century BC, Assyrian, from the Palace of Sargon II, Khorsabad.

7. Votive Punic Stele depicting Priest holding a child, fourth century BC, dark limestone, from the tophet of Carthage.

8. Punic stelae from the tophet of Carthage.

9. Votive Stele depicting
Tanit, goddess of Carthage,
holding a caduceus with a
dolphin and an inscription,
second or first century BC,
Phoenician, from Tophet
El-Horfa, Algeria.

10. Sarcophagus of 'Winged Priestess', fourth or third century BC, marble, from the necropolis of sainte-Monique, Carthage.

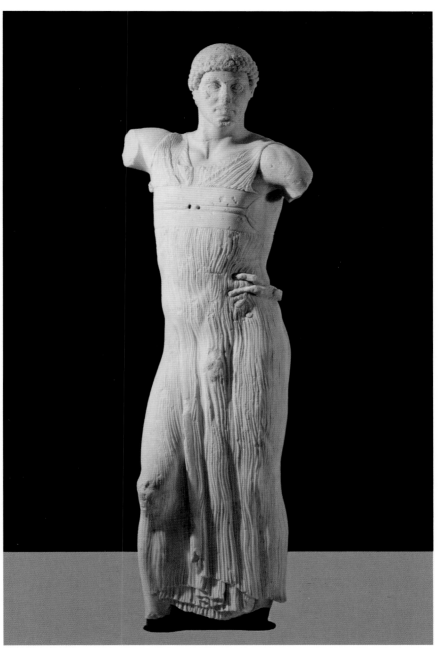

11. Youth of Motya, *c.* 470–450 BC.

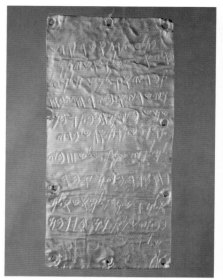

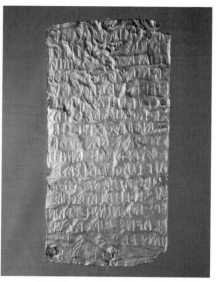

12. Gold sheet with Phoenician text, fifth century BC, from Pyrgi.

13. Gold sheet with Etruscan text, fifth century BC, from Pyrgi.

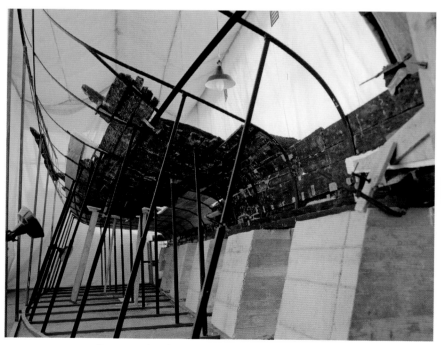

14. Remains of a Phoenician ship, third century BC, Marsala.

15. Stele of Amrit: Melqart on his lion, *c.* 550 BC, from Amrit.

16. Bronze statue of Hercules, second century BC, found in the Forum Boarium, Rome.

17. Silver didrachm showing head of Hercules with she-wolf and twins design, Roman, issued *c.* 275–260 BC.

18. Punic Mausoleum, early second century BC, Sabrata, Tripolitania.

19. Hannibal, first century BC stone bust.

20. Silver double shekel of Carthage showing head of Heracles-Melqart, issued by the Barcid family in Spain, *c.* 230 BC.

21. *Snow Storm: Hannibal and his Army Crossing the Alps*, exhibited 1812, oil painting by Joseph Mallord William Turner.

22. *The Battle of Zama*, 202 BC, 1521, oil painting attributed to Giulio Romano.

23. Scipio Africanus (235–183 BC),
marble bust, Roman.

24. Cato the Elder
(234–149 BC) in a toga,
stone sculpture, Roman.

25. View of the ruins, Carthage.

26. *Apotheosis of Alexandria with Personification of the Four Parts of the World (Or: Dido Abandoned by Aeneas)*, first century AD, mural painting, Roman, from Casa Meleagro, Pompeii.

immediately ordered a Roman withdrawal from the area. Although the Romans managed to delay the Carthaginians' advance by destroying their pontoon over the river, Hannibal quickly found a suitable place on the Po for his engineers to build another bridge. Meanwhile Scipio, feeling increasingly insecure after the desertion of a large contingent of Gallic troops and the betrayal of the town of Clastidium by its Italian commander, withdrew once more, across the river Trebia, and set up camp on high ground overlooking the east bank, where he waited for reinforcements.[37]

Eventually, in mid-December 218, Sempronius Longus arrived with fresh troops. Conscious that his term of office was drawing to a close, and with it the chance of a glorious triumph, Longus was impatient to engage the Carthaginian army in open battle, especially as his own troops appeared to have come off best in a number of minor skirmishes. In fact Hannibal had merely withdrawn his troops to near the Trebia, preferring to conserve his military strength for an encounter of his own choosing. The strategy had worked, because Longus, buoyed by these meaningless victories, was ready to commit his forces to a major confrontation. Scipio attempted to get his consular colleague to reconsider, arguing that their raw troops needed more training over the winter months, and that a period of inactivity would ensure that the notoriously fickle Gauls would start to question their new-found allegiance to Hannibal. Longus, however, was not to be deterred, and Hannibal did everything in his power to encourage a Roman attack.

After boosting Longus' self-confidence, Hannibal now set the trap. Selecting an area between the two camps where plants and undergrowth covered the steep sides of a riverbank, he organized an ambush party of 1,000 horse and an equal number of foot under the command of his brother Mago. The next day at dawn he sent his Numidian cavalry across the Trebia, where they proceeded to provoke the Romans by hurling javelins and abuse at their camp. Predictably, Longus ordered his troops to pursue them. Although the whole Roman force forded the river and drew up into their battle lines in good order, the troops were cold, wet and hungry after being mobilized before they had breakfasted. In contrast, the Carthaginian troops had been well prepared and fed. Both sides appear to have had around 40,000 men each, and, although the heavily armed foot soldiers in the centre were evenly matched, once again Hannibal's superior and more numerous cavalry easily bested their Roman counterparts, leaving the flanks of the Roman infantry exposed to attack. It was then that Mago's small force launched its ambush on the rear of the Roman infantry. Around 10,000 Roman soldiers managed to fight their way out and make it to the nearby town of Placentia, but many others were killed.[38]

Longus escaped and subsequently tried to convince his fellow citizens that the defeat had occurred only because of the extreme weather conditions. However, few if any appear to have believed him.[39] Meanwhile, it took Hannibal little time to persuade the Italian cities to desert the Romans. The Roman and Italian prisoners of war were treated in quite different ways: the former were put on starvation rations; the latter were treated well and eventually sent home. Before they left, Hannibal addressed them and said that 'he had not come to make war on them, but on the Romans for their sakes; and therefore if they were wise they should embrace his friendship, for he had come first of all to re-establish the liberty of the peoples of Italy and also to help them to recover the cities and territories of which the Romans had deprived them.'[40]

The harsh winter of 218/217 granted the Romans some respite, for Hannibal lost a large number of men and horses to the bitter cold, as well as all but one of his elephants.[41] After wintering in Bologna, the Carthaginians moved south and crossed the Apennines into Etruria. They suffered terribly as they spent four days and three nights tramping through terrain so marshy that it was impossible to set up camp. Hannibal, who rode on top of the one remaining elephant, was afflicted by opthalmia, which led eventually to blindness in one eye.[42]

In recognition of the threat that they now faced, the Romans had mobilized over 100,000 fighting men. Concerned that the Carthaginians might launch attacks on Rome's new central-Mediterranean empire, it was decided to send two legions to defend Sicily and another to Sardinia. Two further legions were charged with the defence of Rome itself. The four legions, now under the split command of the two new consuls, Gaius Flaminius Nepos and Gnaeus Servilius Geminus, were reinforced to make up their losses to Hannibal in the previous year.

Flaminius was an impetuous and arrogant man, whom Hannibal immediately tried to goad into rash action by ravaging the agriculturally rich Chianti region where Flaminius and his army were stationed. He consequently managed to lure Flaminius and his army into the Borghetto pass, where on the shore of Lake Trasimene an ambush had been set. The mist of the early morning of 21 June 217 made visibility poor, and the Romans did not see the danger until it was too late. Chaos ensued, and over 15,000 Roman troops were cut down, including Flaminius himself. Some retreated into the waters of the lake, where they drowned in their heavy armour, and 6,000 troops who had survived surrendered when they realized the hopelessness of their situation.[43] In his treatment of them, Hannibal continued his policy of distinguishing between Roman and Italian prisoners, for the latter were sent home without ransom, while the former languished in captivity. The Carthaginian general also had the superior Roman heavy armour and weapons collected up and redistributed to his own Libyan infantry.[44] A few days later the other consul, Geminus, lost virtually all his cavalry as another surprise attack rendered his force virtually worthless.[45]

According to Livy, the news that arrived in Rome after the Carthaginian victory told not only of military defeat, but also of strange and ominous portents in central Italy. Particularly notable are reports that blood had appeared in the sacred spring of Hercules at Caere, an apparent indication of the success with which Hannibal had associated himself with the hero.[46] The Roman reaction, which consisted in offering up prayers at the shrine, certainly suggests an attempt to win Hercules back to the Roman cause.[47] The battle for supremacy was thus being fought on both the temporal and the celestial plane.

Hannibal, recognizing the poor physical shape that his troops and animals were now in, decided to recuperate on the more clement Adriatic coast. According to Polybius, the Carthaginians had by that time captured so much booty that they had grave difficulty transporting it to their new base. After two years away from the sea, Hannibal now had the opportunity to send a message back to Carthage to inform the Council of his victories. The news was met with great celebration in North Africa, and Carthage sent back a message promising support for the campaign both in Italy and in Spain.[48] In contrast, the mood in Rome was one of panic, as news of this latest and most terrible defeat trickled in with the survivors. The populace had thronged around the Forum Romanum and the Senate House, waiting for confirmation from the magistrates. On this occasion the disaster was such that no positive spin could be put on it. One of the praetors climbed on to the speaker's rostrum and simply said, 'Pugna magna victi sumus' – 'We have been defeated in a great battle.'[49] With one consul dead and the other unable to return, the Romans decided to compromise Republican ideology and appoint a dictator, a temporary autocrat allowed by the constitution only in times of intense crisis. The people chose the vastly experienced Quintus Fabius Maximus, twice consul and once censor, with Marcus Minucius Felix to assist him as Master of the Horse.[50]

THE RETREAT OF THE ROMAN GODS?

Fabius, learning from the mistakes of his predecessors, took a very different approach to the war against the Carthaginians. After recruiting two new legions and taking over the two which had been previously commanded by Geminus, Fabius marched to Apulia, where he resisted Hannibal's attempts to induce him into open battle. His Greek biographer Plutarch provides a clear summary of these new tactics:

> He [Fabius] did not plan to fight out the issue with him [Hannibal], but wished, having plenty of time, money and men, to wear out and gradually sap his culminating vigour, his meagre resources, and his small army. Therefore, always pitching his camp in hilly regions so as seem to be out of reach of the enemy's cavalry, he hung threateningly over them. If they sat still, he too kept quiet; but if they moved, he would come down from the heights and show himself just far enough away to avoid being forced to fight against his will, and yet near enough to make his very delays inspire the enemy with the fear that he was going to give battle at last.[51]

Hannibal, appreciating the cleverness of Fabius' tactics, did all in his power to draw his forces out into direct combat by provocations such as the ravaging of the fertile regions of Benvento and Campania. The Romans maintained their discipline, however, shadowing the Carthaginian army and picking off raiding parties when they had the opportunity.[52]

Although effective, Fabius' tactics were very unpopular both in his own camp and on the streets of Rome.[53] Long after his death, the

Romans would come to appreciate their *cunctator* ('delayer' – as Fabius' posthumous epithet would be), but at the time decades of successful aggressive action had enforced the popular perception that such tactics were simply un-Roman.[54] Hannibal himself further stoked up the pressure by sparing the Roman general's own property while burning all the land around it, thus adding substance to a rumour that Fabius had been secretly negotiating with him.[55] Eventually, however, it looked as if Fabius' unpopular strategy had paid off. In the autumn of 217 an increasingly impatient Hannibal made a terrible mistake that left his army at the mercy of the Romans.

> He [Hannibal] wished to draw his army off some distance beyond Fabius, and occupy plains affording pasturage. He therefore ordered his native guides to conduct him, immediately after the evening meal, into the district of Casinum. But they did not hear the name correctly, owing to his foreign way of pronouncing it, and promptly hurried his forces to the edge of Campania, into the city and district of Casilinum, through the midst of which flows a dividing river, called Vulturnus by the Romans. The region is otherwise encompassed by mountains, but a narrow defile opens out towards the sea, in the vicinity of which it becomes marshy, from the overflow of the river, has high sand-heaps, and terminates in a beach where there is no anchorage because of the dashing waves. While Hannibal was descending into this valley, Fabius, taking advantage of his acquaintance with the ways, marched round him, and blocked up the narrow outlet with a detachment of 4,000 heavy infantry. The rest of his army he posted to advantage on the remaining heights, while with the lightest and readiest of his troops he fell upon the enemy's rearguard, threw their whole army into confusion, and slew about 800 of them. Hannibal now perceived the mistake in his position, and its peril, and crucified the native guides who were responsible for it. He wished to make a retreat, but despaired of dislodging his enemies by direct attack from the passes of which they were masters. All his men, moreover, were disheartened and fearful, thinking that they were surrounded on all sides by difficulties from which there was no escape.[56]

Hannibal may have blamed his local guides, but it was Fabius' dogged determination that had allowed the Roman general to capitalize on this error. Hannibal, however, proved himself equal to the challenge. Learning of the Roman ambush prepared for his army, he waited until nightfall and then tied burning brands to the horns of 2,000 captured cattle. The cattle were then driven up to the high ground where the Roman troops were stationed. In the dark, the Romans, thinking that they were under attack, panicked and fled, allowing Hannibal and his army to pass through unimpeded.[57]

This embarrassing incident led to further scorn and derision being heaped on the unfortunate Fabius, though the Carthaginian escape from this seemingly hopeless situation merely highlighted Hannibal's genius rather than the shortcomings of Fabius' tactics. In Rome, a sizeable faction had now decided that the only way of defeating Hannibal was to grant the more aggressive Minucius Felix equal powers to those of Fabius. Despite resistance from Fabius and his supporters in the Senate, the motion was passed, and the Roman forces were thus effectively split between the two commanders.[58] In the wake of his new appointment, Felix immediately attempted to establish his Herculean credentials by dedicating an altar to the hero. Within the context of the Hannibalic campaign, that dedication served to reinforce Roman claims to the Heraclean legend, but it perhaps also represented a challenge by Felix to Fabius' own claim to direct Heraclean ancestry.[59] The battle for Heracles thus now engaged competing generals both between and within the two warring states.

Fabius, indeed, had been the first Roman general to understand the importance of countering the Carthaginian propaganda onslaught. He had Roman priests consult the Sibylline books, a collection of oracular utterances, to find out how the Romans might regain the favour of the gods, and the priests returned with three recommendations: first, the Romans should publicly renew their vows to Mars, the god of war; second, Fabius should dedicate a temple to the goddess Venus Erycina, a Sicilian goddess, and another to the divine quality of *Mens*, 'Composure' or 'Resolution'; finally, the Romans should make the pledge of the 'sacred spring', an ancient rite whereby the entire produce of the next spring was promised to the deity of the spring if victory was achieved within a certain time.[60]

The foundation of a new temple to Venus Erycina on the Capitol, completed in 215, is immediately notable for its links with the Trojan prince Aeneas, represented in Roman myth as the son of Venus, and by this period widely accepted as the forefather of Romulus and Remus. It was thought that Aeneas had married the daughter of Latinus, the eponymous king of Latium, and that upon the latter's death he had ruled over the Latins and his own Trojan settlers. By the time of the Second Punic War, the Aeneas story had become a keystone in the ideological edifice that legitimized Roman domination of Italy, for it located the origins of that domination within a consensual agreement of the shared, mythological past.[61] The interest for the Romans in 217, however, was not simply in a cult of Venus, but more specifically in a cult of Venus *Erycina*. That cult was a relatively recent invention, created after the capture of Sicilian Eryx from the Carthaginians in 248.[62] Although the outer town had soon been retaken by Hamilcar Barca, Hannibal's father, the Roman defenders had withstood several furious assaults and retained the citadel and the sanctuary within.[63] The cult was thus an important symbol of successful Roman resistance against a Carthaginian, and more specifically Barcid, enemy, and its introduction into Rome provided the city with a focal point for resistance to the new Barcid onslaught.[64]

At the same time, the city of Eryx had long been sacred to the Punic goddess Astarte and the Greek goddess Aphrodite.[65] The rebranding of the city's patron deity as Aphrodite/Astarte's Roman equivalent Venus therefore represented an attempt not only to 'Romanize' the cult, but simultaneously to integrate Sicily within the Roman foundational myth associated with Aeneas. Conveniently, the indigenous Elymians, whose capital Eryx was, also claimed a Trojan ancestry, and their city of Segesta (as we have seen) had previously appealed to Rome for intervention precisely on the basis of that shared history. The Roman promotion of the multivalent cult of Venus Erycina thus emphasized resistance to the Carthaginians while simultaneously incorporating the contested island of Sicily within a Roman vision of history. Eryx and its goddess were now as much disputed as Hercules/Heracles/Melqart.[66]

His biographer Plutarch portrayed Fabius' activities on this front as having been driven solely by pragmatism rather than superstition: 'By thus fixing the thoughts of the people upon their relations with heaven, Fabius made them more cheerful regarding the future. But he himself put all his hopes of victory in himself, believing that heaven bestowed success by reason of wisdom and courage, and turned his attentions to Hannibal.'[67] However, there can be little doubt that Fabius' religious activities were informed by a recognition that there was a growing concern among the citizens of Rome that the gods were turning against them.[68] It was as if Hannibal had now turned that most Roman of psychological weapons, the *evocatio*, the ritual through which the gods of Rome's enemies were enticed into defection, against its originators.

Later, Livy described the damaging effect that Hannibal's campaign had had on the collective psychology of the Roman people:

> The longer the war continued, and the more men's minds as well as their fortunes were affected by the alternations of success and failure, so much the more did the citizens become the victims of superstitions, and those for the most part foreign ones. It seemed as though either the characters of men or the nature of the gods had undergone a sudden change. The Roman ritual was growing into disuse not only in secret and in private houses; even in public places, in the Forum and the Capitol, crowds of women were to be seen who were offering neither sacrifices nor prayers in accordance with ancient usage. Unauthorized sacrificers and diviners had got possession of men's minds, and the numbers of their dupes were swelled by the crowds of country people whom poverty or fear had driven into the city, and whose fields had lain untilled owing to the length of the war or had been desolated by the enemy. These impostors found their profit in trading upon the ignorance of others, and they practised their calling with as much effrontery as if they had been duly authorized by the state.[69]

When eventually the Roman Senate was moved to act in this matter by moving these charlatans and their followers out of the Forum Romanum, a riot almost ensued.[70]

This new sense of insecurity also explains the willingness with which the Romans carried out the priests' final recommendation to Fabius: the pledge of a 'sacred spring'.[71] This was one of the oldest and most original elements of Roman religion, and its prescription was clearly no coincidence at a time when those aspects of Roman cultural identity which were shared or contested with other Mediterranean peoples were being so effectively reframed by Rome's enemies. The 'sacred spring', by contrast, was undisputedly a *Roman* religious rite.

THE BATTLE OF CANNAE

In the next campaign year, 216, with the Romans determined finally to defeat Hannibal, a huge army of 87,000 troops was mustered – a number that dwarfed the Carthaginian force of around 50,000.[72] The potency of this impressive mobilization was, however, immediately undermined by the election of two consuls who could not deliver the unity that Rome so sorely needed, for the two men, Gaius Terentius Varro and Lucius Aemilius Paullus, had wildly divergent views on how the war against Hannibal should be waged. Whereas Paullus favoured the old Fabian approach of surrounding Hannibal in his winter quarters and starving him out, Varro was determined to defeat the Carthaginian general in open battle. Even worse, as both consuls went on campaign, each commanded the army on alternate days.[73]

By the end of July, the Roman army had tracked the Carthaginians down to the small Apulian town of Cannae, and set up camp around 16 kilometres away. On 1 August, after a series of skirmishes, Hannibal marched his troops north across the river Aufidus, set up camp, and then offered the Romans open battle. Paullus, who was in command that day, pointedly refused to accept the challenge, much to the consternation of his colleague.[74] The next day, with Varro in command, the Roman army left its main camp on the north bank of the river and crossed to the south, where it drew up in battle formation facing south, with the river to the west. The previous year's consuls, Servilius Geminus and Atilius Regulus (who had replaced the dead Flaminius Nepos), commanded the heavy infantry in the centre, and Paullus led the right wing, where the cavalry and two legions of infantry were situated. Varro himself took command of the left wing, made up of 20,000 infantry and some cavalry.

Hannibal took time to study carefully the Roman battle line before making a move. Although greatly outnumbered in terms of heavy infantry, he noticed that the Roman infantry in the centre were closely packed together, and would therefore find it difficult to manoeuvre. After crossing the river with his army, he set up a highly unorthodox but tactically brilliant formation. In the centre he placed a series of Celtic and Spanish infantry companies in a shallow-stepped line, and

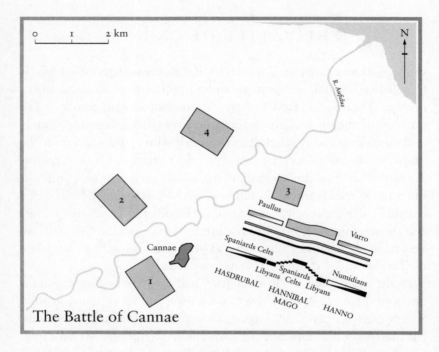

The Battle of Cannae

at the end of each line he placed his elite heavily armoured Libyan foot soldiers, thus leaving a deliberately weakened centre, which he was personally to command with his brother Mago. On both right and left wings he placed his cavalry, under the respective commands of his nephew Hanno and the general Hasdrubal.[75]

The Roman infantry not only had the sun in their eyes, but also the wind blew up great clouds of dust into their faces. When battle started, however, they predictably quickly drove back the Spanish and Celtic foot soldiers, and consequently surged forward into the vacuum at the centre of the Carthaginian formation.

Without a moment's pause they followed up their broken and hastily retreating foe till they took to headlong flight. Cutting their way through the mass of fugitives, who offered no resistance, they penetrated as far as the Africans who were stationed on both wings, somewhat further back than the Celts and Spaniards who had formed the advanced centre. As the latter fell back the whole front became level, and as they continued to give ground it became concave and crescent-shaped, the Africans at either end forming the horns. As the Romans rushed on incautiously between them, they were encircled by the two wings, which extended and closed round them in the rear. On this, the Romans, who had fought one battle to no purpose, left the Celts and Spaniards, whose rear they had been slaughtering, and commenced a fresh struggle with the Africans. The contest was a very one-sided one, for not only were they hemmed in on all sides, but wearied with the previous fighting they were meeting fresh and vigorous opponents.[76]

At the same time, the Carthaginian cavalry on the right wing, which had routed the Roman left, now attacked the rear of the Roman right wing, which was thus effectively surrounded. After defeating this force, the combined Carthaginian cavalry then attacked the beleaguered Roman infantry from behind. The Romans were now surrounded, and a bloody slaughter quickly ensued.

Paullus, who had been seriously wounded by a sling shot, tried to rally his troops, but his courageous efforts would prove to be in vain. After a while he became too weak to manage his horse, so his cavalry escort dismounted to fight on foot. Although offered the chance to escape on the horse of a fleeing cavalry officer, he refused to leave his men and was eventually killed.

Cannae was Rome's greatest military disaster. It is estimated that 70,000 Roman soldiers were killed and another 10,000 captured.[77] Livy has left us with a ghastly description of the immediate aftermath:

The next day, as soon as it grew light, they set about gathering the spoils on the field and viewing the carnage, which was a ghastly sight even for an enemy. There all those thousands of Romans were lying, infantry and cavalry indiscriminately as chance had brought them together in the battle or the flight. Some covered with blood raised themselves from among the dead around them, tortured by their wounds, which were nipped by the cold of the morning, and were promptly put an end to by the enemy. Some they found lying with their thighs and knees gashed but still alive; these bared their throats and necks and bade them drain what blood they still had left. Some were discovered with their heads buried in the earth; they had evidently suffocated themselves by making holes in the ground and heaping the soil over their faces. What attracted the attention of all was a Numidian who was dragged alive from under a dead Roman lying across him; his ears and nose were torn, for the Roman with hands too powerless to grasp his weapon had, in his mad rage, torn his enemy with his teeth, and while doing so expired.[78]

Twenty-nine senior Roman commanders and eighty of senatorial rank had lost their lives. Varro, however, the architect of the disaster, somehow escaped with his life.[79]

For Hannibal, the path to Rome now lay open. According to Livy, Maharbal, the leader of the Numidian cavalry, urged that the army press on to the city while it had the opportunity:

> 'That you may know,' he said to Hannibal, 'what has been gained by this battle I prophesy that in five days you will be feasting as victor in the Capitol. Follow me; I will go in advance with the cavalry; they will know that you are come before they know that you are coming.' To Hannibal the victory seemed too great and too joyous for him to realize all at once. He told Maharbal that he commended his zeal, but he needed time to think out his plans. Maharbal replied: 'The gods have not given all their gifts to one man. You know how to win victory, Hannibal, but you do not how to use it.'[80]

For Livy, Hannibal's delay was in fact to save Rome from destruction, but in reality the Carthaginian troops and animals were exhausted, and Rome was still 400 kilometres away and well served with defensive fortifications that had been rebuilt in 378. Made of tufa blocks, the Roman city wall was over 7 kilometres long and interspersed with towers. Even at its weakest points it was bolstered by earthworks, ramps and ditches. Moreover, the city was defended by two urban legions, smaller groups of marines and other troops, as well as by its inhabitants. The capture of Rome would therefore require a long siege and the deployment of powerful siege engines.[81] In fact the actual taking of Rome does not appear to have been one of Hannibal's key objectives, and he instead sought to continue his policy of marginalizing the city from its Italian and Latin allies, so that eventually, when isolated, exhausted and demoralized, it would surrender and seek terms.[82]

What Hannibal thus sought was a peace in which Carthage could dictate terms, just as Rome had done in the aftermath of the First Punic War. Towards that end, ten representatives were selected from among the Roman prisoners and were dispatched to Rome to make arrangements for the ransoming of the 8,000 Roman citizens that Hannibal was holding. Before they were released, they all had to swear an oath to return once their mission had been accomplished.[83] The ransoming of prisoners was a common feature of contemporary warfare, and was often the first stage on the road to a negotiated peace settlement. The Roman response must therefore have shocked Hannibal, for the Senate refused to see the captured Romans, and a decree was passed which forbade the state or private individuals from paying ransoms. Rome had publicly announced its intention to struggle until the bitter end. Hannibal now had little option but to dispose of the prisoners, for they were a dangerous drain on his already stretched resources. Some were executed, and the majority sold into slavery.[84]

What sort of terms might Hannibal have sought from Rome? According to Livy, Hannibal claimed in an address to the assembled Roman captives that he did not seek the destruction of their city: 'All he was fighting for was his country's honour as a sovereign power. His fathers had yielded to Roman courage; his one object now was that the Romans should yield to his good fortune and courage.'[85] This is perhaps an accurate assessment of Hannibal's intentions in the aftermath of Cannae. In terms of military and propagandistic strategy, the campaign had been a brilliant success. The Roman claims to martial supremacy and to a historical right to rule the Italian peninsula, two of the most important ideological foundations on which Rome's continued expansion had been built, had been utterly undermined. Indeed, the military campaign had been so extraordinarily successful that it is unlikely that even Hannibal's most optimistic advisers would have envisaged the speed of the Carthaginian success. Hannibal's limited objective at this point is thus perhaps easy to appreciate: not the destruction of Rome itself, but rather its relegation to nothing more than a central Italian power, with the Italian cities liberated and Sardinia and Punic Sicily reclaimed for Carthage.

Directly after his greatest military triumph, however, Hannibal had already made his first serious miscalculation, for he assumed that Rome could be forced to negotiate. Hannibal's hybrid education under Sosylus and other Greek tutors might have well prepared him for the intricacies of Hellenistic statecraft, but the contemporary situation now highlighted just how far removed those tutors were from the brutal realpolitik of the age. Two centuries later, the triumph of Roman obduracy was an incontrovertible fact around which the Greek intelligentsia would construct their own version of how the Roman state had come to rule the world. In the final decades of the third century BC, however, the Mediterranean world was only slowly beginning to discover the realities of Roman determination. For Rome, the Italian peninsula was not merely a piece of conquered territory that could be traded or bartered as political circumstance dictated. It would have been a brave politician who suggested that Rome compromise with its enemies or retreat from the hard-won Italian dominions. The Roman senators whom Hannibal faced had been raised on stories that dwelt extensively on their forebears' obstinate refusal to negotiate with the enemy, even in the most desperate of circumstances. That some of these tales concerned examples of heroic Roman grit within living memory, such as Appius Claudius Caecus' refusal to parley with the all-conquering Pyrrhus in 280 BC, only added to their potency. In a society where elite self-representation was so closely associated with *mos maiorum*, the ways of one's ancestors, to give up the land won by the blood of one's forebears was unthinkable.

During the long years of conflict, Carthage had brought Rome to the brink of disaster on more than one occasion. Upon each instance, however, final victory had been snatched from the Carthaginians' grasp by an enemy who would simply not countenance defeat. The Barcid conquest of the Iberian peninsula had in many respects been an excellent preparation for Hannibal's later confrontation with Rome. Twenty years of almost continuous military campaigning against determined and skilled opposition had turned Hannibal into an excellent general, and honed the Carthaginian army into a superb fighting force. However, in his moment of triumph, Hannibal's poor understanding of the Romans' obdurate mentality now stood in stark contrast to his fine appreciation of their military strengths and weaknesses. Expansion into Spain had helped both to alleviate previous Carthaginian defeats and to compensate for lost territory, but at the same time it had robbed the Carthaginian generals of vital military experience against Rome. If Hannibal had gained such experience, he might not have let the wounded Roman beast escape.

12

The Road to Nowhere

THE CARTHAGINIANS ON THREE FRONTS

It was said that when Hannibal was asked whom he considered to be the greatest commander that had ever lived, he put only Alexander the Great above Pyrrhus, king of Epirus.[1] His explanation was that not only had Pyrrhus been a master military tactician, but 'He possessed, too, the art of winning popularity, to such an extent that the nations of Italy preferred the rule of a foreign king to that of the Roman people who had so long held the foremost place in that country.'[2]

Hannibal's wooing of the Greeks of southern Italy placed him very much within the Pyrrhic tradition. As well as offering obvious strategic advantages (through its relative proximity to North Africa and thus also to potential Carthaginian reinforcements), Greek southern Italy must surely have held great cultural allure for one carefully educated in Hellenistic mores but hitherto consigned to the 'barbarous' fringes of the Greek world. Yet if Hannibal had spent a little longer studying the history of Pyrrhus' Italian escapade, he might better have understood the difficulties which swiftly arose between the cities of Magna Graecia and the Epirote interloper. Pyrrhus was not the first Hellenistic adventurer to have found that the warm welcome extended to him on his arrival in southern Italy had quickly evaporated. In 334 BC the citizens of Tarentum had appealed to Alexander, king of Epirus, uncle of Alexander the Great, to protect them from the unwelcome attentions of local Italian tribesmen, but it had soon become clear that Alexander himself was a greater threat to Tarentine autonomy than those he had been summoned to fight, and

Tarentum was saved from Epirote subjugation only by the king's untimely death.

The southern Italian cities had also hailed Pyrrhus as a great defender in their fight against Rome, but relations had again quickly soured. After two dazzling victories against the Roman army, Pyrrhus decided that he wanted to be more than a mere hired hand, and tried secretly to negotiate a deal with the Romans which proposed that Italy be split between them, with him as ruler of Magna Graecia. The Romans, understanding the immense strategic importance of the region, and perhaps sensing that the danger presented by this brilliant but fickle general would fade away, firmly declined his offer. As Peter Green has observed, 'What the locals wanted was a professional general who stuck to his commission; what they got, as with Alexander of Epirus, was an ambitious conquistador, and, worse, this time one who proved no match for the opposition.'[3] After the previous experience of self-proclaimed Hellenistic 'saviours' in the guise of a new Heracles, it was hardly surprising that the cities of Magna Graecia did not immediately flock to Hannibal's banner.

By the end of 216, however, an opportunity to extend Hannibal's influence in southern Italy suddenly presented itself. The wealthy Campanian city of Capua had long been a key Roman ally in the region, and enjoyed the various rights of Roman citizenship as well as the privilege of maintaining its own magistrates. Indeed, many of its elite had close ties with the Roman Senate, often through intermarriage, and a considerable number of the city's young men were serving in the Roman army.[4] With Hannibal now ensconced further north, however, it appears that a number of the ruling elite considered defecting to the Carthaginian cause. Several considerations seem to have influenced their decision. First, worries about the security of the city and its prosperous agricultural hinterland must surely have increased with the news of the disaster at Cannae, and no doubt been further exacerbated by the return home of the Italian prisoners released by Hannibal to spread the news of the Carthaginians' triumph over Rome and generosity to the Italians. Second, there was resentment at the burdens and obligations that an alliance with Rome brought, including the commitment to supply troops for the Roman army, the payment of tribute, and the presence of Roman military officials in the city. Finally, and perhaps most importantly, sections of the Capuan elite appear to have envisioned the restoration both of their previous hegemony over Campania and of lands conceded to the Romans.[5]

The final break came when a Capuan delegation to Rome voiced their concerns about the deployment of 300 of their well-born youths to the Roman army in Sicily. The Roman consul Varro treated their complaint dismissively, and then warned them that they were now effectively on their own, because of a lack of Roman men and resources to protect them. The pro-Carthaginian members of the Capuan delegation then had little trouble persuading their colleagues to approach Hannibal, and an agreement to hand the city over to him was swiftly reached. In exchange for their support, Hannibal agreed that the Capuans would be allowed to keep their own government and laws. In addition, they would not be forced to undergo military service against their will.[6]

The Capuans then returned home, and the rebellion began. All the Roman officials and private citizens in the city were seized and confined in a bathhouse, where they subsequently expired owing to the extreme heat.[7] For Hannibal, Capua was a major catch, and he clearly hoped that its defection would prompt other cities swiftly to follow suit. It was probably for that reason that the Carthaginian general was so generous towards his new allies. According to Livy, Hannibal entered Capua in triumph, and in an address to the Capuan Senate made the ambitious promise that the city would soon be the capital of all Italy, with even Rome subordinate to it.[8] The vast majority of the people and Senate now lent their weight to the Hannibalic cause. While we cannot know the precise basis of the new alliance, only promises as extravagant as those preserved in Livy can have convinced the Capuans to turn against Rome. The dire consequences of defeat must surely have been recognized.

A few Capuans, however, remained unhappy with the new alliance. At a dinner held in his honour, Hannibal was nearly the victim of an assassination attempt by the son of Pacuvius Calavius, one of the leading citizens and a chief supporter of the rebellion, who was only at the last minute dissuaded from carrying out the murder by his father.[9] Another dissident, Decius Magius, who had strongly opposed the new pact on the basis of the precedent of Pyrrhus, was arrested and brought in chains before Hannibal. When ordered by Hannibal to defend himself, however, the feisty Magius refused to do so, citing the very terms of the treaty agreed between the general and the Capuans, which guaranteed the latter's freedom from outside intervention. To avoid further embarrassment, Magius was dragged to a ship bound for Carthage with his head covered, thus preventing his shouts rousing up his fellow citizens against their new allies.[10]

While Hannibal now had a major ally in southern Italy, the alliance had come at some cost. The removal of Roman domination was an immediate motivation for Capua's defection, but broader objectives were the maintenance of the city's political autonomy and the restoration of its traditional authority over the whole of Campania. Indeed, the Capuan desire to be recognized as the dominant city in the region is wonderfully illustrated in the minting of a substantial amount of contemporary local coinage which represents the city as a major, independent power.[11] While Capua was willing to accept Hannibal as the last great bulwark against the encroaching power of Rome, it was willing to do so strictly on its own terms, and only while the alliance accorded with its own regional ambitions. Hannibal had thus been forced to retreat from his promise of Italian liberation in order to ensure the loyalty of a crucial ally. By publicly addressing the issue of Capuan regional hegemony, furthermore, Hannibal had ensured that other Campanian cities were now unlikely to lend him their support. Indeed, subsequent events such as Capua's takeover of the neighbouring city of Cumae, and Hannibal's handing over of the captured city of Casilinum, must only have compounded their fears. Although some smaller allies of Capua did join the revolt, the majority of cities in Campania – such as Nola, Naples, Puteoli and Cumae – did not. As Michael Fronda has recently remarked, 'This pattern suggests that long-standing local inter-city bonds and rivalries persisted under the veneer of Roman rule and surfaced when Hannibal suspended the mechanisms of Roman rule that suppressed them.'[12] Once more the dreams of a foreign general were set to founder through the complex array of agendas that made up the political landscape of southern Italy.

Some cities were now taken by force, but others – most notably Nola – managed to withstand a number of Carthaginian assaults. Livy explained that Hannibal's troops quickly became soft and ill-disciplined once they were stationed in the comfort of Capua, rather than under canvas in the field.[13] A more credible problem was that, in his anxiety to win over the Capuans, Hannibal had absolved them of any obligation to provide him with troops, which left him with a serious recruitment problem. Furthermore, those who did enlist had neither the experience nor the skill of his precious core of African, Spanish and Celtic troops.[14] This lack of manpower would be further compounded when his brother Hasdrubal, who had been instructed to leave his base in Spain and take his army to Italy, was in 216 heavily defeated by a Roman army under the joint command of the brothers Gnaeus and Publius Scipio at Hibera near the river Hiberus. Hannibal was now compelled to ask the Carthaginian Council for reinforcements via his brother Mago, whom he had dispatched to North Africa earlier that year.

Arriving in the Carthaginian Council, Mago dramatically emptied on to the floor a huge pile of gold rings taken from the thousands of dead Roman cavalry who had fallen at Cannae. He then gave an understandably upbeat account of the previous two years of the war, before concluding with a request for fresh troops, supplies and money. His words had the desired effect, for the vast majority of his audience reacted with jubilation. Indeed, one Barcid supporter could not resist a barbed jibe at their old opponent Hanno, mockingly calling for the one Roman senator in the Carthaginian Council to comment.[15] Hanno, however, was far too experienced a political campaigner to be cowed into silence. In a measured but caustic response, he examined the fragile foundations on which Hannibal's great victories had been built:

'But even now, what is it that you are rejoicing at? "I have slain the armies of the enemy; send me troops." What more could you ask for if you had been defeated? "I have captured two of the enemy's camps, filled, of course, with plunder and supplies; send me corn and money." What more could you want if you had been despoiled, stripped of your own camp? And that I may not be the only one to be surprised at your delight – for as I have answered Himilco [a pro-Barcid Carthaginian councillor], I have a perfect right to ask questions in my turn – I should be glad if either Himilco or Mago would tell me, since, you say, the Battle of Cannae has all but destroyed the power of Rome and the whole of Italy is admittedly in revolt, whether, in the first place, any single community of the Latin nation has come over to us, and, secondly, whether a single man out of the thirty-five Roman tribes has deserted to Hannibal.' Mago answered both questions in the negative. 'Then there are still,' Hanno continued, 'far too many of the enemy left. But I should like to know how much courage and confidence that vast multitude possess.'[16]

Hanno followed up this stinging inquisition by asking if the Romans were now suing for peace. Clearly savouring Mago's negative response, Hanno retorted that it was clear that the war was far from won. Despite the obvious power of his words, however, the Council voted to send Hannibal a force of 4,000 Numidians and 40 elephants, as well as 500 talents of silver.[17]

The situation on the island of Sicily was now beginning to look favourable. At Syracuse, the death of Rome's loyal ally Hiero and the subsequent ascension in 215 BC of his teenage grandson Hieronymus to the throne had presented an opportunity for the Carthaginians.[18] Under the influence of pro-Carthaginian advisers, the young king had made friendly overtures to Hannibal, and the latter promptly sent two of his officers of Syracusan origin, the brothers Hippocrates and Epicydes, to Sicily to negotiate an alliance.[19] While Hieronymus was soon dramatically assassinated, and a pro-Carthaginian coup in Syracuse was suppressed, Hippocrates and Epicydes were nevertheless elected to the city's council.[20] As the cities of Sicily wavered between support for Rome and support for Carthage, the brothers used their position to foment anti-Roman feeling among the Syracusan army and citizenry (as well as elsewhere on the island), and were eventually elected as the city's generals.[21]

A Roman army immediately invaded Syracusan territory and set up camp at the city's walls. The Roman general Marcellus then demanded that the Syracusans immediately hand over the brothers, accept back the pro-Roman politicians who had fled, and restore the previous pro-Roman government. With his ultimatum rejected, Marcellus had little option but to attempt to capture the city, and when an initial assault in the winter of 213 failed, a siege that was to last for more than a year began.[22]

The situation would further improve for the Carthaginians when a considerable number of other Sicilian cities also rebelled against Rome in 213, no doubt encouraged by the arrival of a 30,000-strong Punic army on the island.[23] On Sardinia, by contrast, a rebellion in support of Hannibal was swiftly suppressed.[24]

In Spain, the Scipio brothers were enjoying some success against the well-established Carthaginian forces.[25] First they had managed to prevent Hasdrubal from leaving the peninsula to lend support to his brother Hannibal in Italy by inflicting a heavy defeat on his forces at Hibera in 216.[26] And, despite the arrival of reinforcements led by Mago (reinforcements originally earmarked for Italy), the sequence of Carthaginian defeats continued for the next three years.[27] Thus by 212 the Scipios had tied up three Carthaginian armies in Spain.[28]

Despite the setbacks on Sardinia and in Spain, help had now come from an unexpected source. In the spring of 215 an embassy sent by Philip of Macedon had landed at Bruttium and travelled on to Campania to meet with Hannibal and agree a treaty. Polybius claims to reproduce the actual treaty document, a copy of which reportedly fell into Roman hands when a ship carrying both Macedonian and Carthaginian officials was captured on its return to the East. The terms of the treaty bound both sides to protect one another from each other's enemies, with the explicit understanding that the Macedonians would help the Carthaginians in their war against Rome until final victory had been won.[29] Yet it is also clear from the terms that Hannibal was keen to limit Philip's intervention in the conflict and, overall, to keep the Macedonians out of Italy. Once victory was complete, the terms of Carthage's peace with Rome would apply to Macedonia also, with Philip gaining Rome's possessions in Illyria.

The treaty text itself, which appears to have been translated from Punic into Greek by Hannibal's chancery, shows clear associations with the diplomatic language and conventions that had existed in the Near East for millennia, proving that the Levantine roots of the city still exerted a heavy influence on traditional aspects of state business. Appended to the treaty was a list of Carthaginian gods who acted as divine witnesses to the agreement, organized into three (presumably hierarchical) celestial triads. The identities of these deities, who have been transliterated into the Greek divine canon, have been much debated, but it is now generally thought that the top tier was composed of Baal Hammon, Tanit and Reshef.[30] In the second were Astarte, Melqart and Eshmoun, followed by Baal Saphon, Hadad and Baal Malagê in the third.[31] What is particularly interesting about this celestial ordering is that it reflects the divine patrons of the city of Carthage, and not of the Barcids.[32] When it came to negotiating with Philip, king of one of the most powerful of the Hellenistic kingdoms, even Hannibal's reputation as a great general was not enough.[33] This had to be an alliance between Macedonia and Carthage, hence the presence of three named Carthaginian officials – Mago, Myrcan and Barmocar, who were either members of the Tribunal of One Hundred and Four or part of a special commission appointed by that body – as well as other, unnamed, councillors.[34]

This treaty was just one of a number of signs that deference to the constitutional bodies of Carthage had come increasingly to replace the autonomy of action that had marked much of Hannibal's early career. The huge level of financial support that Hannibal received from North Africa in this period demanded the constant involvement of the Carthaginian Council. That support can be ascertained not only from Livy's report – for example, of the monies given to Mago – but also from the large quantity of high-quality-electrum and silver coinage that was minted in this period, much of it clearly aimed for use in Italy. Carthage itself, by contrast, maintained a bronze and debased-electrum currency system.[35] It is striking that it was not until the last years of his time in Italy that Hannibal seems to have produced any coinage himself, meaning that he was relying on booty, promises of pay after victory, and coinage being shipped in from Carthage.[36] All of Carthage's resources were thus thrown at the war effort.

AT THE GATES OF ROME

At Rome also the war effort was causing significant economic strain. After a series of devaluations in 217 and the subsequent emergency production of an issue of gold currency, the coinage system was thoroughly reorganized. Yet even this firm action did not shield the new silver denarius, the centrepiece of the new currency, from two subsequent devaluations. Even a doubling of the tax rates, large loans from Hiero of Syracuse and the establishing of a state bank had not been enough to meet the escalating cost of the war, and by 215 loans with an added risk premium had to be arranged with private tax-gathering syndicates. Furthermore, edicts were passed in 214 and 210 which put in place enforced progressive taxation of Rome's wealthiest citizens specifically to pay for the fitting out of Rome's navy.[37]

The catastrophic defeats of 217/216 forced a reform of the military. The terrible losses in the legions were offset by the recruitment of those who had previously been ineligible for military service. Thus the new legions included slaves and criminals, and there may also have been a lowering of the requisite property requirement in order to include the Roman poor. Indeed, at its peak, it is thought that the Roman army during this period may have numbered as many as 100,000 infantry, 7,500 cavalry and an equal number of allied troops. Most importantly of all, there appears to have been a conscious effort to sustain more continuity in the senior command. Thus Fabius Maximus, who had previously caused Hannibal so many problems, would unusually hold a third, fourth and then a fifth consulship in 215, 214 and 209, while another three veteran commanders held the same office another two or three times between 215 and 209.[38]

Despite such reforms, the city nonetheless remained in the grip of a panic caused by the proximity of the Carthaginian army in southern Italy, a panic compounded by the appearance of a number of menacing religious portents. In 216 the decision had therefore been made to send the senator (and future historian) Quintus Fabius Pictor to the famous sanctuary of Delphi, to discover what prayers and supplications might appease the anger of the gods. The instructions with which Fabius Pictor returned from the oracle specified offerings to particular deities and stipulated that upon final victory the Romans should dedicate a portion of the war booty to Delphic Apollo.[39] The decision to consult the oracle was a clever move on the part of the Senate: not only did it publicly affirm Rome's cultural links with the Greek world (in the face of a Carthaginian attempt to undermine such links), it also made that affirmation at a time when Hannibal was menacing the cities of Magna Graecia. It therefore sought to re-establish firmly Rome's Greek credentials. At the same time, however, the Romans now performed a religious rite which was unmistakably their own. Turning to their Books of Fate, they revived the terrible ritual whereby a Gallic man and woman and a Greek man and woman were buried alive in the Forum Boarium, in what Livy disapprovingly described as 'a sacrifice wholly alien to the

Roman spirit'.[40] Roman human sacrifice was, however, not a crass anachronism, but something first recorded just a few years previously, in 228, when the city was faced by Gallic invasion.[41] Its instigation now was surely a measure of the panic that Hannibal's success had engendered in the city.

Hannibal spent much of 213 in the pleasant surroundings of Apulia and Campania, without making the impact for which he may have hoped. Furthermore, worrying news that the Romans were besieging Syracuse soon arrived. The city was ably defended by the extraordinary range of weapons developed by its chief engineer, Archimedes, the ancient's world's most brilliant geometrician, but by the spring of 212 the Roman commander, Marcellus, had not only managed to bring many rebellious cities to heel, but had also breached Syracuse's outer fortification wall.[42] Later in the summer the Romans also managed to beat off a substantial Punic Sicilian army, which was then further decimated by plague, killing the general Hippocrates.[43] A further Carthaginian force sent to the island in an attempt to retrieve this deteriorating situation failed dismally,[44] and even Epicydes, sensing the increasing hopelessness of the position, slipped away. After botched peace negotiations, Syracuse eventually fell to the Romans through the treachery of some mercenary leaders.[45]

Although the property of pro-Roman citizens was protected, the city was extensively looted and many were killed, including the great Archimedes (despite Marcellus' specific instructions that he should be spared). The fall of Syracuse meant that Carthaginian hopes in Sicily were all but snuffed out, and the failure of the Sicilian revolt was a bitter blow.[46] Not least, Carthage had invested heavily in it, even striking two very large issues of coinage specifically to be used during the campaign.[47]

For Hannibal, the loss of Syracuse and the decline of Carthaginian fortunes in Sicily was only one of a number of pressing problems, of which the most worrying was the Roman seizure of a number of towns in Apulia. And yet now, as so often before, just when the Italian campaign had begun to flounder, fortune decided to smile kindly on the Carthaginian general, for Tarentum, the most important city in Magna Graecia, dramatically capitulated. Both main historical sources for the Second Punic War carry such detailed descriptions of the events surrounding the capture of the city that it is generally accepted that such descriptions derived from the pen of Silenus.[48]

Tarentum had long been a target for Hannibal, but, although there were pro-Carthaginian sympathizers within its walls, they had never been strong enough to deliver the city. By 212, however, feelings were running high against Rome owing to an incident in which a number of Tarentine hostages had been executed by the Romans after trying to escape. Hannibal was at the time camped close to the city, when one evening a group of Tarentine young men left the town and approached the Carthaginian lines. Their leaders, Philemenus and Nicon, were brought before Hannibal and explained that they wished to surrender the city to him. After encouraging them and arranging a secret location for further meetings, Hannibal gave the Tarentine conspirators some cattle so that it would look as if they had successfully stolen them from his camp, thereby alleviating any suspicions on the part of the Roman guard. During a second rendezvous, an agreement was reached with the plotters that on the capture of the city the Carthaginians would respect all Tarentine rights and property.

Now an elaborate plan to capture the city by stealth was set in motion. Over a number of nights Philemenus, who was a renowned hunter, left the city purportedly looking for game. By giving some of his catch to the Roman sentries, he gained their trust enough that they would open the gate at the sound of his whistle. An evening when the commander of the Roman garrison was hosting a party was chosen for the seizure of the city. First, an elite Carthaginian force of 10,000 men left their camp and covered three days' march in one session. Hannibal then carefully disguised this troop movement by sending a squadron of Numidian cavalry ahead so that it appeared that this was nothing more than a raid. Meanwhile, some of the Tarentine conspirators had attended the Roman commander's party and ensured that the celebrations had gone on late into the night. Other plotters gathered around the main gate of Tarentum, and when a fire signal was given from outside by Hannibal they rushed the guards stationed there and killed them before admitting the waiting Carthaginians. At the second gate, which Philemenus had used for his nocturnal forays, Hannibal's troops burst in and killed the sentries while they were admiring Philemenus' catch, a huge boar being carried on a stretcher. After ordering that all the citizens should be spared, Hannibal sent his troops to secure the city. Then at daybreak he summoned all the Tarentines to the marketplace and gave them assurances that they would not be harmed.[49]

While the spectacular capture of Tarentum led to an immediate revival in Carthaginian fortunes,[50] it was however salted by two major difficulties. First, much of the city's Roman garrison, including its commander, had managed to take refuge in the citadel, which stood in an almost unassailable position with access to the sea. There they would remain while Tarentum was in Carthaginian hands.[51] Second, and far more seriously, Capua was now under siege by four Roman legions with orders from the Senate to remain there until the city was taken.[52] In spring 211, after he had failed to break through the Roman encirclement, Hannibal's hand was finally forced. Only one course of action could now draw Roman troops away from Capua. He would march on Rome.[53]

In order to ensure that the Latin cities understood that Rome could not now protect them, Hannibal left a trail of devastation as he marched north.[54] In Rome, panic reigned as news of the Carthaginian advance reached the city, and Hannibal deliberately raised the level of hysteria by sending his Numidian horsemen to terrorize the refugees trying to flee there.[55] Matters only got worse when a squadron of Numidian deserters who had been ordered by the Romans to mobilize against Hannibal's force were mistaken for the enemy by the terrified citizens.[56] Livy reported that 'The wailing cry of the matrons was heard everywhere, not only in private houses but even in the temples. Here they knelt and swept the temple floors with their dishevelled hair and lifted up their hands to heaven in piteous entreaty to the gods that they would deliver the city of Rome out of the hands of the enemy and preserve its mothers and children from injury and outrage.'[57] As a further indication of the seriousness of the situation, the Senate went into emergency sitting and troops were posted around the city.[58]

The panic reached its climax when Hannibal himself – seven years after first entering Italy – finally approached the walls of Rome at the Colline Gate, accompanied by 2,000 Numidian horsemen.[59] If we believe the accounts of Polybius and Livy, however, what transpired next was something of an anticlimax. The former claims (unconvincingly) that the victor of Cannae was dissuaded from attacking the city by the appearance of a legion of battle-ready new recruits.[60] In Livy's account of the episode, however, Hannibal was discouraged by the onset of a severe hailstorm on consecutive days, which he took to be an unfavourable divine omen. He was supposedly further demoralized by the news that the Romans took his challenge so lightly that they were diverting troops to fight in Spain, and that the very land on which his army was camped had been recently sold at auction, with no shortage of Roman buyers, such was the confidence in victory. According to Livy, Hannibal responded by ordering a herald to auction off all the financiers' pitches around the Roman forum.[61]

Both these accounts are based, however, on little more than wilful misunderstandings of Hannibal's true motives. In terms of military strategy the march upon Rome had been a success, because 15,000 Roman troops, under the command of Quintus Fulvius Flaccus, had been summoned back from Capua to defend the city,[62] even if neither Hannibal nor the Roman commanders expected an assault on it (Hannibal had, after all, left most of his heavy infantry and equipment behind at his base in Bruttium). More importantly, Hannibal's presence at the walls of Rome served a crucial propagandistic function. One of the few references to have survived from the history of Silenus, Hannibal's loyal chronicler, gives an extraordinary insight into the significance of the Carthaginian's visit to the gates of Rome. In this fragment Silenus gives an account of Heracles' sojourn in Rome which is markedly at variance with other tales of the hero's visit.

In the Silenian version, Rome's famous Palatine Hill was named after Palantho, daughter of Hyperboreos, the eponymous leader of the Hyperboreans, a mythical northern people. She had enjoyed a romantic liaison with Heracles on that very spot, and hence the hill had gained its name.[63] In another tale, also thought to have derived from Silenus, Latinus, first king and founder of the Latin people, was the product of that same union between Palantho and Heracles.[64] In the charged atmosphere of the Hannibalic war, this seemingly obscure point of history had very serious propagandistic implications. Silenus' version of the prehistory of Rome directly contradicted the generally accepted Roman version of events, which told that Latinus' mother was Fauna, the wife of Faunus, the indigenous king of the region.[65] In Silenus' account, furthermore, the Hyperboreans appear as a metaphor for the Gauls, the barbarous people whom Heracles himself had supposedly tamed on his journey across the Alps. Now Hannibal had crossed that great mountain chain with an army full of Gauls. It therefore looked as if 'history' would repeat itself, as Heracles and his Hyperboreans returned to the Palatine to claim what was rightfully theirs.[66] Part of that Heraclean patrimony included the Latins, the product of the ancient union between the hero and his Hyperborean lover. Silenus' reconception of Roman prehistory and the display of power which the destructive march to Rome represented were therefore part of the same determined campaign to detach the Latins from Rome. It was no coincidence that, as he approached the walls of Rome, Hannibal had first stopped at the temple of Hercules by the Colline Gate.[67] He wanted those who looked on to know that a new Heracles had also journeyed there, with a divine mandate to free the region's people from the heirs of Cacus who had terrorized them for so long.[68]

The decision taken by Fabius Maximus in 209/208 to have the temple of Hercules moved to the safety of the Capitol strongly suggests that Hannibal's visit had been something of a propaganda coup.[69] For all its ideological impact, however, the march on Rome had not achieved its major strategic aim, for at Capua in 211 the demoralized Senate had nonetheless surrendered to the Roman army, and paid a heavy price for its treachery. Anxious to make an example of the city, the Romans rounded up the leaders of the pro-Carthaginian faction and then scourged and executed them. All the other citizens were sold into slavery. The city itself was not completely destroyed, but was allowed to carry on as a humble agricultural market town under the direct rule of Roman officials, a mere shadow of its former self.[70] Indeed, the name of Capua was thereafter associated in the Roman imagination with the conceit of pride and the dangers of ambition.[71]

The impact of the loss of Capua was felt across the region, with a number of other Carthaginian-held towns falling to the Romans. Hannibal continued to enjoy some military success, however, most notably the defeat of a Roman army at Herdonea in 210, which resulted in the death of its general the proconsul Gnaeus Fulvius Centumalus, many of his senior officers and thousands of troops.[72] But by 209 even Tarentum had been lost, and the enormous amount of war booty captured from the city helped rescue Rome from the financial crisis in which it had been embroiled.[73]

The Romans now fought back in other ways. Fabius Maximus, the victorious Roman general, placed a colossal statue of Heracles captured at Tarentum on the Capitol, near to a bronze equestrian statue of himself.[74] The relocation of the statue not only played to Fabius' much trumpeted family connections to the hero, but also reclaimed Heracles for the Roman cause.

It was another member of the Fabii clan, Fabius Pictor, the senator who had been sent to Delphi in 216, who completed the first history of Rome by a Roman historian – his celebrated *Annales* (which has unfortunately not survived). Following the literary conventions of the day, Pictor wrote his opus in Greek. It is clear that he had read the western-Greek historians, such as Timaeus and Philinus, and had accepted the theory that the Romans were the descendants of the Trojans. Yet at the same time Pictor construed his work as a radical departure from the Greek-authored works that had preceded it. This was unashamedly a Roman history.[75] As well as highlighting his use of Roman documentary sources for his research, Pictor also provided careful explanations of archaic Roman customs.[76] The strong emphasis on traditional Roman culture was further underlined by the presentation of the work in the form of annals, a kind of official record traditionally used by the Romans to set down election results, religious ceremonies and other official notices.[77] Despite the Romanocentric hue of his work, however, Pictor, who was a committed philhellene, wrote with a Greek as well as an educated Roman audience in mind.[78] Indeed, one of the major aims of his project was to remind the inhabitants of mainland Greece and Magna Graecia that Rome had a distinguished past which represented far more than a pale reflection of the Hellenic world.[79]

The statement of Rome's cultural equality to Greece was, however, only one part of Fabius Pictor's agenda. He wrote his history during some of the most difficult moments of the war against Hannibal, probably finishing it around 210.[80] The first Roman history was thus written at a time when the Romans were bearing the brunt of a morale-sapping assault not only on the battlefield, but also on their collective identity. Their relationships with their gods, their allies and the wider Mediterranean world had all been called into question by potent

Carthaginian propaganda. Indeed, it is probably the Hannibalic context which explains Polybius' complaint that Pictor showed too much of a pro-Roman bias in his work.[81] In this time of crisis, Pictor attempted to show both Rome and its allies just how spectacularly successful the Romans had been.[82]

After relating the arrival of Aeneas and the Trojans in Italy, Pictor's *Annales* described their first foundation at Alba Longa, the eventual establishment of Rome just to the north of this, and other traditional stories such as the rape of the Sabine women.[83] Those stories stressed not only Rome's antiquity but also its historic and deep-seated ties with the other cities of Latium, key allies in the fight against Hannibal. Furthermore, the cultural links between southern Greeks and Romans were consolidated by reference to Evander, the leader of the Arcadian Greeks who had first settled the site of Rome.[84] Most significantly of all, Pictor is accredited with having given a detailed description of the activities of Hercules, presumably in Italy and specifically at the site of Rome.[85] Within the context of Hannibal's own particular claims to the Heraclean mantle, that description represented an attempt to resituate the legend firmly within Roman foundational history.

A NEW SCIPIO IN SPAIN

In Spain there had been some hope of a revival in Carthaginian fortunes with the defeat and deaths of both Publius and Gnaeus Scipio in 211.[86] The leaderless Roman forces, however, had rallied strongly under Lucius Marcius Septimus, irregularly proclaimed as leader by the troops. Furthermore, the capture of Capua had meant that many of the troops that had been involved in its siege could now be reassigned to Spain, and a new commander to oversee Roman forces in Spain was subsequently elected. The selection was controversial for a number of reasons. The consuls, unusually, brought their nomination before the Popular Assembly for validation, and their candidate should have been disbarred because he had not previously held the requisite senior senatorial post. Indeed, it appears that the powerful Cornelii clan had arranged things so that no one else would stand against Publius Cornelius Scipio, the 25-year-old son and nephew of the two dead generals. Although this may appear little more than nepotism, Scipio's appointment was a shrewd move, for there was no doubt that the Roman armies in Spain would welcome a Scipio as their new commander. It was also apparent, even at this early stage of his career, that the young Scipio was an exceptional man.[87]

Scipio was a member of a younger generation of junior Roman senators who had gained their experience solely against an enemy whose sophisticated use of military and propagandistic strategies was a clear advance on previous opposition. Much of Scipio's genius came from his capacity to borrow and even improve upon many of the strategies that Hannibal himself had deployed to such great effect. This included not only military but also ideological tactics, for Scipio appears to have believed that the most effective way to counter the widely held belief in Hannibal's divine sanction was to encourage the idea that he himself enjoyed heroic status and divine favour.[88] Stories thus went into circulation which connected Scipio's conception and subsequent life with the gods:

> Scipio was believed to be the son of Jupiter; for before he was conceived a serpent appeared in his mother's bed, and a snake crawled over him when he was an infant without doing him any harm. When he went back late to the Capitol, the [temple] dogs never barked at him. He never started out on any course of action without first having sat for a long time in the shrine of Jupiter, as if to receive the god's instruction.[89]

It is, of course, not difficult to see that these stories, which appear in a number of different ancient authors, were designed to create an association both with Alexander the Great and, primarily, with Heracles/Hercules (himself the son of Zeus/Jupiter). This constituted a direct challenge to a Hannibalic campaign that cast the Carthaginian general in the same light.[90]

Another story reported that when his elder brother Lucius stood for the aedileship, Scipio managed to secure election both for his sibling and himself by telling his mother that he had twice dreamt that this would come about, prompting Polybius to comment that 'people now believed that he communed with the gods not only in reality and by day, but still more in his sleep.'[91] Scipio's rumoured quasi-divinity demonstrates the extent to which the Roman people linked political and military success with divine favour (as in the case of Hannibal). While sceptical historians in the mould of Livy or Polybius might dismiss such associations as nothing more than gossip or superstition, it nonetheless seems clear that Scipio himself actively encouraged them.[92] Certainly Livy, despite condemning the tales about Scipio's miraculous birth as nothing more than gossip, strongly suggests that the Roman general did not discourage the impression that he enjoyed divine favour:

> He himself never made light of men's belief in these marvels; on the contrary it was rather promoted by a certain studied practice of neither denying such a thing nor openly asserting it. Many other things of the same sort, some true, some pretended, had passed the limits of admiration for a mere man in the case of this youth. Such were things upon which the citizens relied when they entrusted to any age far from mature the great responsibility of so great a command.[93]

Scipio's strategic manipulation of his heroic reputation is aptly demonstrated by events at the siege of New Carthage in 209. After learning that none of the Carthaginian armies operating on the Iberian peninsula was within ten days' march of the city, Scipio decided to attack. It was a bold but clever move, because if he were successful it would rob the Carthaginian commanders of a strategically important base and, furthermore, seriously weaken the Barcid reputation in Spain. Stationing his fleet opposite New Carthage, Scipio encouraged its defenders to think that an attack was to be mounted from the eastern, landward, side of the city by throwing up earthworks there. In fact the attack would come from the west, for he had learned from local fishermen that the lagoon which bordered that side of the city was fairly shallow, and further that during the ebb of the tide, towards evening, it emptied out through a narrow channel that connected it to the sea.[94] Scipio nevertheless told his troops a very different story, for he related how Neptune, the Roman sea god, had appeared to him in a dream and promised his assistance in capturing the city. The next day, after first launching a fierce assault on the city from the east in order to divert the attention of the Carthaginian defenders, Scipio ordered 500 of his men to cross the lagoon with ladders. After wading through the now shallow waters, the men quickly scaled the unguarded western

CARTHAGE MUST BE DESTROYED ~ Richard Miles
(2010) 373 pp

Book sent for Stanford trip to Tunisia

P. 73 Anatomy of practice of Child Sacrifice

p. 88 Punic was a Levantine dialect

p.127 Ancient tools of warfare

P. 142, 176 First Punic War

239-240 Used elephants in battle

walls. With Roman troops inside the city itself, New Carthage soon fell.[95]

The Neptune incident at the siege of New Carthage conforms to a now familiar model of myth-making as a strategic weapon. Polybius saw this incident as an example of how Scipio 'made the men under his command more sanguine and more ready to face dangerous enterprises by instilling in them the belief that his projects were divinely inspired'.[96] In Scipio, Hannibal thus found an opponent who not only provided a stiff challenge on the battlefield, but also presented himself as a serious rival for the Carthaginian's divine/heroic mantle.

In another indication that he had learned much from Hannibal, Scipio showed mercy to the inhabitants of New Carthage and let many of them return home. He also solved his own manpower problems by promising eventual liberty to the Carthaginian soldiers if they served on his warships and on labour details. The Spanish hostages whom he found in New Carthage were assured of their freedom to return home if their peoples became Roman allies.[97] And the Roman cause in Spain was further boosted by the enormous amount of captured booty: over 600 talents of silver and a vast quantity of war munitions, as well as a fully operational mint with which Scipio could immediately start issuing coinage.[98]

With these considerable resources at his disposal, Scipio now turned his attention to the three Carthaginian armies that were operating in Spain. A mass of defections to the Romans had led Hannibal's brother Hasdrubal to the conclusion that he had to attack Scipio as soon as possible. The two armies met in spring 208 at Baecula, in the north-west of the modern Spanish province of Jaén. Scipio, through bold and decisive action, soon got the better of Hasdrubal's forces, and the Carthaginian consequently put his reserve plan into operation, heading north with the remnants of his army with the intention of joining his brother in Italy.[99]

After this great and decisive victory, however, an embarrassing and potentially dangerous moment occurred when a number of Spanish chiefs acclaimed Scipio as king.[100] This was a title that would not win much favour in Rome, where regal aspirations were hated and feared in equal measure. Scipio, however, responded with characteristic diplomacy: 'He ordered silence to be proclaimed, and then told them that the title he valued most was the one his soldiers had given him, the title of "Imperator". "The name of king," he said, "so great elsewhere, is insupportable to Roman ears. If a kingly mind is in your eyes the noblest thing in human nature, you may attribute it to me in thought, but you must avoid the use of the word."'[101]

Despite Scipio's proclamation (mental or otherwise) as king, the Carthaginians were not yet spent, and had decided on a new course of action. While one army under Hasdrubal Gisco would attempt to hold the only part of the peninsula that remained loyal – the lower Guadalquivir valley and Gades – Mago would travel to the Balearic Islands to recruit fresh troops. Hasdrubal Barca, meanwhile, hurried north with the remainder of the Carthaginian forces, recruiting Gallic mercenaries as he went. After waiting until winter had passed, he and his Carthaginian army crossed the Alps into Italy, taking the easier route through the Durance and Mont Genèvre passes.[102]

With Hasdrubal departed for Italy, the Carthaginian position in Spain became increasingly desperate. A relief army sent from North Africa had been routed, leaving the remainder of the Carthaginian forces holed up in strongholds around Gades and the lower Guadalquivir valley. In the spring of 206, Hannibal's brother Mago, now returned from the Balearics, had joined up with Hasdrubal Gisco and decided to stake all in open battle with Scipio at Ilipa. Although the Carthaginian army was numerically greater (with 60,000 troops compared with the Roman 50,000), Scipio proved himself to be every bit as daring and original a general as Hannibal. After first putting pressure on the Carthaginians by drawing his army up for battle at daybreak, Scipio, rather than placing his crack Roman legionaries in the centre as was customary, stationed them on the flanks, with his less reliable Spanish auxiliaries at the centre. Using similar tactics to those of Hannibal at Cannae, therefore, Scipio let his battle line advance before ordering his legionaries on the wings to turn in on the centre. When the Spanish federates on the enemy flanks had been driven back, pressure was then brought to bear on the Carthaginian centre, which, after a hard fight, was eventually overthrown.[103]

After the final, desperate defeat at Ilipa, Carthaginian resistance in Spain quickly folded, with many of the senior command fleeing to their last real stronghold, Gades.[104] Even the subsequent illness of Scipio, a troop mutiny and a revolt against Rome by the powerful Ilergetes tribes could not revive the Carthaginian cause. By the end of 206, Mago, who had already had to put down an insurrection in the previously loyal stronghold of Gades, left the Iberian peninsula to join Hannibal in Italy and the people of Gades surrendered to the Romans. The once glittering imperial possession that had been Barcid Spain was no more, after little more than thirty years of existence.[105]

ITALY AND THE BATTLE FOR THE GODS

In 207 BC, while the situation in Spain looked increasingly favourable for the Romans, in Italy ominous prodigies had once again been widely witnessed: at Veii showers of stones were reported; at Menturnae the temple of Jupiter had been struck by lightning; and at Capua a wolf had stolen into the city and savaged one of the sentries. Most dramatically, at Frusino a hermaphrodite child was born the same size as a four-year-old. Diviners summoned from Etruria announced that the monstrous infant should be banished from Roman territory without any contact with the earth. After being placed in a box, therefore, the unfortunate child was taken out to sea and thrown overboard. The priests of Rome also decreed that three bands of nine virgins should process through the city chanting a hymn written for the occasion by the Tarentine poet Livius Andronicus. Andronicus was a shrewd choice for two reasons. He had written the first-ever Roman play, which had been publicly commissioned and first performed in 240 in celebration of the victorious conclusion of the First Punic War, and he and his work therefore stood as a symbol of Roman triumph over Carthage. As a Tarentine who wrote in Greek, furthermore, he represented Rome's strong links with the western-Greek world – links put under great strain, and in some cases completely severed, during the course of the war with Hannibal. For the Romans, again, re-establishing proper relations with the gods also demanded recapturing the propaganda initiative from the Carthaginians.

Soon after events at Frusino, the temple of Juno Regina on Rome's Aventine Hill was struck by lightning. In response to her apparent anger, the goddess was propitiated with a solid-gold basin, paid for out of the dowries of the matrons of Rome, and celebrated with solemn sacrifices.[106] Juno's implacable hostility to the Romans (and favour for the Carthaginians) became a very familiar theme in later Roman literature,[107] but this was the first public acknowledgement of that supposed enmity. Contemporary evidence suggests that Hannibal was at least partly responsible for the development of this tradition. While later Roman writers would identify Juno and Tanit, in this period an association had already been drawn in central Italy between Iuni, the Etruscan version of Juno, and the Punic goddess Astarte (on the Pyrgi Tablets).[108] On at least two occasions, Hannibal performed sacred rites at Lake Avernus, a volcanic-crater lake in Campania, widely thought to be the gateway to the underworld and sacred to Avernus, god of death, the husband of the goddess Juno Averna.[109] While it seems likely that Hannibal was worshipping Astarte at Avernus (or perhaps her divine consort Melqart), the Romans may have perceived his actions as an attempt to win over Juno to the Carthaginian cause. The religious rituals conducted at the temple of Juno Regina, therefore, once again point to the success of Hannibal's assault upon the sacred landscape of Italy.

The military situation was similarly portentous, for in the summer of 208 the two Roman consuls, Titus Quinctius Crispinus and Marcus Claudius Marcellus, had been killed.[110] Marcellus' signet ring had, furthermore, fallen into the hands of Hannibal, who then tried to use it to recapture the city of Salapia by sending a letter proclaiming the imminent arrival of the (in fact dead) Roman general. Crispinus, Marcellus' consular colleague, had however managed before his death to warn the surrounding cities, so that when Hannibal arrived at Salapia he could not gain admittance, even with a contingent of Roman deserters placed deceptively in the vanguard.[111] For the Romans it was crucial to prevent Hannibal and Hasdrubal from joining forces, and so Gaius Claudius Nero, one of the replacement consuls, was sent to contain the former in the south while his colleague Marcus Livius Salinator confronted the latter in the north. By early summer 207 Hasdrubal had successfully crossed the Alpine passes and reached the Po valley, with his army in good shape.[112] For Rome this was a particularly dangerous moment, since the Latins, who had hitherto been loyal, had grown increasingly tired of the seemingly endless demands that were placed upon them, and in 208 twelve of the thirty Roman colonies in Latium had refused to provide subsidies and troops for the war effort.

After wasting precious time on a failed siege of the Roman colony of Placentia, Hasdrubal collected more supplies and Gallic troops before marching down the Adriatic coast. In Bruttium, Hannibal made preparations to go north to meet his brother. Although he managed to keep his army on the move, the Carthaginians suffered considerable losses when challenged by Roman forces on a number of occasions. Yet greater disaster awaited, however. A letter sent by Hasdrubal to Hannibal which outlined where the meeting between their respective armies should take place fell into Roman hands after the messengers mistakenly went to Roman-held Tarentum and were captured. After informing the Senate, the consul Claudius Nero secretly marched north with a considerable force, leaving the remaining Roman soldiers to obstruct Hannibal at the Apulian town of Canusium. After a series of forced marches, Nero reached the camp of his consular colleague Salinator at Sena Gallica in Umbria, close to where Hasdrubal was encamped. Despite Roman efforts to conceal the arrival of this new force, the Carthaginian general realized that something was wrong and hastily tried to retreat. However, his guides deserted, and the Romans were soon harrying the lost Carthaginian army as they searched for a place to cross the river Metaurus. The situation soon became so desperate that Hasdrubal was forced to make a stand. After brave resistance the Carthaginian lines were eventually broken, and Hasdrubal, knowing that all was lost, charged into the Roman lines and was killed.[113] Tragically, Hannibal learned of the defeat through the sight of his brother's severed head being hurled before his lines. With the prospect of victory fast disappearing, he mustered his army and retreated to his enclave in Bruttium.[114] There he remained for the next few years living like a minor Hellenistic princeling, surrounded by the wreckage of his Italian dreams.[115]

Hannibal's misery was now compounded by the return of the victorious Scipio from Spain. Despite a masterful stage-managed account of his victories in front of the Senate at the temple of Bellona, and war booty totalling a massive 6,500 kilograms of silver, Scipio nevertheless failed to obtain a triumph, for he had never held a senior magistracy. Such was his popularity, however, that he easily won the election for the consulship in 205.

Scipio now pushed hard to be granted North Africa as his field of operation, for he believed that the Carthaginians would be finished off only if defeated in their homeland.[116] Others, led by Fabius Maximus, wanted to concentrate on first driving Hannibal out of Italy, but eventually, after an increasingly heated debate, a compromise was reached. Scipio was allotted Sicily as his theatre of command, but with the proviso that he could attack North Africa if it served the Senate's interests. His consular colleague, Publius Licinius Crassus, was to remain in Italy and keep the pressure on Hannibal.[117] This arrangement clearly favoured Scipio, and his senatorial opponents therefore tried to hamper his war preparations by refusing him the right to levy troops. Many, however, simply volunteered to fight under him, and a number of loyal Italian states provided timber for ships, as well as corn and munitions. Scipio was thus able to proceed to Sicily to train his army for the battle in North Africa.[118]

Defeated in Spain, Hannibal's brother Mago landed at Liguria in the spring of 205, bringing with him 12,000 infantry and 2,000 cavalry. By that summer, after receiving further reinforcements from Carthage and from among the Gauls and Ligurians, he was ready to move south. The Romans, however, now experienced in dealing with such a threat, simply blocked both sides of the Apennines, meaning that for the next two years Mago and his army were effectively trapped in northern Italy.[119] Hannibal also could do little but wait in his enclave at Bruttium, for he found himself increasingly blockaded both by sea and by land.[120] In the summer of 205 eighty Carthaginian transport ships bound for Bruttium were captured, and no help could be expected from his 'ally' Philip of Macedon:[121] through a series of treaties with Philip's enemies in Greece and Asia Minor the Romans had cleverly ensured that Philip was far too preoccupied at home to contemplate an intervention,[122] and in 205, with the pressure mounting, he had hastily sued for peace with Rome and its allies, thereby jettisoning his previous treaty with Carthage.[123]

The Roman Senate now sensed that the fragile alliance of Carthaginians, Italians and Greeks which Hannibal had constructed was poised to dissolve. It therefore undertook two ideologically charged missions which brilliantly emphasized the cultural links between Rome, Italy and Greece. The Senate now decided to fulfil the promise of a share in the booty for the oracle at Delphi made over ten years previously. Two ambassadors were sent over to Greece with a golden wreath weighing 90 kilograms and other silver trophies from the spoils of the victory over Hasdrubal.[124] Around the same time, a high-ranking Roman delegation was making its way eastward to receive a religious relic from Attalus, king of Pergamum. The object which they were to bring back to their city was a sacred stone of the earth goddess, Cybele (whom the Romans called Magna Mater, 'the Great Mother'). Earlier in 205, continued religious portents had led to another consultation of the sacred Sibylline books. Found within their hallowed pages was a prophecy that foretold the final defeat of Hannibal if the Magna Mater was returned to Rome.[125] Some have puzzled at the timing of this prophecy, particularly as Hannibal was by now a spent force.[126] But great unease still lingered at Rome long after final victory on the battlefield seemed assured.

Indeed, Hannibal's most lasting impact on Rome was not the bloody defeats that he inflicted on its legions at the Trebia, Lake Trasimene or Cannae, but his successful appropriation of much of the mythological legacy (particularly the Heraclean legacy) that had acted as the keystone both in Rome's cultural and political affiliation with the Greek world and in its subsequent claims to the leadership of the central and western Mediterranean. The missions both to Delphi and, in particular, to bring back the Magna Mater therefore marked the beginnings of a protracted exorcism of the doubts and insecurities that Hannibal and his advisers had so skilfully planted in the collective consciousness of the Roman elite. The original home of the Magna Mater had been Mount Ida near Troy, and later myth would claim that Aeneas and his followers had once taken refuge there at the beginning of the journey to Rome.[127] The journey to Pergamum and the negotiations for the sacred stone were thus a very public reaffirmation of Rome's heritage within the wider Hellenistic world, and by extension a reiteration of the historical and cultural connections that Hannibal had worked so hard to dismantle.

13

The Last Age of Heroes

THE TABLES TURN

By 204, after having his proconsular command extended for another year, Scipio was ready to take the war to North Africa. He had spent his time on Sicily carefully preparing for the invasion. As well as undertaking the important task of training and drilling his expeditionary force, he had also found the time to cross back to Italy in 205 and had recaptured the Calabrian town of Locri, thus keeping up the pressure on Hannibal. He had also travelled to North Africa, in order to visit Syphax, the king of the powerful Massaesylian Numidian kingdom, at his capital of Siga. Mindful that they would need friends in North Africa if the invasion was to be a success, the Romans had been assiduously courting this wily political operator since as early as 213. However, Syphax, although continuing to maintain friendly relations with Rome, had clearly calculated that for the time being it was safer to stay in an alliance with Carthage, which was still better placed to have a direct impact on his realm. Now, as the time for the great Roman invasion approached, Scipio made another attempt to detach the king from the Carthaginians. By an extraordinary coincidence, his old Punic opponent from Spain, Hasdrubal Gisco, was also at Siga, having arrived there on his way back to Carthage. Syphax, juggling the competing claims of these two great powers as skilfully as ever, managed to persuade both the Roman general and his Carthaginian adversary to enjoy his hospitality together. Hasdrubal was reportedly so impressed by his Roman counterpart that he left for Carthage in fear for the future of his homeland.[1]

Scipio had nonetheless made the same miscalculation as his

predecessors (including his late father and uncle) when he departed from Siga thinking that he had secured Syphax's support in the up-coming North African campaign. Hasdrubal Gisco, aware of the temptation the Roman overture would present to the Numidian king, had recemented the bonds between Carthage and Syphax by offering his daughter Sophonisba in marriage. Desire would succeed where diplomacy had failed, for the old king fell passionately in love with his lively, intelligent and beautiful young queen. A new alliance between the Massaesylians and Carthage was subsequently signed, after which Hasdrubal persuaded the king to send a message to Scipio in Sicily informing him of the new pact.[2]

Even after this disappointment, the odds were still very much stacked in Scipio's favour. While the Carthaginians had no real standing army in North Africa, and Hannibal's force was languishing in Bruttium, the invasion force of 35,000 men that Scipio had mobilized was a formid-able proposition. At its heart were two legions of battle-hardened veterans who had spent the previous decade in exile, fighting in Sicily as a punishment for fleeing the field at Cannae. This group, we are told, were particularly eager to make amends for their previous transgres-sion. In the spring of 204 the expeditionary force left Lilybaeum to make the crossing to North Africa in a flotilla of 400 transport carriers with a guard of 20 warships. However, unfavourable weather forced Scipio to land the force near the city of Utica, to the north of Carthage, rather than at Syrtis Minor to the south, which would have exposed the fertile region of Cap Bon.[3]

The Carthaginians, although they must have predicted an imminent invasion, were still unprepared and, in an attempt to stall the Roman army while they mustered their own forces and awaited Syphax's Numidian contingents, they sent out two separate cavalry detachments to engage the enemy. Both forces were easily defeated. The Carthagin-ians were nevertheless saved by the close of the campaigning season, and Scipio, after failing to take the well-fortified Utica and conscious that the Carthaginian army was now finally assembled, withdrew and set up camp for the winter.[4]

Realizing that the Carthaginian army would be a much weaker proposition without its Numidian cavalry, Scipio used the lull in fight-ing to make another attempt at luring Syphax over to the Roman side.

The king, clearly concerned about the instability that a war in North Africa could bring to his own realm, was by this time far more anxious to broker a truce between Carthage and Rome (based on mutual withdrawal from the other's homeland). But Scipio, anxious for more personal glory and sensing that a definitive victory could be won, merely feigned interest in this proposition while secretly having an officer reconnoitre the enemy camps. From the information gleaned from this scouting operation, he resolved to launch a surprise attack on the Carthaginian and Numidian positions. One night, after setting up a diversion, Scipio attacked the camps by setting fire to the huts – made out of extremely flammable wood and foliage or reeds – where the Carthaginian and Numidian troops lived, with the result that much of the enemy army of 50,000 infantry and 13,000 cavalry was killed. This disastrous blow to the Carthaginian cause was followed several months later, in 203, by another major defeat at the hands of Scipio, this time in open battle on the great plains south of Utica. The Carthaginian Council of Elders now had little option but to play their final card, and summoned Hannibal back from Italy.[5]

The Carthaginians stalled for time while they awaited Hannibal's arrival. They sent a thirty-man commission to Scipio at Tunes with a mandate to discuss treaty terms. After first prostrating themselves in front him in the Levantine tradition, the envoys proceeded to accept full responsibility for their present predicament, before then laying much of the blame for Carthage's actions on the Barcid clan and their supporters. In response, Scipio offered the following terms: the Carthaginians were to hand over all their prisoners of war as well as any deserters and refugees; they were to withdraw their armies from Italy, Gaul and Spain, and evacuate all the islands between Italy and Africa; they were to surrender their entire navy with the exception of twenty vessels, and provide huge quantities of wheat and barley to the Roman army; and finally they were to pay an indemnity of 5,000 talents of silver. These strictures were undoubtedly harsh, but previously Scipio had been determined to reject any peace proposals and destroy the city of Carthage itself. He had probably changed his mind only after his failure to take Utica, when he had realized that any siege of Carthage would be time-consuming and expensive in terms of both lives and material resources. And a long-drawn-out siege also presented the danger that Scipio himself might be replaced by another magistrate before final victory.[6]

The Carthaginian Council of Elders accepted the terms, and in the late summer of 203 a delegation was sent to Rome to conclude the treaty with the Senate. The ambassadors, apparently following an agreed strategy, once more blamed the Barcids for their present woes: 'He [Hannibal] had no orders from their Senate to cross the Hiberus, much less the Alps. It was on his own authority that he had made war not only on Rome but even on Saguntum; anyone who took a just view would recognize that the treaty with Rome remained unbroken to that day.'[7] After absolving the Carthaginian Council of Elders of any responsibility for the war, the envoys argued that it was not Carthage but in fact Hannibal who had first broken the terms of 241. The purpose of this rhetoric became clear when they proceeded to request that it should be only that treaty that was recognized – a far more advantageous arrangement, because it would have left the Carthaginians free to continue in the Balearic Islands and perhaps even southern Spain. Having ensured that the Roman offensive would be suspended while negotiations were ongoing, therefore, the envoys were now attempting to secure a better deal. Even if that deal was rejected, the longer their discussions continued, the more time Hannibal and Mago would have to return to North Africa.

The Roman senators were no fools, however, and poured scorn on the transparent Carthaginian tactics (not least because it soon became clear that the Carthaginian delegation were too young to remember the actual terms of the 241 treaty). But, incredibly, motivated perhaps by suspicion both of Hannibal and of the ever-successful Scipio, the Senate grudgingly ratified the new treaty, with the proviso that it should come into force only when the armies of Mago and Hannibal had finally left Italy.[8]

Hannibal reacted to the command to evacuate bitterly. The blame game had long since begun in the Council of Elders, but Hannibal quickly showed that he too was not averse to finding an appropriate scapegoat. According to Livy:

> It is said that he gnashed his teeth, groaned, and almost shed tears when he heard what the delegates had to say. After they had delivered their instructions, he exclaimed, 'The men who tried to drag me back by

cutting off my supplies of men and money are now recalling me not by crooked means but plainly and openly. So you see, it is not the Roman people who have been so often routed and cut to pieces that have vanquished Hannibal, but the Carthaginian Senate by their detraction and envy. It is not Scipio who will pride himself and exult over the disgrace of my return so much as Hanno who has crushed my house, since he could do it in no other way, beneath the ruins of Carthage.'[9]

Mutual recriminations continued to fly between the Barcids and their opponents as the fragile accord built on Hannibal's previous success began to fracture. Yet the Council of Elders had never been simply split between pro- and anti-Barcid factions, for many of the latter had been willing to support Hannibal while his aggressive strategy had brought prestige, booty and conquered territory. Once the bad news had started to arrive from the various Carthaginian fronts, the euphoria had quickly been replaced by growing concern and then anger. By 203, many who had previously been content to bask in the glory of Hannibal's achievements had now joined the ever-louder chorus of disapproval emanating from Hanno and his supporters.

Hannibal nevertheless obeyed the command to return. His brother Mago, however, never reached his homeland, for, though he successfully embarked his troops in Liguria, he himself died of battle wounds as the fleet passed Sardinia, and a significant number of his ships were captured by the Romans.[10] Hannibal landed in North Africa with an army composed of 15,000–20,000 experienced veterans. He had left some troops behind to garrison the few towns and cities that still remained loyal to him, and had released others entirely from his service.

The Romans now moved to undermine the memory of Hannibal's considerable support in Italy, as well as the divine favouritism which his cause had claimed. A story was circulated which told how he had massacred his Italian troops when, refusing to embark for Africa, they had sought refuge in the temple of Juno at Cape Lacinium.[11] Although the story was surely apocryphal, it is likely that its setting was carefully chosen by those who sought to blacken Hannibal's name, for it had been at that temple, just 10 kilometres away from his last base at Croton, that the Carthaginian general had sought to secure his Italian legacy by erecting a bronze tablet listing his achievements on the peninsula, in both Latin and Greek. Polybius, a visitor to the temple, proclaimed his trust in the accuracy of the troop and animal numbers that it presented. However, he also intimated that other information it contained, which he did not include, was of a more dubious nature.[12]

This is not the only clue that Hannibal and his advisers, as they whiled away the days in their last stronghold at Bruttium, had come to see this famous sanctuary of Juno as a useful prop in their attempts to secure the lasting legacy of their campaign in Italy.[13] The site was well known for the supernatural happenings that took place: there was, for example, an altar in the entrance court where the ashes were never stirred by the wind.[14] Yet it was also an extremely pleasant spot, with an enclosure surrounded by dense woodland, and its centre blessed with rich pasture on which a variety of different breeds of cattle, sacred to the goddess, grazed. Such was the security and seclusion of the place that the cattle had no need of a cowherd, but simply took themselves back to their stalls at the end of the day. A portion of the huge profits made from the sale of these beasts had been used to pay for the making of a column of solid gold which was then dedicated to Juno.

A story, attributed to the Roman historian Coelius, but thought by most scholars to have originated from Silenus, told of how Hannibal had wanted to carry off the gold column, but first he had a hole bored into it to ascertain whether it was hollow or not. Juno, however, appeared to Hannibal in a dream and warned that she would blind him in his one good eye if he carried out the theft. On waking, not only did Hannibal heed the warning, but he also had a statuette of a heifer fashioned out of the swarf created when the column had been drilled, which was then set upon the top of the column.[15]

Like the other surviving stories detailing Hannibal's dialogue with the gods, it is almost impossible to separate the original sense and aim of this tale from the hostile interpretations subsequently made by Roman and Greek historians.[16] However, as with the other stories, it is most likely that its purpose was to highlight Hannibal's sense of duty and devotion to the gods – in this case Juno/Hera, a goddess already with a reputation for hostility towards the Romans. Once the Carthaginian general was aware of the grave sacrilege that he was about to commit, he not only desisted but also sought to make good the slight that he had afforded the goddess.[17] It was only subsequently that Roman historians turned it into a parable highlighting Hannibal's supposed impiety. In addition, the Cape Lacinium sanctuary may not have appealed to Hannibal only because of its connections with Juno. One tradition had it that the temple had been built by none other than Heracles.[18]

The details of the story also hold other clues as to its Hannibalic provenance. Scholars have long recognized the close parallels between this tale and the claim made by the Greek philosopher Euhemerus, whose ideas had been such a key element of Hannibal's association with Heracles–Melqart, that on an island in the Indian Ocean he had discovered a golden column on which was carved the most ancient history of the world, and particularly an account of the origins of humankind through the earliest Greek gods.[19] The story of the golden heifer, as a final evocation of the euhemeristic creed through which the Carthaginian general had tried to reach out to the Greek world, was as much a testament to the Hannibalic legacy as the inscription that detailed his troop numbers and military campaigns. However, one must imagine that later, under Silenus' skilful pen as he wrote up his account of Hannibal's expedition after its final failure, it became a mournful eulogy to the last great champion of the syncretistic realm of Heracles–Melqart.

Long after Hannibal's departure, the Romans remained wary of the sanctuary and the goddess. When the censor Quintus Fulvius Flaccus removed the tiles from the roof of the temple in 174/173 for use on a temple to Fortune that he was building in Rome, the Senate quickly moved to counter this perceived impiety. During a severe carpeting by his senatorial peers, Flaccus was asked, 'Had he considered that he had insufficiently violated the temple, the most revered in that region, one which neither Pyrrhus nor Hannibal had violated, unless he had foully removed its roof and almost torn it down?' After a careful expiation had been carried out, the tiles were returned to the temple – where they were placed in the building, because none of the masons could master how to secure them back on the roof.[20]

Roman accounts of a massacre of Italian troops at the sanctuary may well have been aimed at countering Hannibalic claims that the temple of Juno at Cape Lacinium represented the final coordinate of the heroic journey that the Carthaginian general had made over the previous fifteen years. Yet even if the accusation was false, what could not be denied was that, in departing from Italy, Hannibal had left his Italian allies to an uncertain future. Indeed, the extraordinary number of coin hoards found in Bruttium, clearly buried by their owners until better times returned, bear mute but tragic testament to the ominous position of those left behind.[21]

In an indication of his lack of trust in the Council of Elders, Hannibal did not proceed directly to Carthage, but camped at the port of Hadrumetum, some 120 kilometres south of the metropolis. He had arrived just in time, because by the spring of 202 the fragile truce with Rome had been broken. When the Carthaginians looted and requisitioned some Roman supply vessels driven ashore by a storm, the Roman envoys sent to demand reparations had been given short shrift, for the Council of Elders had clearly been buoyed by the nearby presence of Hannibal and his troops. The envoys, furthermore, were nearly lynched by a mob and saved only by the timely intervention of the leaders of the anti-Barcid faction, Hasdrubal Haedus and Hanno. The more extreme elements within the Council of Elders nevertheless then attempted an ambush, and while the envoys' ship managed to escape, several fatalities were inflicted.[22]

This deliberate provocation now led Scipio to act decisively. First he summoned his ally the Numidian king Masinissa to join him with his forces, and then, in a clear attempt to force Hannibal into open battle, he started a brutal campaign of attacking and razing to the ground a number of towns situated in the populous and fertile Medjerda valley, selling their populations into slavery. This ruthless tactic soon bore fruit, and representatives from the Carthaginian Council of Elders implored Hannibal to attack Scipio as soon as possible.[23]

Hannibal thus marched north-westward, perhaps with the intention of cutting off Masinissa and his troops before they could join up with Scipio's army. In October 202 he eventually caught up with the Romans at Zama, about five days' march to the south-west of Carthage. Scipio, in a marvellous display of morale-boosting bravado, invited captured Carthaginian scouts sent to reconnoitre the Roman positions to walk freely around his camp and take back their discoveries to their general. This gesture may have been less carefree than it first appears, however, for Scipio relocated his camp to a new position soon after. With the two armies now making the necessary preparations for combat, Hannibal requested a meeting with Scipio. The Carthaginian, whose enormous experience perhaps already told him that military victory against Scipio's forces was unlikely, tried to negotiate new, milder, terms for a treaty. Scipio, however, confident of a victory on the battlefield, refused.[24]

The next morning battle was joined. Although Hannibal's army was more numerous, with now around 50,000 men to Scipio's 29,000, the 6,000 well-trained Numidian cavalry provided by Masinissa gave the Romans a significant advantage. With little cavalry of his own and an untested infantry, Hannibal's battle strategy reflected his rather limited options. Unlike in Italy, where he had often been able to use his advantage in cavalry to encircle the enemy at the wings, at Zama he lined his men up in three lines, with the remnants of his brother Mago's mercenary army in the front rank, a force of Libyan levies and Carthaginian citizens in the second, and his own force of heavily armoured veterans in reserve. His tactics would be simple: he would use brute force to drive a way through the centre of the Roman army, drawn up in a similar formation of three lines (with the most experienced troops at the rear). This was certainly not the most sophisticated battle plan, but considering the resources at Hannibal's disposal it probably represented the most realistic option.

The lack of coherence within the Carthaginian army was highlighted from the beginning of the battle, for Hannibal merely exhorted and encouraged his own veterans in the third row, and the responsibility for rousing the other groups fell to the captains.

In order to make the initial break through the Roman front line, Hannibal relied on a troop of eighty elephants. However, Scipio had already prepared his force for that particular challenge by creating broad corridors through the three massed ranks of his troops. When at last the battle began and the elephants charged, most of those beasts that did not panic and rampage back into their own lines were easily channelled down the lanes that cut through the Roman ranks. Taking advantage of the turmoil, Masinissa's horsemen and the Roman cavalry charged their opposite numbers and drove them from the battlefield.

Among the infantry, the fight was far more even-handed, with both sides standing their ground and inflicting heavy losses on the other before eventually the Carthaginian first and second lines were forced back. After Scipio had reordered his troops into one single massed line, the struggle began against Hannibal's 20,000 battle-hardened veterans, who had been kept in reserve by their commander. The two forces proved evenly matched until the returning Roman cavalry attacked the rear of the Carthaginian lines. Many of Hannibal's famed soldiers were killed, with around the same number captured.[25] It was a crippling blow, both for Hannibal himself, who had managed to escape the battleground, and for Carthage. Zama effectively brought the second great war between Rome and Carthage to an end.[26]

THE AFTERMATH OF WAR

After first fleeing to his base at Hadrumetum, Hannibal then travelled to Carthage for a crisis summit with the Council of Elders. His advice to the assembled grandees was typically blunt: the war was lost, and Carthage's only hope of salvation was now to sue for peace. The Council acted quickly. Ten envoys, including the leaders of the pro-peace party, Hanno and Hasdrubal Haedus, were at once sent to the Romans in a ship decorated with olive branches (the traditional symbols of supplication) and with a herald's caduceus fixed to its prow. Scipio, meeting the ship as his own fleet sailed towards Carthage, ordered the envoys to travel on to Tunes, where he was camped. The peace terms that he proposed there were understandably harsher than those that he had previously offered. In addition to the previous provisions, Carthage was now forbidden from fighting any wars outside Africa, and even on that continent it had first to seek permission from Rome. The indemnity was now set at 10,000 talents (26,000 kilograms) of silver, to be paid over fifty years – nearly ten times the amount demanded in the terms of the 241 treaty. Moreover, Carthage was to hand over all its war elephants, and its fleet was to be reduced to just ten warships.[27]

At Carthage the terms were accepted by the Council of Elders with only one exception. A certain Gisco had stood up to speak against the treaty, but Hannibal, clearly exasperated by this refusal to acknowledge the harsh reality of the situation, manhandled him off the stage. As an indication of the tensions that already existed between Hannibal and many of the elders, the general was forced to apologize for his behaviour. The Council nevertheless accepted Hannibal's advice to accept these terms as relatively lenient. And so, towards the end of 202, Carthaginian envoys led by Hasdrubal Haedus travelled to Rome and declared to the Senate their agreement to the peace conditions, before returning to North Africa, where the treaty was ratified. Carthage's fleet was then dramatically burnt in full view of its citizens, and Latin and Roman deserters were executed. Scipio then embarked his army, as well as 4,000 prisoners of war released by the Carthaginians, and set off for Rome, where he held a magnificent triumph. As a tribute to his extraordinary achievements, he would for ever after be known as 'Africanus'.[28]

According to several Roman sources, Hannibal remained in charge of the remnants of his army and kept them occupied by organizing the planting of a huge number of olive groves.[29] By 196 BC, however, he had apparently tired of semi-private life, and had decided to enter the political arena as a Carthaginian suffete. He would quickly prove himself to be as dynamic a statesman as he was a general.

By exposing and attacking the abuses and corruption that had for so long been a hallmark of Carthaginian political life, Hannibal quickly built himself a reputation as a champion of the common citizenry. He successfully proposed a new law which stated that the Tribunal of One Hundred and Four's membership should henceforth be decided by annual election, and that no one should serve consecutive terms. Such a populist move was never likely to have endeared him to the Council of Elders, which he appears to have circumvented entirely.

Animosities were further heightened when Hannibal then announced an audit of public revenues, which he would personally oversee. After conducting a thorough investigation, he supposedly discovered that large amounts of state funds were being lost due to embezzlement by officials. He then declared in the Popular Assembly that if the duties collected on property and port duties were correctly collected there would be enough to pay the indemnity owed to Rome without recourse to extra taxation. Although this must have further boosted Hannibal's popularity among the people of Carthage, the animosity directed at him by the corrupt officials commensurately increased.[30]

In adopting such a populist agenda, Hannibal appeared to be following the same political strategy that had so benefited Hamilcar and Hasdrubal Barca nearly forty years previously. Indeed, Hannibal's deliberate use of the Popular Assembly to push his measures through and limit the powers of the broader elite placed him on the well-worn path of Barcid demagogy. It has been argued that Hannibal was also the driving force behind an ambitious new construction programme which witnessed the building of new residential quarters and the great improvement of the city in general.[31] Were some on the Council of Elders worried that these populist reforms were building to a bid for autocratic power? Such concerns would certainly explain the Council's subsequent move, which was to send reports to Rome that Hannibal was secretly negotiating with Antiochus, king of the Seleucid Empire. Antiochus, whose realm stretched from south-eastern Asia Minor (Turkey) in the west to the kingdom of Bactria (modern Afghanistan) in the east, was now involved in a tense diplomatic confrontation with the Romans over Greece and the Greek cities of western Asia Minor.[32] When Roman envoys subsequently arrived in Carthage to investigate the claims, in 195, Hannibal was forced to flee east, travelling via Tyre and Antioch and thence on to Ephesus, where Antiochus had his court. Paradoxically, accusations that Hannibal was in collusion with Antiochus left the Carthaginian with little option but to seek the king's protection.[33]

At the court of Antiochus, Hannibal proposed a daring return to Carthage and a subsequent attack on the Italian peninsula.[34] The dispatch of an agent to arrange a prior Carthaginian rebellion with the Barcids in North Africa spectacularly failed, however,[35] and the Carthaginians, nervous of their new overlords' potential reaction, quickly informed the Roman Senate of Hannibal's machinations. Hannibal had grossly underestimated the degree of support which the once lone voice of Hanno now enjoyed at Carthage, and his attempts to secure an opportunity to make good the failures of the past looked increasingly desperate. Snubbed by his own people, the victor of Cannae now found himself on the fringes of Antiochus' court. Indeed, Antiochus and his advisers must have had serious concerns about the strategy that Hannibal reportedly advocated. According to Livy, his plan was 'always one and the same, that the war should be waged in

Italy; Italy would supply both food and soldiers to a foreign enemy; if no disturbance was created there and the Roman people was permitted to use the manpower and resources of Italy for a war outside Italy, neither the king nor any people could be a match for the Romans.'[36] When war between Rome and Antiochus did eventually break out, Hannibal's strategic advice remained equally quixotic and was, unsurprisingly, politely ignored.[37]

Hannibal would, however, have one final fleeting taste of military glory. Recognizing that the general's Punic roots would play well with the Phoenician cities of the Levant, he was dispatched by Antiochus to muster and prepare a small fleet of warships.[38] This Seleucid naval force clashed with the Roman fleet off the coast of Pamphylia in Asia Minor, and for some time the left wing, commanded by Hannibal, managed to hold its own against far more experienced and skilful opponents. Eventually, however, the Seleucid ships were driven back and were effectively blockaded in the port of Side. One can only imagine Hannibal's shock and sorrow to see Carthaginian ships among the Roman fleet.[39]

With the Seleucids eventually defeated at Magnesia in Asia Minor in 189, Hannibal spent the rest of his life wandering the courts of the Hellenistic East. Although his exact itinerary remains a matter of conjecture, anecdotal evidence places him variously on Crete and in Armenia (where he supposedly helped to build a new city).[40] His final refuge, however, was Bithynia, a kingdom in north-western Asia Minor. Here he is said to have continued his career as an urban planner, by creating a new capital, as well as developing the tactic of hurling snake-filled pots on to the decks of enemy ships during battles at sea. Despite the services which he provided for the Bithynian king Pruisas, Hannibal was nonetheless a diplomatic liability. When, in 183, the Roman general Titus Quinctius Flaminius visited Bithynia, he upbraided the king when Hannibal's presence was discovered. Pruisas, concerned about the repercussions of shielding so controversial a guest at a time when Roman power was growing in the region, immediately resolved to surrender Hannibal. When Bithynian soldiers blocked off all exits from his hideout on the coast, Hannibal, realizing that escape was impossible, took the poison that he always carried with him, thus avoiding the humiliation of capture. As he

died, according to Livy, he condemned the Romans for their vindic-
tiveness, impiety and lack of faith.[41] Thus the life of Carthage's
greatest son reached its dramatic end.

THE LAST AGE OF HEROES

The final sad years of Hannibal's life might be viewed as a parable
of Roman vengefulness, but in fact his fate had been largely decided
by his own countrymen. Tired of his egotistical manoeuvrings to
undermine the Carthaginian political system at a time of distinct instability, the majority of the Council of Elders had been desperate to
be rid of him. Hannibal's political failures and misjudgements become
more understandable, however, when one considers that, beyond the
network of loyalties and relationships that were part of his Barcid
inheritance, he was a stranger to the Carthaginian elite, in a way that
Hamilcar and Hasdrubal Barca, who had spent their formative years
in the city, had not been. With his restless energy and inability to
tolerate dissent, Hannibal therefore took his place among that long
line of military heroes who would prove themselves singularly ill-
suited for political office.

In Rome, the news of Hannibal's death received a mixed reaction.
According to Plutarch, some approved of Flaminius' action, because
they 'thought that Hannibal, as long as he lived, was a consuming fire
which needed only to be fanned; for when he was not in his prime,
they said, it was not his body nor his arm that had been formidable
against the Romans, but his ability and experience coupled with his
deep bitterness and hostility'.[42] Others, however, 'thought that the
conduct of Titus [Flaminius] was cruel: for it had killed Hannibal when
he was like a bird allowed to live a tame and harmless life because he
was too old to fly and without tail feathers'.[43] Leading the latter party
was Scipio Africanus – a fact which some have seen as a reflection of
the Roman's high regard for his erstwhile opponent.[44] Scipio was,
however, far too much of a pragmatist to allow such sentimentality to
cloud his judgement. The Roman hero, who knew the political situation
in Carthage better than most, knew that Hannibal now had no chance
of rousing a rebellion against the might of Rome.

It could nevertheless be argued that both sides were right. Although Hannibal was certainly no longer a threat in Carthaginian terms, at the royal courts of the Hellenistic kings his name must surely have still conjured up the seductive image of resistance to Rome. Hannibal himself had been quick to realize this, and had soon produced at least one anti-Roman tract – written in the early 180s, and in the form of a speech addressed to the people of Rhodes – in which he outlined the barbarous outrages committed in Asia Minor by the Roman general Gnaeus Manlius Vulso, with the clear intention of turning his audience against Roman power.[45] Others too were anxious to appropriate the influence still attached to Hannibal's name. In the same period a fake letter, supposedly written by the Carthaginian general after Cannae, was in circulation. In it 'Hannibal' announced his famous victory and foretold that a rebellion among the Greeks would bring an end to Roman domination of the eastern Mediterranean.[46] For many at Rome, therefore, the mere existence of Hannibal, not just at the court of the enemy, but simply as a symbol of resistance, may well have demanded his death.

The reasons for Rome's pursuit of Hannibal, however, extended well beyond any threat that he himself might still represent, for the divisive feelings which he inspired within the Roman Senate made his pursuit a matter of internal politics also. The persecution of Hannibal was therefore also the persecution of his nemesis turned protector Scipio Africanus. The fate of the two men had always been intimately inter-twined, and in the wake of his victories in North Africa the Roman hero had found himself similarly isolated by the political establishment at home. In Rome itself, although a number of his supporters had won elections to high political office, Scipio had achieved very little of worth during his own second consulship, of 194, and he found his ambitions increasingly frustrated by a growing band of opponents in the Senate. Indeed, Scipio's inability to transfer the success that he had enjoyed on the battlefield to the political sphere appeared closely to mirror the disappointments that Hannibal had suffered in Carthage.

For Scipio, decline had begun when he and his brother Lucius were recalled to Rome from their victorious military campaign against Antiochus. Their political enemies, led by Marcus Porcius Cato, had persuaded the Senate to pass a bill whereby consuls should hold commands for only a single year, and had then attempted to prosecute several of their friends and supporters. The Scipios then found themselves under attack when they were called to account for 500 talents of silver given to them by Antiochus as a term of the armistice. Scipio Africanus did not help himself by haughtily tearing up the campaign account books in full view of the Senate. Sensing weakness, Cato and his supporters continued to press the Scipios, and the more the latter refused to account for the money, the more suspicions grew. Finally, in 184, Scipio Africanus suffered the indignity of being prosecuted in the courts on the charge of taking bribes from Antiochus. Realizing that his enemies were in the ascendant, Scipio now opted to leave Rome for his estates at Liternum in Campania, and Cato, his political aims achieved, let the prosecution drop.[47] Within a year, however, the great hero of Zama died a broken man.

That the downfalls of these two great men should follow such similar trajectories is perhaps unsurprising when one considers not only the congruities in their respective political strategies, but also the political systems within which they operated. Scipio, the great hero and a powerful symbol of Roman triumph over Carthage, soon became a dangerous, destabilizing force within a system that centred on the elaborate fiction that all members of its Senate were equal.[48] Hannibal's presence within the political scene at Carthage had proved similarly problematic. His populist reforms, and the concomitant contempt which he showed for fellow members of the Council, presented him to others as a potential autocrat. Confronted with a living hero in their very midst – a hero whose very stature threatened to dwarf those institutions he had been charged to protect – both the Carthaginian Council and the Roman Senate had acted decisively to isolate their former champions. The last age of heroes had come to an emphatic close.

14

The Desolation of Carthage

THE REVENGE OF THE LOSERS

By the 180s BC the benefits of no longer being a great power were becoming increasingly apparent for many Carthaginians. In what has been termed the 'revenge of the losers', Carthage was freed from the burdens and responsibilities of war and empire, and thus staged a remarkable economic recovery. Reportedly, just ten years after the end of the war, the Carthaginians were able to offer to settle, forty years early, the entire indemnity that was owed to Rome, a proposal that the latter refused.[1] How had this economic miracle been achieved? The answer lies in a number of developments that had taken place in the years after the end of the First Punic War.

First, the loss of Sicily and Sardinia had led to a huge expansion of the settlement and agricultural exploitation of Carthage's North African hinterland.[2] The agricultural infrastructure appears to have survived Scipio's African campaign relatively unscathed. Despite the Roman military campaign in the last years of the Second Punic War, North Africa did not suffer the same devastation as certain parts of Italy. Even Scipio Africanus' scorched-earth policy in the Medjerda valley had been a strictly limited operation, designed solely to force Hannibal into open battle. Just one year after the end of the war, therefore, the Carthaginians were able to supply 400,000 bushels of corn to Rome and to the Roman army in Macedonia.[3] This was followed in 191 by the offer of a gift to Rome of 500,000 bushels of wheat and 500,000 bushels of barley for its war with Antiochus.[4] Twenty years after that a further 1 million bushels of corn and 500,000 bushels of barley were sent for Roman forces fighting in Macedonia.[5]

Carthage's thriving trade with Italy was also a significant boon. This trade had first expanded in the period between the First and Second Punic Wars, but had grown enormously in the first decades of the second century BC. Of particular importance are the vast quantities of ceramics and general kitchenware from Campania and other parts of central Italy.[6] This archaeological data paints a picture of a booming Carthaginian agricultural economy able to produce enough surplus not only to provide produce for the Roman military machine, but also to act as a lucrative market for central-Italian merchants. Moreover, there is good evidence that the Carthaginians were involved in the transportation of Campanian wine to Spain, although their own consumption of Italian wine appears to have dropped off, probably because they were now producing large amounts of their own.[7]

Whereas Carthage could continue to rebuild its economy in peace, Rome was involved for much of the first half of the second century BC in a series of draining wars in Greece and Asia Minor, and was reliant on its allies periodically to provide large quantities of money and supplies. Rome's economic exhaustion is also reflected in the vast amount of bronze coinage which was minted to pay its armies, when at the same time very little new silver and no gold issues were being produced.[8] Carthage too had been forced by economic pressures to mint large quantities of bronze coinage in lieu of silver during this period, but, in contrast to the Roman situation, the Carthaginian reliance on bronze coinage should probably not be taken as a sign of economic privation.[9] The Carthaginians had historically paid their mercenary troops with silver, gold and electrum coinage, while primarily using bronze coinage for the domestic market. Therefore, the exclusive usage of bronze coinage in this period may simply be a sign that they had neither an overseas empire to protect nor the need for a standing army.

Further evidence of Carthage's renewed prosperity at this time derives from archaeology, for it was now that a number of ambitious construction and renovation projects were taking place in the city. The most extraordinary of these building works was the new port complex. Appian quotes Polybius' marvellously vivid description of this:

The harbours had communication with each other and a common entrance from the sea 21 metres wide, which could be closed with iron chains. The first port was for merchant vessels, and here were collected all kinds of ships' tackle. Within the second [circular] port was an island, and great quays were set at intervals around both the harbour and the island. These embankments were full of shipyards which had capacity for 220 vessels. In addition to them were magazines for their tackle and furniture. Two Ionic columns stood in front of each dock, giving the appearance of a continuous portico to both the harbour and the island. On the island was built the admiral's house, from which the trumpeter gave signals, the herald delivered orders, and the admiral himself over-looked everything. The island lay near the entrance to the harbour and rose to a considerable height, so that the admiral could observe what was going on at sea, while those who were approaching by water could not get any clear view of what was taking place within. Not even incom-ing merchants could see the docks at once because a double wall enclosed them, and there were gates by which merchant ships could pass from the first port to the city without traversing the dockyards.[10]

Archaeologists have been able to show that this account is remark-ably accurate, although the number of berths for the warships was in reality around 170, rather than 220. That so many vessels could be accommodated in such a confined area was the result of an ingenious use of the space available. On the island itself there were thirty covered dry docks that symmetrically fanned out, separated by a hexagonal-shaped open space with a watchtower on its southernmost side. This area could also be accessed from the north by a narrow gangway. The craft were hauled on to dry land by the use of wooden ramps. Along the circumference of the island, a further estimated 140 boats could have been accommodated.[11] It is, however, very unlikely that the whole fleet would have spent much time in the harbour except during the winter period, when sea travel was considered to be too hazardous. During the rest of the year, the island docks would have been used for repairing and re-equipping craft.[12]

The commercial port also suffered from a certain restriction, with only about 7 hectares of usable space, including its quays. Extra space was created through the construction of a vast platform built out into the sea, in an irregular trapezoid shape near the mouth of the channel that led into the new internal harbour complex, where goods could be loaded, unloaded and stored.[13]

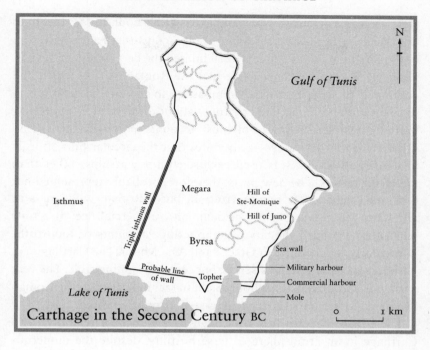

Carthage in the Second Century BC

The creation of these new harbours constituted an enormous investment on the part of the Carthaginians. It has been estimated that around 235,000 cubic metres of earth would have had to have been excavated from what had previously been coastal marshland. Some 10,000 cubic metres of this soil would then have had to have been deposited on the island of dry earth in the middle of the circular basin in order to create enough of a gradient for the ship-sheds. Despite the speed with which one might imagine that these structures were constructed, there is plenty of evidence that they were well built. Even the quaysides of the commercial harbour were built of large sandstone ashlar blocks, with a coffer-dam technique used in the lower courses, whereby parallel wood barriers were created temporarily to exclude the water so that the blocks could be laid.[14]

The design of the harbours, with the external platform sheltering the port from the elements, appears to confirm Polybius' statement that they had been built also to be protected from prying eyes. Indeed, all that one would have seen when approaching the city from the sea were the stout defensive walls and external harbour. In fact the inner dockyards, with their berths for 170 ships, constituted a transgression of the 201 treaty with Rome, which limited the fleet to just 10 vessels. However, it seems inconceivable that the Roman Senate, which had continued to send intermittent embassies to the city to arbitrate in disputes with Numidia, did not know about the existence of this new harbour complex. Besides Polybius' account, moreover, there is no other evidence that categorically states that the circular port, at least in its earliest stages, was used exclusively for warships rather than merchant vessels. The new ports, therefore, probably represented not continued defiance or remilitarization, but a Roman willingness to allow the rebuilding of the Carthaginian commercial fleet at a time when Rome needed the city to supply huge amounts of foodstuffs, particularly to its armies in Greece and Asia Minor. The Carthaginian harbours were built to be discreet, but certainly not invisible. The very existence of the circular harbour might in fact indicate that the Roman Senate no longer saw Carthage as a serious military threat.

The Senate nevertheless continued to conduct its relations with Carthage in an atmosphere of terse hostility, despite the numerous services which the Carthaginians now provided for the Roman cause. Particularly damaging to the Carthaginian cause was the Numidian king Masinissa, who continued to play on Roman insecurities concerning his North African neighbours, perhaps jealous of their new success. Historically dominated by their more powerful neighbour, the Numidians, under Masinissa, took advantage of the result of the Second Punic War by becoming increasingly assertive in their dealings with an economically prosperous but militarily weak Carthage. The third and second centuries BC had witnessed ever-closer ties between the higher echelons of the Carthaginian and Numidian elites, often through inter-marriage, and relations were sufficiently close that within Carthage itself there was a pro-Numidian political faction led by a certain Hasdru-bal.[15] In the religious sphere, Carthaginian deities such as Baal Hammon and Tanit appear to have become increasingly popular with Numidian worshippers,[16] and what remains of Numidian elite material culture from this period often displays a strong Punic influence. A number of royal mausoleums, for example, including the so-called Souma of Khroub, perhaps built for Masinissa himself, all follow the eclectic melange of styles and motifs associated with Punic architecture.[17]

The most striking example of the openness of the Numidian elite to Punic culture is found at the town of Thugga, in modern-day Tunisia, where a three-storeyed funerary monument, put up for a Numidian chief called Atban, sometime around the cusp of the third and second centuries BC, still stands today.[18] Like the mausoleum at Sabratha, the Thugga memorial successfully manages to maintain architectural coherence while including an extraordinarily diverse collection of artistic genres and elements: Aeolic capitals decorated with lotus flowers, decorative fluted Ionic columns, Egyptian moulding, etc. The influence of the Punic world is further proclaimed by its bilingual Libyan–Punic inscription, which states that, although the client and the workmen were Numidian, the architect was Carthaginian.[19]

This cultural assimilation took place against the backdrop of increasingly close economic ties between Carthage and Numidia. Such was the level of interaction that the Numidian kingdom began minting heavy bronze coins that bore a strong enough resemblance to their Carthaginian counterparts to suggest that they were designed to be used in both states.[20] Masinissa was also credited with bringing about an agrarian revolution in his kingdom, probably by copying Carthaginian agricultural techniques.[21] He could in consequence match the Carthaginians in the cereals and other supplies that he sent to his Roman allies.

Masinissa, however, now calculated that the Romans would do little if he seized a greater share of the lucrative North African agricultural and commercial markets for himself. On a number of occasions, tensions and confrontations led to both Carthage and Numidia sending envoys to Rome to argue their respective cases. For the Carthaginians, these appeals often ended in a decision against them, for the Roman Senate was clearly inclined to support the claims of a loyal ally over those of a state which still inspired grave suspicions. An important component of the Numidian strategy was to play on these Roman suspicions of Carthage. Hence, in 170, Gulussa, one of the sons of Masinissa, travelled as part of a Numidian embassy to Rome, where, according to Livy, he warned the Senate 'to beware of treachery from the Carthaginians; for they had adopted the plan, he added, of preparing a large fleet, ostensibly for the Romans and against the

Macedonians; when this fleet should be ready and equipped, the Carthaginians would be free to decide for themselves who should be considered an enemy or an ally.'[22]

The complaint made by the Numidian embassy played not only to Roman military anxiety, but also to negative perceptions of Carthaginians as dishonest tricksters – perceptions that had become firmly entrenched in Roman public opinion since the Second Punic War (and perhaps intensified by the staggering rise in Carthaginian mercantile activity). A fascinating window into the strength of such stereotyping in Rome is provided by a Greek play adapted contemporaneously for the Roman stage by the Umbrian playwright Plautus in 194.[23] The *Poenulus* was a knockabout caper typical of so-called Roman New Comedy. Although it was set in the Greek city of Calydon, four of its main characters were not Greeks but, unusually, Carthaginians. Although it was an adaptation of an earlier Greek play, *The Carthaginian*, it is unlikely that Plautus' decision to use it as the basis for his own work was unrelated to recent political events,[24] and indeed he evidently inserted some original and highly topical dialogue.[25]

The caustic tone of the play is set by its insulting and diminutive title, *The Little Carthaginian*. Much of the play centres on the travails of Hanno, a Carthaginian merchant who has travelled to Greece to search for, and then rescue, his kidnapped daughters, who have been sold into sexual slavery. From his first appearance in the play, Hanno is subjected to xenophobic ridicule. In the prologue he is referred to as deceitful, manipulative and licentious – all characteristics that Plautus sets out as being typically Carthaginian. The audience are told how:

> On arriving at any city, he at once tracks down all the prostitutes at their homes; he pays his money, hires one of them for the night, and then asks where she is from, what country, whether she was captured in war or kidnapped, who her family and parents were. So cleverly and cunningly does he seek out his daughters. He knows all languages too, but, knowing, conceals his knowledge. A Carthaginian to his fingertips! Why say more?[26]

In addition to the more obvious slurs, therefore, is the intimation of potential incest, adding the charges of perversion and sacrilege to an already considerable list of sins.[27] Moreover, Hanno is lampooned for the outlandishness of his dress, for his lack of a cloak and his unbelted tunic were signs of effeminacy to a Roman, as were the earrings worn by his companions.[28]

In an apparent highlight of the play, Hanno pretends that he can speak only Punic to two other characters, Agorastocles, a young gentleman, and his rascally slave Milphio. The latter, after erroneously leading his master and the audience to believe that he is proficient in Punic, proceeds to mistranslate, to great comic effect. Whether the language Hanno speaks is Punic or not (which has never been conclusively demonstrated or disproved), the joke lies in the bizarreness and incomprehensibility of the language to the audience.[29] Furthermore, Hanno, who is in fact a wealthy gentleman, is portrayed by Milphio as a pedlar of a ridiculously diverse range of products, including African mice, cutlery, farming tools, nuts and maybe sewage pipes, all of which was surely a play on the Carthaginian reputation for mercantile trade. In the ensuing farce, Milphio also suggests to Agorastocles that he should be wary of being scammed by the Carthaginian.

Throughout the play, even when the probity of Hanno's intentions has been ascertained, the abuse and ridicule that his character is subjected to continue. In one particularly raucous scene, a soldier mistakes Hanno for a client of his daughters when he comes across the Carthaginian embracing them:

> What's this twosing? What's this twinsing?
> Who's the chap with the long tunics like a tavern boy?
> Eh? Is my eyesight failing? Is that my girl Anterastilis?
> It is! It certainly is! I've felt for a long time that she was making light of me!
> Isn't the wench ashamed to be petting a porter in the middle of a street?
> By the Lord, I'll give him to the hangman this instant for torture from top to toe!
> They're nothing but a set of ladykillers, these dangle-tunics.
> But I'm certainly going to get after this African amorosa.
> Hi, you! I mean you, woman! Have you no shame?
> And you! What is your business with that wench?
> Answer me![30]

Instead of placating the soldier by explaining his familial relationship with the girls, Hanno further winds him up by suggesting that he is in fact a punter looking for some business. The soldier explodes again into another round of racist abuse:

> You shriveled sardine and semi-sarrapian,
> you pelt, saltsouk and olive pulp, yes and stinking of garlic and
> onions worse than a bench of Roman rowers![31]

George Franko has commented, 'Plautus sought to make his audience laugh, and these remarks presumably catered to a racist element in the Roman audience. Veterans of the Hannibalic War might well have enjoyed such anti-Carthaginian abuse. The soldier's remarks indicate that sharing a Carthaginian's joy at the recovery of his daughters will not have precluded laughing at the abuse of that Carthaginian.'[32]

At the same time, however, the *Poenulus* conveyed a far more subtle message, for, despite portraying Hanno as licentious and deceitful, Plautus lays a heavy emphasis on his protagonist's true *pietas*, the recognition and discharge of one's duties to the gods and family. *Pietas* was a particularly Roman virtue, and it was truly extraordinary, and indeed provocative, that it should be ascribed to a Carthaginian, even in a comic context. Hanno's *pietas*, furthermore, is matched by another (perhaps bizarre) accomplishment: his seemingly expert knowledge of Roman law, which he uses to great effect to retrieve his daughters from their pimp. The message of the *Poenulus*, therefore, was that the Roman virtue of *pietas* and the rule of Roman law were the route to success, rather than Punic trickery and deceit – the strategies that Hanno had first used in the play. The *Poenulus* thus not only pandered to popular prejudices against Carthaginians, it also emphasized the superior nature of Roman values and institutions.[33] While the play had been based on a Greek original, its message was unmistakably contemporary.

THE CARTHAGINIAN QUESTION

While the Carthaginians could perhaps cope with their negative presentation within Roman comedy, by the 160s some within the Senate had begun to conceive of more serious anti-Carthaginian action. It is clear that Roman foreign policy now became more aggressive, while continually hiding behind the pretext of 'just war'. In the previous decade, Roman suspicions of King Perseus of Macedonia had led the Senate to declare war. The road to the Third Macedonian War (171–168) had followed an alarmingly familiar path. A series of complaints were laid against Macedon by smaller states favoured by Rome, and diplomatic missions between Macedon and Rome had been quietly hostile. Finally, Perseus' most powerful regional rival, Eumenes, king of Pergamum, had persuaded the Romans that their suspicions about Macedonian aggression were well justified. The final justifications for war were in fact mostly fictitious, including the supposed assassinations of key Roman allies in the region. As Rome mobilized its troops, Perseus' requests for dialogue and information were met by increasing evasiveness and equivocation. A truce was eventually offered to Perseus by the Roman general Philippus, which the young Macedonian naively accepted as a sign of Roman goodwill. Philippus, however, was simply buying time to get the main bulk of his forces to the Balkans. Although some senators balked at this supposedly un-Roman duplicity, their colleagues colluded in it by deliberately delaying Macedon's envoys to Rome from returning home. It was, as one historian has suggested, 'as disreputable a piece of Roman diplomatic duplicity as many senators had ever witnessed'.[34]

Perseus' final defeat, at Pydna in 168, which had spelled the end of the Macedonian monarchy, signalled the adoption of an even harder line against Carthage in the Roman Senate.[35] Indeed, a number of ancient authors saw this as a watershed in Roman attitudes to other Mediterranean states. In a famous passage, Diodorus, who perhaps took the notion from Polybius, wrote, 'In more recent times, the Romans, when they went in pursuit of world empire, brought it into being by the valour of arms, then extended its influence far and wide by the kindest possible treatment of the conquered . . . But once they held sway over virtually the whole inhabited world, they confirmed their power by the wielding of terror and by the destruction of the most eminent cities.'[36]

Although that development was in fact far less clear than Diodorus suggests, it nonetheless appears that, in the wake of Rome's victory over Macedon, the Senate was indeed far more willing to use wars in order to protect its interests. At the same time, however, Diodorus sets out a further feature of Roman foreign policy, which appears, superficially at least, directly to contradict his previous pronouncement: 'The Romans make it a point to embark only upon wars that are just, and to make no casual or precipitate decisions on such matters.'[37] What Diodorus means, however, is that the Roman Senate was *sensitive to the accusation* that it might start a war unjustly. In Roman relations with Carthage, we therefore witness a painfully drawn-out process whereby the Carthaginians eventually provided the Romans with a (weak) justification for further military action.

When, in 162, Masinissa overran the fertile coastal farmland of Syrtis Minor – territory that had been in Carthaginian possession for centuries – the ensuing dispute provided the Romans with the pretext that they required. The real target of this encroachment had been the wealthy trading emporia that dotted the coast, but these were well defended and remained outside Numidian control. What military force had initiated was completed by Roman arbitration. Carthage was ordered to relinquish any claim to the territory seized by Masinissa, and the injustice was further compounded when the former was required to pay the Numidian 500 talents of silver, which represented the revenues the Carthaginians had received from Syrtis Minor since the dispute had begun.[38] Even Polybius clearly highlighted the unfairness of this ruling, writing that 'their [the Carthaginians'] claim to the country was evidently just,' and proved by Masinissa's previous request to enter the territory in order to pursue a renegade general.[39]

While Livy's account of this episode appears to lack the fullness of that of Polybius, it nevertheless includes an interesting detail about the arguments made to Rome by either side. For the Carthaginians, the territory fell within the boundaries set by Scipio Africanus at the end of the Second Punic War, and was therefore indisputably theirs.[40] The Numidians, however, not only disputed the assertion that these lands were included within the 201 agreement, but also countered the Carthaginian claim with much older historical precedent. They asked:

> If one wanted to determine the real origin of a property right, what land in Africa was really Carthaginian? Coming there as strangers, they had been granted as a gift, for the purpose of building a city, as much land as they could encompass with the cut-up hide of a bull; to whatever

extent they had extended beyond their capitol, the Byrsa, they had gained by violence and without right. As to the particular tract of land in question, they could not even prove that they had held it for any considerable length of time, and much less that they had held it continuously from the time that they had begun to claim it. As occasion offered, now they and now the Numidian kings had claimed the right to it, and possession had always remained with the party that was stronger in arms.[41]

Part of the problem was the vagueness with which Scipio had actually set the boundaries in 201, but the Numidian argument actually seemed to confirm the Carthaginian possession of the lucrative trading emporia, for in defence of these Carthage had indeed proved itself 'stronger in arms'.[42] When the Roman Senate decided in favour of the Numidians' dubious and opportunistic claims, it was an ominous warning of what was to come. Within a decade Masinissa employed the same aggressive tactics to seize the fertile Thusca region, which had long been Carthaginian territory. Once more the Carthaginians complained to the Roman Senate, but the subsequent embassy sent from Rome merely compounded their problems, for it was led by a man who was already implacably opposed to the city.[43]

Marcus Porcius Cato was an old man of 81 years, but he had lost little of the hard-nosed political skill and ferocious determination that had driven his rise from relatively humble beginnings to the summit of the Roman political system, the consulship. Famed for his ascetic lifestyle and sense of moral rectitude, Cato had throughout his career rigorously pursued those fellow senators who had failed to meet his own high standards, and it was indeed Cato who had led the successful campaign to drive Scipio Africanus into the political wilderness.[44] Cato's apparent hatred towards Carthage was most probably born from his experiences during the Second Punic War, in which he had served in the Roman army at Capua, the siege of Tarentum and the Battle of the Metaurus in 207.

Arriving in Carthage in 152, the Roman embassy led by Cato decided to leave the seized territory in Numidian hands, but Cato himself was nevertheless alarmed by what he found. According to Plutarch, 'The city was by no means in a poor and lowly state, as the Romans supposed, but rather teeming with vigorous fighting men, overflowing with enormous wealth, filled with arms of every sort and with military supplies, and not a little emboldened by all this.'[45] Moreover, in the countryside crops were growing in abundance to feed the city's burgeoning population.[46] The Roman envoys also found evidence of large quantities of stored timber, which they presumably feared would be used to build a war fleet.[47]

On his return to Rome, Cato set to work lobbying his fellow senators. Although the famous aphorism 'delenda est Carthago' is a later invention, he would nevertheless end all speeches in the Senate with the uncompromising statement that Carthage indeed had to be destroyed.[48] His primary argument was that Carthage not only was restoring itself to its former strength, but had also learned from and corrected the errors of the past.[49] In his desperate efforts to get his senatorial colleagues to back his position Cato proved himself unabashed by a little histrionics. Standing on the speaker's rostrum, he shook out the folds of his toga and revealed a large, juicy African fig. He then told his audience in the Senate House that the fig had been picked in Carthage just three days ago, thereby driving home not only the city's renewed prosperity, but also its proximity to Rome.[50] At the same time, and despite the obvious exaggeration, Cato made his senatorial audience aware of the agricultural riches that could be appropriated if Carthage were destroyed.[51]

Cato's position was opposed by a group of senators led by Scipio Nascia, the son-in-law of Scipio Africanus, who reportedly argued that to destroy Rome's greatest enemy would be simultaneously to destroy its political equilibrium. Without a great enemy like Carthage, they predicted, the common citizenry would refuse to obey the authority of the Senate and, drunk with greed and power, would drag Rome into a series of ill-thought-out and potentially disastrous adventures.[52] Diodorus summarized Scipio's arguments as follows:

> Rome's strength should be judged . . . not by the weaknesses of others but by showing herself greater than the great. Furthermore, as long as Carthage survived, the fear that she generated forced the Romans to live together in harmony and to rule their subjects equitably and with credit to themselves – much the best means to maintain and extend an empire; but once the rival city was destroyed, it was only too evident that there would be civil war at home and that hatred for the governing power would spring up among the allies because of the rapacity and lawlessness to which the Roman magistrates would subject them.[53]

Despite the power of these seemingly prescient observations, we should of course be cautious in accepting them as an accurate reflection of Scipio's objections. Writing a century later, Diodorus already knew that the Roman Republic would indeed be torn apart by political strife and civil war. Livy, by contrast, claims that Scipio's opposition to war was formed on the basis of the lack of adequate justification (and not on aversion to the destruction of Carthage per se).[54] While many senators apparently shared Cato's suspicions of a resurgent Carthage, many also understood that war could not be waged without an adequate pretext.[55] Ever concerned to avoid the charge of transgressing the much-vaunted virtue of *fides*, the Senate decided simply to wait until an opportunity presented itself.

THE DESOLATION OF CARTHAGE

During the last years of the 150s, it became increasingly clear in Carthage that their treaty with Rome offered much by way of obligation, and little by way of protection. The growing exasperation led to the political rise of a democratic faction who, one suspects, were the successors of the demagogic Barcid clique. According to the Greek writer Appian, this group, led by Hamilcar the Samnite and Carthalo, argued that, as no assistance could be expected from Rome, Carthage would have to defend itself.[56] With Carthage's agricultural base being slowly eroded by Numidian infringements, it is not difficult to understand why such a manifesto captured the popular vote in the city.

Once in power, Hamilcar and Carthalo quickly established a more assertive policy towards the Numidians, and drove all pro-Masinissan politicians out of Carthage. Masinissa responded by sending two of his sons to demand the restoration of the pro-Numidian faction, but when the princes were excluded from the city, and then later ambushed by Hamilcar the Samnite, open war between Numidia and Carthage was declared. After an inconclusive battle, the Carthaginians under their general Hasdrubal allowed themselves to be surrounded, and were eventually starved into submission and then treacherously massacred. Only Hasdrubal and a few others escaped back to Carthage.

As a result, yet another sizeable piece of Carthaginian territory in Africa was lost to Masinissa.[57]

The Carthaginians had not only lost the brief campaign against Numidia, by attacking Roman allies they had also violated the terms of the 201 treaty, and thus given their enemies in the Roman Senate a pretext to convince their less belligerent colleagues that another war was justified.[58] Now that the situation in Macedon and Greece had been resolved, and a difficult series of rebellions among the Spanish tribes had been put down, Rome also had the resources to attack Carthage with overwhelming and irresistible force.

It has sometimes been argued that some in the Senate may have feared that the Carthaginian recovery would now accelerate, since in 151 the city had successfully paid off the last instalment of the indemnity from the Second Punic War. It seems equally probable, however, that for some the end of the indemnity signalled not only the end of a lucrative and regular source of revenue, but also the possibility of an even greater payday.[59] War and conquest had brought Rome huge wealth, and all classes of its citizens had benefited.[60] Plutarch recounts how a wealthy young Roman in this period threw an opulent dinner party, of which the centrepiece was a honey cake in the form of a city. The host had then declared it to be Carthage, and exhorted his guests to plunder it.[61] The story, while undoubtedly apocryphal, nonetheless touches upon an important truth: whatever its actual or potential military threat, Carthage, through its mercantile and agricultural wealth, had now become an attractive prospect for slavering Romans who wished it as their own.[62]

In 150 the Romans mobilized an army for North Africa. When the ominous news of this crossed the Libyan Sea, there was widespread alarm. Finding themselves isolated by the desertion of their erstwhile North African allies such as Utica, the Carthaginians desperately tried to appease the Romans by bringing the party of Hanno back into power, and arresting and condemning to death Hasdrubal, the general who had led the Numidian campaign. When Carthaginian envoys arrived in Rome to plead their case, however, they discovered that the Roman army had already left for Sicily, whence it would progress to Africa. Their concerns would not have been eased by the frosty reception that they received in the Senate, where, on informing their audience that Hasdrubal had been apprehended and was awaiting execution, the envoys were asked why this had not been done at the beginning of the conflict. Requests for guidance on how Carthage might atone for its transgressions were simply met by the ambiguous response 'You must satisfy the Roman people.'[63]

Cato, despite his age, did all that he could to maintain the drumbeat of war, and in a speech from which several extracts have survived he reportedly declared, 'The Carthaginians are already our enemies; for the man who prepares everything against me so that he can make war whenever he wants is already my enemy, even if he is not yet taking military action.'[64] Later in the same address, he brought his case to a powerful climax: 'Who are the people who have often broken their treaties? The Carthaginians. Who are the people who have waged war with the utmost cruelty? The Carthaginians. Who are the people who have disfigured Italy? The Carthaginians. Who are the people who ask to be forgiven? The Carthaginians.'[65] In addition to the emphasis on the suffering of Italy, which was obviously an emotive topic,[66] Cato thus played on pre-existent Roman stereotypes of Carthaginians. Punic perfidy was thus set against Roman *fides*, the primary virtue upon which the Roman state increasingly prided itself – to the extent that during the First Punic War the Romans had even built a temple to *Fides*.[67] Cato had in fact established a dossier (now lost, and the subject of seemingly endless historical speculation) of six supposed instances of Carthage's lack of good faith in breaking its agreements with Rome.[68] This strong contemporary emphasis on Punic treachery served, one suspects, not only to strengthen the immediate case for war, but also to mask the Romans' growing awareness of their own diplomatic disingenuousness.

While the Romans continued a diplomatic charade with the Carthaginian envoys, instructions had already been dispatched to the expectant Roman army. Thus in 149, as the Carthaginians, at Rome's behest, handed over 300 noble children as a sign of good faith,[69] the Roman army, made up of 80,000 infantry and 4,000 horse and led by the consuls of that year, Lucius Marcius Censorinus and Marcus Manilius, set off for North Africa. Only once the Roman army was ensconced at Utica were the Carthaginians given the terms under which war could be avoided.

When a trumpet sounded, envoys were brought into the Roman

camp and were made to walk through the massed ranks of Roman legions, who stood to attention fully armed and in complete silence. In front of them, sitting magisterially on tall chairs, were the consuls, with their senior officers standing around them. After a litany of excuses had been curtly dismissed by Censorinus, the Carthaginians were ordered to hand over all their weapons and war machines. The Carthaginians complied, and a train of wagons soon arrived in the Roman camp carrying armour and weapons for 20,000 men, as well as 2,000 giant catapults. Now that the Carthaginians were completely disarmed, a deputation composed of thirty leading citizens was summoned to learn the final peace terms which the Romans were prepared to offer. The Carthaginians would be allowed to live freely under their own laws, and indeed within their own territory (as long as it was at least 16 kilometres inland).[70] But, in order to enjoy that freedom, they had to consent to a dramatic act: the utter destruction of their city.

The destruction of Carthage and its relocation elsewhere was more than a case of simple resettlement. As Serge Lancel has said:

> Such a diktat was the equivalent of a death sentence. There was no precedent in antiquity for a state's surviving the eradication of what constituted it on the sacred plane: the destruction of its temples and cemeteries, the deportation of its cults, were a more surely mortal blow than displacing the population. But that displacement in itself, simply in material and non-religious terms, was the very negation of what had been the vocation and the *raison d'être* of Carthage, a maritime state whose power and wealth relied on the feelers it sent out from its ports across the seas.[71]

The angry and grief-stricken response which the Roman demand elicited from the Carthaginian envoys shows that they understood its full implications. When eventually silence was restored, one of their number, a certain Banno, attempted one last time to intercede on his city's behalf. In his account of the speech, Appian reports that the Carthaginian skilfully highlighted how, in destroying Carthage after promising to leave it free and autonomous, the Romans would transgress a number of the virtues that they proudly claimed to possess. Banno reportedly argued that the obliteration of Carthage, a city founded on the command of the gods, would be an act of gross impiety.

Moreover, to raze to the ground a city that had already surrendered, given up its arms and children, and met all other terms, would be an act of bad faith.[72]

According to Appian, the Roman consul Censorinus responded with a highly selective account of how the Carthaginians' relationship with the sea had brought them nothing but hardship and misery. Even Rome's unjust seizure of Sardinia was presented as the result of Carthage's maritime obsession. The Carthaginians would, he insisted, be far more secure, and indeed content, with the simple joys of agriculture. Then the consul presented the Carthaginians with the brutal logic behind the Roman decision. While the Carthaginians remained in their city they would remember and seek to reacquire the glories of the past: 'The medicine for all evils is oblivion and this is not possible for you unless you put away the sight [of their city and former glory].' Finally, Censorinus, clearly sensitive to the suggestions of impiety and bad faith, proclaimed that, despite the city's destruction, the temples and tombs would be spared. As to the charge of breaking the terms of Rome's own accord with Carthage, the consul was ready with a clever answer: 'We offer you whatever place you choose to take, and when you have taken it you shall live under your own laws. This is what we told you beforehand: that Carthage should have its own laws if you would obey our commands. We considered you to be Carthage, not the ground where you live.'[73]

The Carthaginian ambassadors were now charged with the unenviable task of relaying these unwelcome tidings to their fellow countrymen. First, however, they asked that the Romans send their fleet to within sight of Carthage, so that its citizens should understand the gravity of the situation that they now faced.

In the furore that followed back in Carthage, both those elders who had argued for acquiescence to Rome's demands and hapless Italian merchants were set upon and murdered by the angry mob. At once the city began to prepare for war. It set free its slaves to fight in the army; then Hasdrubal, the general who had been sentenced to death for his part in the war with Masinissa, was reprieved and restored to his old position. After a failed attempt to buy more time by making a request to the consuls for a thirty-day truce while a new embassy went to Rome, the pace of war preparations was stepped up, with all available public space, including temples, being turned into workshops in which men and women worked shifts. Each day 100 shields, 300 swords, 1,000 ballistic missiles, and 500 darts and spears were produced, and the women even cut off their long hair to be used as catapult string.[74] New coins – the first silver issues since the end of the last war with Rome – were also minted, presumably for the payment of troops.[75]

Thanks to extensive excavations since the 1970s, an increasing amount of information about the city in its last years has been gathered. The most extraordinary discovery was made by French archaeologists who uncovered a neighbourhood dating to this period on the southern slopes of the Byrsa hill, the citadel of Carthage and the administrative and religious heart of the city. The 'Hannibal Quarter', named by its excavators after the famous general who held high office in Carthage around the time that it was constructed, is in remarkably intact condition, with some walls still standing to a height of nearly 3 metres, and presents a fascinating snapshot of life for the 700,000 inhabitants of Carthage just before its fall. It is not known for whom these houses were built, although their excavators have speculated that, because of their uniformity, they may have been intended for some kind of governmental cadre.

Although the roads remained unpaved and were clearly unsanitary when it rained heavily, because of their rather rudimentary drainage system, the Hannibal Quarter, with its multi-storeyed blocks uniformly set out on right-angled streets, looked like many others that one might find across the Mediterranean region during this period. Many of the houses were certainly rather small, but they conformed to a basic plan that was found all over the Greek world, with rooms arranged around a central courtyard that acted as the main source of light into the building.[76]

The presence of a large number of cisterns for collecting and storing rainwater gives some insight into the struggle that was waged to collect a sufficient amount when so ill-supplied with natural sources of fresh water. Indeed, these cisterns seem to have collected sufficient water not only for drinking and other household necessities, but also for the bathing and other ablutions performed in washrooms (identifiable by the waterproof plaster on the walls and floor, as well as the outflow drainage). Although only one example has survived, it appears that these washrooms would have possessed free-standing terracotta hip baths (complete with elbow rests) which would have been filled with water from the cisterns in the courtyard.[77]

The stairways and steps that were needed to compensate for the gradient of the slope, and the lack of paved surfaces, made it impossible for vehicles to access its streets, but the area was still a thriving hub for local business. One floor was still covered with coral, obsidian and cornelian chippings from a jeweller's workshop. In another street a miller's yard was found deserted, with parts of a rotary grain mill still lying discarded on the floor.[78]

When the Roman consuls eventually began their siege, what confronted them was a very formidable challenge. Although Appian's account of the fortifications on the isthmus on which Carthage was situated is undoubtedly fanciful – it describes huge walls and fortified towers, as well as barracks and stables large enough to house 20,000 infantry, 300 elephants, and 4,000 horses and their riders – archaeological excavation has proved the existence of triple defences made up of ditches, banks and walls.[79] It was these defences that the Roman consuls tested for the remainder of 149, with very little success. At one point Censorinus used massive battering rams to break down a southern section of the outer walls, but he was once more driven back. The siege dragged on throughout 148, and indeed the Carthaginians, despite the desertion of the old Punic cities of North Africa, had reason to be confident. The reprieved general Hasdrubal was roaming freely around Carthage's hinterland with an army, disrupting Roman communications and supply lines, and the Roman onslaught in general had been repelled with some ease.[80]

In 147 the new Roman consul Lucius Calpurnius Piso attempted a new tactic, and attacked the last towns in the region which still supported the Carthaginians, thus preventing the latter from receiving supplies and reinforcements. His second in command, Lucius Hostilius Mancinus, also led an opportunistic commando assault on a weak section of Carthage's defences, but, after initially breaching the wall, Mancinus and his men were set upon, and were saved only by the timely intervention of the adopted grandson of Scipio Africanus, Scipio Aemilianus, who had just arrived in Africa with reinforcements to take over command of the campaign.[81]

The appointment of the young Scipio Aemilianus, who was underage and without the proper credentials, reflects a general dissatisfaction in Rome with the progress of the war against Carthage. Scipio had been elected consul for 147 not only for his promise as a military commander, but also for the record of his family against the Carthaginians.[82] He had already served with some distinction as a legate on the African campaign, and this experience proved invaluable as he looked to restore the morale, and review the strategy, of his army.[83] Even Cato, the scourge of the Scipios, believed Scipio Aemilianus was the man for the job.[84]

Scipio first made sorties to test the Carthaginian defences at different points, and attacked Megara, a large suburban area of the city. Intended or not, the result of the latter action was that Hasdrubal, still camped with his army in the countryside, was at last sufficiently alarmed to move his forces back inside Carthage. Now all the Carthaginian forces were trapped inside the city, and all Scipio needed to do was to mount an effective blockade, which he did by securing the isthmus with a fortified camp complete with watchtower. His final action to effectively seal off the city from the outside world was the construction of a mole to block the harbour, and thus also the arrival of provisions from the sea.

The Carthaginians, initially sceptical about the possibility of building such a structure, noted its rapid progression and attempted to thwart the project by secretly excavating a new entrance on the other side of the harbour. When it was ready, they sent out at dawn a flotilla of makeshift warships built out of old materials, and launched a surprise attack on the Roman positions.[85] The Romans, completely taken unaware, were at first thrown into confusion, but the Carthaginians failed to take proper advantage of the situation. Three days later an inconclusive sea battle was fought between the two fleets in the old harbour, with the smaller, more nimble, Carthaginian craft having some initial success in damaging the Roman ships. However, when attempting to withdraw so that they could resume battle the next day, some of the Carthaginian ships became entangled at the new harbour entrance, blocking those that followed and leaving them exposed to Roman attack. A number of ships were therefore lost before the Carthaginian naval squadron could retreat inside the city.[86]

With the completion of the Roman mole it quickly became apparent that its purpose had been not merely to block the harbour, but also to provide a thoroughfare along which Roman troops and siege equipment could be brought right up to the harbour fortifications. The target was the large external platform that had been used by the Carthaginians as an external harbour and quayside. In their desperation to keep the Romans at bay, the Carthaginians launched a daring mission in which naked men, carrying aloft unlit torches, swam or waded through the water and, in the face of Roman arrows and spears, managed to set light to and destroy completely the first siege engines that Scipio had dragged up to the walls. The next day, however, the Romans began the process of constructing new machines, which were then dragged forward on to tall mounds. From there torches and vessels full of burning pitch were hurled down on to the Carthaginian defenders, who were subsequently forced to retreat from the platform. Now that his troops held this precious foothold, Scipio knew that it was only a matter of time before the city fell. Leaving a portion of his army to ensure that nobody escaped from the city, he went off with the remainder to mop up the last pockets of resistance in the surrounding towns and countryside.[87]

In Carthage itself the situation was critical, for there was now no food entering the city by land or by sea. The subdivision of many of the houses in the Hannibal Quarter into much smaller living spaces may well be a reflection of overcrowding as Carthage's population was swelled by refugees from the countryside and the suburbs. With the seizure of the last allied cities, there appeared to be little hope of salvation. Now, after centuries of ruthlessly defending their political authority, the Carthaginian elite succumbed to the autocratic ambitions of one among their number.

Hasdrubal had already shown himself well versed in the art of political machination, for he had already engineered the fall from grace of his chief rival, the military commander of the city. (The unfortunate man had been beaten to death with benches in the Popular Assembly, no doubt by supporters of Hasdrubal, after the latter had falsely accused him of treachery.)[88] Once Hasdrubal and his army had taken residence in the city, it was not long before the general revealed his demagogic aspirations.[89] Those among the Council of Elders who dared to oppose him were executed, while Hasdrubal took on the insignia of the city's supreme general, garbed in full armour and a purple robe, and accompanied by a retinue of ten swordsmen. Like the Syracusan tyrants of old, Hasdrubal used a potent mix of populist gestures and brutality to maintain his authority. In a city where supplies were in short supply, food was used as weapon of control, and, as the general citizenry starved, Hasdrubal kept his troops and supporters well fed with banquets and parties.[90] Moreover, by torturing captured Roman soldiers to death in full view of their comrades outside the city, he ensured that the Carthaginians had little option but to stay loyal: after this conspicuous display of barbarity, any chance of mercy from the Romans was gone.[91]

Carthage's lapse into military tyranny was, however, only short-lived. By the spring of 146, Scipio, with his troops mustered, the bridgehead secure, and the rest of Africa subdued, was at last ready to order the fateful final assault with which this book began. Extraordinarily, an eyewitness to Carthage's bloody demise was the most important historian of the Second Punic War, Polybius. Polybius had been a senior official of the Greek Achaean League and, suspected by the Romans of harbouring pro-Macedonian sympathies, had been taken to Italy in the early 160s as a hostage. In Rome he had become a close friend of Scipio Aemilianus, and had consequently travelled with his patron on campaigns in Spain, Gaul and Africa (hence his presence in Carthage in 146).[92] According to Polybius, as Scipio watched Carthage burn he wept, and then:

> After musing by himself a long time and reflecting upon the inevitable fall of cities, peoples and empires, as well as of individuals, upon the fate of Troy, that once proud city, upon the fate of the Assyrian, the Median, and afterwards of the great Persian empire, and most recently of all, of the splendid empire of Macedon, either voluntarily or otherwise the words of the poet [Homer] escaped from his lips:
>
> > The day shall come in which our sacred Troy
> > And Priam, and the people over whom
> > Spear-bearing Priam rules, shall perish all.
>
> Being asked by Polybius in casual conversation (for Polybius had been his tutor) what he meant by using these words, Polybius says that he

did not hesitate to frankly name his own country, for whose fate he feared when he considered the mutability of human affairs. And Polybius wrote this down just as he heard it.[93]

It is, of course, difficult to know if Polybius really did write these words down exactly as he heard them. Whatever the provenance of this anecdote, however, Scipio's tears had little to do with the ghastly horror that the general had unleashed upon Carthage, but were in fact shed for his own city, Rome. With the obliteration of its greatest rival, Rome had arrived as a world power, while at the same time setting in motion the cycle that would eventually lead to its own destruction.

Remarkably, Carthage was not the only venerable, ancient city to be destroyed by the Romans in 146. In the same year a Roman army under Lucius Mummius had captured, looted and destroyed much of the city of Corinth after a revolt by the Achaean League.[94] On the one hand, the fate of Corinth serves to highlight the hypocrisy of Roman claims that a particular fear of Carthage had led to the extraordinarily brutal and unwarranted treatment of the city. On the other, it strongly suggests that there was more to the destruction of Carthage than simple aggression. The sacking of two of the richest port cities in the ancient Mediterranean was, for one thing, a hugely profitable business. Both cities were brutally stripped of their wealth, and their works of art were shipped back to Rome. Scipio Aemilianus could at least partly exculpate himself by the fact that the Greek Sicilian cities were invited to come and reclaim the works that the Carthaginians had previously looted from them.[95] But slave auctions and the seizure of a large swathe of previous Carthaginian territory, which now became public land owned by the Roman state, unequivocally contributed to a massive infusion of wealth into both public and private Roman coffers.[96]

At the same time, the conspicuous destruction of two ancient cities sent an unequivocal message: dissent against Rome would not be tolerated, and past glories counted for nothing in this new world. As Nicholas Purcell puts it, 'Founding, refounding and major embellishment were normal ingredients in rulers' city policy. Destruction was just as effective . . . At Carthage and Corinth in 146 BC the Romans made a carefully considered statement in the old symbolic language, one which went far beyond any recent experience of city war.'[97] The earlier fate of Capua – its people enslaved, its civic status repealed, and its access to the sea removed – had merely been the dress rehearsal for a wider Mediterranean drama.[98] The destruction of Carthage and Corinth now stood as a bloody memorial to the cost of resistance to Rome, and a suitably apocalyptic fanfare for Rome's coming of age as a world power.

THE POWER OVER THE PAST

The escalation in demands by the Senate to the Carthaginians served as a testing ground for the newly acquired power which Rome now wielded. What began with demands for children as hostages ended in total oblivion, and the reversal of centuries of Carthaginian history and tradition. The attempt to justify that act on ethical grounds was patently disingenuous, particularly when measured against the parallel destruction of Corinth and increasing Roman claims to the Mediterranean Sea as *mare nostrum*, 'our sea'.[99] Rome's newly found status was expressed not only in the power to obliterate, but also in the power to justify the unjustifiable. With the destruction of Carthage, therefore, the Romans became the makers of history in more ways than one.[100] Already the Hannibalic wars had played a crucial role in the genesis of Roman historiography, and Fabius Pictor was followed by other senatorial historians keen to document Rome's glorious past.

While Pictor had written in Greek, the seminal *Origines* of (none other than) Cato were composed (tellingly) in Latin. Divided into seven books, the *Origines* set out the history of the Romans up until 149, the year of its author's death.[101] Cato, like Pictor before him, sought to show how particularly Roman virtues such as courage and piety had brought about the rise of Rome as a great power. At the same time, however, he was anxious to emphasize that this success was the result not of the glorious actions of individual generals or statesmen, but rather of the collective endeavour of the Roman citizen body.[102] But the chronological (and geographical) spread of Cato's magnum opus was by no means even. Two whole books were devoted to the origins of the peoples of Italy, perhaps with the intention of emphasizing the peninsula's cultural and historical integrity, as well as the legitimacy of Rome's leadership of it.[103] Much of the first few centuries of Rome's existence were then condensed into one book, while the First and Second Punic Wars were contained within a book each. Finally, two whole books were devoted to the short period from the early 160s until 149.[104] The lack of balance may be explained by the paucity of sources for earlier Roman history, but it also highlights the extent to which the *Origines* was intended as a contemporary manifesto. Not least, the work was perhaps designed to explain (or excuse) both Cato's and the Senate's role in the utter destruction of their greatest enemy. Certainly, it was here that Cato presented the infamous dossier of Carthage's six reputed transgressions of its obligations to Rome.[105] The Carthaginian perspective was, one must imagine, completely erased.

Within the pages of literature, therefore, Carthage remained as unfinished business. However, the Roman attempt both to control and to reshape the past manifested itself in the works not only of historiographers, but also of a new generation of Roman epic poets. These poets self-consciously based their works on Greek precedent, but by emphasizing specifically Roman themes they sought to create their own 'national literary culture'.[106] The first of these writers of epic were in fact not Romans but Italians from the south of the peninsula, where the cultural influence of the Hellenic world was strongest. Coming to Rome during or immediately after the Second Punic War, they established close links with a wide variety of influential Roman senators.[107] Unsurprisingly, the wars with Carthage loomed large in their work. Gnaeus Naevius, a Campanian and a military veteran of the First Punic War, wrote, in the last years of the third century BC, the first Latin epic poem, *The Punic War*, taking that conflict as his subject.[108] Naevius was followed by one of Rome's greatest poets, Quintus Ennius, a Calabrian, who had seen military service against the Carthaginians in the Second Punic War. His epic masterpiece, the *Annales*, took the whole of Roman history as its ambitious theme.[109]

Both Naevius and Ennius explored recent historical events within a broader overarching frame of ancient myth.[110] The history of Roman–Carthaginian relations was forsaken for an epic narrative that emphasized an epic struggle between the two cities for the leadership of the world, a state of affairs divinely ordained from their very foundation. In Naevius' epic, and also one must suspect in that of Ennius (which, like many works from this period, survives only partially, in fragmentary form), the Carthaginian queen and founder Dido (based upon Elissa in the Greek Hellenistic writers) was portrayed as a contemporary of Aeneas. The intention, clearly, was to maintain the fake equivalence between the respective ages of Carthage and Rome, first propounded by Timaeus.[111] For both Naevius and Ennius, it was not the affairs of men but the affections and rivalries of the gods which had brought about the Punic wars. Rome's patron deity and protectress was Venus, the mother of Aeneas, while Juno fulfilled the same role for the Carthaginians.[112] Indeed, it was only when the latter's hatred was placated that a Roman victory was assured.

On one level, such divine partisanship was in no way new, for in the *Iliad*, the great Homeric epic tale, for which both Naevius and Ennius had provided a partial sequel, Hera, the Greek equivalent of Juno, nursed a famous hated of the Trojans (among whom was Aeneas), while Aphrodite, the Greek equivalent of Venus, supported Troy.[113] The mapping of this animosity on to contemporary divisions between Rome and Carthage was, however, a far more recent development, and surely a reflection of the claims to divine favour made by both sides during the Second Punic War. Indeed, the notion of Venus as the ancestress of the Roman people had been securely established only in that period (with the construction of the temple of Venus Erycina on the Capitol), and the acknowledgement of Juno's enmity was made only soon after, with the various ceremonies to appease her.[114] Naevius' *Bellum Poenicum*, written while Hannibal was still in Italy, was thus a further response to the religious propaganda of the Carthaginian general and his entourage.[115]

Ennius, by contrast, wrote the final sections of his *Annales* in the 170s, when Rome's relationship with Carthage had once more deteriorated.[116] Although it took in all of Roman history, the work, like Cato's *Origines*, still displayed a marked bias towards more recent events, in particular the Second Punic War.[117] What survives of the work certainly condemns the Carthaginians, describing them as 'petticoated lads' and 'wicked, haughty foes' and claiming that they sacrifice their own little sons to the gods.[118] Like Naevius before him, Ennius similarly presented the struggle between Carthage and Rome in divine terms, and predicted the triumph of the latter by promise of Jupiter.[119] In both the *Bellum Poenicum* and the *Annales*, therefore, the Punic wars were presented as a divinely ordained battle for supremacy from which only one of the participants could, eventually, emerge intact.

The impact of such ideas on the final decision to destroy Carthage cannot be gauged. Nevertheless, one of the last acts reportedly undertaken by Scipio Aemilianus before the final assault on the city suggests that they represented something far more prescient than mere literary embellishment or fantasy. Before sending his troops upon their final assault, Scipio, according to one later source, performed the solemn religious ritual of the *evocatio*, exhorting the gods of Carthage to desert their city and accept a new home in Rome.[120] The ceremony was significant for a number of reasons. In its immediate context, it meant that the Romans could avoid any charge of sacrilege, for they were now attacking an essentially godless city. More broadly, however, the ritual of the *evocatio* represented a final statement in the long-drawn-out battle for the sacred landscape of the central Mediterranean – a battle which had shaken Roman self-belief to its very core. The ritual was carried out at the moment when Scipio was already assured of his victory, and therefore his appeal for divine favour was certain to appear successful. The divine favour bestowed on the Roman people was now compellingly confirmed by the presence of their legions on the verge of final victory at the enemy city. As the Carthaginian gods supposedly deserted to the Roman cause, Rome's domination of the central and western Mediterranean emphatically received the divine sanction for which it had so long struggled.

15

Punic Faith

THE GHOST OF CARTHAGE

As an intense fire raged on the Byrsa, Scipio ordered his troops to demolish Carthage's walls and ramparts. Following military custom, the Roman general also allowed the soldiers to loot the city, and rewards were handed out to those legionaries who had displayed conspicuous bravery during the campaign. Scipio personally distributed all gold, silver and religious offerings, and other spoils were either sent to Rome or sold to raise funds. The surviving arms, siege engines and warships were burnt as offerings to the gods Mars and Minerva, and the city's wretched inhabitants were sent to the slave markets – with the exception of a few grandees (including Hasdrubal) who, after being led through Rome as part of Scipio's triumph, were allowed to lead a life of comfortable confinement in various Italian cities.[1]

Besides these few commanders, the only Carthaginians who fully escaped their fellow citizens' collective fate were those who had been absent from the city during the siege. One was a well-known philosopher called Hasdrubal, who had relocated to Athens further to pursue his academic career. After arriving in Greece, where he had wisely changed his name to Clitomachus, in 129 he had eventually risen to the headship of the prestigious Athenian Academy. During a long and illustrious career, Clitomachus wrote an astonishing 400 treatises, which earned him praise from a number of prominent Romans. Besides his philosophical works, he reportedly addressed a work to his fellow Carthaginians after the destruction of the city, in which he opined that at such calamitous times much comfort was to be gained from philosophy (a sentiment that would no doubt have been appreciated by his fellow citizens as they were murdered by marauding Roman soldiers or dragged into a life of miserable slavery).[2]

After the initial ravaging of the city by the legions, the Senate sent a ten-man commission from Rome in order to supervise a series of measures designed to ensure that Carthage remained uninhabited. To that end Scipio was ordered to raze the remainder of the city to the ground, and a solemn curse was put on any persons who in the future attempted to settle on the Byrsa or in the Megara district. Moreover, those cities that had remained loyal to Carthage would pay for their loyalty with utter destruction, while Roman allies in the region were rewarded with Carthaginian territory. Those that had remained neutral were placed under the control of a senior senatorial official who would be sent out from Rome each year.[3]

When word of final victory reached Rome, there was an extraordinary outpouring of happiness and relief on the streets of the city. According to Appian, the news was greeted with understandable joy, for 'no other war had so terrified them at their own gates as the Punic wars, which ever brought peril to them by reason of the perseverance, skill, and courage, as well as the bad faith, of those enemies.'[4] While most surviving accounts of the Punic wars contain a high degree of hyperbole, in this instance such extravagant language perhaps accords well with the general reaction of the Roman public. The end of a series of wars which had seen Rome's divine sanction undermined, and the enemy at the very gates of the city, can surely only have brought relief.[5] The extraordinary outpouring of Roman religious and literary activity in the course of the wars, at least, demonstrates the extent to which success or failure on the battlefield was bound up with the Romans' perceptions both of the world and of themselves.

While the Second Punic War was perceived as the confirmation of predestined Roman hegemony, for many it simultaneously signalled the start of a long decline. For Polybius, whose views appear to have been shared by many of the Roman senatorial elite (and the wider intellectual community of the Hellenistic world), it was the unavoidable fate of all great powers that they should eventually fall.[6] Thus, while the well-balanced Roman constitution would help prevent decline for a time, the fate of Carthage also awaited Rome. In Polybian political philosophy, however, future decline lay less in the rise of alternative powers than in destructive internal conflict and the rise of irrationality. The decline, defeat and eventual destruction of Carthage were thus attributed to the demagogy of the Barcids and the increasing influence of popular politics within the city. Even Hannibal, whom Polybius greatly admired as a military commander, was viewed as being fatally flawed by an irrationality and impulsiveness that symbolized the last years of the city.[7] In destroying Carthage, therefore, the Romans had confirmed a theory that forecast the eventual doom of their own city.

In the last decades of the second century BC and into the first, as the Roman Republic plunged into political crisis and bloody civil war, that political philosophy which foretold the decline of Rome must have seemed all the more prescient. As well as providing an ominous blueprint for Rome's troubled future, a fallen Carthage now played a conspicuous role in the genesis of the bitter discord that broke out among the ranks of the Roman Senate. In fact the internal dissension that Carthage would stir within the Roman senatorial elite had become apparent even before the city had fallen. The Roman commander Hostilius Mancinus, piqued at what he perceived as a lack of recognition of his achievements, in contrast to the plaudits and glory showered on Scipio Aemilianus, commissioned an elaborate painting of Carthage and the assaults that he had led against it, which he then erected in the Roman forum. Standing next to this billboard, Mancinus even went as far as to offer onlookers a commentary on how his heroic actions had helped bring about the capture of the city.[8]

Personal glory was not the only disputed spoil of the Third Punic War, however, for the extensive and fertile North African territories that had become Roman land became a major source of tension. Land reform – particularly for the military veterans who had played such a major role in the glittering successes on the battlefield, but afterwards had often indecorously ended up among the growing ranks of disenfranchised poor – became a point of increasingly bitter contention within the Senate. In 123 the senator Gaius Sempronius Gracchus and his supporters in the reformist faction successfully forced through a measure that allowed for not only the settlement of some old Carthaginian territory, but also the establishment of a new colony called Junonia on the site of the old city. The move had met with serious opposition from the conservatives led by Scipio Aemilianus, but Gracchus reportedly won the debate by citing the old argument of Scipio Nascia: that the destruction of Carthage would lead to the emergence of demagogues and would-be tyrants in Rome (a clear reference to Scipio Aemilianus). Aemilianus, understandably sensitive to such accusations, deflected the accusation by blaming factionalism in the Senate on luxury and greed spurred by Rome's conquest of the East.[9] Both sides were nevertheless seemingly agreed: Rome was in moral decline, and conquest was the cause.

The reformers, although they had scored a victory in this particular round of the battle, not long after found their efforts thwarted, for their opponents had turned the tide of public opinion by spreading rumours that the boundary markers of the new colony had been pulled up by wolves (which soothsayers considered an ill omen). The Junonia project was dramatically abandoned soon afterwards.[10] The tensions between reformers and conservatives nevertheless continued, and culminated a year later, in 121, in a bloody putsch perpetrated by the consul Lucius Opimius, whereby Gracchus and 3,000 of his supporters were murdered. In an act of calculated brazenness, Opimius then controversially commissioned a temple on the Capitol to be dedicated to the divine virtue of *Concordia* (Concord).[11] For many it stood as an ironic and unwelcome reminder of the bloody discord that now stalked Rome. The following graffito had been inscribed on the building: 'A work of mad discord makes a temple of Concordia.'[12]

The death of Gracchus did nothing to assuage the tensions between those who wanted to resettle Carthaginian land and those who would not countenance a new Carthage (even a Roman one). In 81 BC the Roman general Pompey, in an attempt to display his conservative credentials, solemnly renewed the curse on the site of Carthage,[13] but in 64 a senatorial party once again attempted a reform by proposing to sell off the territory of Carthage in order to fund land distribution. Once more, however, these plans were successfully rebuffed by the conservatives, who argued that to ignore the curse that had been laid on it amounted to dangerous sacrilege and, furthermore, that a restored Carthage could pose a future threat to Rome.[14]

As the Republic lurched from one political crisis to another, the debate over Rome's decline intensified. In fact the competing arguments earlier advanced by Gaius Gracchus and Scipio Aemilianus had been conflated into the bleak diagnosis that the destruction of Carthage by Rome had catalysed a swift decline fuelled by the greed and ambition of Rome's ruling classes.[15] Indeed, such was the low ebb to which Roman self-esteem had sunk that the story of the Philaeni, Carthaginian brothers who had sacrificed themselves by being buried alive so that Carthage's eastern frontier could be secured, was used by the historian Sallust as an exemplar of selflessness that he saw as sadly lacking among the warring and competing Roman generals of his own time.[16] Thus, only a century after its reduction to a series of uninhabited ruins, Carthage, rather than representing the indefatigable might of the Roman people, stood instead as a brooding monument to the debilitating discord that threatened to tear Rome asunder. Given its controversial status, it is surely unsurprising that the eventual self-proclaimed saviour of the Roman Republic looked finally to resolve the tortured and long-protracted Carthaginian question.

ROMAN VIRTUE, CARTHAGINIAN VICE

By 31 BC, with all his serious rivals for power either dead or neutralized by other means, Octavian, adopted son of Julius Caesar and later, under the name Augustus, to become the first of Rome's emperors, had effectively taken over the reins of Roman government. Augustus was as shrewd a political operator as he was ruthless in his pursuit of power, and he had learned well the lessons of his adopted father's death. Any suspicion that he was aiming for royal power (the persistent rumours of which had led to Julius Caesar's assassination) was assuaged by the new regime's relentless emphasis on Augustus' restoration of the Roman Republic to its former glory, authority and stability. Although his powers came increasingly to resemble those of an autocrat, Augustus preferred to present himself merely as the 'first among equals' in a fully restored and invigorated Republic. The powerful central message of the Augustan regime was that it was only through the restoration of traditional Roman virtues such as *fides* (faithfulness) and *pietas* (duty to one's gods, country and family) that Rome's greatness could be guaranteed.[17] These themes appear frequently in the extraordinary outpouring of artistic and literary endeavour that accompanied the reign of Augustus, often produced by individuals who were broadly supportive of the aims and achievements of the new regime.[18]

The idea of faithfulness and piety as the bedrock of Rome's greatness can be traced back to the Punic wars, and more generally to Rome's increasing military and diplomatic involvement overseas during that period. The first temple to *Fides* in Rome had been inaugurated by Aulus Atilius Calatinus, the first Roman dictator to take troops on active service overseas (in Sicily in 249).[19] Indeed, the ever-increasing emphasis upon good faith as a particularly Roman quality can be mapped on to a growing awareness among the senatorial elite that that same virtue was often the first victim of the realpolitik in which Rome's new position dictated it should now engage. Rome's treatment of Carthage was seen by many, particularly in the Greek East, as evidence of the growing distance between Roman words and Roman actions.

In an excursus towards the end of his *Histories*, Polybius set out the supposed reactions to the destruction of Carthage by certain groups in Greece, two supportive and two unfavourable. While Polybius thus neatly avoided clearly voicing his own opinion on the matter, the fact that he set out the critical views in such great detail gives an important indication of his own disquiet.[20] In particular, he paid considerable attention to the view that the Romans had failed to meet the high standards that they had previously set themselves both in war and in foreign relations:

> Others said that the Romans were, in general, a civilized people, and that their peculiar merit on which they prided themselves was that they conducted their wars in a simple and noble manner, employing neither night attacks nor ambushes, disapproving of any kind of deceit or fraud, and considering that nothing but direct and open attacks were legitimate for them. But in the present case they had used deceit and fraud, offering certain things one at a time and keeping others secret, until they cut off every hope in the city for help from its allies. This, they said, savoured more of a despot's intrigue than of the principles of a civilized state such as Rome and could only be justly described as something very like impiety and treachery.[21]

Such criticisms clearly hit a nerve, and soon apocryphal parables that detailed Rome's adherence to the tenets of good faith, even in the face of extreme provocation, were woven into the fabric of the city's history. The most famous of these stories would, unsurprisingly, involve Carthage. By the 120s BC a fanciful tale began to circulate in which Regulus, the Roman general ignominiously captured during the First Punic War, had returned to Rome with a peace proposal from his captors which he urged the Senate to reject. Then, as faithfully promised, he returned to Carthage and was repaid for his efforts with torture and death.[22] Another historian paints a rather different picture of Regulus' interaction with the Carthaginians. The Sicilian Greek historian Diodorus tells how Regulus' wife, embittered by her husband's continued imprisonment, had starved one Carthaginian to death by locking him in a tiny room with no food or drink. His comrade had been spared from the same fate only because household slaves, alarmed by their mistress's unhinged behaviour, had raised the alarm. So shocking had been the scene that investigating magistrates had supposedly threatened the family with prosecution.[23] Nevertheless, by the last decades of the second century BC the story of Regulus' brave self-sacrifice on the altar of good faith had become a favourite in the canon of Roman history.[24]

It was no coincidence that the reign of Augustus saw the further embellishment of the Regulus legend. In one of his most powerful odes, the poet Horace likened the emperor's uncompromising subjugation of the Britons and the Parthians to Regulus' selfless plea that Rome should reject any peace deal with the Carthaginians, despite the terrible personal consequences for himself:

> It's said he set aside his wife's chaste kisses,
> and his little ones, as of less importance,
> and, grimly, he set his manly face
> to the soil, until he might be able
>
> to strengthen the Senate's wavering purpose,
> by making of himself an example no
> other man had made, and hurrying,
> among grieving friends, to noble exile.

Yet he knew what the barbarous torturer
was preparing for him. Still he pushed aside
the kinsmen who were blocking his way,
and the people who delayed his going.[25]

The Regulus tale is just one example of how during the Augustan period the Punic Wars were presented in increasingly moralistic terms, with a particular emphasis on the Carthaginians as a threat to traditional Roman virtues. Writers who were sympathetic to many of the aims of the Augustan regime, but in no way diehard loyalists, rejected the ambiguities and self-doubt of the past century in favour of the certainties of Roman victory and moral rectitude. In essence, what the work of such writers showed was that Carthage did not need physically to exist to act as the supreme foil to the greatness and virtue of the Romans.

The historian Livy, whom we have encountered on many occasions throughout this book, was one such writer.[26] There was in fact nothing particularly original about the main thesis of Livy's history, which sought to compare the vigour of early Rome with the decline of recent times.[27] Indeed, the familiar emphasis on the corrosive influence of luxury on the Roman character was ever-present in his study.[28] What separated Livy from Polybius and the previous generation of Roman historians, however, was that he saw Roman decline in the wake of the Carthaginian destruction as essentially revocable. According to Livy's estimation, until his time Rome had been through three historical cycles, involving several peaks and troughs. The reign of Augustus represented the start of the fourth such cycle, and with it the opportunity for Rome to become great again. In Livy's programme, it was the responsibility of Augustus, through sometimes unpopular measures, to arrest the current decline and to propel Rome to renewed greatness through the vigorous re-establishment of *fides* and *pietas*.[29]

Carthage's role in Livy's history was far more extensive than to serve merely as Rome's most serious rival for the leadership of the world.[30] In addition to reproducing the Polybian thesis that blamed Carthage's failure on the growing influence of the ill-informed citizenry on its government, Livy also presented the North African city as playing the role of ultimate moral antitype to Rome. While Polybius had argued that Carthage had simply lost its greatness, Livy contended that a morally deficient Carthage had never been great in the first place. Throughout his account of the Punic wars, therefore, Livy continuously juxtaposed Roman virtues and Carthaginian vices.

Although derogatory observations on the Carthaginian national character also appeared in Polybius, Livy's attacks were less considered and even more vitriolic. In one famous passage describing the character of the great Carthaginian general Hannibal, Livy praised Hannibal's physical and military skills, but then followed up with a blistering character assassination that immediately undermined any of the compliments that had preceded it: 'But these great merits were matched by great vices – inhuman cruelty, a perfidy worse than Punic, an utter absence of truthfulness, reverence, fear of the gods, respect for oaths, sense of religion.'[31] Hannibal's vices were thus described as excessive even by the base standards of his race. Indeed, throughout his work Livy placed particular emphasis on Hannibal's faithlessness, including an episode when the Carthaginian general put chains on Roman troops who had been previously promised their freedom by his Numidian cavalry commander. This the historian drily described as an act of 'true Punic' reverence.[32] Thus, although he had not invented the long-standing Roman concept of 'Punic faith', a sardonic expression for gross treachery and faithlessness, Livy did much to entrench it within the Roman mentality, even going so far as to put the expression in the mouth of Hannibal himself, during a fabricated admission that the Roman Senate had little reason to place their trust in Carthaginian peace negotiations.[33]

It is worth reminding ourselves that these representations of impiety, faithlessness and greed were the product of Livy's Roman perspective, fulfilling a particular Roman agenda in both justifying Roman aggression and defining Roman virtue. Despite Livy's protestations to the contrary, the Carthaginians were demonstrably no less faithless than the Romans during the Second Punic War, and many of the charges that Livy laid against Hannibal and his troops in fact served to deflect attention away from Roman breaches of good faith. Thus Livy doggedly portrayed the Carthaginian siege and capture of Saguntum (which had triggered the Second Punic War) as a prime example of bad faith on the part of Hannibal and his countrymen. By contrast, the Roman Senate's failure to protect a sworn ally is completely glossed over.[34]

Much the same can be said for the numerous accusations of impiety that Livy levelled against the Carthaginians. Livy's claims of Punic sacrilege had little to do with actual Carthaginian religious practices and beliefs, and far more to do with those Roman claims to divine favour which had been greatly undermined by Hannibal's military successes and slick propaganda. Livy tackled this awkward point of history by portraying Hannibal's early victories as the result of temporary acts of piety on his part and, more importantly, a simultaneous failure of the Romans to provide due honour to their own gods. By setting out the essential impiety of Hannibal's mission at the beginning of his account of the war, moreover, Livy ensured that his audience understood that any success that the Carthaginians enjoyed would be short-lived. Indeed, Carthage's final defeat was eventually justified by Livy as nothing less than divine retribution.[35] Under Livy's dogmatic but powerful schema, therefore, the fate of Carthage, rather than foretelling Rome's inevitable doom, actually affirmed the superior national virtue of the Romans, the favour of the gods towards them, and their potential for further future greatness.

A NEW HERACLES AND A NEW CARTHAGE

While Livy's ideas were most probably not the product of a state-sanctioned programme, they nevertheless chimed well with prevailing attitudes within the Augustan regime. Hannibal's fifteen-year sojourn on the Italian peninsula had left deep scars on the Roman collective consciousness, and his legacy could not be easily forgotten or erased. Uncomfortable reminders of his mighty achievements and divine associations were now embodied in the very landscape of Italy, courtesy of the epic journey that he and his army had made across the Alps in the footsteps of Heracles. Two centuries after Hannibal had successfully overcome the daunting challenges presented by those mighty mountains, still no Roman had managed to repeat the feat. Indeed, the first-century-BC biographer Cornelius Nepos, who originally hailed from Cisalpine Gaul (in the northern Italian peninsula), reported that the great mountain chain was still called the Greek and Punic Alps, because Heracles and Hannibal respectively had discovered its passes.[36] Now, mindful of the long shadow that the failure to conquer these mountains had cast over Rome, Augustus attempted ownership of the Heraclean Way and thus also of the legacy of its great (and much disputed) hero.

In 29 BC, after his victory in the civil war, Augustus arrived in Rome to celebrate a triple triumph from 13 to 15 August. These dates were carefully chosen, for the festival of Hercules at the Ara Maxima fell upon 12 August, and the arrival of Rome's new saviour thus dovetailed perfectly with that of his heroic predecessor.[37] This dramatic display was but the first stage in the Augustan takeover of the Heraclean tradition, for in 13 BC a new road was constructed, the Via Julia Augusta. Named after the emperor, it followed the path of the old Heraclean Way, from Placentia in northern Italy, over the Alps, and into Transalpine Gaul. At its terminus at La Turbie, just a few kilometres from modern Monaco, a splendid monument, complete with a rotunda of twenty-four columns and a statue of an enthroned Augustus, was built to celebrate the imperial conquest of the Alps. An inscription, furthermore, gave a copious list of all the tribes in the region that the emperor and his two stepsons, Drusus and Tiberius, had pacified.[38]

A few years later this road was followed by the renovation, between 8 and 2 BC, of the 1,600-kilometre stretch of the old Heraclean Way from Gades to the Pyrenees. It was renamed the Via Augusta.[39] That this route was also the one that Hannibal had taken on his march to Italy may have remained unstated, but poetic praise of the Augustan Alpine campaign indicates that the association was implicit in the minds of contemporaries.[40] In a eulogy to the feats of Drusus and Tiberius in the Alps, Horace skilfully weaved into the fabric of his poem a long reference to Hannibal and the defeat at the Metaurus, which had been masterminded by Nero Drusus, an ancestor of the imperial stepsons. In the final lines of the excursus, Hannibal bemoans the failure of his dreams of conquest, as the vigorous youth of Rome finally triumph.[41] The Augustan reappropriation of the Heraclean Way, Horace implies, marks the final defeat for the Carthaginians, and with it the battle for the gods and for the past.

The transformation of the Heraclean Way was, however, insignificant in comparison to the new venture which Augustus now envisioned: the rebuilding of Carthage itself. Other self-proclaimed saviours of the Roman Republic had contented themselves with building and beautifying the temple of Concord in Rome, but for Augustus that would have been a controversial move. While he would indeed eventually remodel the temple, in the early 20s BC his later reputation as *pater patriae*, 'father of the country', was far from secure. Most must surely have regarded him then not as the bearer of concord, but as a brutal butcher who had ruthlessly avenged his adoptive father's murder with the slaughter of political opponents. If Augustus were to construct a monument to Concord, then it would have to be outside Rome, where the risk of hypocrisy was less, and the promise of consensus more. Where better, indeed, to lavish the spirit of reconciliation than on the site of Rome's bitterest enemy?

It was in fact not Augustus but his adoptive father who had first (quite literally) dreamt up the seemingly unthinkable plan of rebuilding Carthage. Appian reports that in 44 BC, while campaigning in North Africa against his fellow Romans, Julius Caesar had a dream in which he had seen the entire army weeping, and upon waking he had immediately issued a memorandum that Carthage should be colonized.[42] The dream itself has been interpreted in several different ways by modern scholars. The most plausible version is that the army represents the dead Carthaginians, so that the reconstruction of their city would illustrate the spirit of *clementia* (clemency) upon which Caesar would pride himself. Alternatively, the army might represent Roman veterans, thereby placing the colonization of the city within the populist Gracchan tradition of land redistribution.[43] The ambiguity may indeed have been deliberately fostered, for a tale so equivocal could represent Caesar's *clementia* both to the defeated and to his own veterans. Although one of Caesar's deputies, Statilius Taurus, was tasked with establishing the new colony, the work undertaken does not appear to have been extensive.[44] Nevertheless, the plan to re-establish Carthage – Rome's most bitter enemy – stood as a potent symbol both of the new Caesarian regime's self-confidence and power, and of the concord brought by Rome to the Mediterranean.[45]

Caesar's infamous murder later in that year postponed much of the new North African project, but by 29 BC Augustus was willing to resuscitate it. From its inception the new city was clearly meant to impress. The street plan was set out with a regularity that was unusually exact even for a Roman city. Each block measured 120 by 480 Roman feet (35.5 by 142 metres), making up precisely one hundredth of the original Roman land allotment.[46] The administrative and religious centre of the new foundation was built on top of the Byrsa, the heart of the old Punic city. The summit of the hill was now crowned by a series of magnificent monumental buildings and grand spaces, including a huge civic basilica, temples and a forum. This dramatic reshaping of the physical landscape, and the construction of a new (Roman) religious and administrative topography, proclaimed not only the absolute supremacy of Rome, but also the unity which it had brought to once hostile states.[47] Thus Carthage was reborn as Colonia Iulia Concordia Carthago, the administrative capital of the Roman province of Africa Proconsularis.[48] Although other Roman colonies had been named in celebration of the concord restored by the Julian clan, the name of the restored Carthage must have had a particularly powerful resonance for the Roman people.[49]

Paradoxically, the rebuilding of Carthage involved a far more extensive destruction of the old Punic city than that achieved by Scipio in the previous century. To prepare the terrain for this monumental building project, the entire summit of the hill was levelled, and an enormous rectangular platform was constructed for the city centre. Over 100,000 cubic metres of rubble and earth – the debris created by this enormously ambitious project – were then pushed down the slopes of the Byrsa. By building a system of retaining walls, a series of terraces was created on the sides of the hill, where residential neighbourhoods and other structures would eventually be built. The new city of Roman Carthage managed to proclaim not only the extraordinary powers of concord and reconciliation possessed by the Augustan regime, but also Roman mastery over an alien landscape. Thus Augustus conquered Carthage with the spade and the trowel with a finality that his predecessors had failed to achieve with fire and the sword.

DIDO AND AENEAS

At roughly the same time that Carthage was being rebuilt, the Italian poet Vergilius Maro had started to write his epic masterpiece, the *Aeneid*. Although Vergil was certainly not an uncritical supporter of the Augustan regime,[50] a number of themes within his work nevertheless dovetailed with the propaganda which surrounded Augustus, for, as one who had lived through the horrors of war, he too must have longed for the new golden age that the regime trumpeted.[51] The *Aeneid* retold the familiar story of Aeneas' turbulent journey from Troy to Italy, where he became the forefather of the Roman people. Within a few lines of the poem's beginning, however, the audience is made aware that Carthage will play a far more important role in this version of the story than it had done previously:

> There was an ancient city, Carthage (home of colonists from Tyre),
> Over against Italy, and the Tiber's mouth afar,
> rich in wealth, and very stern in pursuit of war.
> They say that Juno loved this land above all others,
> even holding Samos less dear. Here was her armour
> and here her chariot, and that here should be the capital
> of the nations, should the fates allow it, was even then
> the goddess' aim and dearest aspiration.[52]

Although the Punic wars themselves receive very little attention in the *Aeneid*, the poem nevertheless self-consciously acts as the sequel (or perhaps prequel) to Ennius' narrative of the conflict.[53] As with the earlier epics of Naevius and Ennius, in the *Aeneid* the enmity between Carthage and Rome is divinely ordained, with each side having its immortal champion: Juno for the Carthaginians and Venus, the mother of Aeneas, for the Trojans. The *Aeneid*, however, was far more than a mere recapitulation of previous Roman poetry. Indeed, the work provided a new and dramatic pre-history for this famous enmity: a doomed love affair between Aeneas and Dido, the respective founders of the Roman and Carthaginian races. Although some kind of meeting between the two had taken place in Naevius' epic, the idea of a romance was in itself a daring and provocative departure.

In the first book of the *Aeneid*, as the Trojan refugees travel away from their destroyed homeland, their ships are caught in a terrible storm instigated by their enemy, the goddess Juno. The survivors eventually wash up on the coast of North Africa, where they are given succour by another group of refugees from the East, the Carthaginians. Venus, fearing that the Carthaginians may do harm to her son, sends Cupid to Dido to ensure that the queen, who has previously resisted all approaches from suitors after the murder of her husband, falls passionately in love with Aeneas. Then Juno, who sees an opportunity to prevent Aeneas and the Trojans from fulfilling their destiny in Italy, suggests to Venus that some kind of marriage should be arranged between the prince and the Carthaginian queen:

> It had not escaped me how, in fear of my city,
> you've always held the dwellings of high Carthage
> under suspicion. But what shall be the end?
> What is the point of all this rivalry now?
> Why do we not strive for everlasting peace
> and a marriage alliance?[54]

Venus agrees to the scheme in order to secure the temporary safety of her son, although she already knows through a prophecy by Jupiter that Aeneas will eventually reach Italy and found the Roman race. Therefore, after the couple have been purposefully separated from the main party by a storm while out hunting, their love is consummated in a cave.

Throughout this episode, Vergil played with knowledge that his audience already possessed: that, despite the apparent amity of the cities' great founders, great conflict would eventually break out between the Carthaginians and Romans. He therefore set up the ultimate 'what if' scenario: what if Aeneas and the Trojans had remained in Carthage and made it their city? Indeed, Vergil even treated his audience to the extraordinary sight of Rome's proto-founder dressed in a cloak of Tyrian purple with gold inlay, and directing the building of that very city that would become Rome's greatest enemy.[55] The poet even ponders the possibility that Rome's foundation will be prevented entirely by the contentment of its champion in North Africa:

It was he who was to rule Italy, a land engorged with empire,
and crying out for war, pass on a race of Teucer's
noble blood, and bring the whole world under its laws.
If the glory of these things does not fire him up,
and for his own celebrity he does not exert himself,
does he begrudge the towers of Rome to Ascanius?
What is his plan? With what hopes does he tarry
among enemy people, forgetting Ausonia and the Lavinian fields?[56]

The reader knows, however, that Aeneas' presence at Carthage cannot last. Beyond the knowledge of the enmity that existed between Rome and the city, Aeneas' destiny has already been ordained. For him to compromise that destiny not only would be impossible, but would furthermore compromise the virtue of *pietas*, a tenet upon which the Roman character had been founded.

Eventually Jupiter sends Mercury, the messenger god, to persuade Aeneas to abandon Carthage. Realizing his inescapable destiny, and the duty which he owes both to the gods and to his (future) homeland, Aeneas gives orders to his men to set sail for Italy. As Aeneas secretly slips away, however, Vergil dramatically confronts his audience with the deserted queen's desperate complaints and scorn. In the climax of the book, as she makes secret preparations for suicide, the grief-stricken Dido issues forth an electrifying curse that foretells the eventual coming of a Carthaginian avenger:

Then, do you, Tyrians, persecute with hatred his whole line
and all the race to come, and offer it as a tribute to my ashes.
Let no love or treaties unite our nations.
Arise some unknown avenger, from my dust, to harry
the Trojan settlers with fire and sword, now, or in the future
whenever might is granted to him.
I pray that shore be opposed to shore, water to wave, arms
with arms: war may they have, them and their children's children.[57]

In the final bitter lament of an abandoned queen, the antiquity and intensity of the hatred that historically existed between Carthage and Rome is represented in uncompromising fashion. Even at the end of the work, when Juno finally accepts the foundation of the Roman race through the intermingling of the Trojans and the Latins, her grievance over Carthage is pointedly and ominously left unresolved.[58]

The *Aeneid* thus provided a powerful reminder of the intractable hatred between Carthage and Rome, while at the same time greatly extending the horizon of its antiquity. The poem, however, simultaneously pre-empted the Augustan revival of the city as the great final act of reconciliation. Indeed, the description of Aeneas' first arrival in Carthage must have had a very particular and vivid resonance for the Augustan audience, for it vividly described the frenetic building activity taking place there:

> Aeneas marvels at the massive buildings, mere huts once,
> marvels at the gates, the noise and paved roads.
> Eagerly the Tyrians press on, some to build walls,
> to raise up the citadel, and roll stones up by hand,
> some to chose a dwelling place and enclose it with a furrow.
> Laws and magistrates they ordain, and a sacred senate.
> Here some are digging harbours, here others lay
> the deep foundations for their theatre and hew out of
> the cliffs massive columns, fitting adornments for the stage.[59]

The resonance for an Augustan audience was thus produced not by an accurate description of the new colony at Carthage (or indeed of its Punic predecessor), but rather by the fact that its new institutions were unmistakably *Roman*.[60]

If the city which Aeneas helped construct at Carthage appeared conspicuously Roman for Vergil's contemporary audience, then his behaviour there surely did not. While Aeneas' departure from Carthage was immediately motivated by the recognition of, and capitulation to, his destiny, the deceitful and clandestine manner in which he abandons his former lover must surely have been unsettling for a Roman, for it reeked of the treachery supposedly characteristic of the Carthaginians. Indeed, contemporary Roman readers were confronted with the uncomfortable and disorientating scene of a Punic woman upbraiding the founder of the Roman people in terms usually reserved for Roman abuse of the Carthaginians:

Faithless one, did you really hope that you could conceal
so base a crime, and steal away from my land in silence?
Does neither our love hold you back, nor the pledge I once gave you,
nor the doom of a cruel death for Dido?
Even in winter do you labour over your ships, heartless one,
so as to journey over the high seas at the height of the northern mael-
strom?[61]

In a further barrage of direct speech which builds up to her eventual
suicide, Dido portrays the Trojan prince as impious and a breaker of
sacred oaths.[62] By contrast, Vergil's Dido is nothing like the duplicitous
oriental queen of earlier Greek and Roman literature. While Venus
may initially fear what the Carthaginian queen will do to her son, Dido
soon proves herself to be everything that the Punic race (in Roman
eyes) was not supposed to be: industrious, honest, pious and charitable.
The deception and trickery that typified the characterization of Elissa
in Timaeus are entirely absent in the *Aeneid*. Famous episodes such as
the theft of Pygmalion's gold or the Byrsa land deal are mentioned to
emphasize not typical 'Punic faith', but rather the queen's courage and
resourcefulness.[63]

In many ways, the Dido and Aeneas episode within the *Aeneid*
concerns the impossibility of reconciliation between Carthage and
Rome. The cruel and faithless rejection of Dido by Aeneas in favour of
his preordained fate functions as a commentary on the brutality of the
Roman quest for empire – a quest similarly ordained by the gods. Just
as Aeneas crushes Dido in order to fulfil his divine mission, so too will
Rome crush Carthage in its pursuit of empire. Nevertheless, just as
Aeneas as a character matures, and comes to regret his treatment of the
Carthaginian queen (whom he later confronts in the underworld), so
too does the *Aeneid* mourn the necessary but nonetheless lamentable
destruction of Carthage, and pre-empt its eventual, Augustan, restoration as a city of the Roman Empire. By subverting centuries of Carthaginian stereotypes (and presenting Dido as more Roman than Aeneas),
Vergil points not only to the impropriety of such stereotypes in the new
Augustan world, but also to the potential of the Carthaginians to be
good Romans. Even at the point at which future enmity is set in train,
therefore, the reader is given a clear sight of future reconciliation. Like

Augustus' new city, the *Aeneid* stood simultaneously as a monument to the restoration of Carthage as a symbol of concord and as a reminder of the discord that had prompted its destruction.

THE TRIUMPH OF NORTH AFRICA

While the refoundation of Carthage undoubtedly represented the most dramatic testament to the reinstatement of concord in Rome by the Augustan regime, a far more striking but less celebrated monument to the gradual development of a rapprochement between Rome and its North African subjects was being constructed almost contemporaneously several hundred kilometres to the east. In 8 BC Hannibal, a wealthy citizen and former chief magistrate of Leptis Magna in Libya, commemorated the construction of a public building put up at his own expense with a long inscription on thirty-one carved blocks. Part of this inscription was written in Punic, the language that still predominated among the inhabitants of the Libyan seaboard, but the remainder of the text was in Latin. Further evidence of the syncretism that had begun to take place between Punic and Latin cultures can be seen in the nomenclature of the benefactor. Although his personal name was Punic, his local family name had been adapted to Tapapius, to make it sound more Roman. His third name, Rufus, was a purely Roman invention.

Even more striking is the substance of the text, in which the Roman emperor Augustus was honoured with his official Roman titles, all carefully rendered both in Latin and in Punic (and not simply transliterated). Hannibal Tapapius Rufus, moreover, proudly proclaimed his role as a priest in the cult of Augustus. This inscription is not a strange anomaly, but merely one of the earliest of a number of often bilingual epigraphic monuments that both highlight the increasingly important contribution of North African elites to the political, economic and cultural life of the Roman Empire and simultaneously proclaim continued local pride in Punic heritage.[64] That gradual integration was expressed also in Tapapius' self-description as 'Lover of Concord', an epithet which resonated both with the imperial rhetoric of his Roman masters and with his Punic inheritance. 'Lover of Concord' had been used as a title by North African elites for centuries.

For the elites who continued to dominate the old Punic cities of the central and western Mediterranean, there appears to have been no sense that their venerable ethnic inheritance and membership of the Roman Empire were in any way incompatible.[65] In North Africa and Sardinia, Punic and neo-Punic continued as spoken and written languages at least until the fourth century AD, and were used by all social classes. Moreover, traditional deities such as Astarte, Baal Hammon and Tanit were still worshipped, and the chief magistrates continued to be called suffetes until at least the second century AD.[66]

The sacred rites that had been performed in tophets across the Punic world also continued, although lambs were now used as sacrificial substitutes for children. It has sometimes been argued that the persistence of Punic traditions in places like Sardinia should be read as a sign of 'silent resistance' to Roman rule. The Punic testimonies of Hannibal Tapapius Rufus and others like him, however, show that such traditions might serve also as a medium through which Punic people could assert their membership of the Roman Empire.[67] Indeed, throughout the first and second centuries AD, the cities of North Africa and their inhabitants were some of the most upwardly mobile in the empire. Ambitious local families began to establish themselves in Italy, where they bought up estates with the vast wealth generated by trade and agriculture, while their sons began to establish themselves among the Roman senatorial elite. Moreover, cities such as Leptis Magna were steadily granted enhanced status by a series of Roman emperors, often leading to the status of colony and the bestowal of Roman citizenship on all of their citizenry.[68]

Despite the political and cultural integration of North Africa within the Roman Empire, therefore, the legend of Hannibal's resistance to Rome continued to exercise the minds of educated Romans, a testament not only to its power, but also to its impact upon the Roman consciousness. The Roman senator Silius Italicus, who wrote in the reign of the emperor Domitian (AD 81–96), thus wrote an enormously long epic on the Punic Wars, the *Punica*, in which he tellingly felt compelled to emphasize the enmity that the god/hero Hercules felt for Hannibal (particularly after the latter's decision to break faith with the Romans and attack Saguntum).[69] The Roman poet Statius indeed imagined that a statuette of Hercules owned by a friend had once been in the possession of Hannibal, but presents the hero less as a divine companion than as a resentful hostage, forced to accompany Hannibal in the form of this statuette. Rather than favour its cause, Hercules despises Carthage for its vicious assault upon Italy.[70]

Statius was nevertheless aware that times had changed. Perhaps conscious of the dangerous associations which might be made between his new epic Hannibal and the North African elites gaining influence at Rome, the poet reminded his Libyan-born friend Septimius Severus of his Roman credentials:

> Your speech is not Punic, nor your dress;
> Your mind not foreign – you are Italian, Italian![71]

What neither the poet nor his friend could have known was that Septimius' grandson and namesake Lucius Septimius Severus would in AD 193 become the first African emperor of Rome. Although they were perhaps too wise to mention it, the more educated of his subjects are unlikely to have missed the fact that the new emperor had won the throne only after embarking with his army on an epic march of some 1,000 kilometres from the Danube to Rome.[72] When he later reburied the remains of Hannibal in a mausoleum of fine white marble, it became obvious not only whom the new Roman emperor had taken as his model, but also how far the Carthaginians had come.[73]

Carthage featured prominently in Roman literature and history throughout antiquity, with successive generations of writers continuing to imbue the Roman city with the same sort of menace and antagonism that had been associated with its Punic predecessor.[74] Equally, the Roman lionization of Hannibal as a hero persisted, to the extent that the nephew of Constantine, the first Christian emperor of Rome, in the fourth century AD, was called Flavius Hannibalianus.[75]

It is impossible to assess the debt that Rome owed to Carthage with the same confidence as for the debt to Greece. We can clearly trace the impact of Greek art, science, literature etc. on Roman culture: indeed, educated Romans were often happy to acknowledge that influence. Carthage, however, was afforded no such place in the Roman cultural canon. This had little to do with any lack of originality, but was at least partly the result of the phenomenal success that the Greeks had in claiming sole ownership of advances that had in fact been the result of centuries of exchange and cross-fertilization. The cultural marginalization of Carthage was a Greek achievement the city's destruction a Roman one.

Carthage did, however, play an important a role in the development of the Roman Empire. Rome hugely benefited from the appropriation of the economic and political infrastructure that Carthage had previously put in place in the central and western Mediterranean. In Sardinia, Sicily, North Africa and Spain, the Romans inherited not wild, virgin lands, but a politically, economically and culturally joined-up world which was Carthage's greatest achievement.

Less tangible, but equally important, was the key role that Carthage played in the creation of a Roman national character. The brutal destruction of the city gave the Romans the freedom to transform Carthage into the villainous antitype against which the 'Roman' virtues of faithfulness, piety and duty could be applauded. As long as the Romans needed proof of their greatness, the memory of Carthage would never die.

Notes

PROLOGUE

1. Rakob 1984, 8. Such was the pace of redevelopment that street levels rose almost to the height of houses' floors, so that if the city had not been destroyed in 146 BC some kind of drastic remodelling would have been required (Rakob 1984, 238).
2. Ibid., 8–10; 1989, 156.
3. Hurst & Stager 1978 on the activities at Carthage's commercial port.
4. Hurst 1994, 33–52, on Carthage's war harbour.
5. Docter et al. 2006, 66–7 on garbage collection in Carthage.
6. Lancel 1988, 85–6 1995, 426. These pits may have also contained the remains of those killed during the final Roman assault.
7. The German archaeologist Friedrich Rakob has tentatively identified this temple (probably the home of the Carthaginian god Reshef, but associated by the Greeks with their own deity Apollo) with a religious sanctuary destroyed by fire that he uncovered near to the ports area (Rakob 1995, 420ff., 432 ff.).
8. Rakob 1984, 3ff.
9. This description of the fall of Carthage is primarily based on the version provided by the Greek historian Appian (8.19.127–31), who had himself extensively used the no-longer-extant eyewitness account of Polybius.

INTRODUCTION

1. Silius Italicus *Pun.* 2.395–456.
2. Starks 1999, 257–60; Prandi 1979. Although a number of scholars have pointed out that the shield scenes pose uncomfortable questions about faithlessness for both Carthaginians *and* Romans – Hannibal is shown breaking his treaty with Rome, while Aeneas callously deserts his lover Dido in order to go off to Italy where his ancestors will eventually found Rome

– the fact is that the whole question of *fides* (faithfulness) was a *Roman* obsession which is here imposed upon the Carthaginians. For further reading on Hannibal's armour see Vessey 1975, Campus 2003a.

3. Huss 1985, 53–5; Dubuisson 1983; Isaac 2004, 325–35.

4. Pliny *NH* 18.22.

5. Timaeus of Tauromenium: see pages 14–15 below for a discussion of this historian.

6. Sallust *Hist.* 1.9; Velleius Paterculus 2.1; Orosius 4.23, 5.8.

7. R. Miles 2003.

8. Velleius Paterculus 2.19.4; Plutarch *Mar.* 40.4.

9. Franko 1994, 154.

10. Brecht 1951.

11. Schmidt 1953, 604–9.

12. As proof of the pervasiveness of the epithet, see W. McGurn, *Perfidious Albion: The Abandonment of Hong Kong* (Washington DC, 1991).

13. *The Jeffersonian Encyclopaedia* 1900, 305; reproduced in Schmidt 1953, 611 n. 35.

14. Bernal 1987, 350–52.

15. Schmidt 1953, 610–11; Bernal 1987, 352–5.

16. Lancel 1995, 441–4.

17. See Green 1982 for a useful contextualization of *Salammbô*.

18. Sainte-Beuve 1971, 437.

19. Cullingford 1996, 225–7, 234; Lennon 2004, 84–5.

20. Byron, *Don Juan*, 8.23.3–7.

21. See for instance Seamus Heaney's *North*, published in 1975 (Cullingford 1996, 228–30), Brian Friel's *Translations* (1980) or Frank McGuinness's *Carthaginians* 1988 (Van Weyenberg 2003).

22. For instance: Emanuel Omoh Esiemokhai, *Iraq the New Carthage: International Law and Diplomacy in the Iraq Crisis* (Ife-Ife, 2003); Richard Gwyn, 'An iron-fisted foreign policy: Bush's hard line on Iraq serves notice that no Carthage will be allowed to rise to challenge today's Rome' (*Toronto Star*, 18 September 2002). Even works such as Alan Wilkins's play *Carthage Must be Destroyed* (London, 2007) that made no explicit reference to the Iraq war attracted reviews that made that connection.

23. Schurmann 1998.

24. In this context it is interesting to note the Tunisian journalist Mezri Haddad's book *Non Delenda Carthago: Carthage ne sera pas détruite* (Monaco, 2002), which attacks the criticism directed at his country by the French press.

25. For the dangers of viewing the Carthaginians as merely passive victims of Roman aggression see Eckstein 2006, 158–76.

26. Rakob 1995, 420ff., 432 ff.
27. Hidden texts = Plutarch *Mor.* 942C; Krings 1991, 654–6. Recently a Carthaginian 'strongbox' was found by excavators, although it contained ritual vessels and ochre rather than traces of religious texts (Docter et al. 2006, 67–75). Punic histories = Servius *Aen.* 1.343, 1.738. Roman claims to have used Punic texts = Sallust *Jug.* 17.7. For modern speculation about an official history of Carthage see Huss 1985, 505. One particular Punic inscription (*CIS* i.5510) has been interpreted as a brief historical description of the conclusion of a Carthaginian military campaign against the Greek Sicilian city of Acragas in the winter of 406 BC. For a discussion of this inscription see Schmitz 1994.
28. Pliny, *NH* 18.22. Two Greek translations were also independently made of the text (Devillers & Krings 1994, 492).
29. Devillers & Krings 1994, 490.
30. Heurgon 1976.
31. He also wrote a history of the war between Pyrrhus, king of Epirus, and the Romans. For a full study of Timaeus see Vattuone 1991.
32. Pearson 1975, 172–8.
33. Pearson 1987, 157–63, 238, 245–50.
34. Diodorus 13.43.6.
35. Ibid. 11.1.4.
36. Ibid. 12.26a–b.
37. Ibid. 20.14.1–7, 13.86.3, 20.65.1.
38. Ibid. 13.3.4.
39. Ibid. 13.57.4–5, 13.86.2–3.
40. Ibid. 13.90.1–6.
41. Hoyos 2003, 212–22; Lancel 1999, 25–8.
42. Livy (21.38.3) had also read the work of Cincius Alimentus, who had actually been a prisoner of Hannibal during the Second Punic War.
43. For studies of Polybius' *Histories* see Champion 2004, Walbank 1957–79.
44. Walbank 1985, 262–79.
45. Ibid., 272, although one of the accusations that Polybius levelled at Timaeus was his own contemptuous treatment of other historians.
46. Walbank 1957–79, I: 63–130; 1985, 77–98; Scuderi 2002, 277–84.
47. Plutarch *Pomp.* 11.3–4.
48. Harden 1939, 12. For other archaeological evidence of the burning down of the city see Docter et al. 2006, 75–6.
49. Lancel 1995, 199–204.
50. Huss 1985, 481–3.
51. Lipiński 1988b, 169–74.

52. Ibid.

53. Dubuisson 1983; Starks 1999, 259–60.

54. Bernal 1987, 352, 355.

55. Like many Punic monuments, the monument has been extensively damaged by earthquakes and later urban development, but enough of it has survived for the building to be painstakingly re-created by archaeologists. The problem that any student of Punic architecture faces is the same as that of the literary scholar: a lack of material. Later Roman urban development and deliberate destruction have left little behind. The few remaining examples that have survived not only ancient but also modern vandalism tend to be located in North Africa on the eastern and western fringes of the Carthaginian territory. For the ongoing controversy over the origins of Leptis Magna, Oea and Sabratha see Longerstay 1995, 828–33. Nor was the Sabratha monument a one-off. A similar structure was excavated a mere 100 metres away from it in Sabratha, and another mausoleum has been found near Oran in western Algeria.

56. Di Vita 1976.

57. For instance the Aeolic style of capital with its scrolled volutes that resembled ram's horns with a palm leaf in between, which had been long unfavoured in the Greek world, was from the fourth century BC very popular in Punic architecture (Lancel 1995, 311).

58. Clothes = Maes 1989. Language = Thuillier 1982; Lancel 1995, 275–6. Literature = Cornelius Nepos *Hann.* 23.13.2; Dio 13.54.3. Philosophy = Diogenes Laertius *Herillus* 7.1.37.3.165; Iamblichus *Pythagorean Life* 27, 36.

59. For a study of archaic Greece's debt to Near Eastern cultures see Burkert 1992.

CHAPTER I: FEEDING THE BEAST: THE PHOENICIANS AND THE DISCOVERY OF THE WEST

1. Grayson 1991, 193–223. (Tr. in Melville et al. 2006, 288–9.)

2. The Assyrian king Tiglathpileser I (r. 1114–1076 BC) had marched into Phoenicia and received a vast amount of tribute from the rulers of the city states there (Moscati 1968, 10).

3. Kuhrt 1995, 483–7.

4. Ibid., 473–8 on Assyrian annals and other historiographical sources. Liverani 1979, 297–317 and Reade 1979 on ideology and propaganda in Assyrian art. Kuhrt 1985, 501–23 on Assyrian imperial ideology and

empire. Oded 1979 on the extensive use of deportation by Assyrian monarchs.

5. Documents exist from as early as the fifteenth century BC recording how the Egyptian pharaoh Tuthmosis III, conscious of the lack of large trees in his homeland, marched his troops into Phoenicia and set about organizing annual wood shipments back to Egypt (Markoe 2000, 15).

6. Aubet 2001, 6–13; Huss 1985, 5ff.; Gubel 2006, 86–7. It is likely that for the Greeks 'Phoenicians' meant the people not just of the Levantine coast but also of the states of northern Syria (Röllig 1992, 93). For recent attempts to distinguish between northern-Phoenician/Syrian and southern-Phoenician enterprises see Fletcher 2004; 2006, 187–92; Peckham 1998. I accept that the coastal cities of northern Syria were also involved in many of the same overseas enterprises as the Levantine states, so I have included them under the Phoenicians' aegis.

7. Aubet 2001, 144–58; Moscati 1968, 27–9. Some experts have argued that the dialect written and spoken in the northern cities of Byblos and Arvad was noticeably different from the Tyro-Sidonian dialect that predominated in the southern coastal region (Krahmalkov 2001, 7–9).

8. Liverani 1990.

9. Horden & Purcell 2000, 10–11. Harris (2005, 15) doubts the ubiquity of this name in the Near East.

10. Ezekiel 27:4.

11. Frankenstein 1979, 264.

12. Kochavi 1992, 8–13.

13. Aubet 2001, 105–14; Frankenstein 1979, 264–8.

14. Isaiah 23:8; Ezekiel 26:16. Aubet 2001, 145–7.

15. Kochavi 1992, 13–15.

16. For a general study of Phoenician material culture see Markoe 2000, 143–66.

17. Against whom spells dated to the seventh century BC have been found written in Phoenician (Clifford 1990, 58).

18. Aubet 2001, 6–9.

19. Moscati 1968, 83–4; Markoe 2000, 163–4.

20. Aubet 2001, 39–43.

21. 2 Samuel, 5:10–11.

22. Josephus *JA* 8.50–60.

23. Ibid. 8.58–60.

24. Ibid. 8. 76–83.

25. Josephus (ibid. 8.57) mentions grain, oil and wine.

26. Frankenstein 1979, 268.

27. Aubet 2001, 43–6.

28. Handy 1994, 3.

29. L'Heureux 1979, 69–79; Handy 1994, 65–102.

30. Clifford 1990, 59–61. She is also known as *Rabbat* (*RBT*), 'The Lady' or 'The Mother' (Krahmalkov 2000, 441).

31. In the Old Testament, the Tyrian king unsurprisingly earns himself a stern rebuke for attempting to elide the temporal and celestial worlds (Ezekiel 28:1–10).

32. Josephus *JA* 8.144–6, citing Menander of Ephesus.

33. Aubet 2001, 150–58; Lipiński 1970. Sacred prostitutes in the temple of Astarte also enacted the ceremony with their clients.

34. Clifford 1990, 61.

35. Ibid., 57.

36. Herodotus 2.44.

37. Nonnus *Dion.* 40.429–68.

38. Ibid., 40.469–534. Other Greek authors also allude to a Tyrian myth that told of how the temple was built at the same time as the city was founded 2,300 years before (Herodotus 2.44).

39. Herodotus 2.44. The emerald pillar is also mentioned in Pliny *NH* 37.75. Evidence from Tyre and Tyrian colonies across the Mediterranean strongly suggests that the twin pillars in the temple represented the olive tree and the eternal flames which appear in Nonnus' foundation tale. Certainly the temple of Melqart at the Tyrian colony of Gades (Cadiz) housed a sacred fire which always burnt and a golden olive tree. It has been argued that the emerald column may have acted as a lighthouse (Katzenstein 1973, 87). However, evidence from other sites suggests that the columns were actually located inside the temple complex.

40. Another Greek myth also attributed the discovery of Tyre's greatest export, purple dye, to the god. It was said that while the god had been strolling along the shell-strewn seashore with his lover, the nymph Tyros, his dog had bitten into one of these molluscs. Quickly realizing the potential of his pet's stained canines, Melqart had a robe dyed to a deep purple and presented it to Tyros as a gift. Another version of the same story had the dog brought before Phoenix, the legendary king of Tyre, who decreed that this purple dye should be manufactured and used as a badge of his royal office. Later Tyrians, shrewd businessmen that they were, would do much to market this story by putting a image of the murex and the purple-toothed dog on their coinage (Aubet 2001, 6–9).

41. Cross 1972a, 36–42.

42. Hiram and then Ithobaal would also take the title of 'king of the Sidonians' (*CIS* 56).

43. Gras, Rouillard & Teixidor 1991, 136.

44. Aubet 2001, 166–75.
45. Ibid., 123–126. Much of this information comes from the Book of Ezekiel, a work written at a considerably later date in the sixth century BC, a period when Tyre no longer ruled the waves. There are sections of the text which many scholars now believe are part of an older document dating to the ninth and eighth centuries BC (Ezekiel 27:9–25; see Aubet 2001, 121–2 for these arguments).
46. Aubet 2001, 50–51.
47. Markoe 1992. Boardman (2004, 154–5) thinks that the perfume enterprise on Rhodes is more likely to be Greek, although he does not take enough account of the Levantine shape of the perfume flasks.
48. Shaw & Shaw 2000; Boardman 1980, 57ff. The considerable quantity of Levantine pottery discovered at the site suggests a great deal of trading activity between Kommos and Phoenicia.
49. Coldstream 2003, 358–66. Röllig 1992, 95 for the idea that these were Phoenicians and other people from the Near East at Athens and Crete, fleeing the conquest of the Assyrian king Sargon II. Burkert 1992, 21–4 for the suggestion that these craftsmen probably travelled over with merchants. On different aspects of the orientalizing phenomenon in the archaic Mediterranean world see the assortment of essays in Riva & Vella (eds.) 2006.
50. Copper ingots as well as considerable quantities of pottery from Cyprus were being exported to the Levantine coast from the fourteenth and thirteenth centuries BC. Cypriots are also listed as residents of the merchant quarters of Ugarit from this period (Kochavi 1992, 10–13).
51. Aubet 2001, 147. An inscription records a Tyrian governor of 'Carthage' on Cyprus (CIS 56). However, it is as yet unclear whether Kition was in fact this Carthage or another, as yet undiscovered, site.
52. Josephus JA 8.146. An early-ninth-century Cypriot inscription has been interpreted by one translator as a memorial to a Tyrian commander who boasts how his troops devastated the island (KAI 30, ll. 1–3). An even earlier inscription, from the twelfth century BC, found near Ghaza proclaims that the god Baal had devastated Cyprus and has been interpreted as showing a history of violent Phoenician intervention on the island (Cross 1980, 2–3).
53. Karageorghis 1998.
54. Aubet 2001, 155.
55. Frankenstein 1979, 269.
56. Postgate 1974.
57. Postgate 1969; 1979, 200–214.
58. Kuhrt 1995, 518–19.
59. Russell 1991.

60. Postgate 1979, 218; Aubet 2001, 90–92; Frankenstein 1979, 272–3.
61. Frankenstein 1979, 286.
62. Aubet 2001, 90–92.
63. Frankenstein 1979, 273.
64. Recent excavations in the south-western Spanish port of Huelva appear to provide strong evidence of Phoenician commercial activity in the ninth century (González de Canales, Serrano & Llompart 2006). For this view see Gubel 2006, 87; Fletcher 2006, 191. For scepticism towards pre-colonizing Phoenician activity in the central and western Mediterranean see Aubet 2001, 200–211; Van Dommelen 1998, 71–5.
65. Giardino 1992; Van Dommelen 1998, 75–6.
66. Van Dommelen 1998, 76–80.
67. Stos-Gale & Gale 1992, 317–37.
68. Fletcher's (2004 & 2006) interesting thesis that such cooperation and incorporation into indigenous communities was the work of Sidonian merchants who would eventually be superseded by Tyrian colonizers is attractive but at the moment unproven.
69. Ridgway 1992, 120.
70. D'Oriano & Oggiano 2005. The settlement seems to have been abandoned in the late sixth century BC.
71. Rendeli 2005, 92–7; Ridgway 2004, 16–19. There has been a long and increasingly rancorous debate over the exact nature of Euboean and Phoenician colonization, trade and interactions in the Mediterranean. For a sample of it see Snodgrass 1994; Papadopoulos 1997; S. Morris 1998; Ridgway 1994; 2000, 183–5; 2004, 22–8; Boardman 2005.
72. Tandy 1997, 66–70.
73. Niemeyer 1990.
74. Nijboer 2005.
75. Markoe 1992, 62–73. In contrast to the enormous appetite for silver in the Near East and Etruria, in Greece there is almost a complete absence of decorated silver work in the seventh century BC. Bronze would remain the precious metal most used for offerings at important Greek sanctuaries. A good deal of orientalizing silver work was produced in Etruria during this time, introducing Near Eastern designs and motifs as well as very particular smithing skills such as granulation, punch-work and filigree, which suggest the presence of Phoenician artisans in central Italy. An orientalizing tradition would become important in areas of Etruscan art (ibid., 78).
76. Malkin 2002.
77. Snodgrass 1971, 304–13; Chadwick 1976, 188–93.
78. Popham, Sackett & Themelis (eds.) 1979. Many of the artefacts display clear Egyptian influences. There is no recorded Greek contact with Egypt

until the seventh century BC. Another important factor is the lack of Euboean staging posts on the long and arduous journey across the open sea to the Levant.

79. Niemeyer 1984, 19.

80. Coldstream 1982; Hudson 1992, 138–9.

81. Coldstream 1988. Considerable quantities of ninth-century-BC Euboean pottery have been discovered at Tyre (Bikai 1978).

82. Strøm 1992, 48–9, 57–60. Particularly popular in Greece were large bronze cauldrons decorated with winged siren and bull-head attachments, many of which originally hailed from northern Syria (Muscarella 1992, 40–43). Others think that they are more likely to have been offerings from Levantine visitors. There is also some suggestion that these cauldrons may have been transported overland through Asia Minor rather than by sea (Röllig 1992, 97–102).

83. There have been many attempts to prove that Al Mina was an Euboean-controlled settlement (e.g. Boardman 2002 & 2005). However, although it is certainly the case that a large quantity of Greek pottery was found at Al Mina, the fact is that a far greater amount of Levantine material was also discovered there – although it never received the same attention as the Greek material, since archaeologists were excited by the possibility of having found evidence of one of the first Hellenic colonies in the Near East. Furthermore, the Greek pottery that has been found covers far too narrow a range to be evidence of a functioning Greek colony. The vast majority of the ceramics is made up of drinking vessels, which suggests that Al Mina was actually a centre for the import and export of luxury rather than subsistence goods (Tandy 1997, 65). There is a distinct possibility that at least some of the pots attributed to mainland Greece were the products of Phoenician-dominated Cyprus, where such 'Greek' styles were already being turned out. Clay analysis suggests that they may have been manufactured in eastern Cyprus. This would also explain the marked difference in quality between real Euboean skyphoi – deep drinking-cups with two handles and a low foot – and those from Al Mina. There is also a question over whether this particular form of skyphos was being produced during this period on the Greek mainland. There is every reason, therefore, to conclude that these were Near Eastern imitations of Greek pottery (Kearsley 1989). Thus, as we have seen in the West, Al Mina may actually show the real strength of an increasingly independent Phoenician Cyprus. Kearsley's interpretation of the dating of the 'Euboean skyphoi' from Al Mina has been criticized by Popham & Lemos (1992, 154–5), who argue that many of them should be given a much earlier dating, putting the Euboeans at Al Mina by 800 BC. However, as Snodgrass (1994, 4–5) has pointed out, the vast majority of

the so-called Euboean skyphoi from Al Mina are dated to after the mid eighth century BC. In fact the first evidence for Greek settlements in the Levant comes from Tell Sukas and Ras el-Bassit in the sixth century BC, but even that evidence is far from convincing (Waldbaum 1997). Furthermore, Al Mina contains none of the particular architectural characteristics associated with the Euboeans, such as thin-wood supported walls, tiled roofs and the apsidal plan (Luke 2003, 23–4). Even more tellingly, there is no evidence of Greek funerary practice in the settlement, or of Greek being spoken there. Only one potsherd has been found with a (poorly executed) Greek inscription upon it. Scholars who have recently studied it point out that the incompetence of the style suggests that the writer was inscribing a non-Greek name or phrase in unfamiliar letters. Analysis of the clay used in the potsherd also suggests that the vessel was not made in Al Mina (ibid., 12, 24). For a convincing set of arguments that Al Mina has to be understood within a north-Syrian context while more generally pointing out the dangers of seeing mercantile activity in the eastern Mediterranean as a bipolar division between Greeks and Phoenicians, see Hodos 2006, 25–88.

84. S. Morris & Papadopoulos 1998.

85. Kopcke 1992, 103–13. Burkert 1992 is the classic study on the relationship between Near Eastern and Greek culture. For the great influence that the Near East had on Greek art see S. Morris 1992. The influence was particularly great on the development of Greek religion in the archaic period. Although a number of the major Greek deities can be traced back to the Mycenaean period, aspects of devotional ritual appear to have hailed directly from the Near East. These included hepatoscopy (the gleaning of omens from the livers of sacrificial victims), purification through blood sacrifice, ecstatic divination where the divinity spoke directly through the mouth of the priest or priestess, and the practice of attempting to soothe the spirits of the dead through gifts and offerings and sometimes invoking them to do others harm through magic spells (Burkert 1992, 46–82). Other fundamental aspects of Greek religious ritual also hailed from the Near East, including the tradition of banqueting at sanctuaries, the use of large altars for the incineration of offerings, and even the building of temples to house the gods and the representation of gods as cult statues (Strøm 1992, 55–6; Burkert 1992, 19–21). In regard to the temples, Kopcke (1992, 110–12) has made the important point that it was the idea of temples rather than the exact architectural/liturgical blueprint that the Greeks received from the Levant. They also adopted the practice of placing offerings in the foundations of religious buildings, which was popular among the Assyrians (Burkert 1992, 53–5). Outside the cultural sphere, some scholars have even speculated that some of the new city states that sprang up around Greece

borrowed their political systems from the Phoenicians. Certainly the very particular constitutional set-up at Sparta appears to have been very similar to the governmental systems of the Phoenician cities (Drews 1979).

86. Coldstream 1982, 269–72; Isserlin 1991; Einarson 1967.

87. Hence the Greek words for their letters (*alpha*, *beta*, *gamma*, *delta* etc.) are also of Semitic origin (Burkert 1992, 28–9).

88. It is generally agreed that the Greek alphabet came into existence in the early eighth century BC. However, some have tried to push this as far back as the fourteenth century BC (Bernal 1990). There is a wide collection of studies on the introduction of the alphabet into Greece in Baurain, Bonnet & Krings (eds.) 1991, 277–371. Greek letters appear at Athens, the Greek island of Naxos and Pithecusa by the mid eighth century BC (Burkert 1992, 26). However, there are some scholars who argue that in fact the Greek alphabet was formulated in the eleventh century BC from proto-Canaanite, the written language from which Phoenician was derived (Naveh 1980). As yet there is no evidence of any Greek writing before the eighth century BC. It was generally accepted by later Greeks that their alphabet had been derived from the Phoenician one, hence the name given to it: *Phoinikeia grammata* ('Phoenician letters').

89. Burkert 1992, 33–40; Lancel 1995, 351–3.

90. Hudson 1992, 134–5. For weights and measures, see Lydus *Liber de Mensibus* 1.9.

91. Lloyd 1975, 54.

92. As well as Thucydides (1.13) there was Diodorus (14.42.1–3) and Pliny *NH* 7.207. However, according to Clement of Alexandria (*Stromateis* 1.16.76), it was the Phoenicians who invented the trireme, and Pliny the Elder (*NH* 7.208) contended that Aristotle believed the Carthaginians to be responsible for the quadrireme. Lloyd is certainly right to contend that it is dangerous to mine Christian polemic for empirical facts, but goes too far in arguing that Clement's claim that the Phoenicians invented the trireme is 'historically worthless' (Lloyd 1975, 49–51; 1980, 197). Some of Clement's claims are certainly correct.

93. That is when Polycrates, ruler of Samos, sent forty triremes to take part in the Persian naval expedition to Egypt (Herodotus 3.44). The arguments of Lloyd (1975, 52–4) that there is good evidence for the trireme being developed by the Corinthians in the seventh century BC rely on a fragmentary source writing during the reign of the Roman emperor Augustus, supported by the somewhat tenuous use of modern precedents to explain why the Greeks take advantage of this technology earlier than the Phoenicians. Furthermore, Thucydides never made the claim that it was the Corinthians who had invented the trireme: merely that they had been

the first Greeks to build one before its designer, a certain Ameinocles, went to Samos, where he built a further four of these vessels (1.13).

94. Despite the ingenuous efforts of Lloyd 1975, 55–7. Lloyd's (1980, 196–7) questioning of Phoenician involvement in the Memphite dockyard of *Prw-nfr* during this period does not undermine this wider point. For the Phoenicians supplying timber to Egypt see Basch 1969, 231ff.

95. Basch 1977, 1–8; 1980, 199.

96. There were clearly differences between the Phoenician and the Greek craft. According to Herodotus (8.118–19), the Phoenician triremes had a continuous deck. Plutarch (*Them.* 14.2) also drew a clear distinction between the light, low Greek ships and their taller 'barbarian' counterparts with higher poops and decks. The Phoenician trireme also appears to have had a slightly different design of stern, carried shields along the gunwale, and had a differently shaped ram (Lloyd 1975, 48).

97. Plato *Phaed.* 109B.

98. Abulafia 2005, 64–9. For a wide-ranging study of the ancient and medieval Mediterranean that explores these ideas see Horden & Purcell 2000, as well as a collection of well-considered responses to the book in Harris 2005.

99. Homer *Iliad* 23.740–45, 6.286–96.

100. Homer *Odyssey* 15.415–16. Capomacchia 1991.

101. Homer *Odyssey* 15.498–615, 14.287–300.

102. Winter 1995.

103. Van Dommelen 1998, 80–81, 111.

104. Trump 1992, 198–203; Bonzani 1992, 210–20. This transformation of the Nuragic landscape is perhaps best reflected in the change in design and function of the nuraghi. In the first millennium BC, some classic nuraghi – usually consisting of a fortified single tower whose existence appears to have been very much concerned with status and ownership within the community – developed into more complex structures. Extra towers and connecting walls were now added, which suggests that these particular nuraghi had become primarily military fortresses. Often these complexes seem to have developed villages around them, suggesting that the population were now living within a complex, socially stratified community (Ugas 1992, 229–30).

105. See the arguments of Rendeli 2005 for an initial considerable Euboean presence in Sulcis.

106. Giardino 1992, 304.

107. González de Canales, Serrano & Llompart 2006.

108. Lipiński 2004, 234–47. There is no consensus on the meaning of the Nora Stone. Peckham (1972) argued that the stele described Milkaton's ship(s) being blown away from Spain in a storm and safely landing in

Sardinia. Cross (1972b) favoured interpreting it as describing a military expedition to Sardinia and 'Tarshish' as a settlement on the island which Milkaton and his troops had captured before the establishment of a truce with the indigenous people of the island. Cross also translated *Pmy* (*-yton*) as Pygmalion, the ninth-century-BC king of Tyre, who had authorized Milkaton's expedition, rather than as the god Pummay. Cross (1987) takes another very fragmentary inscription found at Nora as evidence for Phoenician activity on Sardinia in the eleventh century BC, but this is rather tenuous.

109. Diodorus 5.35.4–5.

110. Frankenstein 1979, 288.

111. Niemeyer 1990, 471–2.

112. Nijboer & Van de Plicht 2006. Phoenician pottery from that period has been found at the port of Huelva.

113. Aubet 2001, 281–3.

114. Strabo 3.5.5.

115. Diodorus 5.20.3.

116. Aubet 2001, 186–91.

117. Herodotus 4.152; Aubet 2001, 279–80, for the ore equivalence.

118. Aubet 2006, 96–105; Van Dommelen 2006, 124–6.

119. Aubet 2006, 106.

120. In some Near Eastern states such as the north-Syrian state of Ugarit, the head of the merchants' guild and some of its members had actually received a regular salary from the royal palace. In return the merchants sometimes acted as the king's envoys (Kochavi 1992, 13–14).

121. Aubet 2001, 116–19.

122. Strabo 3.5.5; Philostratus *Apollon.* 5.4.

123. Strabo 3.5.7. When discussing the spring, Strabo cites Polybius. It is interesting to note that Nonnus also makes much of supposed springs in his Tyrian foundation myth.

124. Aubet 2006, 106.

125. A third-century-AD visitor to the sanctuary, Apollonius of Tyana, asked the temple priests about the meaning of these strange inscriptions, but they could offer no explanation. Apollonius would come up with his own explanation that 'These pillars bind Earth and Heaven together, and he [the creator] inscribed them himself in the house of the Fates, to ensure that there was no strife between the elements, and that they should not neglect the affection that they feel for each other' (Philostratus *Apollon.* 5.4–5).

126. Justin 44.5.2.

127. Silius Italicus (*Pun.* 3.14–44), although writing a rather blowsy and overblown epic for a Roman audience in the second century AD, gives a

useful account of the temple of Melqart at Gades. The doors of the sanctuary on to which, according to Silius, the labours of Heracles were etched must have been a later development or even a product of his extremely lively imagination. For other mentions of sacrificial rites at the sanctuary see Diodorus 5.20.2.

128. In a clear reference to the *egersis* of Melqart, Philostratus stated that the people of Gades were 'the only people to celebrate Death' (*Apollon.* 5.4).

129. Pausanias 10.4.6.

130. Aubet 2001, 273–9.

131. Aubet 2001, 55–7.

132. Moscati 1968, 19–21; Aubet 2001, 57–9.

133. Aubet 2001, 57.

CHAPTER 2: NEW CITY: THE RISE OF CARTHAGE

1. Justin (18.4) calls the exiles 'princes', which may suggest that they were part of that elite group the Tyrian 'merchant princes'.

2. Baurain 1988, 21–2; Scheid & Svenbro 1985, 329, 338.

3. Scheid & Svenbro 1985, 334–8.

4. Bunnens 1986, 124–5, for the parallel with American Thanksgiving.

5. Scheid & Svenbro 1985, 329, 338.

6. Krahmalkov 1981.

7. For the general problem of marrying the literary testimony with the archaeological record see Bunnens 1979, 299–320.

8. New radio-carbon analysis might push this back to around 800 BC (Docter et al. 2006, 39).

9. For convincing arguments against treating Philo of Byblos as a reliable source for the early Phoenician world see Barr 1974 and Edwards 1991.

10. Philistus Fr. 47, *FGH*, IIIB: 564; Appian 8.1.1 (in which 'Azoros' had become 'Zoros'); Lancel 1995, 20–22.

11. Huss 1985, 405–6.

12. Aubet 2001, 227; Bordreuil & Ferjaoui 1988.

13. The linguistic footprint of Punic shows that it was an amalgam of a number of different Phoenician dialects. Certain religious practices such as the use of red ochre in Punic funerary rituals point to a strong native Libyan element (Benichou-Safar 1982, 265–6; Lancel 1995, 53; Docter et al. 2006, 35).

14. Unfortunately, as with the vast majority of public structures in Punic Carthage, no traces of the temples of these deities have been found. However, several smaller temples have been discovered in Carthage as well as at important religious centres in other areas of the Punic West. Melqart temple

inscription = *CIS* i.4894, 5575. Astarte as the consort of Melqart = *CIS* i.250, 2785, 4839, 4850, 5657. The temple of Eshmoun situated on the summit of the Byrsa hill was the most famous temple in Carthage.

15. Diodorus 20.14.2; Polybius 31.12; Arrian *Anabasis* 2.24.5; Quintus Curtius Rufus 4.2.10; Aubet 2001, 157. Some scholars have argued that the potential links with Cyprus revealed in the foundation myth reflect the reality of a strong Cypriot element among the city's early population (Kourou 2002, 102–5). However, the material evidence for an early Cypriot involvement with Carthage is not particularly strong compared with that for other areas of the Greek world (ibid., 90–92; Bisi 1988, 31).

16. Niemeyer 1990, 487.

17. Bunnens (1979) has speculated that Carthage started not as a deliberate colonial venture but as a trading post with a resident group of merchants like the other western Phoenician settlements, and that it was only later that the Carthaginians reinvented their past as an exceptional colonial establishment. There is little doubt that a process of rebranding did take place as Carthage became more powerful, but part of this success was based on the particularity of its circumstances as a planned colonial establishment. Baurain (1988) has ingeniously suggested that this myth may in fact be the result of a misappropriation of a foundation myth relating instead to the city of Carthage on the island of Cyprus. However, this thesis is founded on the mistaken belief that the literary accounts and archaeological evidence need to correlate with each other. There is little reason *not* to believe that the myth does relate to African Carthage.

18. Kourou 2002, 92–7.

19. Niemeyer & Docter 1993; Vegas 1999; Kourou 2002, 92–6.

20. Docter 2000b.

21. Briese & Docter 1992; Kourou 2002, 101–2. However, Boardman's (2006, 199) suggestion that Carthage may well have been originally a 'multi-national comptoir' exaggerates the Euboean influence on the early settlement.

22. Niemeyer & Docter 1993, 213–14.

23. Van Zeist, Bottema & Van de Veen 2001.

24. Van Wijngaarden-Bakker 2007, 846–8.

25. Bechtold 2008, 75–6; Fentress & Docter 2008, 2–3.

26. Docter et al. 2006, 39–43.

27. Ibid., 39–45.

28. For the possible existence of an older, eighth-century-BC, cemetery in Carthage see Docter et al. 2003, 46–8; 2006, 43–5.

29. Lancel 1995, 51–5.

30. Benichou-Safar 1982, 262, 272–85; Tore 1995; Debergh 1973, 241–2; Gsell 1924, 457–8.

31. Fantar 1979, 12–15; Dussaud 1935, 270; Gsell 1924, 457.

32. Virolleaud 1931, 355; Dussaud 1935, 269; Díes Cusí 1995, 413–14.

33. Aubet 2001, 219; Lancel 1995, 45; Docter et al. 2006, 39–40.

34. Lancel 1995, 60–76. The continued strong Levantine influence can also be ascertained by the wide-scale production at Carthage of decorated ostrich eggs, which were exported throughout the western Phoenician world and were often part of grave-good assemblages. The significance of ostrich eggs appears to have been their association with the existence in Phoenician religious thought of a great 'cosmic egg' which when split in two represented the primordial separation between the heavens and the earth. Carthage's location in Africa must have ensured a steady supply of these eggs (Ribichini 1995, 338).

35. Van Dommelen 1998, 81–84; 2006, 127–30. This might also explain Phoenician burials on Sardinia which contained ingots of metal among the grave assemblages (Fletcher 2006, 179–80).

36. Fentress & Docter 2008, 3. In Carthage, archaeologists have discovered considerable numbers of Nuragic amphorae that were used for the transport of food and other raw materials. At the Phoenician settlement of Sant' Imbenia the remains of a metal-workshop store have been found containing 20 kilograms of copper bars, which suggests that this may have been a centre for processing metal ore.

37. Ibid.

38. The most intricate of the tombs that have been discovered consist of a burial chamber with the body housed in a stone sarcophagus or in a niche cut into the walls. Stone slabs formed a kind of pitched roof over the chamber. The frontage of the chamber was usually closed off by a blocked wall. The richest of these tombs were further embellished with fine white plaster on the internal walls and scented-wood panelling on the ceiling. However, most early Carthaginians were buried more simply, in excavated rectangular pits, boxed in by stone slabs (Lancel 1995, 46–51).

39. Herodotus 7.165–6; Diodorus 13.43.5, 14.34.5.

40. Aubet 2001, 229; Huss 1985, 496–7.

41. Sznycer 1978, 567–70.

42. Lancel 1995, 210–11. At the temple of Baal Saphon there were five different price categories: adult cattle, calves, adult sheep, lambs and, lastly, birds. For the less well-off, cheaper offerings of pastries, oil, milk and flour could also be made.

43. In several inscriptions from Carthage the title 'Resurrector of the Divine husband of Astarte' or 'Awakener of the Dead God with the scent of

Astronoë' (depending on the translation) appears (*CIS* i.227, 260–62, 377; i.5510). Most scholars agree that these are references to priests of Melqart (Lipiński 1970, 30–58; Krahmalkov 2000, 308–9; Lancel 1995, 204–7).

44. Lancel 1995, 199–204. She was often addressed on inscriptions as *Rabbat* ('The Lady' or 'The Mother') or *Rabbatenû* ('Our Lady').

45. Le Glay 1966, 440; Lancel 1995, 194–9. Very few examples of any iconography for Baal Hammon have been discovered, however, a fragment of a stele dating to the fifth century BC and found at a coastal settlement some 160 kilometres from Carthage shows a bearded god wearing a conical headdress and a long robe. In one hand he holds a spear, and he appears to be giving a blessing with the other.

46. Exodus 22:29. Sacrifice of kings' sons = 2 Kings 16:3, 21:6. For studies of *molk* sacrifice in the Old Testament see Heider 1985. For backlash, see Deuteronomy 12:31, 18:10; Jeremiah 7:31, 19:5, 32:35; Ezekiel 20:31. For other examples of the sacrifice of sons and daughters in the Old Testament see Aubet 2001, 246–8.

47. Eusebius *Evang. Praep.* 1.10.44. This information was purported to have originally come from the work of Sanchuniathon, a Phoenician who lived in Berytus (modern Beirut) around 1000 BC.

48. Gianto 1987. In addition, a fire temple discovered at Amman in Jordan has produced a large number of human bones which some archaeologists have connected to sacrifice (Ottoson 1980, 101–4).

49. For the fullest studies of child sacrifice in Carthage and the Punic world see Shelby Brown 1991, Benichou-Safar 2004, Stager 1982 and Stager & Wolff 1984. In terms of ancient testament, a fragment of the fifth-century-BC Athenian dramatist Sophocles' play *Andromeda* alludes to 'foreigners' who perform human sacrifice in honour of the god Cronus. The reason why scholars have presumed that this is a reference to the Punic world is that Cronus was the Greek equivalent of Baal Hammon, chief deity of Carthage. However, the first specific mention of child sacrifice in Carthage hails from the fourth century BC (Plato *Minos* 315B–C). The influential Greek philosopher Theophrastus (*c.*371–287 BC) also alleged that human sacrifice was a current Carthaginian practice (Fr. 13.22–6; Porphyry *On Abstinence* 2.27.2). The Sicilian Greek author Diodorus (13.86.3) would claim that a Carthaginian commander had sacrificed a child to Cronus as his forces besieged a city in order to elicit the support of the god. A later Roman author would claim that such was the Carthaginians' barbarity that even the Persians, hardly known for their mildness, ordered that they cease this foul tradition (Justin 19.1.10).

50. Diodorus 20.14.4–7.

51. Cleitarchus *Scholia* 377A. For a similar observation see Plato *Minos* 315B–C.

52. Plutarch *Mor.* 171C–D.

53. Cintas' chapel, which the excavator believed to be the levelling for the first Phoenician structure on the tophet, is most probably just the remains of a number of disturbed urns (Gras, Rouillard & Teixidor 1995, 273).

54. Lancel 1995, 249–50.

55. Aubet 2001, 251–2; Lancel 1995, 248–9.

56. *CIS* i.5507.

57. Aubet 2001, 247.

58. Several of the inscriptions from the Carthage tophet contain the formula 'by the decree of the people of Carthage' (Aubet 2001, 254).

59. Van Dommelen 1998, 116.

60. Van Dommelen 2006, 122–3 for the different settlement models in the far West and the central Mediterranean.

61. Evidence of Carthage's heavy involvement in maintaining the old trading links with Greece and the Levant comes from Malta and its sister island of Gozo, key stopping-off points on the trans-Mediterranean shipping lanes, where there is clear archaeological evidence for a Carthaginian presence on the islands by the late sixth century BC (Sagona 2002, 25–53).

62. Huss 1985, 57–74.

63. Bunnens (1979) in particular presents an imperialist Carthage and erroneously pushes the idea of the Phoenicians themselves as imperialist colonizers rather than traders.

64. Schulten 1922. Most recently Braun (2004, 302) has argued as a likely guess that Carthage destroyed Tartessus around 500 BC and took over its trade.

65. Justin 44.5.1–3. This is not the only story told of tensions between the indigenous Spanish and Gades. Macrobius, a Roman author of the fifth century AD, tells the story of a certain King Theron who attacked the city (*Sat.* 1.20.12). See also Vitruvius 10.1–3. This much later Roman military text asserts that the battering ram had been first been used by the Carthaginians at this siege. Although no date for the incident is given by Vitruvius, he goes on to say that it was before Philip of Macedon's siege of Byzantium of 340–339 BC, where Philip copied the same technique. The story is also mentioned by another treatise written in the earlier period (Athenaeus 4.9.3: Krings 1998, 229–60; Barcelo 1988, 1–22, 38–42).

66. Justin 18.7.1–2.

67. Ibid. 19.1.1–6; Pausanias 10.17.9

68. Van Dommelen 1998, 123–4; Tronchetti 1995, 728–9.

69. There is also clear evidence that during this period the Nuragic people were going through a period of profound social and political transformation (Webster 1996, 179–94).

70. Bechtold 2008, 75; Fentress & Docter 2008, 104.

71. Van Dommelen 2002, 130–37; 1998, 124–5.

72. Barcelo 1988, 46–7.

73. For southern Spain (Toscanos), see Wagner 1989, 150–51. For Ibiza, see Gómez Bellard 1990, 178–83. Supposedly the first Carthaginian colony was Ebusus, founded in 654 BC. However, many scholars now believe that it may initially have been a secondary foundation, possibly set up by settlers from a Phoenician settlement on the Spanish mainland, which came under Carthaginian influence only in the later decades of the sixth century BC, when the region was troubled by the collapse of the Tyrian–Iberian trading route. This change is typified by the introduction of rock-cut burial chambers, steles and statuettes.

74. Whittaker 1978.

75. Ibid., 59.

76. Fruits, cereals and vegetables = Hurst & Stager 1978, 338–40. Analysis of wood used to burn sacrificial pyres also shows evidence that from the fourth century onwards almonds, peaches, apricots and plums were being cultivated in or near Carthage (Stager 1982). Meat and fish = Van Wijngaarden-Bakker 2007, 841, 848. Dogs make up only around 3 per cent of the bone sample, but often show signs of having been butchered.

77. Bechtold 2008, 40–43; Morel 2004, 14; Lancel 1995, 257–302.

78. For evidence from field surveys in Carthage's hinterland see Greene 1983.

79. Diodorus 20.8.3–4. One and a half centuries later, when another invading force tramped its way to Carthage, exactly the same fecundity was there to be witnessed by the awestruck troops (Appian 8.18.117).

80. Kerkouane has often been presented as an anomaly (Van Dommelen 1998, 122), but the lack of evidence for a major Punic presence in other parts of Cap Bon probably has more to do with the limited number of field surveys conducted in the region.

81. For the fullest study of Kerkouane see Fantar 1984. For a short description, Lancel 1995, 280–88.

82. There is also evidence that a number of female deities were worshipped here, including Astarte, Tanit (the mother of Sid) and Demeter.

83. Mezzolani 1999.

84. For a good study of the local Libyan populations in Iron Age North Africa see Hodos 2006, 158–99.

85. Huss 1985, 70–74. In a Greek maritime text dated to the third/second century BC, the influence that the Carthaginians possessed over large swathes of North Africa is made clear in emphatic terms. 'As many townships or emporia as have been written about in Libya, from the Syrtis by Hesperides as far as the Pillars of Heracles in Libya, are all of the Carthaginians' (Pseudo-Scylax 111).

86. It was in this region that the Carthaginians planted huge numbers of olive trees, the crop for which its farmland is still famous for today.

87. Bechtold 2008, 47–48, 75.

88. Greene 1986, 109–16; Fentress & Docter 2008, 105.

89. Fantar 1984.

90. Pliny NH 18.22. Fantar 1998, 118. Mago is in fact cited on 66 occasions by Greek and Roman writers (Devillers & Krings 1994, 490–92). Selection and care of cattle = Columella Agr. 6.1.3; Varro Agr. 2.5.18. On fruit trees = Pliny NH 17.63–4, 131. The Roman writer Pliny the Elder intimated that Mago was not just an agricultural specialist but had also held a generalship, which has led some to speculate that he was indeed the individual whom a Greek source said had 'transformed the Carthaginians from the Tyrians that they had been into Libyans' (Pliny NH 18.22). For the dating of Mago to the fifth century BC see Fantar 1998, 114–15; Lancel 1995, 257–9.

91. Hurst & Stager 1978, 338–40.

92. For evidence of the start of winemaking in Punic North Africa see Greene 2000.

93. Lancel 1995, 269–79.

94. Pytheas supposedly sailed up through the Pillars of Hercules, up the Atlantic coast of France, along the English Channel and up to Scandinavia, the Baltic region, the mouth of the river Don and even the Orkneys, before exploring the Atlantic coast all the way down to Gades. See Dion 1977, 175–222, for a full discussion of the voyage. There is, however, no evidence to back up Dion's assertion (175–6) that the expedition had been commissioned by Alexander the Great. Dion seems to have been heavily influenced by the Hellenocentric claims of Arrian (Anabasis 5.26.1–6) that, after his conquest of Asia, Alexander intended to turn to the West.

95. Pliny NH 2.169 for the idea that they were contemporaneous and sanctioned by the Carthaginian state.

96. Bello Jiménez 2005, 17–34.

97. Festus Rufus Avienus 114–29, 380–89, 404–15. See Picard & Picard 1961, 236–7, for arguments about the veracity of Avienus' claims. Pliny the Elder in his Natural History (2.169) also mentions Himilco's voyage 'to explore the outer coasts of Europe'.

98. Picard & Picard (1961, 239) argue that these monsters were probably

whales, although such sea monsters are a common cliché in Greek and Roman descriptions of northern lands, and acted as a cipher for general wildness and otherness.

99. Herodotus 3.115; Diodorus 5.21.30; Strabo 2.5.15, 3.2.9, 3.5.11, 6.2.5; Pliny *NH* 4.119, 7.197, 34.156-8.

100. Hanno 1; Blomqvist 1979, 5. The voyage of Hanno has been variously dated by scholars to the first half of the fifth century BC (Demerliac & Meirat 1983, 9) or the first half of the sixth century BC (Lacroix 1998, 345). For the single manuscript from which the *Periplus* has been dated to the tenth century AD see Lacroix 1998, 343.

101. Hanno 1-8. The two fullest attempts to track Hanno's voyage are Demerliac & Meirat 1983 and Lacroix 1998.

102. Hanno 9-12. Others have suggested that the site of these mountains was the area around Monrovia, the capital of Liberia.

103. Hanno 13-14.

104. Lacroix 1998, 375-80.

105. Pliny *NH* 6.200.

106. Hanno 15-18. Some have speculated that the premature return of Hanno's mission was a smokescreen for the fact that the Carthaginian fleet secretly carried on their journey and circumnavigated Africa (Lacroix 1998, 380-84). This relies solely on Pliny's assertion that Hanno had successfully sailed from Gades to Arabia by circumnavigating Africa (*NH* 2.169). However, all other sources attest to the fact that Hanno did indeed turn back owing to lack of water, burning heat, and rivers of fire flowing into the sea (Arrian *Indike* 43.11-12; Pomponius Mela 3.89).

107. Bello Jiménez 2005, 56-67, 82-6. Demerliac & Meirat (1983, 64-7) suggest the more realistic number of 5,000 people.

108. J. Taylor 1982; Bello Jiménez 2005, 85-6. The suggestion that this was in fact a secret mission to break the Arab trading monopoly by bringing gold from the mines of the Zimbabwe/Transvaal region of southern Africa via the Strait of Gibraltar is extremely far-fetched (Lacroix 1998, 276-342).

109. Demerliac & Meirat 1983, 49-55.

110. Demerliac & Meirat 1983.

111. Ibid., 46-55, for a possible model of how this North Atlantic trading operation might have worked. The Carthaginians may also have been seeking regular sources of amber and copper from the Baltic and Scandinavia.

112. For the lack of archaeological evidence, Bello Jiménez 2005, 104-5.

113. Lancel (1995, 102-9) argues that the descriptions of the early stages of the voyage in terra cognita along what is now the Moroccan coast were based on historical events, but that accounts of the latter stages that describe

voyaging along the coast of western sub-Saharan Africa were literary fabrications.

114. Desanges 1978, 85. 'On ne peut au Périple arracher son revêtement grec, sans en estomper les détours jusqu'à l'inanité' (tr. Lancel 1995, 108).

115. Lonis 1978, 147–50; Blomqvist 1979, 11. Lancel's (1995, 106) argument against Lonis's thesis is a qualification but not a refutation.

116. Bello Jiménez 2005, 71–81. The Canary Islands are mentioned by the Numidian king Juba II (25 BC–AD 25), who acquired much of his geographical knowledge from Punic sources (Pliny NH 6.37).

117. Herodotus 4.42; Demerliac & Meirat 1983, 30–37. Herodotus (4.43) also mentions a later, unsuccessful, attempt at circumnavigating Africa by a Persian noblemen, Sataspes. Pliny (NH 5.8) actually states that the object of the mission was the circumnavigation of Africa. This is also mentioned as the main aim of the expedition by Pomponius Mela (3.93).

118. Herodotus 4.196.

119. All black Africans were usually collectively described by the Greeks and Romans as 'Ethiopians'.

120. Pseudo-Scylax 112.

121. This is Lancel's (1995, 108) position, although he is sceptical of whether the latter parts of the voyage took place at all.

122. Zimmerman Munn 2003.

123. Aristotle Pol. 6.3.5.

124. Van Dommelen 1998, 115; Campus 2006.

125. Van Dommelen 1998, 124.

126. For instance, at the old Phoenician colony of Motya, in Sicily, the tophet was greatly enlarged and monumentalized with its own wall and sanctuary.

127. This was particularly the case on Sardinia, with the quantity of Attic pottery found on the island quadrupling from the first half to the second half of the fifth century BC (Tronchetti 1992, 364–77).

128. Bondì 1995b, 352.

129. Huss 1985, 498–9. Others have suggested that it may in fact have been a sign of aristocratic privilege. Bordreuil & Ferjaoui (1988, 137–42) discuss an inscription found in Tyre which mentions a 'Son of Carthage', and a number found in Carthage that refer to 'Sons of Tyre'. They see these as merely an admission of the individual's heritage rather than a legal status. Some of the outsiders appear to have been able to hold certain rights in Carthage on account of their citizenship of other Punic and Phoenician city states, with Carthaginians enjoying reciprocal privileges.

130. Peserico 1999. This was particularly true of amphorae, which by the end of the seventh century BC had become very regionally diverse across the

western Phoenician world. For a good discussion of one such Phoenician grave collection found in Sardinia, see Fletcher 2006, 175–85.

131. Moscati 1986, 61–71. The steles produced in some western Phoenician cities, such as Motya and Tharros, do show clear stylistic parallels with Carthage, all displaying a strong preference for simple designs of motifs portrayed symbolically rather than representationally, such as the betyl (sacred stone) and altars and bottle shapes. Architecturally, these cities also stand out for the strong Egyptian architectural influence and the use of cippi, throne-shaped votive monuments (ibid., 74–7). These designs are very much in contrast to those at Sulcis and Monte Sirai, where the steles were decorated with motifs mainly portrayed in a realistic way. However, it is not clear whether the Sardinian and Sicilian cities had been influenced by Carthage or vice versa. There are also stylistic connections between Motya and Tharros, such as the popularity of the motif of a feminine figure clutching a religious sign or artefact to her chest, which is not found in Carthage (Moscati 1986, 78–9). It is also clear from epigraphic evidence that Phoenicians in northern Sardinia had a close relationship with the Phoenician city of Kition on Cyprus, perhaps through colonization. The oldest Phoenician inscription found in the western Mediterranean mentioned that Kition was the mother city of the Sardinian town of Nora (Krahmalkov 2001, 5).

132. Cicero *Scaur.* 42. There are references to ethnic groups created by the intermixing of Phoenician and Punic incomers with indigenous populations in Africa, Spain and Sardinia. On cultural hybridization in the Punic world see Van Dommelen 2006.

133. Van Dommelen 2006, 134.

134. Van Dommelen 1998, 153.

135. This idea was first formulated by Richard White in his study of the interactions between Western settlers and indigenous populations in the Great Lakes region of North America from the late seventeenth to the early nineteenth century (White, 1991). This model has been used extensively by the ancient historian Irad Malkin in relation to the archaic Mediterranean (Malkin 2002, 151–3; 2005, 238–9).

136. Some have assumed that Sid was the founder deity of Sidon (Bernardini 2005, 131), but there is no evidence to support this.

137. Barreca 1969.

138. For the votive inscriptions that they left behind see Fantar 1969.

139. Antas was by no means unique in the Punic world in this respect. The sanctuary to the goddess Astarte at Tas Silg on the island of Malta also clearly witnessed a similar symbiosis with an indigenous female deity.

140. It has been argued that one particularly famous statuette usually identified as Sid is actually of Baal Hammon; however, enough other

depictions of Sid exist showing him as a warrior/hunter deity (Amadasi Guzzo 1969, 99).

141. Barreca 1979, 140.

142. De Angelis 2003, 116–18.

143. Thucydides 6.2.6.

144. Ibid. 6.2.2–6.

145. De Angelis 2003, 122–4.

146. Thucydides 6.2.6; Falsone 1995, 674.

147. Despite maintaining trade networks and establishing some new settlements and bolstering some old ones in the region, keeping the Greeks out of southern Spain was not a priority for Carthage. Indeed, the commercial vacuum created by the abandonment of Phoenician trading stations in southern Spain was increasingly filled by Greeks from Phocaea, on the Aegean coast of Asia Minor, who had established a colony at Ampurias in north-eastern Spain on what is now the Costa Brava (Dominguez 2002, 72–4).

148. Isserlin & Du Plat Taylor 1974, 50–68; De Angelis 2003, 118–20.

149. De Angelis 2003, 110–11. In less exalted indigenous communities there were also signs of growing prosperity and the adoption of some facets of Greek culture. At Monte Iato, another Greek-influenced temple was built during this period. At Segesta, an indigenous city in the western area of the island, the sixth century was a time of rapid aggrandizement and expansion. During this period the elite indigenous families began to take control of centralized institutions in their cities, while also collecting revenues and directing labour. The strong commercial and cultural contacts that the Segestan elite had with the Hellenic world are further underlined by the vast amount of Greek pottery (with some 2,300 shards with Greek writing) that has been found in the city. Yet at other indigenous settlements Greek cultural influence seems to have been strictly limited. At Monte Polizzo, in the rugged interior of western Sicily, a settlement sprang up that at its height was home to up to 1,000 people. Here, while there is some evidence of Greek influence in domestic architecture and pottery styles, this is strictly limited in scope (Morris et al. 2001, 2002, 2003; De Angelis 2003, 107–10). However, the adoption of particular aspects of Phoenician or Greek culture varied markedly from one indigenous community to another (Hodos 2006, 89–157).

150. Pausanias 10.11.3–4. Diodorus (5.9) makes no mention of the Phoenician–Elymian force, but relates that the Cnidian colonists had got themselves involved in an internecine conflict between the Segestans and Selinuntines. Krings (1998, 1–32) points to a number of elements in both texts that suggest doubt as to whether this episode really was one of the starting points for

tensions between Phoenician/Punic and Greek populations. However, despite the usefulness of many of these qualifications, they do not prove that Pausanias' account of a joint Phoenician–Elymian force is incorrect.

151. De Angelis 2003, 128–45.

152. Rocco 1970, 27–33.

153. For archaeological evidence of Carthaginian–Etruscan trade see Macintosh-Turfa 1975. Although only limited amounts of Punic material have been found in Etruscan contexts, it appears that even in the seventh century BC Carthage was supplying luxury goods to Etruria. Etruscan *bucchero* – a type of black pottery – was exported to Carthage in greater numbers. The importation of Etruscan bronze metals and utensils continued to the third century BC. There is little evidence for the scholarly tradition that it was the Greeks who acted as the middlemen in the trade of Etruscan and Carthaginian artefacts. It is also important to note that Etruria was not politically united. It seems clear that Carthage had diplomatic relations with at least the larger kingdoms of Tarquinii and Caere. For Tyrrhenian trade in the archaic period see Gras 1985.

154. Macintosh-Turfa 1975, 176–7.

155. It may have either served as a business card or as a label for commercial stock (Lancel 1995, 85–6; Macintosh-Turfa 1975, 177).

156. Heurgon 1966; Ferron 1972. Some scholars have argued that the dialect used on the third tablet is not Punic but Cypriot Phoenician, and that the architectural decoration in the temple itself also shows strong parallels with Phoenician Cyprus, so that the most likely scenario is that this was actually a grant of a place of worship in an already existing Etruscan temple for a community of Phoenician traders who had originally come from Cyprus (Gibson 1982, 152–3; Verzár 1980). For a summary of the academic debate surrounding the tablets see Amadasi Guzzo (1995, 670–73). However, with our limited knowledge of Phoenician or Punic, and given the close links that existed particularly between Carthage and Phoenician Cyprus, as well as the political alliances between Carthage and the Etruscan kingdoms in this period, the evidence still points towards Punic merchants, although it might very well be both.

157. Aristotle (*Pol.* 3.5.10–11) referred to 'agreements about imports, and engagements that they will do each other no wrong and written articles of alliance' between the Carthaginians and the Etruscans.

158. Aristotle *Rhet.* 1.12.18.

159. Herodotus 1.165–7. Krings' (1998, 159–60) warning about viewing Alalia as part of a wider Mediterranean clash between Carthage and Greeks is, however, surely well founded.

160. Palmer 1997, 23–4. It has been plausibly suggested that this treaty may also have helped regulate Roman purchases of corn from the Punic sector of Sicily when Rome was faced with food shortages in the fifth century BC.

161. For Rome in the sixth century BC see Cornell 1995, 198–214.

162. We are once again indebted to the diligent sleuthing of Polybius, who found the bronze tablets detailing this treaty and two subsequent accords with Carthage in the Treasury of the Aediles at Rome (3.22.3). Polybius even complained of the difficulty of understanding such archaic Latin (3.22–3). For a cogent study of the treaties between Carthage and Rome see Serrati 2006.

163. Polybius 3.22.

164. Cornell 1995, 215–41.

CHAPTER 3: THE REALM OF HERACLES–MELQART: GREEKS AND CARTHAGINIANS IN THE CENTRAL MEDITERRANEAN

1. Dion 1977, 3–82; Malkin 1998, 156–257.

2. Malkin 1998, 156–77; 2002.

3. Particularly in regard to the murder of their leaders. This was true of the southern Italian towns of Croton and Locris (Jourdain-Annequin 1989, 280–81). To spare embarrassment on either side, this was usually explained as being a terrible accident in which the victim had been killed by a mistake while trying to restrain a father-in-law or some other relative who was intent on fighting Heracles or stealing his cattle.

4. Jourdain-Annequin 1989, 311. It was said that the Celts were descended from Heracles after he had slept with the daughter of the king of Galicia and produced a son variously called Galates, Keltus or Kelta, and it was also claimed that he had sired a number of children in Spain and Gaul who had gone on to be kings of various regions there. Such was the popularity of Heracles across Italy that one first-century-BC Greek historian of early Rome wrote, 'In many other places also in Italy precincts are dedicated to this god [Heracles] and altars erected to him, both in cities and along the highways; and one could scarcely find any place in Italy in which the god is not honoured' (Dionysius 1.40.6).

5. Jourdain-Annequin 1992, 35; Malkin 1994, 207.

6. Fabre 1981, 274–95.

7. Malkin 2005, 238–9; 2002, 157–8.

8. Jourdain-Annequin 1989, 273–4.

9. In fact a version of the Geryon story certainly existed in Greece by the eighth and seventh centuries BC. Heracles and Geryon both appear in the work of the eighth-century-BC Greek poet Hesiod (*Theogony* 279.979), and by the seventh century BC a version of the tale was well known enough for vase painters on the island of Samos to use it as a subject. Geryon is portrayed on pottery and texts in a number of different terrifying forms. Stesichorus described him as winged, with six hands and six feet (Stesichorus, *Geryoneis* Fr. S87). Apollodorus (2.107) describes him as having 'the bodies of three men joined into one at the belly, but splitting into three again from the flanks and thighs down'.

10. Malkin 1994, 210.

11. For a detailed account of the development of the Heraclean Way, see Knapp 1986. For Heracles as an ever-evolving phenomenon in the West see Fabre 1981, 274–95; Jourdain-Annequin 1989, 221–300.

12. Dionysius 1.35.2–3; Diodorus 4.22.6, 23.1; Pausanias 3.16.4–5. For the links between Stesichorus and Heracles' Sicilian jaunt, see Malkin 1994, 206–11. The travels of Heracles in Sicily reflected the myriad different experiences and challenges faced by the Greeks who settled on that island. Some scholars even think that the stories of Heracles in Sicily probably contain distant memories of the Bronze Age, when Mycenaean incomers clashed with the local population (Jourdain-Annequin 1989, 282–97). Many of the local leaders whom Heracles fought with could be local indigenous gods. For other possible links between the route of Heracles and the Bronze Age see Martin 1979, who points out that Heracles' journey through mid and southern Italy mirrors the supposed migration route of the Sicels to the island of Sicily.

13. Herodotus 5.43; Diodorus 4.23.2–3; Pausanias 4.36.3.

14. Malkin 1994, 207–8.

15. Herodotus 5.42.

16. Malkin 1994, 192–203; Krings 1998, 189–95.

17. Herodotus 5.43–6; Diodorus 4.23; Pausanias 3.16. 4–5; Krings 1998, 161–215.

18. Malkin 1994, 212. Krings (1998, 202–4) expresses doubts about any self-conscious links between the two expeditions.

19. Krings 1998, 93–160.

20. Malkin 1994, 181–7.

21. Ibid., 186–7. In this case reality self-consciously followed legend (Diodorus 4.17.4–5; Pliny *NH* 5.35). Fifth-century Cyrenean coinage shows Heracles with a Hesperid maiden. Others would argue that in fact the garden of the Hesperides was located much further west, around the mountains of Mauri-

tania. Heracles was also said to have founded a city called Hecatompylon, which had gone on to achieve great success and prosperity until the Carthaginians captured it (Diodorus 4.18.1–4).

22. Asheri 1988, 755.

23. De Angelis (2003, 135–6) thinks that the temple could be a temple of Apollo. For other connections between Motya and Selinus there is the wonderful tufa statue of two lions bringing down a bull at Motya. Some scholars have speculated that it may have formed part of the decoration for the gates of the fortifications. Stylistically it bears such a close resemblance to the metope of the goddess Artemis and Acteon on the famous Temple E at Selinus that many have thought that they must have been created by the same craftsmen.

24. Moscati 1986, 57–8. Their popularity was such that these figurines were soon being manufactured in large numbers in Sardinia and North Africa.

25. Acquaro 1988, 17; Moscati 1986, 51, for the two sarcophagi found at Cannita near the city of Solus and thought to have been made locally sometime in the sixth or fifth century BC. At Cannita a seated goddess flanked by sphinxes was also discovered. Thought to date to the sixth century BC, it too displays clear Greek stylistic influence.

26. Moscati 1986, 72.

27. For Punic attitudes to the nude form see Maes 1989, 22. This interpretation would certainly fit much better with what we definitely know about the statue, namely that it was found in a Punic city. For a discussion of some of the lively scholarly debate surrounding the Motya ephebe, see Lancel 1995, 322–5.

28. Herodotus 2.44.

29. Ibid. Although no archaeological evidence has been found for the Phoenician occupation of the temple of Heracles on Thasos, other Greek authors state that the worship of the hero/god on the island had Phoenician precedents. Indeed, a later Greek travel writer, Pausanias, suggests that the Thasians openly alluded to their own and Heracles' Phoenician origins: 'The Thasians who are Phoenicians by descent, and sailed from Tyre and from Phoenicia generally . . . dedicated at Olympia a Heracles, the pedestal as well as the image being of bronze. The height of the image is ten cubits and he holds a club in his right hand and a bow in his left. They told me that they used to worship the same Heracles as the Tyrians but that afterwards, when they were included among the Greeks, they adopted the worship of Heracles the son of Amphitryon' (5.25.12). Heracles was not the only Greek deity claimed to have had Near Eastern precedents. Pausanias (1.14.6–7) alleged that the worship of Aphrodite was started by the Assyrians, the Paphians of Cyprus and the

Phoenicians. Pausanias, an apparently open-minded man, was well aware of the close links between Greek and Phoenician religion (e.g. 7.23.7–8).

30. Pausanias 7.5.5–8. There was a certainly a strong sense of the duality of Heracles/Melqart in later periods. The third-century-AD Greek writer Philostratus (*Apollon.* 2.33.2) wrote about a gold shield which Heracles had lost while campaigning in India, which 'shows that it was the Egyptian rather than Theban Heracles that reached Gadeira and was the surveyor of the earth'.

31. Jourdain-Annequin 1989, 133–45; Karageorghis 1998, 65–159, *contra* Yon 1986, 147–9, who suggests that in Cyprus the major associations during this period on the island may well have been between Heracles and the Phoenician warrior gods Reshef and Eshmoun (the latter of whom in the Greek world would come to be identified with Asclepius, the god of healing), as well as the Egyptian deity Bes. This clear symbiosis between Heracles and Melqart might explain the strident alacrity with which some later Greek writers aggressively dismissed Herodotus' explanation of the Tyrian origins of the cult of Heracles as nothing more than the perverse prejudices of a writer who had spent too much time with and studying barbarians – in essence, any person who was not a Greek. Yet the fact that these writers felt that they had to address these issues so forcefully hints at grave disquiet over the ambiguous origins of Greater Greece's favourite hero. For instance, see the extraordinary attack on Herodotus by the later Greek writer Plutarch (*De Herodoti malignitate* 13–14), who accused him of 'philobarbarism' – of being a lover of barbarians and a self-hating Greek.

32. Malkin 2005, 246–7.

33. *KAI* 47. Amadasi Guzzo 2005b, 47–8.

34. Malkin 2005, 245.

35. Amadasi Guzzo 2005b, 50.

36. Pausanias 10.17.2.

37. Bonnet 2005, 23–5; Bernardini 2005, 130–33.

38. *CIS* i.256; Bonnet 2005, 25.

39. Grottanelli 1973.

40. Amadasi Guzzo 2005b, 49–50, for arguments which relate the epithet not to Tyre but rather to the outcrop on which the temple at Antas was built. However, this still does not detract from the likelihood that it was a reference to the Tyrian heritage of the god.

41. Bonnet 1986, 210–12.

42. Lipiński 1989, 67–70. Bernardini 2005, 125–6, for arguments that this Carthage was in fact either Tharros or another Punic Sardinian city, Neapolis. However, the case for the North African metropolis is still the most convincing.

43. Bonnet 1988, 399–415.
44. Bonnet 1986, 214–15.
45. M. Miles 1998/9, 1–2, 21–5.
46. Bonnet 1988, 272; Krings 1998, 200.
47. Moscati 1986, 101–5; Galinsky 1969, 70–73.
48. On the association of Melqart and Astarte, see Giangiulio 1983. Long after it had become the Roman cult of Venus Erycina, the cult would maintain much of its Punic character through the continuation of the practice of sacred prostitution and sacrificial rites on an open-air altar in a sacred enclosure (Aelian *On Animals* 10.50; Galinsky 1969, 70–73). Indeed, the site itself had a special connection with another mountain-top sanctuary to Astarte, at Sicca, a Carthaginian-held town in Numidia, where the same religious rites and sacred prostitution took place (Valerius Maximus 2.6.15; Solinus 27.8). It was said that each year the goddess left her sanctuary and travelled to Sicca with the doves that were sacred to her, before returning to Eryx after an interval of nine days (Aelian *On Animals* 4.2; Schilling 1954, 234–9). The same conflation between Heracles and Melqart is found in the work of the sixth-century-BC Greek geographer Hecataeus of Miletus, who wrote that, on his return with the herd of Geryon, Heracles killed Solous, the eponymous king of the Sicilian Punic city of Solus, and received the assistance of a maiden named Motya in getting his stolen cattle back (Hecataeus of Miletus Frs. 71–2, *FGH*, I: 18–19; Malkin 1994, 210–11). In the fifth and fourth centuries BC Solus, which was said by the Greek historian Thucydides (6.2–6) to be a Phoenician foundation, minted a considerable number of coins on which Heracles featured (Bonnet 1988, 272–3).
49. Herodotus 4.8. A number of later Greek writers reported that the tomb of Geryon could be seen at Gades, while others maintained that two trees which dripped blood grew out of the tomb (Philostratus *Apollon.* 5.4). Strabo (3.5.10), citing the second-century-BC Greek polymath Poseidonius, also mentions a tree at Gades which 'if a root is cut, a red liquid oozes forth' (Pausanias 1.35.7). Another stop-off, Abdera, on the eastern coast of Andalusia, was also not Greek but a Phoenician settlement (Apollodorus 2.5.10.)
50. For the merging of Melqart and Heracles in the West, and the earlier syncretism between the hero and the Near Eastern god/heroes Gilgamesh and Sandon, see Fabre 1981, 274–6. There is also some suggestion that the great sanctuary to Venus Frutis at the Latin town of Lavinium may have been connected to the sanctuary at Eryx (Solinus 2.14; Strabo 5.3.5). In two of the manuscripts in which Solinus' work is recorded the designation is not 'Frutis' but 'Ericis', 'of Eryx'. Some have simply put this down to a copying error, but the fact is that, whereas Frutis is an unknown, Aphrodite/Astarte

of Eryx is well attested (Galinsky 1969, 115–18). A further example of the cultural syncretism that defined archaic Sicily can be found in the final episode of the Dorieus tale. Euryleon, the sole survivor of the ill-fated expedition, had taken refuge at the nearby town of Heracleia Minoa. One might assume, especially with the Heraclean undertones of the tale, that the town's name was derived from the Greek hero, whereas in fact the Punic name for Minoa was *Makara*, which simply meant 'City of Melqart' (Malkin 1994, 215–16; 2005, 252–3).

51. Hellanicus of Lesbos Fr. 111, *FGH*, I: 134; Hecataeus of Miletus Frs. 76–7, *FGH*, I: 19; Pearson 1975, 188.

52. It is certainly the case that the vast majority of the later recountings of the activities of Heracles in Rome emphasize the positive and friendly nature of his relationship with the indigenous locals (Fabre 1981, 287). The one dissenting voice is that of Plutarch, who recounts that in fact Heracles had killed Faunus.

53. Dionysius 1.40.1. There has been considerable debate over the provenance of the Cacus myth. It is generally agreed that it owes much to Greek mythology, particularly the story of Hermes' theft of the cattle of Apollo recounted in the Fourth Homeric Hymn and dramatized in the fifth century BC by the Athenian playwright Sophocles in *Ichneutae*. It has also been linked to the story of the theft by Sisyphus of the horses of Diomedes, when Heracles was driving them back to Eurystheus, the king of Mycenae, after the successful completion of his eighth labour (Apollodorus 2.5.8). Dana Sutton (1977) has argued that its most likely source of entry into the Roman mythological canon was through satyr plays written in the early first century BC. However, it is well known that Dionysius heavily used western-Greek Hellenistic-era writers. Taking into account the Greek provenance of the story, one of these authors was surely a more likely source.

54. Bradley 2005, 138–40.

55. Most recently, ibid., 141–143. For the original hypothesis of the Greek roots of Italian, Etruscan and Latin Hercules/Hercle, see Bayet 1926.

56. In other parts of central Italy Heracles was also assimilated with various deities (Bradley 2005, 132).

57. The earliest representation of Cacus is on an Etruscan mirror dated to the fourth century BC.

58. Ritter 1995, 18–23; Bonnet 1988, 296–302.

59. Clear links between the Sant' Omobono temple and Etruria exist through an ivory plaque inscribed with the Etruscan name Araz Silqietanas Spurianas, which was found among the archaeological deposits from the temple (Forsythe 2005, 90). For an overview of the archaeological evidence for temples and sanctuaries in archaic Rome see Smith 1996, 158–65.

60. Forsythe 2005, 90–91.

61. Jourdain-Annequin 1989, 635–6. The identification of the goddess figure has been controversial, with scholars putting forward a number of different deities (on Juno/Hera, see Coarelli 1988, 301–28; on Athena/Minerva, see Colonna 1987). Some have argued that these probable representations of Heracles and Athena, which would have sat on the roof of the temple, were the work of one of the Roman kings who, following the lead of autocratic rulers in mainland Greece, wanted to represent his rule as being divinely sanctioned. They point to a statue in Athens showing the Athenian autocrat Pisistratus as Heracles being introduced to Olympus by Athena, the patron deity of his city, thereby suggesting that he enjoyed divine favour. This might explain the existence of a similar set of statues at the southern Etruscan town of Veii. The later Roman writers Martial (14.178) and Pliny (NH 35.157) both record that Vulca, a sculptor from Veii, was commissioned to produce a sculpture of Hercules by the last Roman king, Tarquinius Superbus (Cornell 1995, 148; Bradley 2005, 130; Ritter 1995, 21 for the connection with Veii). Useful parallels exist between these stories and the sanctuary at Pyrgi, where, within the temple complex where the famous tablets were discovered, archaeologists have pinpointed a specific subterranean space which may have housed the underground tomb of Melqart, before he was brought back to life in the ceremony of the *egersis*. An inscription was found there dedicated to Uni and Tenia, the chief Etruscan deities. As in the context of this temple Uni was associated with Astarte, who was the consort of Melqart, it seems likely that the same kind of religious syncretism was at play here between Melqart and Tenia (Casquero 2002, 89–90).

62. Holloway 1994, 166–7.

63. Van Berchem 1967, 1959–60. There are other similarities, such as the absolute exclusivity of the god in his temple, and the long robes and the crowns of laurels worn on the uncovered heads of the priests (although parallels for these traditions can also be found in the Greek world). It has also been suggested that the Potitii, one of the aristocratic families who were to oversee the cult, were in fact a caste of priests in the Near Eastern tradition (Van Berchem 1967, 311–15). Bonnet (1988, 278–304) is sceptical of the connections between Melqart and Rome. However, her qualifications, although useful, do not discount the appropriation of some of the rites and iconography associated with the god in the archaic city.

64. Torelli 1989, 49–51.

65. Casquero 2002, 86–91.

66. Février 1965.

67. Casquero 2002, 69.

68. At Gravisca, the port of the important Etruscan city of Tarquinii, inscriptions found at a sixth-century-BC temple dedicated to the Greek goddesses Aphrodite, Hera and Demeter show a strong eastern-Greek element (particularly from Samos, Miletus and Ephesus) among its worshippers (Torelli 1989, 48–9; Smith 1996, 146–7). The lack of Phoenician pottery in archaic Roman contexts might argue against the hypothesis of a large Phoenician mercantile presence in Rome (Casquero 2002, 101–2). However, the discovery of large quantities of eighth-century-BC Greek pottery in a deposit underneath the shrine at Sant' Omobono proves very little, as the Phoenicians were often involved in the transportation of Greek goods (Cornell 1995, 68–9).

69. This model for the introduction of Melqart and Astarte into Italy is preferable to the Bonnet thesis (1986, 29) that sees it as the work of the Carthaginians who brought the cult to Etruria. See Smith 1996, 159–62, for an overview of the general issues and how they relate to the Sant' Omobono temple.

CHAPTER 4: THE ECONOMY OF WAR: CARTHAGE AND SYRACUSE

1. For Ibiza, see Gómez Bellard 1990. For Sardinia, Van Dommelen 1998, 125–9. For the idea that Carthage increasingly looked overseas for food and land for its growing population see Ameling 1993, 250 ff.

2. Van Dommelen 1998, 125–9; 2002, 130–3.

3. Mastino, Spanu & Zucca 2005, 103–4; Bechtold 2008, 51–6, 76.

4. Pseudo-Aristotle *Mirab. Ausc.* 100. It is also noteworthy that ears of grain were a common motif on Punic coins minted in Sardinia.

5. Barnett & Mendleson (eds.) 1987, 41–6, for grave goods in Tharros.

6. Barreca 1987, 24–6.

7. Van Dommelen 1998, 127.

8. Bernardini 1993, 173–7.

9. Garbini 1983, 158–60.

10. Van Dommelen 1998, 127–8, must be right in disputing Barreca's claim (1986, 88–9) of a Carthaginian border-defence system across the island, but he in turn does not take enough account of the fortified nature of many of these sites.

11. Gharbi 2004.

12. Bonzani 1992, 215–16.

13. Herodotus 7.165; Brizzi 1995, 308.

14. Polyaenus 1.27.2.

15. Herodotus 7.167.
16. Diodorus, 11.24.4.
17. Ibid. 11.26.1–3.
18. Ibid. 11.25.1–5.
19. Asheri 1988, 776–8.
20. Aristotle *Pol.* 2.8.1–2. Although the actual date of the introduction of the suffeture is vague, Krahmalkov (1976, 153–7) makes the important observation that there is no reference to the suffeture (for an explanation of which see p. 130) in Punic epigraphy before the fifth century BC. Although the suffeture is also recorded in Tyre in the fifth century (Sznycer 1978, 571), there is no evidence that the office hailed from the Levant.
21. Aristotle *Pol.* 2.8.5–6, 2.8.8–9.
22. At Tharros an inscription dated to the third century BC mentions suffetes. However, the inclusion of the ancestral antecedents of the office-holders suggests that the suffeture had existed as a political office in Tharros before this period (Barreca 1987, 26). In addition, suffetes still existed in the first century BC in a number of the old Carthaginian/Phoenician colonies such as Eryx, Bithia, Sulcis, Malta, Gades and perhaps Caralis. Popular Assemblies are recorded at Leptis Magna, Malta, Bithia and Olbia. At a more junior level, many of these colonies also appear to have had officials (who are also attested to in Carthage) whose duties involved administrative matters including the collection of taxes. An inscription (*CIS* i.154.) found in Tharros and dated to the third century BC was originally thought to refer to a Carthaginian official, but it is now thought that he was in fact a local market official.
23. Aristotle *Pol.* 2.8.4, 2.8.8.
24. Herodotus 7.167.
25. It is thought that the temple of Nike, the Greek goddess of victory, at Himera may be one of the two temples. A third clause, that Carthage had to agree to cease the practice of human sacrifice, is thought to be fraudulent.
26. Carthage had resisted other tempting opportunities to reinvolve itself in Sicilian affairs. It had even turned down a call for assistance from the Elymian city of Segesta – locked, as usual, in conflict with its Greek neighbour – and from Carthage's erstwhile ally Selinus (Diodorus 12.82.7). The Carthaginians were perhaps mindful that the Athenians, when matters had been going well for them, had thought more than once about making Carthage their next victim (Aristophanes *Knights* 1302–4; Plutarch *Per.* 20.4).
27. Lancel 1995, 140–41.
28. Ibid., 134–42.
29. Hall 1989.
30. Herodotus 7.163–4.

31. Krings 1998, 276–84.
32. However, there is good evidence for previous friendly relations between Greek and Phoenician people on Cyprus (Snodgrass 1988, 19–20). For the Phoenician kings of Kition see Yon 1992.
33. Pindar, *Pythi. Ode* 1.71–5. For the Deinomenid reinvention of Himera see Krings 1998, 261–5.
34. Herodotus 7.166; Diodorus 11.1.5, 11.20.1.
35. Aristotle *Pol.* 7.2.10; Plato *Laws* 1.637D–E.
36. Aristotle *Poet.* 1459a 24–8: Krings 1998, 284–8.
37. Isaac 2004, 283–98.
38. Aristotle *Pol.* 2.8.1.
39. Ibid. However, later in the *Politics* (5.6.2) Aristotle does make reference to the failed coup of Hanno that marked the end of Magonid political dominance in Carthage.
40. Plato *Laws* 2.674B–C. However, there is plentiful evidence for Carthaginians making, trading and consuming wine (Lancel 1995, 274–6).
41. Morel 1980 & 1983.
42. Athenaeus 1.27e–1.28a (Fr. 63, *PCG*).
43. Bechtold 2007, 65–7.
44. At the city of Thebes someone with the Carthaginian name Nobas (whose real name was probably Annobas) is attested as being granted the status of proxenos, an honorary citizenship bestowed on foreigners for the good service that they had rendered. In Athens around 330 BC two resident Carthaginians are mentioned, and the inventories from the temples of Apollo and Artemis on the island of Delos mention gifts from Punic people (Manganaro 2000, 258).
45. On Antiochus see Luraghi 2002, and on Philistus see Bearzot 2002.
46. Diodorus 13.43.4–5.
47. The successors of Gelon had lacked both his charisma and his ruthlessness, and had been overthrown by the Syracusans, who had grown tired of their excesses. The democratic government that replaced them was no more successful in achieving consensus, for social cohesion had been greatly undermined by the violence and mass deportations that had been such keystones of Gelon's political strategy (Lomas 2006, 102).
48. Whittaker 1978, 66–7.
49. Large quantities of goods from both Italy and Greece were imported into Carthage throughout this period (Bechtold 2007, 54–8, 65–7). For the political independence of the Punic cities in Sicily during this period see Bondì 1999, 39–42.
50. Di Stefano et al. 1998, 88.

51. Diodorus 13.81.5.

52. Whittaker 1978, 81-2.

53. Diodorus 13.43.5.

54. Ibid. 13.43.6-7.

55. Ibid. 13.44.1-6.

56. This was clearly a very sizeable force. However, the figures for its size – either 200,000 foot and 4,000 horse or over 100,000 men – are obviously grossly exaggerated (Diodorus 13.54.5).

57. Ibid. 13.54.6-13.59.3.

58. Ibid. 13.59.4-13.62.6.

59. Jenkins 1971, 29-33. On the mercenaries in Carthage's Sicilian armies see Brizzi 1995, 308-11; Ameling 1993, 212-15.

60. Ameling 1993, 265-6; Visonà 1998, 4.

61. Mildenberg 1989, 7-8; Visonà 1998, 5.

62. On men and supplies, see Fariselli 1999, 59-61; on coinage, Jenkins 1974, 23-6. Wherever the mint was actually physically located, Carthage was certainly the issuing authority (Manfredi 1999, 70).

63. Diodorus 13.63.4-5.

64. Ibid. 13.80.1.

65. Meritt 1940.

66. Diodorus 13.80.1-5.

67. Ibid. 13.80.5-7.

68. Ibid. 13.85.1-13.86.3. Himilcar was also said to have sacrificed a large number of cattle to a sea god by drowning.

69. Ibid. 13.86.4-13.89.4.

70. Ibid. 13.86.90.1-5.

71. Schmitz 1994, 11-13.

72. Diodorus 14.7.1.

73. Ibid. 13.91.1-13.96.4.

74. Ibid. 14.41.1-14.43.4.

75. Ibid. 14.45.2-14.46.5.

76. Ibid. 14.47.5-7.

77. Ibid. 14.52.1-2.

78. Ibid. 14.53.1-5.

79. Ibid. 14.48.1-14.53.4.

80. Ibid. 14.54.2-4.

81. Ibid. 14.54.5-14.63.4.

82. Ibid. 14.71.1-4, 14.63.1-2, 14.70.4-6.

83. Ibid. 14.71.3-4.

84. Ibid. 14.71.1.

85. Ibid. 14.75.2–3. Diodorus/Timaeus also suggested that it was not only greed that lay behind Dionysius' decision, but also the fear that his own citizens might try to oust him if the Carthaginian menace were removed.
86. Ibid. 14.72.1–14.75.3.
87. Ibid. 14.76.3–4; Justin 19.3.1–11. The account of Justin (19.3.12) has Himilco locking himself in his house and committing suicide.
88. Justin 21.4.1.
89. Aristotle *Pol.* 2.11.3; Bondì 1995a, 296–7.
90. The suffetes may have been in existence for some time (Sznycer 1978, 567–70). Prefect of bureau of public works = *KAI* 62.4 k36. Tax collectors = *CIS* i.5547.4/5. Administrators = *KAI* 119.2/3; Aristotle *Pol.* 2.11.3–6; Bondì 1995a, 296.
91. Aristotle *Pol.* 2.11.3–70; Huss 1985, 460–61; Bondì 1995a, 296.
92. Diodorus 14.95.1–14.96.4.
93. Ibid. 15.15.1–2.
94. Ibid. 15.15.3–15.16.3.
95. Ibid. 15.17.5. There were additional clauses such as Selinus and Acragas returning to Carthage's sphere of influence, and Dionysius agreeing to pay Carthage 1,000 talents in reparations.
96. Ibid. 15.24.1–3. The city was in such a state of panic that men were seen to rush out of their houses in full armour and attack their fellow citizens because they imagined that Carthage had come under attack.
97. Ibid. 15.74.2–3.
98. Justin 21.4.1–7.
99. Ibid. 21.4.8ff.
100. Whittaker 1978, 62; Diodorus 13.81.1; Polybius 1.15.10, 1.17.1, 3.24.8, 3.24.12.
101. Panormus, Solus, Thermae Himerae and Eryx were all producing their own coinage in the second half of the fourth century (Jenkins 1971, 53–75).
102. Diodorus 14.16.4; Strabo 6.2.15; Schimtz 1994, 11. Halaisa may have been set up as a base for the recent expeditionary force. On Thermae Himerae, see Diodorus 13.79.8. The population of the city was made up not just of Punic settlers, but also of Greeks from Sicily and southern Italy (ibid. 19.2.2).
103. For a study of Punic Lilybaeum see Di Stefano 1993.
104. Tusa 1984, 36–7, 49–55, 69–71.
105. Ibid., 35.
106. Caruso 2003; Tusa 1984, 24–35; Moscati 1986, 101–5.
107. Tusa 1984, 21–3; Purpura 1981.
108. Jenkins 1977, 8–33.
109. Diodorus 13.59.3; Moscati 1986, 123–9; Tusa 1984, 36–7.
110. Moscati 1986, 127.

111. Ibid., 47.

112. Ibid., 127. Yet, despite the obvious Punic influences, the religious usage of the sanctuary of Malaphorus in the fourth century BC shows clear signs of a reaffirmation of an important indigenous cult which appears to have been held in high esteem by both Greek and Punic populations.

113. Acquaro 1988, 38–9.

114. Moscati 1986, 130–55; Acquaro 1988, 41–3.

115. Morris et al. 2001–2004.

116. Lysias *Olympiacus* 33.3; Plutarch *Tim.* 1.1–2.

117. Cornelius Nepos *Tim.* 3.1.

118. Archaeologists have come to this conclusion as a result of the large number of military coins from the Carthage mint and of Carthaginian transport amphorae found there. For a study of Monte Adranone see Fiorentini 1995.

119. The finds included Carthaginian bronze coins, gaming dice, and large quantities of both wine amphorae and imported Greek pottery (Morris et al. 2001–2002).

120. Anello 1986, 170–72.

121. Fariselli 1999, 62–5. Some have even wished to see this as evidence of the establishment of a kind of 'economic protectorate' whereby mercenary troops were settled on territory under Carthaginian suzerainty and then required to protect it. However, the discernible difference in the material culture of these new sites – where much larger numbers of amphorae from North Africa are found – compared with the old Punic cities of western Sicily, where the vast majority of the amphorae are of local manufacture, appears to show that these new settlements were not part of the thriving local economy (Bechtold 2007, 54–8).

122. Whittaker 1978, 60, 88–90.

123. Bechtold 2007, 65–7; 2008, 56–74, 76.

124. Bechtold 2007, 54–8.

125. Bechtold 2008, 57–8.

126. Docter et al. 2006, 54.

127. Chelbi 1992, 18–20.

128. Bechtold 2008, 49–50.

129. Large numbers of Sardinian 'sack'- and 'torpedo'-shaped amphorae used for the transportation of foodstuffs are found in Punic Sicily during the fifth and fourth centuries BC (Mastino, Spanu & Zucca 2005, 103–4). These amphorae key in with the assertions of Diodorus that the Carthaginian army was fed on Sardinian corn (Diodorus 14.77.6; Fariselli 1999, 59–63).

130. Crawford 1985, 104.

131. Diodorus 16.65.1–9.

132. Ibid. 16.66.5–6, 16.67.1–16.68.8.
133. Ibid. 16.69.3–6, 16.70.4–6, 16.72.2–16.73.3.
134. Ibid. 16.73.3, 16.77.4, 20.10.6.
135. Ibid. 16.79.5–16.81.4; Plutarch *Tim.* 27.2–28.6.
136. Diodorus 16.82.3.
137. In cities, such as Messana, substantial numbers of Campanian and southern-Italian mercenaries had been settled there by Dionysius (Lomas 2006, 112–14).
138. Mildenberg 1989, 6–12.
139. Visonà 1998, 6–7.

CHAPTER 5: IN THE SHADOW OF ALEXANDER THE GREAT: CARTHAGE AND AGATHOCLES

1. Arrian *Anabasis* 2.16.7–2.24.5; Plutarch *Alex.* 24.3–4; Quintus Curtius Rufus 4.2.2–4.4.19.
2. Arrian *Anabasis* 2.24.6.
3. Quintus Curtius Rufus 4.3.19; Arrian *Anabasis* 2.24.5. This visit probably fitted in with the celebration of the *egersis* in February/March. The Tyrians had also sent their women and children to Carthage for safety once the siege had started (Diodorus 17.41.1, 17.46.4; Quintus Curtius Rufus 4.3.20).
4. Justin 21.6.
5. Isaac 2004, 283–303.
6. Diodorus 13.108.3–5.
7. Diodorus 17.2. Arrian (*Anabasis* 2.16.4–7) also states that it was 'not the Argive Heracles, son of Alcmena' but 'Tyrian Heracles'.
8. Diodorus 11.1.4.
9. Ibid. 11.24.1.
10. Ibid. 11.23.2, 11.26.5.
11. Ibid. 20.13.1–3. Hence the Carthaginian general Hannibal who led the 410 expedition is labelled as 'by nature . . . a hater of all Greeks' (ibid. 13.43.6).
12. Plutarch *Tim.* 18.7.
13. Diodorus 13.57, 14.48–53, 14.63.1–3, 14.70.4, 14.73.5, 14.74.4; Athenaeus 12.541A–B.
14. For Greek mercenaries fighting on the Carthaginian side see Diodorus 20.38.6, 20.39.5. For Greeks living in Carthage see ibid. 14.77.4–5. During the Sicilian wars, Carthage had periodically supported Sicilian Greek dissidents who were seeking to bring about regime change in Syracuse (Plutarch *Tim.* 2.1–2; Diodorus 16.67.1–3). This support had also meant that the city had

become a place of refuge for Sicilian Greeks who had been forced out of their own cities. Indeed, Polybius (7.2.3–4) mentions two brothers, Epicydes and Hippocrates, officers in the Carthaginian army, who had been brought up in the North African metropolis after their grandfather had been forced to flee Syracuse after being accused of assassinating one of the sons of Agathocles. For Greeks in Carthage during the third century BC see Galvagno 2006.

15. Diodorus 5.3.1–3; Pearson 1975, 186–7.
16. Diodorus 14.77.4–5.
17. See for instance a dedication in Carthage to 'Lady Ammas [Demeter], the Lady Mistress of the Netherworld' (*KAI* 83): Krahmalkov 2000, 177; Moscati 1986, 73.
18. Jenkins & Lewis 1963, Group III.
19. Moscati 1986, 47–8.
20. Van Dommelen 1988, 151–6.
21. Positioned underneath the god was often a lotus flower, the traditional Phoenician symbol of life and renaissance (Bonnet 1986, 182–6).
22. For instance a ritual razor has been discovered at Utica which shows Heracles fighting against the giant bull. This motif is heavily influenced by the coinage produced by the Greek Sicilian cities of Selinus and Solus (ibid., 195). Several perfume bottles have also been discovered showing Heracles, and in one case Heracles with Achilles.
23. Lancel 1995, 207.
24. Athenaeus 392d.
25. Bonnet 1986, 220–22.
26. Green 1990, 187.
27. Cf. Diodorus 19.2.1–19.9.7 for the early career and rise to autocratic power of Agathocles.
28. Cf. ibid. 17.23.2–3; Zambon 2006 for the association between Agathocles and Alexander.
29. Zambon 2006, 82–3.
30. Plautus *Mostellaria* 775–7.
31. Hoyos 1994, 255–6.
32. Isocrates *Nicocles* 24.
33. Until the third century BC, generals were selected from the political elite and had usually held the suffeture (Drews 1979, 55). Popular Assembly = Aristotle *Pol.* 2.8.9; Diodorus 25.8.
34. Diodorus 20.10.2–4.
35. Pearson 1987, 41.
36. Justin 22.2.
37. Diodorus 19.71.6–7.
38. Ibid. 19.72.1–2.

39. Justin 22.3; Diodorus 19.72.2.
40. Diodorus 19.106.1–4.
41. Ibid. 19.106.5–19.110.5.
42. Ibid. 19.106.5, 20.3.1–3.
43. Ibid. 20.3.3.
44. Ibid. 20.4.1–8.
45. Ibid. 20.5.1–20.7.5.
46. Ibid.
47. Justin 22.5.
48. Diodorus 20.8.1–7, 20.9.2–5.
49. Ibid. 20.10.1–2.
50. Ibid. 20.10.5–20.13.2.
51. Ibid. 20.14.1–7; Lactantius *Div. Inst.* 1.21.
52. *CIS* i.3914.
53. Diodorus 20.31.1–2.
54. Ibid. 20.29.2–20.30.2, 20.33.1–2.
55. Zambon 2006, 82–3.
56. Diodorus 20.33.2–8.
57. Ibid. 20.33.2–20.34.7.
58. Ibid. 20.40.1–20.42.5.
59. Ibid. 20.44.1–6.
60. Ibid. 20.54.1–20.55.5.
61. Ibid. 20.59.1–20.61.4.
62. Ibid. 20.64.1–20.69.3.
63. Justin 22.8.
64. Diodorus 20.69.3–5.
65. Mildenberg 1989, 10–12; Visonà 1998, 7.
66. Visonà 1992, 15; 1998, 9–11.
67. Jenkins 1978, 5–19. For a period these coins had been produced simultaneously at two different mints, before the *mhsbm* issues took over completely.
68. This change has been recognized as significant by a number of scholars. Manfredi (1999, 72) prefers to see it as 'the outcome of the progressive normalization of Punic administration in Sicily which no longer needed any special legitimation'.
69. Jenkins & Lewis 1963, Groups IV to VII. Mildenberg 1989, 10, for these coins being produced from the end of the fourth century.
70. See Zambon 2006, 80–82, for the changes in the coinage of Agathocles, which reflect his new royal status; Diodorus 20.54.1.
71. Diodorus 21.16.4 attributes the disease to poison that was applied through a quill which Agathocles used to clean his teeth.

72. Ibid. 21.16.5. This was said to have been a divine punishment for seizing sacred offerings to the fire god Hephaestus some years previously (Ibid. 20. 101.1–3).

73. Plutarch *Pyrrh.* 14.5.

CHAPTER 6: CARTHAGE AND ROME

1. Eckstein 2006, 131–8.
2. Ibid., 138–47.
3. Harris 1979.
4. Eckstein 2006, 177. More generally, ibid., 118–80.
5. Dench 2003, 307; Lomas 2004, 207–13.
6. Eckstein 2006, 245–57.
7. Cornell 1995, 293–326, 345–68; Harris 1979, 58–67; Crawford 1993, 31–42; Lomas 2004, 201–6.
8. Livy 7.38.2.
9. Polybius 3.24; Livy 7.27.2; Diodorus 16.69.1.
10. Palmer 1997, 15–45.
11. Varro *Lat.* 5.145–59.
12. Palmer 1997, 73–9.
13. Ibid., 118–19.
14. Varro *Lat.* 5.146–7.
15. Palmer 1997, 115.
16. Di Mario 2005.
17. Bechtold 2007.
18. Diodorus 15.24.1.
19. For the strong cultural links between Sicily and Latium see Galinsky 1969, 63–140.
20. Diodorus 15.24.1.
21. Plutarch *Pyrrh.* 13.2–6.
22. Franke 1989, 456–61; Plutarch *Pyrrh.* 2.1–13.1.
23. Plutarch *Pyrrh.* 15.1–17.5.
24. Justin 18.2.1–3; Valerius Maximus 3.7.10.
25. Plutarch *Pyrrh.* 18.1–21.10.
26. Ibid. 22.1–6.
27. Polybius 3.25.1–5.
28. Plutarch *Pyrrh.* 22.4–6.
29. Ibid. 22.1–23.6.
30. Diodorus 22.7.5. Hoyos (1998, 14) argues that there were no Roman participants in this raid. However, the hypothesis put forward by Huss (1985,

212) that Romans were part of the expedition is more convincing, as it appears unlikely that the Romans would have been happy to let such an operation take place on the Italian mainland without their involvement.

31. Plutarch *Pyrrh.* 24.1.

32. Ibid. 25.1–26.1.

33. Zonaras 8.6; Plutarch *Pyrrh.* 34.2–4.

34. Diodorus 22.3; Dionysius 20.4–5.

35. Livy *Epitome* 14; Zonaras 8.8; Lazenby 1996, 34–5; Hoyos 1998, 15–16. One much later Christian writer, Orosius (4.3.1–2), actually described a sea battle between the Carthaginian and Roman fleets that is almost certainly fictitious, although his claim that the Romans sent an embassy to Carthage to complain may be true.

36. Harris 1979, 183–4.

37. Lancel 1995, 365. See Hoyos 1998, 20–21, for a critique of a possible Campanian conspiracy.

38. Bechtold 2007.

39. Livy *Epitome* 14; 21.10.8, Dio Fr. 43.1; Hoyos 1998, 15–16; Lazenby 1996, 38–9.

40. Hellanicus of Lesbos Frs. 31, 83, *FGH*, I: 115, 129 (Dionysius 1.72.13). For scepticism in regard to whether Hellanicus was the source of these claims see Gruen 1992, 17–18. However, see Solmsen's (1986) convincing reiteration of Hellanicus' authorship, which is backed up by Malkin (1998, 199–202). In fact the idea that some non-Greek peoples owed their existence to Greek heroes was not a new one. The claim that the Etruscan and Latin peoples had been ruled over by the sons of Odysseus had been circulating in Greek literary circles since at least the mid sixth century BC, and perhaps earlier. The Etruscans were themselves quite receptive to the idea that their origins were linked to the legendary Homeric wanderer (Malkin 1998 & 2002). These Greek-authored ethnographical studies also acted as powerful exclusionary devices, because, while underlining the 'Greekness' of some peoples, they also highlighted the alien nature of others. These ideas would soon have a significant impact in Italy, where they were enthusiastically adopted and adapted by non-Greek ethnic groups in order to define their superiority over their equally non-Greek neighbours (Dench 2003, 300).

41. Cornell 1995, 63–8. The story of Aeneas, although enormously embellished later, had its roots in *Greek* Homeric epic, and the first references to the Trojan prince travelling to the West are found in a Greek author, the sixth-century-BC Sicilian Greek Stesichorus (Gruen 1992, 13–14). The story of Aeneas in the West was also known in Etruria by the sixth century BC,

as seen on decoration on imported Greek pottery and on locally made ware (Galinsky 1969, 105). However, Gruen (1992, 21–6) has convincingly argued that it was Latium that remained the centre of interest in Aeneas.

42. Gruen 1990, 33; 1992, 31.

43. Gruen 1992, 15–16. The Sicilian Greek writer Callias (Fr. 5A (Dionysius 1.72.5)) argued that Rome had been founded by the twins Romulus and Remus and an unnamed third brother, the offspring of Latinus (king of the Latin people) and Roma (a Trojan woman who had come to Italy with Aeneas, although she was not related to him). Alcimus, another Syracusan historian, produced a slightly different version of this story, which named Romus, son of Romulus and grandson of Aeneas, as the founder of the city (Vattoune 2002, 220). Indeed, such was Rome's increasing profile that, by the fourth century, a number of Greek writers, from both the Aristotelian and Platonic schools, argued that the city was a purely Hellenic foundation (Dionysius 1.72.3–5; Plutarch *Cam.* 22.2). Vattuone (2002, 220) sees the insistence by many fourth- and third-century Syracusan writers that Rome was a Latin and/or Trojan rather than a Greek foundation as a sign that Rome, because of its alliance with the Carthaginians, was seen as an enemy of the western Greeks. However, the fact is that the Greek view of the Trojans was already more nuanced than that, and Timaeus, who clearly viewed Rome in a positive light, also insisted on Rome being a Trojan foundation.

44. The real power of these Greek ethnographical theories lay not only in the ideas themselves, but also in the authoritative rhetoric of scientific investigation in which they were couched. Bickerman 1952a; Momigliano 1975, 14–15; Cornell 1995, 60–63.

45. Strabo 5.3.5.

46. Ovid *Fasti* 2.237.

47. Certainly it has been argued that the Greek Arcadian king Evander, a key figure in the story, was introduced into the Roman mythological past only in that period (Bayet 1926; Cornell 1995, 68–9).

48. Fabre 1981, 287.

49. Franke 1989, 463–6.

50. Pausanias 1.12.1; Gruen 1990, 12.

51. Zonaras 8.9; Gruen 1990, 12–13; Galinsky 1969, 173.

52. Momigliano 1977, 53–8; Walbank 2002, 172–7. For the major influence that Timaeus' views had on Roman perceptions of Carthage see Feeney 2007, 52–7.

53. Dionysius 1.74.1. For Timaeus and his use of synchronisms see Feeney 2007, 43–52.

54. Timaeus explained that the Festival of the October Horse at Rome,

during which a horse was sacrificed, was related to the Greek capture of Troy (Polybius 12.4b.1–12.4c.1). He also stated that the *Penates*, sacred objects supposedly taken by Aeneas from Troy, were kept in the Latin town of Lavinium (Dionysius 1.67.3–4). For evidence of Timaeus' research techniques see Festus Rufus Avienus 190 L. However, Timaeus' claim to accuracy and emphasis on visiting places and interviewing its inhabitants were met with great scepticism and derision by Polybius (12.4d.1–2).

55. Vattuone 2002, 221–2. Pearson 1987, 255–9, for the paucity of surviving Timaean references to Pyrrhus.

56. Diodorus 4.21.6–7, 4.22.1–2; Pearson 1975, 188–92.

57. Ritter 1995, 27–9. The emblems also had personal connections for the victorious Roman generals, one of whom was a member of the Fabii. Both Gaius Fabius and the other consul, Quintus Ogulnius, could boast family associations with the image of Romulus and Remus too. The Fabii were supposedly descended from the group of shepherds who had been supporters of Remus (Ovid *Fasti* 2.361, 2.375). For Ogulnius, the wolf with the twins was an aide-memoire of one of his finest moments, when, nearly thirty years previously, he had successfully brought to trial several detested loansharks. A proportion of the fines had then been used to commission a group of statues, representing Romulus and Remus as infants being suckled by the she-wolf (Livy 10.23).

58. Polybius 1.10.1–2; Zonaras 8.6, 8.8; Diodorus 22.13.5–7; Lazenby 1996, 35–7.

59. Polybius 1.10.7–9.

60. Eckstein 1987, 76–7.

61. Polybius 1.10.3–1.11.4; Lazenby 1996, 37–41.

62. Polybius 1.11.4–5; Diodorus 23.1.3–4.; Zonaras 8.8–9; Lazenby 1996, 43–6.

63. Diodorus 23.1.2; Polybius 1.11.7.

64. Diodorus 23.1.4.

65. Zonaras 8.9; Frontinus *Strat.* 1.4.11; Lazenby 1996, 49.

66. Polybius 1.11.9, 1.20.15.

67. Lazenby 1996, 49–51.

68. Polybius 1.16; Diodorus 23.4; Lazenby 1996, 52–3.

69. Zonaras 8.8.2–3.

70. On Roman acquisitiveness as a cause of the First Punic War, Polybius 1.11.12; Florus 1.18.

71. Hoyos 1998, 51–7.

72. Harris 1979, 9–53. However, Rich (1993, 38–68) highlights the dangers of overplaying Roman bellicosity as the major motivation for Rome's involvement in a significant number of wars during this period. Eckstein

(2006, 181–243) questions how much more militarized, warlike and diplomatically aggressive Rome was compared with its rivals.

73. Eckstein 1987, 92.

74. Although the Roman historian Livy (*Epitome* 14; 21.10.8) alluded to such a treaty, as did the Vergilian scholar Servius (*Aen.* 4.628), Polybius (3.26) vehemently denied its existence. For arguments for there being no 306 treaty, see Lazenby 1996, 33; Eckstein 1987, 77–8. For arguments in favour of the Philinus treaty, see Huss 1985, 204–6; Lancel 1995, 362; Barceló 1988, 140–41; Serrati 2006, 120–29.

75. Lazenby 1996, 33.

76. Eckstein 1987, 93–101.

77. Hoyos 1998, 4–32.

78. Polybius 1.5.1, 39.8.4; Walbank 2002, 172–3.

CHAPTER 7: THE FIRST PUNIC WAR

1. Polybius 1.20.12.

2. Casson 1971, 100–122.

3. Morrison & Coates 1986, 259–60.

4. Goldsworthy 2000, 101–2.

5. Frost 1989, 127–35; Lancel 1995, 131–3.

6. Moscati 1986, 95–6.

7. Polybius 1.20.6–14.

8. Ibid. 1.17.4–1.19.15; Diodorus 23.7.1–23.9.1; Zonaras 8.10.

9. Diodorus 23.9.2.

10. Polybius 1.20.1–2.

11. Ibid. 1.21.2.

12. Ibid. 1.20.10–1.21.2; Lazenby 1996, 63–6.

13. Polybius 1.21.3–1.21.9.

14. Pliny *NH* 8.169; Lazenby 1996, 66–7.

15. Polybius 1.21.8–11.

16. Ibid. 1.23.3–10; Zonaras 8.11; Lazenby 1996, 70–72; Goldsworthy 2000, 106–9.

17. *Corpus Inscriptionum Latinarum* 12.2.25.

18. Diodorus 23.10.1; Dio 11.18; Zonaras 8.11; Valerius Maximus 7.3.

19. Zonaras 8.12. In another version of this story he was stoned to death (Orosius 4.4.4). Polybius (1.24.5–7) merely states that Hannibal was punished for losing many ships and being blockaded in one of the harbours.

20. Polybius 1.24.3–4; Diodorus 23.9.4; Goldsworthy 2000, 82–4; Lazenby 1996, 74–6.

21. Polybius 1.25.4. Some sources suggested that the Carthaginian admiral, Hamilcar, had been tricked by the Romans, who had divided their ships (Zonaras 8.12), or concealed a number of their craft (Polyaenus 8.20). Lazenby 1996, 78–9.

22. Polybius 1.26.1–9. For a discussion of these numbers see Goldsworthy 2000, 110–11; Lazenby 1996, 81–4.

23. Frontinus *Strat.* 2.13.10, although Lazenby (1996, 96) has doubts about whether this incident really took place at Ecnomus.

24. Polybius 1.26.10–1.28.14; Goldsworthy 2000, 109–15; Lazenby 1996, 81–96.

25. Zonaras 8.12; Valerius Maximus 6.6.2.

26. Polybius 1.29.1–1.30.8; Zonaras 8.12; Goldsworthy 2000, 84–6; Lazenby 1996, 97–100.

27. Polybius 1.30.9–1.31.8; Diodorus 23.11–12; Zonaras 8.13; Livy *Epitome* 18; Orosius 4.9.1; Eutropius 2.21.4; Lazenby 1996, 100–102.

28. Polybius 1.36.2–4, *contra* other stories that told of his murder by the Carthaginians (Diodorus 23.16; Zonaras 8.13; Valerius Maximus 9.6; Silius Italicus *Pun.* 6.682; Appian 8.1.4); Lazenby 1996, 106.

29. Polybius 1.32.1–1.39.6; Diodorus 23.14.1–23.19; Zonaras 8.14; Appian 8.1.3; Orosius 4.9.3–8; Eutropius 2.21.4–2.22.3; Lazenby 1996, 102–12; Goldsworthy 2000, 88–92.

30. For the Carthaginians' harsh pacification of the Numidians, see Orosius 4.9.9.

31. The Carthaginians had sent spies into the city, but they were supposedly uncovered by Metellus, who assembled all the citizens and asked them to take hold of all those whom they recognized (Zonaras 8.14). However, it should be said that Zonaras says that the same tactic was used by Mummius at the fall of Corinth in 146 BC.

32. Polybius 1.40.6–16.

33. Polybius 1.39.7–1.40.16; Diodorus 23.21; Zonaras 8.14; Eutropius 2.24; Orosius 4.9.15. The numbers of elephants cited vary from 10 (Polybius 1.40.15) to 142 (Pliny *NH* 8.16). Metellus was said to have offered freedom to any of the captured drivers who could control the elephants, and arranged their transport back to Italy on a series of enormous rafts (Diodorus 23.21). Zonaras (8.14), Pliny (*NH* 8.16) and Frontinus (*Strat.* 1.7.1) all give descriptions of the triumph – after which the elephants were killed. Lazenby 1996, 112–22; Goldsworthy 2000, 92–4.

34. Zonaras 8.14.

35. Polybius 1.41–47; Diodorus 24.1.

36. Polybius 1.49.1–1.54.8; Diodorus 24.3–4; Orosius 4.10.3; Eutropius 2.26.1; Livy *Epitome* 19; Suetonius *Tib.* 2.3; Aulus Gellius 10.6. Publius

Claudius Pulcher would be described by the Roman poet Naevius as a man who 'with pride and contempt ground down the legions' (Naevius Fr. 42). Lazenby 1996, 132–41, Goldsworthy 2000, 119–22.

37. Crawford 1985, 106–7.

38. Visonà 1998, 11–12.

39. Jenkins & Lewis 1963, Groups VIII & IX; Baldus 1982; 1988, 171–6.

40. Baldus 1988, 178–82; Manfredi 1999, 72.

41. Jenkins & Lewis 1963, Group X; Baldus 1988, 176–9; Crawford 1985, 136; Visonà 1998, 14.

42. Appian 5.1.1.

43. Hoyos 2003, 11.

44. For an overly scathing view of Hamilcar's talents as a general see Seibert 1993, 95–106.

45. Hoyos 2001b.

46. Polybius 1.56.1–1.58.6; Diodorus 24.5.1–24.9.2; Zonaras 8.16; Lazenby 1996, 143–50.

47. Goldsworthy 2000, 124.

48. Polybius 1.59–1.61; Diodorus 24.11.1–2; Lazenby 1996, 150–56; Goldsworthy 2000, 122–7.

49. Polybius 1.62.1–1.63.3; Lazenby 1996, 158.

50. Diodorus 24.10.2; Polybius 1.73.1, 1.74.7.

51. Hoyos 2007, 16–19.

52. Greene 1986; Hoyos (2007, 23–4) questions whether Hanno's outlook was exclusively focused on expansion in Africa.

53. Bechtold 2007.

54. They had been illicitly dug up and sold to a private collector. At least one of the tablets (VII) has been exposed as a fake. The recent bibliography for the Entella tablets is understandably very large, and still growing. The clearest general survey is still Loomis 1994. Hoyos's arguments (1998, 28–32) for a possible earlier-fourth-century date seem implausible.

CHAPTER 8: THE CAMP COMES TO CARTHAGE: THE MERCENARIES' REVOLT

1. Polybius 1.62.3–6.

2. Ibid. 1.66.1; Diodorus 24.13.

3. Polybius 3.9.6–7; Livy 21.1.5.

4. Polybius 1.66.12; Appian 5.2.2–3. I have given Hoyos's calculations (2007, 27–31) *contra* Loreto (1995, 48–9, 64–7), who, without any historical justification, argues that the arrears were no more than two months' pay.

5. Polybius 1.66.1–1.67.12. For a detailed account of events at Sicca see Hoyos 2007, 40–50. Hoyos (2007, 46–7) must be correct in his argument (*contra* Loreto 1995, 57–61) that there was no offer from Hanno to re-employ the troops for a further military campaign in Africa.

6. Polybius 1.67.4.

7. Ibid. 1.67.8–11.

8. Hoyos (2007, 53–60) sees many of the mercenaries' claims as being essentially legitimate, if exaggerated.

9. Polybius 1.68.1–1.69.3. Hoyos (2007, 26) is most probably correct in rejecting a story in Appian (5.2.3) that the Carthaginians massacred 3,000 Libyan deserters, who had been handed over to them by the Romans (*contra* Loreto 1995, 89).

10. Acquaro 1989, 137–8.

11. Polybius 1.69.4–1.70.6.

12. Ibid. 1.70.8–9, 1.72.1–5. Hoyos (2007, 93–4) thinks that it is possible that the rebels at the height of the conflict did have this number of troops. See Hoyos 2007, xiii, n. 2, for a list of previous Libyan insurrections and alliances with Carthage's enemies. Loreto (1995, 87–113) makes too much of Libyan disaffection being at the heart of the conflict, while at the same time playing down the role of the mercenaries in the insurgency. Manfredi (2003, 378–404) argues that during the mid third century BC, the Carthaginians were engaged in a campaign of Punicization in the Libyan interior. However, the process of acculturation through a number of different channels, including army service, had probably been taking place over a much longer period.

13. Hoyos 2007, 84–5.

14. Polybius 1.67.7; Hoyos 2007, 6–10, on the ethnic make-up and conditions of service for these mercenaries.

15. Carradice & La Niece 1988; Acquaro 1989. For the various interpretations of the initials M, A and Z also found on the coins see Hoyos 2007, 141–2. The most plausible, but by no means secure, theory is that they stand for the initials of the rebel leaders Mathos, Autaritus and Zarzas. The theory of Manganaro (1992, 93–9) that these coins were minted much later, and based on Sicilian coinage dating to 214–211, is clearly incorrect.

16. There is no real evidence to support the claim, made by Loreto (1995, 112), that Mathos' ambition was to establish a Libyan monarchical state.

17. Carradice & La Niece 1988, 51. The heads of the deities Zeus and (wearing a Corinthian helmet) Athena were both commonly used on Syracusan coinage. The horned bull was the most common emblem for the cities of Campania. The lion was a popular emblem in Punic Sicily. Manfredi (1999, 74) sees this coinage as an opportunity for the different ethnic elements

within the rebel force to proclaim their known autonomy.

18. Carradice & La Niece 1988, 37.

19. There is no evidence to support Loreto's argument (1995, 87–113) that this was essentially a Libyan rebellion, with the other mercenaries in the Libyans' paid employ.

20. Polybius 1.65.6.

21. Carradice & La Niece 1988, 49–50.

22. Polybius 1.71.6–8.

23. Ibid. 1.74.6–7.

24. Ibid. 1.73.1–1.75.2.

25. For a detailed account of the battle see Hoyos 2007, 115–24.

26. For more on Naravas see Hoyos 2007, 146–50.

27. Polybius 1.75.1–1.78.9.

28. Ibid. 1.78.10–1.80.13.

29. Ibid. 1.81.1–1.82.10.

30. Ibid. 1.83.1–11.

31. Ibid. 1.83.6–8, 3.28.3–4; Appian 5.2.3, 8.12.86; Zonaras 8.18; Hoyos 1998, 123–6. Appian's assertion that the Romans also sent mediators to North Africa is very unlikely to have been true (Hoyos 2007, 129). There is no evidence to support the contention of Hoyos (1998, 125) that the Romans agreed to lower or to postpone the indemnity that Carthage had to pay.

32. Crawford 1985, 41–3, 106–9; Polybius 1.58.7–1.59.1.

33. Hoyos 1998, 126.

34. For a study of this arsenical copper-alloy coinage see Carradice & La Niece 1998, 41–5.

35. Polybius 1.84.1–1.85.7. For a reconstruction of events at the Saw see Hoyos 2007, 197–218.

36. Polybius 1.86.1–6.

37. Ibid. 1.87.1–1.88.7.

38. Ibid. 1.79.1–7; Hoyos 2007, 154–9.

39. Polybius 1.79.9–10. Both African and Sardinian rebels used the motif of three ears of corn on their coins, which was not a design found on Carthaginian coins (Visonà 1992, 125–6; Carradice & La Niece 1988, 38–9), which suggests some contact between the two groups.

40. Polybius 1.88.8–12, 3.10.3–5.

41. Ibid. 3.28.1–2; Champion 2004, 119–20.

42. Zonaras 8.18; Appian 6.1.4, 8.1.5. Other later Roman historians would argue that Sardinia was merely ceded to Rome (Livy 21.40.5, 22.54.11). For the lack of evidence for a series of new confrontations between Rome and Carthage in the early 230s see Hoyos 1998, 134–5.

43. Harris 1979, 192–3; Huss 1985, 266–7, *contra* Hoyos (1998, 142), who sees it as a way of protecting Sicily and perhaps Italy.

44. Polybius 1.88.9.

45. Hoyos 1998, 142.

46. Ibid., 135.

47. Lancel 1999, 23.

48. Visonà 1998, 11.

49. Hoyos 1994, 264.

50. Livy 21.1.

51. Polybius 1.82.12.

52. Cornelius Nepos *Ham.* 3.2.

53. Appian 6.1.4. There has been some dispute over the correct dating of the attempted prosecution of Hamilcar Barca. Loreto (1995, 205–10) and Lancel (1999, 28) accept Appian's date of 237, whereas Seibert (1993, 13–14) and Hoyos (2007, 20–21) insist on 241, when Hamilcar's popularity and political power base were at a low ebb.

54. Polybius 6.51.6–8.

55. Aristotle *Pol.* 2.11.1–2.

56. Huss 1985, 496–7.

57. Although around 10 per cent of the votive dedications that have been found in the city were erected by females, it is striking that in most cases female supplicants were identified by their patrilineal descent or by the name of their husband (Amadasi Guzzo 1988, 144–7). Elite families also made joint sacrifices, with father and daughter offering male and female sacrificial victims respectively.

58. Huss 1985, 497–8. On some inscriptions, named individuals are referred to as 'belonging to' (š) another person (Amadasi Guzzo 1988, 143–4).

59. One inscription lists guilds of porters and packers, gold-smelters, smiths, vessel-blowers and even sandal-makers who had contributed to the construction of a new street.

60. Champion 2004, 173–234.

61. Diodorus 25.8.

62. Zambon 2006, 78–85.

63. Polybius 2.1.5; Diodorus 25.8.

64. Polybius 3.24.

65. Wagner 1989, 152. It has been suggested that a series of fortified compounds dating from the fifth to the third century located in eastern Andalusia may have been Carthaginian bases for controlling the mines.

66. Guerrero Ayuso 1989, 101–5.

67. Strabo 3.2.14.

68. Jenkins 1987, 215–16; Visonà 1998, 14–16.
69. Blásquez Martinez & García-Gelabert Pérez 1991, 33–8.

CHAPTER 9: BARCID SPAIN

1. Although those who argue that that Barcid Spain operated as a kind of independent monarchy probably take this argument too far (Blásquez Martinez & García-Gelabert Pérez 1991, 38ff.).
2. For Barcid political domination of Carthage during this period see Hoyos 1994, 259–64.
3. Lancel 1999, 29–30.
4. Appian 7.2, 6.5; Zonaras 8.17.
5. Appian 7.2, 6.5; Hoyos 1994, 270–72.
6. Polybius 2.1.6, *contra* Diodorus (25.10.1), who states that the army sailed from Carthage.
7. Blásquez Martinez & García-Gelabert Pérez 1991, 28–9; Barcelo 1988, 37. There is certainly evidence of later tensions. During the Second Punic War the Carthaginian commander of Gades requisitioned all the valuables from the temple and the city and imposed a war tax on its inhabitants. The city council retaliated by secretly negotiating the handover of Gades to the Romans. Mago, the Carthaginian commander-in-chief, executed them for their treachery.
8. Blásquez Martinez & García-Gelabert Pérez 1991, 33.
9. Diodorus 25.10.1–2.
10. Lancel 1999, 36.
11. Diodorus 5.35–8; Healy 1978, 68.
12. Polybius 34.9.8–11; Strabo 3.2.10; Blásquez Martinez & García-Gelabert Pérez 1991, 33–4.
13. González de Canales, Serrano & Llompart 2006.
14. Diodorus 25.10.3; Lancel 1999, 36–7.
15. Diodorus 25.12.
16. Villaronga 1973, 95–107.
17. Ibid., 98–101. It is now believed that an issue of Carthaginian silver drachmas found in Spain date to well before the Barcid expedition (Villaronga 1992).
18. Villaronga 1973, 124–5. See Lehmler 2005, 60–96, for the coinage of Hiero II.
19. Warships also appear on the coins of Tyre and Sidon during this period (Villaronga 1973, 57).
20. Blásquez Martinez & García-Gelabert Pérez 1991, 48.
21. Villaronga 1973, 61.

22. Ibid., 49–50; Chávez Tristán & Ceballos 1992, 173–5.

23. There is certainly a case for arguing that this design was chosen simply because the Alexander/Heracles tetradrachm was the most ubiquitous silver coinage in the Hellenistic world during that period, and would therefore have been attractive to the mercenary troops in Carthaginian employ. In fact it has been calculated that this same image was being produced on coinage by at least 51 different mints throughout the Mediterranean world and the East in the last quarter of the third century BC (Price 1991, 72–8). Its use may also have been a reaction to Agathocles, who had also put Heracles on his coinage. Just as the 'portrait' of Heracles on some of Alexander's coinage minted after his demise was an idealized likeness of the Great King, there has been some suggestion that the 'portrait' of Heracles on these coins may have borne some idealized likeness to Agathocles (Dahmen 2007).

24. Piccaluga 1974, 111–22.

25. Polybius 2.1.7–8; Diodorus 25.10.3–4; Cornelius Nepos *Ham.* 22.4.2; Appian 6.1.5; Zonaras 8.19.

26. Livy 21.2.4.

27. Polybius 3.8.1–4; Cornelius Nepos *Ham.* 22.3.3. Hoyos (1994, 247–59; 1998, 150–52) argues that Barcid political support in Carthage itself was very secure, and that 'from 237 the Carthaginian republic was in some ways a de facto military monarchy.' My own view follows that of Schwarte (1983) and Huss (1985): that there was in fact a good deal of tension between pro-Barcid and anti-Barcid factions in Carthage.

28. Blásquez Martinez & García-Gelabert Pérez 1991, 48–9. Cf. Crawford 1985, 87, for the lack of a real fiscal structure in Barcid Spain.

29. Diodorus 25.12.

30. Polybius 10.10.

31. For Barcid ambitions in Spain see Barcelo 1988, 145–51; Schwarte 1983, 37–74.

32. Visonà 1998, 15–16; Jenkins 1987, 215–16.

33. Rich 1996, 20; Errington 1970, 37–41, for possible Massilian involvement – an idea strongly disputed by Hoyos (1998, 171). The Massilians had a colonial presence in north-eastern Spain.

34. Dio Fr. 48. Errington (1970, 32–4) and Hoyos (1998, 147–9) both argue that the story was false; however, they have no really strong grounds for such an opinion.

35. Polybius 2.13.7, 3.27.10; Lancel 1999, 40–41. Hoyos (1998, 169–70) subscribes to the idea that Hasdrubal threatened either to ally himself with or to take advantage of the chaos caused by the much anticipated Gallic invasion of northern Italy. This idea had earlier been discounted by Rich (1996, 21–3).

36. Polybius 2.36.1; Livy 21.2.6.
37. Livy 21.3.3–8.
38. Ibid. 21.3.5. See also ibid. 21.4.2.
39. Villaronga (1973, 121) contends that this group of coins (III) were minted during the command of either Hamilcar or Hasdrubal. However Volk (2006), in a closely argued study, has recently put forward the suggestion that this series and the later series XI, which were previously associated by scholars with the Second Punic War, were in fact much closer together in time. As series XI is clearly dated to the correct period, this suggests that series III must be later than Villaronga's dates.
40. There has been much scholarly debate about whether any of these coins portrayed the Barcids (Robinson 1953, 42–3; Villaronga 1973, 45–7).
41. Livy 24.41.7.
42. Polybius 3.13.5–3.14.10; Livy 21.5.1–17.
43. Polybius 3.30.1–2; Harris 1979, 201–2.
44. Polybius 3.15.7.
45. Ibid. 3.15. Livy (21.6) makes no mention of the ambassadors visiting either destination, but merely states that the Roman Senate had decided to send an embassy, but this did not have time to leave before events overtook it. See Rich 1996, 10–12, on why the Roman ultimatum and its rejection occurred long before Hannibal crossed the Hiberus.
46. Pliny *NH* 33.96–7; Blásquez Martinez & García-Gelabert Pérez 1991, 33–4; Villaronga 1973, 97–101.
47. Polybius 3.17.1–11; Livy 21.6–9. There is some debate over whether the Roman embassies mentioned by Polybius and Livy respectively before and during the siege of Saguntum may in fact have been the same incident (Lancel 1999, 50).
48. Livy 21.9.4.
49. See Rich 1996, 13, on opposition to the Barcids in Carthage.
50. Visonà 1998.
51. Greene 1986, 118–51; Bechtold 2007, 65.
52. Morel 1982; Chelbi 1992; Bechtold 2007, 53–4. This black-glaze pottery was so popular that Carthaginian potters began to imitate it.
53. This was certainly the position of the first Roman historian, Fabius Pictor, who, as a senator during this period, was party to the discussions and debates that went on (Polybius 3.8.1–3.9.5).
54. Schwarte 1983, 64–74.
55. Livy 21.10.2–13.
56. Ibid. 21.11.1.
57. Seibert (1993, 58–60) speculates that there may have been some kind of debate before the Carthaginian Council of Elders gave their support to Hannibal.

58. Dio 13.54.11.
59. Zonaras 8.22.2–3; Polybius 3.20.1–5. Rich (1996, 29–30) sees the delay as being for mechanistic and strategic reasons, rather than the result of a real division in opinion among the Roman Senate. Hoyos (1998, 226–232) sees the delay as being primarily caused by dissension within the Senate.
60. Livy 21.11.3–21.15.2.
61. The councillor probably had a valid case, as Hasdrubal's agreement with Rome was a unilateral covenant, pledged by the general on campaign, but never validated later (Bickerman 1952b). For Polybius' rather partisan view of Carthaginian fault in regard to Saguntum, see Serrati 2006, 130–34.
62. Livy 21.16.1–21.18.14; Polybius 3.20–21, 3.33.1–4.
63. Polybius 3.9.1–6, 3.12.7. Two exceptions were Bagnall 1999, 124, and Dorey & Dudley 1971.
64. Goldsworthy 2000, 148.
65. Huss 1985, 288–93.
66. Harris 1979, 200–205; Hoyos 1998, 264, for the idea that after the Carthaginian capture of Saguntum, the Romans 'foresaw a straightforward and no doubt profitable war'.
67. Rich 1996, 31–2.
68. For the most lucid exposition of this argument see ibid., 14–18.

CHAPTER 10: DON'T LOOK BACK

1. Livy 21.21.10–13; Polybius 3.33.5–16.
2. Cornell, Rankov & Sabin (eds.) 1996, 52–3.
3. Polybius 6.52.3–4.
4. Daly 2002, 128.
5. Polybius 9.22.1–4, 9.24.5–9.25.6.
6. Livy 21.11.13.
7. For a detailed breakdown of the different ethnic components and their particular specializations see Daly 2002, 84–112; Lazenby 1978, 14–16; Lancel 1999, 60–61.
8. On Celtic warfare see Rawlings 1996, 86–8.
9. For the most recent research on Hannibal's use of elephants in his campaigns see Rance 2009; Charles & Rhodan 2007. For a general study of the use of elephants in the Graeco-Roman world see Scullard 1974.
10. Lancel 1999, 62–4; Rance 2009, 106–7.
11. Daly 2002, 83.
12. Brizzi 1995, 312–15. On the make-up of Hannibal's army more generally see Goldsworthy 2000, 32–6.

13. Sabin 1996.

14. Polybius 6.52.10–11.

15. Even in the mid second century BC, when Polybius gained his experience of the Roman army, there were still considerable tensions between the Romans and Italians, which eventually led to a terrible civil war.

16. At the Battle of the Trebia, there were 20,000 allied troops, compared with 16,000 Roman citizens.

17. Lazenby 1996, 11–12.

18. Lazenby 1978, 31–2.

19. Livy 21.20.6.

20. Polybius 3.16–19.

21. Polybius 3.20.8, 7.9.1; Walbank 1957–79, I: 334–5, II: 44–5.

22. For an example of the difficulties created by the imposition of a monolithic and modern model of 'propaganda' on the Greek and Roman worlds see P. Taylor 1995, 25–48.

23. Both Sosylus and Silenus wrote accounts of Hannibal's campaigns which, although probably written after the Carthaginian general had eventually been forced to evacuate Italy, undoubtedly drew on earlier accounts. See Diodorus 26.4; Cornelius Nepos *Ham.* 23.13.3; Walbank 1985, 129–30.

24. Spencer 2002, 7–9.

25. Cornelius Nepos *Ham.* 23.13.3. For the debate over the origins of Silenus see Spada 2002, 238. A number of other Greek historians had also quickly realized that Hannibal had the necessary star quality for a major historical blockbuster, although only their names now survive – for example Eumachus of Neapolis, mentioned in Athenaeus 13.576. However, Hoyos (2001a) is surely correct in his assessment that there is no clear evidence that the papyrus fragment P. Rylands III.491, which appears to relate to the peace terms dictated to the Carthaginians in 203 BC and the following breakdown of that truce, should be viewed as a pro-Carthaginian account. Hoyos's argument that the author was in fact the Roman historian Fabius Pictor is impossible to substantiate.

26. Walbank 1957–79, I: 316.

27. Cicero *Div.* 1.24.48.

28. Brizzi 1995, 309.

29. Cornelius Nepos *Ham.* 23.13.3. Those works reportedly included a study addressed to the people of the island of Rhodes on the Roman general Gnaeus Manlius Vulso's subjugation of Asia Minor. The fact that an ancient forger wrote a fictitious letter in Greek from Hannibal to the Athenians shows that it was generally recognized in the ancient world that the Carthaginian general was a well-educated man (Brizzi 1991).

30. Dio 13.54.3.
31. Sosylus, Pap. Wurzburg, *FGH*, IIB: 903–6. Although scholars have long argued over the location of this defeat without any definite conclusions, it is widely believed that it is most likely to have been off the coast of Spain (Krings 1998, 217–60).
32. Krings 1998, 226. Recently it has been tentatively suggested that Sosylus may have been the original source of a small excerpt relating to Hannibal's use of elephants now attributed to Diodorus Siculus (Rance 2009, 108–10).
33. Polybius 3.20.1–5.
34. Spada 2002, 239–40. Surviving excerpts of the work include a description of a garden used by Hieron, king of Syracuse, explanations for the name of a common herb on the island, and the source of the name of the Sicilian city of Palice. Walbank (1968–9, 487–97) perhaps underestimates their significance, although he is probably right that the *Sicilia* was not a conventional history, *contra* La Bua (1966, 277–9).
35. Cicero *Letters to Friends.* 9.25.1; Franke 1989, 456, n. 1.
36. Campus 2005.
37. Pausanias 12.3.4.
38. Picard 1983–4; Rawlings 2005, 164–71; Knapp 1986, 118–19.
39. Polybius 12.28, 3.48.
40. Polybius 14.1; Walbank 1957–79, I: 63–130; Scuderi 2002, 277–84; Hoyos 1998, 42–3, 55–6, 82–3, 95–8, 100–104. Polybius clearly respected Philinus' didactic approach, which closely mirrored his own (Walbank 1985, 77–98). La Bua's (1966) elaborate hypothesis (that Philinus was Polybius' main source for his account of the First Punic War, and that Diodorus' account from the death of Agathocles through to the First Punic War came from Philinus via the later western-Greek historian Silenus) is impossible to prove. It has also been suggested that Philinus was personally influenced by the harsh treatment that his home city received from the Romans on its capture in 261, and that he may have accompanied the Carthaginian army on campaign (Galvagno 2006, 254–6; Scuderi 2002, 275–7). Thus it has also been argued that Polybius' detailed account of the siege of Lilybaeum in 250–249 (41.4ff.) came from Philinus' eyewitness account (Lazenby 1996, 2).
41. Diodorus 23.1.4.
42. Walbank 1985, 90.
43. Broughton 1951–6, I: 229; Badian 1958, 36–43; Hoyos 1998, 122.
44. Polybius 3.28.1–2, 3.15.9–11.
45. Ibid. 7.4.1–2; Livy 24.6.4–8.
46. This can also be seen in the treaties that he later agreed with some Greek cities in Italy, which recognized their political freedoms (Hoyos 1998, 268).

47. De Angelis & Garstad 2006, 213–25; Malkin 2005.

48. Diodorus had extensively used Sicilian Greek authors such as Timaeus, and perhaps also Silenus (La Bua 1966, 249–52, 277–9; Vattoune 2002, 217–22; Pearson 1987, 11–12, 24–5).

49. Dionysius 1.41.1.

50. Fox 1993, 144–5; Rawlings 2005, 169–70.

51. Dionysius 1.41.1–2.

52. Ibid. 1.42.2–3.

53. Ibid. 1.42.4.

54. Twelve inscriptions have so far been found in the Oscan language spoken in these areas. In a recent essay, Guy Bradley (2005) has persuasively argued that many of the commonly assumed reasons for the popularity of Hercules in central Italy, such as Samnite bellicosity and local religious 'beliefs', are heavily influenced by later Roman and modern constructions of what these peoples were like.

55. Villaronga 1973, Series XI.

56. Onasander 10.26, tr. Daly 2002, 137.

57. Daly 2002, 135.

58. Athenaeus 6.246c–d. For Hannibal's skills in motivating and controlling his Celtic warriors see Rawlings 1996, 88–9. For his use of Melqart, Heracles, Hercules and perhaps Gallic and Libyan deities to bring coherency to his ethnically diverse army see Brizzi 1984a, 150.

59. Dio 13.54.4.

60. Vegetius *Pref.* 3. Daly (2002, 88) must be correct in his assertion that there is no evidence of Sosylus fulfilling a military function for Hannibal.

61. Livy 21.21.9.

62. According to the later Greek geographer Strabo (2.145), who himself cited Polybius as the source of his information, the spring flowed inversely to the movement of the sea tide, falling with the flood and filling up at the ebb. Polybius had tried to furnish a scientific explanation for this strange phenomenon, developing a complex argument that revolved around the expulsion of air from the depth of the earth, but his ideas were not accepted by all. Silenus was reported as having his own theory about the workings of the spring, although Strabo fails to tell us what they were, preferring instead to dismiss Silenus as a layman who had no understanding of such complex matters. However, the fact that this spring was associated with Heracles–Melqart strongly suggests that this may have been the root of Silenus' interest in it, and that his theory had some kind of association with the god/hero (Briquel 2004). It is only in a much later fanciful Roman account, Silius Italicus' *Punica*, that we are furnished with any details of Hannibal's visit. It is likely that Silius, with a little poetic licence, was describing what the

temple looked like in his own day, over 250 years after Hannibal's visit. Yet it is striking how the Semitic aspects of the cult had survived. Silius describes how the timber from which the temple was built had never decayed and how neither women nor swine were allowed to cross its threshold. Its shaven-headed, barefoot priests wore long robes and headbands and took a vow of celibacy. In the temple itself the fires by the altar were kept permanently alight, and no statues or images of the gods were allowed.

63. Cicero *Div.* 1.49 (Coelius Fr. 11).

64. Hannibal's dream appears to have intrigued ancient Greek and Roman writers as much as it has modern scholars. There are three other surviving versions of the story: in Livy (21.22.5–9), in Silius Italicus (*Pun.* 3.163–213) and in Dio (13.56.9, copied in Zonaras 8.22). These other versions of the tale appear to have adapted the story to place it in a far more sinister and indeed more hostile light. Modern commentators have understandably focused on the differences between these versions in the context of the role that dreams played in Roman historiography. For Levene (1993, 45–6) the crucial transformation between the Ciceronian and Livian accounts is that, whereas in the former it is the dream that convinces Hannibal to undertake the invasion of Italy, Livy has it that he had already decided on this course of action, meaning that the Carthaginian general's campaign may have been temporally supported by the gods, but was not divinely ordained. Pelling (1997, 202–4) sees the Livian account as clearly signposting divine ambivalence towards Hannibal and his cause ('He must ask no more questions. He should allow destiny to remain in darkness'), with the reader, who already knows what fate has in store for Hannibal, being complicit in this. Stübler (1941, 95–6) takes this idea even further, describing Hannibal's joy at what he is told as a form of blindness. See also Cipriani 1984.

65. Valerius Maximus, 1.7, ext. 1.

66. For the dream offering divine sanction to bolster the resolve of Hannibal's troops see Seibert 1993, 186–7. For the identity of the guide see most recently the very persuasive arguments of Briquel (2004) *contra* the suggestion of Foulon (2003) that the divine messenger was in fact the god Mercury Aletes.

67. Rawlings 2005, 158–61.

68. D'Arco 2002, 160–1.

69. Polybius 3.47.7–9.

70. Livy 21.41.7.

71. More generally on the accusations of impiety levelled at Hannibal see Fucecchi 1990.

CHAPTER 11: IN THE FOOTSTEPS OF HERACLES

1. Polybius 3.34.3–6.
2. Ibid. 3.35; Livy 21.23.4–6.
3. Livy 21.24.2.
4. Ibid. 21.24.5.
5. Archaeological evidence for contemporary conflict and the destruction of native oppida (fortified hilltop settlements) in the region during this period may well be connected to the Carthaginian presence (Barruol 1976, 683). Seibert (1993, 110) has argued for the establishment of garrisons along the route, but Morel (1986, 43) has pointed out that the Carthaginian amphorae and other artefacts found at these sites by archaeologists probably owe more to the activities of Punic merchants in the region. Lancel (1999, 66) argues further that manning garrisons would have quickly depleted Hannibal's troops.
6. I have taken Lancel's excellent study as my guide for Hannibal's route to Italy. For a detailed discussion of the multitude of different scholarly and unscholarly opinions on his itinerary see Lancel 1999, 57–80.
7. Polybius 3.42–3, 3.45–6; Livy 21.26.6–21.28.12.
8. Polybius 3.36.
9. Ibid. 3.48.
10. Polybius claims, by contrast, that it was a new generation of Gallic leaders who had not experienced their forebears' bitter struggles with the Romans who provoked conflict in 225 BC. See Vishnia 1996, 17–18.
11. Polybius 2.13.6. See also Florus 1.19.2.
12. See Vishnia 1996, 13–25.
13. Indeed, it would not be until after the end of the Second Punic War that Rome managed partially to regain control of the region. For a full account of the Roman conquest of Cisalpine Gaul and Liguria see Toynbee 1965, 252–85.
14. For Graeco-Roman stereotyping of the Celtic peoples and other tribal peoples see Rawlings 1996, 84–5.
15. Rawlings 1996, 86–7 on Celtic warfare.
16. Polybius 2.19, 2.21. See Rawlings 1996, 82.
17. Dio 14.6b.
18. Polybius 25.16. For Hannibal's disguises see ibid. 3.78; Zonaras 8.24; Livy 22.1.
19. Polybius 3.40.1–3.41.5; Livy 21.25.1–21.26.5.
20. Polybius 3.44.1–3.45.4; Livy 21.29.

21. Polybius 3.49.1–4; Livy 21.32.1–5.
22. Polybius 3.49.5–3.50.2; Livy 21.31.1–12.
23. Ammianus Marcellinus 15.10.4–6.
24. Polybius 3.50.3–3.53.8; Livy 21.32.6–21.35.3.
25. Livy 21.35.8–9.
26. Ibid. 21.36.7–8. Polybius (3.54.4–3.55.4) also gives an account of the terrible difficulties both men and beasts had with the icy conditions.
27. Livy 21.37.2–3. See Polybius 3.55.6–9 for a similar but far less exciting version of this story.
28. Ammianus Marcellinus 15.10.2.
29. I have once again followed Lancel's sensible suggestions concerning Hannibal's route over the Alps.
30. Ammianus Marcellinus 15.10.9–10.
31. Polybius 3.56.3–4; Livy 21.38.2–5.
32. Polybius 3.60.8–10; Livy 21.38.4.
33. Polybius 3.56.5–6; Livy 21.39.3.
34. Polybius 3.63. See also Livy 21.42.
35. Livy 21.43–4.
36. Ibid. 21.46.10; Polybius 3.65.1–8.
37. Polybius 3.66, 3.67.3; Livy 21.48.10.
38. For a detailed account of Hannibal's tactics at the Trebia see Goldsworthy 2000, 173–81.
39. Polybius 3.68.11–3.75.3; Livy 21.52.1–21.56.8.
40. Polybius 3.77.4. For Hannibal's other efforts, some unsuccessful, to persuade the Italians to desert the Romans see David 1996, 55–60.
41. Polybius 3.74.11. Livy's (21.57–9) account of Hannibal campaigning in that winter is confused and nonsensical (Lancel 1999, 89; Goldsworthy 2000, 181).
42. Polybius 3.79; Livy 22.2.
43. Livy 22.4–6; Polybius 3.82.9–3.84.15. Goldsworthy 2000, 181–90.
44. Polybius 3.85.3–4; Livy 22.7.
45. Polybius 3.86.1–5; Livy 22.8.1–2.
46. Livy 22.1.10.
47. Ibid. 21.62. The celestial consort of Hercules, Juventas, was also invoked, and again a second time in 207 (Livy 36.36.5–6). See also Rawlings 2005, 162.
48. Polybius 3.86.8–3.87.5; Livy 22.9.1–6.
49. Livy 22.7.6–14 (quote = 22.7.9); Polybius 3.85.7–10.
50. Polybius 3.87.6–9; Livy 22.8.6–7.
51. Plutarch Fab. 5.1–2.
52. Polybius 3.88.1–3.92.7; Livy 22.11.1–22.13.11; Plutarch Fab. 5.3.

53. Polybius 3.90.6; Livy 22.14.
54. Livy 30.26.9.
55. Ibid. 22.23.2–8.
56. Plutarch *Fab.* 6.
57. Polybius 3.92.8–3.94.6; Livy 22.15.11–22.18.4.
58. Polybius 3.101.1–3.105.3; Livy 22.23.1–22.27.11.
59. *ILLRP* 118; Rawlings 2005, 161.
60. Livy 22.9.7–11.
61. Gruen 1992, 22–9; Galinsky 1969, 160–63.
62. Polybius 1.55.6.
63. Polybius 1.58.2, 1.58.7–8; Diodorus 24.8.
64. Schilling 1954, 243.
65. Ibid., 235–9.
66. The exploitation of Rome's Trojan 'heritage' may also be seen in the priests' injunction to construct a temple to *Mens*, a quality often associated with clear-headed calculation and composure – those qualities attributed by Greek authors to Aeneas himself. By constructing a temple to *Mens*, Fabius was thus perhaps attempting to convince the Roman public that his patient, unglamorous tactics were in fact deeply rooted in Roman tradition.
67. Plutarch *Fab.* 5.1.
68. Of particular significance in this regard was the goddess Juno, the consort of Jupiter, who was commonly associated with the Punic goddesses Astarte and Tanit, and to whom the Romans made a series of gifts to appease her with regard to both their own city and those in Latium during the terrible run of defeats of 218/217. See Livy 21.62.9, 22.1.
69. Ibid. 25.1.6–9.
70. Ibid. 25.1.10–11.
71. Ibid. 22.10.2–6.
72. Ibid. 22.36.1–5; Polybius 3.107.9–15.
73. Livy 22.38.6–22.41.3.
74. Polybius 3.110.1–3.112.9; Livy 22.41.1–22.45.4.
75. Livy 22.45.5–22.46.7; Polybius 3.113.1–3.114.8.
76. Livy 22.47.
77. Ibid. 22.47.1–22.49.18; Polybius 3.115.1–3.117.12. For detailed descriptions of the actual battle see Daly 2002; Lancel 1999, 103–8; Goldsworthy 2000, 198–214.
78. Livy 22.51.5–9.
79. Ibid. 22.49.16–17. For the escape of Varro see Polybius 3.116.13; Livy 22.49.14.
80. Livy 22.51.1–4.

81. Lancel 1999, 96–7; Lazenby 1978, 85–6. Lazenby (1996, 41) also points out that it would have taken Hannibal's army much longer than the five days that Maharbal suggested to reach Rome.
82. Lazenby 1978, 41–6.
83. Livy 22.58.1–9.
84. Polybius 6.58.1–13; Livy 22.59.1–22.61.10.
85. Livy 22.58.3.

CHAPTER 12: THE ROAD TO NOWHERE

1. Livy 35.14.5–8.
2. Ibid. 35.14.9.
3. P. Green 1986, 231.
4. Livy 23.4.8.
5. Livy 23.6.1–3. Hannibal's promise of freedom for the Italians is treated with scepticism by Erskine (1993), who argues that it was a Greek concept and probably therefore an invention of Polybius. For an analysis of the Capuans' motivations for switching allegiance to Hannibal see Fronda 2007.
6. Livy 23.7.1–2.
7. Ibid. 23.7.3.
8. Ibid. 23.10.1–2.
9. Ibid. 23.8.1–23.9.13.
10. Ibid. 23.7.4–12, 23.10.3–10.
11. Crawford 1985, 62–4.
12. See Fronda 2007 for an in-depth discussion of Capua's relationship with Hannibal. Quote = Fronda 2007, 104–5.
13. Livy 23.18.10–16.
14. Goldsworthy 2000, 222–6.
15. Livy 23.11.7–23.12.7.
16. Ibid. 23.12.13–17.
17. Ibid. 23.13.1–8.
18. Ibid. 24.4.1–9.
19. Polybius 7.2; Livy 24.5.7–8, 24.6.2–3.
20. Livy 24.21.1–24.27.5.
21. Ibid. 24.29.1–24.32.9.
22. Ibid. 24.33.1–24.34.16. For a good summary of events leading up to the siege see Eckstein 1987, 135–55.
23. Livy 24.35.3–24.39.13.
24. Sardinia = Livy 23.32.7–12, 23.34.10–17, 23.40.1–23.41.7.

25. Ibid. 23.26.1–3.

26. Ibid. 23.27.9–23.29.17.

27. Ibid. 23.49.5–14, 24.41.1–24.42.11.

28. Ibid. 25.32.1–5. For the Scipios' campaigns in Spain between 218 and 211 see Eckstein 1987, 188–207.

29. Polybius 7.9; Bickerman 1944 (repr. 1985, 257–72).

30. Barré 1983, 38–64 – *contra* Huss (1986, 228–30), who believes that in the front rank Zeus was identified with Baal Shamen and Hera with Astarte partly because the association between Baal Hammon and Tanit and child sacrifice was considered to be unacceptable by the 'liberals' in Carthage. In his interpretation Tanit is associated with Artemis and Baal Hammon with Cronus. However, I see no reason not to place Baal Hammon and Tanit in the front rank, as they were by this period the most prominent deities in Carthage and there is no evidence for a 'liberal' group there.

31. Barré 1983, 64–86. However, there is some controversy as to whether in fact Iolaos in the treaty text corresponded with the Punic god Sid rather than Eshmoun.

32. Ibid., 12–14, 100–101; Huss 1986, 238.

33. *Contra* Bickerman 1985, 391–4.

34. Lancel 1999, 117.

35. Visonà 1998, 16–19.

36. Crawford 1985, 62.

37. Lancel 1999, 122–3.

38. Tiberius Sempronius Gracchus would be consul in 215 and 213 and Marcus Claudius Marcellus in 214, 210 and 208, while Quintus Fulvius Flaccus was elected in 212 and 209. Furthermore, all these men held pro-consular office throughout this period, meaning that they retained their military commands (Goldsworthy 2000, 226–8).

39. Livy 22.57.5–6, 23.11.1–6.

40. Ibid. 22.57.6.

41. Bellen 1985, 13–23.

42. Polybius 8.37; Livy 25.23.8–25.24.7; Plutarch *Marc.* 19.1.

43. Livy 25.26.1–15.

44. Ibid. 25.27.1–13.

45. Ibid. 25.28.1–25.30.12. For accounts of the siege of Syracuse see Lancel 1999, 124–7; Goldsworthy 2000, 260–68.

46. Eckstein 1987, 177–83.

47. Crawford 1985, 109–10; Visonà 1998, 19.

48. Walbank 1957–79, II: 100–101. It is thought that, whereas Polybius had read Silenus, Livy had taken his account from Coelius Antipater, who had read the original account (Lancel 1999, 128).

49. Polybius 8.24.1–8.34.13; Livy 25.7.10–25.11.20.

50. Two important Italian cities, Metapontum and Thurii, fell to the Carthaginians soon after (Livy 25.15.6–7), and then two heavy military defeats were inflicted on the Roman army: one at the hands of the Lucanian tribes, who had now defected to the Carthaginians, and another at Herdonea in Apulia (ibid. 25.15.20–25.16.24, 25.21.1–10).

51. Polybius 8.34.12; Livy 25.15.4–5.

52. Livy 26.1.2–4, 26.4.1–10.

53. Ibid. 26.5.1–26.7.10; Polybius 9.3.1–9.4.5.

54. Livy 26.9.1–13; Polybius 9.4.6–9.5.3.

55. Polybius 9.6.1–2.

56. Livy 26.10.5–8.

57. Ibid. 26.9.7–8. For a similar description, Polybius 9.6.3.

58. Livy 26.10.1–2.

59. Ibid. 26.10.3.

60. Polybius 9.6.6–9.7.1.

61. Livy 26.11.1–7.

62. Ibid. 26.9.10.

63. Solinus 1.14–15.

64. Dionysius 1.43; Briquel 2000, 126.

65. However, there was some divergence over whether the king or Heracles was his father.

66. Briquel 2000, 126–7. The Gauls were the only people who had sacked Rome, under their king Brennus in 387. Some time earlier a Gallic army under Bellovesus had been the first since Heracles' supposed crossing to traverse the Alps to attack Italy.

67. Livy 26.10.3.

68. Livy's stories, with their emphasis on divine intervention on the side of the Romans and the ownership of land in Latium where Hannibal was camped, perhaps acted as a reaction to this Carthaginian propaganda.

69. Pliny NH 34.40.

70. Livy 26.12.1–26.16.13.

71. See Cicero's character assassination of Capua in his speech On the Agrarian Law (2.76–97).

72. Livy 27.1.3–15.

73. Ibid. 26.38.1–26.39.23, 27.12.1–27.16.9.

74. Plutarch Fab. 22.6.

75. Frier 1979, 268–79. For the structure of the work see ibid., 255–84.

76. Ibid., 266–7.

77. Ibid., 284.

78. This is disputed by Gruen (1992, 231), who views the Annales as being aimed

exclusively at a Roman senatorial audience. Gruen argues that there is little evidence of its being read in Greece and little in the fragments that looks as if it was aimed at a Greek audience. These are strong statements to make when the fragments that we have are so limited. My own opinion is that it was also meant for a Greek audience, but one primarily in Italy and Sicily.

79. Frier 1979, 281; Badian 1958, 3.
80. Frier 1979, 236–46.
81. Polybius 1.14.1–3. On Fabius Pictor's career see Frier 1979, 233–6.
82. Frier 1979, 284; Badian 1958, 6.
83. Gruen 1992, 32–3.
84. Fabius Pictor Fr. 1.
85. This is found in a short description of his and several other Hellenistic historians' work found painted on a plastered wall of a gymnasium fittingly in Tauromenium, the home town of Timaeus (Manganaro 1974; Frier 1979, 230–31).
86. Livy 25.32.1–25.36.16.
87. Ibid. 26.17.1–26.19.9; Scullard 1970, 31.
88. I would argue more strongly than Walbank (1957–79, II: 135–6) does that Scipio encouraged these stories. It is, of course, impossible to ascertain whether he really believed them.
89. *De Vir. Illust.* 49. Birth = Aulus Gellius 6.1.6; Livy 26.19.7–8; Dio 16.57.39; Valerius Maximus 1.2.1. The temple visit = Livy 26.19.5. For a study of the association between Scipio and Alexander the Great see Tise 2002, 45–64.
90. An idea briefly considered by Walbank 1957–79, II: 55. For later Roman comparisons between Scipio and Hercules, see Ennius in Lactantius *Div. Inst.* 1.18; Cicero *Rep.* Fr. 3, Horace *Ode* 4.8.15. For a full discussion see Walbank 1957–79, II: 54–8.
91. Polybius 10.5.5.
92. Scullard 1970, 164–5.
93. Livy 26.19.8–9.
94. For a detailed discussion of this phenomenon see Scullard 1970, 53–7. For the theory that in fact the ebb was caused by the effects of localized wind see Walbank 1957–79, II: 65–6.
95. Livy 26.42.2–26.46.10; Polybius 10.8.1–10.15.11; Goldsworthy 2000, 271–7; Lazenby 1978, 134–40.
96. Polybius 10.2.12–13.
97. Ibid. 10.17.6–10.18.5. For the good relations that Scipio carefully developed with the Spanish tribal leadership see Eckstein 1987, 212–20.
98. Livy 26.47.1–10; Polybius 10.19.1–2.
99. Livy 27.17.1–27.19.1; Polybius 10.34.1–10.39.9; Goldsworthy 2000, 277–9.

100. Livy 27.19.3; Polybius 10.40.2–5.
101. Livy 27.19.4–5. See also Polybius 10.40.4–5.
102. Livy 27.19.1, 27.20.3–8.
103. Ibid. 28.12.13–28.15.16; Goldsworthy 2000, 279–85.
104. Polybius 11.20.1–11.24.11; Livy 28.16.10–13.
105. Livy 28.19.11–28.37.10; Polybius 11.25.1–11.33.7.
106. Livy 27.37.1–15.
107. For the development of Juno as an enemy of the Romans in early Roman epic see Feeney 1991, 116–17.
108. See Dumézil 1970, 680–82, for the Pyrgi inscription.
109. Huss 1985, 235–6.
110. Livy 27.26.7–27.27.14, 27.33.6–7.
111. Ibid. 27.28.1–13.
112. Ibid. 27.39.1–9; Polybius 11.2.1.
113. Livy 27.39.10–27.49.4; Polybius 11.1.1–11.2.2; Goldsworthy 2000, 238–43.
114. Livy 27.51.11–13.
115. Although he had minted currency for his army in Italy, now he had both the time and the necessity (there was little chance any more to acquire war booty) to produce considerable quantities of coinage for the general populace too – usually bearing the prancing horse and head of Tanit associated with Carthaginian coinage (Crawford 1985, 66–7).
116. Livy 28.38.1–11.
117. Ibid. 28.40.1–28.45.11.
118. Ibid. 28.45.13–28.46.1, 29.1.1–14.
119. Ibid. 28.46.7–13.
120. Polybius 15.1.10–11.
121. Livy 28.46.14.
122. Ibid. 28.5.1–28.8.14; Goldsworthy 2000, 253–60.
123. Livy 29.12.8–16.
124. Ibid. 28.45.12.
125. Ibid. 29.10.4–29.11.8, 29.14.5–14; Ovid *Fasti* 4.247–348.
126. Gruen 1990, 6–7.
127. Ibid., 17–19.

CHAPTER 13: THE LAST AGE OF HEROES

1. Livy 28.17.10–28.18.12; Appian 7.9.55.
2. Livy 29.23.2–29.24.2.
3. Ibid. 29.24.10–29.27.15.

4. Ibid. 29.28.1–29.29.3, 29.34.1–29.35.15.

5. Ibid. 30.3.1–30.12.4.

6. Ibid. 30.16.1–15; Eckstein 1987, 246–9.

7. Livy 30.22.2–3.

8. Polybius 15.1–4; Livy 30.22.1–30.23.8.

9. Livy 30.20.1–4.

10. Ibid. 30.19.

11. Ibid. 30.20.5–9; Appian 7.9.59.

12. Polybius 3.33; Livy 28.46.16. For Livy's treatment of Hannibal's association with the sanctuary at Cape Lacinium see Jaeger 2006.

13. Campus 2003b.

14. Livy 24.3.3–7, 28.46.16.

15. Cicero *Div.* 1.24.48. Cicero stated that his source was Coelius Antipater, who later he states used Silenus for his information on Hannibal.

16. For Livy's selectiveness in using Coelius and other sources so that the moral schema of his work remained unchallenged see Levene 1993, 68; Jaeger 2006, 408–9.

17. Wardle in Cicero, *Div. 1* (2006), 229.

18. Servius *Aen.* 3.552.

19. Brizzi 1983, 246–51; Lancel 1999, 155–6.

20. Livy 42.3.4.

21. Crawford 1985, 66.

22. Livy 30.24.5–30.25.8, 30.29.1. A papyrus fragment from Egypt (P. Rylands III 491) dated to sometime before 130 BC appears to give a very different account of the diplomatic wrangling that went on at this time. In particular it makes no mention of the seizure of the Roman cargo ships or the attempted ambush, and has therefore led to the suspicion that these events may have been exaggerated or even completely falsified by Polybius and perhaps other pro-Roman writers (Hoffman 1942). Eckstein (1987, 253–4) has nevertheless convincingly argued that on balance Polybius' account, although perhaps embellished to portray Scipio in as positive a light as possible, is probably to be trusted. See Hoyos 2001a for the suggestion that the papyrus fragment may in fact have been part of an epitome of the Roman historian Fabius Pictor.

23. Livy 30.29.1–4.

24. Ibid. 30.29.5–30.31.9.

25. Lazenby 1978, 221–7.

26. Livy 30.32.4–30.35.3.

27. Ibid. 30.35.4–30.37.6.

28. Ibid. 30.37.7–11, 30.42.11–30.43.9.

29. Cornelius Nepos *Hann.* 7.1–4; Aurelius Victor *De Caes.* 37.3.

30. Livy 33.46.1–33.47.5.

31. Lancel 1995, 404.

32. Livy 33.45.6–8. For general historical accounts of Rome's wars with Antiochus see Grainger 2002; Errington 1971, 156–83.

33. Livy 33.48.9–33.49.8.

34. Ibid. 34.60.4–6. The plan to attack Italy was most probably designed to persuade Antiochus to buy into Hannibal's grand strategy for a new war against Rome; see Grainger 2002, 143–5.

35. Grainger 2002, 143–5.

36. Livy 34.60.3–4.

37. See ibid. 36.7. The unrealistic nature of the proposals for attacking Italy has led some scholars to speculate that they were a later fabrication (Lancel 1999, 200; Grainger 2002, 223–4).

38. Grainger 2002, 270.

39. Livy 37.8.3, 37.23.7–37.24.13.

40. For Crete, see Cornelius Nepos *Hann.* 9.1; Justin 32.4.3–5. For Armenia see Strabo 11.14.6; Plutarch *Luc.* 31.4–5.

41. Livy 39.51.

42. Plutarch *Flam.* 21.5.

43. Ibid. 21.1.

44. De Beer 1969, 291.

45. Cornelius Nepos *Hann.* 13.2. For the outrages committed by the Romans, particularly against the Galatians, see Polybius 21.38; Livy 38.24.

46. Brizzi 1984b, 87–102; Momigliano 1977, 41.

47. For an account of the Scipios' legal difficulties see Scullard 1970, 219–24.

48. See Levick 1982, 57–8, for the wider context of the tension between individual ambition and equality within the Roman Senate after the Second Punic War.

CHAPTER 14: THE DESOLATION OF CARTHAGE

1. Livy 36.4.8.

2. Greene 1986, 109–16.

3. Livy 31.19.2.

4. Ibid. 36.4.5–9.

5. Ibid. 43.6.11.

6. Morel 1982, 1986; Lancel 1995, 406–8; Bechtold 2007, 53–4.

7. Bechtold 2007, 53–4, 66–7; Lancel 1995, 408–9. This view of Carthaginian renewed prosperity as built on agriculture and trade is confirmed by Appian (8.10.67).

8. Crawford 1985, 72.

9. Visonà 1998, 20–22; Crawford 1985, 136–8. Crawford argues that Carthage's last two issues of pure silver coinage were the result of its economic renaissance, whereas Visonà views them as the money that the Carthaginians had to mint to meet their war expenses at the outbreak of the Third Punic War.

10. Appian 8.14.96.

11. For an extensive study of this harbour see Hurst 1994, 15–51.

12. Lancel 1995, 181–2.

13. Ibid., 180.

14. Hurst & Stager 1978, 341–2.

15. Appian 8.10.68.

16. For the sanctuary at El Hofra, see Berthier & Charlier 1952–5, II.

17. Rakob 1979, 132–66. Others include the Medracen, the mausoleum of the Massylian royal dynasty, near Batna, and the funerary monument built for their Massaesylian counterparts at their capital of Siga.

18. However, it had to be heavily restored after being all but demolished during the nineteenth century by the British consul at Tunis, who was anxious to get his hands on the bilingual Libyan and Punic inscriptions (Lancel 1995, 307).

19. Ibid. 307–9.

20. Alexandropoulos 1992, 143–7; Visonà 1998, 22; Crawford 1985, 140.

21. Polybius 36.16.7–8; Appian 8.16.106.

22. Livy 43.3.5–7.

23. Leigh 2004, 28–37.

24. Arnott 1996, 284–7.

25. Franko 1996, 439–40, 442, 444. Many of the observations that follow are taken from this particular study.

26. Plautus *Poen.* 104–33.

27. Franko 1996, 429–30.

28. Plautus *Poen.* 975–81, 1008, 1121.

29. Gratwick 1971; Adams 2003, 204–5.

30. Plautus *Poen.* 1297–1306 (based on tr. Nixon, pp. 131–3).

31. Plautus *Poen.* 1312–14 (based on tr. Nixon, p. 133).

32. Franko 1996, 445.

33. Clark 2007, 96–7. For the same prejudices in Plautus' broader canon see Leigh 2004, 23–56.

34. Errington 1971, 202–12 (quote = 210); Harris 1979, 227–33.

35. Errington 1971, 260–62.

36. Diodorus 32.4.4–5.

37. Ibid. 32.5.

38. Polybius 31.21; Livy 34.62. I agree with Lancel (1995, 411) that Polybius' account and dating of this episode are to be favoured.

39. Polybius 31.21.7–8.

40. Livy 34.62.9–10.

41. Ibid. 34.62.11–14.

42. Lancel 1999, 178, for the ambiguity of the terms.

43. Appian 8.10.68–9.

44. For Cato's hounding of the Scipios see Scullard 1970, 186–9, 210–24.

45. Plutarch *Cat. Maj.* 26.2.

46. Appian 8.10.69.

47. Livy *Epitome* 47.15.

48. Pliny *NH* 15.74–5; Thürlemann-Rappers 1974; Little 1934.

49. Plutarch *Cat. Maj.* 26.2–3.

50. Ibid. 27.1.

51. Baronowski 1995, 27–8; Lancel 1995, 277–8. See also the comments of Pliny (*NH* 15.76) on how Carthage 'was destroyed by the testimony of one piece of fruit'.

52. Plutarch *Cat. Maj.* 26.2.

53. Diodorus 34/35.33.5.

54. Livy *Epitome* 48. For a discussion of the Scipio Nascia position see Vogel-Weidemann 1989, 83–4.

55. Polybius 36.2; Appian 8.10.69.

56. Appian 8.10.68.

57. Ibid. 8.10.70–73.

58. Baronowski 1995, 20–21; Diodorus 32.1; Livy *Epitome* 48; Zonaras 9.26.1–2.

59. Adcock 1946, 120.

60. Harris 1979, 54–104.

61. Plutarch *Mor.* 200.11.

62. Baronowski 1995, 28–9. For the attack on Carthage as related to the rise of Numidian power, and the forthcoming succession of Masinissa, see also Adcock 1946, 119; Vogel-Weidemann 1989, 85.

63. Appian 8.11.74.

64. *Oratorum Romanorum Fragmenta* 78–9.

65. *Rhetorica ad Herennium* 4.14.20; Quintilian *Or. Ed.* 9.3.31. See Baronowski 1995, 24–5, n. 22, for a discussion of its context.

66. See Cornell's (1996) convincing thesis that Brunt (1971, 269–77) seriously underestimates the damage that the war inflicted in southern Italy.

67. Scheid & Svenbro 1985, 334–8; Cicero *Nat. Gods* 2.61. For the suspected influence of Timaeus on Cato see Astin 1978, 228–9.

68. Aulus Gellius 10.1.10.

69. Appian 8.11.76.

70. Ibid. 8.11.78–8.12.81.

71. Lancel 1995, 413.

72. Appian 8.12.81–5.

73. Ibid. 8.12.86–9.

74. Ibid. 8.13.90–93.

75. Visonà 1998, 22.

76. Lancel 1995, 156–72.

77. Mezzolani 1999, 108–16.

78. Lancel 1995, 158–9.

79. Ibid., 415–19.

80. Appian 8.13.94–8.16.110.

81. For the early career of Scipio Aemilianus see Astin 1967, 12–61.

82. Ibid., 62–9.

83. Appian 8.16.110–8.18.117.

84. Polybius 36.8.7; Livy *Epitome* 49; Diodorus 32.9a; Plutarch *Cat. Maj.* 27.6.

85. Appian 8.18.117–21.

86. Ibid. 8.18.122–3.

87. Ibid. 8.18.124–6.

88. Polybius 38.7.1–38.8.10.

89. Ibid. 38.8.13.

90. Ibid. 38.8.7, 38.8.11–12.

91. Appian 8.18.118.

92. For a succinct account of Polybius' life see Champion 2004, 15–18.

93. Appian 8.19.132. For the Scipio quote, see Homer *Iliad* 6.448–9.

94. Harris 1979, 240–44, who sees it as yet another diplomatic incident largely provoked by the Roman Senate. Errington (1971, 236–40) lays much of the culpability on the inexperience and impetuosity of the new leadership of the Achaean League.

95. Eutropius 4.12.2; Diodorus 13.90; Cicero *Verr. Or.* 2.2.86–7, 2.4.72–83; Valerius Maximus 5.1.6.

96. Although there is no evidence of large-scale Roman appropriation of Carthaginian territory for over twenty years after the destruction of the city, it has been pointed out that an in-depth survey of the land began almost immediately: see Wightman 1980, 34–6.

97. Purcell 1995, 133.

98. The association is clearly made by later writers such as Cicero (*Agr.* 2.87), and Livy (26.34.9).

99. Purcell 1995, 134–5. For the half-heartedness of later Roman apologia for the fate of Carthage see ibid., 145–6.

100. Ibid., 143.

101. In many ways Cato would build on the historiographical foundations laid by Fabius Pictor. He would also follow the myth of Aeneas and the Trojan origins of the Romans (Gruen 1992, 33–4).

102. Astin 1978, 217.

103. Ibid., 227–31. Despite his legendary contempt for some aspects of Greek culture, Cato appears to have followed the model of Timaeus in this respect, although with one important difference. Whereas the Sicilian Greek had sought to place Italy and Rome within a wider central-Mediterranean context, Cato wished to highlight the centrality of Rome to Italy.

104. Astin 1978, 213–16.

105. Aulus Gellius 10.1.10.

106. Feeney 1991, 99.

107. Goldberg 1995, 52.

108. Gruen 1990, 92–106; Goldberg 1995, 32–6.

109. On the biographies and work of Naevius and Ennius see Gruen 1990, 106–22; Goldberg 1995, 114–22; Jocelyn 1972, 991–9.

110. Such is the intertwining of myth and recent events in the work of Naevius that it has been suggested that a famous section describing a battle between giants and heroes was in fact a description of a frieze on the eastern pediment of the temple of Zeus at Acragas in Sicily (Fraenkel 1954, 14–16; Feeney 1991, 118).

111. Wigodsky 1972, 29–34, for a discussion of what role Dido may have played in Naevius' epic. The fiction of Rome as an established and venerable central-Mediterranean power was further aided by the historical conceit of transforming Romulus, the founder of Rome, into the grandson of Aeneas: see Goldberg 1995, 95–6.

112. Feeney 1991, 109–10.

113. In Ennius this is confirmed by the testimony of Servius *Aen.* 1.281 (Feeney 1991, 126–7), whereas in Naevius it is merely suspected (ibid., 116–17). Certainly, Rome's increasing political and military involvement in Greece and the Hellenistic East during the late third and early decades of the second century BC had played its part, for the Roman senatorial elite sought to explain not only the extraordinary success that they had enjoyed, but also their relations with the wider Hellenic community (Gruen 1990, 121–3; Goldberg 1995, 56–7).

114. Feeney 1991, 109–10.

115. Goldberg 1995, 162, n. 5. Feeney (1991, 110 n. 58) also entertains the idea that Naevius wrote it after the end of the Second Punic War.

116. Jocelyn 1972, 997–9.

117. Ibid., 1006. Ennius, out of respect for Naevius, wrote very little about the First Punic War, even though he also appears to have been dismissive of Naevius' literary talents (ibid., 1013–14).

118. Aulus Gellius 6.12.7 (E. Warmington 1935, 270: 98–9); Paulus 439.7 (E. Warmington 1935, 282: 104–5); Festus Rufus Avienus 324.15 (E. Warmington 1935, 237: 84–5). Later writers would recognize Ennius as being strongly partisan, particularly in downplaying the disasters that were suffered by the Romans (Cicero *Pomp.* 25).

119. Servius *Aen.* 1.20. For Naevius and prophecy see Feeney 1991, 111–13.

120. Macrobius *Sat.* 3.7–9.

CHAPTER 15: PUNIC FAITH

1. Appian 8.20.134; Orosius 4.23.5–7; Florus 4.12. Other sources claim that Scipio completely demolished the city (Velleius Paterculus 1.12; Eutropius 4.12; *De Vir. Illustr.* 58; Zonaras 9.26–30). However, archaeologists have discovered that some of Carthage was certainly still standing after the onslaught (Lancel 1995, 428–30). For Hasdrubal's retirement see Eutropius 4.14.2; Zonaras 9.30; Orosius 4.23.7. For a general discussion of these references see Ridley 1986, 140–41.

2. Geus 1994, 150–53; Krings 1991, 665–6; Diogenes Laertius *Clitomachus*.

3. Appian 8.20.133. For other evidence of a form of curse being placed on the site to prevent its reoccupation see Cicero *Agr.* 1.2.5; Plutarch *C. Gracch.* 11; Appian *CW* 1.24; Tertullian *De Pallio* 1. On ploughing the ground and sowing it with salt see Modestinus, in Justinian *Dig.* 7.4.21; Stevens 1988, 39–40; Purcell 1995, 140–41. The surveying and reorganization of Carthage's old territory = Wightman 1980, 34–6.

4. Appian 8.20.134.

5. Bellen 1985.

6. Polybius 6.9, 6.57; Champion 2004, 94–8. Walbank (2002, 206–8), while acknowledging the Polybian view that Rome's decline was inevitable, in my view underplays the importance of this in Polybius' general historical thesis. Indeed, Cato's mention of Carthage's mixed constitution in his *Origines* might well reflect that this was a position that he held (Servius *Aen.* 4.682). It was certainly a view held in Stoic philosophical circles a little later (Champion 2004, 96–7).

7. Polybius 6.51–2; Champion 2004, 117–21; Eckstein 1989.

8. Pliny *NH* 35.23.

9. Lintott 1972.

10. Appian *CW* 1.3.24; Plutarch *C.Gracch.* 11; Orosius 5.12; Livy *Epitome* 60. In 111 an agrarian law was passed that made provision for the North African public land but forbade any resettlement of the site of Carthage.

11. Appian *CW* 1.26.

12. Plutarch *C. Gracch.* 17; Clark 2007, 133–4. Unsurprisingly, this building would long remain a symbol of the fragility of Roman political cohesiveness. It was an association that a talented political operator such as Marcus Cicero knew how to use to his own advantage. When in 63 BC, as consul, he chose the temple as the venue for the trials of those who had been involved in an unsuccessful *coup d'état*, Cicero, clearly wishing to distance his own actions from the bloody events that had prompted the temple's construction, was careful to emphasize that his own successful attempt to defend Roman concord had not ended in terrible bloodshed, a clear reference to Opimius' own purge. See Clark 2007, 172–6; Cicero *Cat.* 3.21; Sallust *Cat.* 9.2. Cicero would also use the temple as a place to launch a vitriolic attack on Mark Antony and the hypocrisy of his speech on concord after the murder of Caesar (Cicero *Phil.* 3.31, 5.20).

13. Tertullian *De Pallio* 1.

14. Cicero *Agr.* 1.5. The cynical use of the curse story is highlighted by the fact that elsewhere Cicero actually appears to discount any threat of religious sanction (*Agr.* 2.51). Harrison (1984, 96–101) argues that, even if the tradition of the curse was true, its impact was very minimal in terms of subsequent Roman senatorial decisions made about Carthage. A restored Carthage a threat to Rome = Cicero *Agr.* 2.33.90.

15. See in particular the historian Sallust (Gaius Sallustianus), *Cat.* 10.1–3 and *Jug.* 41.2; Lintott 1972.

16. Wiedemann 1993, 54–6; Sallust *Jug.* 79.1. A later Christian writer, Orosius (4.23), described Carthage as the necessary whetstone on which Rome's greatness could be kept sharp.

17. Piccaluga 1981; Freyburger 1986 for studies of *fides* during the Augustan period.

18. There is an extensive literature on the question of Augustan propaganda and the literary culture of the period. See Kennedy 1992; White 1991; Galinsky 1996 and more generally the essays in Woodman & West (eds.) 1984; A. Powell (ed.) 1992.

19. Clark 2007, 59. Atilius also vowed a temple to *Spes* (Hope).

20. Champion 2004, 163–6, 196 – *contra* Walbank (1985, 168–73), who sees the ordering of the opinions as evidence of Polybius' pro-Roman stance on this matter.

21. Polybius 36.9.9–11.

22. Livy *Epitome* 18; Eutropius 2.25; Florus 1.18.23–6; Orosius 4.10.1; Dio 11.26; Zonaras 8.15. A major pointer to the later invention of the tale is that it is not mentioned by Polybius.

23. Diodorus 24.12; Clark 2007, 61–2.

24. The story first appears in the work of the Roman historian Sempronius Tuditanus, who wrote in the last decades of the second century BC.

25. Horace *Ode* 3.5.41–52. For another hostile reference to the Punic threat and the challenge that it presented to traditional Roman virtue see Ovid *Fasti* 6.241–6.

26. Livy, who started writing his great history of Rome from its foundation to his own times in around 29 BC, was certainly not a slavish admirer of Augustus. However, he did recognize that the self-proclaimed restorer of the Roman Republic probably constituted Rome's best chance of lifting itself out of the morass into which it had fallen. On Livy's complex attitudes towards Augustus see Mineo 2006, 112–17, 134–5.

27. G. Miles 1995, 76–94.

28. Ibid., 78–9.

29. Mineo 2006, 293–335, 102–11. In fact Livy traced this decline back to Marcellus flooding Rome with the riches looted from Syracuse in 212.

30. The battle for universal hegemony = Livy 29.17.6.

31. Ibid. 21.4.9.

32. Ibid. 22.6.11–12.

33. Ibid. 30.30.27. The actual expression *fides Punica* occurs for the first time in surviving Latin literature in Sallust *Jug.* 108.3. However, as we have seen, Punic faithlessness was a very old trope that is found in both Greek and early Latin literature.

34. Livy 21.6.3–4, 21.19; Mineo 2006, 275.

35. Levene 1993, 43–7. For an example of Hannibal's temporary piety see Livy 21.21.9. For the impiety of Hannibal's attack on Saguntum see ibid. 21.40.11. Carthage's final defeat as divine retribution = ibid. 30.31.5, 30.42.20–21.

36. Cornelius Nepos *Hann.* 3.4.

37. Gransden 1976, 16. It was also surely no coincidence that in 29 BC Augustus should choose as his consular colleague Potitus Valerius Messalla, supposedly an ancestor of Potitius, chief priest of the Ara Maxima, and mentioned by Vergil in his rendering of the Cacus episode (*Aen.* 8.269, 281). See Galinsky 1966, 22, for the argument that the reference in the *Aeneid* to

a saviour arriving in Rome may have referred equally to Hercules or to Augustus. For a discussion of the use that Vergil later makes of the Hercules and Cacus incident to display the monstrosity of civil war see Morgan 1998, 175–85; Lyne 1987, 28–35.

38. Pliny *NH* 3.136–7.

39. Knapp 1986, 121–2.

40. Horace *Ode* 4.4. Part of this association was also clearly mediated through the young Augustus' close connection with Alexander the Great. As well as the clear borrowings from the Alexandrian iconography – especially in the earlier Augustan portraiture – it was said that such was his fascination with the Macedonian king that he had the corpse of Alexander embalmed and had his portrait on his signet ring (Suetonius *Aug.* 18.1.50; Zanker 1988, 145).

41. Horace *Ode* 4.4.

42. Appian 8.20.136.

43. Carthaginians = Harrison 1984, 99. Veterans = Wightman 1980, 36. For Caesarian clemency see Clark 2007, 84–5. A temple to *Clementia Caesaris* had been built in Rome in 45 BC (Galinsky 1996, 82, 84).

44. Wightman (1980, 37–8) probably overstates the case for the progress made in terms of the Caesarian colony.

45. Certainly this was how some later Roman commentators perceived this initiative: see Dio 43.50.4–5.

46. Wightman 1980, 38–9.

47. Gros 1990.

48. Rakob 2000.

49. Hadrumetum in Africa was named 'Concordia Iulia', and Apamea in Bithynia 'Colonia Iulia Concordia' (Clark 2007, 251).

50. Although the late-antique literary commentator Servius would write that 'the intention of Vergil is to imitate Homer and praise Augustus through his ancestors' (Servius *Aen.* 1, proem), Vergil's relationship with the regime that he wrote under was clearly more complex than that. For a critique of viewing Vergil as an Augustan propagandist see Thomas 2001, 25–54.

51. Morgan 1998, 181–2.

52. Vergil *Aen.* 1.12–19.

53. Feeney 1991, 131. The Punic wars are heavily alluded to but rarely directly mentioned in the *Aeneid*. One important exception is the procession of future Roman heroes which is pointed out to Aeneas in the underworld, which includes Cato, the Scipios, Fabius Cunctator and Marcellus (Vergil *Aen.* 6.841–859).

54. Vergil *Aen.* 4.96–9.

55. Ibid. 4.259–63.

56. Ibid. 4.230–36. Teucer, a legendary archer, fought alongside his more famous half-brother Ajax in the Trojan War. Ascanius, the son of Aeneas, was the first king of Alba Longa, the forerunner of Rome. Ausonia was a region of southern Italy

57. Ibid. 4.622–9.

58. Ibid. 12.826–8; Feeney 1991, 146–9.

59. Vergil *Aen.* 1.421–9.

60. Feeney 1991, 101–2; Harrison 1984, 96, for the dangers of seeing this piece as an accurate description of the Augustan settlement.

61. Vergil *Aen.* 4.305–10.

62. Starks 1999, 274–6.

63. Ibid. 267–71.

64. *KAI* 120; Adams 2003, 222; Birley 1988, 9–10. The same process can also be seen on the coinage that these cities produced during this period (Adams 2003, 207–9). For the same process in the Numidian city of Thugga see Rives 1995.

65. For the strong Punic influence on the region around Gades in the first and second centuries AD see Fear 1996, 225–50. On Sardinia see Van Dommelen 1998, 174–7. Africa = Millar 1968.

66. On Punic language see Jongeling & Kerr, 2005; Adams 2003, 209–30. On the suffetes see Lancel 1995, 430–31; Van Dommelen 1998, 174; Birley 1988, 16. Religious continuities = Lancel 1995, 432–6.

67. Van Dommelen 1998. It has even been recently argued that Pomponius Mela, the author of *De Chorographia*, a geographical work written in the first half of the first century BC, may have been of Hispano-Punic descent, and that his work was aimed at a population that was still heavily imbued with Punic culture, being designed as a reaction against the prevailing Romano-Greek mapping of the world (Batty 2000).

68. On the rise of Leptis Magna see Birley 1988, 8–22.

69. Silius Italicus *Pun.* 2.149–270, 4.4.72, 11.136ff., 2.475, 9.287–301; Rawlings 2005, 153–5.

70. Statius *Silv.* 4.6. See also Martial *Epigr.* 9.43 for similar speculations about Hannibal and the statuette.

71. Statius *Silv.* 4.5.45–6.

72. Birley 1988, 89–107.

73. Tzetzes *Chil.* 1.798–805; Birley 1988, 142.

74. R. Miles 2003.

75. 'Hannibalianus 2', in Jones, Martindale & Morris 1971, 407.

Bibliography

ABBREVIATIONS

AJP   *American Journal of Philology*
ANRW   *Aufstieg und Niedergang der römischen Welt*
AWE   *Ancient West and East*
BaBesch   *Bulletin antieke Beschavung*
BASOR   *Bulletin of the American Schools of Oriental Research*
CP   *Classical Philology*
CQ   *Classical Quarterly*
G&R   *Greece and Rome*
JHS   *Journal of Hellenic Studies*
JRS   *Journal of Roman Studies*
MAAR   *Memoirs of the American Academy in Rome*
MDAI(R)   *Mitteilungen des Deutschen Archäologischen Instituts Römische Abteilung*
OJA   *Oxford Journal of Archaeology*
RSA   *Rivista storica dell'antichità*

ANCIENT TEXTS

Aelian, *On the Characteristics of Animals*, ed. & tr. A. Scholfield. 3 vols. Cambridge, Mass., 1958–9

Ammianus Marcellinus, *History*, ed. & tr. J. Rolfe. 3 vols. Cambridge, Mass., 1935–9

Apollodorus, *The Library*, ed. & tr. J. Frazier. 2 vols. Cambridge, Mass., 1913

Appian, *Roman History [inc. Civil Wars]*, ed. & tr. H. White. 4 vols. Cambridge, Mass., 1912–13

Aristophanes, *Acharnians, Knights*, ed. & tr. B. Bickley Rogers. Cambridge, Mass., 1930

Aristotle, *The Art of Rhetoric*, ed. & tr. J. Freese. Cambridge, Mass., 1947

—— *Poetics*, ed. & tr. S. Halliwell. Cambridge, Mass., 1995

—— *Politics*, ed. & tr. H. Rackham. Cambridge, Mass., 1932

Arrian, *The Anabasis of Alexander*, ed. & tr. P. Brunt. 2 vols. Cambridge, Mass., 1976–83

—— *Indike*, ed. & French tr. P. Chantraine. Paris, 1927

Athenaeus, *The Deipnosophists [The Learned Banqueters]*, ed. & tr. S. Olson & C. Gulick. 7 vols. Cambridge, Mass., 1927–41

Aulus Gellius, *Attic Nights*, ed. & tr. J. Rolfe. 3 vols. Cambridge, Mass., 1961–8

Aurelius Victor, *De Caesaribus [On the Caesars]*, tr. H. Bird. Liverpool, 1994

Cicero, *On the Agarian Law against Rullus*, in *Pro Quinctio [etc.]*, ed. & tr. J. Freese. Cambridge, Mass., 1930

—— *On Behalf of Scaurus*, in *Pro Milone [etc.]*, ed. & tr. N. Watts. Cambridge, Mass., 1992

—— *On Catiline*, in *In Catinilam [etc.]*, ed. & tr. L. Lord. Cambridge, Mass., 1937

—— *On Divination Book 1*, ed. & tr. D. Wardle. Oxford, 2006

—— *Letters to Friends*, ed. & tr. D. Shackleton Bailey. 3 vols. Cambridge, Mass., 2001

—— *M. Tulli Ciceronis de imperio Cn. Pompei ad Quirites oratio [etc.] [On the Command of Gnaeus Pompey]*, ed. C. Macdonald. London, 1966

—— *On the Nature of the Gods*, in *De Natura Deorum [etc.]*, ed. & tr. H. Rackham. Cambridge, Mass., 1933

—— *Philippics*, ed. & tr. W. Kerr. Cambridge, Mass., 1969

—— *The Republic, Laws*, in *De Re Publica [etc.]*, ed. & tr. C. Keyes. Cambridge, Mass., 1994

—— *The Verrine Orations*, ed. & tr. L. Greenwood. 2 vols. Cambridge, Mass., 1928–35

CIS = *Corpus Inscriptionum Semiticarum. Pars Prima Inscriptiones Phoenicias Continens*. Paris, 1881

Cleitarchus, *Scholia Platonica*, ed. W. Greene. Chicago, 1981

Clement of Alexandria, *Stromateis [Miscellanies]*, ed. O. Stählin. 2 vols. Leipzig, 1906–9

Columella, *On Agriculture*, ed. & tr. E. Forster & E. Heffner. 3 vols. Cambridge, Mass., 1941–55

Cornelius Nepos, *Hamilcar, Hannibal, Timoleon*, in *Lives of Eminent Commanders*, ed. & tr. J. Rolfe. London, 1929

Corpus Inscriptionum Latinarum. Berlin, 1863–

Corpus Iuris Civilis, vol. 1, ed. T. Mommsen & P. Krueger. Berlin, 1954; ed. & tr. A. Watson. 4 vols. Rev. edn. Philadelphia, 2009

De Viris Illustribus [Deeds of Famous Men], ed. & tr. W. Sherwin. Norman, Okla., 1973

Dio Cassius, *Roman History*, ed. & tr. E. Cary. 9 vols. Cambridge, Mass., 1917–27

Diodorus Siculus, *The Library of History*, ed. & tr. C. Oldfather et al. 12 vols. Cambridge, Mass., 1960–67

Diogenes Laertius, *Clitomachus, Herillus*, in *Lives of the Eminent Philosophers*, ed. & tr. H. Hicks. 2 vols. Cambridge, Mass., 1925

Dionysius of Halicarnassus, *The Roman Antiquities*, ed. & tr. E. Cary. 7 vols. Cambridge, Mass., 1948–50

Epitome of the Philippic History of Pompeius Trogus, ed. & tr. J. Yardley & R. Develin. Atlanta, Ga., 1994

Eusebius of Caeserea, *Evangelica Praeparatio [Preparation for the Gospel]*, ed. H. Gifford. Oxford, 1903

Eutropius ('Eutrope'), *Abrégé d'histoire romaine [An Abridged History of Rome]*, ed. & French tr. J. Hellegouarch. Paris, 1999

Fabius Pictor, *Fragments*, in H. Beck (ed.), *Die frühen römischen Historiker. Band I: Von Fabius Pictor bis Cn. Gellius*. Darmstadt, 2001. 55–136

Festus Rufus Avienus, *Ora Maritima or Description of the Seacoast*, ed. & tr. J. Murphy. Chicago, 1999

FGH = F. Jacoby et al. (eds.), *Die Fragmente der griechischen Historiker*. Leiden/Berlin, 1923–

Florus, *Epitome of Roman History*, ed. & tr. E. Forster. Cambridge, Mass., 1984

Frontinus, *Stratagems, Aqueducts*, ed. & tr. C. Bennett. Cambridge, Mass., 1925

Hanno the Carthaginian, *Periplus or Circumnavigation [of Africa]*, ed. & tr. A. Oikonomides & M. Miller. Chicago, 1995

Herodotus, *The Persian Wars*, ed. & tr. A. Godley. 4 vols. Cambridge, Mass., 1920–25

Hesiod, *Theogony*, ed. & tr. G. Most. Cambridge, Mass., 2007

Homer, *Iliad*, ed. & tr. A. Murray & W. Wyatt. 2 vols. Cambridge, Mass., 1999

—— *Odyssey*, ed. & tr. A. Murray. 2 vols. Cambridge, Mass., 1984

Horace, *The Complete Odes and Epodes*, tr. D. West. Oxford, 2000

Iamblichus, *On the Pythagorean Life*, tr. G. Clark. Liverpool, 1989

ILLRP = *Inscriptiones Latinae Liberae Rei Publicae*, ed. H. Degrassi. 2 vols. Florence, 1957–63

Isocrates, *To Nicocles*, ed. & tr. S. Usher. Warminster, 1990

Josephus, *Jewish Antiquities*, ed. & tr. H. Thackeray et al. 13 vols. Cambridge, Mass., 1930–65

Justin, *Apologies*, ed. A. Blunt. Cambridge, 1911

Justinian, *Digest*, ed. T. Mommsen, tr. A. Watson. Philadelphia, 1985

KAI = H. Donner & W. Röllig (eds.), *Kanaanäische und aramäische Inschriften*, 3rd edn, 3 vols. Wiesbaden, 1964

Lactantius, *Divine Institutes*, ed. & tr. A. Bowen & P. Garnsey. Liverpool, 2003

Livy, *History of Rome [inc. Epitome]*, ed. & tr. B. Foster et al. 14 vols. Cambridge, Mass., 1961–7

Lydus, Ioannes Laurentius (John Lydus), *Liber de Mensibus [On the Months]*, ed. R. Wuensch. Leipzig, 1898

Lysias, *Olympiacus*, ed. & tr. W. Lamb. Cambridge, Mass., 2000

Macrobius, *The Saturnalia*, ed. & tr. P. Davies. New York, 1969

Martial, *Epigrams*, ed. & tr. D. Shackleton Bailey. 3 vols. Cambridge, Mass., 1993

Naevius, *Belli Punici Carminis Quae Supersunt [The Punic War]*, ed. W. Strzelecki. Leipzig, 1964

Nonnus, *Dionysiaca*, ed. & tr. W. Rouse. 3 vols. Cambridge, Mass., 1940

Onasander, *The General*, ed. & tr. Illinois Greek Club. Cambridge, Mass., 1923

Oratorum Romanorum Fragmenta Liberae Rei Publicae, ed. H. Malcovati. Paravia, 1955

Orosius ('Paul Orose'), *Histoires contre les païens [History against the Pagans]*, ed. & French tr. M.-P. Arnaud-Lindet. 3 vols. Paris, 1990–91

Ovid, *Fasti [The Festivals]*, ed. & tr. J. Frazer. Cambridge, Mass., 1931

Pausanias, *Description of Greece*, ed. & tr. W. Jones & R. Wycherley. 5 vols. Cambridge, Mass., 1918–35

PCG = Poetae Comici Graeci, ed. M. Kassel & C. Austin. Berlin, 1983–

Philostratus, *The Life of Apollonius of Tyana*, ed. & tr. C. Jones. 2 vols. Cambridge, Mass., 2005

Pindar, *Nemean Odes, Isthmian Odes, Fragments*, ed. & tr. W. Race. Cambridge, Mass., 1997

—— *Olympian Odes, Pythian Odes*, ed. & tr. W. Race. Cambridge, Mass., 1997

Plato, *Euthyphro, Apology, Crito, Phaedo, Phaedrus*, ed. & tr. H. North Fowler. Cambridge, Mass., 1914

—— *Laws*, ed. & tr. R. Bury. 2 vols. Cambridge, Mass., 4th repr. 1967–8

—— *Minos*, in *Charmides [etc.]*, ed. & tr. W. Lamb. Cambridge, Mass., 1927

Plautus, *Mostellaria [The Haunted House]*, in *The Merchant [etc.]*, ed. & tr. P. Nixon. Cambridge, Mass., 1924

—— *Poenulus* in *The Little Carthaginian [etc.]*, ed. & tr. P. Nixon. Cambridge, Mass., 1932

Pliny, *Natural History*, ed. & tr. H. Rackham, W. Jones & D. Eichholz. 10 vols. Cambridge, Mass., 1962–7

Plutarch, *De Herodoti malignitate [On the Malice of Herodotus]*, ed. W. Goodwin. Boston, 1878

—— *Moralia*, ed. & tr. F. Babitt et al. 15 vols. Cambridge, Mass., 1927–69

—— *Parallel Lives*, ed. & tr. B. Perrin. 11 vols. (*Camillus, Cato Major, Lucullus, Themistocles* – vol. 2. *Fabius Maximus, Pericles* – vol. 3. *Marcellus, Pompey* – vol. 5. *Timoleon* – vol. 6. *Alexander* – vol. 7. *Marius, Pyrrhus* – vol. 9. *Gaius Gracchus, Flaminius* – vol. 10.) Cambridge, Mass., 1914–26

Polyaenus, *Stratagems of War*, in E. Woelfflin (ed.), *Polyaeni Strategematon Libri Octo*. Leipzig, 1887; tr. P. Krentz & E. Wheeler. Chicago, 1994

Polybius, *The Histories*, ed. & tr. W. Paton. 6 vols. Cambridge, Mass., 1922–7

Pomponius Mela, *De Chorographia [Description of the World]*, tr. F. Romer. Ann Arbor, 1998

Porphyry, *On Abstinence from Killing Animals*, ed. J. Bouffartigue, M. Patillon & A.-P. Segonds. 3 vols. Paris, 1979–95; tr. G. Clark. Ithaca, NY, 2000

Pseudo-Aristotle, *Mirabiles Auscultationes*, in A. Westermann (ed.), *Paradoxographoi. Scriptores rerum Mirabilium Graeci*. Amsterdam, 1963

Pseudo-Scylax, *Periplus*, in J. Hudson & J. Gail (eds.), *Geographi Graeci Minores*. Paris, 1831

Quintilian, *The Orator's Education*, ed. & tr. D. Russell. 5 vols. Cambridge, Mass., 2001

Quintus Curtius Rufus, *History of Alexander the Great*, ed. & tr. J. Rolfe. 2 vols. Cambridge, Mass., 1946

Rhetorica ad Herennium, in (formerly attrib. Cicero) *Ad C. Herennium [etc.]*, ed. & tr. H. Caplan. Cambridge, Mass., 1954

Sallust, *War with Catiline, War with Jugurtha, Selections from the Histories*, ed. & tr. J. Rolfe. Cambridge, Mass., 1931

Sempronius Tuditanus, *Historicorum Romanorum Reliquiae*, ed. H. Peter. Leipzig, 1906, 1914. 143–7

Servius, *Commentary on Book Four of Virgil's Aeneid*, ed. & tr. C. McDonough, R. Prior & M. Stansbury, Wauconda, Ill., 2004

Silenus, in K. Müller (ed.), *Fragmenta Historicorum Graecorum*, vol. 3. Paris, 1849. 100–101

Silius Italicus, *Punica*, ed. & tr. J. Duff. 2 vols. Cambridge, Mass., 1934

Solinus, *Collectanea Rerum Memorabilium*, ed. T. Mommsen. Berlin, 1864

Statius, *Silvae*, ed. & tr. D. Shackleton Bailey. Cambridge, Mass., 2003

Stesichorus, *Geryoneis*, in *Greek Lyric*, vol. 3, ed. & tr. D. Campbell. Cambridge, Mass., 1991

Strabo, *Geography*, ed. & tr. H. Jones. 8 vols. Cambridge, Mass., 1917–67

Suetonius, *Augustus, Tiberius*, in Suetonius, *Lives of the Caesars*, vol. 1, ed. & tr. J. Rolfe. Cambridge, Mass., 1914

Tertullian, *De Pallio*, in *Opera*, pt 4, ed. V. Bulhart & P. Borleffs. Vienna, 1957

Theophrastus, in *Theophrastus of Eresus: Sources for his Life, Writings, Thought and Influence*, ed. W. Fortenbaugh et al. 2 vols. Leiden, 1992

Thucydides, *History of the Peloponnesian War*, ed. & tr. C. Smith. 4 vols. Cambridge, Mass., 1919–23

Tzetzes, *Chiliades*, ed. T. Pressel. Tübingen, 1851

Valerius Maximus ('Valère Maxime'), *Faits et dits mémorables [Memorable Deeds and Sayings]*, ed. & French tr. R. Combès. 2 vols. Paris, 1995–7

Varro, *On Agriculture*, ed. & tr. W. Hooper & H. Ash. Cambridge, Mass., 1934

—— *On the Latin Language*, ed. & tr. R. Kent. Cambridge, Mass., 1938

Vegetius, *Preface* in *Vegetius: Epitome of Military Science*, tr. N. Milner. 2nd edn. Liverpool, 1996

Velleius Paterculus, *Compendium of Roman History*, ed. & tr. F. Shipley. Cambridge, Mass., 1924

Vergil, *Aeneid*, ed. & tr. H. Rushton Fairclough. 2 vols. Cambridge, Mass., 1916–18

Vitruvius, *On Architecture*, ed. & tr. F. Granger. 2 vols. Cambridge, Mass., 1931–4

Zonaras, *Epitome of History*, ed. L. Dindorf. Leipzig, 1868–75; tr. T. Banchich & E. Lane. London, 2009

MODERN STUDIES

Abulafia, D. 2005 'Mediterraneans', in Harris (ed.) 2005, 64–93

Acquaro, E. 1983–4 'Su i "ritratti barcidi" delle monete puniche', *Ritratti storici dell'antichità*, 13–14: 83–6

—— 1984 *Arte e cultura punica in Sardegna*. Sassari

—— 1988 *Gli insediamenti fenici e punici in Italia*. Rome

—— 1989 'Les émissions du "soulèvement libyen": types, ethnies et rôles politiques', in Devijver & Lipiński (eds.) 1989, 137–44

Acquaro, E., Manfredi, L., & Cutroni Tusa, A. 1991 *Le monete puniche in Italia*. Rome

Acquaro, E., et al. (eds.) 1969 *Ricerche puniche ad Antas*. Rome

—— 1991 *Atti del II Congresso internazionale di studi fenici e punici: Roma, 9–14 novembre 1987*. Rome

Adams, J. 2003 *Bilingualism and the Latin Language*. Cambridge

Adcock, F. 1946 'Delenda est Carthago', *Cambridge Historical Journal*, 8: 117–28

Africa, W. 1970 'The One-Eyed Man against Rome: An Exercise in Euhemerism', *Historia*, 19: 528–38

Alexandropoulos, J. 1992 'Contributions à la définition des domaines monétaires numides et maurétaniens', in Hackens & Moucharte (eds.) 1992, 133–48

Amadasi Guzzo, M. 1969 'Note sul dio Sid', in Acquaro et al. (eds.) 1969, 95–104

—— 1988 'Dédicaces de femmes à Carthage', in Lipiński (ed.) 1988, 143–9

—— 1991 '"The Shadow Line". Reflexions sur l'introduction de l'alphabet en Grèce', in Baurain, Bonnet & Krings (eds.) 1991, 293–311

—— 1993 'Divinità fenicie a Tas-Silg, Malta, I dati epigrafici', *Journal of Mediterranean Studies*, 3: 205–14

—— 1995 'Mondes Étrusque et Italique', in Krings (ed.) 1995, 663–73

—— 2005a 'Cultes et épithètes de Milqart', *Transeuphratène*, 30: 9–18

—— 2005b 'Melqart nelle iscrizioni fenicie d'occidente', in Bernardini & Zucca (eds.) 2005, 45–52

Ameling, W. 1993 *Karthago. Studien zu Militär, Staat und Gesellschaft.* Munich

Anello, P. 1986 'Il trattato del 405/4 a.C. e la formazione della "eparchia" punica di Sicilia', *Kokalos*, 32: 115–79

Arnott, W. 1996 *Alexis: The Fragments: A Commentary.* Cambridge

Asheri, D. 1988 'Carthaginians and Greeks', in J. Boardman et al. (eds.) 1988 *The Cambridge Ancient History*, vol. 4: *Persia, Greece and the Western Mediterranean c.525 to 479 B.C.* Cambridge. 738–80

Astin, A. 1967 *Scipio Aemilianus.* Oxford

—— 1978 *Cato the Censor.* Oxford

Aubet, M. 2001 *The Phoenicians and the West: Politics, Colonies and Trade.* 2nd edn, tr. M. Turton. Cambridge

—— 2002a 'Notes on the Economy of the Phoenician Settlements in Southern Spain', in Bierling & Gitin 2002, 79–98

—— 2002b 'The Phoenician Impact on Tartessos: Spheres of Interaction', in Bierling & Gitin 2002, 225–40

—— 2006 'On the Organization of the Phoenician Colonial System in Iberia', in Riva & Vella 2006, 94–109

Badian, E. 1958 *Foreign Clientelae (264–70 B.C.).* Oxford

Bagnall, N. 1999 *The Punic Wars: Rome, Carthage and the Struggle for the Mediterranean.* London

Baldus, H. 1982 'Unerkannte Reflexe der römischen Nordafrika-Expedition von 256/5 v. Chr. in der karthagischen Münzprägung', *Chiron*, 12: 163ff.

—— 1988 'Zwei Deutungsvorschläge zur punischen Goldprägung im mittleren 3. Jh. v. Chr', *Chiron*, 18: 181–8

Balmuth, M., & Tykot, R. (eds.) 1998 *Sardinian and Aegean Chronology: Towards the Resolution of Relative and Absolute Dating in the Mediterranean*. Oxford

Barceló, P. 1988 *Karthago und die Iberische Halbinsel vor den Barkiden*. Bonn

—— 1991 'Mercenarios hispanos en los ejércitos cartagineses en Sicilia', in Acquaro et al. (eds.) 1991, 21–6

Barnett, R., & Mendleson, C. (eds.) 1987 *Tharros: A Catalogue of Material in the British Museum from Phoenician and other Tombs at Tharros, Sardinia*. London

Baronowski, D. 1995 'Polybius on the Causes of the Third Punic War', *CP*, 90, 1: 16–31

Barr, J. 1974 'Philo of Bylos and his "Phoenician History"', *Bulletin of the John Rylands University Library*, 57: 17–68

Barré, M. 1983 *The God List in the Treaty between Hannibal and Philip V of Macedonia: A Study in Light of the Ancient Near Eastern Treaty Tradition*. Baltimore

Barreca, F. 1969 'Lo scavi del tempio', in Acquaro et al. (eds.) 1969, 9–46

—— 1979 *La Sardegna fenicia e punica*. Sassari

—— 1985 'Il giuramento di Annibale. Considerazioni storico-religiose', in G. Sotgiu (ed.) 1985 *Studi in onore di Giovanni Lilliu per il suo settantesimo compleanno*. Cagliari. 72–81

—— 1986 *La civiltà fenicia-punica in Sardegna*. Sassari

—— 1987 'The City and the Site of Tharros', in Barnett & Mendleson (eds.) 1987. 25–6

Barruol, G. 1976 'La résistance des substrats préromains en Gaule méridionale', in *Editura academiei Romậne Les Belles Lettres*. Bucharest. 389–405

Bartoloni, P., et al. (eds.) 1983 *Atti del I Congresso internazionale di studi fenici e punici: Roma, 5–10 novembre 1979*. 3 vols. Rome

Basch, L. 1969 'Phoenician Oared Ships', *Mariner's Mirror*, 55: 139–62, 227–45

—— 1977 'Trières grecques, phéniciennes et égyptiennes', *JHS*, 97: 1–10

—— 1980 'Outriggers and Galleys', *Mariner's Mirror*, 66, 4: 359–66

Baslez, M. F., & Briquel Chatonnet, F. 1991 'De l'oral à l'écrit: le bilinguisme des Phéniciens en Grèce', in Baurain, Bonnet & Krings (eds.) 1991, 371–386

Batty, R. 2000 'Mela's Phoenician Geography', *JRS*, 90: 70–94

Baurain, C. 1988 'Le Rôle de Chypre dans la fondation de Carthage', in Lipiński (ed.) 1988, 15–28

Baurain, C., Bonnet, C., & Krings, V. (eds.) 1991 *Phoinikeia Grammata: Lire et écrire en Mediterranean.* Leuven

Bayet, J. 1926 *Les origines de l'Hercule romain.* Paris

Bearzot, C. 2002 'Filisto di Siracusa', in Vattuone (ed.) 2002, 91–136

Bechtold, B. 2007 'Nuovi dati basati sulla distribuzione di ceramiche campane e nordafricane/cartaginesi', *BaBesch*, 82, 1: 51–76

—— 2008 *Observations on the Amphora Repertoire of Middle Punic Carthage.* Ghent

Bellen, H. 1985 *Metus Gallicus, metus Punicus. Zum Furchtmotiv in der römischen Republik.* Mainz

Bello Jiménez, V. 2005 *Allende las columnas: la presencia cartaginesa en el Atlántico entre los siglos VI y III a.C.* Las Palmas

Benichou-Safar, H. 1982 *Les tombes puniques de Carthage: topographie, structures, inscriptions et rites funéraires.* Paris

—— 2004 *Le tophet de Salammbô à Carthage: essai de reconstitution.* Rome

Bernal, M. 1987 *Black Athena: The Afroasiatic Roots of Classical Civilization,* vol. 1. Piscataway

—— 1990 *Cadmean Letters: The Transmission of the Alphabet to the Aegean and Further West before 1400 B.C.* Grand Rapids

Bernardini, P. 1993 'La Sardegna e i fenici. Appunti sulla colonizzazione', *Rivista di studi fenici,* 21: 29–81

—— 2005 'Melqart di Sardò', in Bernardini & Zucca (eds.) 2005, 125–43

Bernardini, P., & Zucca, R. (eds.) 2005 *Il Mediterraneo di Herakles. Studi e ricerche.* Rome

Berthier, A., & Charlier, R. 1952–5 *Le Sanctuaire punique d'El Hofra à Constantine.* 2 vols. Paris

Bickerman, E. 1944 'An Oath of Hannibal', *Transactions of the American Philological Association,* 75: 87–102; repr. in Bickerman 1985, 257–72

—— 1952a 'Origines gentium', *CP*, 47: 65–81, 375–97

—— 1952b 'Hannibal's Covenant', *AJP*, 73: 1–23

—— 1985 *Religions and Politics in the Hellenistic and Roman Periods.* Como

Bierling, M., & Gitin, S. (eds.) 2002 *The Phoenicians in Spain: An Archaeological Review of the Eighth–Sixth Centuries B.C.E.* Winona Lake

Bikai, P. 1978 *The Pottery of Tyre.* Warminster

Birley, A. 1988 *Septimius Severus: The African Emperor.* 2nd edn. London

Bisi, A. M. 1988 'Chypre et les premiers temps de Carthage', in Lipiński (ed.) 1988, 29–42

—— 1991 'Les plus anciens objets inscrits en phénicien et en araméen retrouvées en Grèce: le typologie et leur rôle', in Baurain, Bonnet & Krings (eds.) 1991, 277–82

Blázquez Martinez, J. 1976 'Consideraciones historicas en torno a los supuestos retratos bárquidas en las monedas cartaginesas', *Numismatica*, 26: 138–43

Blázquez Martinez, J., & García-Gelabert Pérez, G. 1991 'Los Bàrquidas en la Peninsula Iberica', in Acquaro et al. (eds.) 1991, 27–50

Bloch, R. 1975 'Hannibal et les dieux de Rome', *Comptes rendus de l'Académie des Inscriptions et Belles-Lettres*, 119: 14–25

—— 1983 'L'alliance étrusco-punique de Pyrgi et la politique religieuse de la république romaine à l'égard de l'Etrurie et de Carthage', in Bartoloni et al. (eds.) 1983, 2: 397–400

Blomqvist, J. 1979 *The Date and Origin of the Greek Version of Hanno's Periplus*. Lund

Boardman, J. 1980, *The Greeks Overseas*. 3rd edn. London

—— 2002 'Al Mina: The Study of a Site', *AWE*, 1, 2: 315–33

—— 2004 'Copies of Pottery: By and For Whom?', in Lomas (ed.) 2004, 149–62

—— 2005 'Al Mina: Notes and Queries', *AWE*, 4, 2: 278–91

—— 2006 'Early Euboean Settlements in the Carthage Area', *OJA*, 25, 2: 195–200

Bondì, S. F. 1995a 'Les Institutions, l'organisation politique et administrative', in Krings (ed.) 1995, 290–302

—— 1995b 'La Société', in Krings (ed.) 1995, 345–53

—— 1999 'Carthage, Italy and the Vth Century Problem', in Pisano (ed.) 1999, 39–48

Bonnet, C. 1986 'Le culte de Melqart à Carthage. Un cas de conservatisme religieux', in Bonnet, Lipiński & Marchetti (eds.) 1986, 209–22

—— 1988 *Melqart: cultes et mythes de l'Héraclès tyrien en Méditerranée*. Leuven

—— 2005 'Melqart in occidente: percorsi di appropriazione e di culturazione', in Bernardini & Zucca (eds.) 2005, 17–28

Bonnet, C., Lipiński, E., & Marchetti, P. (eds.) 1986 *Religio Phoenicia*. Namur

Bonzani, R. M. 1992 'Territorial Boundaries, Buffer Zones and Sociopolitical Complexity: A Case Study of the Nuraghi on Sardinia', in Tykot & Andrews (eds.) 1992, 210–20

Bordreuil, P., & Ferjaoui, A. 1988 'A propos des "fils de Tyr" et des "fils de Carthage"', in Lipiński (ed.) 1988, 137–42

Bradley, G. 2005 'The Cult of Hercules in Central Italy', in Rawlings & Bowden (eds.) 2005, 129–51

Braun, T. 2004 'Hecataeus' Knowledge of the Western Mediterranean', in Lomas (ed.) 2004, 287–347

Brecht, B. 1951 Letter eventually published in *Offener Brief an die deutschen Künstler und Schriftsteller*. Frankfurt, 1997

Breglia Pulci Doria, L. 2005 'La Sardegna arcaica e la presenza greca: nuove riflessioni sulla tradizione letteraria', in Bernardini & Zucca (eds.) 2005, 61–86

Briese, C., & Docter, R. 1992 'Der phönizische Skyphos: Adaption einer griechischen Trinkschale', *Madrider Mitteilungen*, 33: 25–69

Briquel, D. 2000 'La propagande d'Hannibal au début de la deuxième guerre punique: remarques sur les fragments de Silènos de Kalèaktè', in *Actas del IV Congreso Internacional de Estudios Fenicios y Púnicos, Cádiz, 2 al 6 de octubre de 1995*, vol. 1. Cadiz. 123–7

—— 2003 'Hannibal sur les pas d'Herakles: le voyage mythologique et son utilisation dans l'histoire', in H. Duchene (ed.) 2003 *Voyageurs et antiquité classique*. Dijon. 51–60

—— 2004 'Sur un fragment de Silènos de Kalèactè (le songe d'Hannibal, F Gr Hist 175, F 8). À propos d'un article récent', *Ktêma*, 29: 145–57

Brixhe, C. 1991 'De la phonologie à l'écriture: quelques aspects de l'adaptation de l'alphabet cananéen au grec', in Baurain, Bonnet & Krings (eds.) 1991, 313–56

Brizzi, G. 1983 'Ancora su Annibale e l'Ellenismo: la fondazione di Artaxata l'iscrizione di Era Lacinia', in Bartoloni et al. (eds.) 1983, 1: 243–51

—— 1984a *Annibale, strategia e immagine*. Perugia. 1984

—— 1984b *Studi di storia annibalica*. Faenza

—— 1991 'Gli studi annibalici', in Acquaro et al. (eds.) 1991, 59–65

—— 1995 'L'Armée et la guerre', in Krings (ed.) 1995, 303–15

—— 2000 *Annibale*. Rome

Broughton, T. 1951–6 *The Magistrates of the Roman Republic*. 2 vols. New York

Brunt, P. 1971 *Italian Manpower 225 BC–AD 14*. Oxford

Bunnens, G. 1979 *L'expansion phénicienne en Méditerranée*. Brussels

—— 1986 'Aspects religieux de l'expansion phénicienne', in Bonnet, Lipiński & Marchetti (eds.) 1986, 119–25

Burkert, W. 1992 *The Orientalizing Revolution: Near Eastern Influence on Greek Culture in the Early Archaic Age*, tr. M. Pinder & W. Burkert. Cambridge, Mass.

Byron, George Gordon, Lord 1988 *Don Juan*, ed. T. Steffan. London

Camps, G. 1979 'Les Numides et la civilisation punique', *Antiquités Africaines*, 14: 43–53

Campus, A. 2001 'Considerazioni su Melqart, Annibale e la Sardegna', *La Parola del passato: rivista di studi antichi*, 56: 419–435

—— 2003a 'Silio Italico, Punica, II, 391–456: Lo scudo di Annibale', in *Atti della Accademia nazionale dei Lincei. Rendiconti Classe di scienze morali storiche e filologiche*. Rome

—— 2003b 'Annibale ed Hera Lacinia', *La Parola del passato: rivista di studi antichi*, 58: 292–308

—— 2005 'Herakles, Alessandro, Annibale', in Bernardini & Zucca (eds.) 2005, 200–221

—— 2006 'Circolazione di modelli e di artigiani in età punica', *Africa Romana*, 16, 1: 185–96

Capomacchia, A. 1991 'L'avidità dei Fenici', in Acquaro et al. (eds.) 1991, 266–9

—— 1995 'Le anfore di Hannibal', in *Actes du troisième congrès international des études phéniciennes et puniques, Tunis 11–16 Novembre 1991*. Tunis. 249–53

—— 2000 'Hannibal e il prodigio', in *Actas del IV Congreso Internacional de Estudios Fenicios y Púnicos, Cádiz, 2 al 6 de octubre de 1995*, vol. 2. Cadiz. 569–71

Carradice, I. A., & La Niece, S. 1988 'The Libyan War and Coinage: A New Hoard and the Evidence of Metal Analysis', *Numismatic Chronicle*, 148: 33–52

Caruso, E. 2003 'Lilibeo–Marsala: le fortificazioni puniche e medievali', in *Atti di Quartet Giornate Internazionale di Studi sull'area Elima*. Pisa. 173–226

Casquero, M. 2002 'El exótico culto a Hércules en el Ara Máxima', in *La Revista de Estudios Latinos*, 2: 65–106

Casson, L. 1971 *Ships and Seamanship in the Ancient World*. Princeton

Chadwick, J. 1976 *The Mycenaean World*. Cambridge

Champion, C. 2004 *Cultural Politics in Polybius' Histories*. Berkeley

Charles, M., & Rhodan, P. 2007 '*Magister Elephantorum*: A Reappraisal of Hannibal's Use of Elephants', *Classical World*, 100, 4: 363–89

Chávez Tristán, F., & Ceballos, M. 1992 'L'influence phénico punique sur l'iconographie des frappes locales de la Peninsule Ibérique', in Hackens & Moucharte (eds.) 1992, 167–94

Chelbi, F. 1992. *Céramique à vernis noir de Carthage*. Tunis

Cipriani, G. 1984 *L'epifania di Annibale. Saggio introduttivo a Livio Annales, XXI*. Bari

—— 1986 'Plutarco, Annibale e lo statuto del comandante guercio e fraudolento', in *Annali della facoltà di lettere e filosofia*, 29: 19–38

Clark, A. 2007 *Divine Qualities: Cult and Community in Republican Rome*. Oxford

Clifford, R. 1990 'Phoenician Religion', *BASOR*, 279: 55–64

Coarelli, F. 1988 *Il foro Boario dalle origini alla fine della Repubblica*. Rome

Coldstream, J. 1982 'Greeks and Phoenicians in the Aegean', in Niemeyer (ed.) 1982, 261–72

—— 2003 *Geometric Greece*, 2nd edn. London

Coldstream, J., & Bikai, P. 1988 'Early Greek Pottery in Tyre and Cyprus: Some Preliminary Comparisons', *Report of the Department of Antiquities of Cyprus*, 1988/2: 35–44

Colonna, G. 1987 'Etruria e Lazio nell'eta dei Tarquinii', in M. Cristofani (ed.) 1987 *Etruria e Lazio Arcaico*. Rome. 55–66

—— 1989–90 'Le iscrizioni votive etrusche', *Scienze dell'antichità*, 3–4: 875–903

Cornell, T. 1995 *The Beginnings of Rome: Italy and Rome from the Bronze Age to the Punic Wars, c.1000–264 BC*. London

—— 1996 'Hannibal's Legacy: The Effects of the Hannibalic War on Italy', in Cornell, Rankov & Sabin (eds.) 1996, 97–117

Cornell, T., Rankov, B., & Sabin, P. (eds.) 1996 *The Second Punic War: A Reappraisal*. London

Crawford, M. 1985 *Coinage and Money under the Roman Republic: Italy and the Mediterranean Economy*. London

—— 1993 *The Roman Republic*. 2nd edn. Cambridge, Mass.

Cristofani, M. 1979 'Recent Advances in Etruscan Epigraphy and Language', in D. Ridgway & F. Ridgway (eds.) 1979 *Italy before the Romans*. London. 373–412

Cross, F. 1972a 'The Stele Dedicated to Melcarth by Ben-Hadad', *BASOR*, 205: 36–42

—— 1972b 'An Interpretation of the Nora Stone', *BASOR*, 208: 13–19

—— 1980 'Newly Found Inscriptions in Old Canaanite and Early Phoenician Scripts', *BASOR*, 238: 1–20

—— 1987 'The Oldest Phoenician Inscription from Sardinia: The Fragmentary Stele from Nora', in D. Golomb (ed.) 1987 *Semitic and Egyptian Studies Presented to Thomas O. Lambdin*. Winona Lake. 65–74

Cullingford, E. 1996 'British Romans and Irish Carthaginians: Anticolonial Metaphor in Heaney, Friel, and McGuinness', *Proceedings of the Modern Languages Association of America*, 111, 2: 222–39

Cutroni Tusa, A. 1993 *La circolazione in Sicilia*. Naples

D'Arco, I. 2002 'Il sogno premonitore de Annibale e il pericolo dell'Alpi', *Quaderni di storia*, 55: 147–62

Dahmen, K. 2007 *The Legend of Alexander the Great on Greek and Roman Coins*. London

Daly, G. 2002 *Cannae: The Experience of Battle in the Second Punic War*. London

David, J. 1996 *The Roman Conquest of Italy*. Oxford

De Angelis, F. 2003 *Megara Hyblaia and Selinous: The Development of Two Greek City-States in Archaic Sicily*. Oxford

De Angelis, F., & Garstad, B. 2006 'Euhemerus in Context', *Classical Antiquity*, 25: 211–42

De Beer, G. 1969 *Hannibal: The Struggle for Power in the Mediterranean*. London

Debergh, J. 1973, 'La libation à caractère funéraire à carthage: état de la question et direction de la recherché', *Revue Belge de Philologie et d'Histoire*, 51: 241–2

Demerliac, J.-G., & Meirat, J. 1983 *Hannon et l'Empire Punique*. Paris

Dench, E. 2003 'Beyond Greeks and Barbarians: Italy and Sicily in the Hellenistic Age', in A. Erskine (ed.) 2003 *A Companion to the Hellenistic World*. Oxford. 294–309

Desanges, J. 1978 *Recherches sur l'activité des Mediterranéens aux confins de l'Afrique*. Rome

Devijver, H., & Lipiński, E. (eds.) 1989 *Punic Wars*, Leuven

Devillers, O., & Krings, V. 1994 'Autour de l'agronome Magon', *Africa Romana*, 11: 489–516

Di Mario, F. 2005 *Ardea, il deposito votivo di Casarinaccio*. Rome

Di Stefano, C. 1982–3 'I Cartaginesi in Sicilia all'epoca dei due Dionisi. Lilibeo', *Kokalos*, 28–9: 156–65

—— 1993 *Lilibeo punica*. Marsala

Di Stefano, C., et al. 1998 *Palermo punica*. Palermo

Di Vita, A. 1969 'Le date di fondazione di Leptis e di Sabratha sulla base dell'indagine archeologica e l'eparchia cartaginese d'Africa', in J. Bibauw (ed.) 1969 *Hommages à Marcel Renard*, vol. 3. Brussels. 196–202

—— 1976: 'Il mausoleo punico-ellenistico B di Sabratha', *MDAI(R)*, 83, 1: 273–85

Diana, B. 1987 'Annibale e il passaggio degli Appennini', *Aevum*, 61: 108–12

Díes Cusí, E. 1995 'Architecture funéraire', in Krings (ed.) 1995, 411–25

Dion, R. 1962 'La voie héracléenne et l'itinéraire transalpin d'Hannibal', in *Mélanges à A. Grenier*. Brussels. 527–43

—— 1977 *Aspects politiques de la géographie antique*. Paris

Docter, R. 2000a 'East Greek Fine Wares and Transport Amphorae of the 8th–5th Century B.C. from Carthage and Toscanos', in P. Cabrera Bonet &

M. Santos Retolaza (eds.) 2000 *Ceràmiques jonies d'època arcaica: centres de producció i comercialització al Mediterrani occidental. Actes de la Taula Rodona celebrada a Empúries, els dies 26 al 28 de maig de 1999*. Barcelona. 63–88

—— 2000b 'Carthage and the Tyrrhenian in the 8th and 7th Centuries B.C. Central Italian Transport Amphorae and Fine Wares Found under the Decumanus Maximus', in M. Aubet & M. Barthélemy (eds.) 2000 *Actas del IV Congreso Internacional de Estudios Fenicios y Púnicos, Cádiz, 2 al 6 de octubre de 1995*, vol. 1. Cadiz. 329–38

Docter, R. et al. 2003 'Carthage Bir Massouda: Preliminary Report on the First Bilateral Excavations of Ghent University and the Institut National du Patrimoine (2002–2003)', *BaBesch*, 78: 43–70

—— 2006 'Carthage Bir Massouda: Second Preliminary Report on the Bilateral Excavations of Ghent University and the Institut National du Patrimoine (2003–2004)', *BaBesch*, 81: 37–89

Dominguez, A. 2002 'Greeks in Iberia: Colonialism without Colonization', in Lyons & Papadopoulos (eds.) 2002, 65–95

Dorey, T., & Dudley, D. 1971 *Rome against Carthage*. London

D'Oriano, R., & Oggiano, I. 2005 'Iolao ecista di Olbia: le evidenze archeologiche tra VIII e VI secolo a.C.', in Bernardini & Zucca (eds.) 2005, 169–98

Drews, R. 1979 'Phoenicians, Carthage and the Spartan Eunomia', *AJP*, 100: 45–58

Dubuisson, M. 1983 'L'image du carthaginois dans la littérature latine', in E. Gubel, E. Lipiński & B. Servais-Soyez (eds.) 1983 *Redt Tyrus = Sauvons Tyr. Histoire Phénicienne = Fenicische Geschiedenis*. Leuven. 159–67

Dumézil, G. 1970 *Archaic Roman Religion*. Chicago

Dussaud, R. 1935 'La notion d'âme chez les israélites et les phéniciens', *Syria*, 16: 267–77

Eckstein, A. M. 1987 *Senate and General: Individual Decision-Making and Roman Foreign Relations 264–194 B.C.* Berkeley

—— 1989 'Hannibal at New Carthage: Polybius 3.15 and the Power of Irrationality', *CP*, 84: 1–15

—— 2006 *Mediterranean Anarchy, Interstate War, and the Rise of Rome*. Berkeley

Einarson, B. 1967 'Notes on the Development of the Greek Alphabet', *CP*, 62, 1: 1–24

Edwards, M. 1991 'Philo or Sanchuniathon? A Phoenicean Cosmogony', *CQ*, 41, 1: 213–20

Errington, R. 1970 'Rome and Spain before the Second Punic War', *Latomus*, 29, 1: 25–57

—— 1971 *The Dawn of Empire: Rome's Rise to World Power*. London

Erskine, A. 1993 'Hannibal and the Freedom of the Italians', *Hermes*, 121: 58–62

Fabre, P. 1981 *Les Grecs et la connaissance de l'Occident*. Lille

Falsone, G. 1995 'Sicile', in Krings (ed.) 1995, 674–97

Fantar, M. 1969 'Les Inscriptions', in Acquaro et al. (eds.) 1969, 47–93

—— 1979 *Eschatologie phénicienne punique*. Tunis

—— 1984 'A Gammarth avant la conquête romaine', *Histoire et archéologie de L'Afrique du Nord (Actes 1 Colloque I International Perpignan 1981)*. Paris. 3–19

—— 1998 'De l'agriculture à Carthage', *Africa Romana*, 12: 113–21

Fariselli, A. 1999 'The Impact of Military Preparations on the Economy of the Carthaginian State', in Pisano (ed.) 1999, 59–68

Fear, A. 1996 *Rome and Baetica: Urbanization in Southern Spain c.50 BC–AD 150*. Oxford

Feeney, D. 1991 *The Gods in Epic: Poets and Critics of the Classical Tradition*. Oxford

—— 2007 *Caesar's Calendar: Ancient Time and the Beginnings of History*. Berkeley

Fentress, E., & Docter, R. 2008 'North Africa: Rural Settlement and Agricultural Production', in P. Van Dommelen & C. Gómez Bellard (eds.) 2008 *Rural Landscapes of the Punic World*. London, 101–28

Ferron, J. J. 1966 'Les relations de Carthage avec l'Etrurie', *Latomus*, 25: 689–709

—— 1972 'Un traité d'alliance entre Caere et Carthage contemporain des derniers temps de la royauté étrusque à Rome ou l'évènement commémoré par la quasi-bilingue de Pyrgi', *ANRW*, 1, 1: 189–216

Février, J. 1965 'L'inscription punique de Pyrgi', *Comptes rendus de l'Académie des Inscriptions et Belles-Lettres*, 109: 9–18

Fiorentini, G. 1995 *Monte Adranone*. Rome

Fletcher, R. 2004 'Sidonians, Tyrians and Greeks in the Mediterranean: The Evidence from Egyptianising Amulets', *AWE*, 3, 1: 51–77

—— 2006 'The Cultural Biography of a Phoenician Mushroom-Lipped Jug', *OJA*, 25, 2: 173–94

Foley, J. 1900 *The Jeffersonian Cyclopedia*. London

Forni, G. 1992 'Riflessioni sulla presenza di Annibale nell'italia meridionale e sulle conseguenze', in Marangio (ed.) 1992, 9–23

Forsythe, G. 2005 *A Critical History of Early Rome from Prehistory to the First Punic War*. Berkeley

Foulon, E. 2003 'Mercure Aletes apparent en songe a Hannibal', in P. Defosse (ed.) 2003 *Hommages à C. Deroux*, vol. 4. Brussels. 366–77

Fox, M. 1993 'History and Rhetoric in Dionysius of Halicarnassus', *JRS*, 83: 31–47

Fraenkel, E. 1954 'The Giants in the Poem of Naevius', *JRS*, 44: 14–17

Franke, P. 1989 'Pyrrhus', in Walbank et al. (eds.) 1989, 456–85

Frankenstein, S. 1979 'The Phoenicians in the Far West: A Function of Neo-Assyrian Imperialism', in Larsen (ed.) 1979, 263–94

Franko, G. 1994 'The Use of *Poenus* and *Carthaginiensis* in Early Latin Literature', *CP*, 89: 153–8

—— 1996 'The Characterization of Hanno in Plautus' *Poenulus*', *AJP*, 117, 3: 425–52

Freyburger, G. 1986 *Fides. Étude sémantique et religieuse depuis les origines jusqu'à l'époque augustéenne*. Paris

Frier, B. 1979 *Libri Annales Pontificum Maximorum: The Origins of the Annalistic Tradition*. Rome

Fronda, M. 2007 'Hegemony and Rivalry: The Revolt of Capua Revisited', *Phoenix*, 61: 83–108

Frost, H. 1989 'The Prefabricated Punic Warship', in Devijver & Lipiński (eds.) 1989, 127–35

Fucecchi, M. 1990 'Empietà e titanismo nella rappresentazione siliana di Annibale', *Orpheus*, 11: 21

Galinsky, K. 1966 'The Hercules–Cacus episode in *Aeneid* VIII', *AJP*, 87: 18–51

—— 1969 *Aeneas, Sicily, and Rome*. Princeton

—— 1996 *Augustan Culture*. Princeton

Galvagno, E. 2006 'Sicelioti in Africa nel III secolo a.C.', *Africa Romana*, 16, 4: 249–58

Garbini, G. 1983 'Iscrizioni funerarie puniche in Sardegna', *Annali dell'Instituto Universitario Orientale di Napoli*, 42: 463–6

—— 1999 'The Phoenicians and Others', in Pisano (ed.) 1999, 9–14

Garnand, B. 2001 'From Infant Sacrifice to the ABC's: Ancient Phoenicians and Modern Identities', *Stanford Journal of Archaeology*, 1: http://www.stanford.edu/dept/archaeology/journal/newdraft/garnand/index.html

Geus, R. 1994 *Prosopographie der literarisch Bezeugten Karthager*. Leuven

Gharbi, M. 2004 'Frontières et échanges en Sardaigne à l'époque punique', *Africa Romana*, 15, 1: 791–804

Giangiulio, M. 1983 'Greci e non-Greci in Sicilia alla luce dei culti e delle leggende di Eracle', in *Modes de contacts et processus de transformation dans les sociétés anciennes. Actes du colloque de Cortone (24–30 mai 1981)*. Pisa. 785–845

Gianto, A. 1987 'Some Notes on the Mulk Inscription from Nebi Yunisc (RES 367)', *Biblica*, 68: 397–401

Giardino, C. 1992 'Nuragic Sardinia and the Mediterranean: Metallurgy and Maritime Traffic', in Tykot & Andrews (eds.) 1992, 304–16

Gibson, J. 1982 *Textbook of Syrian Semitic Inscriptions III. Phoenician Inscriptions*. Oxford

Goldberg, S. 1995 *Epic in Republican Rome*. Oxford

Goldsworthy, A. 2000 *The Punic Wars*. London

Gómez Bellard, C. 1990 *La colonizacion fenicia de la Isla de Ibiza*. Madrid

González de Canales, F., Serrano, L., & Llompart, J. 2006 'The Pre-Colonial Phoenician Emporium of Huelva ca. 900–770 BC', *BaBesch*, 81: 13–29

Grainger, J. 2002 *The Roman War of Antiochus the Great*. Leiden

Gransden, K. 1976 *Aeneid VIII*. Cambridge

Gras, M. 1985, *Trafics tyrrhéniens archaïques*. Rome

Gras, M., Rouillard, P., & Teixidor, P. 1991 'The Phoenicians and Death', *Berytus*, 39: 127–76

—— 1995 *L'Univers phénicien*, 2nd edn. Paris

Gratwick, A. 1971 'Hanno's Punic Speech in the *Poenulus* of Plautus', *Hermes*, 99: 25–45

Grayson, A. 1991 *Assyrian Rulers of the Early 1st Millennium BC*, vol 1. Toronto

Green, A. 1982 *Flaubert and the Historical Novel: 'Salammbô' Reassessed*. Cambridge

Green, P. 1990 *Alexander to Actium: The Hellenistic Age*. London

Greene, J. 1983 'Carthage Survey', in *British Archaeological Reports, International Series*, 155: 130–38

—— 1986 'The Carthaginian Countryside: Archaeological Reconnaissance in the Hinterland of Ancient Carthage'. Unpublished PhD dissertation, University of Chicago

—— 2000 'The Beginnings of Grape Cultivation and Wine Production in Phoenician/Punic North Africa', in P. McGovern, S. Fleming & S. Katz (eds.) 2000 *The Origins and Ancient History of Wine*. London. 311–22

Gros, P. 1990 'Le premier urbanisme de la colonia Julia Carthago: mythes et réalités d'une fondation césaro-augustéenne', *Collection de l'Ecole française de Rome*, 134: 547–73

—— 1992 'Colline de Byrsa: les vestiges romains', in *Pour sauver Carthage. Exploration et conservation de la cité punique, romaine et byzantine*. Paris. 99–103

Grottanelli, C. 1973 'Melqart e Sid fra. Egitto, Libia e Sardegna', *Rivista di studi fenici*, 1: 153–64

Gruen, E. 1984 *The Hellenistic World and the Coming of Rome*. 2 vols. Berkeley

—— 1990 *Studies in Greek Culture and Roman Policy*. Leiden

—— 1992 *Culture and National Identity in Republican Rome*. Ithaca, NY

Gsell, S. 1924 *Histoire ancienne de l'Afrique du nord*. Paris

Gubel, E. 2006 'Notes on the Phoenician Component of the Orientalizing Horizon', in Riva & Vella 2006, 85–93

Guerrero Ayuso, V. 1989 'Majorque et les guerres puniques: données archéologiques', in Devijver & Lipiński (eds.) 1989, 99–114

Hackens, T., & Moucharte, G. (eds.) 1992 *Numismatique et histoire économique phéniciennes et puniques*. Louvain

Hall, E. 1989 *Inventing the Barbarian: Greek Self-Definition through Tragedy*. Oxford

Handy, L. 1994 *Among the Host of Heaven: The Syrian-Phoenician Pantheon as Bureaucracy*. Winona Lake

Harden, D. 1939 'The Topography of Punic Carthage', *G&R*, 9, 25: 1–12

Harris, W. 1979 *War and Imperialism in Republican Rome: 327–70 B.C.* Oxford

—— 2005 'The Mediterranean and Ancient History', in Harris (ed.) 2005, 1–42

Harris, W. (ed.) 2005 *Rethinking the Mediterranean*. Oxford

Harrison, E. 1984 'The *Aeneid* and Carthage', in Woodman & West (eds.) 1984, 95–116

Healy, J. 1978 *Mining and Metallurgy in the Greek and Roman World*. London

Heider, G. 1985 *The Cult of Molek: A Reassessment*. Sheffield

Herrmann, W. 1979 *Die Historien des Coelius Antipater*. Meisenheim am Glan

Heurgon, J. 1966 'The Inscriptions of Pyrgi' *JRS*, 56: 1–15

—— 1976 'L'agronome carthaginois Magon et ses traducteurs en latin et en grec', *Comptes rendus de l'Académie des Inscriptions et Belles-Lettres*, 441–56

Hodos, T. 2006 *Local Responses to Colonization in the Iron Age Mediterranean*. London

Hoffmann, W. 1942 *Livius und der Zweite Punische Krieg*. Berlin

Holloway, R. 1994 *The Archaeology of Early Rome and Latium*. London

Horden, P., & Purcell, N. 2000 *The Corrupting Sea: A History of Mediterranean History*. Oxford

Hoyos, B. D. 1994 'Barcid "proconsuls" and Punic politics, 237–218 B.C.', *Rheinisches Museum für Philologie*, 137: 246–74

—— 1998 *Unplanned Wars: The Origins of the First and Second Punic Wars*. Berlin

—— 2001a 'Polybius and the Papyrus: The Persuasiveness of P. Rylands III 491', *Zeitschrift für Papyrologie und Epigraphik*, 134: 71–9

—— 2001b 'Identifying Hamilcar Barca's Heights of Heircte', *Historia: Zeitschrift für Alte Geschichte*, 50: 490–95

—— 2001c 'Generals and Annalists: Geographic and Chronological Obscurities in the Scipios' Campaigns in Spain, 218–211 B.C.', *Klio: Beiträge zur Alten Geschichte*, 83: 68–92

—— 2003 *Hannibal's Dynasty: Power and Politics in the Western Mediterranean 247–183 BC*. London

—— 2006 'Crossing the Durance with Hannibal and Livy: The Route to the Pass', *Klio: Beiträge zur Alten Geschichte*, 88: 408–65

—— 2007 *Truceless War: Carthage's Fight for Survival, 241–237 BC*. Leiden

Hudson, M. 1992 'Did the Phoenicians Introduce the Idea of Interest to Greece and Italy – and if so, When?', in Kopcke & Tokumaru (eds.) 1992, 128–43

Hurst, H. 1994 *Excavations at Carthage: The British Mission*, vol. 2, pt 1: *The Circular Harbour, North Side: The Site and Finds Other than Pottery*. Oxford

Hurst, H., & Roskams, S. 1984 *Excavations at Carthage: The British Mission*, vol. 1, pt 1: *The Avenue du President Habib Bourguiba, Salammbo: The Site and Finds Other than Pottery*. London

Hurst, H., & Stager, L. 1978 'A Metropolitan Landscape: The Late Punic Port of Carthage', *World Archaeology*, 9: 334–46

Huss, W. 1985 *Geschichte der Karthager*. Munich

—— 1986, 'Hannibal und die Religion' in Bonnet, Lipiński & Marchetti (eds.) 1986, 223–30

Isaac, B. 2004 *The Invention of Racism in Classical Antiquity*. Princeton

Isserlin, B. S. J. 1991 'The Transfer of the Alphabet to the Greeks: The State of Documentation', in Baurain, Bonnet & Krings (eds.) 1991, 283–91

Isserlin, B. S. J., & Du Plat Taylor, J. 1974 *Motya: A Phoenician and Carthaginian City in Sicily*. Leiden

Jaeger, M. 2006 'Livy, Hannibal's Monument, and the Temple of Juno at Croton', *Transactions and Proceedings of the American Philological Association*, 136: 389–414

Jenkins, G. 1971–8 'Coins of Punic Sicily'. Parts 1–4 in *Swiss Numismatic Review*, 50: 25–78 (1971); 53: 23–41 (1974); 56:5–65 (1977); 57: 5–68 (1978)

—— 1987 'Some Coins of Hannibal's Time', in *Studi per Laura Breglia, Bollettino di numismatica*, 4: 215–34

Jenkins, G., & Lewis, R. 1963 *Carthaginian Gold and Electrum Coins*. London

Jocelyn, H. 1972 'The Poems of Quintus Ennius', *ANRW*, 1, 2: 987–1026

Jones, A., Martindale, J., & Morris, J. 1971 *The Prosopography of the Later Roman Empire*, vol 1. Cambridge

Jongeling, K., & Kerr, R. (eds.) 2005 *Late Punic Epigraphy*. Grand Rapids

Jourdain-Annequin, C. 1989 *Héraclès aux portes du soir: mythe et histoire.* Besançon

—— 1992 *Héraclès–Melqart à Amrith. Recherches iconographiques: contributions à l'étude d'un syncrétisme.* Paris

—— 1999 'L'image de la montagne ou la géographie à l'épreuve du mythe et de l'histoire: l'exemple de la traversée des Alpes par Hannibal', *Dialogues d'Histoire Ancienne*, 25: 101–27

Karageorghis, V. 1998: *Greek Gods and Heroes in Ancient Cyprus*. Athens

Katzenstein, H. 1973 *The History of Tyre: From the Beginning of the Second Millennium B.C.E. until the Fall of the Neo-Babylonian Empire in 538 B.C.E.* Jerusalem

Kearsley, R. 1989 *The Pendent Semi-Circle Skyphos*. London

Kennedy, D. 1992 '"Augustan" and "Anti-Augustan": Reflections on Terms of Reference', in A. Powell (ed.) 1992, 26–57

Knapp, R. 1986 '"La Via Heraclea" en el occidente, mitho, arqueologia, propaganda, historia', *Emerita*, 54: 103–22

Kochavi, M. 1992 'Some Connections between the Aegean and the Levant in the Second Millennium BC: A View from the East', in Kopcke & Tokumaru (eds.) 1992, 7–15

Kopcke, G. 1992 'What Role for Phoenicians?', in Kopcke & Tokumaru (eds.) 1992, 103–113

Kopcke, G., & Tokumaru, I. (eds.) 1992 *Greece between East and West: 10th–8th Centuries BC*. Mainz

Kourou, N. 2002 'Phéniciens, Chypriotes, Eubéens et la fondation de Carthage', *Cahier du Centre d'études Chypriotes*, 32: 89–114

Krahmalkov, C. 1976 'Notes on the Rule of the Softim in Carthage', *Rivista di studi fenici*, 4: 171–7

—— 1981 'The Foundation Date of Carthage, 814 B.C., the Douimes Pendant Inscription', *Journal of Semitic Studies*, 26: 177–91

—— 2000 *Phoenician–Punic Dictionary*. Leuven

—— 2001 *A Phoenician–Punic Grammar*. Leiden

Krings, V. 1991 'Les Lettres grecques à Carthage', in Baurain, Bonnet & Krings (eds.) 1991, 649–68

—— 1998 *Carthage et les Grecs c.580–480 av. J.-C.* Leiden

Krings, V. (ed.) 1995 *La Civilisation phénicienne et punique: manuel de recherché*. Leiden

Kuhrt, A. 1995 *The Ancient Near East c.3000–330 BC*. 2 vols. London

La Bua, V. 1966 *Filino, Polibio, Sileno, Diodoro: il problema delle fonti, dalla morte di Agatocle alla guerra mercenaria in Africa.* Palermo

—— 1992 'Il Salento e i Messapi di fronte al conflitto tra Annibale e Roma', in Marangio (ed.) 1992, 43–69

Lacroix, W. 1998 *Africa in Antiquity: A Linguistic and Toponymic Analysis of Ptolemy's Map of Africa.* Saarbrücken

Lancel, S. 1988 'Les Fouilles de la mission archéologique française à Carthage et le problème de Byrsa', in Lipiński (ed.) 1988, 61–89

—— 1995 *Carthage: A History*, tr. Antonia Nevill. Oxford

—— 1999 *Hannibal*, tr. Antonia Nevill. Oxford

Larsen, M. T. (ed.) 1979 *Power and Propaganda: A Symposium on Ancient Empires.* Copenhagen

Lazenby, J. F. 1978 *Hannibal's War.* Warminster

—— 1996 *The First Punic War: A Military History.* London

Le Bonniec, H. 1969 'Aspects religieux de la guerre à Rome', in J. Brisson (ed.) 1969 *Problèmes de la guerre à Rome.* Paris. 102–15

Le Glay, M. 1966 *Saturn africain.* Paris

Lefkowitz, M. R. 1996 'Introduction: Ancient History, Modern Myths', in Lefkowitz & MacLean Rogers (eds.) 1996, 3–23

Lefkowitz, M. R., & MacLean Rogers, G. (eds.) 1996 *Black Athena Revisited.* Chapel Hill

Lehmler, C. 2005 *Syrakus unter Agathokles und Hieron II. Die Verbindung von Kultur und Macht in einer hellenistischen Metropole.* Frankfurt

Leigh, M. 2004 *Comedy and the Rise of Rome.* Oxford

Lennon, J. 2004 *Irish Orientalism: A Literary and Intellectual History.* Syracuse, NY

Levene, D. 1993 *Religion in Livy.* Leiden

Levick, B. 1978 'Concordia at Rome', in R. A. G. Carson & C. M. Kraay (eds.) 1978 *Scripta Nummaria Romana: Essays Presented to Humphrey Sutherland.* London. 217–233

—— 1982 'Morals, Politics and the Fall of the Roman Republic', *G&R*, 29: 53–62

Lewis, S. (ed.) 2006 *Ancient Tyranny.* Edinburgh

L'Heureux, C. 1979 *Rank Among the Canaanite Gods: El, Ba'al and the Repha'im.* Missoula

Lintott, A. 1972 'Imperial Expansion and Moral Decline in Rome', *Historia*, 21: 626–38

Lipiński, E. 1970 'La fête de l'ensevelissement et de la résurrection de Melqart', in A. Finet (ed.) 1970 *Actes de la XVIIe Rencontre assyriologique internationale.* Ham-sur-Heure. 30–58

—— 1988a 'Sacrifices d'enfants à Carthage et dans le monde seditious oriental', in Lipiński (ed.) 1988, 151–62

—— 1988b 'Stèles carthaginoises du Musée National de Cracovie', in Lipiński (ed.) 1988, 162–82

—— 1989 'Carthaginois en Sardaigne à l'époque de la première guerre', in Devijver & Lipiński (eds.) 1989, 67–73

—— 2001 'Gorillas', in K. Geus & K. Zimmermann (eds.) 2001 Punica–Libyca–Ptolemaica: Festschrift für Werner Huss. Leuven. 87–98

—— 2004 Itineraria Phoenicia. Leuven

Lipiński, E. (ed.) 1988 Carthago. Leuven

Little, C. 1934 'The Authenticity and Form of Cato's Saying "Carthago Delenda Est"', Classical Journal, 29: 429–35

Liverani, M. 1979 'The Ideology of the Assyrian Empire', in Larsen (ed.) 1979, 297–317

—— 1990 Prestige and Interest: International Relations in the Near East ca. 1600–1100 B.C. Padua

Lloyd, A. 1975 'Were Necho's Triremes Phoenician?', JHS, 95: 45–61

—— 1980 'M. Basch on Triremes: Some Observations', JHS, 100: 195–198

Lomas, K. 2004 'Italy in the Roman Republic, 338–31 BC' in H. Flower (ed.) The Cambridge Companion to the Roman Republic. Cambridge. 199–224

—— 2006 'Tyrants and the Polis: Migration, Identity and Urban Development in Greek Sicily', in Lewis (ed.) 2006, 95–118

Lomas, K. (ed.) 2004 Greek Identity in the Western Mediterranean: Papers in Honour of Brian Shefton. Leiden

Longerstay, M. 1995 'Libye', in Krings (ed.) 1995, 828–44

Lonis, R. 1978 'Les conditions de la navigation sur la côte atlantique de l'Afrique dans l'Antiquité: le problème de retour', in Afrique noire et monde méditerranéen. Dakar. 147–70

Loomis, W. 1994 'Entella Tablets VI (254–241 B.C.) and VII (20th cent. A.D.?)', Harvard Studies in Classical Philology, 96: 127–60

Loreto, L. 1995 La grande insurrezione libica contro Cartagine del 241–237 A.C. Una storia politica e militare. Paris

Luke, J. 2003 Ports of Trade: Al Mina and Geometric Greek Pottery in the Levant. Oxford

Luraghi, N. 2002 'Antioco di Siracusa', in Vattuone (ed.) 2002, 55–89

Lyne, R. 1987 Further Voices in Vergil's Aeneid. Oxford

Lyons, C., & Papadopoulos, J. (eds.) 2002 The Archaeology of Colonialism. Los Angeles

Macintosh-Turfa, J. 1975 Etruscan–Punic Relations. Ann Arbor

—— 1977 'Evidence for Etruscan–Punic Relations', American Journal of Archaeology, 81: 368–74

Maes, A. 1989 'L'habillement masculine à Carthage à l'époque des guerres puniques', in Devijver & Lipiński (eds.) 1989, 15–24

Malkin, I. 1994 *Myth and Territory in the Spartan Mediterranean*. Cambridge

—— 1998 *The Returns of Odysseus: Colonization and Ethnicity*. Berkeley

—— 2002 'A Colonial Middle Ground: Greek, Etruscan, and Local Elites in the Bay of Naples', in Lyons & Papadopoulos (eds.) 2002, 151–81

—— 2005 'Herakles and Melqart: Greeks and Phoenicians in the Middle Ground', in E. Gruen (ed.) 2005 *Cultural Borrowings and Ethnic Appropriations in Antiquity*. Stuttgart. 238–58

Manfredi, L. 1999 'Carthaginian Policy through Coins', in Pisano (ed.) 1999, 69–78

—— 2003 *La politica amministrativa di Cartagine in Africa*. Rome

Manganaro, G. 1974 'Una biblioteca storica nel Ginnasio di Tauromenion e il *P. Oxy* 1241', *Parola del passato*, 29: 389–409

—— 1992 'Per la cronologia delle emissioni a leggenda Libuvwn', in Hackens & Moucharte (eds.) 1992, 93–106

—— 2000 'Fenici, Cartaginesi, Numidi tra i Greci. IV–I secolo', *Quaderni ticinesi di numismatica e antichità classiche*, 29: 255–68

Marangio, C. (ed.) 1992 *L'età annibalica e la Puglia romana*. Mesagne

Markoe, G. 1992 'In Pursuit of Metal: Phoenicians and Greeks in Italy', in Kopcke & Tokumaru (eds.) 1992, 61–84

—— 1996 'The Emergence of Orientalizing in Greek Art: Some Observations on the Interchange between Greeks and Phoenicians in the Eighth and Seventh Centuries BC', *BASOR*, 301: 47–67

—— 2000 *Phoenicians*. Berkeley

Martin, R. 1979 'Introduction à l'étude du culte d'Héraclès en Sicile', *Recherches sur les cultes grecs et l'Occident*, vol. 1. Naples. 11–17

Mastino, A., Zucca, R., & Spanu, P. 2005 *Mare sardum: merci, mercati e scambi marittimi della Sardegna antica*. Rome

Medas, S. 1999 'Les équipages des flottes militaires de Carthage', in Pisano (ed.) 1999, 79–106

Meister, K. 1971 'Annibale in Sileno', *Maia*, 22: 3–9

Melville, S., et al. 2006 'Neo-Assyrian and Syro-Palestinian Texts I', in M. Chavalas (ed.) 2006 *Historical Sources in Translation: The Near East*. Oxford. 280–330

Meritt, B. 1940 'Athens and Carthage', in *Athenian Studies Presented to William Scott Ferguson*. Cambridge, Mass.

Mezzolani, A. 1999 'L'espace privé chez les Puniques: remarques sur les salles d'eau', in Pisano (ed.) 1999, 107–24

Mildenberg, L. 1989 'Punic Coinage on the Eve of the First War against Rome:

A Reconsideration', in Devijver & Lipiński (eds.) 1989, 5–14

Miles, G. 1995 *Livy: Reconstructing Early Rome*. Ithaca, NY

Miles, M. 1998/9 'Interior Staircases in Western Greek Temples', *MAAR*, 43–4: 1–26

Miles, R. 2003 'Rivalling Rome: Carthage', in C. Edwards & G. Woolf (eds.) 2003 *Rome the Cosmopolis*. Cambridge. 123–46

Millar, F. 1968 'Local cultures in the Roman Empire: Libyan, Punic, and Latin in North Africa', *JRS*, 58: 126–34

Mineo, B. 2006 *Tite-Live et l'histoire de Rome*. Paris

Moeller, W. 1975 'Once More the One-Eyed Man against Rome', *Historia*, 24: 402–8

Momigliano, A. 1975 *Alien Wisdom: The Limits of Hellenization*. Cambridge

—— 1977 'Athens in the Third Century B.C. and the Discovery of Rome in the Histories of Timaeus of Tauromenium', in A. Momigliano, *Essays in Ancient and Modern Historiography*. Oxford. 37–66

Morel, J.-P. 1980 'Les vases à vernis noir et à figures rouges d'Afrique avant la deuxième guerre punique et le problème des exportations de Grande-Grèce', *Antiquities africaines*, 15: 29–90

—— 1982 'La céramique à vernis noir de Byrsa: nouvelles données et éléments de comparaison' in *Actes du colloque sur la céramique antique*. Carthage. 43–61

—— 1983 'Les importations des céramiques grecques et italiennes dans le monde punique', in Bartoloni et al. (eds.) 1983, 3: 731–40

—— 1986 'La céramique à vernis noir de Carthage, sa diffusion, son influence', *Cahiers des études anciennes*, 18: 25–68

—— 2004 'Les amphores importées à Carthage punique', in E. Sanmartí Grego et al. (eds.) 2004 *La circulació d'àmfores al Mediterrani occidental durant la Protohistòria (segles VIII–III aC): aspectes quantitatius i anàlisi de continguts*. Barcelona. 11–24

Morgan, L. 1998 'Assimilation and Civil War: Hercules and Cacus (*Aen.* 8.185–267)', in H.-P. Stahl (ed.) 1998 *Vergil's Aeneid: Augustan Epic and Political Context*. London. 175–97

Morris, I., et al. 2001 'Stanford University Excavations on the Acropolis of Monte Polizzo, Sicily, I: Preliminary Report on the 2000 Season', *MAAR*, 46: 253–71

—— 2002 'Stanford University Excavations on the Acropolis of Monte Polizzo, Sicily, II: Preliminary Report on the 2001 Season', *MAAR*, 47: 153–98

—— 2003 'Stanford University Excavations on the Acropolis of Monte Polizzo, Sicily, III: Preliminary Report on the 2002 Season', *MAAR*, 48: 243–315

—— 2004 'Stanford University Excavations on the Acropolis of Monte

Polizzo, Sicily, IV: Preliminary Report on the 2003 Season', *MAAR*, 49: 197–279

Morris, S. 1998 'Bearing Greek Gifts: Euboean Pottery on Sardinia', in Balmuth & Tykot (eds.) 1998, 361–2

Morris, S., & Papadopoulos, J. 1998, 'Phoenicians and the Corinthian Pottery Industry', in R. Rolle, K. Schmidt & R. Docter (eds.) 1998 *Archäologische Studien in Kontaktzonen der antiken Welt*. Göttingen. 251–63

Morrison, J., & Coates, J. 1986 *The Athenian Trireme: The History and Reconstruction of an Ancient Greek Warship*. Cambridge

Moscati, S. 1968 *The World of the Phoenicians*, tr. Alastair Hamilton. London

—— 1986 *Italia Punica*. Milan

Muscarella, O. W. 1992 'Greek and Oriental Cauldron Attachments: A Review', in Kopcke & Tokumaru (eds.) 1992, 16–45

Musti, D. 1991 'Modi e fasi della rappresentazione dei fenici nelle fonti letterarie greche', in Acquaro et al. (eds.) 1991, 161–8

Naveh, J. 1980 ' The Greek Alphabet: New Evidence', in *Biblical Archaeologist*, 43, 1: 22–5

Niemeyer, H. G. 1984 'Die Phönizier und die Mittelmeerwelt im Zeitalter Homers', *Jahrbuch Des Römisch-Germanischen Zentralmuseums, Mainz*, 31: 3–94

—— 1990 'The Phoenicians in the Mediterranean: A Non-Greek Model for Expansion and Settlement in Antiquity', in J.-P. Descœudres (ed.) 1990 *Greek Colonists and Native Populations: Proceedings of the First Australian Congress of Classical Archaeology Held in Honour of Emeritus Professor A. D. Trendall*. Oxford. 469–89

—— 2002 'The Phoenician Settlement at Toscanos: Urbanization and Function', in Bierling & Gitin (eds.) 2002, 31–48

Niemeyer, H. G. (ed.) 1982 *Phönizier im Westen: Die Beiträge des Internationalen Symposiums über 'Die phönizische Expansion im westlichen Mittelmeerraum' in Köln vom 24. bis 27. April 1979*. Mainz

Niemeyer, H. G., & Docter, R. F. 1993 'Die Grabung unter dem Decumanus Maximus von Karthago', *MDAI(R)*, 100: 201–44

Niemeyer, H. G., et al. (eds.) 2007 *Karthago. Die Ergebnisse der Hamburger Grabung unter dem Decumanus Maximus*, vol 2. Mainz

Nijboer, A. J. 2005 'The Iron Age in the Mediterranean: A Chronological Mess or "Trade Before the Flag", Part II', *AWE*, 4, 2: 255–77

Nijboer, A. J., & Van de Plicht, J. 2006 'An Interpretation of the Radiocarbon Determinations of the Oldest Indigenous-Phoenician Stratum Thus Far Excavated at Huelva, Tartessos (South-West Spain)', *BaBesch*, 81: 31–6

Oded, B. 1979 *Mass Deportations and Deportees in the Neo-Assyrian Empire*. Wiesbaden

O'Gorman, E. 2004 'Cato the Elder and the Destruction of Carthage', *Helios*, 31: 97–122

Ottoson, M. 1980 *Temples and Cult Places in Palestine*. Uppsala

Paladino, I. 1991 'Marcii e Atilii tra fides romana e fraus punica', in Acquaro et al. (eds.) 1991, 179–85

Palmer, R. 1997 *Rome and Carthage at Peace*. Stuttgart

Paoletti, O., & Perna, L. 2002 'Etruria e Sardegna centro-settentrionale tra l'età del Bronzo Finale e l'arcaismo', in *Atti del XXI Convegno di Studi Etruschi ed Italici. Sassari–Alghero–Oristano–Torralba, 13–17 ottobre 1998*. Pisa and Rome

Papadopoulos, J. 1997 'Phantom Euboians', *Journal of Mediterranean Archaeology*, 10: 191–219

Pearson, L. 1975 'Myth and *archaeologia* in Italy and Sicily – Timaeus and his Predecessors', *Yale Classical Studies*, 24: 171–95

—— 1984 'Ephorus and Timaeus in Diodorus: Laqueur's Thesis Rejected', in *Historia*, 33: 1–20

—— 1987 *The Greek Historians of the West: Timaeus and his Predecessors*. Atlanta

Peckham, B. 1972 'The Nora Inscription', *Orientalia*, 41: 457–68

—— 1998 'Phoenicians in Sardinia: Tyrians or Sidonians?', in Balmuth & Tykot (eds.) 1998, 347–54

Pelling, C. 1997 'Tragical Dreamer: Some Dreams in the Roman Historians', *G&R*, 44: 197–213

Peserico, A. 1999 'Pottery Production and Circulation in the Phoenician and Punic Mediterranean: A study on Open Forms', in Pisano (ed.) 1999, 125–35

Picard, G. 1963 'La religion d'Hannibal', *Revue de l'histoire des religions*, 162: 123–4

—— 1983–4 'Hannibal hegemon hellenistique', *RSA*, 13–14: 75–81

Picard, G., & Picard, C. 1961 *Daily Life in Carthage*. London

—— 1964 'Hercule et Melqart', in M. Renard & R. Schilling (eds.) 1964 *Hommages à J. Bayet*. Brussels. 569–78

Piccaluga, G. 1974 'Heracles, Melqart, Hercules e la penisola iberica', in *Minutal. Saggi di storia delle religioni*. Rome. 111–31

—— 1981 'Fides nella religione romana di età imperiale', *ANRW*, 17, 2: 703–35

—— 1983a 'Urbs Trunca: passato mitico ed espansionismo contro la Capua del "dopo Hannibal"', *RSA*, 13: 103–25

—— 1983b 'Fondare Roma, domare Cartagine: un mito delle origini', in Bartoloni et al. (eds.) 1983, 2: 409–24

Pisano, G. 'Remarks on Trade in Luxury Goods in the Western Mediterranean', in Pisano (ed.) 1999, 15–30

Pisano, G. (ed.) 1999 *Phoenicians and Carthaginians in the Western Mediterranean*. Rome

Pomeroy, A. 1989 'Hannibal at Nuceria', *Historia*, 38: 163–76

Popham, M., & Lemos, I. 1992 'Review of Kearsley: The Pendent Semi-Circle Skyphos', *Gnomon*, 64: 152–5

Popham, M., Sackett, L., & Themelis, P. (eds.) 1979 *Lefkandi*. London

Postgate, J. 1969 *Neo-Assyrian Royal Grants and Decrees*. Rome

—— 1974 *Taxation and Conscription in the Assyrian Empire*. Rome

—— 1979 'The Economic Structure of the Assyrian Empire', in Larsen (ed.) 1979, 193–221

Powell, A. (ed.) 1992 *Roman Poetry and Propaganda in the Age of Augustus*. Bristol

Powell, B. 1991 'The Origins of the Alphabetic Literacy Among the Greeks', in Baurain, Bonnet & Krings (eds.) 1991, 357–70

Prandi, L. 1979 'La "Fides punica" e il pregiudizio anticartaginese', *Contributi dell'istituto di storia antica*, 6: 90–97

Price, M. 1991 *The Coinage in the Name of Alexander the Great and Philip Arrhidaeus: A British Museum Catalogue*. London

Purcell, N. 1995 'On the Sacking of Carthage and Corinth', in D. Innes, H. Hine & C. Pelling (eds.) 1995 *Ethics and Rhetoric: Classical Essays for Donald Russell on his Seventy-Fifth Birthday*. Oxford. 133–48

Purpura, G. 1981 'Un graffito di nave in un cunicolo delle fortificazioni puniche di Lilibeo', *Sicilia Archeologica Trapani*, 13, 44: 39–42

Rakob, F. 1979 'Numidische Königsarchitektur in Nordafrika', in *Die Numider: Reiter und Könige nördlich der Sahara*. Cologne. 119–71

—— 1984 'Deutsche Ausgrabungen in Karthago. Die punischen Befunde', *MDAI(R)*, 91: 1–22

—— 1989 'Karthago: Die frühe siedlung. Neue forschungen', *MDAI(R)*, 96: 155–94

—— 1995 'Forschungen im Stadtzentrum von Karthago. Zweiter Vorbericht', *MDAI(R)*, 102: 413–61

—— 2000 'The Making of Augustan Carthage', in E. Fentress (ed.) 2000 *Romanization and the City: Creation, Transformations, and Failures: Proceedings of a Conference Held at the American Academy in Rome to Celebrate the 50th Anniversary of the Excavations at Cosa, 14–16 May, 1998*. Portsmouth, RI. 72–82

Rance, P., 2009 'Hannibal, Elephants and Turrets in *Suda* 438 [Polybius FR.162 B] – an Unidentified Fragment of Diodorus', *CQ*, 59, 1: 91–111

Rankov, B. 1996 'The Second Punic War at Sea', in Cornell, Rankov & Sabin (eds.) 1996, 49–58

Rawlings, L. 1996 'Celts, Spaniards and Samnites: Warriors in a Soldier's

War', in Cornell, Rankov & Sabin (eds.) 1996, 81–95

—— 2005 'Hannibal and Hercules', in Rawlings & Bowden (eds.) 2005, 153–84

—— 2007 'Army and Battle during the Conquest of Italy (350–264 BC)', in P. Erdkamp (ed.) 2007 *A Companion to the Roman Army*. Oxford. 45–62

Rawlings, L., & Bowden, H. (eds.) 2005 *Herakles and Hercules: Exploring a Graeco-Roman Divinity*. Swansea

Reade. J. 1979 'Ideology and Propaganda in Assyrian Art', in Larsen (ed.) 1979, 329–43

Rendeli, M. 2005 'La Sardegna e gli Eubei', in Bernardini & Zucca (eds.) 2005, 91–124

Ribichini, S. 1983 'Mito e storia: l'immagine dei Fenici nelle fonti classiche', in Bartoloni et al. (eds.) 1983, 2: 443–8

—— 1985 *Poenus Advena: gli dei fenici e l'interpretazione classica*. Rome

—— 1995 'Les Mentalités', in Krings (ed.) 1995, 334–44

Rich, J. 1993 'Fear, Greed, and Glory: The Causes of Roman War-Making in the Middle Republic', in J. Rich & G. Shipley (eds.) 1993 *War and Society in the Roman World*. London. 46–67

—— 1996 'The Origins of the Second Punic War', in Cornell, Rankov & Sabin (eds.) 1996, 1–37

Ridgway, D. 1992 *The First Western Greeks*. Cambridge

—— 1994 'Phoenicians and Greeks in the West: A View from Pithekoussai', in Tsetskhladze & De Angelis (eds.) 1994, 35–46

—— 1998 'L'Eubea e l'Occidente: nuovi spunti sulle rotte dei metalli', in M. Bats & B. d'Agostino (eds.) 1998 *Euboica: L'Eubea e la presenza Euboica in Chalcidice e in Occidente*. Naples. 311–22

—— 2000 'The First Western Greeks Revisited', in D. Ridgway et al. (eds.) 2000 *Ancient Italy in its Mediterranean Setting: Studies in Honour of Ellen Macnamara*. London. 179–91

—— 2004, 'Euboeans and Others along the Tyrrhenian Seaboard in the 8th Century B.C.', in Lomas (ed.) 2004, 15–33

Ridley, R. 1986 'To be Taken with a Pinch of Salt: The Destruction of Carthage', *CP*, 81: 140–46

Ritter, S. 1995 *Hercules in der römischen Kunst von den Anfängen bis Augustus*. Heidelberg

Riva, C., & Vella, N. (eds.) 2006 *Debating Orientalization: Multidisciplinary Approaches to Processes of Change in the Ancient Mediterranean*. London

Rives, J. 1995 *Religion and Authority in Roman Carthage from Augustus to Constantine*. Oxford

Robinson, E. 1956 'Punic Coins of Spain and their Bearing on the Roman

Republican Series', in R. A. G. Carson & C. H. V. Sutherland (eds.) 1956 *Essays in Roman Coinage Presented to Harold Mattingly*. Oxford

—— 1964 'Carthaginian and Other South Italian Coinages of the Second Punic War', *Numismatic Chronicle*, 7, 4: 37–64

Rocco, B. 1970 'Morto sotto le mura di Mozia', *Sicilia Archaeologica*, 3: 27–33

Röllig, W. 1982 'Die Phönizier des Mutterlandes zur Zeit der Kolonisierung', in Niemeyer (ed.) 1982, 15–30

—— 1992 'Asia Minor as a Bridge between East and West: The Role of the Phoenicians and Aramaeans in the Transfer of Culture', in Kopcke & Tokumaru (eds.) 1992, 93–102

Russell, J. 1991 *Sennacherib's Palace without Rival at Nineveh*. Chicago

Sabin, P. 1996 'The Mechanics of Battle in the Second Punic War', in Cornell, Rankov & Sabin (eds.) 1996, 59–79

Sagona, C. 2002 *The Archaeology of Punic Malta*. Leuven

Sainte-Beuve, C.-A., 1971 'Articles de Sainte-Beuve sur Salammbô', in Gustave Flaubert, *Salammbô*, Œuvres complètes de Gustave Flaubert, vol. 2. Paris

Scheid, J., & Svenbro, J. 1985 'Byrsa, la ruse d'Elissa et la fondation de Carthage', *Annales (économies, sociétés, civilisations)*, 328–42

Schilling, R. 1954 *La religion romaine de Venus, depuis les origines jusqu'au temps d'Auguste*. Paris

Schmidt, H. 1953 'The Idea and Slogan of "Perfidious Albion"', *Journal of the History of Ideas*, 14, 4: 604–16

Schmitz, P. 1994 'The Name "Agrigentum" in a Punic Inscription (*CIS* i.5510.10)', *Journal of Near Eastern Studies*, 53, 1: 1–13

—— 1995 'The Phoenician Text from the Etruscan Sanctuary at Pyrgi', *Journal of the American Oriental Society*, 115, 4: 559–75

Schulten, A. 1922 *Tartessos. Ein Beitrag zur ältesten Geschichte des Westens*. Hamburg

Schurmann, F. 1998 'Delenda est Iraq – Why U.S. is on Warpath against Saddam'. http://www. pacificnews.org/jinn/stories/4.04/980216–iraq.html

Schwarte, K.-H. 1983 *Der Ausbruch des Zweiten Punischen Krieges. Rechtsfrage und Überlieferung*. Weisbaden

Scuderi, R. 2002 'Filino di Agrigento', in Vattuone (ed.) 2002, 275–99

Scullard, H. 1970 *Scipio Africanus: Soldier and Politician*. London

—— 1974 *The Elephant in the Greek and Roman World*. London

Seibert, J. 1993 *Hannibal*. Darmstadt

Serrati, J. 2006 'Neptune's Altars: The Treaties between Rome and Carthage (509–226 B.C.)', *CQ*, 56, 1: 113–34

Shaw J., & Shaw, M. (eds.) 2000 *Kommos*. Princeton

Shelby Brown, S. 1991 *Late Carthaginian Child Sacrifice and Sacrificial Monuments in their Mediterranean Context*. Sheffield

Smith, C. 1996 *Early Rome and Latium: Economy and Society c.1000 to 500 BC*. Oxford

Snodgrass, A. M. 1971 *The Dark Age of Greece*. Edinburgh

—— 1988 *Cyprus and Early Greek History*. Nicosia

—— 1994 'The Nature and Standing of the Early Western Colonies', in Tsetskhladze & De Angelis (eds.) 1994, 1–10

Snowden, F. M., Jr, 1996 'Bernal's "Blacks" and the Afrocentrists', in Lefkowitz & MacLean Rogers (eds.) 1996, 112–28

Solmsen, F. 1986 'Aeneas Founded Rome with Odysseus', *Harvard Studies in Classical Philology*, 90: 93–110

Spada, S. 2002 'La storiografia occidentale di età ellenistica', in Vattuone (ed.) 2002, 233–73

Spencer, D. 2002 *The Roman Alexander: Reading a Cultural Myth*. Exeter

Stager, L. 1982 'Carthage: A View from the Tophet', in Niemeyer (ed.) 1982, 155–66

Stager, L., & Wolff, S. 1984 'Child Sacrifice at Carthage: Religious Rite or Population Control?', *Biblical Archaeology Review*, 10: 30–51

Stampolodis, N., & Kotsonas, A. 2006 'Phoenicians in Crete', in S. Deger-Jalkotzy & I. Lemos (eds.) 2006 *Ancient Greece from the Mycenaean Palaces to the Age of Homer*. Edinburgh. 337–60

Starks, J. 1999 'Fides Aeneia: The Transference of Punic Stereotypes in the *Aeneid*', *Classical Journal*, 94: 255–83

Stevens, S. 1988 'A Legend of the Destruction of Carthage', *CP*, 83, 1: 39–40

Stos-Gale, Z. A., & Gale, N. H. 1992 'New Light on the Provenience of the Copper Oxhide Ingots Found on Sardinia', in Tykot & Andrews (eds.) 1992, 317–46

Strøm, I. 1992 'Evidence from the Sanctuaries', in Kopcke & Tokumaru (eds.) 1992, 46–60

Stübler, G. 1941 *Die Religiosität des Livius*. Stuttgart & Berlin

Sumner, G. 1972 'Rome, Spain and the Outbreak of the Second Punic War', *Latomus*, 31, 2: 469–80

Sutton, D. 1977 'The Greek Origins of the Cacus Myth', *CQ*, 27, 2: 391–3

Sutton, J. 2007 'West African Metals and the Ancient Mediterranean', *OJA*, 2, 2: 181–8

Sznycer, M. 1978 'Carthage et la civilisation punique', in C. Nicolet 1978 *Rome et la conquête du Monde Méditerranéen 264–27 avant J.-C.*, vol. 2, Paris. 545–93

Tandy, D. 1997 *Warriors into Traders: The Power of the Market in Early Greece*. Berkeley

Taylor, J. 1982 'A Nigerian Tin Trade in Antiquity?', *OJA*, 1: 317–24

Taylor, P. 1995 *Munitions of the Mind: War Propaganda from the Ancient World to the Nuclear Age*. Manchester

Thomas, R. 2001 *Virgil and the Augustan Reception*. Cambridge

Thuillier, J.-P. 1982 'Timbres amphoriques puniques écrits en lettres grecques', in *Actes: Colloque sur la Céramique Antique. Carthage 23–24 Juin 1980*. Tunis

Thürlemann-Rappers, S. 1974 'Ceterum censeo Carthaginem esse delendam', *Gymnasium*, 81: 465–75

Tise, B. 2002 *Imperialismo romano e imitatio Alexandri: due studi di storia politica*. Lecce

Tore, G. 1995 'L'art, sarcophages, reliefs, stèles', in Krings (ed.) 1995, 471–93

Torelli, M. 1989 'Archaic Rome between Latium and Etruria', in Walbank et al. (eds.) 1989, 30–51

Toynbee, A. 1965 *Hannibal's Legacy: The Hannibalic War's Effects on Roman Life*. 2 vols. Oxford

Tronchetti, C. 1992 'Osservazioni sulla ceramica attica di Sardegna', in Tykot & Andrews (eds.) 1992, 364–77

—— 1995 'Sardaigne', in Krings (ed.) 1995, 712–42

Trump, D. 1991a 'The Nuraghi of Sardinia, Territory and Power: The Evidence from the Commune of Mara, Sassari', in E. Herring, R. Whitehouse & J. Wilkins (eds.) 1991 *The Archaeology of Power: Papers from the Fourth Conference of Italian Archaeology*. London. 43–77

—— 1991b 'Nuraghi as Social History: A Case Study from Bonu Ighinu, Mara (SS)', in B. S. Frizell (ed.) 1991 *Arte e Architectura Nuragica: Nuragic Architecture in its Military, Territorial and Socio-Economic Context*. Stockholm. 163–8

—— 1992 'Militarism in Nuragic Sardinia', in Tykot & Andrews (eds.) 1992, 198–203

Tsetskhladze, G. R., & De Angelis, F. (eds.) 1994 *The Archaeology of Greek Colonisation*. Oxford

Tusa, V. 1982/1983 'I Cartaginesi nella Sicilia occidentale', *Kokalos*, 28–9: 131–46

—— 1984 *Lilibeo testimonianze archeologiche dal IV sec. a.C. al V sec. d.C.* Palermo

Twyman, B. 1987 'Polybius and the Annalists on the Outbreak and Early Years of the Second Punic War', *Athenaeum*, 65: 67–80

Tykot, R., & Andrews, T. (eds.) 1992 *Sardinia in the Mediterranean: A Footprint in the Sea*. Sheffield

Ugas, G. 1992 'Considerazioni sullo sviluppo dell'architettura e della società nuragica', in Tykot & Andrews (eds.) 1992, 221–34

Van Berchem, D. 1959–60 'Hercule Melqart à l'Ara Maxima', *Rendicanti della Pontifica academia Romana di archeologia*, 32: 61–8

—— 1967 'Sanctuaires d'Hercule-Melqart: contribution à l'étude de l'expansion phénicienne en Méditerranée', *Syria*, 44: 73–109, 307–38

Van Dommelen, P. 1998 *In Colonial Grounds: A Comparative Study of Colonialism and Rural Settlement in First Millennium BC West Central Sardinia*. Leiden

—— 2002 'Ambiguous Matters: Colonialism and Local Identities in Punic Sardinia', in Lyons & Papadopoulos (eds.) 2002, 121–47

—— 2006 'Colonial Matters. Material Culture and Postcolonial Theory in Colonial Situations', in C. Y. Tilley et al. (eds.) 2006 *Handbook of Material Culture*. London. 267–308

Van Weyenberg, A. 2003 'Ireland's Carthaginians and Tragic Heroines', *Xchanges*, 2, 2: *Confrontation, Conflict, and Negotiations of National Space*. http://infohost.nmt.edu/~xchanges/xchanges/2.2/weyenberg.html

Van Wijngaarden-Bakker, L. 2007 'The Animal Remains from Carthage, Campaign 1993', in Niemeyer et al. (eds.) 2007, 841–9

Van Zeist, W., Bottema, S., and Van der Veen, M. 2001. *Diet and Vegetation at Ancient Carthage: The Archaeobotanical Evidence*. Groningen

Vattuone, R. 1991 *Sapienza d'Occidente: il pensiero storico di Timeo di Tauromenio*. Bologna

—— 2002 'Timeo di Tauromenio', in Vattuone (ed.) 2002, 77–132

Vattuone, R. (ed.) 2002 *Storici greci d'Occidente*. Bologna

Vegas, M. 1999 'Eine archaische Keramikfüllung aus einem Haus am Kardo XIII in Karthago', *MDAI(R)*, 106: 395–435

Verzár, M. 1980 'Pyrgi e l'Afrodite di Cipro', *Mélanges de l'école française. Antiquité*, 92: 35–86

Vessey, D. 1975 'Silius Italicus: The Shield of Hannibal', *AJP*, 96: 391–405

Villaronga L. 1973 *Las Monedas Hispano-Cartaginesas*. Barcelona

—— 1992 'Les monnaies hispano-carthaginoises du système attique', in Hackens & Moucharte (eds.) 1992, 149–52

Virolleaud, C. 1931 'The Gods of Phoenicia', *Antiquity*, 20: 404–15

Vishnia, R. 1996 *State, Society and Popular Leaders in Mid-Republican Rome 241–167 BC*. London

Visonà, P. 1988 'Passing the Salt: On the Destruction of Carthage Again', *CP*, 83, 1: 41–2

—— 1992 'Carthaginian Bronze Coinage in Sardinia', in Hackens & Moucharte (eds.) 1992, 121–132

—— 1998 'Carthaginian Coinage in Perspective', *American Journal of Numismatics*, 10: 1–27

Vogel-Weidemann, U. 1989 '*Carthago delenda est*: aitia and prophasis', *Acta classica*, 32: 79–96

Volk, T. 2006 'The "Mazzarrón" hoard (ICGH 2325) revisited', *Numisma*, 250: 205–28

Wagner, C. G. 1989 'The Carthaginians in Ancient Spain: From Administrative Trade to Territorial Annexation', in Devijver & Lipiński (eds.) 1989, 145–56

Walbank, F. W. 1957–79 *A Historical Commentary on Polybius*. 3 vols. Oxford

—— 1968–9 'The Historians of Greek Sicily', *Kokalos*, 14–15: 476–98

—— 1972 *Polybius*. Berkeley

—— 1985 *Selected Papers: Studies in Greek and Roman History and Historiography*. Cambridge

—— 2002 *Polybius, Rome, and the Hellenistic World: Essays and Reflections*. Cambridge

Walbank, F. W., et al. (eds.) 1989 *The Cambridge Ancient History*, vol. 7, pt 2: *The Rise of Rome to 220 B.C.* Cambridge

Waldbaum, J. 1997 'Greeks *in* the East or Greeks *and* the East?: Problems in the Definition and Recognition of Presence', *BASOR*, 305: 1–17

Warmington, B. 1960 *Carthage*. London

Warmington, E. 1935 *Remains of Old Latin*. London

Webster, G. 1996 *A Prehistory of Sardinia 2300–500 BC*. Sheffield

White, R. 1991 *The Middle Ground: Indians, Empires, and Republics in the Great Lakes Region, 1650–1815*. Cambridge

Whittaker, C. R. 1978 'Carthaginian Imperialism in the Fifth and Fourth Centuries', in P. D. A. Garnsey & C. R. Whittaker (eds.) 1978 *Imperialism in the Ancient World*. Cambridge. 59–90

Wiedemann, T. 1993. 'Sallust's Jugurtha: Concord, Discord, and the Digressions', *G&R*, 40, 1: 48–57

Wightman, E. 1980 'The Plan of Roman Carthage: Practicalities and Politics', in J. Pedley (ed.) 1980 *New Light on Ancient Carthage*. Ann Arbor. 29–46

Wigodsky, M. 1972 *Vergil and Early Latin Poetry*. Wiesbaden

Winter, I. 1979 'North Syria as a Bronzeworking Centre in the First Millenium BC: Luxury Commodities at Home and Abroad', in J. Curtis (ed.) 1979 *Bronzeworking Centres of Western Asia, c.1000–539 B.C.* London. 193–226

—— 1995 'Homer's Phoenicians: History, Ethnography, or Literary Trope? [A Perspective on Early Orientalism]', in J. B. Carter & S. P. Morris (eds.) 1995 *The Ages of Homer: A Tribute to Emily Townsend Vermeule*. Austin. 247–72

Woodman, A., & West, D. (eds.) 1984 *Poetry and Politics in the Age of Augustus*. Cambridge

Wonterghem van, F. 1992 'Il culto di Ercole tra i popoli osco-sabellici', in C. Bonnet & C. Jourdain-Annequin (eds.) 1992 *Héraclès: d'une rive à l'autre de la Méditerranée: bilan et perspectives: actes de la Table Ronde de Rome, Academia Belgica – Ecole française de Rome, 15–16 septembre 1989.* Brussels. 319–51

Yon, M. 1986 'Cultes phéniciens à Chypre: l'interprétation chypriote', in Bonnet, Lipiński & Marchetti (eds.) 1986, 127–52

—— 1992 'Le royaume de Kition', in Hackens & Moucharte (eds.) 1992, 243–60

Zambon, E. 2006 'From Agathocles to Hieron II: The Birth and Development of Basileia in Hellenistic Sicily', in Lewis (ed.) 2006, 77–94

Zanker, P, 1988 *The Power of Images in the Age of Augustus*. Ann Arbor

Zecchini, G. 2003 'Annibale prima e dopo il Trasimeno. Alcune osservazioni', *RSA*, 33: 91–8

Zimmerman Munn, M. L. 2003 'Corinthian Trade with the Punic West in the Classical Period', in C. Williams & N. Bookidis (eds.) 2003 *Corinth: The Centenary, 1896–1996*. Princeton. 195–217

Index